AN INTRODUCTION TO MORMONISM

D0364793

The Church of Jesus Christ of Latter-day Saints is one of the fastest growing religious movements in the world. It is highly visible, with a massive missionary programme, yet it remains a mystery in terms of its core beliefs and theological structure. This timely book provides an introduction to the basic history, doctrines and practices of The LDS – the 'Mormon' Church. Written by a non-Mormon, it seeks neither to prove nor to disprove the truthfulness of the religious claims of that faith but rather to describe them in ways that non-Mormons can understand. Particular emphasis is given to sacred texts and prophecies as well as to the crucial temple rituals of endowments, marriage and baptism for the dead, through which human beings may achieve their divine potential. This rich comparative study offers a new understanding of Mormon theology and ideas of humanity.

DOUGLAS J. DAVIES is Professor in the Study of Religion at the Department of Theology at the University of Durham. He is the author of numerous books including *The Mormon Culture of Salvation* (2000) and *Death, Ritual and Belief* (2002).

AN INTRODUCTION TO MORMONISM

DOUGLAS J. DAVIES

CAMBRIDGE
UNIVERSITY PRESS

CAMBRIDGE UNIVERSITY PRESS
Cambridge, New York, Melbourne, Madrid, Cape Town, Singapore, São Paulo, Delhi

Cambridge University Press
The Edinburgh Building, Cambridge CB2 8RU, UK

Published in the United States of America by Cambridge University Press, New York

www.cambridge.org
Information on this title: www.cambridge.org/9780521520645

© Douglas J. Davies 2003

This publication is in copyright. Subject to statutory exception
and to the provisions of relevant collective licensing agreements,
no reproduction of any part may take place without the written
permission of Cambridge University Press.

First published 2003

A catalogue record for this publication is available from the British Library

Library of Congress Cataloguing in Publication data
Davies, Douglas James.
An introduction to Mormonism / Douglas J. Davies.
p.   cm.
Includes bibliographical references and index.
ISBN 0 521 81738 2 (hardback) – ISBN 0 521 52064 9 (paperback)
1. Church of Jesus Christ of Latter-day Saints – Doctrines.   2. Church of
Jesus Christ of Latter-day Saints – History.   I. Title.
BX8635.3D38   2003
289.3 – dc21   2003043582 CIP

ISBN 978-0-521-81738-7 hardback
ISBN 978-0-521-52064-5 paperback

Transferred to digital printing 2009

Cambridge University Press has no responsibility for the persistence or
accuracy of URLs for external or third-party Internet websites referred to in
this publication, and does not guarantee that any content on such websites is,
or will remain, accurate or appropriate. Information regarding prices, travel
timetables and other factual information given in this work are correct at
the time of first printing but Cambridge University Press does not guarantee
the accuracy of such information thereafter.

Contents

Abbreviations

D&C	Doctrine and Covenants
EM	*Encyclopedia of Mormonism*, ed. Daniel H. Ludlow (New York: Macmillan, 1992)
FARMS	Foundation for Ancient Research in Mormon Studies
HC	*History of the Church*
JD	*Journal of Discourses*
JHC	*Journal History of the Church*
LDS	Church of Jesus Christ of Latter-day Saints
MS	*Millennial Star*
RLDS	Reorganized Church of Jesus Christ of Latter Day Saints
TPJS	*Teachings of the Prophet Joseph Smith*

Introduction: vision, plan and church

A vision, a plan and a church: these are three major elements of Mormonism. The first vision produced a prophet, the plan of salvation a blueprint of doctrine, and the Church an organization through which vision and plan are realized. This threefold basis of the religious movement founded by Joseph Smith is outlined in this introduction alongside the two notions of 'relations' and 'principles' that run throughout this book as interlinked perspectives underlying the Latter-day Saint way of life.

The Church of Jesus Christ of Latter-day Saints, the formal name of the movement popularly called Mormonism, is often abbreviated to LDS or the LDS Church, and members often simply refer to the Church. Its members can, similarly, be called Saints, Latter-day Saints, LDS, or Mormons. When using 'Mormon', this book does so as a simple description of the Church or its members and not in any derogatory sense even though I acknowledge that Saints themselves do not prefer that title. Occasionally, reference will be made to the Utah Church in order to distinguish it from the Reorganized Church of Jesus Christ of Latter Day Saints (RLDS), whose headquarters is at Independence, Missouri, and which now calls itself the Community of Christ. These name-related issues, associated with changing identities are discussed in chapter 9.

This book focuses on Mormon beliefs, doctrine and opinions in relation to the Church's sacred texts, epics and revelations. Together these primary sources offer a broad tradition of Mormon theology as the means by which Latter-day Saints have approached God and the meaning of life. Secondary streams of opinion come from a small number of books by central church leaders that have gained something of an official status (e.g. Talmage 1915), or have been accepted with appropriate amendment (e.g. McConkie, B. R. 1966), or even with caution (e.g. Roberts, B. H. 1994). Others interpret LDS thought in a more directly personal way (e.g. McMurrin 1959, 1969; White 1987). Still, Mormonism has by no means developed as formal an academic tradition of theology as is present in many other major Christian denominations. This is largely because it possesses prophetic revelations from the past and a living prophet in the present, both of which constrain the exploratory tendencies of theologians in other churches. What Mormonism has come to possess is a relatively large group of historians who are sometimes thought to substitute for theologians, but that is only partially true.

The account of Mormon belief in the following chapters is not written by a Latter-day Saint and cannot be taken as any form of 'official' doctrinal statement. Its goal is to describe beliefs and practices that many, both within and outside the Church, would regard as important in the history of the movement and in the lives of current members. This book does not argue the truth or falsity of beliefs. Sometimes it presents material from the perspective of any LDS believer convinced that revelations have all come from God, at other times it echoes the critical opinion of those who see them as the product of prophetic imagination and social circumstances. It is only by reflecting both perspectives that those inside and outside this church may gain some sense of what each other believes, and this is especially important since most readers are likely not to be Latter-day Saints. So I begin with what can be regarded today as two pillars of Mormonism – the vision and the plan. Each will be encountered by new converts: the vision offering its own direct appeal to religious experience and the plan opening doors to deeper reflection by dedicated church members.

THE VISION

The vision tells how Joseph Smith, a boy of twelve years of age, began a religious quest for certainty, forgiveness and salvation amidst the Christianly informed culture of New York State. When Joseph was reading his Bible, the Epistle of James spoke powerfully to him: 'If any of you lack wisdom, let him ask of God' (James 1: 5). Now fourteen years old, he enters some woods to pray, thereby making prayer foundational for himself as for subsequent generations of LDS seekers. Kneeling there he becomes engaged with evil; 'seized upon by some power which entirely overcame me...I could not speak...Thick darkness gathered around me...it seemed...as if I were doomed to sudden destruction' (*JHC* vol. 1, 1: 15). A pillar of light, shining like the sun, descends upon him from over his head and frees him from the oppressive darkness. He now sees two figures, identical in appearance until one identifies the other as his Beloved Son. Recovering himself before this appearance of the divine Father and Son, Joseph asks the prime question that had set him upon his quest, namely, 'which of all the sects is right, so that I might know which to join?' Forbidden to join any, he is told that all are wrong. In language taken straight from the Bible the divine figure – who is in fact the Heavenly Father – judges contemporary religious adherents as insincere believers. Exhausted after the vision, Joseph recovers, returns home and tells his mother that he now knows that 'Presbyterianism is not true.' Days later he tells a Methodist minister of his vision but is rejected and told that such visions are of the devil. Joseph ponders his relative insignificance, being economically poor and but a teenager and yet one to whom people should pay so much attention.

Then, rather like the Apostle Paul in his conversion drama, Joseph awaits further divine communication but, even so, he feels that his own form of life is not entirely consonant with that of someone to whom God has spoken so directly. Then, in a repentant state, on 21 September 1823 he receives three visionary visits from the angel Moroni, who tells Joseph that he will be a most significant person, that a book written on gold plates will be obtained and translated and that a priesthood will be revealed to him; a 'turning of hearts' of fathers and children will also take place to avoid a calamity of judgement upon the earth. Ideas of getting rich through all this religious activity also come to Joseph's mind, aware as he is of his poverty, but the angel forbids that temptation, directing him to glorify God and build up his kingdom (*HC* 1: 46). Moroni sets his message amidst Old and New Testament texts and the whole atmosphere is one of promise and fulfilment. Joseph is exhausted the following day and collapses, Moroni reappears and encourages Joseph to tell the visions to his father. This he does and is believed. He then goes to the place of the buried book and finds it, but as the time for translation is not right for a further four years, he is to come annually to meet the angel at that spot. Ultimately, he receives the metal plates and is enabled to render them into English, and the book is published in 1830, the same year as the Church is formally established.

THE PLAN

'The plan of salvation', a phrase running throughout LDS belief, provides a prime frame within which Mormon theology is best understood, because it gives relatively little priority to any single doctrine. In theological terms the plan of salvation is a kind of doctrine of doctrines. In terms of the study of religion it is the overarching myth that embraces all aspects of belief and of ritual, providing them with their ultimate reference point. While specific elements of this plan will be studied in detail in later chapters, the following brief sketch will help to introduce them.

Devised by Heavenly Father, the plan of salvation decreed that the spirit children of heavenly parents should not only exist as spirits in their pre-mortal existence, or first estate, but be given the opportunity to possess a body in which to demonstrate their obedience to God through the exercise of their personal agency on earth in their second estate. Since this would involve temptation and sin, which would alienate them from God, some means was needed to bring them back to him. A Council in heaven considered this possibility and Jesus was chosen as the saviour; Lucifer, the other candidate, rebelled, and there was a war in heaven resulting in Lucifer being cast out along with other disobedient spirits. Then came creation or, more accurately, an organization of pre-existing matter, to form the earth and all other worlds. Adam's and Eve's bodies are also formed from pre-existing material and would have lived in a state of changelessness had not they succumbed to Satan's temptation. Their fall, however, resulted in the positive advantage that they could have children to provide bodies, allowing innumerable pre-existing spirits to take flesh and exercise their own agency. Despite that, there remained as one major negative effect of the fall the plight of spiritual death: the prevention of any future life with God. It is to deal with this that Jesus Christ comes to earth as Saviour and by a divine act of grace atones for the sin of the world; he does this not only on the cross but especially in the Garden of Gethsemane, where he takes the sin of the world upon himself and bleeds at every pore. The outcome of this is the unconditional benefit of resurrection. This gospel message must be heard and accepted and result in baptism and confirmation at the hands of Melchizedek-priesthood holders of the Church. Individual Latter-day Saints now become deeply responsible for their own eternal future and for that of their family and, in this, they should seek the assistance of the Holy Ghost. The unconditional salvation from spiritual death is now replaced by the conditional possibility of exaltation in the celestial kingdom, which is one of three major degrees of glory experienced after death. This should be sought through marriage, parenthood, temple ritual for oneself and for one's own dead relatives and through ethical living. Through specific rites performed in temples married Saints are provided with the means of conquering death and pursuing an eternal existence in which they, themselves become gods.

THE CHURCH OF SALVATION

This composite version of the plan of salvation is not presented in exactly the same way as it might be told by Mormon missionaries. The addition of the terms Melchizedek-priesthood holders, celestial kingdom and degrees of glory make it more obvious that it is a scheme of belief rooted in a particular church, one reckoning itself to be the one true church through which the highest form of salvation – exaltation – is possible. This makes it clear that theology and church belong together and shape each other. Belief affects ritual and ritual affects belief, so this book will pay particular attention to historical events and distinctive individuals who have caused an interplay between the two. Although the following chapters accentuate the more formal elements of Mormon thought, they will avoid the temptation of presenting an overly systematic version of doctrines. This is important in a relatively young church whose doctrine is still in a process of development and change, but it is also important in terms of the way in which individuals live their religious lives. Some early ideas have faded into insignificance in today's church, even though occasional opponents of Mormonism still rehearse them with vigour; others may be in the process of re-establishing themselves in contemporary LDS spirituality.

Contemporary LDS theology combines its original Protestant-like doctrines of atonement, grace, resurrection, repentance, faith, baptism and salvation with its subsequent, distinctive, scheme of priesthood ordination, endowments, merit, baptism for the dead and exaltation. This dual configuration is also evident in the double format of the local-chapel and regional-temple form of church organization. At the outset Mormonism offered salvation from sin and a call to prepare for the Second Coming of Christ; in its transformation it conferred powers for humans to conquer death and become gods in the world to come; today both features are combined through basic missionary work and the subsequent desire to transform converts into temple-active members. Historically speaking, Mormonism promised salvation before it offered exaltation: today both are possible. To its opening rituals of baptism, confirmation and Sacrament Meeting its metamorphosed state added baptism for the dead, marriage for eternity and endowment rites. Initially the Saints congregated in homes, halls, public places and meeting houses familiar to all Protestants, where sermons were preached, prayers offered and hymns sung; later they added temples for their distinctive rites and for fuller expression of developing doctrine. So it is that contemporary Latter-day Saints now gather weekly at their meeting-houses for congregational purposes and periodically at temples for the work of exaltation of their family group. Mormon religious architecture – with its sharp distinction between numerous local chapels and a regional temple – marks this theological difference between 'salvation' and 'exaltation'. No such distinctions exist in other major Christian traditions: Catholic, Anglican or Lutheran parish churches and cathedrals, for example, are not different in kind from each other and do not reflect any difference in theology or ritual; only by being alert to these differences will clarity be gained between traditional Christian doctrinal schemes and those of the Church of Jesus Christ of Latter-day Saints. The historical development of LDS doctrine and forms of ritual can, in one sense, be thought of almost as two different styles of religiosity, practically two different churches, existing in a developing and mutual relationship with each other but involving tensions, conflicts and discrepancies as well as coherence and advantage. Accordingly, LDS theology involves what might be viewed as the theologies of two churches: Protestant millenarian Mormonism and symbolic temple Mormonism. Born out of a Protestant concern with forgiveness and God's true word, Mormonism developed into a moral quest for perfection under the influence of a ritualized conquest of death. Jan Shipps has also described a development in LDS belief but preferred to view it in terms of 'three distinct layers': an initial focus on the Book of Mormon and restoration of the priesthoods, a secondary gathering together through a growing sense of self-identity as a kind of latter-day 'Hebrew' people and, finally, a more esoteric church associated with a 'powerful group mystical experience' (Shipps 2000: 296). Despite this the present study will be conducted rather in terms of different elements of Mormonism which exert themselves at different times and places.

RELATIONS AND PRINCIPLES

Earliest Mormonism developed through a strong sense of relationships: some were amongst divine agents, some between divine and human agents, and others between human beings, and they strongly reflected many aspects of the theological world underlying the Book of Mormon. As the Mormon movement grew, it soon developed a philosophical outlook grounded in 'principles' – rules that controlled and governed the universe. One way of interpreting the life and thought of the Church of Jesus Christ of Latter-day Saints is in terms of the way 'relations and principles' affect each other at different times and in terms of differing circumstances.

In tracing these trends and evaluating the interpretation given of Mormon thought in this book, it is important for the reader to know that the author is not and never has been a member of the Church of Jesus Christ of Latter-day Saints or any other restoration movement. This book is written, very largely, for those who are not Latter-day Saints but who want some understanding of their way of thought. Even so, it is hoped that active Latter-day Saints might also engage with the interpretation of Mormon theology offered here, albeit by one who is not a fellow Saint but who seeks to understand the nature of this world of faith that means so much to those who live by it.

CHAPTER I

The birth and growth of Mormonism

The Mormon Church was officially founded by six individuals in 1830; by 2002 there were approximately 11 million members. When the first prophet, Joseph Smith Jnr, died in 1844, he had gathered some 26,000 followers and these had grown to some 115,000 when his successor, Brigham Young, died in 1877. The middle and later decades of the nineteenth century witnessed a large part of this growth through migration of converts from Great Britain and Scandinavia. Such emigration largely ceased with the beginning of the twentieth century and growth was relatively slow to 500,000 members by 1919. The Church had increased to 2 million members by 1963; this doubled to 4 million by 1979 and to 8 million by 1991. The quickening growth in the closing decades of the twentieth century was due to rapid expansion in South America, which helped to produce the 11 million or so in the opening years of the twenty-first century. These patterns of growth reflect the changing nature of this church, the early years being a time of 'calling to Zion', gathering converts in America to prepare for Christ's Second Coming. Then followed a steady state when the Saints became consolidated in their North American heartland, especially in Utah. After defending themselves from opposition by the Federal Government on the issue of polygamy, they finally capitulated, officially abandoning the practice in 1890 whilst continuing to emphasize the importance of family life. From the middle of the twentieth century renewed missionary endeavours established the Church across the world, leading some to predict that new levels of growth will make Mormonism the next new world religion after Islam.

One major task of any formal study of a religious tradition is to describe its changing pattern of doctrine and ritual, identifying its dominant features and marking any significant changes in direction that are brought about by events and circumstance. In doing this I will give due attention to both historical and contemporary aspects of the faith while presenting information in a way that compares and contrasts it with elements in Protestant and Catholic traditions of Christianity. When using this method of comparative theology, I will deal with topics, whether Mormon, Protestant or Catholic, in a way that assumes each to be true, as would theologians within those traditions. This, obviously, means that I will not follow those who might regard Mormonism as some strange and false American cult, where the very word 'cult', and to a lesser degree, the word 'sect', indicates disapproval: even Joseph Smith used 'sect' to describe the numerous religious denominations of his day (*HC* 1: 18). Certainly, that kind of evaluation finds no place in this book.

Comparison of patterns of theology invites the question of what excites religious believers to give their lives to a church and its teachings in the first place. Why are religious ideas important? Is the excitement of the first generation the same as the excitement in later centuries? Would first-century Christians, for example, have been in the least interested in some current Christian debates about the ordination of women or the celibacy of the priesthood? Are many twenty-first-century Christians worried about what food to eat or whether or not boys should be circumcised, as were the Christians in the Acts of the Apostles? To study these things is to enter into the enthusiasm of others and to seek to understand a whole world of meaning in which people come to live and have their being. It is also to appreciate that different teachings have been influential at different periods of a church's life, and this is certainly true for the Latter-day Saints.

BELIEF AND RITUAL: DOCTRINE AND COVENANTS

The Church of Jesus Christ of Latter-day Saints came into being 'for the purpose of building up my church and kingdom on the earth, and to prepare my people for the time when I shall dwell with them, which is nigh at hand' (D&C 104: 59). This text from the Doctrine and Covenants (D&C) indicates the millenarian nature of early Mormonism and exemplifies the way in which Joseph Smith, as prophet, gave expression to the voice of Jesus Christ. The very title of this source text, the Doctrine and Covenants, is of crucial significance in understanding Mormon theology because it integrates two aspects of religion. On the one hand, it deals with doctrine, the articulated and shaped beliefs of religious devotees, and, on the other, with covenants, the enacted forms of religious commitment. In an overly simplified sense we might say that doctrines deal with belief and covenants with practice. Certainly, as far as Latter-day Saints are concerned, doctrine is an important part of individual religious life just as it is of the historical development of the Church of Jesus Christ of Latter-day Saints, but it would remain abstract and uninfluential apart from the Church's ritual, through which believers commit themselves to that doctrine by entering into forms of covenant relationships with God. Covenant is not a neutral term in LDS theology. It is dynamically enlivened through personal ritual experience framed by Mormon history and the architectural arena of Mormon temples. More immediately still, covenants have their consequences within the family, which is itself the springboard for eternity and destiny's fulfilment.

EXCITEMENT

Excitement is one answer to the question of why people give their lives to religion. It is one of the more neglected aspects of religious experience. Excitement stirs group worship in waves of passion, brings teenagers the force of unique identity, sustains the middle aged during years of responsible duty, and to the aged brings memory and hope. Just as falling in love can, for a time, foster an intense sense of being alive, so can the awareness of being in contact with God. Richard van Wagoner cites Joseph Smith's sermon of 14 May 1843 when the prophet tells how 'Excitement has almost become the essence of my life. When that dies away, I feel almost lost.' Wagoner links this with 'the frenzied tempo' of Smith's life in 1843 and with the fact that Smith was 'sealed to at least nine Nauvoo women' in that year (van Wagoner 1994: 299). Such prophetic excitement helps to fuel the charisma which attracts followers; it promises drama in the personal life of believers, as, for example, in the case of Sidney Rigdon, Joseph's early assistant, who came from a Baptist background with an 'exciting sense of discovery, the thought that an ancient treasure of divine truth was just now being brought to light after having been lost for centuries' (van Wagoner 1994: 44). Many converts to today's religious movements are similarly moved by the sense of excitement of being where the divine action is, of being with people who possess an explicit purpose that gives firm shape to their lives. Often this contrasts with the relatively humdrum life of families whose sense of purpose in life is implicit and can relatively easily fall apart if placed under pressure or close scrutiny.

For the early generation of Latter-day Saints the expectation that the end of the world was near fired just such an excitement of faith, motivating arduous migration to the United States from Europe and equally perilous trekking to designated US destinations. Despite no predicted date of the return of Christ, there was a firm expectation, held out by Joseph Smith and after him by Brigham Young and others, that the end would be within the first generation of believers, as told in many patriarchal blessings – special utterances made when a patriarch lays hands on a Saint's head and speaks under the influence of the Holy Spirit (van Wagoner 1994: 151–5). For contemporary Mormons too, excitement still comes through temple ritual for themselves, for their dead and when serving two years of missionary work away from home. Missions, in particular, provide opportunity lacking in the religious life of many other churches: for nineteen-year-olds it adds fuel to the fire of faith. Still, Joseph Smith's own young life was not all excitement. Bushman talks of Joseph Smith's family being like many others whose 'contemporary religious situation presented a picture of dead fallen timber in a landscape dreary, silent and devoid of life'; here was a religious disillusionment and no 'American optimism and romantic nationalism' (Bushman 1984: 139).

RELIGIOUS AND CULTURAL BACKGROUND

Joseph's boyhood was set in a mixed world where tedium engaged with dynamic 'mystic excitement', a phrase that intentionally blurs the distinction many make between formal religion and superstition. Many accounts of Mormon origins stress, for example, the revivalistic religion of New York State that had led to its popular description as the 'burned-over district', a name reflecting the 'fire' of the Holy Spirit that had swept through it in a series of religious revivals (O'Dea 1957: 11, 20). This powerful backdrop sets off Joseph's own account of his early teenage life and his sense of confusion about which church was the true one. Other accounts single out various activities that are described in terms of popular magic and are associated with seeking out buried treasure through the use of crystal-gazing and the like. While drawing sharp lines between these activities is useful for analytical academic ends, it can all too easily imply a false division in people's lives, thoughts and actions. 'Mystic excitement' retains something of the integration of diverse factors in life. In the more traditional history of Roman Catholic spirituality, for example, much attention has been paid to the delicate balance between official Catholic teaching and revelations reported by mystics. It is no easy task for religious traditions to foster intense individual pursuit of God and at the same time to moderate the excess that such personal zeal can readily generate. Even acknowledged saints in the Catholic Church can produce revelations that are not fulfilled, as did, for example, St Norbert, who founded the Premonstratensian Order in the twelfth century. He was thought to have been very sure, because of revelation, that Antichrist would come in his generation, but this did not impress St Bernard, nor did it come to pass (Poulain 1921: 326).

At the beginning of the twenty-first century there is in many modern western societies a degree of renewed interest both in conservative aspects of established religions and in a whole series of religious innovations that are often described as new-age movements. Indeed, if one compares the revivalist aspect of modern charismatic groups and the crystal-gazing of modern pagans with parallel activities at the commencement of the nineteenth century in the United States, a degree of similarity can be found. The use of crystals has, after all, been one of the most widespread of human activities in relation to mysteries (Besterman 1924). To see Christian revivalism as quite different from crystal-gazing says more about the scholar than about a population with an interest in what can, broadly, be called 'spiritual' aspects of life. Indeed, by the early twenty-first century the very words 'spiritual' and 'spirituality' had come into wide popular use and have practically stolen the concept from its ecclesiastical home.

So it was that in Joseph Smith's world individuals lived amidst ideas, beliefs and practices that merged with each other in terms of mystical forces. While there is no established way of talking about the links between social events and personal psychological experiences, we can nevertheless appreciate how social change prompts psychological change. In high-risk contexts individuals often employ activities that are not empirically verifiable in the hope that they may affect the outcome of events, such as when athletes practise mini-rituals before a game, wear a particular article of clothing, or dress in a particular order to gain luck. To have 'good luck' is the 'dynamic-mystical' way of saying that they wish for success and to achieve a desired goal. Much the same happens when people set out on hazardous journeys or engage in new activities; they try to set some kind of success-frame around their life. And something similar seemed to be happening in Joseph Smith's day, when religious beliefs relating to salvation existed alongside popular practices of seeking good luck and fortune. In the terms of the early anthropologist of religion, Bronislaw Malinowski, these rites were various examples of an attempt at ritualizing human optimism (Malinowski 1974: 90).

Two streams of thought that helped to swell the Mormon current were Adventism and popular magic. Adventism proclaimed that Christ would soon return to the earth, dramatically and powerfully, to establish divine rule, beginning with the millennium – a thousand-year period of special events. Popular magic, by contrast, included the search for buried treasure and employed crystals or seer-stones as search-aids. While relatively easy to describe in historical terms, these topics can become problematic because, as is understandable, many ordinary Mormons today do not associate the origin of their religion with either Adventism or magic and 'popular superstition'. While it is wise to be alert to these sensitivities, it is also important to try to interpret people's activities in the context of their own day and not only in terms of our own. This has been done in Christian theology for some time, as when, for example, scholars interpret the role of Jesus as a wonder-worker or as an exorcist in the culture of his own day. With that in mind I first consider Adventist millenarianism and then popular magic, always recalling the dynamic-mystical frame that enlivened each of them.

ADVENTISM AND MILLENARIANISM

Christian millenarianism, the belief in a thousand-year reign of Christ associated with the final chapters of God's dealing with humanity, is basic to early Mormonism. The 'tradition' of millenarianism – if it is not too paradoxical to speak of a 'tradition' when referring to repeated announcements concerning what is supposed to be a final event – has its roots in Judaism, especially within the prophetic-apocalyptic streams of spirituality represented, for example, in the Book of Daniel, Second Esdras and various writings associated with the figure of Enoch. Earliest Christianity was itself a prophetic movement, believing that the end of this world would come in and through the activity of Jesus as the specially appointed and anointed one, the Christ of God. This strand of religious faith is represented in some New Testament writings, especially the Book of Revelation and, for example, in the two Letters to the Thessalonians. It was echoed by the Montanists in the second century, Anabaptists in the sixteenth and numerous Protestant Independent groups from the seventeenth to the early nineteenth centuries, most especially the Adventists. The very fact that the Bible contains these apparently strange books has always provided the opportunity for believers in search of new truth to find it by interpreting these texts in relation to their own day and age. The Bible provides one example of what I have described elsewhere as a 'pool of potential orientations' to the world, a reservoir of ideas always available for development and elaboration as occasion and needs demand (Davies 2000: 247). William Miller (1782–1849) was amongst the most renowned of Adventists and established his own denomination in New York State in 1831, only a year after the LDS Church was founded. By then, ideas of a Second Coming of Christ, which

Miller dated to 1843–44, were already widespread. Adventism involves an excitement with time: it makes the present a time of hope and challenge, bringing an intense sense of meaning to passing moments and events. It focuses and engenders religious excitement by highlighting the theological ideas of resurrection and judgement and an imminent transformation of the world into a new divine realm.

Adventism speaks of the activity of God and of human activity in response to it and in preparation for it. Adventism is activist religion and Mormonism was Adventist from its outset. It is, however, more usual to speak of Mormonism as millenarian in order to focus on the millennial reign of Christ for, in LDS terms, the core faithful are to be resurrected at the outset of the millennium and will live somewhere apart from the earth, but with the capacity to visit it. The faithful who live and die on earth during this millennium will be instantly resurrected to join their fellows elsewhere. Others who die will have to await the 'second resurrection' that will take place at the end of this thousand-year period. During that thousand years the earth will 'rest' (Moses 7: 64), but still be inhabited, not least by sinners still in need of the true message of salvation. This will be brought to them because the millennium will be a period of intensified missionary activity. In LDS terms it will also be a time of extensive temple work on behalf of the dead. At the close of the millennial age the three heavenly kingdoms – to be described later – will be fully furnished with their appropriately deserving inhabitants. Then will emerge the place and state of perdition, the closest LDS concept to that of hell in other denominations. This state of being finally separated from the influence and effect of God in any form will be dreadful; indeed, there is some LDS speculation whether the resurrected unity of spirit and body will be able to survive for ever when the body is not itself 'glorified'. Some people hint at a kind of regression of that unified entity into its constituent parts with 'spirit' returning to its 'native element' (see Turner, R. 1992: 1391–2). Such a reversal would, of course, involve depersonalization in the LDS scheme of thought. Grant Underwood has described Mormonism's millenarian and premillennialist nature, regarding these as practically synonymous terms in a form of salvation that was largely 'collective, terrestrial, total, imminent and miraculous' (Underwood 1993: 5–6).

POPULAR MAGIC

From a less 'total' perspective there were others in Joseph Smith's day who approached life's problems and desires not in terms of a divinely caused cataclysm but in more humanly practical terms. This outlook of practical magic rather than cosmic magic is small-scale and not universal in scope. A great deal has been made of the belief that Joseph and his family employed popular magic to find buried treasure and, in particular, used special 'seer' stones or crystals through which they could identify the location of hidden things. Some set these activities against the background of European alchemy and its Hermetic traditions, rooted in Gnostic views of the second and third Christian centuries that sought a ritual transformation of the human into the divine. The Renaissance, between the fourteenth and sixteenth centuries, marked a revitalization of human interest in human affairs and sparked renewed interest in these ancient mystical ideas, linking them with human creativity and, later, with attempts at science-like projects in alchemy. One idea was that base metals could be transformed into gold and, as a kind of analogy, human beings could be transformed into gods. The identification of humanity and deity outside and beyond the formal Christian doctrine of the incarnation was a feature of this Hermetic tradition. By the time of the Reformation, following on the tail of the Renaissance and itself being a kind of theological renaissance, this sort of idea and the texts that gave rise to it were increasingly rendered unorthodox and passed out of intellectual favour. The subsequent rise of empirical science in chemistry and physics as part of the Enlightenment of the seventeenth and eighteenth centuries further marginalized Hermetic alchemy, even though individuals such as Isaac Newton could still employ some of its thoughts. One strand of this thinking passed into the Rosicrucian movement of the early seventeenth century, which was itself related to the emergent Freemasonry of the eighteenth century – originating in Europe and passing rapidly into the United States, it was present in Joseph Smith's cultural background. This has been argued in some detail by John L. Brooke in his study *The Refiner's Fire* (1994).

Whatever may have been the precise content of ideas surrounding Joseph Smith's youth, it is wise to heed Bushman's judgement that 'the power of Enlightenment scepticism' had little influence on Joseph Smith, whose world was not 'created by Enlightenment rationalism with its deadly aversion to superstition', indeed 'rationalism had not penetrated Smith family culture very deeply' (Bushman 1984: 184). Bushman notes how Smith prized 'the seerstone' and 'Urim and Thummim' and never repudiated them, not even when accused of seeking buried treasure through such means. Mention of the seer-stone in the same breath as the Urim and Thummim is helpful in illustrating just how Joseph was able to link aspects of ancient biblical texts with life in his own day.

TRUTH

This act of association was a hallmark of Smith as a prophet of the Restoration and as one who believed in revelation as a medium of truth, for, whatever else Mormonism was at its inception, it was a search for truth. But 'truth' is no easy concept. While philosophical issues of truth have their place in Mormonism, so does the part played by personal experience in the individual's knowledge of God. Greater still is the sense of authority that frames teaching. In practice these domains merge as an individual gains a personal sense of the truthfulness of doctrine within the context of the Church. It was, in particular, the personal sense of confusion about which church amongst so many was the true church that set the young Joseph Smith upon his religious quest that resulted in his heading a new religious movement in 1830. Its truth was to be grounded in the revelation that he believed came to him from God, validating him as a prophet and his Church as the one true Church.

RESTORATION AND RELATIONS

For Joseph this church was no innovation, nor a later version of other denominations: it was a restoration of doctrines and practices that were, in effect, ages old. Richard Bushman uses the phrase 'reunion with the deep past' when approaching the particular direction that Mormonism took as a restoration movement rather than as a Protestant biblicist movement keen only to affirm a particular set of familiar doctrines and to elicit a renewed commitment to them (Bushman 1984: 185). This powerful phrase indicates that at its outset Mormonism was not fundamentalist in nature – not seeking to 'retrieve fundamentals' – but was a more creative and innovative endeavour, grounded in persons and personalities rather than in sharply focused doctrine (Marty and Appleby 1993: 3). This person-focused or relational aspect needs emphasis because it is easily overlooked in sociological studies and often entirely ignored in theological analyses, as we will see in chapters 2 and 3.

Joseph Smith's teenage question as to which church was the true church was itself answered relationally. The persons underlying these relationships were both divine and human; they visited Joseph in visions and as characters making a literary appearance throughout the Book of Mormon and numerous parts of the Doctrine and Covenants. As named individuals from both the mythical-historical past and from Joseph's own day they play leading roles in the divine plan of salvation. This is not to say that doctrine and more formal ideas were not important to Mormonism – they were and are – but it is to note how doctrine was often presented through persons and their actions. Joseph was set within an intense network of relationships both with human beings and with the divine personages who he believed had called him to his task. His successors in the prophetic office also maintained this network of interpersonal relations, albeit more focused on the human rather than the divine agents, and, with the growth of the Church, developed it through the hierarchy of leaders. This is one reason why Mormon texts read more like biblical narratives of person-engaged events than any formal theological treatise rooted in abstract logic. Similarly, a great deal of contemporary Mormon literature, whether pondering doctrine or the management style of church leaders, includes stories, accounts and reports of people and their relationships with others (e.g. Toscano 1994; Mangum and Yorgason 1996). This relational element of Mormonism is particularly deep seated and helps to constitute one of its practical foundations.

MASONRY

One highly significant 'reunion with the deep past' that would practically transform the Latter-day Movement was Freemasonry. Today, in the twenty-first century, Freemasonry involves a relatively closed group of men with social and ethical interests, which are pursued in convivial company, and a bond of mutual commitment. Some of them also engage in the pursuit of knowledge to foster their way of life and destiny, and frame their endeavour within special rituals performed in a temple that is generally open only to the initiated. While interpretations of the origin of Masonry vary, it is safe to say that in the seventeenth century some intellectuals became interested in aspects of the guilds associated with practising stonemasons of the medieval period, the very people who built the great cathedrals and churches of Europe. The newcomers developed what has been called speculative Masonry, which furnished a kind of focus for scientific and philosophical reflections upon the nature of the world and of human destiny. Elementary science combined with interests in mystical aspects of human life and religion that sometimes ran at cross-currents to mainstream religion. Numerous beliefs jostled with each other in this world of creativity and excitement over knowledge. 'The deep past' erupted into the present through Masonic life; the cabalistic mystical beliefs of Jewish rabbis were fostered and myths thought to be derived from biblical accounts of the building of Solomon's temple came to the fore amongst individuals with independent means that enabled them to hold opinions separate from official Christendom. Such ideas passed freely between England and western Europe on the one side and the East Coast of the United States on the other. They provide modern historians with a rich source of potential influences upon people, even though it is sometimes hard to be sure just how influential they might have been, particularly on early Mormons. The issue of the relationship between Masonry and Mormonism is very long-standing and, for present purposes, it is best simply to identify the two major explanations of this resemblance.

Masonry was increasingly popular in parts of the United States by the 1790s, not least where Joseph Smith's family had lived (Brooke 1994: 97). A Masonic lodge was established in the essentially LDS town of Nauvoo in March 1842; Joseph Smith and about three hundred Saints became Masons in its first year of operation. Just weeks after his initiation into Masonry Joseph Smith introduced 'temple ordinances' into church life, rites that are discussed in chapter 8. The significant point is that there is considerable similarity between the Masonic and Mormon rites and, accordingly, critics interpret the LDS rites as derived from Masonry; the LDS response, which acknowledges similarity, argues that Masonic rites had been given to the world in very ancient times, perhaps even to Adam, and had become corrupted over the years whereas the LDS rites came as part of the restoration of truth to the world through Joseph Smith (Buerger 1994: 40). Because this LDS interpretation grounds itself in the primary Mormon concept of restoration, it is able not only to explain the similarity between Mormon and Masonic rites but also to affirm the superior authenticity of the Mormon rites. The period of LDS and Masonic alliance was, however, relatively short-lived, for when a new Masonic Hall was opened in April 1844, just months before the prophet was killed, it functioned for only about a year; activity then decreased and the Saints migrated from Nauvoo in 1846. It is thought that about 1,500 Saints had become Masons in this period in Illinois (Godfrey 1992: 527–9).

This positive acceptance of Masonry is quite different from the picture painted in the Book of Mormon of some secret groups who were accused of being Masons because of their oaths and vows, such as, for example, those described as the Gadianton robbers. Their leader Giddianhi, writing to a Nephite leader, described his 'society and the works thereof' as 'good' and 'of ancient date and they have been handed down to us' (3 Nephi 3: 9). When these Gadianton robbers finally came to do battle against the Nephites, they came wearing a 'lamb-skin about their loins', which could be taken as a reference to the Freemasons' aprons (3 Nephi 4: 7). Still, Gadiantons remained firm enemies of the Nephites, which would, symbolically, reflect hostility between Masons and Mormons rather than their unity. If there is any truth in this interpretation, then a marked difference exists between the Book of Mormon and the later sections of Doctrine and Covenants concerning the status and identity of Freemasonry within Mormonism's ritual world. Bushman is sceptical about too close an identification of Gadianton groups with Masons, observing that 'people who knew anti-Masonry and the Book of Mormon in the 1830s made less of the connection than critics today' (Bushman 1984: 131). Still, it is worth drawing attention to parts of the Book of Moses set within the Pearl of Great Price and internally dated as a translation of part of the Book of Genesis made by Joseph Smith between June and October 1830, after the publication of the Book of Mormon. This refers to one Lamech, who enters into some kind of wicked covenant with Satan and becomes 'Master Mahon', which is not far removed from the technical term Master Mason in general Freemasonic parlance. This covenant involved taking an oath on pain of death and conferred a secret knowledge of the members of a brotherhood, a group that is viewed negatively and as an abomination by those who trust in God (Moses 5: 49–52).

Generally speaking, Masonry involved an intellectual quest combined with fellowship of Masons. Given the particular context and differing personnel, the weighting placed on each could vary a great deal. Doubtless this was as true in Joseph's day as it is today when some Masons gain most from the sense of corporate membership and some from the intellectual satisfaction that comes from combining speculation about life with ritual events related to its mysteries. One feature of Masonic engagement that may have been significant for Mormonism when it took its distinctive turn into ritualized activity lies in the visual domain. Whilst all human activities involve the visual sense, it becomes particularly important in Masonry when, for example, the initiate for the first degree is brought blindfolded into the lodge as one in darkness seeking the light of truth and, at another point, is made to lie upon a symbolic grave while the lodge is in darkness except for a single light thrown upon both a sacred book and the Master of the lodge, seated towards the feet of the candidate. In another rite illustrations in the form of wall hangings or pictures illustrate the mythical history of the temple at Jerusalem and the origin of Masonic secrets in a protective guild. To this day an instructor may use a pointer to indicate the personnel and events represented in illustrations that are quite naturalistic for some of the narrative and are entirely symbolic for others. Each Masonic lodge is replete with overt symbolism of the status and function of each office holder as well as illustrations of the heavenly formations of stars and the like. So it is that the initiate in the lodge sees things he will never have seen before, just as he will use words and names that he has never heard before. The lodge is a place of mysterious novelty. Visual and auditory stimuli alongside special clothing have their place in a new fellowship with others who have committed themselves to a search for wisdom and ethical living through vows and promises that are not to be divulged to outsiders.

Whatever brought Joseph Smith to Masonry, including the facts that several of his key associates were already in the brotherhood, and that it promised a community affording a degree of security against enemies, it is hardly possible that he could have been left unimpressed by the experience. Joseph Smith was a highly intelligent and creative man whose mind was able to make connections between many ideas and practices and, whether one speaks in terms of creativity or of revelation, his encounter with Masonry was very soon followed by the new ritual direction he brought to the Church. While this is important for endowment ceremonies, which will be described in chapter 8, it should be noted, along with Buerger, that 'nowhere did Smith leave a direct statement of how the endowment ceremony came to be' (1994: 40). When, in 1853, Brigham Young described endowments as conferring the knowledge allowing priesthood holders to 'walk back to the presence of the Father, passing the angels who stand as sentinels' and as giving them appropriate words and signs, his account would have been familiar to Freemasons, whose gatherings and initiations also involve giving words and signs to various guardians of access. There is a form of 'literalism' involved in some accounts of endowments which may derive its power more from these actual experiences, whether in Masonic lodges or Mormon temples, than from any written text. This confers upon Mormonism a pragmatic and ritually based dimension of experience that is additional to any insight gained simply from reading texts.

POPULAR INTELLECTUALISM

It is easy for critics to overplay the secretive ritualism of Masonry and to use it against Mormonism, just as it is with divination and treasure digging. Much more germane to an understanding of early Mormon devotees is to grasp the eclectic nature of their life-quest. Many of these partially educated or uneducated men and women sought to learn to read and write and, along with some educated people, kept journals of their lives and had a strong open-minded attitude to knowledge of many kinds. This can easily be forgotten when contemporary opponents of Mormonism interpret the movement in terms of the popular idea of a fundamentalist cult. The idea of fundamentalism, which did not emerge in any formal sense until the early twentieth century, is often anachronistically read back in time and applied to groups that it ill fits. This is not to say that there have not been religious groups – including LDS groups, as I show in chapter 9 – that have responded to their own religious and social worlds in ways that we would now regard as fundamentalist; it is to say that early Mormonism was not that kind of movement. Bushman makes this point, albeit indirectly, when he argues that 'the Book of Mormon did not become a handbook for doctrine' for, instead of the Saints seeking 'to pore over the record to extract policy and teachings' they found that it came day by day through revelations to the prophet (Bushman 1984: 142). Though they believed their restored gospel to be rooted in the past, its power lay in its promise for the future. Bushman is right in identifying Joseph Smith as one who stood on the line dividing 'the yearning for the supernatural from the humanism of rational Christianity', a boundary that, like many others, is fraught with danger (Bushman 1984: 79). In Joseph's thought, these domains can be represented, on the one hand, by his magical use of seer-stones and his capacity for prophecy and, on the other, by his attraction towards underlying principles or laws governing the universe and its religion.

EGYPTIAN AND HEBREW

One example that, in a sense, combined the mystical and the rational lay in Joseph's developing interest both in Hebrew and in Egyptian hieroglyphics. Hebrew came on the LDS agenda within the programme of the School of the Prophets in the period 1833–36 and it appears that Joseph was introduced to the language in 1835 (Widmer 2000: 80). This same year his interest in ancient Egypt, originally prompted by biblical narratives and taken up in the Book of Mormon (e.g. Mosiah 1: 4), was fostered by one Michael Chandler who toured with an exhibition of mummies and papyri (Widmer 2000: 70). This was, of course, at a time prior to any popular understanding of Egyptian hieroglyphics and their translation (Brodie 1995: 170). Joseph's engagement with the mummies and papyri from Chandler underlay the Book of Abraham which, as I discuss in chapter 3, is now published as LDS scripture and described as a translation of some 'ancient records...from the catacombs of Egypt'. The combination of Joseph's initial familiarity with Hebrew and his engagement in an attempt at translating Egyptian hieroglyphics was, in some way, associated with his growing conviction in a belief in the plurality of gods. This gave the Book of Abraham quite a

different theological meaning from the Book of Mormon, published prior
to Joseph's engagement with his new orientalism. It was not only Joseph
who had become impressed by the intriguing objects of antiquity: Wilford
Woodruff, for example, records a visit to the Kirtland Temple in November
1836 in whose upper rooms he 'viewed four Egyptian Mummies and also the
Book of Abram Written by his own hand', all objects that made 'a lasting
impression upon the mind which is not to be erased' (Woodruff 1993:
8). When considering the development of Mormon theology in terms of
pragmatic history, the sheer influence of 'events' cannot be ignored, not
least the event of Chandler's bringing 'Egypt' to Joseph.

PRINCIPLES

Joseph's engagement with new experiences typified Mormonism from approximately the 1830s to the 1890s: it was often open-minded and ready
to accept new ideas and to develop them into concepts or principles, as
witnessed by the change in Joseph's revelations on the nature of deity.
At a practical level, for example, some key Saints enjoyed debate, as was
demonstrated by the establishment of The Deseret Theological Society, in-
augurated by Brigham Young in April 1855 (Woodruff 1993: 165). (Deseret
was the term used by the Saints to designate their new territory.) Mark
Leone interpreted early Mormon speculation as a world-view that, in its
own way, preceded the intellectual developments of social and historical
science. 'Joseph Smith and his peers', says Leone, 'glimpsed the createdness
of truth, its capacity to change, and its ultimate locus in the individual, not
the church or class of specialists' (1979: 221).

  This period of open-ended and speculative curiosity continued until the
late decades of the nineteenth century when Federal opposition to plural
marriage not only curtailed Mormonism's experiment in kinship arrangements but also had the effect of making the Church more defensive by
adopting a wider range of American ways. Throughout the twentieth century, however, especially from the 1930s, the Church adopted a version
of attack as its mode of defence. Armand Mauss has pursued this renewed
activism through a whole series of forms of retrenchment including continuous revelation through the prophet, the work of temples and genealogical
research, an expanded missionary programme, the strengthening of families and an extensive educational movement focused on learning doctrine
(Mauss 1994: 85).

  Most of these exemplify one enduring aspect of the early decades of the
Church's speculative life, namely its commitment to the idea of 'principles',

the fundamental laws that underlie the universe. 'Principles' came to be of essential significance to LDS theology and, in some respects, to play as important a role as the notion of deity itself. It could even be argued that they played a more important role. It was by gaining access to these principles that Mormonism saw itself as a restoration of truth and, from an analytical standpoint, this involved a different process from any simple 'retrieval of fundamentals', which is sometimes used when defining 'fundamentalist' groups. Mormonism both did and did not wish to go back to some golden age of the faith and to restore its ritual and practice. It wished to go back because it believed that by doing so it could avoid the contamination of the truth that Christian history had brought to the purity of the time of Christ but, equally, it did not wish only to 'retrieve fundamentals', because it believed that God still had much to reveal in the present and in the future. This was why Mormonism was no 'back to the Bible' movement but saw new truth coming to life in the Book of Mormon and in the growing material of the Doctrine and Covenants.

The formal 'principles' fostered by early Mormonism were unlike biblical or other textual ideas that describe the uncreated aspects of the universe, for they constituted the very matrix of causality upon which all life operated. Principles also furnish a background rationale against which doctrinal discussion and teaching function. Although I will explore the basic LDS notion of agency in chapter 3, it is worth offering as an example here McConkie's treatment of that topic in his influential, though at times controversially conservative, *Mormon Doctrine*, in which the first two sentences of a relatively long account read thus: 'Agency is the ability and freedom to choose good or evil. It is an eternal principle which has existed with God from all eternity' (McConkie, B. R. 1979: 26). He continues: 'four great principles must be in force if there is to be agency'; indeed, he formulates his entire argument in terms of 'principles'. Similarly, when discussing 'doctrine' he speaks of 'Gospel doctrine' as including 'the principles and precepts, and revealed philosophies of pure religion' (McConkie, B. R. 1979: 204). Principle and 'law' come to be almost synonymous when accounting for the foundational basis of thought. 'Principle' and 'law', in this sense, comprise a category of LDS thought: they are ideas necessary for thinking about everything else and are themselves non-reducible to other ideas. I will offer another example, concerning 'justification', in chapter 9, while in chapter 3 the issue recurs in relation to the LDS notion of heaven, highlighting the idea of 'principles' as the basis for grading heavenly domains.

'Principles' thus furnish both the hallmark of LDS philosophical theology and its distinctiveness from the wider Christian tradition. Eternity is governed by such principles, and those principles have a certain imperson-ality: they resemble scientific laws more than the outcome of any one divine intention. The gods themselves, including Heavenly Father, have had to learn these principles, so that divine wisdom consists in precisely such an ever-growing knowledge. Although it is too easy to press this description to a logical conclusion, one might differentiate between the traditional Christian scheme, in which God creates absolutely everything, including the laws of the cosmos, and the LDS perspective in which those laws have always existed and were even prior to the divine personages with whom current human beings 'have to do'.

'Laws', in the LDS view, can also refer to ultimate principles and are not simply, as many traditional Christians might expect, the divine laws of the Ten Commandments and other 'laws' of the biblical books. So, when Brigham Young asserts, 'The gospel is a set of laws and ordinances', he goes on to speak of the 'principles of the gospel', acknowledging that not all people understand them, nor do the Twelve Apostles 'understand them all' (1992: 139, 141). When referring to the 'ordinances of the House of God', Brigham describes them as 'the Celestial Law' and tellingly he also raises the issue of ultimate damnation in terms of 'principle' when he poses the question: 'Is there any such principle as annihilation? No. There is no such principle in heaven or upon earth or under the earth.' As a final example, Brigham Young equates 'the mysteries of the Kingdom of God' with 'the Principles of Eternity (Young 1992: 87, 138, 88). One very particular example of such a principle is enshrined in two neologisms, both of which refer to some eternal factor: 'Gnolom', coined in a revelation (Abraham 3: 18), and 'gnolaum' in Joseph Smith's King Follett Sermon. Joseph is said to have transliterated 'gnolaum' from an Egyptian text as an adjective synonymous with 'eternal', while 'Gnolom' is a noun referring to a form of hell where those who commit the unpardonable sin of murder dwell 'worlds without end' (McConkie, B. R., 1979: 315–16). Similarly, in association with the very notion of the reckoning of time, Joseph Smith's interpretation of the Book of Abraham speaks of the star 'Kolob', which is 'nigh unto the throne of God', with one of its revolutions being the equivalent of a thousand years (Abraham 3: 9, 4). The same text refers to a moment when God touches Abraham's eyes and he is told the names of the sun 'Shinehah', of the two stars 'Kokob' and 'Olea' and of the stars in general 'Kokaubeam'. As this new grammar of discourse develops it allows the Lord to tell Abraham that 'Kolob is the greatest of all the Kokaubeam' (Abraham 3: 16). It is in this same third chapter of the Book of Abraham that an account is also given of the divine 'organization' of spirits and, afterwards, the 'organization' of the earth. This is where the LDS plan of salvation originates, set as it is within a discourse favouring a logical and reasonable rationale for all things.

PRINCIPLE OF OPPOSITION

One idea that reaches the status of a principle in early Mormonism concerns the opposition between factors. This principle of opposition comes to sharp expression in the Book of Mormon text: 'For it must needs be, that there is an opposition in all things' (2 Nephi 2: 11). Because it becomes especially important for ethical issues I deal with it in chapter 6, but its importance for the freedom to do what one wills as the basis for eternal benefits runs throughout this book. The very chapter description introduced into the Book of Mormon for this important section of the Second Book of Nephi reads, 'Freedom of choice (agency) is essential to existence and progression.' As I will mention in chapter 2, these few descriptive words add a theological direction to the text that is not there in the original; it shows how later LDS thinking has been introduced into earlier texts and highlights the growing power of principles in LDS reflection.

As far as the principle of opposition is concerned, verse 13 of 2 Nephi 2 is a positive *tour de force*, justifying the rationale of opposition as the very basis of logic and the possibility of truth. If there is no law, there is no sin, and if no sin, there is no righteousness, and if no righteousness, there is no happiness. Without righteousness and happiness there is no punishment or misery. 'And if these things are not there is no God.' Here the rhetorical style is highly reminiscent of Paul's treatment of belief and doubt about death and resurrection in 1 Corinthians 15. For Joseph Smith the pivotal point (the equivalent of 1 Corinthians 15: 20 – 'But in fact Christ has been raised from the dead') is his affirmation 'for there is a God, and he hath created all things' (2 Nephi 2: 14). This assertion sets in train the basic account of the Plan of Salvation including the 'misery' of the devil after his fall, with his subsequent desire to make 'all men . . . miserable like unto himself' (v. 27). That was the purpose of the devil in tempting Adam. Adam and Eve in their pre-fall state would not even have known what joy was, 'for they knew no misery' (v. 23). The fall resulted in children and in a world that could now change. Change is part of the fall, but change is also the arena within which joy becomes possible once people come under the influence of the redeeming action of Christ and come away from the devil's influence. To be controlled by the devil is to know misery, but to be redeemed by Christ is to know joy. Joy is a form of controlled happiness just as its goal is exaltation, as we see in chapters 6 and 8.

In terms of doctrine and theology LDS thought must be set against this background of eternal laws and principles, to which all beings must be subject, even deities. When Brigham H. Roberts (1857–1933), one of the most penetrating thinkers of his generation and the most prolific of all LDS authors, addressed himself to the attributes of God, for example, he worked on the assumption that God's 'immutability should be regarded as... adherence to principle' though he goes on to wonder whether even God might gain 'new thoughts... new adventures and enterprises that will yield new experiences, advancement and enlargement, even for the Most High' (Roberts, B. H. 1994: 476). This language would not have appeared strange, for example, in the writings of Brigham Young, yet a special review committee set up to evaluate Roberts' work said that despite their belief in 'eternal progression' they were unhappy with the idea that God might be in 'quest of hidden truth or laws'; Roberts thought their criticism 'meaningless' (Roberts, B. H. 1994: 477). Still, the point for Roberts, as for other LDS thinkers, is that even God operates under the constraints of ultimate reality. This leads him, and others, to affirm what Sterling McMurrin identifies as 'the crucial idea that more than anything else determines the character of Mormon theology', namely the 'nonabsolutistic or finitistic conception of God'; this is the point in Mormon theology that 'so radically undercuts the chief foundation of Christian orthodoxy' (McMurrin 1994: xv). It is an issue to which I return in later chapters.

For practical Mormonism, only by aligning a morally pure life with these principles that control all reality is it possible for a person to progress into an ever-increasing glory in the realms to come. For many traditional Christians this is an important concept to grasp, for it differs from established views that set God the Holy Trinity as the ultimate source and frame of all that is, without any principle 'behind' God, or in relation to which God must operate. This is the foundational difference between LDS theology and historical Christian traditions. Within Mormonism there are many gods even though it is the business of men and women to focus on the God 'with whom we have to do' in this world of ours. An early Mormon hymn – 'If you could hie to Kolob' – muses on that star mentioned above and develops this theme: 'If you could hie to Kolob in the twinkling of an eye, And then continue onward with that same speed to flie, D'ye think that you could ever, Through all eternity, Find out the generations where Gods began to be?' (*Hymns* 1978: 257). It answers that just as one would find no such beginning so, too, one would find no end. In fact one would find 'no end to virtue, might, wisdom, light, union, youth, priesthood or truth'. Given such immensities, it was no wonder that, for example, Brigham Young should be especially emphatic on the aspect of reality that does impinge upon us, not least the God from amongst the Gods 'with whom we have to do' (Young 1992: 93). As in that hymn, existence was, for Brigham Young, an immense reality. Worlds without number 'are from eternity to eternity in their creations and redemptions' and every one of them 'has had an Adam and an Eve'; the worlds have known the reality of good and evil, and each 'has been created on the same principle'. In an interesting gloss Brigham adds that the Saints would feel astonished and amazed if they once realized the extent of the 'Exaltation of the Gods': like Isaiah in his vision of the Lord of Hosts they too would say, 'Woe is me, I am undone, I am of unclean lips' (Young 1992: 93. Cf. Isaiah 6: 5).

PRINCIPLES AND RELATIONS: RELATIONS AND PRINCIPLES

The principles are implicitly accepted by many Latter-day Saints, who will often not be aware of their importance as a category of thought that informs and drives all other discussions, whether relating to justification, to the heavens or to marriage. To grasp the underlying power of 'principles' in LDS thought is, then, as important as understanding the foundational nature of the divine Trinity in traditional Christianity. And precisely the same point needs to be made for the relational nature of Mormonism. Earlier in this chapter I drew attention to the significance of relationships in the emergent LDS understanding of God and of other members of the Church. This, too, operates as a kind of category of thought within Mormonism and needs to be brought into a clear juxtaposition with the notion of 'principles'. Indeed, one of the underlying themes of this book operates on the understanding that 'relations' and 'principles' serve as a combined element in directing and motivating LDS thought. This will become particularly apparent in chapter 6 when I analyse the nature and function of grace in Mormon theology, for there I will argue that there is an inherent tension present between the idea of 'relations' and that of 'principles'. While, in certain contexts, that tension can work in a very positive way, in others it produces negative effects. From a theoretical standpoint, it is important to be clear that this 'relations and principles' pairing is introduced into this book as one way of reflecting upon Mormon theology and practice; the notions are not paired by Latter-day Saints.

GATHERING TO ZION

The context within which the 'principles' element emerged and came to a controlling position within Mormon thought included a strong missionary drive. Joseph Smith's personal religious quest, combining a 'magical mysticality', Adventist millenarianism and popular intellectualism resulted in a mass movement of people, and many converts were made within North America, with many more drawn from Europe, especially from Great Britain and Scandinavia. The Latter-day Saints called this 'the gathering' or 'gathering to Zion', and in all probability it ensured the long-term survival of the Church.

This gathering offers one of the clearest examples of a theological idea influencing social action: the Second Coming of Christ prompted the social response of migration and settlement. Neither was unique to Mormonism; Adventism was a long-established Christian revitalization of Protestantism, and migrations of people to North America were a feature of the days of the Pilgrim Fathers and into the later eighteenth and early nineteenth centuries. In Mormonism these theological and social elements so united in a person, a book and a missionary message that they yielded a powerful religious compound that would contribute significantly to Mormonism's success. Converts migrated to be with the prophet and his successors as they prepared a place and a community fit for the coming of Christ.

Theological belief can also affect geography as much as it did Mormon social action. The history of the world has been marked not only by the association of religious ideas with particular secular authorities but also by the emergence of groups dedicated to their religious ideals and seeking to manifest them within communities established as separate from others. Buddhism, Christianity, Hinduism, Islam, Judaism, Sikhism and Zoroastrianism, for example, have all had their periods of geographical-political-religious power. So too, in its own way, has Communism. Mormonism is no exception. Joseph Smith's early teaching announced that Jesus would soon come again and that it was necessary for believers to gather together to prepare for that advent. That was hardly a new teaching. But Joseph linked that second advent with North America, allowing secular and religious desires to unite in a drive that was more than the sum of its parts. For Jesus was to come again not to Jerusalem, as the great majority of biblically influenced religious innovators argued, but to a sacred place in North America.

REVALUING AND RELOCATING ZION

This idea of Zion as an American Zion allowed a redefinition of other places by revaluing their religious significance. In traditional biblical theology Jerusalem was the Holy City and it would be to Jerusalem that Jesus as the Messiah (or Christ) would return. From there he would rule the new world order. Details varied to some degree in what are called premillennial and postmillennial traditions. Premillennialists think that the thousand years of bliss will begin with the Second Coming of Christ, while postmillennialists think that there will be a thousand-year period of preparing for the Second Coming of Christ. Grant Underwood has fully explored the Mormon position making use of the historian Robert Clouse, who saw two very different styles of religious outlook underlying pre- and postmillennialism in general (Underwood 1993). Premillennialists really believe in a doubling of events with two comings of Christ, two sets of resurrections and two judgements. The first of these would be the coming of Christ for the resurrection and 'judgement' of true believers, who would then spend the millennium with him prior to the resurrection and judgement of others before their final separation into the afterlife of heaven and hell. Postmillennialists, by contrast, see only one of everything: a single coming of Christ to judge all resurrected people. Underwood is convinced that Mormonism corresponds most clearly to the premillennialist stance (Underwood 1993: 6). Significantly, the Gathering to Zion would include the ten lost tribes of Israel as they reappeared, gained the necessary blessings and benefits of the LDS Church and moved to their final inheritance in the Holy Land, as interpreted from Doctrine and Covenants (see D&C 133: 26–32) by Underwood with additional references to Parley Pratt, an important early Mormon authority (Underwood 1993: 179). The plain text of the Doctrine and Covenants, however, could be interpreted to mean that these tribes would find their fulfilment in the new Zion of America. Certainly, an interest in the lost tribes of Israel as the possible source of the indigenous populations of America had been on the intellectual agenda both in Europe and America from the seventeenth century (Bushman 1984: 134–90). The Book of Mormon refocused that interest in the light of both its millennial teaching and its missionary practice.

For the moment, at least, there was no need for those of ancient Jewish origin to migrate east to Jerusalem, for the call to Zion was now a westward vocation. Section 133 of the Doctrine and Covenants – a document to be discussed much more fully in chapter 2 – addresses itself to this movement of the faithful from all the 'nations, islands of the sea' and 'foreign lands' that are now reclassified in a theological way as 'Babylon'. In biblical theology Babylon stands as a symbol of evil and wickedness and of all that opposes the goodness and righteousness of God, which are themselves symbolized by Jerusalem or Zion, names that are synonymous. Evil Babylon confronts Holy Zion and people must chose their location as an expression of their religious commitment; a call to separation was clear in a kind of communal purity, as many parts of the Book of Mormon testify (e.g. Alma 5: 57).

A MOVING FAITH

Earliest Mormonism thus demanded movement and the preparation of a place, showing how faith should manifest itself. Many twenty-first-century Christians, rooted in static denominational churches and neighbourhoods, may fail to see the significance of this. As an urban religion Christianity in the twentieth century increasingly developed an ecumenical attitude – different churches worked together to some degree, even though it may have been relatively limited in scope. By contrast, in many rural areas, as in parts of France, Italy, Spain, Ireland, Greece, Germany, England and some Scandinavian countries, one church, whether Catholic, Orthodox, Anglican or Lutheran, often tended to be the dominant Christian presence. These territorial presences often originated for political reasons, largely related to the history of Christianity, its great eastern and western schism in the eleventh century and the internal transformation of western Christianity in the Reformation of the sixteenth century.

One development of Christianity is particularly important for understanding the relationship between this Christianity of place and worldwide Christianity. As argued by Peter van Rooden, Christianity in the very late eighteenth and early nineteenth centuries developed a new dynamic and, in effect, almost adopted a new form through its strong missionary activity conducted by missionary societies throughout the world (1996: 65ff.). This has relevance for Mormonism in that while it was born out of Adventism, 'magical mysticality', popular intellectualism and Masonry' its earliest life took the form of a missionary movement. In fact it exemplifies van Rooden's thesis in a novel form. Unlike missionary societies that were formed by people within or from established denominations, the LDS movement was a combination of Church and missionary society. So it was that the prophet could announce the word of the Lord as basic to the Church's venture and nature: 'Send forth the elders of my church unto the nations...the islands of the sea...unto foreign lands...and this shall be their cry, and the voice of the Lord unto all people: Go forth unto the land of Zion... Awake and arise and go forth to meet the Bridegroom...prepare for the day of the Lord' (D&C 133: 8–10). I will return to this issue in chapter 9 when considering further Mormonism's current and future development.

The practical spirituality of early Mormonism viewed the world at large as evil, symbolized by Babylon, from which they should flee to Zion both to avoid disasters that God would bring upon the evil world and to prepare for the coming of Christ. Despite this stress on the American Zion and the fact that hundreds of thousands responded to the call to gather, there remains within LDS texts an ongoing commitment to the Holy Land and to Jerusalem as Zion. Within the crucial Doctrine and Covenants Section 133 there are several key verses referring to the final day of Christ's coming when he will 'stand upon the mount of Olivet, and upon the mighty ocean...and upon the islands of the sea, and upon the land of Zion' (D&C 133: 20). At that time all lands will reunite, the seas will be driven back and 'the land of Jerusalem and the land of Zion shall be turned back into their own place, and the earth shall be like as it was in the days before it was divided' (D&C 133: 24). Still, in the mid nineteenth century, the LDS message was to gather, and many did so in the belief, as it came to be expressed in the tenth Article of Faith of the Church: 'We believe in the literal gathering of Israel and in the restoration of the Ten Tribes; that Zion [the New Jerusalem] will be built upon the American continent.'

ZION IN HEART

Much more specific than this are revelations in the Doctrine and Covenants announcing that Independence, Missouri, will be the key site for the ultimate city of Zion (D&C 57: 1–3). The Church of Jesus Christ of Latter-day Saints was based in Independence for only about a year before being driven out in 1833, and their 'centre place' of prophecy is now owned by the Reorganized Church of Jesus Christ of Latter Day Saints, to which I return in chapter 9. As the nineteenth turned into the twentieth century it was apparent that Christ had not come and a shift in general views of Zion began to occur. Zion would now be the pure in heart wherever they dwelt, whether in Utah, other parts of America, Europe or elsewhere. The fact that migration had practically ceased meant that some of these remnant churches needed a rationale for their life and faith and such did develop but only with time. For the last two decades of the nineteenth century and first two of the twentieth century, Utah Mormonism had its work cut out in self-defence against central US authorities over the issue of polygamy, and it was only through the formal Manifesto abandoning the practice 'for the temporal salvation of the Church' that it was able to survive as a self-sustaining social institution. That passage from the nineteenth into the twentieth century involved something of a change of mindset as new generations were produced who, especially after the First World War and even more so after the Second World War, were citizens of a world that witnessed a tremendous development in North American social life, as separate States developed into a new form of Federal democracy. Meanwhile, the wider world had also moved away from European imperialism and colonialization with the rise of many newly independent countries. In intellectual and scientific terms the world had also changed a great deal.

In its early phase, as an Adventist and premillennialist group believing in a relatively imminent end of the world, Mormonism's sense of urgency in missionary activity was high, fostered by its great expectations. Grant Underwood has detailed this attitude, rehearsing as he did so Orson Hyde's enthusiastic hope that 'While kind heaven shall lend me breath, I'll sound repentance far abroad, And tell the nations to prepare, For Jesus Christ, their Coming Lord' (Underwood 1993: 6). His zeal as an early and influential LDS apostle was not so apparent by the close of the nineteenth century when early Mormonism missionary expansionism gave way to the need to survive political pressure on the very centre of the Church itself. But survive the Church did. Its doctrinal commitments to plural marriage, tied to temple rites and underpinning the hope of death's conquest, underwent transformation, as a new focus on the family dwelt more on its quality of life and mutuality than on its sheer quantity of earthly members. Missionaries would, however, remain vital, for as Mormonism shifted from its centripetal to its centrifugal phases from the mid nineteenth to mid twentieth centuries, so the armies of young missionaries would find themselves gaining new experiences of the world as they also gained a new sense of their faith. It is likely that Mormonism revitalized itself as much through the personal conversion of its own inborn missionaries as through the converts won by those missionaries.

CHURCH ZION

The very word 'Church' is fundamental to the essential nature of Mormonism. Here, as elsewhere in this book, a word that is widely shared throughout Christendom and beyond must be given its distinctive LDS signification. Many Christian denominations, in their theology at least, make some sort of distinction between Christianity as such and their own denominational version of it. Many Christian believers do not find it impossible to worship in churches other than their own and can, with relative ease, move from one denomination to another even though the broad boundaries of Catholicism, Orthodoxy and Protestantism do serve as natural and powerful barriers to individual movement. The Church of Jesus Christ of Latter-day Saints, under the constraint of its own sense of being a restorationist group, limits movement in much the same way as these clearly defined outer boundaries. The account of the religious lives and experiences of the peoples filling the entire Book of Mormon is formed by a grammar of discourse of Church and churches (e.g. Alma 6: 2–3). From its outset the Book of Mormon discusses truth and falsehood not in abstract terms of philosophy or theology, nor in the relational terms of mystical love but of churches and their obedient or disobedient membership (1 Nephi 1: 26). This grammar includes the rise of a 'great and abominable church' founded by the devil, which is given high profile in the very first prophetic book in the Book of Mormon, internally dated as the sixth century BC (1 Nephi 13: 5–6).

This is one example of the relative absence in the Book of Mormon of the division present in the Bible between the Old and New Testaments, an issue which I pursue more specifically in chapter 2. In terms of the rationale of social life the Old Testament functions on the distinction between numerous tribes and nations, with God's people emerging as a chosen people with a promised land, while the New Testament establishes a major division between the Jewish temple and synagogue and the emergent Christian church, which is open to all humanity everywhere. The Book of Mormon depicts an ongoing conflict between true Church and false churches, working towards the final triumph of Christ and the establishing of the true Church as the divine kingdom, a view which runs in a relatively homogeneous fashion throughout the entirety of its text. This division between true and false churches provides a powerful echo of Joseph Smith's boyhood desire to know which church was the true church, a desire that was met with his emergence as a prophetic voice of divine veracity.

CHAPTER 2

Prophets and texts

Joseph Smith's true Church, born through his visionary experience, was established in the same year as the Book of Mormon was published. Church and book confirmed Joseph as a prophet as he engaged in the numerous relationships that mark a charismatic leader and his followers. At the outset, prophet and texts emerge together as the basis of Mormon religion. Still, today, while teachers, preachers and priests hold significant offices, their work is ultimately constrained by the prophet-leader who can, in a moment, render previous interpretations of past writings quite redundant.

All theology depends upon a particular source of authority and for Mormonism that authority comes from the belief that God has established the Church of Jesus Christ of Latter-day Saints as the restored source of true teaching and ritual practice needed for ultimate salvation, the state described as exaltation. This restoration itself depends upon a committed belief in prophets, especially Joseph Smith Jnr, and in the scriptures produced through prophecy as God's chosen method of communicating the truths of the Restoration. This chapter explores both the key texts of Mormonism and its view of prophecy.

A TEXTUAL CONTINUUM

The earlier text of Mormon theology emphasizes 'relations' whereas the later ones emphasize 'principles'. The early text – the Book of Mormon – was published in 1830 and expressed a general Christian doctrine of salvation rooted in repentance, faith and baptism, all framed by a dynamic millenarian expectation of an imminent return of Christ. For this Christians should prepare by gathering together. The later texts – the Doctrine and Covenants (1835) and the Pearl of Great Price (1851) – take Mormonism into the new theological territory of covenant-making temple ritual, the conquest of death by persons set on the eternal path of apotheosis or of becoming divine.

There is nothing surprising or novel in religious groups developing theological ideas in new directions. Early Christians, for example, took Jewish religious traditions of God, creation, sin, the fall, redemption, a saviour figure, resurrection, and a people of God, and reconfigured them all in relation to Jesus of Nazareth identified as saviour and lord. Christianity also brought a very open boundary to that previously, largely controlled community of Jews and talked not only about a spirit power that qualified people for inclusion but also asserted the belief that the resurrection had already begun in the person of Jesus. It was not long before a variety of other ideas, especially Greek ideas, helped ongoing generations of Christians to express their growing sense that Jesus was also divine and needed to be included in a new view of God as a Holy Trinity. The early Christian idea that Christ would soon return to transform the world was itself transformed into an ongoing commitment to develop and expand the Christian community itself.

Similarly, Mormonism developed many pre-existing ideas into a new pattern in which the total picture yielded more than the sum of its parts. Unlike many other prophetic groups, from the seventeenth through to the twentieth centuries, the LDS configuration proved successful. The sense of truth associated with this new pattern impelled Joseph Smith in his proclamation of new revelation while its acceptance by others resulted in a church. Through the committed engagement of prophet and hearer the Latter-day movement came alive and distinguished Mormonism from other groups. The Latter-day Saints believed this new configuration of belief and practice to be a divine restoration of truth to the earth, with prophecy as its means and a prophet as its leader.

PROPHECY AND PROPHETS

While the sixth and seventh of Mormonism's Articles of Faith – more fully described in chapter 3 – refer to prophets and prophecy, it is the fifth Article that gives prophecy pride of place within church organization, affirming that 'a man must be called of God, by prophecy, and by the laying on of hands by those who are in authority, to preach the gospel and administer in the ordinances thereof'. Similarly, the Book of Mormon is rooted in accounts of ancient American prophets and filled with extensive quotations from biblical prophets who speak of and for God, telling the past and predicting the future. They also serve as judges and pastors of believers in their day.

The very name 'Mormon' was that of a prophet thought to have lived between AD 310 and 385 in America where, according to LDS tradition, he wrote the plates that ultimately became the Book of Mormon. His son, Moroni, also a prophet, completed his father's account of human disobedience and the demise of God's people in America and – described sometimes as a resurrected being and sometimes as an angel – was believed to have been sent to the boy Joseph Smith in 1823 to tell of records hidden some fourteen hundred years before on a hill not far from where young Joseph lived. This figure of Moroni (for there is also another Moroni, who appears in the Book of Alma within the Book of Mormon) is of considerable symbolic interest, for he serves as the bridge between the Book of Mormon with its claimed account of ancient American history and the America of Joseph Smith in the 1820s. It is as a prophet who produced the records that he now calls a new prophet to discover, translate and use them as the basis for a new message of divine salvation. Prophets are the LDS focus for and undercurrent of religious activity. This prophetic activism is continued in Joseph Smith's own life as he tells of when Jesus, who in Mormon belief is the Lord Jehovah of the Old Testament, appeared in the Kirtland Temple on 3 April 1836, forgave him his sins and validated the building as a place of blessing. Immediately afterwards there followed three visitations, of Moses, Elias and Elijah. These conferred upon Joseph and Oliver Cowdery 'the keys of this dispensation' (D&C 110: 15). This important text unites the notion of a prophet with that of a distinctive 'time' – a dispensation – a specially designated period of human history within which Joseph Smith would be the agent of change. 'Prophet' and 'dispensation' become inseparably interfused concepts, each a facet of divine activity, with 'dispensation' framing a period of marked divine endeavour within which the 'prophet' is the means of new revelation and of organizing human response to the divine plan. Accordingly, LDS texts are dispensationally prophetic, even when they deal with various events of the sacred past that might otherwise be regarded as historical.

This sheds some light on the relative homogeneity of LDS texts when compared with the Bible: while Judaism's scriptures give due weight not only to prophetic books but also to books of law and wisdom, Mormonism's sacred texts are very largely prophetic utterances and, within themselves, give priority of place to prophetic figures. Though resembling both the prophetic books of the Old Testament and much of the New Testament, in so far as the texts possess nothing like the Psalms or Proverbs the Book of Mormon does not reflect an established worshipping community. The Doctrine and Covenants, by contrast, does take account of the ritual life of an emergent worshipping group that created and borrowed many hymns and songs, leading to various editions of a Latter-day Saint Hymnbook (see D&C 20: 75–9; 124: 24–41). In this, Mormonism followed the pattern of most Christian churches, especially in Protestantism, where practical spirituality came to demand two books, a scriptural text – normally the Bible – plus a worship-book of some kind. In practical terms the Hebrew scriptures of Judaism come to be replicated in Protestant Christianity in a combination of Bible plus hymn-book. In Anglicanism, for example, the *Book of Common Prayer* even includes the Psalms of the Old Testament as a basic resource for Christian worship: sometimes a hymn-book section was also bound into that book of Anglican worship. When Mormonism developed its temple rituals (see chapter 8), it too generated forms of words and rites that furnished radically important patterns of action but these never emerged as official public texts due to the sacred secrecy surrounding those rites.

AUTHORITY

As already intimated, Christian theology is always grounded in some specific kind of authority, and for Mormonism it is prophetic. Catholicism claims that Christ founded a church in and through his immediate apostles, especially St Peter, and vouchsafed its authority through the apostolic succession until the present day. The pope stands as the prime symbolic embodiment of that foundation and continuity in a worldwide church held together by bishops of whom he is first amongst equals. Catholic priests are responsible for the sacraments, which are the means of grace, most especially the Mass as a symbol of the death of Christ for the salvation of the world. Doctrine in Catholicism lies under the scrutiny and interpretation of central church authorities and is not left open to each member's views. It is no accident that Catholicism developed in and through a closed hierarchy of priests within a church that, when in its medieval prime, took the form of a holy empire.

The Protestant Reformation dramatically questioned this view of authentic power and moved its focus to the Bible as the prime authority in religion. Believing that the Bible contains the revealed word of God, made real to believers through the internal witness of the Holy Spirit, Protestants developed the doctrine of the priesthood of all believers, in which each man and woman is held responsible before God for their own religious lives.

There is no special corps of priests to do it for them. By democratizing religious expertise Protestants made salvation free for all, but that salvation demanded commitment from each believer. It is no accident that Protestantism fostered theology as a way of understanding God both through a detailed study of biblical texts and through the construction of systems of interpretations based on them.

Yet another form of religious authority is that of mysticism. There is no 'church of mystics' but only a style of religion periodically seen in distinctive individuals for whom religiosity is entirely personal and experience is self-authenticating. Catholicism and Protestantism, along with other great religious traditions of the world, have always possessed individual members of this mystical type and have quite often been successful in retaining them as part of the overall life of their church. Catholicism, in particular, has allowed mystics to influence the growth of particular spiritual traditions and orders within the church. Mysticism is seldom without its cues and sustaining channels of religious resource. In Catholicism the Mass, together with forms of devotional love related to it, has fostered the sense of mystic union, while in Protestantism the Bible has furnished a world of symbolic attraction for the individual creativity of mystics. Still, mystics are always potentially dangerous precisely because their sense of authority is inward and it cannot be guaranteed that liturgical or scriptural resources will contain their creative endeavours.

Simply speaking, we can say that, as far as authority is concerned, apostolic authority stands over the Bible in Catholicism and the Bible stands over the church in Protestantism, while in mysticism the personal inward vision determines truth. While all affirm God as the source of their authority, these three positions could be characterized as locating authority in church, Bible or self, with Mormonism displaying all three. This is evident when Joseph Smith Jnr is viewed (i) as a new apostle, commissioned through latter-day appearances of Jesus and other biblical figures, (ii) as the prophetic source of new scriptural revelation and (iii) as a mystic emerging from the Protestant cultural world.

Formally, the leader of the Church of Jesus Christ of Latter-day Saints is widely acknowledged to be a prophet, seer and revelator or, as the Doctrine and Covenants has it, 'seer, revelator, translator' and 'prophet' all expressing the gifts God 'bestows upon the head of the church' (D&C 107: 93). Another text adds the titles of 'apostle of Jesus Christ' and 'elder of the church' to his other designations as 'seer, translator and prophet' (D&C 21: 1). This reinforces the fact that prophets and prophecy lie at the heart of LDS theology. As we saw in chapter 1, a sense of mystery and of discovering esoteric knowledge through distinctive techniques played an important part in the formative stages of Joseph's development, in what we might call the pre-prophetic period of his calling. This is reflected in the title 'seer and revelator' and, to a degree, in that of 'translator', since his translations were grounded more in a sense of spiritual insight than of linguistic expertise. The titles of elder and apostle, by complementary contrast, indicate something more of the authority and organizational capacity of the leader. While the idea of being a prophet can be used to embrace all these more particular elements, it also establishes the firmest of all links between Joseph Smith, the Bible and the Book of Mormon, a link of profound significance given the notion of Mormonism as a restoration movement.

PROPHETS AND DISPENSATIONS

The ideas of 'prophet' and 'prophecy' are so well established in general theological terms that it is easy to ignore the way in which they relate to divinely appointed periods of time and of special activity called dispensations. Prophets can be viewed as representing acts of divine disclosure, with their lifetime marking a period of special favour. Prophets embody dispensations as their message proclaims divine acts within these times of deep significance. In LDS discourse this uniting of person and period is symbolized in the notion of a person possessing the 'keys' of a dispensation.

The wider Christian notion of 'dispensations', which influenced some Adventist movements, was particularly associated with the Protestant group of the Plymouth Brethren, first formed in England in the 1830s at almost exactly the same time as the LDS Church was established in the United States. Though details vary, dispensationalism involves dividing world history into different phases or stages in which divine activity emphasizes some distinctive aspect of salvation. This division is based upon very specific interpretations of biblical texts and often takes a sevenfold form beginning with human life prior to the fall of humanity. There man and woman are typified by a kind of innocence followed by a world in which conscience holds sway. With the figure of Noah, human government then emerges, prior to the era of promise rooted in Abraham but soon passing into the era of law extending from Moses to Christ. With Christ comes the dispensation of grace and the history of Christian churches which lasts until the millennium.

Latter-day Saint dispensationalism takes its own distinctive form by associating particular eras with individual figures who were responsible for bringing certain tasks to completion. Some, for example, refer to seven

LDS dispensations, which match the wider Protestant number but are represented by the figures of Adam, Enoch, Noah, Abraham, Moses, Jesus and Joseph Smith. LDS teaching identifies each of these with an aspect of life and salvation that ranges across the ages and is not strictly confined to any one stage. Still, there is a developing and cumulative sense that they complement each other to ensure the ultimate benefit of human beings. In fact the LDS approach to dispensations renders redundant any strict succession of truths since it argues that in each era of human existence the cluster of truths and practices necessary for salvation have been present, even if largely unrecorded. It is even argued, for example, that doctrines concerning the fall, faith in Christ, and the need for atonement 'were taught in each era from Adam's day onward whenever there were living prophets selected by the Lord' (Lasseter 1992: 389).

This is a telling quotation for it raises the issue of anachronism in the Book of Mormon, a topic regularly advanced by critics of Mormonism who pinpoint Book of Mormon references to Christ generations before Jesus was born (1 Nephi 11: 13–24). While Mormon theology values these dispensational eras it brings a different content to them. The implicit assumption of most Christian groups is of a progressive revelation with the Old Testament leading up to the life of Christ and, after his death and resurrection, to the New Testament and a new age of Christian church life. Then, though different groups espouse various ideas of resurrection and judgement, they generally assume that in the afterlife believers will attain everlasting joy and felicity. Relatively little is said about that afterlife and, in general terms, after the end of the nineteenth century it was increasingly avoided as a topic of theological investigation. Some twentieth-century non-LDS theology even focused on the lifetime of Jesus as a period of realized eschatology, as the crucial point in time when the profoundest expression of God had been gained in Christ. In broadest terms, the Christian tradition restricted prophets to the Old Testament and interpreted their work as pointing forward to Christ, well in advance of the historic birth of Jesus of Nazareth. After Christ's birth prophets are almost rendered redundant, their place being taken by apostles of Jesus, teachers of his message and pastors of those who believe.

For Joseph Smith to see himself as a prophet, then, alerts us to distinctive theological possibilities regarding this division of time. In practice, Latter-day Saints taught that Jesus died to atone for Adam's sin, that it is now up to converts to repent and be baptized for the remission of the sin involved in their fallen state, and that it is up to them to begin to take responsibility for themselves in relation to their exaltation in the afterlife (as fully described in chapters 3, 4 and 8). All this can only be done through observing church ordinances or rituals as revealed by Joseph the prophet in his new period of the restoration of truth. Through him were brought to light utterly vital rites that are not contained in the Bible, making his prophetic identity foundational for ultimate exaltation – the highest form of salvation. Behind this picture lies the LDS belief that these rites were present in earlier periods of human history and would have been known to Jesus and his disciples, as also to Adam and Eve, who were given the gift of the Holy Spirit; Adam was also given to understand that his sacrifices were symbolic of the ultimate sacrifice of Christ (Smith, J. 1985: 15). Indeed, it is part of traditional LDS thought that 'the gospel, with its ordinances and the holy priesthood, was taught to Adam and was had among all the early patriarchs, from Adam to Abraham' (Matthews 1985b: 276). It was just such knowledge that was removed from the earth by God sometime after the earliest Christian period so that, for example, although some Christian thinkers may have pursued truth, it would have been with the disadvantage of not having access to these ritual truths. The Reformation is one case in which the Latter-day Saints are happy to see individuals pursuing truth according to the best light available to them, but it was not until these vital factors were restored through Joseph Smith that any real religious advance was possible.

KEYS AND PERSONS

Here 'restoration' itself becomes the theological idea of restoration, highlighting the fact that Mormonism speaks of itself as a restoration movement through which soteriological highways are reopened through particular individuals – reaffirming the major theme of the relational nature of Mormon theology – and highlighting the covenantal values of LDS thought and practice that come to frame those relationships. Relational and covenantal factors come to expression in the lives of particular prophets as they pursue distinctive dispensational goals.

Although the motif of 'key' is found in the New Testament (Matthew 16: 19; Luke 11: 52; Rev. 1: 18; 3: 7; 9: 1; 20: 1), its relatively low profile is far from that accompanying the subsequent development of the image of 'the keys' in Roman Catholic ecclesiology. The LDS approach, by contrast, is even more developed, though it took time to emerge and is not, for example, present in the Book of Mormon. Given the way in which biblical passages often either recur or are echoed within the Book of Mormon, one might expect to find 'keys' occurring in relation to passages about the 'rock', or

Peter, as the foundation on which God would establish the church. But it is not so. In fact Jesus and his teachings are identified as the rock: he 'who is the Christ, the Son of God' is the prime focus (Helaman 5: 12; 3 Nephi 14: 24–6).

However, once we pass from the Book of Mormon to the Doctrine and Covenants a major change takes place and 'keys' now emerges as a predominant expression of religious significance, with particular 'keys' associated with particular individuals for very particular purposes. These Doctrine and Covenants passages begin with a revelation to Oliver Cowdery as well as to Joseph Smith informing them that they are being given the 'keys of this gift': none other than the ability to translate the plates that will furnish the Book of Mormon itself (D&C 6: 28). Another text finds the biblical figures of Peter, James and John being given the 'keys of this ministry' until Christ comes (D&C 7: 7). Then a whole series of texts relates persons, keys and goals: the keys of records to Moroni, restoration to Elias, of 'turning the hearts' of fathers to children and children to fathers to Elijah, and the gathering of Israel to Moses (D&C 110: 11). To Hyrum Smith were given the keys of patriarchal blessing (D&C 124: 92). Finally, Christ commits to Joseph Smith the 'keys of my kingdom and a dispensation of the gospel for the last times; and for the fullness of times' (D&C 27: 5–13). Many other 'keys' could be cited, including Joseph's 'keys of the mysteries of the kingdom' (D&C 64: 5) and keys that belong to Joseph and always to the 'Presidency of the High Priesthood' (D&C 81: 2).

'Keys' came to be an all-embracing term invested with diffuse religious significance and, in effect, 'keys' became a way of bringing theological ideas of power and divine authority to bear upon organizational aspects of church life. There is also a sense of special knowledge associated with 'keys', as when devotees are told of 'three great keys' that enable them to detect the difference between angels, resurrected beings and the devil. Angels can shake hands, resurrected beings do not have bodies and will not proffer their 'hands' to be shaken, while the devil – being a deceiver – will offer a hand but the recipient will feel nothing (D&C 129: 1–9). The very use of the word can also, for example, convey a meaning to the initiated that is not accessible to others. Public use of the word 'keys' can thus carry a message to Mormons who have undergone temple education and ritual but would mean little to those who have not. Such 'keys' do not simply refer to the historical past and the contemporary organization of the Church; they also hold prospective power associated with the afterlife and the conquest of death, as we see in chapters 4 and 8. Keys and the dispensation for the fullness of times belong together, for they explain Mormonism's notion of prophet and prophecy, of its own restoration and of the continuous revelation that underpins its sacred texts.

There are four primary texts of Mormonism, often called the Standard Works: the Bible, the Book of Mormon, the Doctrine and Covenants and the Pearl of Great Price. LDS practice has retained the use of the King James Version of the Bible despite the fact that Joseph Smith indicated a degree of error in it due to improper translation and transmission over time; he even produced his own version in which some of these errors were removed. This 'Joseph Smith Translation' (JST) was never published during his lifetime and the manuscript was left with his widow, Emma, who gave it to the Reorganized Church of Jesus Christ of Latter Day Saints, of which she became a member (see Nyman and Millet 1985). It was the Reorganized Church that first published the Joseph Smith Translation in 1867, renaming it the Inspired Version in 1936 (see Matthews 1985a). During much of the time that Joseph spent rendering the King James text into his own version he worked very closely with Sidney Rigdon, a former Baptist minister, who was far more deeply versed in the Bible than Joseph and who influenced Joseph Smith a great deal (van Wagoner 1994: 71–4). A feature of this work lay in the way in which biblical texts prompted Joseph to ponder hitherto ignored issues. These included ideas of the innocence of children relating to sin, the plan of salvation, and ideas of priesthood as well as reflections on the enigmatic figure of Enoch – with whom Joseph can be seen to have closely identified himself – and on the city that Enoch was said to have founded before it was translated into heaven prior to its future reappearance on earth (Matthews 1992: 763–9). Because most of these topics were simultaneously taken up and developed in the Doctrine and Covenants, and because it was the Reorganized and not the 'Utah' Church of Jesus Christ of Latter-day Saints that fostered the Inspired Version, I will not devote any more time to it here; suffice it to say that one of the Articles of Faith acknowledges belief in the Bible as 'the word of God as far as it is translated correctly' (Article 8). When Smith set out to produce his own 'translation', it was based not on expert knowledge of the biblical languages but on a revelation or spiritual insight into the proper meaning of the text of the King James Version, about a tenth of which he changed.

Apart from the fact that it does not own the copyright to the Joseph Smith Translation, a significant practical reason why the Church has retained the use of the King James Version and not, for example, opted for a more

modern version of the Bible is because both its language and a great number
of its actual passages are reflected and contained in the other Standard
Works. In other words it is retained for purposes of coherence, mutual
reinforcement and unity of ethos, since both the Book of Mormon and the
Doctrine and Covenants follow the style of King James English (Barlow
1991). Saints are encouraged to read these sources for their spiritual good and
probably do benefit from dwelling upon one world of thought and feeling
rather than jumping between different literary styles when moving between
volumes. For the few who may wish for a simple and contemporary style
Lynn Matthews Anderson, herself a lifelong Latter-day Saint, published
what she calls the *Easy-to-Read Book of Mormon*, originally written for her
own children (1995). Though in no way official, her version shows the
continuing, and perhaps even growing, commitment of Latter-day Saints
to the message in the Book of Mormon's texts.

Indeed, texts are important for Mormonism. Joseph Smith's life was
much caught up in them, from the metallic plates, through the basic text of
the King James Version of the Bible to, for example, the Apocrypha, which
is itself of interest because Smith devotes a revelation to it, now appearing
as Doctrine and Covenants Section 91. Its brief six verses attest that some
of the Apocryphal writings are true and correctly translated and that others
are flawed due to 'interpolations by the hands of men'. The Lord reveals
that while 'it is not needful that the Apocrypha should be translated' by
Joseph, if people do read it they may gain some understanding 'for the Spirit
manifesteth truth' (D&C 91: 5). Historically speaking, Catholic traditions
have favoured the Apocrypha and included it in their translations of the
Bible, while the Protestant Reformation accorded it less than full canonical
status. As useful as the Apocrypha might be for general edification, it was
not valid for doctrinal debate and formulation. Early Mormonism, then,
echoed the Protestant trend over these texts and went so far as to possess a
revelation on the topic.

In more general contemporary study there are some LDS scholars who
pursue forms of textual analysis of the Book of Mormon that are a direct
extension of some scholarly analyses of the Bible (Parry 1992). Their intention is, largely, to demonstrate the authenticity of the Book of Mormon text
and not, as with some biblical scholars, to engage in what believers would
see as faith-reducing critical studies. Finally, and as a non-biblical element,
when the new and curious 'texts' of Egyptian hieroglyphics fell into Joseph's
hands in 1835, he eagerly set about 'translating' them too (Widmer 2000:
70–4).

PERSONAL IDENTITY

One characteristic feature of many religious leaders lies in their sense of personal vocation grounded in a relationship with the divine, and for Joseph divine visitations and promises of texts to be translated went hand in hand. This sense of direct contact with God possesses numerous consequences of both positive and negative kinds. Positively, it can produce figures so firmly set upon a virtuous path that no forces can hinder their advance. Negatively, it can yield a bigotry and stubbornness that brooks no contradiction and heeds no friendly advice. The formation of human identity is an extremely complex process but, amongst its conscious elements, the sense of possessing divine truth at the heart of life turns a career into a mission. Given appropriate circumstances, such conviction can be of tremendous advantage to leaders. Joseph Smith and Sidney Rigdon have been likened to each other because of their 'powerful belief in their own correctness', alongside an unreadiness to concede 'personal error or misconduct'; they were linked in generating some of Mormonism's most influential texts (van Wagoner 1994: 192).

One of the most obvious and yet controversial examples of this certitude lies in the very revelations of the Doctrine and Covenants. It is controversial because, to most Latter-day Saints, these revelations are precisely that: messages from God delivered through the medium of Joseph Smith. For those who are not believing Latter-day Saints, however, revelations can be accounted for as reflections of the prophet's own mind. Whether or not he was conscious of these as his own thoughts, couched in terms suggesting that they came directly from God, we cannot say. To non-Mormons, however, it is obvious that these revelations served numerous purposes, including that of social control over his followers. For those who treat revelations as the imaginative product of a religious leader's mind they become a valuable means of understanding something of their motivation and intention.

THE BIBLE IN THE STANDARD WORKS

While Joseph Smith, like many of his contemporary core-leaders and thousands of early Mormon converts, had been brought up in a world familiar with the Bible, this familiarity should not always be over-accentuated as some golden age of popular biblical knowledge. Formal school education was often sporadic and literacy not always widespread but much was possible and, as we see below, B. H. Roberts, a naturally gifted individual, learned to read by about the age of thirteen (Roberts, B. H. 1990: 46). The Bible was amongst the most familiar reading matter and, obviously, much emphasized in the widespread Protestantism of early nineteenth-century North America. Those who were literate helped to spread the word to those who were not, yet Roberts, for example, could also tell of Latter-day Saints who preached in public and who committed extensive biblical passages to memory precisely because they could not read (Roberts, B. H. 1990: 12).

This background knowledge of the Bible must have furnished a degree of elective affinity between a prospective convert and the LDS message, not least because a great deal of biblical material and, certainly, of biblical-style language pervaded LDS texts. So, whether in terms of form or content, there was a great deal of the Bible in both the Book of Mormon and the Doctrine and Covenants. Many parallels of biblical texts are found in the Book of Mormon including Malachi and, for example, a third of the Book of the Prophet Isaiah (Ludlow 1992: 106). To explore the relationship between these biblical texts and their Book of Mormon context is a study in its own right; here attention is drawn to a different feature, namely, to the occasional addition made to a biblical text or a gloss added to a text in a way that expresses an additional idea, reflects a different literary style or simply adds a personal religious insight. In 2 Nephi, for example, there is an echo of the Christian idea from the Sermon on the Mount concerning the narrow gate and the hard way that leads to life (Matthew 7: 13–14); it is expressed thus, 'Behold the way for man is narrow, but it lieth in a straight course before him, and the keeper of the gate is the Holy One of Israel: and he employeth no servant there' (2 Nephi 9: 41).

JOHANNINE WITNESS

One clear theme in the early part of the Doctrine and Covenants is an emphasis upon the Johannine mystery that is to be revealed, and the light that shines in darkness. This mirrors an account of Jesus, who, after his ascension into heaven, makes a special descent to the Nephites in AD 34, according to Book of Mormon chronology. He teaches the nature of baptism in the name of the Father, the Son and the Holy Ghost in order to stress the unity of these three and does so in the language of John's Gospel (John 17: 20). Other material in this chapter of Nephi also reflects further Johannine passages concerning the Father bearing witness to the Son (cf. verse 32 and John 8: 18). In the next chapter of 3 Nephi we find Jesus repeating to the Nephites the Sermon on the Mount, largely in the words of Matthew's

Gospel (cf. 3 Nephi chs. 12–15, and Matthew 5: 3 – 7: 26). Yet, even when concluding this repeat sermon, Jesus continues with the Johannine promise to raise believers up on the last day (3 Nephi 15: 1; cf. John 6: 44) and goes on to speak of himself as the good shepherd (cf. John 10: 11).

TEMPLE AND MOUNT SERMONS

One LDS interpretation of 3 Nephi 12–15, described as the Sermon at the Temple, compared it with the Sermon on the Mount (Matthew 5–7), arguing that the Book of Mormon text could be used to shed light upon the biblical parallel precisely because the Mormon version was set in the context of a temple and, accordingly, should be interpreted in the light of LDS temple teaching. For example, when Jesus blesses the children brought to him in the biblical account, he is in effect 'sealing' them to their parents for time and eternity. Similarly, when he calls his disciples to be 'perfect' as their Heavenly Father is perfect, he is 'expressing his desire' that they become fulfilled through 'their instruction and endowment' (Welch 1990: 58, 80). This exercise in biblical hermeneutics by Jack Welch shows how some LDS scholars are prepared to engage in some aspects of textual criticism drawn from wider biblical scholarship even if the final interpretative thrust derives from Mormon doctrine.

JOHANNINE MYSTERY

Returning to the Doctrine and Covenants, we find the figure of John being given distinctive appreciation in Section 7, which describes how he, as the beloved disciple, when asked by Jesus what gift he wanted, asked for 'power over death' with the ability to win souls for Christ. This he was granted with the result that he would not die but, rather, 'tarry until I come in my glory' (D&C 7: 3). Another, and most significant, link between death and John the beloved disciple, who is assumed by Latter-day Saints to be the author of John's Gospel, comes in Doctrine and Covenants Section 76, which records that, while Joseph and Sidney Rigdon were engaged in the translation of John's Gospel, they came to John 5: 29 and its account of the resurrection of the just and of the unjust. This prompted a question and affords an example of the process mentioned earlier in which engagement with the text leads Joseph to elaborate upon a variety of theological ideas. In this case it was a form of theophany exposing the future destiny of humanity, echoing some central ideas on sealing, and discussing Melchizedek priests and the divine nature of human beings. Amongst other passages that show a Johannine character are Doctrine and Covenants 92: 45, with its simple 'I will call you friends because you are my friends' (cf. John 15: 15). Similar features occur in the Book of Mormon, for example, 3 Nephi 19: 20–9, in which Jesus prays in much the same words as the high-priestly prayer of John's Gospel (John 17). Similarly 3 Nephi 27: 30–3 shows a mixture of Johannine and Synoptic elements. Within the Doctrine and Covenants a similar Johannine presence is felt, such as when Jesus describes himself as 'the same that came unto mine own and mine own received me not. I am the light which shineth in darkness, and the darkness comprehendeth it not' (cf. D&C 6: 21 and John 1: 11, 8: 12). Many minor points of similarity also occur – for example, Ammon in Alma 18 as a clear mirror of the biblical Daniel.

EVALUATING THE BOOK OF MORMON

Only now, having established the primacy of the prophet, prophecy and texts in the LDS movement, do I address the Book of Mormon and its explicit content. Indeed some might argue that the following treatment of themes is excessive, a view that might surprise some non-Mormons, especially if they assume that the book's position within Mormonism is fully analogous to, say, the Bible in Protestant churches. In fact the Book of Mormon occupies a rather ambiguous position in LDS culture, for although it was of crucial importance in the earliest years of the Church as a medium through which numerous converts gained a sense that a new revelation had taken place through the prophet Joseph Smith, practically no new doctrine came from it. But, as I intimate later in this book, since it is possible, and perhaps even likely, that the Book of Mormon will assume an increasing significance in twenty-first-century Mormonism, it is important to have a grasp of its basic narrative and dominant themes.

The Book of Mormon is primarily a text that plays and replays established biblical ideas of obedience and disobedience to God within an omnipresent engagement with Jesus Christ, whose kingdom will soon be established after people have gathered together from evil society to prepare for it. There is little theological novelty in that. Both the life of the early Mormon Church and accounts of early converts seem to indicate that what inspired people was 'the very idea of a new revelation' rather than the content of the book itself (Bushman 1984: 142). Taking that point further we can see that the book was one form of embodiment of the ideal of revelation: it focused and manifested the belief that God had spoken through prophets in the past and was speaking again through Joseph Smith in the present. The fact that

Joseph Smith, as a prophet, seer and revelator, was alive and leading the group meant that members could seek new truth from his lips and need not go back to a text in the way that so many other Christians had to do with the Bible. In this sense the Doctrine and Covenants became a more immediate source of religious direction as it documented the words of the prophet addressed to each new situation. Within the ongoing history of Mormonism the Book of Mormon has continued to stand in this ambiguous position. On the one hand, it is the foundational document, validating Joseph Smith as the chosen prophet and, in the later twentieth century, fostering forms of textual, historical and archaeological studies as well as dramatic pageants, while, on the other hand, its profile in respect of active configuration of belief and practice has been very much less significant. The inspiring of pageants involving very many performers is, perhaps, one of the Book of Mormon's more unusual theological influences, most especially in the case of the Cumorah Pageant held near Rochester, New York since 1937. Such pageants offer a powerful example of narrative theology in action as they take thousands of visitors on an imaginative journey into the epic world of the Book of Mormon accounts of ancient groups. There are few better ways of stirring imaginations and of linking what some would see as fictional or mythical events with a sense of their actual historicity. It is, then, with these observations and cautions in mind that I offer an account of the Book of Mormon's thematic content.

TEXTS AND DIRECTION

The Book of Mormon, as now set out, contains a brief description of topics at the head of each chapter. This parallels the custom that emerged in Bible translation, with the growth of printing presses and publication of newly translated versions of the Bible associated with the Reformation. Translators and editors could easily introduce a new level of interpretation to the plain meaning of the text through glosses, which serve, in effect, as theological guidance-notes. One example will suffice. In the second chapter of 2 Nephi there is a long address to Jacob concerning the Messiah and the atonement that he will effect for the sin of humanity, occasioned by the fall. It describes the original fallen angel, the temptation of Adam and Eve, the principle of atonement to remove the effect of the fall that allows each person their own subsequent freedom of choice and the important 'principle of opposition' between concepts that fundamentally structure a logical world. It employs standard Christian concepts of grace, Holy Spirit, heaven and hell. What it does not do is assert that this freedom of choice is related to 'progression'. In context, not even the chapter's final phrase in verse 30 – the 'everlasting welfare of your souls' – refers to anything other than ordinary Christian notions of an afterlife. However, once a reader sees the introductory guidance invoking the notion of 'progression' the chapter can then easily be read in a distinctly different way. Although the word 'progression' is used three times in the entire Book of Mormon, it is never used in the LDS theological sense of eternal progression in the process of deification but only in the everyday sense of journeying or developing (e.g. Alma 4: 10). Some non-LDS biblical scholars have, in their own churches, objected to such chapter headings in the Bible precisely because they intrude ideas that are not present in the text. Others, of course, see them as a helpful direction, as a means of using the developed theology of a church to assist ordinary believers in their devotional and studied use of the text.

BOOK OF MORMON THEMES AND CONTENT

As it stands today the Book of Mormon is subdivided into fifteen books, each named after a prophetic figure: Nephi (4 books), Jacob, Enos, Jarom, Omni, Mormon, Mosiah, Alma, Helaman, Ether and Moroni. It is thought to span the period of approximately 600 BC to AD 420 in a narrative account that tells of migration from the ancient Holy Land of Jerusalem to America, of the many vicissitudes of these migrant groups as they flourish, divide and war amongst themselves, largely in rebellion against divine law despite the many prophets amongst them. Jesus appears in America, paralleling his Holy Land resurrection. A period of peace ensues but is soon followed by further division, disobedience and warfare resulting in a final battle at the end of which the records of all these events, which have been devotedly kept by the prophets, are secreted away for some future hand to find.

From this brief sketch we can spell out this narrative in a little more detail by following one of the two groups who are thought to have made the journey from the Middle East to America. We begin in Jerusalem with the figure of Lehi and his family, who are warned to leave before their city is destroyed. They are led through a wilderness aided by a wonderful compass-like object called the Liahona (Alma 37: 38) – a brass ball of curious workmanship containing two spindles (1 Nephi 16: 10). There is much discontent between Lehi and his fellows, which highlights the theme of one man who obeys God whilst others rebel in hard-hearted disobedience and faithlessness. This becomes a theme that will run to the end of the entire story and echoes the biblical-historical and prophetic books that also frame the account of human rebellion against the divine will and of the presence of prophets who remind them of God's commands. They now build a ship not 'after the manner of men' but according to divine instruction received when Lehi visits the Lord on a mountain (1 Nephi 18: 2–3). Here, in both the Liahona compass and the direction for boat building we encounter the theme of mysterious guidance and disclosure that recurs throughout many subsequent events.

When they finally set sail, driven by a providential wind towards their new promised land, 'rude' behaviour and disobedience escalate into mutinous action and Nephi, Lehi's well-behaved son, is tied up. This, however, is completely counter-productive because the compass fails to work until he is released, after which they finally arrive in the promised land of America. On arrival, God commands Nephi to make metal plates and begin inscribing a history of events. In what is to become another Book of Mormon theme this history is not only to be of 'sacred' material but will also contain a strong emphasis upon prophecy and the future. This special knowledge of what is to come is disclosed to the prophets through the Spirit, sometimes described as the 'voice of the Spirit' for 'by the Spirit are all things made known unto the prophets' (1 Nephi 22: 2). Here a distinction is drawn between the things of the flesh and the things of the Spirit, with the accent falling upon the Spirit as the only reliable source and medium of truth.

THE FUTURE CHRIST

By spiritual prophecy Nephi foretells that the 'God of Israel' will come 'in six hundred years' in the figure of none other than Jesus (1 Nephi 19: 5, 8). This announces the prime theme of the Book of Mormon: prophecies involving discussions upon and arguments about Christ's future appearance and message in the new world of the promised land and not simply in the old world of Jerusalem. Here too, at the outset, there is clear reference to one who will be spat upon and crucified, the one who in LDS theology – as chapter 3 will demonstrate – is 'the God of Israel' (1 Nephi 19: 13). And Israel, in the form of its twelve tribes, is far from irrelevant, for another telling theme in the Book of Mormon focuses upon the ten lost tribes of Israel and their final inclusion in God's plan of salvation for humanity. In terms of what might be called spiritual demography the Book of Mormon sees ancient Israel as scattered across the earth prior to being 'nursed'... and...'nourished by the Gentiles' and finally gathered together again (1 Nephi 22: 6, 8).

The idea of a relationship between the lost tribes of Israel and Christ's Second Coming and millennial reign had been a significant element in broader British Christianity from the later seventeenth century and certainly entered into American millenarian thought in the eighteenth and nineteenth centuries (Underwood 1993: 64, 178). In LDS life 'the Gathering' played a central part in the growth of the early church, not least through migration from Britain. Its own grammar of spiritual discourse took the distinction between Jew and Gentile as a model for that between Latter-day Saint and Gentile. With time Saints even came to identify themselves with Jewish tribes not simply as some kind of 'spiritual Israel', as in part of Paul's theology of Christianity developed in his Epistle to the Romans, but in a much more literal sense, as we see in chapter 7. This final Gathering would take place in Zion, not in the ancient Jerusalem, but in North America, the new land of promise, 'a land of liberty', which God would preserve from being overrun by all and sundry nations and into which he would call his special people (2 Nephi 1: 7, 8).

That calling together, however, would take place at a time when there would be many other calls upon people and their commitments, not least from all those 'churches which are built up to get gain' and are 'popular in the eyes of the world', including 'that great and abominable church which is the whore of all the earth' (1 Nephi 22: 23, 13). Alongside this institutional concern with other churches the Book of Mormon is given to the constant flux of rebellion, disobedience, unbelief and individual hardness of heart. It constantly calls for repentance in the knowledge that blessing attends repentant obedience as surely as cursing follows rebellion. One of the major consequences of these spiritual dynamics is the rift that occurs between two of Lehi's sons, Laman and Nephi. Laman, one of the mutineers who had bound Nephi aboard the vessel to the promised land, continued in rebellion with the result that his descendants, the Lamanites, became a 'wild and a hardened and ferocious people', entrenched enemies of Nephi's descendants, the Nephites, and much given to tying up their enemies (Alma 17: 14, 20). This division increases throughout the Book of Mormon, despite brief periods when some Lamanites submit to divine truth and live in accord with the Nephites (Alma 17: 4). Some soundly converted Lamanites were even given a name-change to indicate their transformed identity, as with the Anti-Nephi-Lehies (Alma 23: 17). Generally, however, the Lamanites are the opponents of the Nephites. One popular LDS tradition identifies the Lamanites with Native Americans and sees the Book of Mormon as furnishing an explanation of the origin of those inhabitants of America as a 'remnant' of 'the Jews' (D&C 19: 27).

The Lamanite–Nephite grouping is not, however, the only population discussed in the Book of Mormon. Another group is thought to have migrated from east to west, leaving Jerusalem at the 'time that Zedekiah, king of Judah was carried away captive into Babylon'. Identified with the figure of Mulek, who survived the sacking (Helaman 8: 21), they were guided 'across the great waters' and settled at Zarahemla which is the name of both a place and a person (Omni 1: 13–16). They were discovered by Mosiah, who found that they had also experienced their share of war. Their language, too, 'had become corrupted'. They denied their creator and they possessed no records. Mosiah teaches them the language of the Nephites and then finds that Zarahemla can rehearse his own genealogy from memory. This, in turn, seems to indicate yet another population group, the people of Coriantumr, who originated at the Tower of Babel (Omni 1: 21, 22). Ultimately these groups merge into the broad Nephite–Lamanite grouping and share the conflict it experiences in the period that matches the historical time of the life of Jesus.

THE LIFETIME OF JESUS

The period when Jesus was historically active, as reported in the New Testament, is interesting as far as the Book of Mormon is concerned because it raises the question of the religious life of the people then depicted in America. What was happening to them while Jesus was in Palestine? In answering this question through the Book of Mormon texts it is worth recalling Grant Underwood's classification of early Mormonism as pre-millennialist, as was discussed in chapter 1. He noted the doubling-up of religious features in a premillennialist scheme of thought, and this is something we can press further for the Latter-day Saints, not least when the life of Jesus is presented through two sets of resurrection appearances.

It is important for me to focus on this part of the Book of Mormon, which deals with the earthly ministry of Jesus, as a way of commenting upon the observation made in chapter 1 that the Book of Mormon possesses no division matching that of the Bible's Old and New Testaments. My suggestion was that this is due to the epic's theme of an omnipresent Christ. The figure of Jesus runs throughout the Book of Mormon and is guaranteed in its 'pre-Christ' phase by prophets and their explicit reference to him. Some detail about his lifetime is, then, unavoidable.

The Third Book of Nephi is the textual base for the human birth of Christ and includes, in its first chapter, the pre-birth Jesus announcing the day on which he will be born, a day marked by miracle in that after 'sunset' the earth remains light until the following morning's sunrise (3 Nephi 1: 13–15). All of this took place in the American world of the Nephites, who began dating their calendar anew from that night of light (3 Nephi 2: 7–8). During this period – in fact in its thirteenth year – wars and popular discord continued in America and some of the Lamanites, those who were faithful to divine commands, joined with the Nephites 'and their curse was taken away from them, and their skin became white like unto the Nephites' for, as an earlier reference explains, 'the skins of the Lamanites were dark' because of a curse – 'a skin of blackness' – placed upon them for their transgression and rebellion (3 Nephi 2: 15; 2 Nephi 5: 21 [cf. Alma 3: 6]). Mormon, the one said to be the author of 3 Nephi, describes himself as a 'disciple of Christ, the Son of God' at a time when Jesus was still a man in his mid twenties.

JESUS' DEATH AT JERUSALEM

At approximately the time when Jesus was engaged in his public ministry in the ancient Holy Land something similar takes place in the American world. There, once more, the people have a degree of peace even though in their heart they are 'turned from the Lord'. There, the prophet Nephi is visited both by angels and 'by the voice of the Lord' and is enabled to preach 'repentance and remission of sins through faith on the Lord Jesus Christ' (3 Nephi 7: 15–16). Again, in parallel with New Testament accounts, miracles occur: the dead are raised and unclean spirits cast out but, even so, only a few are actually 'converted' and are baptized (3 Nephi 7: 19–21, 24).

One of the most dramatic parts of the Book of Mormon covers the time of the death of Jesus at Jerusalem. Instead of anything like the flow of the traditional passion narratives, considerable emphasis falls on natural catastrophe, abnormal experience of darkness, and a divine voice. Earthquakes and fires destroy cities and roads, and social communications are disrupted and many die, all in the space of three hours. Indeed the text is emphatic, noting that some reckoned it took longer but affirming that 'all these great and terrible things were done in about the space of three hours – and then, behold, there was darkness upon the face of the land'; this was no ordinary darkness – it could be felt as a 'vapor of darkness' and as 'mists of darkness' (3 Nephi 8: 19–22). This darkness lasted three days. The tactile, sensible, nature of darkness is powerfully portrayed. In symbolic terms the three hours of catastrophe followed by three days of darkness might be regarded as equivalent to the three hours Christ was on the cross followed by the period leading to his resurrection 'on the third day', as tradition expresses it. Though the three hours of a day's darkness mark the death of Christ, that is not explicitly stated in the text but has been added by later Church authorities in the chapter heading. It is a period that balances the entire night of light that marked his birth. The place of darkness and light deeply underscores these texts in a way that is reminiscent of the place of light and darkness as motifs in the Gospel of John, which, as already observed, has a marked underlying presence in this part of 3 Nephi. Here, after the darkness ends, the divine voice announces itself as 'Jesus Christ, the Son of God', one who is 'in the Father' and the Father in him, and one who was 'with the Father from the beginning'. More than that, mirroring the prologue to St John's Gospel, this is the one who 'came unto his own' and was not received, the one who is the 'light of the world' and who makes people 'sons of God' (3 Nephi 9: 15–18). After the voice of Christ there is a mighty silence in the land and, once more, some believe and turn to God.

ASCENSION AND AMERICA

After Christ's ascension, as described in the New Testament, 'he did truly manifest himself unto them – showing his body unto them (3 Nephi 10: 18–19). This appearance begins with the voice of the heavenly Father attracting the attention of people; it was neither a harsh voice nor loud, and yet in its smallness it pierced them. The words, 'Behold my Beloved Son, in whom I am well pleased, in whom I have glorified my name – hear ye him', take words from the Synoptic Gospels associated with Jesus' baptism and transfiguration and unite them with a similar Johannine theme of God's glorification of Jesus (Matthew 3: 17, 17: 5; John 12: 12). The people look upwards and a man in a white robe descends and announces himself as Jesus Christ who has suffered for the sins of the world, has drunk from the bitter cup, bears the marks of nails and now calls all to repentance and baptism. In fact repentance and baptism are repeatedly affirmed as the foundation for believers' responses to him. This practical action is what is important and not 'disputations among you concerning points of doctrine' (3 Nephi 11: 28). Jesus commissions twelve people to conduct these baptisms before repeating the words widely known in Christianity as the Sermon on the Mount from St Matthew's Gospel. This is largely, but not entirely, verbatim from the King James Version of the Bible. Occasionally there is a difference, such as in the inclusion of the word 'senine' for 'penny' (3 Nephi 12: 26), 'senine' being part of an entire nomenclature of weights and measures outlined in the Book of Mormon (Alma 11: 3–19). The command to be perfect 'as your heavenly Father is perfect', as the Bible says (Matthew 5: 48), carries the inclusion of 'be perfect even as I, or your Father who is in heaven is perfect' (3 Nephi 12: 48), thus emphasizing the perfection of Jesus Christ. One major part of his message concerns the relationship between Jews and Gentiles and, in particular, the lost tribes of Israel, to whom Jesus also had a mission (3 Nephi 17: 4). Jesus teaches the importance of the rite of eating bread and drinking wine in remembrance of him, and finally commissions twelve disciples, speaking to each personally, before ascending into heaven only to reappear the following day to reinforce his teaching in words that are very extensively derived from St John's Gospel.

One feature of the words of Jesus in his American appearance focuses on the future and on the preparation for a coming day of the Lord. Here a future-oriented 'Second Coming' is strong but so is a time of preparation for it, a time associated with Elijah the prophet (3 Nephi 24: 1; 25: 5). Here an absolutely key verse, one that subsequent Mormon spirituality would echo time and time again, is drawn from the biblical book of Malachi: 'Behold I will send you Elijah the prophet before that great and terrible day of the Lord comes. And he will turn the hearts of the fathers to their children, and the hearts of children to their fathers, lest I come and smite the land with a curse' (Malachi 4: 5). I return to this verse, perhaps the single most significant text in Mormonism, in chapter 8 when dealing with temple ritual, for it came, increasingly, to have deep theological significance for Latter-day Saints. Within the Book of Mormon, however, that last day would be one of judgement and separation of those going to heaven and those to hell (3 Nephi 26: 4–5).

Another distinctive feature of Jesus' appearance lies in his validation of the records kept by the Nephites. Jesus is said to have called Nephi, as keeper of the records, to have 'cast his eyes upon them', to have found something missing and to command inclusion of this absent reference to people who had risen from the dead according to prophecy (3 Nephi 23: 7–13). To have the figure of Jesus himself scrutinise and thereby validate the scriptures of the Book of Mormon is to reinforce the LDS sense of potential errors in scripture that have now been corrected by latter-day revelation.

A final act of validation comes in yet another post-resurrection appearance to his twelve committed disciples when he asks what gifts they want. Nine ask for an immediate transition into heaven when they die and are granted it; three have an unspoken desire – but one that is 'read' by Jesus – and are granted that they will not die until the final return of Christ (3 Nephi 28: 1–10). This desire is related to John's Gospel and the saying amongst some early Christians that John would not die until Christ came again; in fact, the Johannine text is much more direct and is addressed to Peter, telling him to look after his own affairs and not to be concerned about Christ's will for John. Accordingly the biblical text runs 'If it is my will that he remain until I come, what is that to you?' (John 21: 23). It also adds as a point of clarification that 'Jesus did not say to him that he was not to die' but simply 'If it is my will'.

QUESTION–REVELATION TEXTS

For LDS spirituality, however, this intriguing text comes to be the basis for one element of ongoing popular LDS mysticality in the notion of the Three Nephites who wander the earth until Christ comes again. It is one of the many Doctrine and Covenants 'question–revelation' texts, as they will be called in this book, and derives from Joseph Smith's preparation of his revised version of the Bible. These texts caused Joseph often to ponder some biblical passage that lacked any directly obvious answer or which was partly rhetorical, and they became the occasion for Joseph to receive a revelation by way of an answer or solution. One other significant case, for example, involved a revelation on plural marriage, grounded in a question over Abraham, Isaac and Jacob and their marriages (D&C 132: 1). Here, however, our attention returns to the lifetime of Jesus.

THE AMERICAN RESURRECTION

In Christ's post-resurrection period there was an era of considerable unity and peace when there was no distinction, 'neither were there Lamanites, nor any manner of -ites; but they were one, the children of Christ, and heirs to the kingdom of God' (4 Nephi 1: 17). This interesting cameo in which the category distinction between Nephite and Lamanite falls away is slightly reminiscent of the Acts of the Apostles and the unity of all believers following the Day of Pentecost (Acts 2: 43–7). Yet it was but short lived, as people 'began to be divided into classes; and they began to build up churches to themselves to get gain' so that, in Book of Mormon chronology, by AD 210 'there were many churches in the land' (4 Nephi 1: 26). An absolutely intense religious hatred emerged, for these churches were false to the divine message and abused the few of Christ's disciples who were still alive as immortal witnesses upon earth. Then, in the year AD 231, 'there arose a people who were called the Nephites' who now appeared as 'the true believers in Christ' and, once more, they lived alongside the Lamanites (4 Nephi 1: 36). The evil increased in number, set up secret societies, and even the Nephites now began 'to be proud in their hearts', and it is from this period that those continuing disciples of Christ 'began to sorrow for the sins of the world' (4 Nephi 1: 44).

At this point there was no distinction between Nephite and Lamanite – all were evil, as recorded on tablets that were then buried by Ammaron. He told the ten-year-old boy Mormon what he had done and gave him instruction for the future keeping of records, a story taken up in the section of the Book of Mormon called 'The Book of Mormon' reckoned to date from AD 322. The escalation of evil in warfare now became so great that even the mysteriously present beloved disciples of Christ 'were taken out of the land', leaving Mormon alone to witness to the truth (Mormon: 1: 16). In many respects it is easy to see in Mormon a reflection of the biography of the boyhood of Joseph Smith. Somehow, Mormon finds himself leading a group of Nephites against the rest in a 'complete revolution throughout the face of the land' (Mormon 2: 8). Yet again there is a repentance, this time on the part of Mormon's Nephites, but it is not genuine and, accordingly, it is turned into 'the sorrowing of the damned'; 'the day of grace' has passed them by. All this Mormon now writes down upon the earlier plates of Nephi, which he has recovered. He addresses himself in these texts to the twelve tribes of Israel, and to all, calling them to repent (Mormon 3: 14). The overall purpose of the Book of Mormon now comes to be enshrined in its closing verses as Moroni exhorts those who will read it at some future date to know of the mercy of God 'from the creation of Adam' to the present and, more particularly still, to ponder all this, sincerely asking God to validate the truthfulness of the accounts (Moroni: 10: 4). It is this very challenge to test the truthfulness of the Book of Mormon through personal prayer that remains a key feature of LDS life and missionary work in the twenty-first century.

CHRISTOLOGICAL THEOLOGY

Testing truthfulness is closely related to the Church's desire to be a witness for Jesus Christ; one easily overlooked aspect of this concerns the dynamic way in which Christ appears throughout the fifteen books that comprise the Book of Mormon's unfolding story. He is there as a kind of eternal presence even when, paradoxically, he has yet to be revealed. Examples could be chosen almost at random. One early case, reckoned to come from approximately 66 BC, has Lehi tell of the Messiah, his baptism, death, resurrection and the coming of the Spirit (1 Nephi 10: 11). Another, from approximately 550 BC, describes Nephi telling how he glories in 'plainness... in truth: I glory in my Jesus, for he hath redeemed my soul from hell' (2 Nephi 33: 6). In Mosiah, internally dated to approximately 124 BC, the good King Benjamin of Zarahemla, father of Mosiah, gave a final address to the people before he died. This he did from a specially built tower in a context that describes each family dwelling in their tents all pitched around the temple with each family receiving the message in their 'home', though some receive it in printed form because not all could hear the actual words. In this 'Tower Sermon', as we might call it, he speaks of the Messiah who is to come, who will 'dwell in a tabernacle of clay', perform miracles and undergo temptations. Indeed, in his temptation, his anguish for the 'wickedness and abomination' of people will cause him to bleed at every pore (Mosiah 3: 7). 'And he shall be called Jesus Christ, the son of God, the Father of heaven and earth, the Creator of all things from the beginning: and his mother shall be called Mary' (Mosiah 3: 8). This particular text reinforces the crucial fact, which will be explored again in chapter 3, that Jesus is identified with what ordinary Christians regard as the God of the Old Testament. Mainstream Christianity, guided by its traditional division of the Old Testament and the New Testament and by its doctrine of the Holy Trinity, implicitly associates the God of the Old Testament with the Trinitarian 'Father'. In the New Testament they still identify 'God' with the Father and, while the precise status of Jesus of Nazareth remains open to question, he is definitely not equated with the God of the Old Testament. In the Synoptic Gospels Jesus is a teacher with a question mark over his identity as the Messiah; in John's Gospel and in some of the Epistles his divine identity begins to be much more evident, as we see in chapter 3.

TESTAMENTAL UNITY

If there is no division within the Book of Mormon analogous to the Bible's Old and New Testaments, it is because the Bible is not a Christological document from beginning to end, even though some Christians do interpret what they call the Old Testament to make it appear so. The Book of Mormon, by contrast, is much more of a unity and is Christologically driven; indeed it can be read as an example of narrative theology with Christ present from beginning to end. A slight case could be made for a distinction between a period before and after the appearance of Jesus Christ in America, in that there is a brief text referring to the short golden age after his appearance when all lived happily together and 'did not walk any more after the performances and ordinances of the law of Moses; but they did walk after the commandments which they had received from their Lord and their God' (4 Nephi 1: 12). But, even that is not pressed heavily into any account of radically distinctive beliefs and practices, for the 'new' behaviour of fasting, prayer, meeting, praying and hearing the word of the Lord had always been part of the religious life of the Nephites during their obedient phases or when conscience-stricken. The Book of Mormon is not, however, always clear as a flowing narrative: the 'Words of Mormon' is thought to be a form of editorial interpolation from approximately AD 385 and lies between the Book of Omni, dated 279–130 BC and the Book of Mosiah, dated about 130 BC.

A REDUCTIONIST OPENNESS

For non-Mormons who regard the Book of Mormon as largely or exclusively the product of Joseph Smith's creative mind, its texts provide access to his own spirituality. In one important example, from Mosiah, King Benjamin could be taken to represent Joseph Smith (Mosiah 2: 8 – 4: 30). Here we find a man for whom religious ideas are no mere 'trifle' but relate directly to 'the mysteries of God' (Mosiah 2: 9). He is aware of himself as an ordinary human being who has not sought wealth but, as one 'kept and preserved' by God's 'matchless power', has sought to serve others and sees service as a central component of life (Mosiah 2: 17). He is a man who can 'tremble exceedingly' when engaged in the Lord's message (Mosiah 2: 30) but who knows that what he has is true because it comes through an angel (Mosiah 3: 2). Many similar examples could be adduced.

ORIGIN OF THE BOOK OF MORMON

But what of the origin of the Book of Mormon? Is it Joseph's own design? Is it a document originating in approximately 600 BC in Jerusalem and ending in approximately AD 420 in North America or is it a product of some other creative mind writing in the early nineteenth-century United States? This is an issue for any concerned with the book and its impact on life, but it is also a matter of faith. At the outset it is important to emphasize this matter of personal belief, not simply because it is a major issue for theology, but also because it is easily overshadowed by authors who wish to claim some historical or textual basis for proving or disproving the identity of the document. Two brief accounts will describe the issue at stake before I go on to consider each in more detail.

For earliest Latter-day Saints there was a strong belief that God had directed the writing of a historical account of groups who, as we have seen, had migrated from Jerusalem to America where a civilization emerged in which some obeyed divine laws and others did not. A series of prophets and battles surrounded these acts of obedience and disobedience that led to a final battle, after which these long historical records were written on metal plates and buried on a hillside. There they lay until the 1820s when God called the boy Joseph Smith and caused him to find them and, ultimately, to render them into English by means of a special instrument. The result was the Book of Mormon, published in 1830, the same year as the establishing of the Church of Jesus Christ of Latter-day Saints. For the earliest, as for later critics and opponents of Mormonism, this book was, by contrast, nothing of the sort. Rather than being grounded in any actual accounts of real peoples over a thousand-year period, it was some form of epic or romance, someone's creative writing of the later eighteenth or very early nineteenth century. Debates exist whether Joseph Smith took over an entire document written by someone else and passed it off as a divine phenomenon or whether he wrote it himself in a sustained act of personal creativity which he may have genuinely believed to be coming from a divine source: certainly numerous editorial and textual changes have occurred over time (Bushman 1984: 115–42; Givens 2000; Widmer 2000: 28–36).

AUTHORITY, TRUTH AND FAITH

It is easy to argue for an either-or position in this debate, whether as a Latter-day Saint using the book as the basis for the truthfulness of Mormonism or as opponents of the movement who wish to undermine the validity of the movement by finding flaws in the book. The drive for the either-or stance is largely rooted in the personal faith and ideological politics of individuals. The opposition between the two has been great and is particularly attributable to the Bible itself. For many Christians, most especially Protestants, the Bible stands as the foundational basis of Christianity. Here the notion of authority, already discussed at length above, comes to the fore, especially since Protestant Christians will not allow another source of authority to compete with the Bible. This is why Protestants have traditionally opposed Roman Catholicism because of its rooting of authority in the Church and not in the Bible. For such Protestant critics, Mormonism and Catholicism are both wrong in setting up some additional source of religious authority other than the Bible. Catholics, in turn, see the LDS Church as a false source of authority in its claim for the Book of Mormon, given the Catholic Church's claim to be the true source of religious authority. For the same reason Roman Catholicism questions the validity of Protestant churches and their ministries.

It is often difficult for people from any one of these traditions to see the point of view of the others. The personal sense of truth that many possess comes from their whole life within a community of faith and can easily be directed towards one specific point when the argument demands it. For such believers it is sometimes difficult to imagine how a sacred text or rite can speak powerfully to others, especially if they run the risk of having their own texts and rites devalued. It appears that some religious people find it difficult to share a sense of truth. Latter-day Saints, for their part, have often related the validity of the Book of Mormon to a personal religious experience associated with reading it and many speak of a feeling or sensation of its truthfulness as it speaks some personal message to them.

TESTIMONY AND TRUTH

Members of the Church testify to this inner feeling. Indeed, the very idea of 'testimony' underpins Mormon spirituality and validates its theological view of authority. As noted earlier, missionaries are likely to challenge potential members to read the Book of Mormon and to pray sincerely and ask God if the book is true or not. This challenge to personal experience marks the normal route of LDS encounter with its prime book. Converts, too, speak of similar experiences, and phrases such as 'a burning in the breast' are used to describe this inner sense of new conviction. Such testimony has been important for the Book of Mormon from the very outset, as is apparent at the front of each current copy, where there are three sets of testimonies, one from three witnesses, another from eight witnesses and the third from Joseph Smith himself. All affirm the book's divine source and witness to having seen the metallic source plates with their inscriptions.

These earliest of testimonies feed into a wider 'testimony' genre within the LDS movement that was perfectly expressed by the fifteenth prophet-leader, Gordon B. Hinkley, in closing the first chapter of his book *Faith: The Essence of True Religion*:

With certitude I give you my witness of the truth. I know that God our Eternal Father lives. I know that Jesus is the Christ, the Savior and Redeemer of mankind, the author of our salvation. I know that this work of which we are part is the work of God: that this is the Church of Jesus Christ. (Hinckley 1989: 6)

Most Saints would hear in those words strong echoes of testimonies given at the monthly Fast and Testimony Meeting when they tell how God has influenced their lives, often through family, friends and church leaders and describe incidents and events illustrating this. Speakers express gratitude and thankfulness and often testify that they know that God lives, that this is the true church and that Joseph Smith is a true prophet of God. Such testimonies are, frequently, emotional occasions on which the speaker's voice expresses their feeling. In all of this the church community serves as the framework for beliefs in the divine restoration, in the sacred texts, in the prophetic leadership and in a believer's personal involvement in all of these things. It is within this community of testimony that the Book of Mormon gains its own status and identity and, through such events, the printed and historical witnesses to the book come into a relation with contemporary believers.

CRITICISM AND FAITH

Believers do not, generally, ponder critics' arguments about inner contradictions or the historical anachronisms of the Book of Mormon as something separate from their wider life of faith. No more do Christians of other churches as far as the Bible is concerned. This is as important an issue for theology in general as it is for Mormon theology in particular, especially since biblical scholars have, from the nineteenth century, examined the text of the Bible in greater detail than any other single book. They have explored the historical situations in which its constituent books were written and the ways in which its many authors have employed different sources and marshalled cultural idioms to express particular theological ideas. In other words, the question of 'interpretation' has become central to the critical understanding of the Bible and embraces not only the way scholars 'read' the past but also how people receive the texts today.

Not all Christians have appreciated these developments. In the early part of the twentieth century, for example, there emerged in the United States a group who regarded much of what was called biblical criticism as a negative process that undermined what they took to be the simple truth of the Bible. These came to be called Fundamentalists because they published a series of pamphlets on Christian Fundamentals, including their view of and belief in the divine inspiration of the Bible; I will return to them in chapter 9. For many of these Christians biblical criticism ignored divine inspiration and produced an understanding of the Bible that was too open to diverse and divergent readings that discounted miracles and the more obviously supernatural aspects of faith. During the course of the twentieth century an entire spectrum of different forms of interpretation has emerged from a strong fundamentalism through to an extreme liberalism. This means that today there are some Christians who take practically every word in the Bible to be factually true in a historical and archaeological sense, while others accept a great deal of biblical material as the expression of belief in and through myth, story and theologically interpreted versions of history. Some think biblical statements are applicable for all time, while others want to understand rules and ideas within their cultural contexts. Within LDS cultural life, for example, there is a group called the Foundation for Ancient Research in Mormon Studies (FARMS) that follows the more traditional line, just as there are relatively small groups of liberal Saints who hold conferences and publish articles in journals such as *Dialogue* and *Sunstone*.

It is important to bear these variations in mind when thinking about the place of the Book of Mormon in Latter-day Saint life. Some of the more conservative members resemble other Christian fundamentalists in believing that the Book of Mormon really is a record of ancient Jewish and American peoples and prophets. They believe that Joseph was led to the plates and through the means of special spectacle-like instruments was enabled to produce the Book of Mormon in English. Some particularly liberal Latter-day Saints take quite a different view and are prepared to accept the book as a creative and, in that sense, inspired product of Joseph Smith's own mind. This position is possible for people who have been brought up as Latter-day Saints and have a firm identity in their life and their church community even though it might seem quite unacceptable to more conservative believers. Certainly, it is not a position that the great majority of church leaders would accept and it could hardly be the basis for the missionary work of the Church, not least because more recent Mormon theology has come to describe the Book of Mormon as 'Another Testament of Jesus Christ', setting it alongside the Bible as a collection of complementary texts telling of God's dealing with humanity. As important as these texts are, it remains true that the prophet-leader may at any time produce a revelation, such as that which removed the ban on Negro ordination (discussed in chapter 5), and thereby reverse former doctrine. It is this complex relationship between prophet and text that makes the hermeneutic situation of Mormonism unlike that of other contemporary Christian churches.

CHAPTER 3

Divine–human transformations

Prophecy and sacred texts provide the medium and the message that together helped to forge Mormonism's doctrines of deity, humanity and the relationship between the two. Although very early Mormonism viewed God much as other Protestants did, it also developed the idea that God had undergone a process of progression and that, through special rituals and ways of life, human beings could also undergo a process of transformation or apotheosis to become gods in the next world. In this chapter I explore core doctrines that work together to bring this about, paying special attention to ideas of God, Jesus Christ, Holy Spirit, covenant and deification as well as sin, salvation and the various levels of heaven. Each is related to the others in the overall quest for religious understanding that culminates in exaltation.

CREDAL SHADOW

Although there have been numerous lists of LDS doctrines and principles, the closest the Latter-day Saints come to possessing a creed is in two sets of texts, the document called the 'Articles of Faith' and a text in the Doctrine and Covenants; here I consider each but with an emphasis upon the first because it has assumed a greater distinctive identity over the years.

Originating in 1842 as a direct response to John Wentworth, editor of the *Chicago Democrat*, the Articles of Faith underwent various changes before its inclusion in the Pearl of Great Price in 1880 (Whittaker 1992: 67–9; cf. 'The Wentworth Letter', *EM*, 1992: 1750–5). It is not a creed in the wider Christian sense of the word, is not rehearsed in worship and does not have to be learned or assented to in any formal fashion. As with most other 'restorationist' groups of Protestants originating in the early nineteenth-century United States the Latter-day Saints did not take kindly to formal creeds; indeed, one reference to creeds in the Doctrine and Covenants is entirely negative, describing 'the creeds of the fathers' as part of 'inherited

lies' and related to the filling of 'the world with confusion' (D&C 123: 7).
Richard Bushman's biography of Joseph Smith also observed this LDS
avoidance of creeds; he viewed it as due, in part at least, to a strong preference for actual events rather than for the theological rationalization or
schematization that were often present in other groups such as the Disciples,
a movement founded by Alexander Campbell, which was well known in
Smith's day and was related to Smith through Campbell's former associate,
Sidney Rigdon (Bushman 1984: 188).

An early revelation in Doctrine and Covenants Section 20 provides just
such an action-related description of the Church and its organization in
what might be read as its founding charter. Set amidst its description of
restoration events surrounding the 'Church of Christ in these last days',
there is one section, namely verses 17–36, that does take a credal form.
Many, but not all, of its phrases echo elements of the Apostles' Creed most
strongly. Reflecting this in paraphrase, it affirms belief in an eternal and
infinite God in heaven, 'from everlasting to everlasting the same unchangeable God, the framer of heaven and earth, and all things which are in them'.
He created male and female 'after his own image' and gave them commandments to love and serve him. By 'transgression of these laws man became
sensual and devilish' and this occasioned God to give his 'Only Begotten
Son' to suffer temptations 'but not to heed them. He was crucified, died
and rose again the third day; And ascended into heaven, to sit down on
the right hand of the Father.' Those who believe and are baptized – even
those born before these events took place – may have eternal life. The Holy
Ghost, who bears witness to all this, is also involved in the process: 'which
Father, Son and Holy Ghost are one God, infinite and eternal, without
end. Amen'. One reason why this text has not assumed greater currency
in the Church may be because creeds, as such, were not preferred as a ritual form, but another reason may lie in the potential dissonance between
the Church's traditional Christian view of an eternal and changeless God
and the idea of God as a progressing agent, which soon came to prominence in the developing LDS cosmology. Still, the text remains a cultural
resource of the Church and could be developed if the Church decided to
stress the changeless nature of God, which is often favoured by Christendom at large, rather than its evolving deities that were much in favour
during Brigham Young's leadership of the Church in the mid nineteenth
century.

Another formal LDS statement of belief is found in Doctrine and
Covenants Section 134 and described there as a 'declaration of belief regarding governments and laws in general'. Though hardly theological in

any strictly doctrinal sense, these twelve verses assent to governments as instituted of God and as having a right to promulgate laws and enforce them. A sharp distinction between state and churches is advocated, as is the right of churches to discipline their own members. A final document, entitled *Lectures on Faith,* will also be considered in some detail in chapter 4 in connection with Mormonism's doctrinal interpretation of salvation. I now return to the Articles of Faith as a more often specified text of LDS belief and, given their sharp doctrinal focus, I will use several of them in both this and subsequent chapters to highlight basic LDS theology and to observe some historical aspects of doctrinal development.

GOD

The Articles open with the assertion: 'We believe in God, the Eternal Father, and in His Son, Jesus Christ, and in the Holy Ghost.' This simple affirmation echoes the doctrine of the Trinity, which gradually became the mark of orthodoxy during the first four hundred years of Christianity and sets the mark for all subsequent debates about the nature of God. Whilst reflecting early Christian creeds the affirmation does not express the rationale of LDS thought, especially its later development, for it does not operate on the same philosophical principles. Though some LDS writers have tried to describe LDS accounts of God in relation to the official creeds of Christendom, the venture is seldom fruitful, because the worlds of thought and of ritual action associated with them are markedly different (Hale 1989: 7–14). In fact the LDS approach to God is not always easy for members of other Christian denominations to grasp, because of the distinctive value given to the relative status of 'God', 'Father' and 'Son'. Jesus Christ, for example, is identified with the Old Testament figure of Jehovah and was the God of Israel. This immediately draws a distinction between LDS and most other Christian traditions, which would identify the God of the Hebrews as 'the Father', and Jesus as the Father's Son. There are, in fact, some other dramatic complexities in the Mormon doctrine of God, symbolized in the expression 'Adam-God theory', but I will return to these below, after dealing with a more straightforward and more widely accepted picture of deity.

God the Father

At the outset the very word 'Father' demands close attention. Many ordinary Christians would, in popular terms and in practical spirituality, identify

God the Father with the God of the Old Testament, often referred to as Jehovah. For them the link between Father and Jehovah is assumed and they would not anticipate the counter-intuitive LDS view that equates Jesus with Jehovah. For ordinary Christians it is important to stress this fact: in Mormon terms Jesus is Jehovah and Jehovah is not the Father. In Mormon terminology the source responsible for all spirits, including that of Jesus, is *Elohim*. This Hebrew plural noun of majesty or intensity is usually used with a verb in the singular and, biblically, describes the single identity of God the Father. In the opinion of Latter-day Saints and in their traditional ritual, however, *Elohim* becomes particularly important in relation to creation stories, in which it is given a full plural designation – the Gods (Abraham 4: 1). This marks a clear distinction from historical Christian doctrine for two reasons.

First, speaking of 'Gods' instead of 'God' sets the notion of a plurality of gods against Christianity's emphatic monotheism. As we saw in chapter 1, this idea emerged with the Book of Abraham and, as Fawn Brodie indicates, was concurrent with Joseph Smith's engagement with Hebrew when, in the winter of 1835–6, he learned that *Elohim* was a plural form (Brodie 1995: 170–2. cf. Kirtland 1989: 36–7; Widmer 2000: 36). It was also shortly after Joseph had become much engaged with Egyptian papyri and mummies that he had set about producing a 'translation' of one of these that would emerge as the Book of Abraham. This element of what we might call Joseph's 'orientalism' included the fact that Joseph Smith seems to have identified himself, to some degree at least, with the biblical figure of Joseph, sold into slavery in Egypt. Indeed, Brigham Young is reported to have clearly stated that Joseph's descent was 'from Joseph that was sold into Egypt . . . and the pure blood was in him' (see Swanson 1989: 98).

Certainly, Egypt and its mysteries were important to Joseph and this period of study was crucial in his thinking, the Book of Abraham being of importance as the first to present a published expression of the idea of a plurality of Gods in 1842, though it was not officially established as a doctrinal feature until the 1880s. Here the primal organization of the earth is accomplished by the Gods (plural), suggesting a connection in understanding between *Elohim* as a plural form and an actual plurality of agents (Abraham 4: 14–27). *Elohim* 'organized' pre-existent matter; they 'certainly did not create it' (*The Father and the Son: Doctrinal Exposition by the First Presidency*, 1916; see *EM*, 1992: 1670).

This notion of 'organization' introduces the second major difference between traditional Christian and LDS theology: whether by single or multiple agency, this 'organization' contrasts with the general Christian doctrine often expressed in the Latin phrase *creatio ex nihilo*. This idea carries the double connotation of God creating everything from nothing – what now exists once did not exist – and of God as being independent of the 'created order' – God is not of the same 'stuff' as the universe. This emphasis upon 'organization' over 'creation' will become particularly significant in chapter 5 with regard to the underlying ideological rationale of LDS church and community life: there, too, we also see the Hebrew plural of *Elohim* rendered as a direct plural – 'Gods'. This difference of perspective between LDS and mainstream Christian tradition must, then, be kept in mind when using words such as 'creation' or 'creator', not least because this pattern of ideas generated what would become Mormonism's overarching doctrinal mythology – the plan of salvation – outlined at the very start of this book. This image of God reinforces Dan Vogel's argument that 'Mormonism was never trinitarian but consistently preferred heterodox definitions of God' (1989: 17).

God the Son

More traditionally, perhaps, Jesus is taken to be the 'Son of God', and this in the most direct sense of God the Father engaging with Mary to engender his Son. This allows Latter-day Saints to speak of the divine and the human nature in Jesus without becoming involved in the technical debates of the early period of Christian history. The Articles of Faith, for example, do not refer to the human and divine natures of Jesus, nor yet to his mother being a virgin, nor to a virgin birth. Brigham Young was clear on the subject, 'the Being whom we call Father was the Father of the spirit of the Lord Jesus Christ, and he was also his Father pertaining to the flesh. Infidels and Christians, make all you can of this statement': Mary was impregnated by God the Father to produce Jesus in the same way as Brigham's father had sired him (Young 1992: 127, 137).

To make the situation slightly more complex, however, there are occasions when Jesus is called 'The Father' and this association is only partially resolved by arguing that this is when his own 'Father' decides that Jesus should represent him (see Vogel 1989: 22–23). In this representative role Jesus may be called 'Father' by human beings even though, in general, when Latter-day Saints speak of God as 'Heavenly Father' their prime reference is to God the Father. This becomes very clear in one of the very few set church prayers used at the sacrament service, as described in chapter 7.

There are further cases in which there is a strong potential for confusing the identities of these divine agents, as, for example, in the dedicatory prayer used at the Kirtland Temple and explicitly furnished as being of divine revelation in Doctrine and Covenants. Forms of address used in the prayer are to the Lord God of Israel, also addressed as the Lord (D&C 109: 1, 3), God (D&C 109: 79), the Lord God Almighty (D&C 109: 77), who is further identified as the Holy Father (D&C 109: 4, 10, 14, 22, 24, 29, 47). He is also addressed as Father of Jesus Christ (D&C 109: 4), and as the Most High (D&C 109: 9). Without any apparent shift of person addressed, the prayer also directs itself to Jehovah (D&C 109: 34, 42, 56) in a setting where a wide usage of 'Lord' seems to embrace the divine focus of the prayer (D&C 109: 3, 4, 9, 31, 33, 43, 46, 47, 48, 49, 50, 51, 54, 60, 68, 69, 71, 72, 75, 78). In verse 68 however – in one of those elements of prayer in which the divine focus is reminded of an aspect of the religious life of the supplicant – a distinction is made between persons in a particularly individual part of the prayer: 'O Lord, remember thy servant Joseph Smith, Jun., and all his afflictions and persecutions – how he has covenanted with Jehovah, and vowed unto thee, O Mighty God of Jacob...' This particular prayer is, then, but one example of the way in which the names and the identity of persons of the godhead can, potentially at least, be confusing. This should not, however, be taken as a unique feature of LDS prayers since those of many denominations, especially when they are grounded in the emotional experience of a particular event, can easily blur the distinctions that are made and held in formal theology.

In more formal terms, God the Father, or 'God the Eternal Father' as he is often addressed in worship, is particularly important because, along with a heavenly mother figure, he is the source of all spirit children. Jesus, too, was produced as a spirit child in this way in the pre-existent world prior to his taking a human body through Mary, in a human birth that was the outcome of a form of union between Mary and the Eternal Father. As the Prophet Ezra Taft Benson explained it: 'Jesus was not the son of Joseph, nor was he begotten by the Holy Ghost. He is the Son of the Eternal Father' (1983: 4, cited by Millet 1992: 725).

As far as the LDS doctrine of the godhead is concerned – and 'Godhead' is a term much preferred over 'Trinity' – much is driven by Joseph Smith's first vision, when he was fourteen years of age. Joseph described a great pillar of light in which two divine beings came to him: the one was assumed to be God the Father because he called the other his Son. It is precisely because these two 'personages', as they are usually called, were perceived by Joseph to be distinct entities that Mormonism set itself on the path to a notion of godhead which some stress as being twofold but others as threefold, albeit with the qualification that two of the three possessed actual bodies.

This visionary presence of Jesus is at least as important as the doctrine of the Incarnation as the foundation for belief in the divine engagement with human bodies.

One minor aspect of early LDS thought, or perhaps it might better be called speculation, and one that is rarely formally discussed today, is the idea that Jesus did, in fact, marry, and that he married both Mary and Martha, the sisters of Lazarus, whom he raised from the dead (see Buerger 1994: 67; Kraut 1969). This idea would probably be viewed as impious by many ordinary Christian traditions, not simply because the Bible says nothing about it, but because marriage, sex and sin often seem to combine in a negative way in everyday Christian mentality, despite theological protestations to the contrary, and Christians do not associate Jesus with sin of any sort. In LDS spirituality, however, sexuality is largely positive and in early Mormonism marriage, especially plural marriage, became the route to exaltation rather than to hell.

Holy Ghost

After affirmation of the Son and the Father, Latter-day Saints include the Holy Spirit but do so from a distinctive perspective. Usually referring to the Holy Ghost rather than the Holy Spirit, Saints describe this aspect of the divine as 'a spirit man, a spirit son of God the Father' (McConkie, J. F. 1992: 649). Once more, the Spirit is accorded a clear gender status but the distinctive difference between him and the figures of the Father and the Son, according to the Doctrine and Covenants, is that while each of them possesses flesh and bones, 'the Holy Ghost has not a body of flesh and bones, but is a personage of Spirit', with the functional advantage of being able to 'dwell in us' (D&C 130: 22). Exactly what the 'personage of Spirit' meant was debated, as some Saints pondered whether the Spirit had a spirit body that rendered him more definitely a distinct entity or whether he was only an influential power. Other beliefs of folk-speculation, firmly negated by church leaders, were variously that Joseph Smith might have been the Holy Spirit incarnate or that Adam or Michael or even the 'Mother in heaven' might answer to that identity (Swanson 1989: 97–8).

In more practical terms, too, the Holy Ghost is a striking feature of LDS theology and yet a feature that can easily be overlooked because its significance lies in the emphasis the Saints place upon experience. This affects the foundation experiences of the prophet and key church leaders as well as of individual Saints. Though many texts from the Standard Works illustrate this point, one, from the Book of Mormon, will suffice to illustrate the Spirit's centrality. In an important section dealing with the organization and practice of believers the Book of Moroni tells how 'their meetings were conducted by the church after the manner of the workings of the Spirit, and by the power of the Holy Ghost: for as the power of the Holy Ghost led them whether to preach, or exhort, or to pray, or to supplicate, or to sing, even so was done' (Moroni 6: 9). Later in Moroni comes a passage that has emerged as something of a proof text in practical Mormon life, especially employed by missionaries when inviting inquirers to test the truth of the Book of Mormon for themselves. As Moroni concludes what is to be the Book of Mormon and, before hiding it away in his war-ridden days until it would be found by Joseph Smith, he addresses later generations:

and when ye shall receive these things, I would exhort you that ye would ask God, the Eternal father, in the name of Christ, if these things are not true: and if ye shall ask with a sincere heart, with real intent, having faith in Christ, he will manifest the truth of it unto you by the power of the Holy Ghost. And by the power of the Holy Ghost ye may know the truth of all things. (Moroni 9: 4)

This exemplifies the much wider Protestant theological idea of the interior witness of the Holy Spirit, a driving feature of a religious world in which individual responsibility and a sense of private authenticity underlie each person's approach to God. It also reflects the status given to the biblical text in Protestant thought, for this prayer too requests a sense of the truthfulness of the texts Moroni committed to the future. Here, it is through a strong belief in the Holy Ghost that earliest Mormonism is setting a sacred text alongside personal experience in the anticipation that they will become bound together in a unified demonstration of the validity of divinely sourced truth. This single text is also interesting in that it enshrines something of the early threefoldness of Mormonism when referring to engagement with deity, for, in many respects, the Book of Mormon treats Father, Son and Spirit in terms reminiscent of mainstream Christianity, often because it reflects or directly echoes biblical texts. The real problem with discussing 'the Trinity' in Mormonism is that once one passes from a general reference to any detailed consideration of the 'nature' of 'individuals', all classical descriptions of the Trinity are rendered redundant in documents that are later than the Book of Mormon (Vogel 1989; Kirtland 1989).

Still, the Holy Spirit remains profoundly important for practical religion and the experience of individual Saints. This, too, raises questions, for, as LeGrand Richards explains, the Holy Spirit is a 'male personage... in the form of a man' and, therefore 'confined to a limited space', which, inevitably, raises the issue of how he can influence people at a distance (1969: 120). Richards addresses this problem by making a distinction between the gift of the spirit, which comes only by the rite of the laying on of hands by accredited priests, and the wider 'influence' of the 'Spirit of God or the Spirit of Christ', which God may employ without any earthly agent to achieve his own purpose (1969: 126–30). But these are issues of the divine presence that are seldom fully systematized in any form of Christianity and reflect changing emphases over time.

Adam-God

Such differences between doctrines enshrined in the Book of Mormon and doctrines that emerged later in the Church can be profound. No single case is probably as clearly significant as that which has come to be called the Adam-God doctrine. It is included here as a separate section because it holds a questionable place within Mormon thought, not least because of its paradoxical nature. Indeed, seldom is the word 'paradoxical' more appropriately used, for its doctrinal position lies alongside others in a way that strikes contradictory chords. In doctrinal terms the God of the Book of Mormon is not the same God as appears in the Adam-God theory. This caused much debate in nineteenth-century Mormonism and sometimes causes embarrassment today.

Doctrinal issues that mainstream Christianity takes to be rooted in established tradition are in no way so binding in LDS thought, because the prophetic commitments of the faith always make revelation a possibility. For Joseph Smith this revelatory religion embraced a sense of the secret, and secrecy was part of its attraction, prompting the excitement, sketched in chapter 1, that helped to motivate commitment to what might lie ahead (see Buerger 1994: 49). Indeed the ninth Article of Faith reflects this in seeing 'all that God has revealed' and 'all that He does now reveal' as a background to the belief that 'He will yet reveal many great and important things pertaining to the Kingdom of God'. It was in what has been called the King Follett Sermon of April 1844 that Joseph Smith disclosed just such a 'secret', outlining some of his most advanced ideas relating to God as an evolving being who had organized pre-existing matter and helped pre-existing intelligences on their path to becoming gods. All this was in the context of a funeral sermon and highlights the vital importance of death in Mormon theology and religion, as I show in later chapters. The principal message of that sermon was that 'the core essence of God and man was co-equal' (Widmer 2000: 129). Joseph announced that God (the Eternal Father) is an exalted man and once was as we now are: 'God himself was once as we are now, and is an exalted man and sits enthroned in yonder heavens! That is the great secret' (*TPJS*, 1938: 345). This view of God raised many questions, especially the key issue of how God could have evolved from man but, because Joseph Smith died shortly after this sermon, it was left to others, not least to Brigham Young, to try to answer them. In one of his sermons Brigham says, 'I tell you, when you see your Father in the Heavens, you will see Adam: when you see your Mother that bear your spirit, you will see Mother Eve' (Young 1992: 99). This Adam-God doctrine, as it came to be called, developed in the 1850s and one example of it appeared in the *Millennial Star:* 'Jesus our elder brother was begotten in the flesh by the same character that was in the Garden of Eden and who is our Father in Heaven...Adam...Michael the Archangel, the Ancient of Days. He is our Father and our God and the only God with whom we have to do' (*MS*, 1853: 770). The plan of salvation serves, once more, as the motivating frame for this doctrine which, as Kurt Widmer describes it, begins in the Council of the Gods, who decide that one of their number, a lesser God named Michael, along with his wife, is sent to earth to furnish bodies for pre-existing spirits (Widmer 2000: 130–42). This discloses Adam's true identity: Adam was Michael who, in the pre-existence, had also produced spirit offspring including Jehovah and Lucifer.

This means that Michael, though a lesser God in the ultimate Council of the Gods, was the one who fathered the spirit children in the pre-existence and also made it possible for them to come to earth, because he and one of his wives had already come to earth to begin the human race. In fact it was their 'fall' that enabled them to become human. Through subsequent development and progression Michael, who was also Adam, then evolves to take his place as God the Father, the only God 'with whom we have to do'. If these separate ideas are pressed into some logical conclusion, we have to see the nature of reality as possessing Gods above and behind the single identity of Michael-Adam-Father whilst retaining him as 'the God with whom we have to do'.

One reason why this Adam-God theory was historically important in approximately 1850–1900 was that it came to be expressed at significant parts of the temple-ritual drama and reinforced the developing Mormon doctrines of plural families and the eternal future of family members as persons evolving into godhood. Special lectures portrayed the Council in Heaven, the organization of earth, the arrival of Michael and his wife, their being tempted by Lucifer and their subsequent parenting of earthly children. This was complemented by accounts of how current Mormons should covenant with God and, by receiving their own endowments, could regain a heavenly identity after death. These formal lectures were in some contexts accompanied by formal ritual drama that rehearsed the plan of salvation in dramatic form. Some elements of this teaching and drama continue to play a part in LDS temples even though the Adam-God theory and the notion of Gods above and beyond Heavenly Father are given little formal status in today's church. In the mid and later nineteenth century Brigham's view was far from accepted by all: for example, he had some considerable debate with Orson Pratt over the Adam-God doctrine. Pratt was an important exponent of LDS doctrine with a philosophical sense that some think was fostered by his time spent in Scotland in the 1840s. Brigham even went so far as to ban some of Pratt's published work because many Saints tended to align themselves with it. Pratt preferred to speak, for example, of many Gods in the sense that individuals could become the temples of vehicles for truth: 'TRUTH is the God, that dwells in them all' (Widmer 2000: 136).

Indeed, the potential for confusion over these various ideas of and terms describing God was recognized not in a revelation but in a 'Doctrinal Exposition' on 'The Father and the Son', which was published by the First Presidency and the Council of the Twelve Apostles in June 1916 and to which I made an earlier reference concerning creation. Its basic affirmation is that 'Jesus Christ was Jehovah, the God of Israel, and that Elohim was his father'; as Boyd Kirtland argued concerning this issue, 'Little biblical support for these ideas could be given, as the exposition mainly dealt with problems inherent in early LDS scriptures and the theology of Joseph Smith and Brigham Young' (Kirtland 1989: 47). Contemporary LDS views of God tend more, if anything, to the wider Christianity already present in the Book of Mormon.

God's body

Despite earlier debates, the notion of the development of divine identity is inextricably bound up with the LDS belief that God possesses a body. To speak of God's body is not just some metaphorical reference for Latter-day Saints but is an expression of the profoundest symbolic expression of Mormon spirituality, for in it the Saint acknowledges a likeness with God, a likeness that is rooted in their ultimate kinship and speaks of the possibility of what lies open to one's own destiny. The Latter-day Saint conviction remains that 'the Father has a body of flesh and bones as tangible as man's' (D&C 130: 22). Just how God developed and evolved lies beyond current knowledge and involves speculation whether there were worlds before the current universe. It is the focused belief that God possesses a body that remains of paramount importance to LDS thought and it has, for example, been firmly defended in terms of philosophical theology by LDS philosopher David Paulsen (Paulsen 1996: 204–12). In so speaking of God the use of gender language referring to 'him' is perfectly intelligible since God's body is gendered, indeed that is the reason why human beings are male and female, because they are modelled after the divine Father and, by implication and by some explicit reference, a divine mother, as I show in chapter 7.

Godhead, triune or dual?

So it is that, as Mormon thinking about the deity developed, the Father, Son and Holy Ghost were described as constituting the godhead, with 'godhead' coming to be the strongly preferred LDS term for this grouping of identities rather than 'Trinity'. This is not accidental, because Latter-day Saints increasingly distanced themselves from the mainstream of Christianity, its extensive philosophical reflections and the formulae that allowed theologians of the first five Christian centuries to speak of the three persons as sharing one 'substance'. To say, with early orthodoxy that Father, Son and Holy Spirit were 'homoousios' – Greek for 'of one substance' – did not make sense to Joseph Smith. To say that God was 'three in one and one in three' is to indicate a 'strange God': for him each was a distinct 'personage', a distinctive term in LDS thought, and as such was also a 'distinct God' whose basic unity lay in a unity of purpose and intent (Dahl 1992: 552–3). This 'agreement' was an important term for Joseph Smith, so much so that he sought to render part of the Greek text of John's Gospel as expressing agreement rather than 'oneness' (John 17: 11, 21). And this agreement was itself grounded in an 'everlasting covenant...made between' these 'three personages before the organization of this world' (*TPJS*, 1938: 190). Brigham Young, for example, approaches a similar issue, that of the relationship between God and humanity, by arguing that the 'father of our spirits in the eternal world... is a being of the same species as ourselves' (Young 1992: 106). In traditional Christian terms this would set humanity and God as being of 'one substance'. Brigham, in characteristic jocular mode, comments on traditional Christian Christology of the two natures of Christ by likening it to the mule as a hybrid beast, though he begs pardon for the analogy.

If Young's views introduced new streams of thought into Mormonism, or at least developed Joseph Smith's partly formed ideas, another source that has held a paradoxical place in Mormon thought is that known as *Lectures on Faith* (Smith, J. 1985). Originally intended as class lectures for the elders in 1834–35 in Kirtland, they were included in the 1835 edition of Doctrine and Covenants and remained until the 1921 edition had them removed. They are problematic in presenting doctrinal ideas that differ from later LDS revelations. It is likely that they were written or much influenced by Sidney Rigdon, though most LDS sources tend only to speak of his assisting in their preparation: in fact, as we see in chapter 5, he left the Church after a failed attempt to assume its leadership on the martyrdom of Joseph (van Wagoner 1994: 162, 174). An original convert to the Baptist Church, he had later joined Joseph Smith and worked closely with him during his lifetime. Some contemporaries and many later writers deemed him a headstrong and relatively unstable individual, fervent and belligerent on occasion. He later attempted to set up his own prophetic group, as described in chapter 9. His background and training may explain why the lectures read more like a Protestant Catechism than an LDS revelation; it is hard to see much of Joseph Smith's visionary theology in them, except perhaps on the issue of faith as a principle and as an attribute of deity (see Vogel 1989: 27). Certainly their commitment to the notion of deity as unchanging is difficult to reconcile with the later LDS views of eternal progressive development, as discussed above with regard to the Adam-God theory. What is important for present purposes is that its fifth lecture – part of the Standard Works of the Church for the best part of ninety rather formative years – deals with the topic of the godhead. It emphasizes the Father and the Son as the 'two personages who constitute the great, matchless, governing, and supreme power over all things' and, while including the Holy Spirit in the central threefold group, describes that aspect of deity in terms of being the 'mind of the Father'. The description of the relation between the Father and the Son is also more credal than most other LDS texts, and it is noteworthy for this description of the Holy Spirit (not the 'Holy Ghost' as in most LDS texts) as the 'mind of the Father'. These *Lectures on Faith* are, then, conceptually odd, for, whilst they introduce a notion of faith that will have distinctive consequences, as I show in chapter 4, and while they are more Binitarian than Trinitarian, their general tenor, as far as faith in a broad sense is concerned, remains generically Protestant with a rational rather than pietist inclination; more Deist or Unitarian than Methodist or Presbyterian. Certainly they differ from the Book of Abraham with its plural notion of deity and it would be theologically impossible to construct the plan of salvation from the *Lectures on Faith*.

COVENANT SPIRITUALITY

This is particularly true as far as the crucial LDS notion of covenant is concerned, for there is practically nothing on the notion of covenant in the *Lectures on Faith*, yet for Joseph and for the Church after his death the idea of covenant became radically more significant than in mainstream churches. They took 'covenant' to distinguish between the Old Covenant or Old Testament of the religion of Jews before the coming of Jesus and the New Covenant or New Testament that covered God's dealing with humanity after the birth of Jesus and leading into the era of Christianity.

Often certain words serve a profound purpose within religions, acting as symbols that unite and enhance ideas and practices, as I have explored elsewhere for such Mormon concepts as 'the mantle', the 'keys', 'the brethren' and 'calling' (Davies 2000: 175–80). To these I would add 'covenant'. If anything, Joseph's emphasis on covenant reflects a religious attitude more reminiscent of the Jewish religious thought underlying the Hebrew Bible than of the Christian perspective inherent in much of the New Testament. In an important study of LDS theologies of Israel, Steven Epperson has shown that Joseph's commitment to 'Israel's example and integrity' led him to 'foster its covenantal role in the redemption of the world' (1992: 125). This differential emphasis colours much LDS thought and practice and affords a major point of departure between LDS and traditional Christian theology. When members of different religious traditions disagree with each other they often tend to argue the merits of one doctrinal case over another; text is debated against text and idea against idea but without much effect upon each other. What is often lacking in such debates is any real sense of how their ingrained way of life, the respective lives of faith, give meaning to their existence and underlie their arguments. The word 'spirituality' is a useful shorthand for the mixed bundle of formal and informal beliefs, practices and customs that animate and inform a people's religious way of life, which was why, for example, I entitled an earlier study *Mormon Spirituality* (Davies 1987).

Throughout its history the Mormon Church has maintained a firm root within a spirituality of covenant, one in which there is a sense of mutual agreement between God and the individual believer and also between the individual member of the Church and its prophet-leader. The strength and nature of this covenant agreement is unlike the spirituality of most other Christian churches and it goes far in explaining the difference of perspective on Christianity that obtains between them. One of the most frequent points of debate between Mormons and others focuses on the very nature of salvation as related to the notion of 'grace', which I explore in some detail in chapters 4, 7 and 8, and it is in preparation for those discussions that 'covenant' is emphasized here. Mormon covenant is a binding agreement entered into ritually and with due solemnity and reflects the covenant agreement entered into by the divine personages of the godhead prior to the creation of this world in which we live. Covenant also underlies the LDS theological scheme because of the divine promise expressed through prophets and their prophecy (e.g. 3 Nephi 29: 1–3).

HUMAN DEIFICATION-APOTHEOSIS

When current Saints enter into their own covenant agreements through the symbolism of the endowment temple-ritual, they explicitly enter upon a way of life that leads to 'godhood', a distinctive LDS term. The LDS aphorism that we are all 'gods in embryo' is meant to be taken literally and as an encouragement to live ethically and ritually in fulfilment of religious covenants in order to progress from one's present human condition into divine status. The entire LDS theory of the individual within the total cosmos is one of a developmental shift from eternal intelligence, to personalized intelligence as a spirit child of God the Father, then as a human being and then as a resurrected being. Throughout this progression the 'self' is increasingly engaged in growing numbers of relationships and responsibilities. In this the Church shows itself to have been, as it were, one of the earliest of American 'human potential' movements, not least a potential for godhood. As we see in chapters 4, 6, 7 and 8, this move into the future depends upon holding both marital and priesthood status. It also takes place against a background of belief that heaven is a complex and layered set of domains within which each person can gain the rewards resulting from different levels of life achievement.

There is, then, an apotheosis, a making of gods, at the heart of LDS spirituality, as would be revealed in the notion that there be 'many gods' (D&C 121: 28). What is of importance in LDS theological history is that this element of apotheosis was deeply welded to the practice of making covenants with God in the context of endowment rituals. Covenant and apotheosis are usually, within religions, concepts of quite different types but, in the development of LDS thought they have combined to yield a spirituality that is more than the sum of its parts; it was by 1843 that this began to take effect in Mormonism when small numbers of married couples were receiving a 'second anointing', ensuring that they would become divine kings and queens in the afterlife.

While the notion of covenant is deeply familiar to historic Christianity, that of apotheosis is far less so, and it becomes decreasingly familiar as one moves from Greek Orthodoxy, with its recognition of 'theosis' as a process in which people may be transformed through becoming united with God, to Roman Catholicism, whose 'saints' are Christians closer to God within the overall 'body of Christ'. Protestantism, for its part, has rendered such ideas redundant through its emphasis upon the fallen sinfulness of humanity and upon the Incarnation as Christ's assumption of human nature – sin excepted – in the overall process of salvation. Heaven, for the Protestant, is to be with God and not to be a god, despite biblical texts that can be read as a description of human transformation into the image of Christ (e.g. Romans 8: 29). Generally speaking, it is difficult for the majority of mainstream Christians to understand how people may 'become gods', precisely because credal orthodoxy sets a sharp distinction between God and humanity. As we have seen, the Holy Trinity's members being of 'one substance' with each other sets them apart as 'God' from the 'human substance' of being human. Indeed the great debate in early Christianity lay precisely in trying to find a language to explain how the divine nature of God and the human nature of people could, in some way, come together in the person of Jesus. The 'two-natures' argument over Jesus' identity still remains of interest to contemporary Christians, because he is sometimes made so divine as to lose contact with humanity, whilst at other times he is represented as so human as to lose the divine status. For Latter-day Saints this is not a problem, for every individual shares the same 'substance', everyone is a spirit person at some stage of developing their potential as divine, and in this sense Jesus is simply an elder brother who is further along the path of divine development.

HEAVEN AND HEAVENS

In traditional Christian thought such a fulfilment of human development comes not in this life but in the life of the world to come when, freed from sin and its influences, the believer is transformed through the possession of a spiritual body and is set free to worship God. But such traditional and popular Christian ideas of heaven still foster the idea of difference be-tween God and humanity by interpreting heaven as a place of worship, for worship involves a radical distinction between God and worshippers. It is this distinction that makes worship possible. Even when in the more pietistic forms of Christian devotionalism heaven is portrayed as a form of loving intimacy with God, there remains a difference between divine and human persons. Charles Wesley's extremely popular hymn 'Love divine all loves excelling' exemplifies this when he speaks of being 'changed from glory into glory, till in heaven we take our place: Till we cast our crowns before Thee, Lost in wonder, love and praise'. Here the believer has received the victor's crown only to lay it before God, who remains the central focus of being. Here, by the grace of a divine light of glory dawning upon the saved person, the full benefit of the Beatific Vision of God is known. Many other Christian hymns across two millennia reflect a similar sense. The heavenly vision of God is the final attraction and absorption of the faithful. Whatever transformation may have taken place in Purgatory – in the Church Expectant of Catholic theology – or through the direct transformation wrought by the resurrection – for most Protestant thought – believers now come to the fulfilment of their being within the full complement of the Communion of Saints Triumphant. Here salvation in the communal presence of the redeemed is embraced by the presence of the undivided Holy Trinity of God.

The LDS scheme presents a different picture, in which the process of proceeding to godhood involves the ongoing plan of salvation moving from the pre-existence, through obedience in this life into the post-mortal life. The afterlife is formally divided into three kingdoms, or three 'degrees of glory', the telestial, terrestrial and celestial. Each is internally subdivided in such a way that each individual gains a reward according to achievement on earth. The celestial kingdom is also internally divided into three, with the highest reserved for those who have been fully obedient to all the revelations and rites of the Church. Fundamentally this means married Melchizedek priests who have experienced all available temple ceremonies.

The basic features of these heavenly realms are disclosed in the Doctrine and Covenants described as a revelation given to both Joseph Smith and Sidney Rigdon on 16 February 1832. This is one of the more powerful and theologically poetic sections of the Doctrine and Covenants, and includes the joint testimony of Joseph and Sidney to Jesus that 'he lives' (D&C 76: 22). Though an apparently innocuous religious utterance, this has assumed some prominence within LDS spirituality as an expression commonly heard at LDS testimony meetings. This whole section was occasioned by Joseph's pondering the nature of heaven in terms of the varied rewards due to different degrees of human effort on earth; it was prompted by the reference to the resurrection of life and resurrection of judgement in John's Gospel (John 5: 29). It also explains the origin of the devil as one who held prominence in heaven but rebelled against 'the Only Begotten Son whom the Father loved'; the outcome of that rebellion was his being 'thrust down from the presence of God and the Son' (D&C 76: 25). Along with Satan – son of the morning – are other sons of perdition and evil angels who deny the Son and the Holy Ghost; they end in the 'lake of fire and brimstone' and will not ultimately be redeemed. Indeed they are 'the only ones who shall not be redeemed in the due time of the Lord' (D&C 76: 38). There then follows an account of different levels of religious response and the benefits accorded them. Heading these is the 'church of the Firstborn' (D&C 76: 71) whose 'bodies are celestial, whose glory is that of the sun, even the glory of God, the highest of all' (76: 70). Then come those 'of the terrestrial', a mixed group who 'died without law' or died before the time of Christ – which, indeed, he visited after his death – and those who are honourable men but were blinded by the 'craftiness of men'. In their afterlife world they gain the presence of the Son but not of the Father; their glory is that of the moon compared with that of the sun. Then there follows a third degree of glory, that of the 'telestial', lesser still than the sun or moon but important for LDS belief because it encompasses a great number of humanity. The language used of them can, unless carefully interpreted, be confusing to Christians at large because those of the telestial domain are 'thrust down to hell' and are with the devil 'until the last resurrection, until the Lord, even Christ the Lamb, shall have finished his work' (76: 84–5). This period in hell for those who will, in due course, experience their own form of heaven is potentially confusing for non-LDS Christians, for whom hell and heaven are entirely distinct categories. Even Catholic theology with its provision of a purgatorial state does not equate it with hell neither does it internally divide heaven.

In the Doctrine and Covenants these people, who had neither received the gospel of Christ nor denied the Holy Spirit (D&C 76: 82–3), were of obvious import to the author for they receive double treatment in a form of coda provided by verses 99–112. This describes people who are 'of Paul, Apollos and Cephas' and, echoing Paul's diatribe against divisions within early Christianity (1 Corinthians 1: 12), can be interpreted as referring to religious divisions in Joseph's own day. At least that is the case if one takes the Doctrine and Covenants to be a form of commentary on Joseph Smith's own life and times. This group, then, also includes the morally suspect who 'suffer the vengeance of eternal fire' (D&C 76: 105), at least until the fullness of times when, in their afterlife, they receive the beneficial presence of the Holy Spirit but neither that of the Son nor that of the Father. Yet, even this third degree of glory 'surpasses all understanding' (D&C 76: 89). As one example of a 'clarification' passage, Doctrine and Covenants interprets 'eternal' punishment not in terms of time or duration but as something done by God: 'eternal punishment is God's punishment. Endless punishment is God's punishment', because God 'is endless' (D&C 19: 10–13). The overall rationale of post-mortal states is such that each 'shall be judged according to their works, and every man shall receive according to his own works, his own dominion, in the mansions which are prepared' (D&C 76: 111).

RESURRECTIONS

Remembering that Section 76 of Doctrine and Covenants was prompted by Joseph Smith's engagement with John's Gospel concerning the resurrection of the just and of the unjust (John 5: 29), we can see that what emerges is a distinction between two resurrections as the mode of entry into the heavenly domains. The distinction between the first and second resurrections is important in formal LDS thought because it provides a distinct framework for the notion of the millennium, itself a much more important feature of early Mormonism than of its current, twenty-first-century manifestation. The first resurrection populates the celestial and terrestrial kingdoms while the last resurrection, with its numbers like 'the sand upon the seashore', fills the telestial heaven (D&C 76: 109). Brigham Young would develop this model of divided heavens still further to argue that 'there are millions of such kingdoms... as many degrees of glory as there are degrees of capacity' (Young 1992: 140). Brigham also argued that believers would experience the resurrection through the authority of Joseph Smith, whom he describes as 'the President of the Resurrection pertaining to this generation': Joseph gives permission for all to enter the kingdom of heaven and, in particular, to be exalted. Joseph will be the first to be resurrected, then his apostles to whom Joseph will commit the 'keys of the Resurrection' to enable them to complete the resurrection of everyone else (Young 1992: 99). Such reflections mirror the day in which Brigham spoke, one when LDS thoughts struck notes radically different from traditional Christianity and, in so doing, emphasized the power of prophetic knowledge in the restoration movement. Today it would be very rare indeed for LDS leaders to speak in this way; resurrection is aligned much more directly with Jesus Christ and is discussed in ways that are far less different from traditional Christianity.

The LDS division of the afterlife is based on two broad bases, one biblical and one philosophical. Biblically it follows Paul's answer to the question as to what the resurrection body would be like. His response was to reflect on the nature of differences: the differences between the flesh of fish, birds, animals; between the sun, moon and stars; and between seeds and the plants grown from them (1 Corinthians 15: 39–41). His point is that there will be a difference between the earthly bodies of believers and their transformed heavenly bodies given through the resurrection. Joseph Smith's revelation develops this emphasis into a scheme of the afterlife by adding the 'telestial' domain and relating each to the presence of Father, Son or Spirit, indicating a degree of hierarchy amongst these three personages. This grading of heavens in terms of the divine personage present in each is in marked contrast to the unified focus grounded in the worship of the undivided Trinity of traditional Christianity.

There is, however, yet another distinctive feature for, if anything, the LDS heavens are characterized not by a concluding fulfilment in worship but by an ongoing activity. This was expressed, for example, in one of Joseph Smith's revelations, in which he saw that after death 'faithful elders... continue their labors in the preaching of the gospel... among those who are in darkness... in the great world of the spirits of the dead' (D&C 138: 57). This idea can be extended further, through the belief that in the future worlds exalted men and women, becoming gods and goddesses as husbands and wives, are forever extending their own kingdoms and producing their own spiritual offspring. In other words the traditional Christian idea of either a heavenly 'rest' or an eternal singing of the praise of God does not correlate with the LDS ethos of activism and ethic of achievement so tellingly portrayed in Joseph Smith's vision within which, to repeat, 'faithful elders... continue their labors in the preaching of the gospel... among those who are in darkness... in the great world of the spirits of the dead' (D&C 138: 57). In other ways, too, the speculative element in Mormonism sees eternity as a dynamic venture. Wilford Woodruff's diaries, for example, refer to speculative discussions between him, Brigham Young and Orson Pratt, with Pratt asking whether 'Adam or any God' would 'continue to make worlds people them taste of Death to redeem them?' Young answered that it would be their privilege so to do but that he rather doubted it; he countered Pratt's follow-up query about how it would be possible for such a deity to have 'his seed increase to all Eternity' by arguing that it could be achieved 'through the increase of his posterity [*sic*]' (Woodruff 1993: 167).

The LDS division of the heavens is based on both biblical and philo-sophical foundations. As I have considered the biblical element, it remains simply to emphasize the philosophical element, which was specified in chapter 1 concerning the principles governing the operation of the cosmos, including just rewards for appropriate achievement. While this cosmic reci-procity closely resembles Indian notions of karma and reflects something of the wider Christian notion of reward, it should not simply be read as an example of such religious reciprocity – itself a concept I have fully explored elsewhere (Davies 2002: 53–80, 195–210) – but also as an expression of those principles that govern all things. The essential difference between heaven in Christian theology and the heavens in LDS belief is that the former derives its entire rationale from God's being, while the latter is grounded in eternal principles of development to which even the divine is subject. In many respects traditional Christianity's heaven has the divine Trinity at the focus of all activity, while in Mormon thought the evolving godhood of the married human pair plays a significant role, framed though it may be by the presence of the divine Father and, indeed, possibly by his divine con-sort. But, behind the married Melchizedek priest and his developing family there lie eternal principles of development and progression, of obedience to covenants and of dedicated action.

This distinctive way of thinking can make it difficult for LDS and other Christians to communicate with each other at any depth, for while such words as 'Father', 'Son' and 'Holy Ghost' are held in common their particu-lar meanings are derived from two different sets of rationales, two different ways both of contemplating and of interacting ritually with ideas. For Latter-day Saints, the goal of godhood, as a prompting challenge to live the covenanted life, can almost appear as a blasphemy to other Christians. Yet, in practical terms, ordinary Latter-day Saints do view God and Christ with considerable reverence in much the same way as many believers from other traditions. It is the logical nature of their respective systems that pulls in different directions rather than the sense of person, piety and devotion.

The Mormon 'self'

This background of human destiny now allows us to focus in greater detail on Mormonism's theological anthropology, the doctrine of what constitutes a 'self' and underlies 'personhood'. Apart from the physical body itself, the crucial topics are those of 'spirit', 'soul' and 'spirit body', with additional significance coming from the notions of 'matter' and 'agency'.

Body

The physical body is of considerable import to LDS thought because, as a central feature of the plan of salvation, it is the vehicle through which a person comes to gain experience on earth and live in obedience to God. It is to be cherished as such and treated with respect and according to the food rules of the Word of Wisdom, as discussed in chapter 7. Exercise and sport are commended for fitness, and sexual health is encouraged through pre-marital chastity, avoidance of masturbation, and marital fidelity. Contemporary Latter-day Saints in the United States show very positive statistics on physical well-being in areas that are largely Mormon. But the body also carries a strong symbolic value through the belief in its future resurrection, even though it is believed that each body will receive the degree of glory merited by individuals during their earthly life (Callister 1992: 1223). Despite its virtues, the body, on its own, is nothing: it demands the presence of spirit, whether in this or a future world, before it can serve as the medium for anyone's mortal or immortal life.

Spirit

As for 'Spirit', according to Joseph Smith it is a kind of 'matter' and is eternal. Smith wanted it to be clear that he disagreed with the widespread Christian assumption that body and spirit were two quite different entities. For him, the distinction between spirit and matter was one of degree and not of kind. In the Doctrine and Covenants Spirit is described as 'more fine or pure' than matter; the difference seems to be one of density (D&C 131: 7–8). The entirety of the cosmos is both spiritual and 'material' in this sense, and parts of it can be distinguished only in terms of the degree of density or 'fineness' of spirit. As far as human beings are concerned, spirit can, and does, exist within the body just as it existed before the body was engendered and will exist after the human body has decayed in the grave. Human life thus becomes a form of embodied life, in which two different degrees of what we might call spirit-matter become intimately related, though it must be noted that the term 'spirit-matter' is used here to make the point and is not used by Latter-day Saints themselves.

This is but one example of the relational nature of Mormon thought to which I draw attention throughout this book, though for one particular reason some care is needed in its use in this case. Much mainstream Christianity sets up a distinction between spirit and body in a way that assumes a radical distinction between the two, and makes it easy to speak of the relations between two entities, spirit and body. This is reflected, for example, in the Book of Mormon when King Benjamin addresses his people just before his death as he is 'about to go down to my grave' but when his 'immortal spirit' is itself about to 'join the choirs above in singing the praise of a just God' (Mosiah 2: 28). However, according to LDS thought as it developed after the Book of Mormon, it becomes deceptive to set spirit and matter over and against each other and then to speak of their relation, precisely because they are, intrinsically, the same 'stuff' at different levels of density. Yet, having said that, the relational element still exists, for it is the relationship between spirit-matter and body-matter that makes a human body live. The presence of spirit gives life to the body. Life is, in fact, both the basis for and the symbol of the relation between the two.

Certainly, the LDS notion of 'spirit' has much in common with the almost universal notion of some life-force that animates the body. Widely described in terms of a 'soul' such a spirit-force has been deemed a dynamic aspect of human life for much of antiquity. In eastern religion the processes of *karma* underlie the reincarnation of this essential self depending upon its merits, while, for example, in the Christian tradition, Origen's third-century outworking of Neoplatonic philosophy could suggest that it was very reasonable that the soul be introduced into a body on the basis of its former actions (Roberts and Donaldson 1869).

Still, Latter-day Saints speak of spirit in a way that can sometimes appear to cause a problem when different aspects of concern are brought together in a decontextualized way. This is particularly apparent with regard to the origin of spirit, for on the one hand spirits are said to be 'self-existent, organized matter' that are 'governed by eternal laws', while on the other, 'human spirits are the literal offspring of perfected, exalted parents, a father and a mother in heaven', as I discussed earlier for the plan of salvation (Jensen 1992: 1403–4). I will return to the father and mother god idea in chapter 7, here the interest lies in the relationship between a self-existent entity and something that is an 'offspring' of parent figures.

Intelligence

Some LDS thinkers do identify this problem and one, Jay E. Jensen, who wrote the *Encyclopedia of Mormonism* entry on 'Spirit', noted that while 'the Lord has revealed much ... about spirit matter and spirit beings, many unknowns remain' (1992: 1404). In particular he drew attention to three additional terms, 'intelligence', 'light' and 'truth' and these are instructive in disclosing the heart of both LDS philosophy and spirituality. 'Intelligence' stands out amongst these, for intelligence, according to the Doctrine and Covenants, was neither created nor made (D&C 93: 29). This leads to a difference of interpretation as to whether intelligence refers to a self-existent basic kind of 'matter' in general, in the LDS sense of a less-dense material existing from eternity, or to a more personalized attribute of this very fine matter. The problem derives from two convictions of early Mormon thought. The first focused on 'intelligence' – a combination of a philosophical view of the universe as progressively developing matter and the human capacity for thought and potential to achieve great things. The second was more directly religious and appealed to the idea of a self-revealing deity from whom humanity derived and to whom people were responsible.

These dual concerns are expressed through two rather diverse grammars of discourse that are not entirely at ease with each other. This is exemplified in two further terms, 'light and truth', and in their textual affirmation that 'Man was also in the beginning with God. Intelligence, or the light of truth, was not created or made, neither indeed can be' (D&C 93: 29). Some LDS put this dissonance down to the fact that revelation has not been given on these issues. What is clear, and it is manifest in the fact that the *Encyclopedia of Mormonism* includes separate entries for 'intelligence' and 'intelligences', is that Mormon thought contains two closely related strands of thought on the issue of fundamental origins of the very stuff of human life.

The easiest way to understand this problem is to see one as relating to the philosophical questing of Joseph Smith and later LDS thinkers such as B. H. Roberts, and the other to the more explicitly religious convictions set within a more traditional Christian perspective. The major point of contact between the two comes to sharp focus in the plan of salvation and its divine Council that lie behind the emergence of the earth, humanity, and the interplay of good and evil within human life. Before clearly asserting that 'no formal pronouncements have been made by the leading councils of the Church to clarify what additional meanings and attributes may be assigned to the word "intelligences," beyond that which identifies intelligences as spirit children of God', the *Encyclopedia of Mormonism* provides examples from Spencer W. Kimball, Marion G. Romney and Bruce R. McConkie, all leading Saints in their day, describing how self-existing and intelligent matter came to be organized into a focus of personhood through its 'birth' into distinct children of God in the pre-existent world and prior to birth through human parents into this world (Hyde 1992: 692–3). This resolves the diverse discourses in different LDS texts by presenting a scheme in which 'intelligence' moves from being some kind of general property of uncreated matter to a capacity that comes increasingly under the control of what Mormons call 'agency'. It is through an increase in agency that an ever-increasing intensity of relationship may be experienced. That eternal intelligence that was once co-existent with God becomes increasingly related to God by being transformed into spirit children of God and then, through human birth, by becoming obedient human children of God. Here the relational aspect of Mormon thought appears yet again.

Agency

Agency is the LDS way of describing the increasing awareness of responsibility that is inherent in the obligation of relationships; it requires a context in which choice may be both implemented and developed. In this sense the original 'intelligence' of primal 'spirit' had but little scope for action compared with intelligence resulting from the divine generation of spirit children. So it was that, in the pre-existent world of spirit beings in the company of God the Heavenly Father, the agency of these spirit beings and their capacity for intelligence increased. It was in that arena of heavenly communion that some spirit beings decided to act against the Heavenly Father, following the biblical notion of a rebellion in heaven as a result of which Lucifer or Satan became a 'fallen' being. More particularly, the Pearl of Great Price specifically states that he was cast down from his position with God precisely because he 'sought to destroy the agency of man' (Moses 4: 3).

Here the part played by the fall in heaven, behind and prior to the fall on earth, is crucial. For, even if Satan failed to destroy the agency of humanity, his fallen status brought about the temptation that allowed human agency to disobey God, and that became the positive means used by God to permit spirit beings to take human flesh upon them and to face the challenge of obedience amidst that more 'dense' material realm. So it is that spirit-matter united with what, almost redundantly, needs to be called 'material-matter' and, in that domain, had the opportunity for demonstrating obedience to divine principles. In chapter 6 I will develop this issue of obedience as an outcome of agency in relation to LDS ethics.

Soul

Closely associated with that ethical plane is the distinctive LDS use of the word 'soul' when referring to the combined relationship of the spirit and the body (D&C 88: 15–16). Such a soul refers to the whole human person, embracing its earth-derived and its pre-existence-derived aspects, and adds weight to the LDS theology of this life and the life to come. In other words, the 'soul' is the relational basis of human life in which spirit relates to body: together they exercise the agency that belongs to intelligence in this world. By obedience to divine laws and ordinances the individual lives in a way that prepares himself or herself, his or her being, as a 'soul' for the post-mortem future. Though I explore this more fully in chapter 4, it is worth grasping here that death occurs when the spirit and the body separate. The spirit goes to the spirit world, also referred to as paradise, there to await the resurrection. And the resurrection is particularly important for the Saints because it is through the resurrection that the spirit comes together again, re-relates one might say, with the body as a transformed and eternal form of matter with divine potential. The textual basis for this configuration of elements lies in the LDS version of Genesis 2: 7, namely Abraham 5: 7, where man becomes a 'living soul' once the Gods place 'spirit' into the body that originates from dust. Having detailed something of Mormonism's philosophical anthropology, I am now in a position to turn to the destiny that awaits it.

CHAPTER 4

Death, faith and eternity

Latter-day Saint theology is, above all else, a theology of death's conquest. While that might be said of Christianity in general, it by no means reaches the same degree of complexity or ritual enactment as it does in Mormonism. Here the LDS Church, once more, develops ordinary Christian ideas to the point where they transform into a unique configuration of belief and action. Christianity takes death, with its root cause of sin, as the major flaw in existence that has to be overcome if salvation is to be achieved; in this chapter we see how Latter-day Saints have realigned basic notions of sin, atonement, repentance, faith, resurrection and exaltation to produce a powerful theological basis for a ritual life that relates life to death in a particularly appealing fashion. Here, 'relations and principles' come to cohere in a dramatic way through baptism for the dead: family relationships are framed by the principle of ritual performed on earth resulting in benefits available in the heavens.

A THREEFOLD CONQUEST

Mormonism has approached death in at least three ways; they are not mutually exclusive and have historically influenced each other at different times. One concerns the millenarian response of preparing for the coming of Christ, which I will consider but briefly. Another is through belief in the resurrection, which in Mormonism is associated with the doctrine of the atonement, and with the fact that it is through divine grace that everyone will receive a resurrection from the dead. This I will consider at length in the present chapter along with allied issues and ritual practices, including baptism for the dead. One profound aspect of the LDS theology of atonement, that of Christ's suffering in the Garden of Gethsemane, will be explored in chapter 6 in its particular relevance to Mormon ethics. The third approach to death concerns what Latter-day Saints call exaltation, which is intimately bound up with early LDS beliefs concerning polygamy or plural marriage and will be discussed both here and when dealing with temples in chapter 8.

Although Mormonism's earliest millenarian engagement with salvation was deeply significant for the founding generation of Saints, it is to the subsequent themes grounded in the distinction between salvation and exaltation that I will pay most attention. To grasp the import of this difference it is important to know that resurrection is the outcome of grace, which has been effected by the atonement wrought by Christ's engagement with evil, so that all will be resurrected, irrespective of individual merit. Exaltation, by contrast, is the outcome of dedicated human endeavour on the part of the Latter-day Saint. Salvation involves freedom from death achieved through resurrection and exaltation, the freedom for the opportunity to obtain the glories of the highest heaven through personal dedication.

GATHERING FOR CONQUEST

As we saw in chapter 1, early Mormonism was millennial and Adventist, calling the faithful to Zion in America to await the coming of Christ. Its initial focus was on the process of gathering, of sacred migration, and this was the basis for interpreting death and offering a salvation from it. People could do something about death: they could answer the call to Zion and move towards the prophetic source of their faith. They could go to where Joseph Smith was. When Christ came, the living would be immediately transformed, as would the resurrected dead. The very process of transformation was in accord with wider Christian teachings on eschatology, on the doctrine of the Last Things. The cherished LDS hymn 'Come, Come Ye Saints' expresses this well in its final verse:

> And should we die before our journey's through,
>   Happy day! all is well!
> We then are free from toil and sorrow, too:
>   With the just we shall dwell!

When it became increasingly obvious that the end had not come and was, perhaps, far from coming, Mormons increasingly focused not on the process of migration but on building a church community and, very soon, also on developing temples and temple rites grounded in a new theology of human ethical endeavour and guaranteeing eternal life. In an overly simplistic way we might describe this as an ultimate shift from migration to mystery. What is certain is that in the Gathering, as in community building and then in temple building, Latter-day Saints were active and their varied approaches to salvation and death were similarly activist.

VALUED DEATHS

More directly, it was, as we saw in chapter 3, in the King Follett Sermon preached at a funeral that Joseph Smith explicitly engaged with death and salvation. He did so by outlining some crucial theories on the evolution of God and the potential for godhood inherent within every human being. This firmly established the importance of death and its conquest at the heart of Mormon theology, albeit not in any simple sense. Certainly, the suffering and death of Jesus were vital, interpreted as they were as an act of sacrifice atoning for humanity's sin.

Though not at all of the same order of magnitude, Joseph Smith's death also came to be understood as a form of martyrdom, while the death of each human being too was not ignored but seen as a dramatic transition to another world. Mormonism's origin within Christian religion naturally ensured that death would have a high profile, since Christianity, above all religions, is rooted in death and gains much of its theological rationale of salvation from its conquest. The death and resurrection of Jesus furnished the basis for this not only through the experience of what early believers described as his resurrection, but also through the community that emerged from those initial believers and in which they reckoned still to encounter his mysterious presence. All subsequent Christian-sourced groups have, in one way or another, grounded both their theology and their ritual practice in Christ's conquest of death. For Joseph Smith, the broad Christian theology of death was but a starting point from which he went on to introduce distinctive rituals – ordinances as Latter-day Saints call them – that purposefully conferred upon believers personal power over death. This demanded a theology all of its own.

DEATH AND PRIESTHOOD

In fact Mormonism set its theology of death not only within an extensive ritual established to master it but also in the priesthood itself. Brigham Young, for example, talks of the very 'particles composing these bodies', bodies that have decayed, as having 'been made subject and obedient, by the law of the everlasting Priesthood, and the will and commandment of the Supreme Ruler of the Universe' (Young 1992: 128). The distinctive Mormon notion of obedience is here applied even to the elements of the decayed body. These are to be obedient to the power of the priesthood which will ensure their reuniting in the resurrection to furnish a transformed yet definite body ready to join with the spirit in rendering a full identity for eternal progression.

When these ordained men received endowments, they were enabled to assume the power that properly belongs to their priesthood. Brigham Young explained these temple endowments – to be described more fully in chapter 8 – as imparting all that is necessary 'for you, after you have departed this life, to... walk back to the presence of the Father, passing the angels who stand as sentinels, being enabled to give them the key words, the signs and tokens, pertaining to the Holy Priesthood, and to gain your eternal exaltation' (Backman 1995: 111, citing Brigham Young's *Journal of Discourses* 2: 31 for 6 April 1853). These words, signs and tokens refer to elements learned in temple rituals. When such endowed Saints died, they were, and are, buried in their special temple clothes and laid to rest until the resurrection. It is that resting which made any disturbance of the grave, most especially grave robbing, a particularly serious offence for Mormons (Woodruff 1993: 269). Commitment to the resurrection also underlies the strong preference for burial over cremation that impressed itself upon Church leaders in the twentieth century for, as it happens, their predecessors of the nineteenth century were more willing to contemplate cremation: for them it mattered little to God and the power of the priesthood whether body-particles had received their apparent dissolution through decay or flame. Either way, they would be reconvened and transformed.

PREDICTIVE EVANGELISM

Mormonism addressed not only the post-mortem destiny of the living but also the destiny of the dead, taking up one of the long-standing theological questions of many Christian traditions about those who lived and died before the gospel of salvation was enacted by Jesus, preached by his apostles and extended into the world through subsequent evangelism. For Joseph Smith's tradition, however, this did not remain a marginal and largely irrelevant topic, nor did it foster ideas of hell and punishment, but moved to a central place within the Church's theological scheme in the rite of baptism for the dead.

While it would be relatively easy to argue here that baptism for the dead was a late development in Joseph Smith's thought, as the revelations in the Doctrine and Covenants imply, and to use that evidence to reinforce the argument that there is a significant difference between the content of the Book of Mormon and the Doctrine and Covenants, it would be misleading to do so. For, while this is strictly true in a literal sense, there runs throughout the Book of Mormon what might be called a predictive or prophetic evangelism. According to its internal chronology, and much as we have seen in chapters 2 and 3, for some six hundred years before the human birth of Jesus, there existed prophets after the Old Testament model who foretold the coming of Christ and who called people to belief in him (e.g. 2 Nephi 10: 2–3, of 559–545 BC). In many Book of Mormon passages the name Jesus Christ is invoked in association with salvation, deliverance or promise (e.g. 2 Nephi 25: 24–7) – the 'Tower Sermon', which was described in chapter 2, being a very fine example (Mosiah 2–4). To read the Book of Mormon is to see the Nephites, Lamanites and others, all being confronted with some form of the gospel of Jesus Christ long before that gospel had actually been preached. This allowed those who had died earlier an opportunity to encounter the gospel, albeit in embryonic form. However the evidence is interpreted, the Book of Mormon does disclose a concern over the message of Jesus Christ, knowledge of it and its reception in relation to salvation.

DYING WITHOUT KNOWLEDGE

Despite the Book of Mormon background, the question of those dying without knowledge of the gospel is formally and explicitly raised by Joseph Smith in his Doctrine and Covenants revelation on 'the salvation of the dead who should die without a knowledge of the gospel' (D&C 128: 5). The possibility of being baptized on behalf of someone who was already dead was very real for the prophet and its feasibility depended, very largely, on five factors, all grounded in biblical texts. Though presented here in list form, they should not be read as a logical progression, because contextually each is related to the others in a cluster of mutual significance. They all occur in Doctrine and Covenants Section 128, internally dated to 6 September 1842, and are sketched here along with the biblical reference provided by the Doctrine and Covenants text. The first is Paul's rhetorical question, asking why people are baptized on behalf of the dead (1 Corinthians 15: 29). The second addresses the progression from earthly to heavenly forms of reality (1 Corinthians 15: 46–8). The third describes Peter's being granted the keys of the kingdom of heaven with the power so to bind events on earth that they will be bound in heaven (Matthew 16: 18–19). The fourth concerns the books of records in heaven that Joseph regards as records of records kept on earth (Revelation 20: 12). The final and fifth point is grounded in the notion of the turning of the hearts of fathers to children and children to fathers (Malachi 4: 5–6).

THE SPIRIT WORLD

Throughout LDS history the influence of the notion of records is of singular significance, showing how this core teaching of the Doctrine and Covenants resembles the motif of record-keeping that runs throughout the Book of Mormon. In chapter 8, for example, I take up the element of progression from earthly to heavenly realities, noting the apparently pragmatic fact of record-keeping and its underlying rationale that accurate records establish a firm bond between earth and heaven. This link assumes its primacy in relation to the vicarious work done by the living for the dead, especially in the ordinance of baptism. Behind this rite is the belief in a place where human spirits go after death, where they are much more active and full of endeavour than the broad Christian idea of a post-mortem sleep or rest in the Lord might ever indicate. Baptism for the dead operates with an eye to an afterlife realm in which the deceased are conscious and aware of what is being done or not being done for them on earth. Here LDS thought posits a dynamic interplay between the living and the dead in a theology that pervades several aspects of everyday LDS life including genealogical research, family history, and in the implementing of that research in baptism and other vicarious rites on behalf of the dead.

The link between living and dead can be so intense that it is difficult to describe the individuals concerned as 'dead' when that word carries the connotation of lifelessness and inertness of being. 'Dead' and 'death' do become problematic words in the light of LDS theology, given its conviction that the departed are conscious. Though their spirit is separated from their body until the day of their resurrection, they are still alert and as self-aware as they can be. The theological reason for this active self-awareness of the dead lies in a specific and highly significant revelation contained in Doctrine and Covenants Section 138. This derives not from Joseph Smith but from his nephew Joseph F. Smith (1838–1918), who became the prophet-leader of the Church in 1901. To explore this material is to see just how LDS doctrine develops and is elaborated over time.

THE PARADOXICAL BROTHER

In the present Doctrine and Covenants there are very few entries indeed that are not given through Joseph Smith Jnr. Key exceptions are Section 134 on politics and law expressed as a collective Church decision, Section 135 by Elder John Taylor describing the martyrdom of Joseph and his brother Hyrum, and Section 136 by Brigham Young calling the Church to faith as it journeyed on after the martyrdom of Joseph. Between this poignant reflection on the death of Joseph and the revelation to Joseph F. Smith comes Section 137, which reverts to a revelation of Joseph the Prophet and is dated back to January 1836, when Joseph sees the heavens opened and in a vision of glorious dimension views 'the transcendent beauty of the gate through which the heirs of that kingdom will enter, which was like unto circling flames of fire'. He sees the heavenly streets paved with gold and the 'blazing throne of God whereon was seated the Father and the Son'. There, too, is father Adam and Abraham and with them his own father and mother and, most paradoxically, Alvin, his long dead, long lost and dearly loved brother. This causes him to question deeply how it was that Alvin could be there, in such exalted company, given that he had died before the Restoration had emerged, with the result that Alvin 'had not been baptized for the remission of sins' (D&C 137: 7).

Though the relationship between Joseph and all his brothers can be viewed as a theme that mirrors elements in the Book of Mormon, as Fawn Brodie suggested in her influential and much-debated study of the prophet entitled *No Man Knows My History*, the place of Alvin does indeed 'deserve more attention' than Brodie came to realize she had given him (Brodie 1995: 415). Indeed, it may even be that Alvin's death influenced Joseph a great deal and, in more psychological terms, may go some way to explain why Joseph's movement came to be the most observant of all Christianly sourced groups as far as benefiting the dead is concerned (Davies 2000: 86–100). In the context of his vision, however, Joseph's questing quandary is resolved by a divine voice, the Lord telling him that all who died without knowing the gospel will become 'heirs of the celestial kingdom', if they are such as would have received it had they lived at the right time. The Lord says he will judge on the basis of the 'desire of their hearts', adding that, as far as children are concerned, those who die 'before they arrive at the years of accountability are saved in the celestial kingdom of heaven' (D&C 137: 1–10). Here Joseph sees a dynamic afterworld and begins to dwell upon the destiny of the dead in relation to their hearing or not hearing the gospel, as well as upon that of children who lived in an age when infant mortality weighed upon most families. In the Doctrine and Covenants this revelation of Joseph Smith Jnr sets the scene for yet another revelation that would come to his nephew Joseph F. Smith some eighty-two years later, which I pursue in chapter 9 where it is peculiarly appropriate as part of an analysis of the Mormon theology of polygamy. It is noteworthy that the editorial process behind the Doctrine and Covenants places these two revelations together and not apart as its normal chronological method would demand.

GRIEF

Joseph F. Smith, like his uncle Joseph, had been no stranger to death in his close family. He was five years old when his own father was killed alongside Joseph the Prophet and only thirteen when his mother died too. So there were some seventy-five years between his last seeing his father and uncle and then 'seeing' them again in his vision. The Prophet Joseph had also experienced a gap, in his case of thirteen years, between seeing his brother Alvin, who died in 1823, and receiving the vision of Alvin in heaven. In fact death was no stranger to many early Latter-day Saints, as to others of their day, and it is perfectly possible to see how their religion was not simply a comfort to them, as it might be to any Christian believer in an afterlife, but a distinctive support in the light of the strong LDS belief in the unity of families after death. Wilford Woodruff, for example, had lost his mother before he was two years of age, while one of his wives and thirteen of his children died during his lifetime (Jesse 1992: 1580–3). In the case of Brigham Young, for example, Arrington drew attention to his sense of joy and discovery in his new-found faith, which paralleled the death of his first wife and possibly allowed 'his previously unexpressed grief over his mother's death' to force a 'catharsis, marking a dividing point he would never forget' between his old life and his new vocation (Arrington 1986: 32). Joseph and Brigham would not have found it hard to share a commitment to a church dedicated as much to the salvation of the dead as of the living. If there is any truth in the hypothesis that early grief can be a factor in forging a charismatic personality in adults, then all of these leaders would be potential candidates (Aberbach 1989: 125; Brodie 1995: 415; Davies 2000: 102–3.). But even if that hypothesis cannot be sustained, these individuals, like thousands of others in the early LDS movement, had every reason to see some benefit in a church that attended to the dead of its members, whether or not they had themselves been members.

TRANSFORMING BODIES

Church members were able to help their dead because of their emerging theory of the relation between time, eternity, human bodies and the role of ritual in relating all of these. We have already seen in the previous chapter how bodies are central to Mormon theology in the relationship between the various elements that constitute the Mormon 'self' at different phases within the total scheme of salvation. This can be further exemplified with a textual example that shows just how important the principle of transformation of matter is to LDS soteriological processes, each related to a period of time. The source is the Book of Mormon, chapter 28 of 3 Nephi. The internal context is that of the resurrected Jesus making an appearance to disciples in America shortly after his death in Jerusalem and his resurrection appearances there. He chooses twelve 'American' disciples and before departing from them asks them what gifts they would like to receive from him. Nine ask that when they die they might 'speedily' go to be with Jesus in his kingdom and he tells them this will be so after they have attained their seventy-second birthday. Turning to the remaining three, Jesus asks what they desire. When they make no response he tells them that he can read their thoughts and knows that they want the same as did John the beloved disciple (John 21: 20–3). I have already alluded in chapter 2 to the LDS interpretation of that event but develop it further here because it was of some importance to Joseph Smith, as is clear from the fact that it recurs in one of his Doctrine and Covenants revelations (D&C 7: 1–8). The disciples' gift is never to experience the pain of death but to live on in the world from about AD 34 until Jesus comes again and a new world order is established. These Three Nephites will travel the world and anonymously furnish people with many spiritual gifts. They have become part of a general LDS folklore, many stories being told well into the twentieth century of unusual or dramatic events in which LDS have been helped by mysterious strangers who render some powerful service before vanishing from sight. A similar theme, to which it is explicitly related, occurs in the Doctrine and Covenants (D&C 7: 2) when Jesus asks John the beloved disciple what gift he would like to receive. John replies 'Lord, give unto me power over death, that I may live and bring souls unto thee.' He too holds a place in popular LDS tradition as one who lived on. These ideas are found in one of a set of what might be called 'biblical query sections' of the D&C, where Joseph addresses issues and points in the Bible that did not seem to him to be clear when he was reflecting upon biblical texts, in this case the Gospel of John (21: 20–3). This expresses something of the prophet's concern about death and its conquest but it also draws attention to the significance of the Mormon theology of the body and attitude to time.

While a great deal has already been said in chapter 3 concerning the LDS theology of the body in relation to both the pre-existence of spirits and the plan of salvation, I take up this topic here precisely to explore the changing nature of the body within each phase of the LDS categorization of time, in this case the significance of the period between the post-resurrection appearance of Jesus in America and his Second Coming. The text asks whether or not their bodies had undergone some form of change, given that they had, momentarily, been taken into heaven and shown wonderful things that they should never tell others. This had given them a sense of having been 'changed from this body of flesh into an immortal state' (3 Nephi 28: 15). But the text asks just what that change might have been and answers in a revelation to the effect that 'there was a change wrought upon their bodies' to save them from pain and to prevent Satan from having power over them. Still, this was not the same kind of change that 'shall take place on the last day' (3 Nephi 28: 36–9, 28–9). These bodily changes, reflecting early Mormonism's sense of mysticality, symbolize the transitional nature of the millennial age between Christ's First and Second Coming.

The Three Nephites, in particular, stand as transition symbols. In certain respects they stand in a similar symbolic position to that of committed Latter-day Saints who participate in temple ritual and who, in a sense, are also partially transformed by that encounter with divine sources of power although they still await a final transformation. But there are many other cases in the Book of Mormon of individuals and groups who have become, in the LDS use of the term, 'translated beings', whose immediate destiny is not that of some heaven but of some more practical ministry, even serving perhaps as 'ministering angels unto many planets' as Joseph Smith once suggested (see McConkie, M. L. 1992: 1486).

Even these 'translated beings', along with all other humans, will need the benefit of resurrection, whether at the first resurrection of the LDS faithful or at the second, general, resurrection in order to receive the type of 'body' in which to face divine judgement and their ensuing eternal destiny. The resurrection is also important for it produces bodies that are freed from the negative element which earthly life entails. Sometimes Mormonism is described in overly positive terms as ignoring the negative features of Protestant notions of the fall. This needs to be corrected because some have described the fall in terms of its effect upon the body, as does Brigham Young, who, following Paul's argument in the Epistle to the Romans, speaks of the 'constant warfare' between the body and the spirit that comes to it, given that Satan has influenced the world for ill (1992: 145).

SPIRIT WORLD AND SPIRITUALISM

Given that many Saints speak of the dead as being in a spirit world that, at times, seems to impinge upon the earthly world of the living, it is inevitable, perhaps, that the question of the relationship between Mormonism and Spiritualism should be raised. Historically speaking, the cultural ethos of the mid and late nineteenth-century United States fostered widespread interest in the ongoing life of the dead. It was an interest that coexisted with and fed upon notions of spiritual power that were also interpreted in a semi-scientific way. Ideas of Animal Magnetism and Mesmerism, for example, described a power that could lead practitioners to exert considerable influence over others, whether in curative contexts or, more dangerously and subversively, in conversion. When the *Millennial Star*, which was the longest running of all LDS journals and was published in Britain from 1840–1970, was considering church work in Britain from the standpoint of 1903, it warned LDS missionaries not to learn hypnotism lest it be misconstrued by the Church's critics (*MS*, 1903: 90). In the United States too opponents saw such mysterious powers as potentially dangerous in the hands of Mormon elders, especially regarding women converts; these powers easily overlapped, in the popular mind, with an interest in the spirit world (Givens 1997: 140). By the end of the nineteenth century Spiritualist Churches, which originated with the Fox sisters in the later 1840s, were well known and attempts to make scientific-philosophical studies of psychical activity had also been established in the 1880s.

But there is one important difference between Mormonism's 'spirit world' and the 'other side' spirit world of Spiritualism. It concerns what might best be called the nature or 'the direction of flow' of the mode of interaction. Mormonism's interest is more centrifugal while that of the Spiritualists is centripetal. Before 1848, when Spiritualism burst upon upstate New York with the Fox family, the Latter-day Saints had already possessed knowledge of the afterlife through the plan of salvation, which had been revealed to the prophet, and were already engaged in rites for the dead. As we have already seen and I will show in greater detail in chapter 8, Joseph Smith had introduced firm ideas of the relationship between the living and dead through vicarious baptism. With time, this work would grow and, if members did experience a sense of the presence of the dead, as they most surely did, they need take no recourse to Spiritualist channels of explanation. More than that, they did not need a ritual form through which to engage with such ideas. It is always too easy for academic studies to focus on realms of ideas and to forget the more practical ways in which people engage with concepts. In Spiritualism, for example, it is the séance and the ritual virtuoso who is given to forms of trance-mediumship that provide an arena within which the seeker may encounter the spirit world. To go to a séance, to contact a medium, these are ritual acts that bring ideas of a spirit world to life. Latter-day Saints possessed their own form of engagement with the spirit world; it was also through ritual, but it demanded no virtuoso performance and no trance. The active work of genealogical research and the use of the data gained in vicarious temple ritual provided opportunity enough for a sense of the other world to impinge upon this one. The temple itself afforded a meeting place, and one that was conceptually 'safe'.

Still, Spiritualism did offer its attractions and, even in the 1870s LDS women were counselled not to attend séances; this was shortly after a period of difficulty in the Church when several otherwise respectable and well-informed individuals were felt to oppose the leadership and seek a degree of personal freedom in doctrinal interpretation rather than accept what core leaders said (Bitton 1994: 92). One William S. Godbe spearheaded this group, which reckoned it had been visited by the spirits of some dead Saints who had encouraged them to purge the Church of overly authoritarian leaders; economic factors were also involved in their disquiet but ultimately the Godbeite faction was dispelled (Arrington 1986: 355).

Ann Taves' excellent study of religious experience in the eighteenth and nineteenth centuries marks something of this open, liberal, vision of the world that went with Spiritualism, despite its use of trance states (1999: 167). What is crucial in the distinction between Spiritualism and Mormonism concerning the spirit world is that Mormonism's knowledge was thought to come by revelation and was part of an authoritative doctrinal and ritual system that was increasingly becoming formalized and controlled just when Spiritualism was emerging. If elements of Spiritualism might attract the Saints, they could be brought to see that a fuller truth existed within the LDS Church just as, if Freemasonry attracted them, a fuller realization of its ideals was available in the Restoration. The temple took precedence over the Spiritualists' séance and over the Masons' lodge.

ATONEMENT

From these wider and historical aspects of the dead and the afterlife I now focus the discussion on how LDS theology addresses the foundational possibility of salvation and eternal life in and through the pivotal doctrine of the atonement. Salvation, as already observed, is a central topic of Christianity yet its precise meaning has varied in the major traditions throughout history. Indeed, although Jesus is central to salvation there is no single Christian doctrine of salvation. Sometimes the goal of God's endeavour in relation to human need and fulfilment – itself, perhaps, a general definition of salvation – falls upon a church's ritual power to bring an individual into salvation and sometimes upon the individual's responsibility through personal commitment and decision. Some speak of salvation history and play upon the progressive outworking of the divine will over time, while others prize the mystical insight of a glorious moment of understanding. Within these theological considerations of salvation the focal point regularly falls upon the idea of atonement as a restoration of ruptured relationships between God and humanity. Even so, there is no single doctrine of atonement, but a series of theories that have developed century after century, often influenced by the philosophical and social factors of their day.

In one reliable account of the atonement written for non-theologians Paul Fiddes, an Oxford theologian, provides a creative overview of these theories that are so often expressed in 'images and metaphors created through the ages... in pictures drawn... from the temple, the battle-field, the law-court, the slave-market, courtly love, family life and medicine' (1989: 4). He shows how doctrine itself can also be a form of worship, 'a celebration by the mind, returning words of praise to God', an insight that flows from his own complementary scholarship in English literature. His prime task was to show that what Jesus did on the cross affected history and has been passed down to the present in and through complex images and metaphors – expressions that engage with the life of faith of believers of each age. From his own foundation in the Baptist tradition of Protestantism he speaks simply and directly of the cross as the absolute centrality of atonement. It simply does not occur to him to attend to the one issue that became foundational for the LDS theology of atonement, namely, Christ's endeavour in the Garden of Gethsemane, an issue to which I return in chapter 6.

IMMORTALITY AND SALVATION

Whilst leaving the precise nature of Christ's engagement with evil until chapter 6, I can here simply accept that for Latter-day Saints the outcome of atonement is expressed in the two ideas of immortality and salvation. Immortality comes to all; it refers to life after death but is not immediately aligned with 'heaven', as generally understood in Christianity. Salvation refers to the forgiveness of sins that is in the LDS view conditional upon repentance and faith; this makes LDS atonement conditional atonement. The work of Christ brings individuals to a realization of their sin, and of the fact that he has so engaged with it that forgiveness is possible and the way opened for immortal life. In Mormon soteriology, however, atonement does not stand alone but is partnered by and fulfilled through the idea of exaltation. Exaltation is the quality of life that may be obtained in the highest of the eternal heavens but it too is conditional. Exaltation is conditional upon several factors, especially ordination into the Melchizedek priesthood, marriage, and temple rituals, particularly endowments.

CONDITIONALITY

Both salvation and exaltation are, then, conditional: salvation is conditional upon repentance and faith, both expressed through baptism and confirmation, and exaltation is conditional upon ordination, marriage and endowment rites. In Mormon spirituality this conditionality frames the entirety of cosmology, theology and ethics and is grounded in 'principles', the causal laws that direct the nature of all matter, as already considered in chapter 1. The conditional nature of eternity, along with the idea of the principles by which all things operate, reinforces a general attitude of cause and effect in Mormon thought, which in turn bears upon the LDS approach to ethics and to the practicalities of life. At one level this is reflected in the Mormon preference for being busy, which will be discussed in chapter 6 and again in relation to family duties in chapter 7.

These themes of conditionality, principle and causality help to constitute a cluster of theological ideas that does not easily correlate with clusters in some other churches that favour unconditionality through motifs of grace, acceptance and love. This is not to say that grace, acceptance and love are not ideas and realities encountered within LDS religious experience but it is to say that they are so framed by the 'conditional cluster' that their significance alters, making them appear at different points on the Mormon theological map. These very issues merit more detailed reiteration and exploration precisely because the themes of atonement and salvation lie at the heart of all Christian traditions and because any form of dialogue or engagement of one tradition with another demands an awareness of the nuances of usage of each.

Both salvation and exaltation, as formal doctrines, entail further theological concepts that influence ritual and pervade daily life. Atonement involves repentance, faith, baptism and confirmation, while exaltation embraces obedience to divine principles in social and ethical worlds, as well as the performance of temple rites including marriage, baptism for the dead and endowments. Mormonism's emphasis upon atonement reflects its earlier Adventist-millenarian period and its Protestant root, so evident in the Book of Mormon, while exaltation reflects the later, more ritually mystical form of Mormonism reflected in the Doctrine and Covenants and the Pearl of Great Price. Organizationally, atonement relates more directly to the regular activities of local chapel and stake (see page 172), while exaltation centres on the more periodic work of temples. That distinction should not be pressed too far, however, because both atonement and exaltation underpin ordinary LDS life, not least family life, as will be shown in chapters 6 and 7.

In this present chapter the prime concern is atonement and its allied features of repentance and faith; exaltation will be retained until chapter 8, while chapter 6 will consider atonement in the context of LDS ethics. While the topic of death could also find its natural home in any of those chapters, it has already been addressed here because atonement and exaltation pave the believer's way from the sin of Adam, through the individual's life in this world, through death, through resurrection and into the eternal realms of glory that lie beyond. Nowhere is the relationship between atonement and exaltation more apparent than in this phenomenon of baptism for the dead, which has already been analysed above and which unites within itself two basic elements: (i) baptism as an expression of repentance and faith in Christ, who has atoned for the original sin of Adam and (ii) a rite performed on earth through the Melchizedek priesthood with the potential for eternal consequence in the realms beyond this earth.

THEORIES OF ATONEMENT

The core of Christian theology emerges from the belief that the death of Jesus was in some way a sacrifice for sin and that his resurrection was both a vindication of his life-commitment and the basis of life after death for his followers. As already intimated, one of the longest-standing Christian doctrinal beliefs identifies Christ's death as bringing about a change in the relationship between God the Father and mankind at large. Following the Book of Genesis, the picture of the fall ruptures divine–human relationships, and numerous theological doctrines emerge to explain how this breach was repaired and reconciliation effected. These theories of atonement will be sketched here as a way of relating Mormonism's theological map of salvation to that of Christendom at large.

Atonement is often interpreted against the Jewish background of temple sacrifices and takes Jesus' death to be a sacrifice for sin. In the Judaism of the early Christian centuries atonement for sin was often associated with suffering and especially with the death of ordinary Jews. The very process of dying and of the subsequent decay of the flesh was seen as part of the personal suffering that brought about atonement with God (Kraemer 2000: 34–5). Early Christianity united such notions of suffering for sin in the single focus of Jesus: his passion and death, and not those of each believer, became the source and focus of atonement. Accordingly, atonement is wrought by an expiation, a removal of sin, through his death as a blood offering, as the biblical Epistle to the Hebrews strongly argues.

The Catholic theology of the Mass reflects these issues in the representation of a sacrifice, while Protestantism dwells on the cleansing blood that removes the guilt-stained conscience. The LDS view refocuses the nature of the blood element and develops the idea of Christ's agony in the Garden of Gethsemane, when he sweated blood in an act of supreme obedience that was the act of atonement. This theme I reserve until chapter 6 in order to emphasize its profound motivational significance within LDS ethics. Suffice it to say that it was the suffering of Christ, both in Gethsemane and on the cross at Calvary, that furnished the basis of atonement for the sin of Adam. This means that every other human being can gain forgiveness for the original sin of Adam, and for their own personal sins, if they repent, believe and are baptized. It is also this atonement that furnishes the basis for the resurrection of all people, a resurrection that will be the prelude to judgement and to the further directing of people on a positive or negative path into eternity. LDS theology has decisively invested in the resurrection the idea of grace that mainstream Protestantism has reserved for eternal life. It would be unusual, for example, for a Protestant theologian to describe the resurrection of the dead as 'a free gift to all men' rather than as 'the result of the exercise of faith or accumulated good works' (Callister 1992: 1222). It is this relocation of grace to resurrection instead of the spirituality of forgiveness and redemption experienced on earth and the bliss of heaven that establishes a major distinction between LDS and Protestant theology.

One exception to this general principle of atonement and resurrection is the early LDS idea of 'blood atonement'. This argues that those who shed blood in an act of murder cannot avail themselves of divine forgiveness until their own blood is shed. This, too, will be developed in chapter 6 because it highlights crucial theological issues underlying LDS ethics. Bruce R. McConkie's account of atonement as the prime and fundamental church doctrine hints at numerous earlier traditional Christian theories: his summation of atonement's meaning is 'to ransom, reconcile, expiate, redeem, reclaim, absolve, propitiate, make amends, pay the penalty' (McConkie, B. R. 1979: 62). What is of real interest in McConkie, as in other LDS sources, is that 'atonement' is used as a higher-order term in places where many Protestant theologians would use 'the cross'.

A brief sketch of traditional theories of atonement will help to provide a further perspective on the LDS case. Origen's third-century view saw the atonement in terms of Christ being a ransom paid to the devil, acknowledging the rights he had come to possess over fallen humanity. In the eleventh century Anselm answered his famous question *Cur Deus Homo* – Why did God become Man? – by saying it was to satisfy God's honour, outraged through human disobedience. But Anselm also indicated that Jesus was an example of how people ought to live in voluntary offering to God, and one of his younger contemporaries, Abelard, pressed this exemplary aspect much further, urging people to see how much their lives should be excited by Christ's example. For Abelard the cross reveals love just as it creates a responsive love in the believer. Fiddes is one Protestant theologian who has sought to recover this Abelardian position, pursuing the theme of love as it pervades other aspects of atonement in order to show how believers are influenced as they tell the story of their salvation from age to age (Fiddes 1989). During the Reformation of the sixteenth century the emphasis upon love in atonement gave way to the conquest of evil, a topic reinforced in the early twentieth century by the Swedish Lutheran Gustav Aulén. Often described as the 'Dramatic Theory' of atonement, Aulén's view portrays Christ doing battle and triumphing over evil, as the Latin title, '*Christus Victor*', of his book indicates (Aulén 1953). Later twentieth-century attitudes to salvation often talk of atonement in more psychological terms, developing later nineteenth-century liberal views of a human Christ who increases the humanity of his followers, but with an added emphasis upon therapeutic terms of healing.

Earliest LDS theology expressed a classic form of Protestant thought on the atonement, which reached careful and comprehensive expression in the Book of Mormon in a theologically significant cameo, a sermon-like description of the Holy Messiah who is 'full of grace and truth', who offered himself as 'a sacrifice of sin, to answer the ends of the law' for those who 'have a broken heart and a contrite spirit' (2 Nephi 2: 6–14). This, continues the text, is something that must be made known to the world:

no one can 'dwell in the presence of God, save it be through the merits, and mercy, and grace of the Holy Messiah', who laid down his life and took it up again through the resurrection 'by the power of the Spirit' and is able to 'bring to pass the resurrection of the dead'. Belief in this figure will lead to salvation. It is only as Mormonism develops that the idea of atonement comes to be increasingly focused upon Christ's mental engagement with evil in the Garden of Gethsemane.

REPENTANCE

While repentance is easily taken for granted as a widely shared Christian concept, it would be a serious mistake to take it for granted in LDS theology, because repentance lies at the heart of LDS spirituality, ethics and texts. The entire Book of Mormon narrative is filled with periods of disobedience and hard-heartedness followed by some degree of guilty conscience that leads to repentance, in cycle after repeated cycle. Sometimes the emphasis is placed upon an entire group and sometimes upon an individual; either way, disobedience is an evil. The classic example of group rebellion is that of the Lamanites, as described in chapter 1, whose skin was turned dark as a curse-mark, singling them out as a disobedient people and providing a visible boundary between them and the Nephites (Alma 3: 6–11). The promise of a light skin was held out to them should they repent and become an obedient people.

A clear example of an individual is 'unbelieving Alma', the son of the devout Alma who faithfully served God and was promised eternal life (Mosiah 26: 20; 27: 8). This idolatrous individual who 'was going about to destroy the church of God' bears a strong resemblance to the biblical Apostle Paul in that each experienced a profound religious conversion. Unlike Paul, who was struck blind by the vision of Christ, Alma is not only rendered dumb by the angel of the Lord but falls weak and has to be carried to his father (Mosiah 27: 8–19). For two days the faithful pray for him and then, receiving back his voice and strength, he announces that he has repented of his sins, been redeemed by the Lord and has been born of the Spirit (Mosiah 27: 24). He describes the depth of his repentance as having been 'nigh unto death' and his soul as having been 'racked with eternal torment'. This is but one of very many cases of repentance that together furnish the bedrock religion of the Book of Mormon. Those who repent are expected to have a humility of spirit and not to be haughty. Haughtiness, pride, and the pleasure of possessions are all negative attributes in the Book of Mormon, whose implicit good life is one of relative simplicity (Alma 4: 6–8).

FAITH AND *LECTURES ON FAITH*

Although repentance and faith should be conducive to humility, faith is not an easy concept to grasp in Mormon thought. While LDS authors often point to the *Lectures on Faith* as a foundational resource, that work too is not entirely clear, at least if one approaches 'faith' from a general background in wider Christian theology. This is because a distinctive feature of 'faith' is that, rather like the LDS notion of 'priesthood', it refers to or expresses a 'principle'. A major problem emerges in the *Lectures on Faith* when the nature of such a principle is combined with biblical references to something that appears to belong to a different logical type. A dissonance emerges that tends to confuse the ongoing explanation.

This can be clarified by reference to the biblical Epistle to the Hebrews, a key text cited by the *Lectures*. Basic to the argument of the Epistle to the Hebrews is the idea of faith as an inward hope that impels and inspires the servants of God in their life. Part of the appeal of Hebrews to the authors of the *Lectures* is probably that it appears to give a firm definition of faith: 'Faith', it says, 'is the assurance of things hoped for, the evidence of things not seen' (Hebrews 11: 1, as cited in *Lectures*, 1985: 6). The *Lectures* then state: 'And being the assurance which we have of the existence of unseen things, must be the principle of action in all intelligent beings.' Once identified, this 'principle' is extended to various aspects of divine activity, for 'It is the principle by which Jehovah works, and through which he exercises power over all temporal as well as eternal things. Take this principle or attribute – for it is an attribute – from the Deity, and he would cease to exist' (*Lectures*, p. 3). This distinctive idea emerged from a direct reading of Hebrews 11: 3 in the King James Version (KJV) of the Bible. As the *Lectures* read: 'Through faith we understand that the worlds were framed by the word of God.' The text offered Joseph and his colleagues the plural of 'world', worlds, which accords with the developing LDS ideology of a multiplicity of worlds.

This text is interesting in that the Greek word αἰῶνας, which has the rootmeaning of 'age' in the sense of period of time or a generation of people, not of 'cosmos', in the sense of an entity or place, has offered various translators scope for their theological opinion. For example, the Revised Standard Version (RSV), renders the text in the singular as 'world' and says 'the world was created' giving a direct sense of the creation of this world in which we live. The New English Bible (NEB) broadens the picture with 'the universe was fashioned', while J. B. Phillips in his more popular version offers 'the whole scheme of time and space was created'.

John Wesley, writing for ordinary believers, retained 'worlds' but in his commentary interprets it as 'Heaven and earth and all things in them, visible and invisible' (Wesley 1831). He dwells on faith, in this context, as referring not, primarily, to the faith that justifies a person before God, in the typical Reformation sense, because it is not used in direct association with Christ as the one in whom such faith gains this effect. Rather, Wesley sees faith, in this context of Old Testament characters, as 'a course of steady obedience amidst difficulties and dangers of every kind'.

A complementary picture emerges in Brunner's twentieth-century Protestant account of faith; he gives a clear and ethically demanding description of the way, manner and reality in which faith walks, in contrast to doctrine, which is simply a 'good map' that ever tempts the individual into believing that the map is itself the reality of the journey. Similarly, and appropriate for this chapter, Brunner argues that 'the doctrine of the Atonement is not a "theory of sacrifice", but it is the unveiling of our guilt in its truly fatal character, and of the incomprehensible Act of Grace by which God has taken our part' (1934: 599–600). The essentially heart-groundedness of 'faith' in Brunner comes out when he portrays the difference between thinking 'about' these doctrines and submitting ourselves to them; he says that when doctrines become 'objects to us' and not we to them, then 'our attitude becomes wrong'. In all this, so much depends upon the style of thinking, the method of approach, and that is precisely the point being made in this chapter about the way in which different Christian traditions engage with 'faith'. It must be said, however, that in the Book of Mormon there is a connection between ideas of faith and of conversion, and the idea of having a 'change of heart', a 'mighty change wrought' in the heart, holds a relatively high profile (Alma 5: 7, 14, 26).

Still, in the *Lectures on Faith* 'faith' is interpreted in an unusual and distinctive way to refer to 'the principle of power which existed in the bosom of God, by which the worlds were framed' rather than to some attitude of mind or heart by which people viewed the created order of things. Almost all translators see the 'faith' element as referring to human beings and to the attitude by means of which humans come to understand that created things came about through the 'word of God' (KJV, RSV and NEB) or 'by God's command', as Phillips puts it. Westcott's influential nineteenth-century commentary emphasizes 'the direct exercise of faith', the 'act of faith' by which the believer learns 'to recognize that there is a divine power behind' the things that we see and, for Westcott, this 'conclusion is the fundamental triumph of faith' (1899: 353). Here, the attitude of faith in believers relates to the creative capacity of the divine word, which itself was often used in the Old Testament to describe God's creative command.

LDS thought, as portrayed in the *Lectures* (1: 16) not only argues, as mentioned above, that faith 'is the principle by which Jehovah works' but that 'had it not been for the principle of faith the worlds would never have been framed'. Faith comes to be a principle of power, power that exists in God but which can also exist 'in men', for, as point 24 of the first *Lecture* puts it: 'Faith, then, is the first great governing principle which has power, dominion, and authority over all things.'

GRASPING FAITH

The significance of this portrayal of faith cannot be stressed highly enough as a basis for understanding LDS theology, belief and practice in the dynamic-mystical, post-Book of Mormon, form of this religion: it is of fundamental importance for anyone from mainstream Christianity seeking to understand Mormon spirituality. 'Faith' is a topic that is both ever present in and often absent from the work of theologians. What I mean by this apparent contradiction is that while they often speak much of 'faith', their extensive considerations work and remain within the grammar of discourse of their own church. As such, 'faith' is a term with very real built-in assumptions that are not always shared across denominations. It is the ignoring of that fact that underlies the relative absence of talk about 'faith' in many theologies. The obvious potential for confusion is great in contexts like this when people try to talk to each other using common words but investing them with differing nuances or even with a quite different significance.

The historian of religion Wilfred Cantwell Smith, for example, showed how the very word 'religion' had differed and changed in meaning from the world of classical antiquity through the medieval and Reformation periods into the present. In his enduringly significant study *The Meaning and End of Religion* he was keen to establish the profound variation between 'religion' as a term referring to the whole combination of the architectural and doctrinal culture history of a group on the one hand and the intimate realm of individual experience that appropriated and embodied aspects of that history in a living present on the other. He even wished to abolish the single word 'religion', replacing it with the two expressions 'cumulative tradition' and 'faith', to reflect these two dimensions (Smith, W. C. 1963: 61ff.). I stress Cantwell Smith's contribution because his concern about the meaning of religion-related words is of profound significance for Mormonism both as part of its own internal dialogue and for discussion between Latter-day Saints and others.

I have considered some LDS words and their contextual meaning in an earlier study, drawing attention, for example, to what I call 'definite article words' such as 'the mantle', 'the Church', 'the keys' and 'the brethren' (Davies 2002: 175–9). Much the same can be said of 'faith'. Risking brevity I will suggest that, essentially, 'faith' in Protestant spirituality describes a perceived quality of personal existence in relation to God. John Calvin's staunchly Protestant theology, for example, roots faith in 'a steady and certain knowledge of the Divine benevolence towards us, which being founded on the truth of the gratuitous promise in Christ, is both revealed to our minds, and confirmed to our hearts, by the Holy Spirit': then, to reinforce the experiential dimension of this mental revelation and cordial confirmation, he adds that 'faith is absolutely inseparable from a pious affection' (*Institutes*, III.II.VIII). As much of Luther's theology also argued, faith is the root of an individual's existence; it acts before it even ponders how to act, but it is always and inevitably grounded in a relationship with Christ: faith cannot exist simply as an entity in and of itself; it is relational (e.g. Luther 1961: 155). The Catholic approach to faith, while essentially more corporate, is also relational and sets the believer in communion with Christ. It does so by framing this relation with the authority of the Catholic Church as God's chosen medium of receiving, interpreting, teaching and handing on the divine word of revelation and the sacraments of salvation (see Catechism, 1994: 26–8.).

While Protestant and Catholic traditions share many theological words they, too, often approach them from these different perspectives, one from the individual to the institution, the other from the institution to the individual. The Catholic theologian Yves Congar, considered that a shift 'from the spiritual man' to 'hierarchical privilege... guaranteed and understood in a juridical manner' actually took place between the eleventh and thirteenth centuries (Congar 1966: 506). A similar Catholic point was made by Schillebeeckx when discussing the 'encounter with Christ in the Church': he spoke in terms of the rise of the official sacraments as both a means to encounter Christ and yet a possible hindrance to so doing when purely legal forms of authority take precedence over individual spirituality (1963: 194–5). Schillebeeckx also pursued these particular reflections whilst discussing sacraments and the development of the idea of a seal from being a mark of recognition or possession to an effect – or 'character' – made upon the inner being of a recipient of a sealing or sacramental act (Schillebeeckx

1963). Here the Catholic theology of official actions that foster salvation parallels the LDS notion of 'sealing' that is intrinsic to exaltation, as described in chapter 8.

While re-emphasising the stress placed upon the relation between individual and church institution, and the way these operate within these respective churches, it is possible to identify the LDS position on faith as located somewhere between the Protestant stress on the individual and the Catholic stress upon the institution. The individual must repent of sins and accept the forgiveness that comes with Christ's act of atonement but must then become obedient to the ordinances of the gospel, including the temple rites of 'sealing' in eternal marriage bonds, in order to attain the higher realms of exaltation.

In a wider sense, however, Mormons also refer to faith as a general attitude, as in the second of the *Lectures* (*Lectures* 2: 33), which speaks of the existence of God as 'an object of faith' that emerged amongst mankind following the days of Adam, to whom God had revealed himself; Adam's descendants maintained a degree of knowledge even though they were now separated from any more intimate sense of relationship with God. This lecture furnishes a genealogy from Adam to Abraham to indicate the flow of knowledge in 'rational beings' (*Lectures* 2: 55). If the second lecture dwelt on a kind of natural knowledge of God through the tradition of generations, the third and fourth lectures emphasize revelation as a way of describing the divine attributes, and do so in a way that any Christian tradition could accept. The fifth lecture has already been considered in chapter 3 in relation to Christology but the sixth lecture is particularly appropriate to the present consideration of death and salvation, for it underscores the significance of certain knowledge rather than 'mere belief or supposition' over one's final entry 'into eternal rest' and participation in 'the glory of God'. What is more, it links this certainty of knowledge to a sacrificial attitude to life. This embraces a pragmatic form of ethics. It is by actually sacrificing all that one has for the sake of truth that one knows that the foundations of faith are firm. Nowhere is anything said about the nature of what has to be sacrificed; it is as though the challenge over what is to be sacrificed is known to all. Certainly, this was the period when the Doctrine and Covenants revelations (D&C 104–7) were dealing with the two priesthoods and their duties in the new religion, not least in the context of the building of the temple at Kirtland. Traditional Christian views were being pressed into a new form and it is relatively easy to associate the sacrifice mentioned in the *Lectures* with the certainty of belief that banishes doubt. So it is that 'doubt and faith do not exist in the same person at the same time' (*Lectures* 6: 12). This reflects the fact that 'faith' was categorized less as some form of existential experience than as a philosophical and quasi-scientific schema. It would appear that the core elders for whom these lectures were written were, in fact, being called into serious dedication to the new revelations even if, and especially if, this meant sacrificing older doctrines they had held previously when they were members of other churches. The final lecture reinforces this interpretation for it defines faith as an endeavour of 'mental exertion' rather than physical exertion. Mental exertion is described for the angels and all beings who achieve anything. Faith is, once more, described as the mode of operation energizing anything that is achieved. What is more this achievement embraces salvation; people will and act and this assists their salvation. It is particularly important to observe that, though not formally expressed in the *Lectures*, it was just such a mental exertion that operated in Christ when engaging with evil and effecting atonement in the Garden of Gethsemane; I will return to this in chapter 6.

It is the seventh lecture, however, which pinpoints salvation as an 'effect of faith'. In posing the question of the difference between someone who is saved and someone who is not, the radical distinction between LDS and Protestant thinking is clearly manifested, albeit in a subtle expression that demands careful interpretation. The text answers that the saved are 'persons who can work by faith and who are able, by faith, to be ministering spirits to them who shall be heirs of salvation'. Here, again, the element of action grounded in a principle comes to the fore rather than the existential domain centred on notions of hope or trust or the like. To be able to 'work by faith' might be interpreted as a play on words intended to echo the long-standing Christian theological debate concerning 'works' and 'faith', which has roots in the New Testament and an extension in Augustine and Luther. And, while there might well be an element of that involved in this formulation, it is more likely that the dominant desire is to stress the idea of faith as a principle upon which one can work. To 'work by faith' could then apply to the new rituals associated with the Melchizedek priesthood, whose organization and duties were being announced at the same time; so, too, with the notion of faith enabling people to 'be ministering spirits' to the potential 'heirs of salvation'. In other words, it is those who have grasped the power inherent in the restored priesthood who will have the power to be involved in the ritual work for the dead that was associated with the idea of 'turning the hearts' of the father to children, as will be fully explored in chapter 8.

JESUS AS A SAVED BEING

In order to make the nature of faith quite clear, the text asks for some example, some 'prototype' or paradigmatic case of a faith-filled person, and finds its answer in Jesus. Then, in what will appear to be a theologically curious expression to most non-LDS Christians, it also describes Jesus as 'a saved being' on the basis that 'if we can find a saved being, we may ascertain without much difficulty what all others must be in order to be saved'. The distinctiveness of this approach to Jesus is particularly marked because mainstream Christian traditions speak and think of Jesus within the context of Christology, that is, of the theological study of Jesus as the Christ, as the one who is the very source and medium of salvation, and not one who needs salvation. In strict terms of biblical theology, however, it can be argued that, for example, Christ was 'made perfect through suffering', something that is a theme of the Epistle to the Hebrews, the book that is influential in this early LDS approach to faith (cf. Hebrews 2: 10; 11: 1). But, interestingly, that is precisely not the interpretative path followed in this lecture; on the contrary 'salvation consists in the glory, authority, majesty, power and dominion which Jehovah possesses and in nothing else'. These LDS notions of faith and salvation, embedded as they are in a theology of death's conquest, only come into operation through the structures and organization of the Church, and it is to its embracing ecclesiology that I turn in the next chapter.

CHAPTER 5

Organization and leaders

Mormon theology is essentially an ecclesiology. It is a theology of the Church established by prophecy through its two major priesthoods and its wider supporting organization. The deep underpinning of this ecclesiology lies in the doctrine of the Restoration itself, the teaching that God has, once more, given power to humanity to achieve divinity. With that in mind, this chapter explores the ways in which the Church's organization has related to economic and political aspects of life through distinctive ideals, institutions and individual leaders. In particular it shows how the relational element of Mormonism is subject to the principles inherent in the LDS attitude to 'organization'.

'Organization' is a word whose theological significance for Mormonism pervades church and wider cultural life. Its theological source appears as a variant of the biblical account of creation in the Book of Abraham, itself the most distinctive of all LDS texts. It rehearses a form of the Genesis creation story by speaking of the Gods – in the plural – who, at the beginning, 'organized and formed the heavens and the earth' (Abraham 4: 1). These gods 'organize' the growth of plants, sun and moon and everything else ready for the moment when they, similarly, 'organize man' in their own, divine, image (Abraham 4: 27). So it is that men and women, in their turn, rightly and properly have the task of organizing what falls to their duty and responsibility, not least the organization of the Church and of the family units that help to compose it and the wider community. In turn, all necessary bureaucratic church tasks are an extension of divine activity and human responsibility and not some irksome inevitability. To discuss organization is not, therefore, to fill in some background activity that supports the major venture of preaching prime doctrinal messages but is to identify organization as the dynamic matrix within which human agency extends and develops itself.

Given such a theological formatting of organization, it is not surprising that the early Mormon attitude towards church and community governance should take the explicit form of theocracy, especially since the two further doctrines, of prophecy and priesthood, also emerged as fundamental complements in the LDS view of the world. Early Mormonism's theological commitment to a complementarity of prophecy and priesthood contributed fundamentally both to its nineteenth-century ideal of theocracy, attempted but unrealized, and to its subsequent establishment of an extensive ecclesiastical bureaucracy. Prophecy and priesthood would also engender a ritual system to help to sustain that bureaucracy just as it also furnished the basis of salvation. The birth of the Church lay in Joseph Smith's prophetically charismatic millenarian message, which was complemented by the publication of the Book of Mormon, itself a prophet-filled volume; the Church's survival and subsequent flourishing were fuelled by a growing population who were sustained by values generated by formal ritual, which was introduced after the founding of the Church and was informed by ideas that came to fruition, for example, in the Book of Abraham in the 1840s. That eclectic community, largely focused in Utah in the nineteenth and early twentieth centuries and energized by thousands of European converts, became the basis for an increasingly expanding missionary programme that, in its turn, fostered a worldwide Mormonism rooted in local congregations. And missionaries were produced by and sustained through LDS family life.

ADVENT, PLACE, ETERNITY

These first Mormons, like the earliest Christians, expected the world soon to end with the Second Coming of Christ. While the ultimate responsibility for renewing the world and establishing the new order of things would fall to God, the Latter-day Saints had much to do to prepare for its inauguration. Joseph Smith, unsure about just when the end-time would be, set about organizing a church structure to proclaim the divine truths and to practise the new ritual that increasingly occupied his creative mind. Just before he died in 1844 the Mormons were already a church in process of becoming a community, but one still geographically on the move. Joseph's message of millennial hope and gathering to Zion resulted, at his martyrdom, in a large number of people gathered together with, as it were, nowhere to go.

With the greatest of good fortune, as far as the survival of the Church was concerned, Brigham Young and not Sidney Rigdon prevailed in the leadership succession. A dependable pragmatist with a strong commitment to the notion of prophecy, and dedicated to developing what he had learned from Joseph, Brigham possessed a spirituality that was concerned as much with agriculture and social welfare programmes as with building temples and practising their rites. He also had a prevailing sense of where the Saints should go and a real intimation of when they had arrived there. The ensuing community that Brigham helped to forge in the Salt Lake Valley had to take responsibility for organizing itself politically, economically and ethically. In the most real way LDS political and economic theologies, along with its ethics, resulted from the fact that Christ's Second Coming did not come. The awaiting congregation became a community. Purity of heart needed to become rooted in ongoing social relationships and would have to be shaped and reshaped as changing social forces were encountered over the next century and a half and beyond.

These community dynamics were driven by that notion of a 'church' that had, from the outset, been Joseph Smith's goal. A 'church' was no afterthought, no accidental outcome of some personal religious experience that simply happened to be accepted by others. Joseph Smith's enthusiasm was precisely for a church, for the one, true, church. This motive had set his teenage spirituality upon its quest, and the arrival of the Restoration was as significant as any desired 'end of the world'. When Jesus did not come upon the clouds and bring the wicked world-order to judgement, the Church did not dissolve, despite fragmentation at the time of Joseph's murder in 1844. Though seriously fragmented, the fourteen-year-old Church survived for a variety of reasons. Many aspects of its organization had been both outlined through Joseph's revelations in the Doctrine and Covenants and implemented in the 1830s by those who had invested their limited means and life commitment in migrating and gathering together to the prophet, despite opposition and much hardship. Crucially, sufficient core members had also become involved with the priestly, ritualized, domain of Mormonism to ensure that it would become the generative heart of the new Church, which would, itself, combine a sense of mystery with a status invested with power and with promises to overcome death and inherit eternal kingdoms of glory.

Just as the Book of Mormon reflected Mormonism as a prophetically millenarian movement of salvation grounded in repentance, faith and baptism, so the Doctrine and Covenants expressed its priestly control of an organized ritual process of exaltation symbolized in baptism for the dead and endowments. In theological terms of eschatology – the doctrine of the last things – Mormonism passed from its hope of an imminent fulfilment of the divine will for the world to a confidence in a transcendent fulfilment in eternity. After the primal Mormon message had called people together to await the coming of Christ from heaven to earth, its developing strategy prepared them to progress from earth to heaven. The diligence needed to carry out the metamorphosis inherent in this reversed process fell to Brigham Young; its success depended on the people coming to possess a land of their own for a sufficiently long period to establish the temple organization that was the ritual substructure for the eternal work. In practical terms, he headed a complex mix of people from several US states and many other countries, people whose communal life, amidst adverse ecologies and politics, demanded the development of new forms of integrated economic, political and social attitudes and practices. And he headed them for thirty years, a sustained leadership of consolidation that produced a viable society.

ZION'S DYNAMICS

While Brigham Young would never have talked of economic, political or social 'theologies', a great deal of his thinking, and the subsequent practice of the Saints, was concerned with just such theological issues. This was inevitable in a religious group that became a powerful community and which some might even view as a sub-culture within the United States. In this chapter we approach the political elements of the Church's life through the LDS notion of theocracy and approach its economic dimensions through the idea of the United Order, terms that typically indicate the early Mormon interfusing of religious ideas and pragmatic necessity. Other aspects of social theology will be covered in chapters 6 and 7 in the context of ethics, education and family. The one idea that brings all these domains together is that of Zion. Zion, grounded in a theocracy and organized as a United Order, serves as a metaphor for Mormonism, for its restoration of ancient biblical places and events, its identification with Israel and its hope for future fulfilment.

Theocracy-bureaucracy

Though Zion in its fullness would be led by Jesus Christ, until his Second Coming leadership would be exercised by the prophet, seer and revelator of the Church, assisted by his counsellors and intermediary priesthood groups. The very fact that the call to Zion produced an increasingly sizeable community, often at odds with its neighbours, raised political issues especially when, for example, the Saints decided that Independence, Missouri, would be the 'center place' and the location of Zion city (D&C 57: 1–3). For Joseph, this location in Jackson County had been the location of the original Garden of Eden (*JD* 10: 235). However, one year after the Saints had begun to gather and settle at Independence political hostilities occasioned their removal. While the LDS still hold out hope for this 'center place', it is now under the control of the Reorganized Church of Jesus Christ of Latter Day Saints, as described in chapter 9. Joseph then led his growing church as it settled, as it thought, in Kirtland, Ohio, establishing a temple there in 1836 and swamping the existing population. The rise in Mormon political power, with its Democratic tendency, caused opposition that resulted in waves of departing Saints and came to its climax in 1838.

The 'repeat migrants' found their new home in an area and settlement that Joseph named Nauvoo – the beautiful. Despite receiving its own charter, it, too, proved to be a temporary dwelling. Politically speaking, in both Kirtland and Nauvoo, Joseph Smith's intentions had been to develop a 'theocratic kingdom' and he had, in March 1844, set up a special group of key leaders as the 'Grand Council or Council of Fifty' to serve 'as a legislative body for the theocratic society' and these were active after his death, in fact until Utah's territorial government was established in 1851 (Arrington 1986: 108–9). This Council of Fifty, which included several non-Mormons, witnessed Joseph's 'installation as "king" of the earthly Kingdom of God', an event that was kept profoundly secret at the time, for obvious political reasons (Quinn 2001: 141). It was as a result of a degree of internal dispute that non-Mormons also set themselves against this potentially powerful political society and that unrest led to Joseph's murder by a mob in Carthage gaol in 1844. A later, and much more organized form of political opposition also brought about the abandonment of polygamy in the 1880s, as church leaders sought to save the Church by acceding to popular demands.

In religious and ritual terms, Mormonism's geographical pauses at both Kirtland and Nauvoo were socially and religiously significant as staging posts to Utah and the final development there of what would become permanent temples. The dedication services of Kirtland's temple were accompanied by forms of visionary and ecstatic religion as well as the rites of anointing and washing of feet, both of which would become significant in later days. At Nauvoo baptism for the dead was introduced, first in rivers and then in the new temple, as were the crucial rites of endowment and eternal marriage. Nauvoo was the geographical focal point for the Saints, a creative centre where Joseph's revelations on eternal marriage, the dead and the afterlife were implemented. In particular this was a time when inner circles of devotees came to accept the developing Mormonism of plural marriage even though that did not become public knowledge and practice until the early 1850s when the Saints were safe in Utah. In Nauvoo, too, in the early 1840s numerous Saints became engaged in Freemasonry and a Masonic lodge was built, a fact of considerable consequence for the development of LDS temple rites. Yet again, however, disaster struck when the prophet was killed in 1844, and the people set once more on the migrant trail by early 1846, but only after serious effort to complete the temple and receive their endowments. This pattern of possessing increasingly significant religious rituals but, initially, having to perform them in temporary locations whilst awaiting the completion of a temple re-emerged when the Saints reached the great Salt Lake Valley. After settlement in 1847, work on the temple commenced in 1853 to be completed in 1893 but endowments – the cornerstone of LDS theology and hope of eternity – were received in temporary accommodation, especially in the Endowment House which served, from 1855, as a form of LDS temple, at least as far as endowments for the living were concerned. The dead would not be embraced until temples proper were consecrated. This constant shift in location allowed ritual to develop and change in an adaptive way that served the Saints well.

The territory of Utah was established by the US Congress in 1850, but statehood came only in 1896, after protracted conflicts with the Federal Government over polygamy. Anti-polygamy laws were passed in 1862, and in 1882 the Edmunds Act disenfranchised polygamists, forbidding them from holding public office, including legal office. Then, in 1887, the Edmunds–Tucker Act virtually dissolved the Church as a legal entity and appropriated much of its property. Polygamy had come to be the symbol of LDS difference for anti-Mormon sentiment just as it had become the focus of Mormon ideas of salvation, and, as we saw in chapter 4, President Woodruff decided to act 'for the temporal salvation of the Church' and formally abandoned polygamy. This was the period when the Church's earlier commitment to a theocratic rule in Zion ended, as Saints became clear members of a state that was subject to the same earthly rule as all the others in the United States. From this conflict there emerged a church community dedicated to the ideals of liberal democracy but prepared to encourage its members to support either the Democratic or the Republican parties in the United States (see Alexander 1986; Hill 1989). In other countries the Church went on to encourage its members to be subject to official governments and to be loyal citizens; this was nothing more or less than an appropriate application of the Article of Faith stating belief 'in being subject to kings, presidents, rulers and magistrates, in obeying, honoring, and sustaining the law' (Article 12).

Perpetual Emigration Fund

The migrant community that had constituted Mormon Utah was now having to reverse its vision and see the world not only as a mission field but as an entire world within which the faith could grow. This transition can only be fully understood against the background of that earlier call to Zion and the migration that brought it about. Migration, especially from Europe to America, was of fundamental importance to early Mormonism and it is probable that the early Church would not have survived without it. This 'gathering to Zion' was thoroughly based in and motivated by the theological belief that a people must come together to prepare for the Second Coming of Jesus Christ. But the 'gathering' was, itself, soon subjected to the LDS ideal of 'organization'.

As converts were called to journey to a central place church leaders sought their general welfare through the Perpetual Emigration Fund, which ran from 1849 until the Church's conflict with the US Government over polygamy led to the Fund's dissolution in 1887. Over its thirty-eight-year lifespan, including some years when it was suspended, the Fund is reckoned to have facilitated the migration of more than thirty thousand church members, offering them loans for the journey and, almost as important, organizing details of both sea and land travel (Boone 1992: 1075). In another example of welfare, the United States' Great Depression of 1936 led to the Church Security Programme, which became the Welfare Programme in 1938 and operated farms and factories feeding into the organization of bishops' storehouses created to help those in need (Hartley 1992: 1041). Many other community-focused welfare programmes have also been instituted by the Church, extending from the local bishop and his responsibility for needy people to international welfare programmes that developed, particularly in the later twentieth century, to respond to crises and disasters across the world (Mangum, G. L. 1992: 1554–8). The close attention paid by the Church to the economic well-being of members has to be understood against the background of the social history of the nineteenth and the first half of the twentieth centuries when most members were relatively poor. Mutuality and community support is proverbial in Utah Mormonism and still has a part to play in the development of the Church in economically impoverished societies, not least in parts of South America. It is an attitude with strong textual support as, for example, in the 'Tower Sermon', which has already been mentioned in chapter 2 in connection with ideas of salvation, but which also expounds a strong communal ethic. King Benjamin preaches his sermon to an entire society: the picture is reminiscent of the ancient Hebrews, with each family inhabiting its own tent, 'being separated from each other' yet all arranged to face the temple (Mosiah 2: 6). His call to believe and repent, having reduced his hearers to literal humility, exhorts them to live in peace with each other, and to ensure that nobody goes without basic necessities (Mosiah 4: 13. Cf. Mormon 8: 37–9). What is more, the rich must not think that the poor have brought poverty upon themselves, for, as the theological rhetoric expresses it, 'behold are we not all beggars? Do we not all depend upon the same Being, even God, for all the substance which we have...?' If one's own resources are exhausted then it is best simply to admit it, acknowledging that one would give if one could. Above all, welfare provision should be 'done in wisdom and order', echoing early LDS commitments to community organization and directed leadership as well as to principles of action (Mosiah 4: 27).

United Order

Another background concept informing the Church's adaptation to life in the twentieth century concerns its economic base. It is not hard to see how the theology of Mormonism includes an intense desire for a people who are unified in their social and economic activities as well as in the general doctrinal aspects of life. Such a unity was a particular concern of Brigham Young; it was his vision for the Saints throughout their changing circumstances, not least when the number of non-Mormons increased as the railroad was brought to Utah in 1869. Members of these community-focused groups would ensure, through their physical commitment to work and through a form of co-operative social and economic organization that the people could experience an overall unity of purpose: they would be as one large family. Brigham sought to implement this kind of co-operative venture under a variety of named 'United Orders', such as the Order of Enoch when, once more, that Old Testament prophet who had been a favourite of Joseph Smith (e.g. D&C 76: 67; 107: 57) made his presence felt in LDS thought (Arrington 1986: 376–81). In some of these Orders members were rebaptized and engaged in new covenants agreeing to be 'energetic, industrious and faithful... to abstain from all selfish motives and actions... to seek the interest and welfare of each other: and to promote the special good of the Order and the general welfare of mankind' (Arrington 1995: 308). Some of these co-operative communities were established in Utah in the 1870s to 1890s but they did not, ultimately, come to prominence. Still, the fact of their brief economic and social existence left an important theological mark on LDS thinking as a symbolic expression of an ideal society whose religious teaching pervaded work and social ethics to yield a perfect community.

A similar ideal, though more focused on money itself, occurred in earlier LDS social history when, in 1837, the Kirtland Safety Society Bank failed. This had been established late in 1836 on the basis, as some believed, of nothing less than revelation (van Wagoner 1994: 182–7). A considerable minority of the Kirtland LDS community left or were excommunicated after these events, and included in their number were the three original witnesses to the truthfulness of the Book of Mormon and four of the Quorum of the Twelve Apostles, showing just how serious the situation had been.

Today some contemporary Saints see the theological commitment to a democratic sharing of goods and service under divine leadership as a major alternative to either communism or socialism rooted in a market economy that is stained by human imperfection. Lucas and Woodworth, a lawyer and a management consultant, respectively, have addressed this issue with some vigour in a call advocating that 'each Saint must act as a moral agent of Zion' (Lucas and Woodworth, 1996: 354). They see the power of a moral community, grounded in shared wealth and in succouring the less able, not as an end in itself, as worthy as that would be, but as part of the process of fully developing the theological idea of Zion. For them it is no simple matter of a 'top-down' implementation of some standard church directive but more of a 'roots-up' endeavour, triggered by local circumstances and fostered by local Saints and the possibilities open to them. Work and self-reliance are integral to this scheme, as is the LDS application of the idea of the stewardship of that which one consecrates to God. Ultimately, Lucas and Woodworth root the basis of any united order in a two-word sentence: 'God works.'

Church administration

As the twentieth century began, Mormon theology was in the process of changing, not least because of the simple fact of 'events'. Although the practice of polygamy ended through political necessity, it was replaced, in one sense, by a strengthening of other aspects of family life, including genealogy and temple work for deceased ancestors. Similarly millenarian beliefs had to adapt to the fact that Christ's Second Coming had not taken place. By taking stock of itself both as an American sub-cultural group undergoing personal reassessment, and as a church expanding throughout the world, this movement came to organize itself in increasingly self-conscious ways.

Having begun as a prophetic movement, it maintained its commitment to prophetic leadership albeit exercised through an increasingly extensive bureaucratic form of organization that expressed the prime doctrinal idea of establishing Zion.

Most fundamentally, as Mark Leone adroitly argued, Mormonism moved into the twentieth century by 'emerging as a church after its destruction as a political entity', but it was a church in which most people held church offices for only limited periods of time with the consequence that theological ideas often varied with these individuals (Leone 1979: 213). Leone, writing as an anthropologist, argued another profoundly significant point as far as religious belief is concerned. For him, not only did this shifting of personnel through many church offices train people to adapt to change and, in a sense, prepare them to understand the very changeable world that the twentieth century created around them, but it also made anything like a systematic theology quite redundant. Indeed life came to be lived in the present in such a way that both history and theology, if understood as a formal and critical division of the past and of religious ideas into formal eras or schemes, played little part in ordinary life. People focused on the present and taught that change was part of the eternal nature of things: they 'had no use for segmenting the past and thereby making history out of it, nor the conceptual apparatus to conceive a coherent theology' (Leone 1979: 213). Still, the Church was committed to the two poles of prophecy and bureaucracy as may be exemplified through two cases: the ordination of Negro males and the Church's correlation programme. The one involves a sudden and dramatic theological change and the other a long and slower development with occasional speedy transformations.

Negro ordination

The early LDS Church developed a strong theological argument about why Negro males could not hold the priesthood, and many nineteenth-century Saints adhered to the belief that the Lamanites of the Book of Mormon epic had been marked with a dark skin because of their disobedience to God. This was despite evidence that Joseph Smith himself held positive views of individuals with a Negro ancestry, as in the case of Elijah Abel, who was ordained to the priesthood and anointed in Kirtland's temple in 1836. Joseph also had it in mind to 'abolish slavery by the year 1850' (Quinn 2001: 141). Brigham Young's discourses did not follow a similar vein; he not only describes the mark of Cain as present in the Negroid features of flat nose and black skin but notes that they are 'seemingly deprived of nearly all the blessings of intelligence that is generally bestowed upon mankind', and will be 'servants of servants' despite what 'Abolitionists' might say, until such time as the curse is removed – that time will come only when 'the last residue of Adam's children' are saved (Young 1992: 132–3). In the event, it was not until 1978 that a revelation was announced to the effect that all worthy males could be ordained. This radically important message had come, it was said, 'after extended meditation and prayer in the sacred rooms of the holy temple' where the prophet-president Spencer W. Kimball, deeply aware of the faithfulness of some who had joined the Church but could not be ordained because of the Negro element of their identity, had 'pleaded long and earnestly in behalf of these, our faithful brethren' (D&C, Official Declaration 2). He had spent 'many hours in the Upper Room of the Temple supplicating the Lord for divine guidance' and the Lord had 'heard our prayers, and by revelation confirmed that the long-promised day has come' when all faithful males might be ordained. This revelation did not come too soon for some black Africans who had, in a sense, become Mormons of their own accord and had been in contact with the church leadership for some time, seeking missionaries to come to them. Brigham Young had sent missionaries to white South Africa in 1853, but it had taken 125 years for revelation to allow black Africa such contact (LeBaron 1996: 80–90).

Structure, leader and decision

The way in which the Declaration on Negro ordination was produced illustrates the theological belief controlling church organization. The prophet, seer, and revelator of the Church disclosed his revelation to his two counsellors, then to the Twelve Apostles and then, in turn, to 'all other General authorities'. Having been accepted by them, it was only then brought before the semi-annual conference of the Church on 30 September 1978 for acceptance by the traditional method of raising the right hand; it was unanimously accepted. Here the prophetic and bureaucratic elements of LDS life combined in effecting a major change in custom and opened the way for missionary work amongst many people and countries where none had been fostered before, especially in Africa and the Caribbean. The revelation's vehicle, Spencer Kimball, the twelfth leader of the Church of Jesus Christ of Latter-day Saints, had come to office unexpectedly when his predecessor Harold B. Lee died of a heart attack after only a year as leader. Kimball himself had already been seriously ill and was seventy-eight when he assumed leadership but, rather unexpectedly for the Church at large, the early years of his twelve-year presidential tenure assumed a dynamic force. His previous duties in the Church had included prime responsibility for Native American Indians and he had long been hostile to all forms of racial prejudice. Some see this as the underlying personal commitment behind his deep concern for the ban on Negro ordination and the ensuing revelation reversing it.

In terms of Church organization his tenure also illustrates the potential problem of always having the most senior of the Twelve Apostles as a president who continues until death, a scheme derived from historical precedent. This 'longevity principle' as the non-LDS author Jan Shipps describes it, is a problem in that such a man is likely to be old on assuming office, especially in a community whose way of life fosters good health and old age (Shipps 2000: 380). During his last three years or so Kimball was practically unable to function due to operations on his brain, and the responsibility for running the Church fell to his two counsellors. Joseph Smith, by sharp contrast, had founded the Church when aged twenty-five and was killed when thirty-eight years old. The following list of prophets shows the age when appointed, age at death, approximate years as prophet and year of death.

Presidential tenure of prophets of the Church of Jesus Christ of Latter-day Saints

Prophet	Age during tenure	Years of tenure	Year of death
Brigham Young	46–76	30	1877
John Taylor	71–78	7	1887
Wilford Woodruff	82–91	9	1898
Lorenzo Snow	84–87	3	1901
Joseph F. Smith	62–80	18	1918
Heber Jeddy Grant	62–88	26	1945
George Albert Smith	75–81	6	1951
David Oman McKay	77–96	19	1970
Joseph Fielding Smith	93–95	2	1972
Harold B. Lee	73–74	1	1973
Spencer Wooley Kimball	78–90	12	1985
Ezra Taft Benson	86–94	8	1994
Howard William Hunter	86–87	1	1995

It will be interesting to see if in the nearer future the Church receives a revelation relieving very old prophets of their leadership responsibility or admitting younger men for limited periods. This might be a considerable advantage as the Church grows in size and the need for high leaders to travel the world might increase. In itself that might be the kind of revelation that underlay the changing features of church organization related to the correlation programme.

Correlation programme: organizing authority

Unlike the revelation on Negro ordination the 'correlation' approach, by contrast, demonstrates a slower form of organization and change yet it is one that can have far-reaching effect. Just as the Doctrine and Covenants, itself a book of revelations through prophecy, possesses many sections dealing with management and organization, the correlation approach of church management relates decisions of the First Presidency to practical aspects of church life. At the beginning of the twentieth century a Committee of Correlation and Adjustments was established. It underwent a series of name changes but its task was to institute shifts in church organization, as with the Family Home Evening in 1965 and the 1980 change to holding all Sunday morning activities in a consolidated block of three hours. From 1987 all documentation for church activities and programmes needed to pass through the Correlation Department (May 1992: 325).

As I will intimate again in the final chapter, these important changes ensure that nothing occurs without the permission of central authority; accordingly, correlation fosters a uniformity of doctrine and practice and guarantees a controlling power within the Church. In one of the more tellingly human verses of the Doctrine and Covenants comes the revelation that 'we have learned by sad experience that it is the nature and disposition of almost all men, as soon as they get a little authority, as they suppose, they will immediately begin to exercise unrighteous dominion' (D&C 121: 39). This idea came to Joseph while he was in prison and, though his situation was far removed from today's church, it provides an echo of the concern that must ever be in the mind of contemporary religious leaders.

In chapter 2 I described hierarchical, scriptural and mystical forms of authority found in major forms of Christianity and now I take up one element of this, namely the relationship between formal organization and spiritual awareness. In the Articles of Faith (already introduced in chapter 3) the fifth Article explicitly relates prophecy and authority: 'we believe that a man must be called by God, by prophecy, and by the laying on of hands by those who are in authority, to preach the Gospel and administer in the ordinances thereof'. While this emphasizes both the divine source of inspiration and the direction of human activity, it also circumscribes a person's activity through the 'authority' of others. One of the successes of LDS life in fostering both a bureaucratic organization and the personal life of interior spirituality lies in this juxtaposition of prophecy and authority, and in the way a supernatural frame is brought to surround bureaucracy. The Doctrine and Covenants, as a book of revelations derived from prophecy, includes many sections dealing with church organization. Here I will consider but two of them, Sections 107 and 124, the former dealing with the Aaronic and Melchizedek priesthoods of the Church and the latter with the office of Patriarch.

PRIESTHOOD, RESTORATION AND LEADERSHIP

The Melchizedek priesthood is said to have been present on earth from Adam to Moses, after whose lifetime it was withdrawn, leaving human religion to operate only in terms of the lower or Aaronic priesthood. This is why the Old Testament ritual system of the temple is grounded in Aaronic descent (Richards, A. L. 1992: 587–8). That withdrawal is mirrored by a similar removal of authority sometime after the death and resurrection of Jesus. Only with Joseph Smith was it restored and in two ways: one through the priesthoods and the other through temple ordinances. The priesthoods came first, in both the Aaronic and Melchizedek forms and then, over a period from approximately 1836 to 1844, but especially in an intense period of activity between December 1843 and April 1844, Joseph Smith inducted nine of the Twelve Apostles, along with their wives, into the inner mysteries of knowledge expressed in the endowment and other rites that brought added status to the basic Melchizedek office. This exerted a double effect: on the one hand, it bequeathed to them everything that Joseph believed could be provided for the ultimate conquest of death and the hope of future exaltation, while, on the other, it established these apostles as fully capable of leading the Church on earth.

This double power over mortality and Church organization is symbolically summarized in the LDS expression 'the keys' (already described in chapter 2), keys that would be used more rapidly than any of the apostles could have imagined when the prophet died only months after the completion of these rites. His lynching sprung upon them the fundamental issues of leadership, organization and mission and, as things transpired, the group of the Twelve Apostles assumed responsibility for the Church under the strong leadership of Brigham Young. After migration and settlement in Utah the First Presidency was re-established in December 1847, with Brigham Young as prophet (Backman 1995: 117). In what was a deeply symbolic architectural fact the Saints were left, at the death of Joseph, with only a partially completed temple at Nauvoo. Its destiny, in a sense, would signal the outcome of Mormonism, for after a brief interruption it was completed and, with extensive and exhausting effort, more than five thousand Saints received their endowments there. Latterly, this was all done in the knowledge that this temple would be left behind as the Saints migrated westwards, which they did in the spring of 1846. It suffered from arson and tornado and is only now, at the commencement of the twenty-first century, being rebuilt.

Theologically speaking, the population that left Nauvoo was not the same as the one that arrived there in 1839, neither in its leadership nor in its membership at large. Of the original Twelve Apostles one had died and five had left in apostasy; yet this was, also, the moment when Joseph Smith sent eight of the full number to England on an evangelistic campaign (Allen, Esplin and Whittaker 1992: 1–19). This testing point of core men and future leaders was also a turning point in that it yielded as many as five thousand English converts. These migrants to Nauvoo had 'gathered' for the Second Coming of Christ but, by the time they gathered their possessions to migrate further westwards, they did so in the power of their endowments and with a hope of glory that did not depend simply or solely upon Christ's imminent return. In sociological terms, this transformation of religious goals saved church members from that kind of cognitive dissonance that sometimes attends groups whose prized belief fails to materialize. In Nauvoo a majority of Saints – and not just a very small core group – had experienced the transformation of a readily understandable form of Christian Adventist-millenarianism into a symbolically rich form of ritualized faith; this faith did not simply await the inbreaking of the divine future into the present but allowed dedicated believers to engage in a covenantal religion that conferred blessings upon them, allowing them to break into the divine future, whether at the Second Coming of Christ or when they themselves died.

Patriarchal blessing

One form of divine inbreaking for individual Saints lay in patriarchal blessings. These offer a window into the highly significant LDS theological world of divine communication, the regulation of inspiration, and the nature of personal relationships with God. Today the Church appoints a patriarch or patriarchs for each stake and, once members gain a 'recommend' from their bishop, they can visit them for a blessing. In a rite of the laying on of hands they receive a personal blessing believed to come by direct inspiration of the Holy Spirit; it is written down and copies are kept by the individual and the Church. Saints do not talk about blessings with any other than very close relatives or friends, since they are deemed to be strictly personal. In this respect patriarchal blessings resemble temple rites, which are also regarded as secret because they too are sacred. Indeed, although patriarchal blessings are given in the stake or ward context and not in the temple, there is something about them that echoes temple rites in that each depends upon an attitude towards the power of words spoken under divine guidance or under oath in a formal covenant with God, but in the blessings it is God who 'speaks' powerful words through the patriarch.

The blessing informs the individual of the tribe of Israel to which they belong, itself a reminder of early Mormonism's strong identification both with Israel and with its lost tribes. Many are told that they belong to the tribe of Ephraim, to which the task of leading the latter-day restoration has been committed, but other tribes can occur. Further information, often couched in broad terms, can be read by individuals in quite personal and intimate ways, sometimes indicating possible avenues of work for God or some feature of character and personal life in the future. Wilford Woodruff's patriarchal blessing of 15 April 1837, conferred by the prophet's father, Joseph Smith Snr, is not unlike many others. He too was of 'the blood of Ephraim'; he would visit 'many barbarous tribes of the earth', would gain many spiritual experiences and his intellectual powers would be preserved. He was also told that he would 'remain on the earth to behold thy Saviour Come in the Clouds of heaven', and be 'numbered with the one hundred forty and four thousand' (Woodruff 1993: 17–18). It is of some interest that the Church as such is not mentioned or named in the blessing. It is as though the entire LDS venture is so great that the individual's call and life transcends any institutional cause as he becomes engaged with angels and supernatural powers. Today, Saints often seek patriarchal blessings at crucial moments in life, such as, perhaps, when setting out on their two-year mission. For many it confirms the reality of God and of his working through an official of the Church. Patriarchs are the real point of contact between a Latter-day Saint and that aspect of the Church that has to do with intimate divine–human relationships. They express the mystical authority of Mormonism and can in some respects be contrasted with bishops, who also have major responsibility for order and discipline in the Church and, in that sense, hold legal authority.

As we will see below in Brigham Young's informal account of how patriarchal blessings emerged, the first official patriarch appointed by Joseph Smith Jnr in 1833 was none other than his father, Joseph Smith Snr, so he really was a patriarch in heading the prophet's family. For much of its subsequent history the formal office of patriarch to the Church was held by descendants of the Smith family until 1979 when the office was ended because so many stake patriarchs had by then been appointed. The fact that Joseph's father had been made patriarch reflects the LDS belief that while stake patriarchs provide a major channel of blessings, any father of a family who holds a Melchizedek priesthood is, by his very fatherhood, a patriarch to his family and can bless his children with a father's blessing: there is a strong overlap of duty and responsibility at this point.

Theologically speaking, the office of patriarch, together with the act of giving and receiving a patriarchal blessing, offers another firm expression of the relational nature of Mormonism and of its commitment to the idea of direct communication between God and human beings. Formally speaking, the patriarchal blessing is not prophecy, yet, functionally speaking, it does serve as a kind of prophecy for individuals. In so doing, it continues and fosters the LDS belief in the deeply personal nature of God and in each individual as someone who is known to God and who, within the overall plan of salvation, has a part to play in the development of Zion.

CHURCH WITHIN A CHURCH

The existence of such patriarchal blessings, along with the rites of the temple, would not generally be familiar to newcomers to Mormonism – those who had become acquainted with the regular meetings at the local ward chapel. Indeed, it might surprise them to discover that there was another dimension to the faith located within LDS families and also in the regional or national temple. This would be particularly true outside the LDS heartland of Utah, where there are numerous temples and a culture in which temples and patriarchal blessings are familiar to many. For such converts it is the relational aspect of Mormonism that is likely to be encountered before its system of 'principles'.

Where the Church of Jesus Christ of Latter-day Saints operates in full accord with its ideals the local chapel and regional temple are fully complementary to each other, and in an ideal world all Saints would be married, pay their tithes, live satisfactory ethical lives, accept all church doctrine and support its leaders unreservedly. After an interview with their local bishop such individuals would be granted a certificate – a temple recommend – qualifying them to attend the temple, be married there for time and all eternity, be baptized for the dead and receive their own endowments – rites that will be described in later chapters.

It would also be possible for someone to approach Mormonism through books that so played on the ideal Mormon life of temples and eternal exaltation as to ignore the reality of relatively inactive church members or others devoid of temple recommends. While statistics are not easily accessible on this topic it is likely that a well-established area may have, say, 70 percent of its members qualified for temple activity, while mission areas or more peripheral branches of the Church may have only about 15 percent. In mission areas where individual families or persons are converted, it may take a considerable period of time before temples are built and the culture of temple ritual develops within the local 'chapel'-minded congregation. Even when it does develop, numerous reasons arise that can prevent members from being active either at the local chapel or, even more so, at the temple.

In the introductory chapter I suggested that Mormonism's history and doctrine can, at times, give the impression of there being two different styles of church within the overarching LDS structure. The earliest Church of the 1830s was, as it were, a single body, a form of Adventism with an essentially Protestant millenarian message. When Joseph Smith first added the temple rites of endowment, allied with plural marriage, he did so for only a select group of close leaders: that period marked a distinction between the millenarian church – albeit one that had its share of popular magic – and the birth of the ritual-mystical mode of Mormonism. The ongoing distinction between these modes, symbolized in the difference between chapel and temple, would only develop as the nineteenth century turned into the twentieth and the twenty-first, and, as we will see in the final chapter, there may be some real advantage built into this distinction as far as evangelism and church expansion are concerned.

Those holding recommends for temple or for blessings are likely to be the core leadership of the local congregation, who constitute a kind of church within a church. Because the temple ritual is held to be sacred, it is not talked of outside the temple, not even at the local chapel, except that leaders encourage individuals and families to reach such a level of commitment that they may engage in temple activity. This distinctive LDS organization into temple and chapel life is quite different from all other Christian churches and does not parallel, say, the difference between parish church and cathedral in Anglican or Catholic life. Symbolically speaking, it is better to compare the LDS temple and its rites with the Eucharistic form of worship in parish churches and the LDS chapel with the other, non-Eucharistic, services held, whether in parish churches or cathedrals. This analogy benefits from the distinction that is often, though unofficially, made by some Anglican clergy between the core members who faithfully attend the Eucharist and the others who only come to other morning or evening forms of worship. The fact that a Sacrament Meeting, the strict LDS equivalent of the Eucharist, takes place in the chapel and not the temple should not be allowed to confuse the distinction just made between temple and chapel: it is the distinction between core and peripheral members that is important. The LDS rite that commemorates the atonement of Jesus is, in effect, open to all – even if they are not Latter-day Saints themselves. All churches tend to draw boundaries around that which they regard as the most theologically significant aspect of their ritual and, for the Saints, this is the temple and not the chapel nor any of the events within it. When it is also remembered that Mormonism does not possess a paid and professional clergy which can serve as the core organizational group, it becomes all the more important that there should be some defining characteristic of the dedicated membership. Similarly, the Church provides a *General Handbook of Instructions*, whose first edition of 1899 dealt primarily with tithing but now deals with all aspects of church life. It is supplied to all priesthood holders in positions of particular responsibility, enabling them to respond to changing circumstances within the Church as well as in dealing with long-established practices. It is not generally available to the membership at large.

DOCTRINE, EVENT AND SALVATION

Behind all such handbooks, Church directives and the committees that produce them, stand individual leaders. Indeed, the organization of the LDS Church, as well as its history, is a faith-history of great men, and of some great women, but the men predominate. To grasp the Church's doctrine is to see how these individuals with all their hopes and difficulties engaged with visions of God and felt themselves called both to lead and to follow. Doubtless, as in all churches, they experienced the combined influence of the desire to serve God and neighbour as well as to advance themselves and responded to each to differing degrees. Here, however, I leave such imponderables of spirituality and power to consider two well-established notions of theology at large – salvation history and narrative theology. These complementary perspectives on the nature of human life in relation to God and destiny possess one subtle difference that is determined by their direction of interest.

In narrative theology abstract ideas are rendered practical through events as people evaluate their own identity, align themselves with groups of earlier believers and enact their response to God (Stroup 1981). In this sense contemporary Mormon spirituality can relate itself to Nephites in their periods of obedience, while human rebellion can always find its parallel in Lamanite hard-heartedness. Narrative theology begins, as it were, with a contemporary Christian group and develops as that group reads the Bible and comes to interpret its own experience in terms of the experience of earlier generations of God's people. It makes the Bible its own by coming to identify with, for example, the ancient Hebrews in Egyptian or Babylonian captivity, or in journeying as a pilgrim people through its own wilderness hardships to its own promised land. Similarly, a group may relate to the earliest Christian communities by seeking to live communally or under the direct inspiration of the Holy Spirit. In such a narrative theology there is a strong sense of the current day, of the present moment, of God being active in the here and now, and this gives a sense of hope and purpose amidst political and economic difficulties, as was the case in the use of narrative theology in the Liberation Theology amongst oppressed Catholic groups in South America from the 1960s.

Salvation history, with its development in nineteenth-century theology, and already a largely dated theological idea, starts from a more abstract and decontextualized perspective, concerned as it is with God's plan for the world and for the salvation of humanity. Though scholars have their own nuanced interpretation of this notion, it is rooted in divine action and sets a frame around events that encourages believers to view them as possessing an ultimate purpose. In LDS terms the plan of salvation is a form of salvation history coming, as it were, from above downwards, while the history of the Saints, telling of early revelations, evangelism, conversion, migration, hostility, the trek to and settlement of Utah, is its narrative theology emerging from the people 'upwards'. Underlying much Mormon folklore is the sense of God's direction and providential care, which feeds into the personal testimony of today's Saints and their own lives, as well as into their relatively limited knowledge of senior church leaders through stories of them or brief references to something they have said or written. Against this background the Book of Mormon, complemented by the Doctrine and Covenants, appears to be an extensive example of salvation history but, at the same time, both books display a strong narrative theology, especially the Doctrine and Covenants, in which divine response and divine initiative engage with immediate individual and community needs. Indeed, from one perspective the entire Book of Mormon could be interpreted as an extended case of narrative theology. Standing out within these narratives are certain key individuals who dramatically manifest the values which LDS theology prizes.

JOSEPH SMITH, JNR (1805–1844)

Bringing together the perspective of salvation history in the form of the plan of salvation and narrative theology as Mormonism's interpretation of their own history makes it easier to see how doctrine affects experience and how experience moves into doctrine. The focal point at which salvation history and narrative theology most specifically cohere for Latter-day Saints is in Joseph Smith, especially in his first vision (already outlined in chapter 1), whose date is a subject of contention; some locate it in 1820 and others in 1823 but it was not written until 1832 (Bushman 1984: 56, 204). Historians have pondered the various phases of this vision's evolution and tend to see its present form as a 'late development', only gaining an influential status in LDS self-reflection late in the nineteenth century (Widmer 2000: 92–107). Jan Shipps described the first vision, which Joseph reckoned to have occurred in 1823 but did not discuss at all widely until about fifteen years later, as having been 'later canonized by believers' (2000: 290). Despite the fact that a considerable amount of historical and literary critical analysis has already been brought to bear on this vision, I presented it rather simply in chapter 1, in its developed form, as an overview of LDS spirituality. As I indicated there, this first vision has, in a sense, come to be for Joseph Smith's life what the plan of salvation is for the Church itself. The one serves as a charter of and for an individual's mission, and the other for the mission of the Church.

Whatever view is taken of Joseph's first and successive visions, there is no doubt that his life was as eventful as that of any religious founder. From obscurity he finds himself both famous and infamous, from poverty he comes to control relative wealth but, above all, from wondering and pondering about which sect is true he establishes a Church that he knows is from God and is the sole means of the fullest truth available to humanity. One of the most insightful descriptions of Joseph comes from himself when he says: 'deep water is what I am wont to swim in'. This reflection, in a revelation dated 1 September 1842, discloses something of the inner life, or at least of the self-understanding of Joseph Smith, at a time when the Church had grown but only under much conflict from many sources (D&C 127: 2). Here is a man who uses the language of being both called and ordained to describe his own destiny and the destiny of humanity. His life, he says, is something mysterious to himself: he asks his readers to judge whether his life has been for good or ill. He describes the discord, envy and tribulation he has experienced as having become 'second nature' to him. Yet his conviction remains that God is on his side. Fawn Brodie's challenging reflections on the many streams of thought that moved Joseph Smith remain as influential now as when she first wrote under the enigmatic title *No Man Knows My History* in the 1940s (1995 [1945]).

A PRISON PRAYER

One insight into Joseph's spirituality comes in a prayer from prison (D&C 121). An editorial gloss describes the text as dealing with 'prayer and prophecies' written by Joseph Smith while a prisoner at Liberty, Missouri. This is apposite because the elements of prayer and prophecy are intimately entwined: prayer in the sense of human speech to God and prophecy in the sense of God's speech to a man. The first six verses show Joseph calling upon God, asking where he is and why oppression has fallen upon his Saints. In verses 7 and 8 God replies and refers to himself in the third person. By verse 15 it is difficult to know if God is speaking or if Joseph, as prophet, is speaking for God. By approximately verse 33 it is clear that the prophet is speaking to fellow believers. What is of stylistic interest is the way in which Joseph's speech passes from prayer to prophecy to reflection without any apparent break. This affords an apt, condensed, example for those who view the Book of Mormon as well as the Doctrine and Covenants as the work of Joseph's own religious creativity.

It will always remain a matter of personal religious faith whether someone believes that Joseph was a prophet or not, as with any other religious founder or leader; even so Joseph thought of himself as a prophet and so have millions of others. What is more, it was within and through his prophetic role that Joseph not only established a Protestant-like Adventist movement but also a deeply ritualized mystical tradition of death-conquest and apotheosis. Inherent in that vocation to divine character was plural marriage, as we see in chapters 8 and 9. His death, in 1844, gave his followers a final image of him not only as a martyr, sacrificed in a powerful ending to a dramatically influential life, but as one who had invested a core leadership with authority and power to continue his work, all within an overriding divine plan of salvation.

SIDNEY RIGDON (1793–1876)

While it was Brigham Young who spearheaded the leadership and ensured Mormonism's survival after the death of its founding prophet, there was a competition for primacy and Joseph's close associate Sidney Rigdon was the major contender. I briefly describe Rigdon not only because of that challenge but, more significantly, because of his great influence on Mormonism during the lifetime of the first prophet and despite the fact that he subsequently left the movement.

After some years as a Baptist minister, much influenced by the teachings of Alexander Campbell, Rigdon, already thirty-seven years old, was converted to Mormonism in 1830 through the impression that the Book of Mormon made upon him. He soon became Joseph Smith's right-hand man. The fact that his contact with Mormonism followed the publication of the Book of Mormon is important because one early criticism of the book was that Rigdon, steeped in biblical texts, in preaching on them and disputing them against diverse interpretations, had been its author, or at least had highly influenced it. What Rigdon did bring to Joseph was his persuasion that some form of communitarian lifestyle was important for any contemporary form of Christianity that claimed authentic relations with earliest Christianity. Indeed, Richard van Wagoner tells how Smith's 'communal vision began evolving within days of meeting Rigdon'; he also described them as inseparable during the Mormon period of residence in Kirtland, Ohio from 1831–39 (van Wagoner 1994: 79, 160). Not only did Rigdon bring friendship and comradeship but he was a real convert, made by the new book, and importantly an individual who had been a practising and successful minister of an ordinary Christian denomination. Since one of Joseph Smith's major concerns as a boy and young man had been about which church to join, it is likely that the conversion of a minister of one of those churches would have encouraged the prophet in his commitment to the new way he had set himself.

Rigdon fostered education amongst the largely poorly or uneducated Saints and himself became the chief teacher in Kirtland's 1833 School of the Prophets. It is very likely that he was the author of the *Lectures on Faith* used in that school and placed in the Doctrine and Covenants until removed in 1921 (van Wagoner 1994: 162). The publisher's preface to the present edition of *Lectures on Faith* describes them as 'prepared chiefly by the Prophet Joseph Smith (with perhaps some assistance from other brethren)' (Smith, J. 1985: v). Rigdon disappears from view here in but one example of how history can obscure events. In the Kirtland days, however, he was dramatically important, not least in promoting the publication of Joseph Smith's revelations in what became the Doctrine and Covenants. On the occasion of the dedication of the Kirtland Temple on 27 March 1836, Rigdon's profile was practically as high as that of Joseph Smith. Only after preaching an extremely impressive sermon did Rigdon introduce the prophet, who read the dedicatory prayer. When the Saints decided to put Joseph Smith forward as a candidate for the Presidency of the United States in 1844, Rigdon was to serve as his vice-president in the Mormon Reform Party.

Rigdon's place in Mormon history became most apparent and problematic at the death of Joseph. As a life-long opponent of plural marriage Rigdon had left Nauvoo on LDS business and arrived in Pittsburgh on 27 June 1844, the day of the prophet's death. He wished that the Twelve Apostles, largely scattered on LDS business themselves, should join him in Pittsburgh to plan for the future. There is no doubt that Rigdon expected to assume Joseph's place, though there was no established form of succession since Smith was still in his prime. Back in 1837–38, when the financial disaster of the United States embraced and magnified the problems of the Kirtland Safety Bank led by Joseph Smith and Sydney Rigdon, Rigdon had become a focus of discontent amongst a considerable number of core believers. His famous address on the Fourth of July 1838 at Far West was itself a kind of affirmation of Mormon independence, but it also set Rigdon apart as 'the symbol of Mormon militancy in Missouri': it prepared him as a 'scapegoat within the church for all the misfortune' that the church experienced over this devastating period (van Wagoner 1994: 221). It may also have sown the seeds of his later rejection as leader when Joseph died in 1844 and a virtual challenge arose between Rigdon and Brigham Young, which Young won out. Rigdon soon disappeared from the main Mormon movement and sought to establish his own following, as I describe in chapter 9.

BRIGHAM YOUNG

Brigham Young remained and grew in stature as a leader. He had been baptized in the spring of 1832 and first met the prophet later that summer. On the very evening of their meeting, when all were together in Joseph's house, Brigham Young spoke in tongues. He had being doing so since his conversion, a time that seemed to signal an outburst of positive life-energy in him. There had been a division of opinion over whether this was a divine gift or not and this first meeting with the prophet provided a good opportunity for gaining a definite answer. Not only did the prophet say it was from God but it seems as though this was the first time Joseph had heard 'tongues'. Later that very night he, too, spoke in tongues. Arrington noted the strangeness of Brigham speaking in tongues, since he was 'a practical and rather staid person' and seldom spoke in this way after 1832 (Arrington 1986: 34). But that moment was one when both Joseph and Brigham sensed that they participated in the divine work with which they were familiar in the biblical accounts of the Day of Pentecost (Acts 2). Certainly, as Arrington notes, the Book of Mormon had played a major part in Young's conversion, much as it had for Sidney Rigdon.

It is interesting that research into current religious groups in which speaking in tongues occurs on a regular basis shows that 'The adulation accorded the leader was the most obvious characteristic of tongue-speaking groups. At no time was this degree of reverence for a leader observed in non-tongue-speaking groups' (Kildahl 1972: 51). This may help to explain why glossolalia only occurred in the earliest years of real LDS 'charismatic leadership' – in its sociological sense – but not in the later years of bureaucratic leadership under Brigham Young. From an early age, and before his conversion to Mormonism, Brigham Young reckoned it 'his duty to control all passions' and, to a very great extent, managed to do so (Arrington 1986: 23–4). When he was twenty-three years of age, he became a Methodist, though he was dissatisfied with its general teachings. Brigham continued to experience that religious longing which lies at the heart of much spirituality yet which takes different forms, sometimes seeking self-sacrifice, sometimes moral perfection and sometimes a doctrinal scheme or ritual practice. Brigham Young reflected something of Joseph Smith's longing for a system of sincere faith that is grounded upon a divine revelation devoid of human interpretation and the agglomeration of long human tradition.

Brigham Young's discourses are many and could provide the basis for a very extensive theology of Mormonism in and of themselves. Here I draw attention to their creativity, general open-mindedness and strong advocacy of that LDS ideal of intelligence, itself a hallmark term of Mormonism bearing both a general and a specific meaning. Chapter 3 has already accounted for its specific sense with regard to human identity and here I simply press its general and popular sense of the pursuit of learning and its transformation into wisdom. In a sermon of October 1859 Brigham Young spoke on 'intelligence' as the subject that interested him more 'than any other pertaining to the life of man' (Young 1992: 122–33). He talks of doctrinal disputes between religious denominations which ignore what they do possess as truth. It is the purpose of LDS elders, he says, 'to gather up all the truths in the world pertaining to the life and salvation of man . . . and to bring it to Zion'. It is obvious that Brigham is entranced by the mystery of life, of the very air we inhale as 'the greatest source of life'. He tells how God organized matter to make the earth and human beings, and he intimates that he knows other things that had, perhaps, better not be revealed. Still, he discloses the information that 'the seeds of every plant... were brought from another world'. 'This', he says, 'would be news to many of you' (Young 1992: 126). News indeed, but also an expression of Brigham's curious openness to knowledge and to life and to the sense that revelation was related to need and to the capacity to grasp ideas as opportunity presented itself.

One instructive example comes in his description of how patriarchal blessings originated almost accidentally. In a sermon of 1873 Brigham tells how his own brother – Joseph Young – had asked the Prophet Joseph Smith if the Young family might receive a blessing from their father. The prophet thought it a good idea and, when attending the event himself, not only suggested that the old man had better be given an 'ordination' to allow him to bless the family but also duly ordained him for that task. This event, according to Brigham Young, not only prompted the prophet to think that the same thing should occur in his own, Smith, family but that, 'in the course of a few weeks... Joseph Smith received a revelation to ordain patriarchs' (Young 1992: 213). So it was, argued Brigham, that Joseph Smith was instructed 'little by little... for the Lord never reveals all to a person at once'.

THE PROPHET'S MANTLE

One episode of Brigham Young's life exemplifies the relationship between church organization and Mormon spirituality in its earlier years, and it is not without some echo still. The event has been called the day of the prophet's mantle. The day was 8 August 1844, when the Saints, heavily mourning Joseph's death, held a large meeting at which Sidney Rigdon claimed to be leader on the basis that he was still a mouthpiece for the dead Joseph. Though often eloquent, on this occasion he failed to carry his audience. Brigham Young, by contrast, when he rose to speak was thought by some to physically resemble the dead prophet and to speak in the prophet's very tone of voice. Not all had this experience, some only referred to it years later, but there were contemporary references to some form of impressive experience (Quinn 1994: 166). Whether this perception was due, as Leonard Arrington suggests, 'to the downcast spirits of the Saints... their disappointment with Rigdon... the surprise presence of Brigham', who was thought to be *en route* from Boston, or to Brigham's noted 'talent for mimicry', it led to Brigham's acceptance and Rigdon's demise (Arrington 1986: 113–15). The instructive element of this event is that it is slightly reminiscent of Joseph

Smith's first vision and the plan of salvation. This needs careful explanation because, though it is far less significant than either of those, it stands as part of the mythical-historical framework of LDS reflection. It implies a divine influence in the leadership and in the direction of events associated with the survival of the Church and, thereby, of human destiny. If the vision and the plan serve as two dominant symbols within Mormonism, explaining its reason for existence and the basis of its mission, then the 'prophet's mantle' furnishes an intensification of each, sustaining them and helping to weave the fabric of spirituality that is the LDS movement.

MISSION AND MOVEMENT

So it is that, over time, the Church of Jesus Christ of Latter-day Saints developed a changing sense of what its mission was as its message spread out from an Adventist-millenarian gathering, through a crisis of leadership into nation building, to engaging with the dead and to an expansionist programme that was interpreted by some as the emergence of a new world religion. In concluding this chapter it is important to show mission not simply as a vehicle for a religious message but as part of the very message itself. Mission and missionaries have penetrated and motivated LDS life throughout its history. But 'mission' is not quite as simple a term as it may at first appear, for a broad and general awareness of Christianity can easily give the impression that Jesus gathered a group of disciples who, subsequently, became missionaries of the message of salvation as depicted in the Acts of the Apostles. Certainly it is the case that early Christianity attracted many adherents, resulting in what became the Christian Church, and once Christianity was adopted as an official religion by Constantine in the fourth century, it was set on a course for influencing, and at times dominating, entire cultures. Yet, all that did not necessarily make for a missionary religion. Not even the Reformation, viewed by many as a watershed in the development of Christianity, involved a missionary movement, but more of an internal transition from Catholicism. In chapter 9 I will follow the idea that a new kind of Christianity emerged in the late eighteenth and early nineteenth centuries, one grounded in missionary societies and missionary endeavour, and that Mormonism was one early example of this dynamic trend.

Such mission demands movement, and spatial movement was and is an integral feature of LDS mission organization. Much LDS theology is dynamic, with its source and goal being more related to practice than to theory. This emerges in the present context in the case of the Seventy and further series of Seventies, men whose task is 'to travel among the nations', as opposed to those whose task is for the more local and residential organization of the Church (D&C 107: 98). Joseph Smith was extremely alert to this dual need for travelling missionaries as well as for resident pastors. The outward movement of missionaries and the inward migration of converts established a dynamic demography within Mormonism. In the twentieth century this shifted more to a dynamic of movement in the sense that missionaries and other church leaders travelled extensively but converts no longer migrated to Zion. Zion was to be everywhere. This would even be symbolized, for example, by LDS chaplains serving in the armed forces of the United States.

Contemporary missionaries are called from among young adults who serve the Church for two years at their own expense. After a brief period of training they may be sent anywhere in the world, often after having received basic language training. Such a period can help to convert the missionaries themselves, especially if they have been brought up in staunch LDS communities and need to come to a point of appropriating their faith for themselves and not simply accepting what others believe. In that process of gaining a testimony of the truth, as fellow Saints would call it, the individual can grasp something of what might have happened to Joseph Smith as he entered into a sense of divine vocation. Through their mission, individuals come to engage at a significant level both with the authority of the Church and with their obedience to it, for authority and obedience are two cardinal features within Mormon ecclesiology. But, mission work does not end there; it even extends beyond life and into the realm of the dead, as I will argue in the final chapter. At that point ecclesiology, with its roots firmly in prophecy and priesthood, passes into an even wider cosmology, within which human agency is a vital component in benefiting from Christ's atonement and in taking forward the human pursuit of eternal glory.

CHAPTER 6

Ethics, atonement and agency

The two theological ideas of agency and atonement underpin the ethical life and destiny of Mormons. Agency describes human responsibility, atonement accounts for sin, while destiny sets the goal within which redeemed individuals may reap the eternal rewards of their own ethical endeavour. Much has already been said on agency in chapter 3 and on atonement in chapter 4, so it now remains to develop each in terms of LDS ethics. This is particularly true for the theology of atonement because LDS ethical theory is fundamentally related to the Church's understanding of Christ's suffering and its consequences for the way in which believers should live. Because that understanding differs, quite significantly, from the views of most traditional Christians it will be treated here by comparing it with some specific examples of Protestant theology. Some of the consequences of these ethical views, especially on agency, will be developed still further in chapter 7.

Unsurprisingly, ethics, in the formal sense of a philosophical consideration of how to live a good life, plays a relatively small part in Mormon belief because the growth of doctrine has provided the Saints with a practical ethics. Mormons are much more likely to think of the 'principles of the gospel' than of 'ethics'. Bruce McConkie, for example, argues that ethics derives directly from doctrine and that those with the 'highest ethical standards' will be those with the greatest number of 'gospel doctrines' (McConkie, B. R. 1979: 240). In his extremely brief consideration of ethics McConkie goes on to say that 'the only real superiority of the apostate sects of Christendom over their more openly pagan counterparts' lies precisely in their having 'preserved many of the ethical teachings of Christ and the apostles'. This appreciation of Christian churches at large, in one who could be very negatively inclined towards them, illustrates the power of ethical teaching for Mormons. In another comment, as illuminating as it is brief, Neil Brady explains the traditional philosophical distinction between the teleological and deontological approaches to ethics – the former dealing with the purpose of actions and the latter with one's response to laws – as being more problematic for Christianity at large than for Latter-day Saints, who gladly combine, 'obedience to divine imperatives and pursuit of ultimate happiness' (Brady 1992: 467). In this chapter I excavate beneath this particular foundation to discover what the 'self' is that may decide to be obedient to laws that may confer happiness.

HAPPINESS AND JOY

Brady's guidance is helpful here, for the two ideas of 'happiness' and 'imperatives' stand at the very core of LDS ethical reflection and application, albeit expressed in different terms with 'happiness' as 'joy' and 'imperative' as 'principle'. A key LDS text, used a great deal when describing human life, asserts that 'men are, that they might have joy' (2 Nephi 2: 25). This half-text is drawn from one of the Book of Mormon's prime reflections on salvation involving the pre-mortal fall of Satan, the subsequent temptation of Adam and Eve and their disobedience. The full text runs, 'Adam fell that men might be; and men are, that they might have joy.' This is an LDS expression of the *felix culpa* theme of wider Christian theology, the idea that the fall of humanity was a blessing precisely because it resulted in the Incarnation and redemption wrought in Christ. In one of the more robust carols of Christendom, 'Adam lay ye bounden', worshippers express this in the lines, 'blessed be the time the apple taken was, e'er had ne'er Our Lady 'a been Heavenly Queen'. Here Mary, Our Lady of the carol, has become Queen of Heaven, having mothered the Redeemer of Mankind. While that particular association is not made in Mormonism, the 'happiness' element in relation to the fall remains a strong undercurrent of the Book of Mormon, not least because it is the opposite of misery, and misery is directly associated with evil and the devil.

This association of ideas is, once more, derived directly from the LDS affinity with the concept of 'opposition of all things', which has already been documented in chapter 1. So it is that 2 Nephi 2 verse 10 sets happiness in opposition to misery and parallels the way in which the devil is opposed to Christ and damnation to salvation. 'Punishment...is in opposition to... happiness.' One of the outworkings of this sense of opposition is found in Brigham Young's reflections on the outcome of Adam's sin: 'The whole plan was previously calculated' to eat the forbidden fruit 'to reduce his posterity to sin, misery, darkness...and to the power of the Devil, that they might be prepared for an Exaltation, for without this they could not receive one' (Young 1992: 97).

SELF: RELATIONS AND PRINCIPLES

These features of happiness and joy also bring us back to the issue of 'relations and principles' raised in chapter 1, where I indicated that LDS theology is both relational and grounded in principles: the former more and the latter less 'personal' in ethos. This pair of clustered values – relations, happiness and joy, on the one hand, and principles and imperatives, on the other – underlies a considerable field of LDS life, not least ethics.

On the relational front, it is absolutely fundamental to appreciate that even a person's ultimate salvation depends upon his or her relationship to someone else. It was common for early Mormon leaders to stress that nobody is 'saved' alone, indeed, this is a distinctive feature of LDS theology, for exaltation is a corporate venture. This broad perspective quite contradicts the growing individualism of the West from the end of the twentieth century into the twenty-first century when, for example, increasing numbers of people live alone and follow a lifestyle in which self stands at the heart of everything. When it comes to human relationships, the individual decides how much to become involved with others and in what way. In terms of religion, individuals are very likely to focus on self-development and self-fulfilment. Indeed 'self-religion' has been one of the clearest descriptions of this way of thinking and quite inverts the LDS scheme of things (Heelas 1996). In general theological terms the earliest Christians, portrayed in the New Testament, seemed to combine Jesus' teaching on the personal and sincere responsibility of people towards God as their heavenly father with the teaching of the apostles, which emphasized the unity of all believers within the Christian congregation. Paul's Epistles develop the idea that the community that Christians joined was a kind of corporate group that could even be described as the 'body of Christ'. This remarkable description portrays living individuals as continuing the work that Jesus started when alive as a man. Paul's theology argues that Jesus had been resurrected from the dead and that his physical body had been transformed into a spiritual body, now in heaven with God, and would reappear when Jesus came in glory to establish God's kingdom of righteousness on earth. But he also argued that the Holy Spirit, a power or force that came from God and exerted a transforming influence upon people, had already come to the earth and was the dynamic power that united individuals together into a community of believers. And it was that community, inspired and enlivened by the Holy Spirit, that comprised the 'body of Christ' on earth.

Paul already possessed something of a model for this image in the people of Israel, the Jewish community that was itself believed to be God's chosen people. For Paul, this powerful image yielded its own problem: it seemed as though God could really only have one 'chosen people', and that Christians were taking over this identity from the Jews. Much of his Epistle to the Romans is devoted to this issue, the outcome of which is that Christians comprise the new community in which God's covenant promises to Israel are fulfilled and in which membership is thrown wide open to all who believe in Jesus: it is not restricted only to those who are Jews by birthright. The idea of a church as the vehicle for God's divine activity through Jesus developed from this community of believers and it is one that has deeply influenced the notion of what constitutes an individual. In particular, it stresses the corporate and communal nature of human life marked by baptism, a ritual of incorporation into the death and resurrection of Jesus, and by some rite marking the coming of the Holy Spirit. The subsequent ritual of the breaking of bread further emphasized the communal integrity of believers. In later church life these rites were formalized as baptism, confirmation and Eucharist, often within a wider sacramental system covering the whole of life and making it quite clear that people existed as part of a divine community. Salvation itself, as the ultimate goal of existence, was dependent upon belonging to this group, and the ultimate punishment for transgression was excommunication, being formally cut off from the benefits of group membership. This description covers the great majority of subsequent Christian churches even though their theologies may tailor the ideas in one direction more than another, as was the case for LDS thought.

Against this strong relational background, the LDS view of the individual affirms and extends the mainstream Christian view of community while also affirming the necessity for individuals to employ their own decision-making capacity or 'agency'. This means that the Mormon 'self' must be understood as an interplay of community and agency: the self is more relational than essential despite the 'eternal' nature of underlying 'intelligence'. In one sense it is easy to argue that Mormonism is radically individualistic, given its strong emphasis upon individual responsibility in the process of attaining salvation, but that would be a mistake because, as vital as that personal responsibility is, and as much as it may be advocated by church leaders, it demands a community of endeavour to achieve its goal. As I will show in chapter 8, Mormons require the services of each other if they are to attain anything like that fullness of salvation described as exaltation. More practically still, within church life considerable benefit accrues to those who conform to its expectations.

The significance of that individualistic element within LDS ethics becomes all the more obvious when the relational factor is set alongside the theme of 'principles' as advanced in this book. The relational view of self when associated with the need for adherence to the principles by which the universe operates produces a potential paradox, for the logic of relationships is not entirely coherent with the logic of adherence to principles. The one tends to stress trust and operates on the basis of love, while the other functions on obligation and obedience. This is not simply a restatement of the traditional Protestant division between gospel and law, although it does involve some of the conflict inherent in that interpretation of religion; far more important is the fact that LDS life actually provides a basis for each. There is much in family, community and congregational life that fosters love, affection and trust and inspires the relational attitude to life. But there is also much in the operation of the church organization and the formal rationale of temple rites that bespeaks obedience to principles whatever that might mean for an individual. Ironically, it is the family that has to bear the weight of both of these dimensions, a weight that is likely to increase, the more dedicated a family becomes to the ideals of Mormonism. Obedience is enacted through agency, itself a power of personal intelligence embodied in priesthood. It is expressed in vows and covenants and manifested through marriage and parenthood. Its goal lies in attaining the highest possible exaltation in eternal realms of glory as detailed in the plan of salvation. Freedom to engage in it only really begins when, after repentance and faith, someone is baptized and gains the benefit of Christ's atonement, as we have seen in chapter 4. Once in the Church's baptized membership, believers must use their agency in obeying divine commands in order to avail themselves of all ritual benefits of the Church.

FROM CALVARY TO GETHSEMANE

The single most influential example of agency and freedom within LDS thought comes to expression in Jesus, and here one cannot simply think of him, as might be natural for many Christian theologians, as Jesus of Nazareth. For agency and freedom first appear in the pre-existence when the divine Son offers to undertake the task of coming to earth precisely to atone for human sin, and to ensure that the divine plan of salvation, stretching from pre-mortality through this life and into ages to come, is accomplished. Christ's exercise of his agency is nowhere more directly apparent than in the very purpose of his coming to earth, dramatically portrayed in the arena of atonement, an arena embracing both the hill of Calvary with its cross, and the Garden of Gethsemane with its trial of will and demonstration of obedience. While much has already been said about the distinctions between these locations and their theological significance in chapter 4, much remains to be developed in relation to ethical issues because what Jesus did in Gethsemane stands as a model of how Latter-day Saints should themselves live. The narrative of Christ's engagement with evil, with all its pain and anguish, is the occasion for seeing how the key LDS concepts of agency, freedom and obedience are related. Latter-day Saint ethics is rooted in this implementation of atonement because it is the foundation upon which resurrection rests and from which the Saint sets out on a life of dedicated endeavour and achievement that leads to exaltation.

One approach to this distinctive tradition is through a revelation dated March 1830, just when the Book of Mormon was being published and the Church established. Following from a passage of chastisement and call to repentance addressed to one named individual – Martin Harris – this text discloses the mystery that, for example, 'eternal punishment' should be interpreted as 'God's punishment' precisely because God is eternal: 'Endless is my name' (D&C 19: 10). It then describes how Jesus Christ suffered to bring about atonement and to save others from suffering, if they only but repented. Not to repent would be to endure the 'sore...and exquisite' suffering that God had even brought upon himself as witnessed when Jesus did 'tremble because of pain' and did 'bleed at every pore' (D&C 19: 18).

This expression, 'bleed at every pore' came to assume distinctive significance for Latter-day Saints and brought LDS theology to diverge from practically all other theological opinions that limit their concern to the sacrificial blood of crucifixion. By the time when James Talmage (1862–1933), then one of the Twelve Apostles, wrote *Jesus the Christ* in 1915, the image of atonement in the Garden was already well developed. Talmage depicts Christ's suffering as not being simply 'physical pain, nor mental anguish alone...but a spiritual agony of soul such as only God was capable of experiencing' (1962 [1915]: 613). As part of his explanation of this suffering Talmage draws a conceptual difference between God and man that is highly analogous to mainstream Christendom. 'No other man...could have suffered so', he argues, and explains that in some 'incomprehensible' way 'the Savior took upon Himself the burden of the sins of mankind from Adam to the end of the world'. This conflict of Gethsemane, and its 'bitter anguish', from which Christ emerges as victor, would not even be matched by 'the frightful tortures of the cross' that would follow on Calvary. The element of incomprehensibility of Christ's engagement with sin in Gethsemane is a significant feature of LDS atonement doctrine that is often mentioned by later authors. It becomes the means of asserting and affirming the profundity and extent of atonement in LDS thought – in part because this 'infinite atonement' guarantees the 'infinite' resurrection of all people, irrespective of their moral state. More significantly, this incomprehension serves as a frame for events that cannot be reduced to a single explanation. One aspect of atonement is relatively clear in LDS thought, namely, that mercy and justice come to cohere in Christ's suffering and death, yet this is but a mirror of one standard Protestant interpretation of atonement as sacrifice. Mormonism is not, however, totally content with that interpretation: it wants more, even though it may not know, explicitly, exactly in what that 'more' would consist. In trying to express a sense of the extent and wonder inherent in the life, passion and death of Jesus, LDS theologians have alighted upon and remained with 'infinite atonement'. Increasingly, however, the cross and Calvary are being aligned with the suffering in the garden as part of the single LDS view of atonement (e.g. Robinson 1992: 120).

THEOLOGICAL CROSS-CURRENTS

Many non-LDS Christians do not engage in any form of serious discussion with Latter-day Saints, or vice versa, for numerous reasons, political and religious, but one of them lies in the fact that they seldom grasp the real significance of the ideas underlying apparently familiar and shared words. One of these is 'the cross'. Because the 'cross' is so basic both to LDS and to Protestant, Catholic and Orthodox positions, it is wise to sketch something of its significance in each world. As an exercise in relating them I will take one specific debate about the place of the cross in salvation, showing two sides of an argument present in non-LDS traditions and then seeing how the arguments relate to LDS theology.

Often described in terms of the opposition between the theology of glory and the theology of the cross, this distinction is frequently used when considering the theology of the Reformation. The theology of glory represents God as the God of all power and might, attended by angelic beings and receiving the worship of humanity. Grounded in the model of kingship and princely courts, it portrays human duty as the offering of worship to God. It is a model that, for example, fosters the theory of atonement offered by Anselm when he argues that sin offends our Lord God to whom we owe proper duty and allegiance. Our sin outrages his honour and full reparation must be made, just as it was by Jesus. His death provides satisfaction for the outrage of God. This model of salvation, grounded in a strongly hierarchical and, indeed, feudal form of society, matched a church set in power as an earthly kingdom that reckoned to represent the divine king. It was not the society of Joseph Smith's boyhood.

CRUCIAL THEOLOGY

The theology of the cross, by sharp contrast, sees God's glory revealed in Jesus as the divine Son. More particularly, it is a glory revealed in Christ's suffering. Because Martin Luther's Reformation theology was grounded in the idea of human sinfulness before a righteous God whose work of salvation through his divine Son takes its fullest expression in his sacrificial death by crucifixion, it was that death, and the passion framing it, that became the prime arena of salvation. Following a strong motif in John's Gospel, Christ's crucifixion becomes the focus of and magnetic appeal for believers (John 12: 32). This tradition has grown within Protestant theology and has been, for example, much elaborated through the twentieth-century experience of the two world wars. Two individuals will serve as examples, the first now almost forgotten and the second very well-known, but each speaking from the depths of his own experience and in a way that ensures that theology is a real 'life-science' and no abstract ideology.

Geoffrey Studdert Kennedy died in 1929. He had been a minister of the Church of England and came into his own as a chaplain in the First World War. Some of his most poignant theological reflection on pain and the nature of God took the form of poetry, and the poem 'High and Lifted Up' is the prime example of this passionate insight into the deaths of so many in such dire circumstances as he had witnessed as a chaplain. It is impossible to convey briefly the power of his sixty-four-line engagement with love, suffering and God. He rehearses visions of divine glory told by preachers and sets them against 'a million mothers sitting weeping all alone', only to conclude that he hates 'the God of Power on His hellish heavenly throne'. His only hope comes to lie in 'God, the God I love and worship,' who 'reigns in sorrow on the Tree, Broken, bleeding, but unconquered, very God of God to me'. Studdert Kennedy is moved to speak to God: 'Thou hast bid us seek Thy glory, in a criminal crucified. And we find it – for Thy glory is the glory of Love's loss, And Thou hast no other splendour but the splendour of the Cross.' As it ends, the poem brings into a few lines entire volumes of Protestant theology on the saving death of Christ, just as it also echoes many hymns that have entered into the Protestant heart.

For in Christ I see the martyrs and the beauty of their pain,
And in Him I hear the promise that my dead shall rise again.
High and lifted up, I see Him on the eternal Calvary,
And two piercèd hands are stretching east and west o'er land and sea.
On my knees I fall and worship that great Cross that shines above,
For the very God of Heaven is not Power, but Power of Love.

(Studdert Kennedy 1983: 42)

The spiritual intensity and heartfelt insight that come with these lines have led generations of Christians to a position that gives the cross a centrality they cannot easily ignore. Certainly, it also furnishes an almost unconscious attitude that makes it hard to shift the theological centre of gravity anywhere else, not even to Christ's passion in the Garden. It is, perhaps, by rehearsing such a theology in poetry that the power of this perspective will be appreciated by Latter-day Saints, who otherwise might align a simple Protestant notion of substitutionary atonement too easily with 'cheap grace' or with a 'born again' conversion on the part of the believer.

One of the most influential of later twentieth-century and early twenty-first-century Protestant theologians, Jürgen Moltman, learned much from Studdert Kennedy's writing, as he did from his own experience as a German prisoner of war in England during the Second World War. He developed his own theology of divine suffering that is so explicitly expressed in the title of one of his books: *The Crucified God: The Cross of Christ as the Foundation and Criticism of Christian Theology* (Moltmann 1974). Moltmann is one theologian who opens up the difficult issue of the Holy Trinity in relation to the suffering and death of Jesus. Just how is the divine Father implicated in the death of Jesus, his son? Is he a legalistic and hard-hearted Father who is more concerned that justice be done than love expressed? How is the very 'inner' life of the Trinity disrupted by the death of Jesus? These and many other questions have become deeply significant in the Christian theology of the death of Jesus. It is, in fact, a melting-pot of theological concerns, not least because each age has its own social and political concerns as well as its philosophical predilections. In the twentieth century, Liberation Theology, with its concern for the poor and disinherited, asked its own questions of the cross, for example, Leonardo Boff's insight that the Father may have come to learn the nature of abandonment through what happened to Jesus and, through that, be able to become the Father of all who are abandoned (see Fiddes 1989: 192–5).

This kind of thinking about the cross has, in one form or another, been characteristic of evolving Protestant theology for some five hundred years. Before and after that, in Catholic spirituality too the cross has played a dramatically central role in worship, church architecture and practical piety, crucifixes being the dominant mode of representing both the death of Christ and the love of God. The Mass itself, as the foremost Catholic rite, takes place 'beneath' the cross and as a representation of the events of Christ's sacrificial death. Within the Mass this theological focus upon Christ's sacrificial death becomes refocused upon the bread and wine as they become the body and blood of Christ to the believer. As I have fully explored elsewhere, this very act of eating and drinking brings home to individuals their own participation in the dramatic events of salvation as they come to embody theological ideas (Davies 2002: 82–4).

This Catholic and Protestant engagement with the cross is radically paradoxical within Mormonism. Indeed the cross is the theological symbol, almost above all others, that typifies the differences of theology, spirituality and ethics between Mormonism and other Christian traditions. This needs great care because the difference lies upon emphasis and nuances of usage: while LDS church leaders do not use the cross on or in chapels or temples and see the bare symbol as rather negative by contrast with their strong emphasis upon life and resurrection, no Latter-day Saint would ever say or believe that the cross of Christ was not a vital element within the total plan of salvation. To reiterate, significance and difference lie in the way each tradition frames, grasps and interprets the cross. In my *Mormon Culture of Salvation* I gave an account of the LDS approach to the cross, showing how some significant church leaders, such as Joseph Fielding Smith, argued against seeing the cross as 'an emblem of torture' rather than as a sign of victory (Davies 2000: 41). From what has been said above it will be apparent that much hangs on the notion of 'victory', not least depending upon the relative influence of a theology of glory or theology of the cross.

THE INNER CRUCIFIXION

The Book of Mormon reflects a Mormonism rooted in the Protestant theology of the cross (e.g. 1 Nephi 11: 33; 2 Nephi 6: 9), often employing Old Testament texts that were regularly used in Protestant theology to relate prophecies to the life of Jesus (Mosiah 14: 5; cf. Isaiah 53: 5). This also occurs in significant passages in the Doctrine and Covenants (D&C 38: 4; 45: 4; 76: 69) where there is reference to the biblical injunction to 'take up your cross, follow me', addressed to the Twelve Apostles (D&C 113: 14). But, from this foundation, LDS doctrine developed one of its most extensive theological superstructures by drawing from the allied gospel narrative of the betrayal and temptation of Christ in the Garden of Gethsemane and pinpointing this moment of inner struggle and sweating of blood. Here I describe this feature as a kind of 'inner crucifixion'. This is not a Mormon term, indeed it is precisely because LDS thinkers would almost certainly not choose to use it that I do, thereby drawing attention to the Mormon preoccupation with the Gospel of Luke's account of Jesus in the Garden of Gethsemane on the night before he was crucified. As Jesus engages in ardent prayer asking that, if possible, his great trial might be removed from him an angel comes to strengthen him and 'being in an agony he prayed more earnestly: and his sweat was as it were great drops of blood falling down to the ground' (Luke 22: 44). This is the King James Version, for in some subsequent translations verses 43 and 44 are relegated to a footnote since the account is only in some ancient biblical texts. For Joseph Smith however, as for others grounded in the King James Version, this is a text full of the obedient suffering of Jesus. Later church leaders would develop this theme, as the pore-bleeding in Gethsemane came to parallel and perhaps even to predominate over the crucifixion of Calvary as the prime scene of the act of atonement for the sin of Adam. This is a dramatic shift, given the strong Christian piety that had long surrounded the crucifixion of Jesus as enshrined in many writings and devotional works. The mid and later nineteenth century would also witness the growth of many hymns dwelling on the theme of the cross, Christ's shed blood upon it, and the significance of the cross in the life experience of forgiveness of the believer.

I have documented some of these developments elsewhere citing, for example, President Ezra Taft Benson's view that 'it was in Gethsemane that Jesus took on Himself the sins of the world' (Davies 2000: 46–52; Brown 1992: 542). There I also developed the idea of Jesus as the 'proactive Christ' of Mormon theology, an interpretation that helps to make sense of many other aspects of LDS thought and life, especially its ethical code. This needs further elaboration, building on the discussion of atonement in chapter 4. Essentially, atonement in Mormonism comprises two complementary elements: blood and obedience. The blood factor combines both the crucifixion on Calvary and the bloodshed, sweat-like, in Gethsemane. The obedience factor underlies the dedicated commitment of Jesus to implementing the divine plan of salvation through a self-conscious life of doing good and opposing evil. That pointedness of action comes to its most explicit expression in Gethsemane, when Christ takes upon himself the sin of the world, not as a passive sacrifice but by an act of will. Here the Mormon notion of agency comes fully into play. There is a sense in which the crucifixion can give the impression that Jesus is a passive recipient of the anger of men and the divine wrath of God. He is led, as the Old Testament background has it, as 'a lamb to the slaughter'. While such passivity is reflected in the Book of Mormon, it is the activity, the enacted agency, of Jesus that increasingly predominates in early Mormonism. And that is precisely why the Garden scene became so important. It is the quintessential expression of agency, obedience and goodness: the holy one who possesses agency, employs it obediently.

At this point Mormon theology reveals the depth of its view of Jesus as it portrays him engaged in a kind of mental battle with evil. It is an internal conflict with the evil of all times and places that, in some divinely wonderful way, floods the inner being of Jesus. As Stephen Robinson, a modern LDS theologian expressed it, 'In that infinite Gethsemane experience, the meridian of time, the center of destiny, he lived a billion billion lifetimes of sin, pain, disease and sorrow' (1992: 123). This 'mystical atonement', as we might designate this event, sees Christ as encountering 'a kind of mystical participation in evil at the level of embodied mind' (Davies 2000: 52). That is, I think, a useful way of drawing the attention of non-Latter-day Saints to a feature of theology and spirituality that is relatively undeveloped in wider Christianity. The problem with theories of passive sacrifice is that atonement becomes a kind of legal penalty, a price that has to be paid rather than the intensely personal engagement with evil of a more deeply psychological kind.

Within both Catholic and Protestant Christianity relatively little theological attention has been paid to this moment of Christ's life. The gospel narratives of Christ's last days dwell upon his death and, as far as Gethsemane is concerned, they tell the basic story of Christ going apart to pray, of his asking that the 'cup' of his trial be taken from him, of the angel strengthening him, not least because the disciples keep falling asleep. As we have seen, they do tell of his stress and anguish and of sweat appearing as drops of blood, but I have also noted that even that text is glossed as only being in some ancient sources and has been relegated to a footnote in some modern translations. Tellingly, however, biblical commentators spend most of their time on the active betrayal of Jesus by Judas, his kiss and Christ's subsequent arrest. Even more tellingly, perhaps, Christian art has followed the theological tradition, devoting its paintings and stained-glass windows to the betrayal by Judas and, most certainly, to Calvary and Christ's crucifixion. LDS art, by sharp contrast has several important works on the sweating-blood feature but very few of the crucifixion (Davies 2000: 52–4). So it is that art expresses the LDS philosophical theology of the divine encounter between good and evil. It is a battle that takes place within Christ's consciousness. It is not between Christ and the betrayal by Judas or Christ and his arrest by soldiers. It is, in one sense, not a conflict restricted to one particular and localized set of events. It is not, as it were, this Judas here and now but the betrayals of all time. There is a cosmic dimension to Christ's engagement with evil. Indeed it is cosmic because some LDS sources see the effect of Christ's atonement as extending beyond this earth. McConkie summarizes this view by linking Christ as creator of many worlds (Moses 1: 33; D&C 76: 24) with his role as their redeemer too: 'the atonement of Christ, being literally and truly infinite, applies to an infinite number of earths' (McConkie, B. R. 1979: 66).

The element of personal commitment, so evident in this interpretation of a pro-active Christ, highlights the very idea of personal responsibility; it echoes my point in chapter 4 that Mormonism frames the atonement as one distinctive form of exemplary theory. One, final, example that will conclude my analysis of LDS atonement concerns 'blood-atonement'. This very phrase will, at first, seem to indicate the issues that have already been analysed at some length. But that is not the case. It is a phrase that introduces a distinctive LDS idea, one that not only marks a sharp divide between Christian thought at large and this Mormon outlook, but also underlines the fundamental LDS conception of the relation between Christ's atonement and the responsibility of individuals for their own progression from salvation to exaltation.

BLOOD ATONEMENT

Chapter 4 introduced the idea that murder, for example, required the shedding of the murderer's blood if that criminal was to receive ultimate forgiveness. This is the doctrine of blood atonement, referring to the sinner's own blood and not to the blood of Christ. It was widely known to earlier generations of Saints and was even discussed in, for example, the *Millennial Star* (*MS*, 1891: 148). One social consequence of this was that in the State of Utah a murderer condemned to die through capital punishment could elect to be shot, thereby having his own blood shed and opening the way for forgiveness through the atonement of Christ (Gardner 1979: 9–25). This notion is, largely, of historical significance and would not be known to many current church members, though McConkie in his *Mormon Doctrine* has an entry on the topic, using it to rebut early anti-Mormon accusations that church leaders had certain people killed on the basis of blood-atonement. Far more important for the present theological discussion is McConkie's clear affirmation that 'under certain circumstances there are some serious sins for which the cleansing of Christ does not operate, and the law of

God is that men must then have their own blood shed to atone for their sins. Murder, for instance, is one of these sins' (1979: 92). But, in addition to murder, McConkie adds a further comment, and it is one that readers unfamiliar with LDS thought might find confusing. It is worth explaining the issue here because it has far-reaching consequences for LDS belief and practice, especially that of the temple. Although a fuller account of temple rites will be given later (in chapter 8), let it be said here that there are rituals that confirm an individual with a high and responsible status after death. In effect, a person is given power over death and a self-empowered authority to conquer mortality. What if such a person commits murder after being so endowed? The answer is that his own blood must be shed if forgiveness is to be attained. Using terminology that indicates LDS commitment to covenants and blessings entered into and gained by one who has, 'so progressed in righteousness that his calling and election has been made sure', McConkie rehearses the words of an earlier prophet, Joseph Fielding Smith, to the effect that 'Man may commit certain sins that – *according to his light and knowledge* – will place him beyond the reach of the blood of Christ. If then he would be saved, he must make sacrifice of his own life to atone – so far as in his power lies – for that sin, for the blood of Christ alone under certain circumstances will not avail' (McConkie, B. R. 1979: 93). The original emphasis on 'light and knowledge' is a marker of the ritual undergone by the one now perilously placed.

This most instructive situation highlights the ethical paradoxes that churches sometimes encounter when one doctrinal development finds itself under unintended constraints. In other words, Joseph Smith developed rituals for core leaders who were expected to be ethically committed and, because of their earlier and proven obedience, had been admitted into a ritual status associated with their identity as kings and priests to God involving their own growing potential as divine beings. Here we are at the core of temple theology and of Mormonism's philosophical anthropology, where humans can become divine. Human beings are 'gods in embryo' and, through their obedient lives, that embryo may develop both through personal living and through temple rites. Development requires earthly ritual to ensure a heavenly consequence. The status accorded to such individuals within the church hierarchy was great but what if such an individual, on the path to godhood and invested with privileges of high priesthood endowments, committed a grave sin? The answer was blood atonement: as LDS theology developed away from its base-line Protestantism its evolving theology of human glory demanded a compensating ethics of human failure. The logic of Protestant atonement in the blood sacrifice of Christ as full and complete in itself, and to which no human could add anything, could not contemplate any sin for which Christ's blood could not atone. Because Mormonism introduced a formal difference between, on the one hand, the atonement of Christ, which counteracted the original sin of Adam and allowed each Saint freedom to set out upon his own path of obedience to divine laws and ordinances, and, on the other, the capacity of the individual to achieve godhood, it also made itself subject to the problems that might ensue if and when that individual radically failed in that life course.

Once the spotlight falls upon human effort and its glories in success it is also ready to fall, equally, upon the highly endowed person who fails. And the failure is doubly great because of the ritual and symbolic height from which he falls. The theological divide between Christ's blood atonement and an individual's own priestly endeavour in his post-atonement life leads to the logic of a person's own need to cope with a personal fall through major sin. This explains the theological logic of personal blood atonement. It also explains why it would make no sense to have such a murderer killed. It is self-willed and self-conducted death that alone would lead to a new forgiveness.

BLASPHEMY AND MURDER

Related to blood atonement was the idea of the unforgivable sin against the Holy Spirit, an issue which was raised in the Gospels of Matthew (12: 31–2), Mark (3: 28–30) and Luke (12: 10), and which was of concern to Joseph Smith. Biblically, in the context of Mark's Gospel in particular, it refers to those who thought that Jesus possessed an unclean spirit rather than, by implication, the Holy Spirit. The other two Synoptic Gospels leave that assumption unvoiced. For Joseph Smith this reference to the unforgivable sin plays a relatively central part in Doctrine and Covenants Section 132 dealing with the new revelation on eternal marriage. Joseph's revelation adds to the gospel accounts the clear interpretation that the shedding of innocent blood in murder is, in fact, the blasphemy against the Holy Ghost (D&C 132: 27). The text also refers to an 'assent unto my death' along with the committing of murder after having received this 'new and everlasting covenant' of eternal marriage. Just whose death is assented to is far from clear. It could refer to the death of Christ and to some sort of betrayal of it, or it could refer to the death of Joseph Smith. Either way this reference to the unforgivable sin serves to highlight the import of the new revelation on eternal marriage by framing it with the possibility of curse and damnation.

ETHICAL RESPONSIBILITY

While the example of unforgivable sin is far removed from the life and experience of contemporary Latter-day Saints, it nevertheless raises in sharp profile a principle that is experienced, albeit in feint shadow, by many devout church members. It is the issue of perceived failure: their own sense of failure within an ethical system of high expectation and demand and within an active community of many obligations. In terms of practical spirituality the question is where the forgiveness inherent in Christ's atonement stops and the necessity for self-achievement begins.

Once more, the distinction between salvation and exaltation becomes apparent, echoing chapter 4, where we saw that salvation comes through atonement and is appropriated by repentance and faith. Thereafter a committed Saint should be set on the path to exaltation through the temple ritual of endowments as well as through the performance of vicarious rites for the extended family. It is now clear that Mormonism's ethical system has to be understood in relation to this development from salvation to exaltation. We might, for example, speak of the ethics of salvation and the ethics of exaltation, and of what is involved in each. More particularly we need to draw attention to a certain dissonance that can emerge between the two.

MORMON ETHIC

It would be easy, but not entirely accurate, to interpret Mormonism's sense of social responsibility in terms of Max Weber's Protestant ethic. Much of his sociology of religion concerned the way in which values informed action; his much debated work *The Protestant Ethic and the Spirit of Capitalism* is the prime example of ideas of salvation influencing practical action (Weber 1976). His reference to Mormonism as a movement half-way between 'monastery and factory' is itself a telling description of a spirituality that is deeply engaged with intense activity framed by an otherworldly goal (Weber 1976: 264). For it is true to say that LDS social ethics are quite extensively related to soteriology. In classical terms the Protestant ethic was impelled by the Calvinist doctrine of double predestination, in the belief that God had predestined some people to eternal life and some to damnation. Because none could know, in doctrinal terms, to which they belonged, they sought more indirect routes of confirmation of their positive status. Since it was believed that God blessed his own, it was not pointless to see one's own flourishing as something of an indication of one's being predestined to life. One could also view the spiritual quandary of the classic Protestant as a kind of cognitive dissonance set up between the firm belief in predestination and the uncertainty of one's own condition. The Protestant ethic then becomes a kind of escape route from dissonance. By husbanding one's goods, by being a good steward of God's gifts, by investing one's profits and not spending wastefully on frivolous ventures, one increases in wealth and that, surely, is a sign of grace, of being counted amongst the redeemed. One LDS biblical scholar, when exploring issues of justification by faith, observes, for example, that 'practical Protestantism acts as if men and women are free agents' despite belief in predestination (Anderson, R. L. 1983: 167).

That background is useful, for Mormonism took the logic of Protestant predestination and deconstructed it through a common-sense view of causality and of God. For early Mormons, God was reasonable and human agency was of prime importance; predestination was abandoned, for it could not cohere with agency. God, and it was a male gender that was envisaged, acted according to eternal principles of justice which included a direct sense of reciprocity. He expected human beings to do the same. What people earned and deserved was precisely what they received: accordingly, they were to work at their religion in a very practical way. This highlights the extremely important LDS commitment to specific and discrete actions and to the way in which the Mormon approach to ethics is grounded in choosing to perform particular acts, an issue to be taken up again in chapter 7. Brigham Young, the second prophet, governed the Church for some thirty years and was renowned for his pragmatism. Leonard Arrington, one of the most influential of all Mormon historians, identified the task of 'working out one's salvation' in a this-worldly commitment to productive farming and community development as one of the major legacies Young left to the Church (Arrington 1986: 404). Arrington (1917–99) was himself a prime example of industry as a leader amongst LDS church historians and a mentor of an entire generation of younger scholars. He typified LDS scholars from rural and small-town backgrounds who entered higher education with a commitment to knowledge and the search for truth that fully reflected some mid and later nineteenth-century church leaders. Men like Arrington represented the best of this Mormon character, in which a mature civility and a love of scholarship and of fellow human beings forbad the tendency often inherent in hierarchical institutions to encourage defensive boundaries around itself. In Arrington's splendid biography of Brigham Young he identifies as one of Young's legacies to the Church 'an attitude or mind-set that held Mormonism to be synonymous with truth, incorporating scientific and philosophical as well as doctrinal truth' (1986: 405). And this applied as much to ethics as to other aspects of church life.

But, Brigham Young's strong this-worldly orientation to practical church organization must also be set alongside his commitment to the endowment ceremonies conducted at the Endowment House in Salt Lake City prior to the completion of the great temple there. Brigham knew, as did later prophets and most especially Wilfred Woodruff, that the basic survival of the Church through practical community action was the foundation for its other-worldly activity. There would be no temple without chapel, no basis for engaging in work to conquer death if there was no shared community in which to live both in this life and beyond. It is precisely these endowments and other temple rites – to be detailed in the next chapter – that gave Mormonism its own otherworldly agenda and admits a parallel between the Protestant ethic and what we might, similarly, call the Mormon ethic. Like its Protestant cousin, the Mormon ethic relates salvation to action in the world but does so with a sense of certainty rather than uncertainty. If the Protestant ethic was typified by a dissonance resulting from a firm belief in predestination combined with an uncertainty as to whether one was in the saved group, the Mormon ethic is typified by a dissonance between a firm belief that endowments can guarantee exaltation but uncertainty as to whether one is properly fulfilling one's vows and obligations to the highest degree.

Both Protestant and Mormon 'ethics' result from the interplay in the relative emphasis placed, respectively, upon grace or endowment in establishing the believer's spiritual status. Each 'ethic' is, in effect, the resulting dissonance. Puritans worked hard to demonstrate to themselves that they were children of grace, Mormons know the possibility of being kings and priests through endowment but must work hard to ensure the highest grade attainable in the afterlife. Some have even argued that Mormons have 'substituted hyperactivity for insightful inquiry' with the result that they depend upon the insights of others rather than upon their own engagement with LDS ideas (Shoemaker 1989: 1). If and when such 'activity' is reckoned to decrease it can give church leaders cause for concern. Indeed, there have been moments in Mormon history when church leaders have felt that the people at large had slipped in their level of commitment. Such was the case during what has been called the Mormon Reformation of 1856–57 in Utah. An extensive missionary programme was triggered to recall the Saints to their religious duties; many were rebaptized and schooled in their moral duties through the use of specially constructed catechisms (Peterson 1989:

68–71), for if their earthly duties failed their eternal reward could not be guaranteed.

Continuity between this and the next world is also important in Mormonism with regard to the idea of 'work' itself. Work holds a high status amongst the Latter-day Saints, not just as a development of the Utah frontier demand for survival but also as a way of life that will extend beyond death. Unlike some broad Christian notions of heaven as a place of rest, the LDS afterlife is active and full of endeavour. It is interesting that when some Latter-day Saint leaders and thinkers address themselves to issues of work, they see associations with the Protestant ethic but do draw a distinction between work and worship; they are also likely to remind members not to be become overactive and 'some measures in the Church are taken to take the commandment to work from being misconstrued to encourage "workaholism", or a frantic compulsion to be constantly busy' (Cherrington 1992: 1586).

RECIPROCITY

Moving from the sociologically rather narrow notion of a Protestant and a Mormon 'ethic' to ethics as more generally conceived, we cannot escape the issue of reciprocity, the theory of exchange between individuals. This is a fundamental feature of all human societies and plays a major role in their theological systems. It can even be argued that this topic plays as significant a part in religions as does any idea of God, not least because it is, for example, as germane to practical Buddhism as to Christianity, while the idea of the divine is problematic in any comparison of the two.

The history of Christianity is replete with debates on reciprocity: from the parables of Jesus to Paul's theology, from the tradition associated with Augustine amongst the early Church Fathers to Luther at the Reformation. Typically Augustine argues against Pelagius that human effort plays no part in salvation. Luther came to argue the same basic point. This was not to condone any lack of spiritual endeavour or service of neighbour but simply to argue that endeavour and service resulted from an experience of grace and did not cause one's entry into a state of grace. Despite the simplicity of the logical argument, the impact on life of the doctrine of salvation by grace resulting in a life of happy servitude to God and neighbour has not been easy to ensure. Many Protestant traditions possess the doctrine but it is not easy for such a value-inverting idea to become embodied in religious believers.

I have explored this domain of grace in terms of gift-theory and love in a previous study and mention it here simply because of the complexity involved in ideas of grace and salvation in all Christian traditions (Davies 2002: 53–80, 195–210). The LDS engagement over divine initiative and human endeavour is nothing new; it represents but one variation on the theme composed by the earliest Christians as they sought to interpret Jewish law in the light of their new inclusive church community. In the LDS context, however, there is a sense in which the committed belief that 'God works', becomes highly significant because it clearly expresses the deepest root of the Mormon ethic – agent motivated activism. This 'work' must be set against the backcloth of what all temple-going Saints learn in and through their endowment education, namely, that the plan of salvation is an exercise in divine activity. The organization of matter into worlds is the primal theological act. God's work is to bring about ultimate salvation; in a quintessentially Mormon expression Lucas and Woodworth affirm that, 'He leads an eternal enterprise to bring exaltation to the universe's intelligences' (1996: 151).

Here we come close to that kind of knife-edge that exists in many religious traditions where true intent is easily toppled if undue emphasis is placed on either of two balanced concepts. Here issues turn on the nature and purpose of exaltation. From what I have said in chapter 4, for example, it would be easy to see exaltation as a state of pleasure and delight gained through the ultimate conquest of death. This image could easily be parodied as one of eternal hedonism, as could the exhausting activism needed to sustain its achievement. Each of these over-emphases probably finds a place within the history of Mormonism though, in practice, the stress of effort overtakes the presumption of some easy eternal pleasure. A different note is struck by some contemporary Saints who see exaltation in far from a blatantly self-directed fashion. 'Eternal progression is expanding our and others' capacity to serve', argue Lucas and Woodworth, and this is to set a firm moral foundation for Mormonism's transcendent optimism (1996: 151).

LAW AND GOSPEL

Theological and pastoral discussions about grace and law will always be a constituent element of any church that follows the Bible, because they touch upon the absolutely fundamental element of obligation within human experience. Obligation will always appear with differing shades of emphasis because, the grace–law complex is ever influenced by the structure and organization of its parent church, as indeed of the society within which it exists. It is worth dwelling on the issue embraced by this paradox of how God relates to people and they to God because it is not as simple as the shorthand label of grace and works implies. Members of different churches should seek to understand the way of belief and of living it out that each tradition follows, and to recognize that they give different values to words, as I repeatedly emphasize throughout this book.

At the heart of the grace–works system of spirituality, for example, there is often much talk about 'conversion', a word generally avoided in Mormonism from the later nineteenth to the later twentieth centuries, not least because it was a word favoured by Protestants. Since words can be as strong a boundary marker as rules about food and drink, this is a telling point. Protestant 'conversion' was problematic to Latter-day Saints because it was too easily identified with a certain kind of evangelistic experience of an emotional 'born-again' type, as thoroughly familiar to contemporary Americans as to Joseph Smith's generation. There is no guarantee that such an experience of forgiveness of sin will involve an intellectual grasp of the fact that the rules that govern ordinary social relationships do not apply to God. At this point many Protestant preachers use the language of 'free-gift', yet even this attempted explanation can fail because it, too, remains engaged with ordinary reciprocity instead of making a conceptual leap, leaving giving and receiving behind and moving, for example, to the language of love, which does not measure its mutualities. Mystics often make that leap with vigour to talk of rapture and not of what they have done to gain it: they know that divine love is beyond telling.

In this particular tradition from Paul to Wesley, to be converted involves a conceptual reorganization: it does not mean that things are now free that once had to be bought. It means living in a world where the language of cost has lost its currency. It is particularly interesting that the key players in this grace concept have tended to be people who have, for some considerable time and with some immense effort, played the ordinary game of reciprocity, and played it as the means of being religious. Paul, Augustine and Luther are good examples of individuals who had engaged diligently in rule-based forms of spirituality until they came to a crisis point. Only when their endeavours were found radically wanting did the breakthrough come. The very notion of 'merit' involved in their former style of religious life echoes the concept of money. It is something that can be both obtained and accumulated. Indeed, it was the very concept of the treasury of merit whose wealth could offset a penitent's poverty through the purchase of an indulgence from the Catholic Church that catalyzed Luther's Reformation. The basic theological distinction between those Catholic and Protestant eras lay in the means of production and expenditure of merit. Both agreed that merit was vital for salvation but Protestant theology saw Christ as the only means of its generation – through his sinless life and obedience to divine law – while Catholic views, though stressing Christ, also added the faithful lives of Mary, the martyrs and other Christians. Accordingly, when it came to 'spending' merit, Protestants saw God as lavishing the merits of Christ upon meritless sinners through the motive of divine love. Catholics added to this the possibility of seeking the prayers of the meritorious saints and even being granted special merit from the treasury of merit of the church through the good office of the Pope.

Latter-day Saint theology could not possibly escape this whole debate, given the seriousness with which it took the Bible, not least as a volume 'by which a people felt they had encountered the sacred' (Barlow 1991: 156). As we have seen earlier, a great deal of the Book of Mormon deals with grace in an essentially Protestant way but, as the LDS Church later developed into its ritual-mystical form, it established a clear distinction between two forms of 'salvation'. As we have seen several times already, the very word 'salvation' becomes problematical and it means different things to Latter-day Saints, Catholics and Protestants. In LDS terms 'salvation' came to apply to the essentially Protestant view of learning about the Christian message, of repenting of one's sins, being baptized and having the promise of a resurrection. This is where LDS ideas of atonement, as elaborated in chapter 4, also belong. But, then, Mormonism developed the idea of 'exaltation' to apply to the ultimate benefits and rewards that could be achieved in the celestial heavens on the basis of having been obedient to the distinctive laws and ritual associated with priesthood and temple endowment. Given this dual scheme, Mormon theology came to possess a theological place for both grace and works: grace related to resurrection-salvation and works to exaltation.

But, as I have already shown when identifying the dissonances associated with the Protestant ethic and the 'Mormon ethic', there are some dedicated Latter-day Saints who do wonder whether they can ever do enough to ensure that they will gain the highest exaltation. The relative restriction of grace-language to what we might call baptism-Mormonism and its absence in endowment-Mormonism allows this problem to emerge. Yet this is precisely the point at which some contemporary Latter-day Saints are reconsidering their own overall spirituality in relation to 'grace' and are seeking to bring the 'baptism' and 'endowment' elements into closer relationship (Millett 1994: 116). But it is a problematic consideration because, though the Mormonism of the Book of Mormon period shared in this Protestant appreciation of grace as the basis of salvation, and it was one that lasted in some streams of Mormonism for some time, the rise of rite-related endowment-Mormonism fostered the notion of covenantal promises and of the need for achievement in order to attain the highest realm of exaltation in the celestial kingdom. The language of Christian Evangelicalism that speaks of simply asking Jesus into one's heart and 'being saved', whilst bearing some kinship with early Mormonism's call for repentance and faith, runs counter to the developed scheme of endowment-exaltation with its obligation to increased knowledge and ritual participation.

But, and this is a crucial feature, exaltation also came to involve action and not simply 'belief', echoing the foundational place of 'action' and 'activity' in LDS thought. In this context I do not simply refer to temple rites, the wearing of special clothing and the learning of key words but to marriage. This aspect of LDS ethics in relation to exaltation cannot be ignored, because it brings into play the whole spectrum of issues around family life and the links between family and community and local church life, which I discuss in greater detail in the next chapter. Even so, these are among the numerous domains in which a Latter-day Saint needs to be productive. Certainly, no Protestant or Catholic Church has ever made ultimate salvation dependent upon marriage. If anything, Catholicism and parts of Greek Orthodoxy have favoured celibacy, which in many respects is a much easier form of life as far as multiple commitments and obligations are concerned. Non-LDS Christianity has tended to focus salvation upon an individual's belief, on acceptance of formal creeds and, to a degree, have required baptism and some other sacraments. Marriage, however, involves a commitment of a different type and, for core Mormon leaders around Joseph Smith the acceptance of plural marriage as part of the status of being a Melchizedek-priesthood holder was no mean or simple task. Most had come from traditional Protestant culture, with its monogamy and sense of moral purity in marriage, and this made the revelations on priesthood and its allied polygamy far from easy to accept. These new covenants magnified the notion of reciprocity underlying church membership and conducted Mormonism into a domain of obligations that became a world of its own. At the same time the church was developing as an institution whose leadership roles were related to success in achievement. It was quite understandable that in later generations some Saints could speak of the 'easy grace' of Christian Evangelicalism, for to ask Jesus 'into one's heart' was simplicity itself compared with the preparation for and engagement in endowment, marriage, and life lived in a church organization that made high demands. But, as with Paul and Luther, there are some dedicated Saints who feel the strain of obligation and advocate the need for using the language of grace within the Church.

ETHICS AND AESTHETICS

Whatever the theological drives of the past, Mormonism's commitment to endeavour helped to ensure that of the hundreds of movements that sprang up and ultimately failed within Christianity in the nineteenth century it not only survived but also produced a subculture of its own. While a church, as such, may focus on doctrine, ritual practice and self-organization, anything resembling a subculture, as with Utah-based Mormonism, will inevitably generate wider circles of customary behaviour embracing educational and leisure activities and many other aspects of life within which ethics and aesthetics become mutually influential.

Mormons have long fostered art, for example, whether in the painting and sculpture of amateur or more professional Saints or, for a very brief period in the 1890s, in the small band of 'art missionaries' (Davies 2000: 117). These were sent to Paris to foster their talent, on the understanding that they might return to beautify temple interiors, to nurture human skills and express achievement. The Saints encourage art for those and other reasons, not least that the family home, itself a kind of microcosm of temple and the afterlife, be adorned appropriately. The very fact that the Utah desert came to 'blossom as the rose' in an agricultural sense might indicate the blessing of God upon the activism of his people, but the fact that townships might flourish and raise architecture to the glory of God and as a place to foster the salvation of others made the presentation of those places of more than passing concern.

In other words LDS aesthetics are soteriological, expressing both the development of the artist and the significance of places of spiritual endeavour. Pictorial art, for example, is not just 'art for art's sake'. Neither is music, singing or dancing, all forms of performance practised and enjoyed by Saints and seen as both expressing the joy of the heart towards God and strengthening the community of Saints. Even pragmatic Brigham Young had one of his daughters, Vilate, go to stay with relatives in Salem for her schooling and to learn to play the piano (Arrington, 1986: 110).

This is not to say that each form of activity has not changed, sometimes dramatically, over the history of the Church, nor that each has not come to possess different values placed upon them. Music, for example, followed the Protestant pattern of communal hymn-singing for much of the nineteenth and twentieth centuries but in the later twentieth century music and singing played a decreasing part in formal temple and chapel ritual though it was retained in the public chapel services and in the major public interface of the Mormon Tabernacle Choir (Kear 2001: 77–93). Similarly with regard to dancing, while more formal styles of ballroom dances have been fostered, the apparently less organized styles of disco and certainly rave dancing are not encouraged. Indeed some sorts of loud popular music, often enjoyed by teenagers at large, are regarded as potentially evil. Since aesthetics is intrinsically soteriological in Mormonism, it is to be expected that such negative evaluation may be passed on some boundary-breaking styles. The decision as to which is which is inevitably in a hierarchical movement decided by central church leaders even though they are usually very much older than the generations for which they take cultural decisions.

AESTHETICS AND PERSONHOOD

The decline of music and singing in temple rites was directly related to the increased significance of those rites and the power of words within them; much the same happend in chapels, where, at the sacrament service, for example, members were encouraged to focus on the words of the prayers used and not to be distracted by organ voluntaries. This reflects Mormonism's sense of control over emotions that complements its strong emphasis upon formal principles.

In a community of this kind aesthetics is not to be taken as a distinctive sphere of activity in which expert opinion pronounces on 'fine art' or the like. The measure of beauty is also the measure of how some work expresses community values, of how a picture, statue or piece of music catches the communal sentiment and reproduces it. A great deal of LDS art is descriptive of historical events, of the settlement of Utah, of particular families and individuals rooted in the faith, as well as portraying the prophet-leaders and other core members. Mormonism comes to be enshrined in art just as it is embodied in persons: and the two may reflect each other. In 2001, for example, a statue was unveiled at Liverpool's quayside to commemorate the thousands of European migrants who had set sail from that port. It portrayed a nineteenth-century father and mother with two children: he stands looking into the future.

WELFARE

Although welfare and aesthetics are not often associated, the LDS world-view tends to bring them together because Mormonism's idea of the 'individual' is essentially 'communal'. It is quite obvious that welfare issues are grounded in collective ideals but this may not be so immediately apparent for aesthetics. Yet, it is so because Mormonism has, historically, not favoured the emergence of elite groups controlling matters of taste. One reason for this is that, formally speaking, Mormon church-life is itself 'lay' in the sense that it does not possess a professional priesthood or cadre of theologians. And that property of being a 'lay' organization extends to other aspects of LDS life, including aesthetics. Each person should cultivate their own taste and sense of what is good, true and beautiful but will do so within the broad ethos of what the community and its core leadership tends to accept as such. Here we are dealing with a form of creative constraint, for while the Saints were traditionally told to pursue all knowledge (see D&C 93: 53; 128: 14), to study and read good books (D&C 88: 118) and to sing and dance (D&C 136: 28), they were still expected to remain within the broad traditional interpretations of cultural life that have prevailed within the Church. In terms of cultural mood, Mormonism addresses itself to both welfare and aesthetic issues with a certain controlled exuberance grounded in the hope of community development. That is particularly clear, for example, in the work of The Relief Society which, under a variety of names, has been the main organization for LDS women throughout much of the Church's history and which fosters food supplies as well as care for the sick – as in its early Nurse School – alongside intellectual and personal development (Cannon and Mulvay-Derr 1992: 1199–207). The Relief Society's grain storage programme, which ended when it sold large quantities of wheat to the US Government at the close of the Second World War, was one pragmatic expression of early Mormonism's desire for self-sufficiency, demonstrating just how community survival lay at the heart of Mormon ideas of and plans for welfare.

EDUCATION

As with economics so with education. From the very early days the Latter-day Saints fostered education whether at home or in the local community. This led to the emergence of colleges and the flagship institution of the Brigham Young Academy of 1875 that became Brigham Young

University in 1903. Based at Provo, Utah but with associated campuses elsewhere, this institution has gained eminence in numerous academic fields. It has occasionally experienced minor crises with members of staff concerning doctrinal orthodoxy in historical and sociological issues, which is, perhaps, to be expected given the nature of critical scholarship and the very particular view of the past held by central authorities. The students are themselves expected to maintain a clear honour-code as members of a distinctly church-sponsored institution. At the local level the Church seeks to encourage religious education through an extensive 'Seminary programme' for young people aged fourteen to eighteen that runs in parallel with ordinary education. In some parts of the world this involves people in early morning study prior to ordinary schooling, and reflects a high degree of commitment on the part of students as well as on their families and the organization of the local and regional Church, whose organization I pursue in the next chapter.

CHAPTER 7

Priesthood, stake and family

It is the Church's theology of the family that underpins the practicalities of daily life, weekly church activities and periodic LDS temple rites. Not only does the family provide the integrating link between chapel and temple activities but it also furnishes the background for the Church's plan of salvation. Together the family, chapel and temple make calls upon individual commitment which, when all works well, provides the energy that makes the LDS Church a great success but they can also demoralize some Saints through sheer volume of activity and high level of expectation. With that in mind, this chapter will not only describe some of these fundamental aspects of LDS church and community life but will also briefly revisit the broad Christian theological issue of grace in relation to the occasional sense of failed endeavour. At the outset, it is important not to over-romanticize the Mormon family, for while it is easy to describe this aspect of LDS life as though it always functions perfectly and is fully co-ordinated through the Church's doctrine, very few Saints would wish to ignore the problems that emerge in their families, as in most families. It is no accident that The Proclamation on the family made by the First Presidency in 1995 (see below), alluded to the violation of chastity, to abuse of spouse and children and to the disintegration of the family. Still, this awareness of difficulty and the desire that church leaders should seek the best underlies this chapter, which will conclude with a brief account of the way in which husband and wife are united through a special temple ritual demonstrating the centrality of family and eternity in the quest of exaltation.

FAMILY LINK

Chapter 5 showed how the total church organization can be viewed as a kind of church within a church, with the chapel and temple forms of life being in many ways distinct from each other. As forms of ritual activity and as expressions of particular kinds of doctrine they are rather separate but the uniting feature, the underlying factor that welds them together, is the Mormon family. The family provides the key link between these two worlds as the fundamental unit at the local and regional levels of organization. It is also the basis of exaltation. In other words, Mormonism's ultimate salvation is rooted in the family: salvation becomes a corporate affair. This is why the family is also the research base for genealogical work, for discovering the family tree is the basis for conducting rites for the family's ancestors. In long-established Mormon families this attitude fosters family associations engaged in kinship research and expressed in occasional family reunions of large groups of people. Accordingly, in this chapter I link the family and its home life with the local congregation and LDS community and I reserve description of temple activity for chapter 8.

REGIONAL CHURCH ORGANIZATION

At the local level a 'ward' holds between three hundred and seven hundred individuals with several wards grouped into a 'stake' of approximately two thousand members. The stake reflects the Church in microcosm, with a president and counsellors, a high council and other officers. It also holds regular conferences for all members and, theologically, these conferences are significant as indicators of Mormonism's Protestant root and democratic spirit. From the outset the Saints received revelations instructing them to hold regular conferences (D&C 20: 61–4). In some respects this practice mirrors both the annual conference established by the Methodists in the 1880s as the basis for their own church governance and, to a limited degree, the place of the General Assembly in Presbyterianism. The LDS General Conferences held at Salt Lake City are often televized to stakes around the world, enabling many members to share in the talks of leaders and others. Even so, some from the central leadership or General Authorities – which is the basic and paid formal core of church administration consisting of the First Presidency, the Twelve Apostles, and some of the Quorums of the Seventy – seek to visit stakes over a period of time but, with the rapid growth of the Church, that kind of contact becomes less viable. Still, at conferences the whole group votes, or 'sustains', decisions and appointments made by the leadership. While this expresses the democratic ethos of early Mormonism, it also manifests its theocratic leadership since it is the decision of a small group of leaders, believed to be spirit-guided, that is agreed to by all. It is very rare for a single member not to sustain a proposed vote.

While it is through the ward that members engage with the universal Mormon Church, their family life on a daily and weekly basis revolves around the ward, whose leader is the bishop. He is roughly the equivalent of a parish priest but is unpaid and sustains his family through ordinary secular employment. He has two counsellors, is responsible to the stake president for the many activities located in his ward and supervises the numerous individuals who are called to lead the numerous subsections of each ward, including the Presidents of the Sunday School, Young Women, Elders and Aaronic Quorums and Relief Society. The main Sunday morning 'consolidated meeting' focuses many of these in a three-hour event, which is subdivided into three parts and was devised in 1980 to maximize the benefit of church attendance. These three elements consist of the Sacrament Meeting, Sunday-school classes according to age groups and then divisions into age and sex groups for the various focused activities of priesthood holders, Young Women's Group and Relief Society for older women. In all of this there is a general expectation that members are married with families and that a sexual division of labour in the church and family is the basis of ordinary life. In wards with significant numbers of single adults special events are organized; there are even Singles' Wards where circumstances demand. Involvement with organizations such as the Boy Scouts also takes up ward time on other days.

The bishop is expected to be a pastor to the people as well as to maintain good order and discipline. He interviews people who are seeking temple recommends as well as discussing tithing or any breaches of discipline. As already mentioned, this very time-consuming task is unpaid. Not only will he hold the Melchizedek priesthood but he will also have been ordained as a high priest within it; this unites him with other high priests, all of whom hold or have held higher office within the Church, and demonstrates the wider network of church organization with which the local church maintains constant links.

OBEDIENCE AND AGENCY

Behind all these activities lies the theology of agency, obedience and priest-hood. In chapter 3 I began to explore the LDS notion of agency and its relationship to the spirit that has existed eternally, to the spirit children of God into which spirit has been transformed and now, in this chapter to the human beings that result from the relationship between those spirit children and the human bodies into which they come at birth. As indicated earlier, these spirits do not come in a morally neutral condition. They have already proved themselves, to a degree, within the constraints of the pre-existent world and now, in the 'more dense' domain of material reality, they have an even greater opportunity to demonstrate their obedience to God. What is more, the arena of earthly life offers an enhanced kind of freedom through the atonement of Christ and it is precisely here that Mormonism's elimination of the doctrine of original sin becomes most apparent: there is no 'contagion of sin' lurking in human babies as there is in the broad Augustinian tradition, described by Bruce McConkie as amongst 'the wicked heresies prevailing in modern Christendom', for, through the grace of Christ revealed in his atonement 'all spirits begin their mortal life in a state of innocence and purity without sin or taint of any sort' (McConkie, B. R. 1979: 673–4). Indeed, babies and children under the age of discretion – reckoned to be eight years of age – are admitted straight into the celestial kingdom in heaven. The Church also holds a strongly pastoral view, reflecting the importance of the family, in respect of stillbirths and, while it has no absolute revelation on the topic, there is teaching enough to indicate that a foetus is the home of its life-giving spirit from the time the mother can feel its movements. While records of stillbirths are not kept on church records, individual families may record them in their own family records (McConkie, B. R. 1979: 768). One fascinating insight into this topic occurs in Wilford Woodruff's diary for 16 October 1857 when he records that Brigham Young said that premature babies who die after only a few hours of life can be blessed and named; Woodruff adds that he does not do that himself because, in his own words, 'I think that such a spirit has not a fair Chance for I think that such a spirit will have a Chance of occupying another Tabernacle and develop itself.' He adds that 'this is a new doctrin yet it looks Consistent. What period of Demarkation or age the spirit would take another Body we were not informed [*sic*]' (Woodruff 1993: 204). His comments reflect that early period in church life when ideas were still developing and it is possible to see him as someone operating in terms of basic theological logic, in this case the idea that embodied life is a time for eternal spirits to gain bodily experience 'to develop itself' through its use of agency.

In essence LDS theology of agency stems from the Book of Mormon argument that the Messiah redeemed humanity from the fall, as a result of which not only have they 'become free forever, knowing good from evil' but they are also free 'to act for themselves and not to be acted upon', exemplifying the principle of opposition that was described in chapter 1 (2 Nephi 2: 26). Obedience runs throughout LDS ethics, motivating

local church and family life and becomes of ultimate significance in relation to temple marriage and its consequence for the highest form of
salvation.

PRIESTHOOD, CALLING AND MEMORY

It is in and through priesthood that agency and obedience come to their
fullest focus: Mormons often refer to 'priesthood' as shorthand for the
principle through which the overall church is organized. The significance
of priesthood in Mormonism can be glimpsed indirectly through one proposal that emerged in Dietrich Bonhoeffer's powerful post-war Protestant
engagement with the purpose of human life when he argued that 'Luther's
return from the monastery to the world, to the 'calling' is, in the true New
Testament sense, the fiercest attack and assault to be launched against the
world since primitive Christianity' (Bonhoeffer 1955: 223). Bonhoeffer argued this as part of his trenchant analysis of 'the place of responsibility'
and it finds a very particular application within the present account of
Mormonism for which responsibility is integral to 'agency', to the power
to act that is inherent in LDS life and which finds its direction through
the 'calling' made by church leaders. Here the Protestant notion of 'calling'
comes to be explicitly applied to church members at large, indicating as
it does so the radical relational nature of LDS life. Utilizing Bonhoeffer's
terms, we could see this as part of Mormonism's 'assault against the world'
and its own form of manifestation of 'primitive Christianity'.

While agency is directed through a whole series of 'callings' throughout
someone's life, it is for men also given form and structure through 'priesthood' and for women through the priesthood of their husbands, fathers
and sons and, organizationally, through offices they may be called to fill
in the Church's auxiliary organizations. Here, the Protestant theological
theme that Mormonism takes and presses to a theological conclusion is
that of the priesthood of all believers, but it develops it in a most distinctive
fashion. There are two basic forms of priesthood, the Aaronic or lower and
the Melchizedek or higher priesthood and, over time, they have come to be
age-related. They also mark the internal distinction between the Protestant
style of LDS religiosity and the ritualism of temple-Mormonism that are
embraced by the history of the movement. The Aaronic priesthood is internally divided into the age-related offices of deacon (12–13), teacher (14–15)
and priest (16–18). If boys serve well in their tasks and show appropriate
responsibility, they are then ordained to the Melchizedek priesthood when
about nineteen years old. This will always happen before they serve their

two-year mission when they go out as 'elders', a distinctive title used for young missionaries and for the most senior of central church leaders, but not for all the intermediary levels of church organization. Theologically speaking, the missionary and the core leaders seem to be counted together as very special agents of the Church's message.

While it is theologically tempting to interpret Mormonism's commitment to its form of the priesthood of all believers as but another expression of the early Christian idea that each member of the Christian community is one element of the 'body of Christ', that temptation must be avoided. This is because the image of the body of Christ is inappropriate to the LDS pattern of thought, and is so precisely because of the way in which Mormonism approaches the relationship between human beings and God. This is a subtle but significant point grounded in the fact that Mormonism's relational nature, mentioned throughout this book, is shaped through covenants and consecration rather than through a generalized sense of participation. This becomes particularly clear through its theology of the Sacrament Meeting and through the fact that Mormonism does not speak of sacraments at all, except for that one rite. While valuing baptism, confirmation, marriage and ordination very highly, LDS theology presses Protestantism to breaking point essentially by redefining sacraments as ordinances – the generic term for all rites that are significant for this life and for ultimate destiny. Furthermore, by insisting upon rebaptism of any convert already baptized in another church, Mormons demonstrate their sense of absolute difference in matters of authority and their commitment to the notion of restoration of that which had been lost and absent in those other churches. In terms of practical Christianity, of previous life-experience and forms of response to the new message, it was this issue of baptism that focused the mind and challenged the attitudes of many early converts, as of converts today who may have been, and are often likely to have been, members of other churches. Richard Bushman, for example, pressed this issue, arguing that 'no single teaching caused the early missionaries more trouble than the requirement of rebaptism, with its implication of universal Christian apostasy' (Bushman 1984: 153); though it should be recalled that early Mormonism is also known to have practised rebaptism within its own ranks at periods of religious rededication (Davies 1987: 67; Peterson 1989: 66).

What then, characterizes priesthood for Latter-day Saints? Historically and in an almost abstract sense the Aaronic priesthood resembles many aspects of 'ministry' in numerous Protestant Churches. It relates to congregational life and order as well as to a broad-scale pastoral care, and this made considerable sense at the foundation of the Church when those ordained to its offices were adults. Over time, the rise in temple Mormonism ensured that the Melchizedek priesthood would come to be vastly more significant than the Aaronic, not least because it was composed of adult members. The age issue apart, the Aaronic priesthood is, in general theological terms, more identifiable with Protestant 'ministries', while the Melchizedek priesthood is more reminiscent of Catholic forms of priesthood, especially in its authority to perform certain rites intrinsic to ultimate salvation, that is, to exaltation. While Mormon and Catholic traditions are at one in strongly affirming the authority conferred by ordination and while, in a sense, they each have their own form of 'apostolic succession', there remain three fundamental distinctions between them, and it is these that ultimately define priesthood in Mormonism: God's priesthood, the power of 'the keys', and commitment to principles or laws.

Priesthood is seen as an attribute of God, has been evident amongst humanity from the days of Adam and is eternal, except if and when God removes it from the earth. Its restoration to Joseph Smith – the Aaronic priesthood through John the Baptist and the Melchizedek through Peter, James and John – becomes the foundation for the description of the Church as a restoration movement. By coming to hold the Melchizedek priesthood a man begins to participate in something that is related to the divine governance of the universe. This is only possible because Joseph Smith – and after him all prophet-leaders of the Church – possesses the 'power of the keys'. Power is a distinctive aspect of priesthood and 'the keys' is an extensive theological metaphor for numerous forms of church service and activity. 'The keys' is a significant term because it enshrines a degree of mystery grounded in formal authority and links the divine and particular church officers through the First Presidency. Here 'the keys' overlap with the theme of commitment to principles, to the underlying rules that govern the universe. Reflecting its nineteenth-century ancestry, Mormon theology possesses a strong pragmatic current of belief in a scientific-like sense of the organizing principles by which the universe is governed and controlled. It is through the power of the keys, restored to and through Joseph Smith, that the Church has not only come to know these principles but, in and through the priesthood, comes to hold and use them. They are as important in organizing local church life as they are in the family and in the ultimate domain of death conquest, which I explored in chapter 4 regarding salvation and will explore in chapter 8 regarding exaltation. In the power of the keys we see the Melchizedek priesthood press the idea of ministry far beyond any known in Protestantism and even in Catholicism. And, ideally, every family has such a priest to head its household.

As already intimated, the Aaronic priesthood more closely resembles a Protestant form of ministry, as is apparent in and through the Sacrament Meeting, which itself offers a further example of a Protestant religious idea pressed to its theological conclusion in that a 'lay' priesthood engages in a fundamentally memorialist rite. The Sacrament rite extends Protestant ideas of the Lord's Supper into a clear and affirmative memorialist position. Part of the historical debate over the Mass, Lord's Supper, Holy Communion or Eucharist – variant names that all express some theological interpretation of the event – has focused on how the bread and wine must be thought of in relation to Christ's body and blood. In the twelfth and thirteenth centuries traditional Catholicism developed the idea of transubstantiation as a philosophical way of arguing that the real nature of the bread (its substance) was changed into the real nature of Christ's body, while its appearance to the senses (its accidents) remained those of bread. Some Protestants, with Luther, argued for consubstantiation, the idea that the real substance both of bread and of Christ's body were co-present in the bread but others, with John Calvin, stressed that Christ was in heaven and that the hearts of the faithful needed to be raised to him there in worship whilst sharing in the real bread on earth. Zwingli, the Swiss Reformer, argued firmly that it was precisely through faith that the individual was related to Christ and that the bread and wine were solely symbolic.

This memorialist element is highly visible in Mormonism, where the use of water rather than wine stresses the importance of the memory of the believer, as the dedication prayer below shows. This rite is administered not by the Melchizedek priesthood but by members of the Aaronic priesthood and is focused not in the temples but in local chapels. This tellingly marks the distinction between the local church life that is focused on salvation and the regional temple activity that is focused on exaltation. The Sacrament Meeting takes place each Sunday as part of the three-hour morning session. It is one of the few rites of the Church that involves set and formal prayers, which originated as revelations in Section 20 of Doctrine and Covenants. Given its distinctive place in church life it will be given in full, not least because it typifies a major form of LDS spirituality in capturing a sense of how Latter-day Saints approach God in the chapel and domestic context.

The officiant is instructed to 'kneel with the church and call upon the Father in solemn prayer', saying:

O God the Eternal Father, we ask thee in the name of thy Son, Jesus Christ, to bless and sanctify this bread to the souls of all those who partake of it, that they may eat in remembrance of the body of thy Son, and witness unto thee, O God the Eternal Father, that they are willing to take upon them the name of thy Son, and always remember him and keep his commandments which he has given them: that they may always have his Spirit to be with them. Amen. (D&C 20: 76–7)

A similar prayer refers to 'this wine ... in remembrance of the blood of thy Son, which was shed for them' (D&C 20: 79). For historical reasons of obtaining uncontaminated supplies of good wine the Church uses water and refers to it as such and not to wine. The bread and water are kept covered by a cloth during the service and are exposed for these prayers before being passed around the congregation; even infants may partake.

TESTIMONY

On the first Sunday of the month the meeting is also a fast and testimony meeting when the money for the missed meals goes to the Church and opportunity is given for individuals to give their verbal testimony before the congregation at large. I mentioned in chapter 3 the importance of gaining a sense of certainty about the truthfulness of Mormonism and it is here, in this special meeting, that full expression can be given to it. This important aspect of LDS congregational life allows for a demonstration of restrained yet deep emotion as people talk about what they have learned from God or from other members of their family or church. Each testimony ends with an assertion including some reference to a certain knowledge that 'God lives', that Joseph Smith is a prophet and that this is the true Church. Although testimonies can be, and sometimes are, rather formulaic they do offer opportunity for an expression of a believer's sincerity of purpose and, in one sense, demonstrate the LDS theological idea that the Holy Ghost can and does influence individual lives when they are lived in obedience to Church teaching. The impact of this regular event upon LDS children and converts should not be overlooked as part of the learning process of faith that is found both in the ward and family. While everyone knows that certain members are likely to become emotional and perhaps say very similar things in a repetitive way, it remains a time when people learn that experience is a dynamic influence on others. Individuals come to appreciate the kinds of relationships and values that deeply touch members of the community and the particular day inevitably arrives when even the more cynical youth comes to feel the influence of the Holy Ghost through the thoughtful act of kindness of parent, teacher or friend.

The experience of the testimony meeting is but one occasion when the LDS teaching on the power of the Holy Ghost – the preferred title used by Latter-day Saints – becomes manifest. It echoes Mormon advice given to potential converts that they should read the Book of Mormon and pray that God will show them its truthfulness by an inner 'burning in the breast', a conviction that these things are true. Though the founding Saints experienced the more dramatic aspects of speaking in tongues when the Kirtland Temple was dedicated in 1836, later generations did not follow that path but increasingly linked the Spirit with a personal conviction aligned with an individual's position and responsibility within the Church. Some even interpret 'speaking in tongues' as being able to learn foreign languages in preparation for missionary work.

LAY PRIESTHOOD

Latter-day Saints often stress the fact that theirs is a lay priesthood, by which they mean that there is no paid priestly caste divided from a laity. Additionally, apart from the highest level of central leadership, all identifiable local church leaders are unpaid. When teenage boys say the sacrament prayers and administer to all present, the Church makes it clear that there is no distinctive and separate 'priesthood' within the Church. The 'lay' nature of the LDS priesthoods also carries the particular sense that there is no formally trained cadre of theological experts: all are expected to become familiar with church texts and doctrine. Each is taught the necessity of seeking from God appropriate insight and guidance for their 'calling', or particular office within the Church. The availability of such inspiration – 'that they may always have his Spirit to be with them' – reinforces the high value placed upon individual character and the responsibility borne by each to fulfil their calling. While the Church does give status to people by virtue of the office they hold, it also places high value on the manner in which they hold it. In other words, achievement derived from agency dedicated to its task counts for more than the simple name of the office held. What is more, except for the central authorities, members are called to serve in a particular office for relatively limited periods, after which they are 'released' from it. This can easily mean that someone holds a lower office after having held high office, in the sense that some tasks obviously have a higher profile than others. In this kind of church, however, the most prized attitude is one that asks each person to give of their best whether in the highest or lowest of jobs. Character and its development is prized over status in the service of God and of the Church.

ACTIVITY

Chapter 6 raised the issue of service as a feature of Mormonism's communal life and it now remains to describe such service in relation to the general idea of 'activity' as worked out in the domains of practical behaviour. 'Activity' is itself a much-used word with a distinctive LDS connotation: it describes one who is engaged in many different kinds of church events and who links family and church life. Similarly, 'inactive' people are the less engaged. Activity, as such, is part of the cosmic endeavour of God and of those seeking their own divine identities in the worlds to come when, in a continuing process, they will still be actively involved in fostering the salvation and exaltation of others. Apart from parenthood and these general forms of church service there are two aspects of LDS life, namely the 'Word of Wisdom' and tithing, that provide a distinctive, focused and identifiable expression of activity. These channels also furnish the prime opportunity for the development of personal agency and obedience.

WORD OF WISDOM

The term 'Word of Wisdom' comes from a revelation of 1833 and is found in Doctrine and Covenants Section 89, where it is described as a revelation that came to Joseph Smith when he was pondering the propriety of fellow leaders smoking during meetings at his home. The outcome has formed the basis of Mormonism's dietary code and, in a more general sense, a widespread attitude to health and well-being. It included a prohibition on drinking alcohol, except in the sacrament service, though even that has now been abandoned in favour of water. Tobacco is also forbidden though both alcohol and tobacco are, nevertheless, reckoned to be useful as medicines if rubbed on the body. Hot drinks were also proscribed; in 1842 these were further defined as tea and coffee (Lyon 1992a: 288) and later their caffeine content was identified as the crucial factor – in an informal way the ban was extended to include Cola drinks when they appeared on the market. Additionally, the revelation advocates the use of grain, different sorts for humans and animals, and sees meat as an occasional food, especially in winter. Observance results in both 'temporal and spiritual' benefits, an expression that describes both daily life and its eternal outcome; the latter is emphasized by the final verses which promise 'health in their navel and marrow to their bones', and assure that 'the destroying angel shall pass by them' (D&C 89: 18, 21). These phrases echo ideas inherent in the endowment ceremonies.

In historical terms, however, many continued with these prohibited items and it was not until the early twentieth century that church leaders began to highlight this aspect of LDS life. Only in the 1930s did observance become a requirement for gaining a temple recommend (Lyon 1992b: 1585). Another feature of family life that is related to food but has nothing to do with the Word of Wisdom in any direct sense lies in the family food store, a supply of food to sustain the family in any time of trouble; this is an ongoing practice from Mormonism's original frontier experience in Utah.

Theologically speaking, the Word of Wisdom is one way of expressing the value that the Latter-day Saints place upon the human body as the arena of exercising agency and obedience to God and of preparing for the resurrection and the life to come. Given the food rules of ancient Israel and modern Jewry, the Word of Wisdom also marks out the Saints from others and provides an echo of their own sense of identity as God's own people; indeed the Latter-day Saints have long interpreted their own history and destiny in terms of that of Israel. They have had their own prophets, period in the wilderness, plagues and promised land and, as we saw in chapter 2, also claimed to have ancestry in the Holy Land itself.

TITHING

As with the Word of Wisdom so with tithing, its basis lies in a revelation (D&C 119) dated July 1838, a day of several revelations dealing with money and property (D&C 117, 118, 119, 120). Although the precise sum involved has varied over time, contemporary Saints interpret 'tithe' as one tenth of their actual income. In a 1970 directive from the First Presidency, however, members were told that they needed to make their own decision as to what a proper payment should be. It is important for active Saints to engage with this issue because they have an annual meeting with their bishop to agree whether they are full tithe payers or not; only those paying what is regarded as proper, given their circumstances, can be given their recommend to attend the temple and engage in its rites of exaltation: a requirement dating from 1881 (Swainston 1992: 1481).

Tithing is important because it introduces the importance of money to religious life in general and to LDS commitment in particular. This is a highly significant topic that has been very largely ignored in the broad stream of Christian theology and is often absent from formal systematic theologies. In earliest Christianity money was one significant means both of expressing religious sincerity and of 'deceiving the Spirit' as in the case of Ananias and Sapphira in the Acts of the Apostles (5: 1–11). I have explored some of those issues elsewhere and here simply draw attention to the monetary-economic base of LDS temple life and to the exaltation that proceeds from it (Davies 2002: 199). In other words, money and exaltation are directly related. In saying this, one is, quite explicitly, not making the kind of criticism often levelled against some religious movements that equate money with gain and the manipulation of people. Far from it. Even within the Church there is a sense of realism about money and wealth, for, while tithing may help to make a church rich, 'the prosperity of any people was not positive evidence of their being right', as Brigham Young once judged (Arrington 1986: 107).

What is of real theological interest is the way in which many groups define money and its uses, often with the assumption that money is somehow intrinsically evil, despite the biblical injunction that it is the 'love of money' that introduces the negative factor (1 Timothy 6: 10). Mormonism developed an important sense of money as part of the commitment of church members through its early period of migration and settlement. Unlike many major churches, Mormonism emerged as a community-in-construction, one in which goods and service needed to be mutually shared if that community was to survive; because of this, money as such was not the single most significant medium of exchange or of relation between member and church. It was, however, as in earliest Christianity, a potent symbol of commitment to the cause, used to express both sincerity and deceit. Still, money is a fundamental means by which family and church are related. Partners need to discuss their tithing and to discuss it with their bishop; they also need to budget with care. For many core LDS families this means making allowance for supporting their sons or daughters if they are called to serve a mission, often prior to their going into higher education. In all this a family needs to gain a sense of common values that cannot ignore Church membership.

FATHERHOOD, PRIESTHOOD AND BLESSING

At the heart of family organization lies the theology of priesthood, ideally of the Melchizedek father with Aaronic sons and of the wife and daughters who share the benefits of such priesthood. As I show at the close of this chapter and in another way in chapter 8, the pairing of husband and wife and the sealing of their children to them underlie the ultimate state of salvation or exaltation. In more immediate and temporal terms the father is also to be a patriarch to his family, with the authority and responsibility to bless them, pray for them and anoint them if they are sick. His role in giving what is called a father's blessing mirrors at the family level the task of the formal patriarchs to the Church (described in chapter 5). Blessing is, itself, a central LDS concept, which I mentioned in chapter 6 when discussing the United Order and which is even more important in relation to the Word of Wisdom, tithing and family life.

Though easily overlooked, the significance of 'blessing' demands attention, as two verses of the Doctrine and Covenants show. In connection with the United Order the prophet announces that a 'promise immutable and unchangeable' governs the fact that 'the faithful should be blessed with a multiplicity of blessings' while, 'inasmuch as they were not faithful they were nigh unto cursing' (D&C 104: 2, 3). Blessing is aligned both with covenant and obedience to furnish the prime grammar of discourse of Mormon ethical theory and its daily application in family and church life. The Book of Mormon offers a clear textual example of the relation between obedience, success and blessing in King Mosiah's words: 'if ye do keep his commandments he doth bless you and prosper you' (Mosiah 2:22). Many Latter-day Saints would testify to such a link between faithfulness in tithing, in the Word of Wisdom and the flourishing of their family.

ETERNAL KINSHIP

Lessons learned within the family are also of eternal consequence since it is the family group that will provide the basic medium for eternal life. But that itself will only come about if the husband and wife have been married and their children sealed to them through temple ordinances. In this way the several levels of LDS life are intertwined, from the family through the local ward to the temple. The Family Home Evening, instituted in 1965 and reaffirmed in 1999, ensured that Monday evenings were free of other church activities so that parents and children could share various activities aimed at fostering bonds whilst being educative. This is a good example of LDS theology affecting social organization, for it is often recognized in other churches how leaders are so caught up in running congregations that their own families suffer as a result. Many Latter-day Saints would acknowledge that bishops and many other office-holders benefit from this family time, given their otherwise extremely busy church life conducted in addition to their ordinary employment.

While the nuclear family is the primary group as far as regular activity within the Church is concerned, the ultimate theological focus lies with as broad an extended family as possible. Accordingly, the Church encourages its members to establish as extensive a genealogical record as possible as the basis for engaging in temple ritual on behalf of their dead and to make it possible for them to be both saved and exalted in the worlds to come. If the home is the nursery of good family relations where children begin to learn responsibility, the ward offers a temporal extension of that on a community basis, while the temple affords eternal scope for developing relationships.

The inclusion of the dead within the ritual processes granting eternal identity after death became increasingly formalized in the later nineteenth century, at the very time when the Church was undergoing serious Government opposition over polygamy. George Durrant describes how the Genealogical Society of Utah was established in 1894, was renamed the Genealogical Society of the Church of Jesus Christ of Latter-day Saints in 1944, The Genealogical Department of the Church in 1976 and The Family History Department in 1987 (Durrant 1992: 537). These name changes show the increased focusing on genealogy both in the Church's organizational structure and the family itself. A great deal of effort has been expended by the Church throughout the world in copying records of births, marriages and deaths as well as by individual family members in seeking their own ancestors. The Church's commitment to gaining copies of such records, especially parish registers of major denominations has sometimes drawn a critical response on the basis that proxy work done for the dead somehow compels the dead to become Mormons in the afterlife. This could not be further from the truth because, in theological terms, the crux of the matter lies in agency and in the decision any individual might take, whether in this world or the next. All that vicarious ritual does is provide the opportunity – itself a key LDS concept – for those who had never heard the LDS form of the Christian message to hear it, and to respond to it as they will. Family members of the Church are taught to fulfil their responsibility to their dead by searching out their identity and undergoing ritual on their behalf. If and when their ancestors in the spirit domain accept these benefits, then the living really do become 'Saviours in Zion', as the LDS phrase has it, expressing the unified world of the 'pure in heart' who have entered into divine truth through the Restoration, its doctrines and its rites or, as the Saints would say, through the gospel and the ordinances of the gospel. The larger the eternal family unit the greater the benefit that accrues to each member.

DIVINE PARENTHOOD

Behind the LDS commitment to families lies the ultimate family in the form of divine parents, the Father-God and Mother-God in heaven. This is not often discussed in contemporary Mormonism although some LDS feminist writers draw upon its implications to ask whether the mother in heaven fully shares in the deity of God the Father or is simply some sort of wife needed for the production of spirit children (Anderson, L. 1996: 159–65). The highly popular LDS hymn 'O My Father', written by Eliza R. Snow, an early Mormon poet and a co-wife of Joseph Smith and, after Joseph's death, of Brigham Young, poses the question, 'In the heav'ns are parents single?' and gives a firm 'No' in response. The very idea of their being single 'makes reason stare'. She continues, 'Truth is reason, truth eternal, Tells me I've a mother there.'

Lest this be taken to refer simply to Eliza's own earthly parents, which is not the interpretation most Saints would give to it, we might add as evidence the well-known assertion of the Church's First Presidency in 1909 that 'man as a spirit, was begotten and born of heavenly parents, and reared to maturity in the eternal mansions of the Father...as an offspring of celestial parentage', so that 'all men and women are in the similitude of the universal Father and Mother, and are literally the sons and daughters of Deity' (Anderson Cannon 1992: 961). In LDS theology it is easy to both overplay and underplay this element of divine destiny in celestial realms of glory. Ward-involved Saints who are not active in temple rites – a proportion varying from some 30 per cent in established Utah wards to 85 per cent in some British contexts – are seldom exposed to explicit accounts of temple-related theological ideas. Indeed, it would be easy for non-LDS Christians to attend Mormon meetings and begin to wonder just what the difference is between this and other churches, since the Book of Mormon, other Standard Works and references to temples are not always present in talks or readings, which are often related to the human endeavour of daily life.

PRAYER

As in many other churches, prayer is, in fact, a significant element in congregational, family and individual life. Saints are taught to pray about many things, and newcomers who are interested in Mormonism and often described as investigating the gospel are also encouraged to pray as they read the Book of Mormon to enable God to give them a sense of its truthfulness. Church members pray about their family life and church life and about many other things, just as church leaders pray over all aspects of organization and management, not least when calling people to and releasing them from specific posts. Whilst it is easy to identify the commonplace nature of LDS prayer as but one feature of religious practice running throughout Christendom, it is wise not to overlook the example and influence of Joseph Smith upon subsequent generations. Joseph's first vision, described in chapters 1 and 5, establishes prayer as the medium for serious engagement with God and as the opportunity in relation to which God responds. In the Book of Mormon, for example, when Jesus appears in America there is a great emphasis on both individuals and whole groups of people falling upon their knees to pray (see 3 Nephi 19: 6–18). This occasion prompts an entire section in which Jesus also prays in a way that amazes the people (3 Nephi 17).

Today children learn from seeing their family pray whether at meals, the Family Home Evening or in church. With time, prayer becomes increasingly important, not least when young people serve their mission and are thrown upon their own spiritual resources more than ever before. For some this is a time when prayer either becomes rather difficult or breaks through into a new level of significance. In all these contexts prayer reflects the relational nature of Mormonism, as God is explicitly, intentionally, and emotionally designated as 'Heavenly Father'. The whole plan of salvation, within which the earthly family plays a pivotal role, furnishes an entire relational network that stretches from the heavenly Father and Mother in heaven, who procreate spirit children in the first place, through earthly mothers and fathers, who provide bodies for these spirit children, and on to future generations who will join their ancestors in an eternal domain of glory. To pray to 'Heavenly Father' becomes perfectly natural, in full accord with Joseph's eager prayer and with the prayerful dimension of church organization.

FAMILY PROCLAMATION

The plan of salvation was reiterated with considerable force by President Gordon B. Hinkley in September 1995 when speaking for the First Presidency and the Twelve Apostles. In what was described as a 'solemn proclamation' he stressed the centrality of the family, human origins in 'heavenly parents' and the individual's 'divine nature and destiny'(Hinkley 2001: 592). In this full-blown affirmation of the pre-existence and current mortal life in which experience may be gained 'to progress towards perfection' marriage is affirmed as essential to what is, tellingly, called the 'divine plan of happiness'. The division of labour according to gender is also stressed, with the father responsible for providing 'the necessities of life' and the mother 'the nurture of the children'. Addressing those who break their vows of chastity or who abuse spouse or children, the proclamation warns them of their accountability to God and calls upon all, both individual citizens and government, to foster the family 'as the fundamental unit of society', warning 'that the disintegration of the family' will bring about 'the calamities foretold by ancient and modern prophets'. Within these powerful affirmations one hears responsive echoes to various elements and events in the Church that have touched on sexual irregularity of many kinds. Above all it is a clear statement of traditional LDS values.

GRACE: PASTORAL AND CRITICAL

Against this background of obligation and duty I return to the major theological issue of grace by comparing what I shall describe as 'pastoral grace' with O. Kendall White's notion of grace, which I will designate 'critical grace'.

Pastoral grace

The pastoral model takes up the sense of inadequacy that some Saints develop in the face of high levels of performance expected in family responsibilities, church activity and daily work. Many find it hard enough to achieve a minimum level of performance without beginning to think in terms of exaltation. The ideal language of celestial glory can, at times, seem distant from the chores of family and local congregational life; indeed, the language of grace, in the sense of divine love and acceptance of the failing sinner, has a certain attraction to exasperated believers who are trying their best but are haunted by a sense of failure.

But it is at this very point that LDS theology encounters a very particular problem concerning the nature of sin, and of grace in relation to sin. In traditional Christian theology men and women are described as sinners in the sense that they participate in the very nature of Adam, who disobeyed God and whose descendants, in some way, carry the infection of this fallen nature. Whether this is interpreted in historical, mythical or existential

terms, humanity is accounted morally weak and helpless. An extreme view –
total depravity – was developed in some Protestant traditions to describe the
complete human inability to do or think anything that pleases God. The
crucial element here is the view of human nature as being deeply affected
by evil. Even if the human will does find itself desirous of doing good, there
is something about the totality of that person's life that thwarts the desire.
In other words sin comes to refer to the flawed core of human nature and
accounts for human failings and failure: existentially humanity is sinful. In
this perspective it is perfectly understandable that the things that people
do will also be sinful. Sinful acts spring from a sinful nature.

Mormonism's developed theology of agency, opportunity and achievement works in a completely different direction from this. As we have already
seen, Mormonism adopted a positive view of the fall of Adam for, while that
fall brought death to Adam's descendants, the atonement of Jesus Christ
restored immortality through a guaranteed resurrection. What people do
about their forthcoming resurrection depends on their own sense of responsibility, for – and this is the crucial feature of LDS theology – human
nature itself is not infected by any negative inevitability. The spirit that
comes to each new baby-body possesses at its core that 'intelligence' that is
itself uncreated. The 'spirits' that have been engendered by heavenly parents
prior to their coming to take a body through human parents have, in one
sense, already proved their positive orientation to God, the heavenly father,
long ago in their pre-existence. It is now a question of individuals exerting
their agency to decide to do good or evil. And it is here that sins, in the
plural, may take place. It is when someone chooses to do something wrong
that they sin. Sins exist in the plural; they are the actual acts performed. Sin
does not exist in the singular as a description of the givenness of human
nature.

Herein lies the sharp division between LDS and other Christian views
and it is of fundamental significance when considering the theological idea
of grace, not least in terms of what I am calling the pastoral model of
grace. The pastoral model of grace is the key operating feature of Protestant spirituality and brings hope to the hopeless. Allied with the doctrine of
justification by faith and new-birth through the Holy Spirit that is emphasized in Protestantism, grace becomes a dynamic feature that revivifies the
spiritually dead and gives them new life within an ongoing frame of grace.
The LDS case is not entirely consonant with this even though several of
White's neo-orthodox thinkers are close to it. The LDS pastoral model of
grace would assume that there are individuals who really wish to be good
and who try and strive to do what they believe is right but that they still

come to a point of self-confessed inability. It is at this point that the disjunction between Protestant and neo-orthodox thinkers emerges, for while the Protestants emphasize a sinful nature, the LDS stress the sense of failure that attends the life of deep endeavour. LDS authors Robert L. Millett (1994) and Stephen E. Robinson (1992) offer clear examples of this form of spirituality and come to speak of grace more in terms of a divine love that embraces the whole of life than in terms of having the strength to decide to do 'good things'. Millett even uses language normally associated with Protestant Evangelicalism when talking about 'new birth' as an element in spiritual development, including his own 'immersion into the heavenly element' of love and care (1994: 81).

Crisis grace

Having briefly outlined these types of grace, I can consider more formally Kendall White's thesis on grace in a crisis theology as expounded in his study *Mormon Neo-Orthodoxy: A Crisis Theology* (White 1987). His argument depends upon a sociological interpretation of how certain groups respond to periods of crisis, especially in the case of secularization as a challenge to received ways of constructing the religious world. How do people respond when their cherished certainties seem to be undercut at the root? First, he takes the basic shift in Protestant theology associated with Karl Barth, Emil Brunner and Reinhold Niebuhr's Protestant Neo-Orthodoxy of the early twentieth century. Living in a world of liberal challenge and political confusion, these turn to God as the one ultimate source of unchanging truth and tell how he addresses the human condition and, through the divine communication of grace, saves mankind from its plight. White takes up a series of LDS thinkers including Stirling McMurrin, Thomas G. Alexander and T. Edgar Lyon, who have shown, much as in earlier chapters of the present study, how earliest Mormonism shared a strong family resemblance with basic Protestantism and how this changed with the development of temples, endowments and theories of exaltation. These also turn to an idea of an all-mighty and unchanging deity in the face of challenges to belief and to the Church, especially in the 1960s, and, in so doing, they began to diverge from the LDS view of God as one in a process of development and who is, philosophically, not almighty.

White's thesis is relatively straightforward as an exercise in the sociology of religion and there is likely to be some truth in arguing that in periods of profound secularization of society, when cultural values are no longer influenced by religious ideas and when the sense of meaning becomes eroded, one response of religious believers is to seek ever more conservative forms of leadership and firmer sources of religious authority. Accordingly, he regards the 'Protestant Reformation and neo-orthodox theologies' as 'sophisticated rationales for helplessness and the necessity for divine intervention'; so too with the LDS shift to a view of God as the one from whom all must come, given the hopelessness of humanity left to its own devices (White 1987: 7).

MORAL MEANING

There is, however, a potential gap in White's thought between two different kinds of 'meaning', namely, cognitive meaning and moral meaning. His emphasis is upon the cognitive and rational meaning of the world and on the fact that when, due to secularization, 'the cognitive foundations that endow social structures with meaning were challenged and undermined', devotees opted for an all-powerful deity who could save them from meaninglessness. Indeed, his crisis model of grace lies precisely here. His sociological interpretation sees the desire for grace as the outcome of conceptual helplessness. This is an appropriate form of argument given White's use of Max Weber, whose sociology of religion argued that there are different forms of salvation appropriate to the needs of different groups of people. It is the intellectual who, largely, takes centre stage in White's argument. But there is another kind of meaning, moral meaning, that may well embrace intellectuals but which also encompasses a much larger group of people who are deeply motivated by the ideals of their religion and highly responsive to its demands across the spectrum of their lives. Their concern about what we might call 'moral meaning' touches the desire to feel in accord with the moral claims of their church and community and to sense doctrinal truth in and through their religious practice: these 'feel' their doctrine as much as 'think' it. And it is just such individuals who take precedence in the theological thinking of people such as Robert Millett and Stephen Robinson, whose books of the 1990s were far more concerned with the pastoral power of grace than with any abstract intellectual view of it (Millett 1994, 1995; Robinson 1992). In LDS terms they are concerned with the 'testimony' people have and on how people's experience of God shapes their lives.

It is at this point that the crucial difference between the critical and pastoral models of grace becomes apparent because I follow White's own sociological model: it is on his own terms that I want to distinguish between differing needs and the differing values given to 'grace'. My distinction lies in the assumption that – agreeing with White – the critical type of grace comes from the intellectual need for certainty on the part of thinking people who are aware of, and even afraid of, the confusion wrought by secular forces outside the Church but, diverging from White, I would argue that the pastoral form of grace comes from forces inside the Church. These internal forces involve pressures to succeed in family and work life, to engage in very active congregational lives and to pursue temple work. This endeavour is, inevitably, complex for each individual and may involve the pressure of time, responsibility, sense of capability, unworthiness, weakness and a whole series of comparisons with other people who seem to cope with everything and still be able to do more. Within this matrix of self-judgement people may also feel guilt, and guilt is one human sentiment that fits ill in developed Mormon theology. The atonement of Christ is regarded as dealing with humanity's original guilt in Adam (Moses 6: 54) but guilt as such plays a relatively small part in LDS theology: there is no direct reference to guilt, for example, in either McConkie's *Mormon Doctrine* or in *The Encyclopedia of Mormonism*. Guilt is, however, firmly located in the Protestant configuration of grace and in its conception of human nature as itself sinful. So it would seem that the pastoral model of grace, as a response to internal church pressures upon an individual's life and the guilt it may induce, is its own form of LDS adaptation to the pressures of its own organization. It is a home-grown theological necessity.

One overlap between the pastoral and critical notions of grace lies in the sense that something 'comes' to the believer from an external and authoritative source. The subtle distinction between them, however, lies in the perceived need to which that 'gift' of grace is the required benefit. In the one it is intellectual guidance and a call to follow powerful leaders who will serve as bulwarks against the encroaching secular tide, while in the other it is emotional guidance sensed as coming from the supernatural source of God.

White's model serves a very useful theological purpose in describing how the word 'grace' is used in Mormon history and, in so doing, how it has diverged from wider Christian usage. In what I have described as critical grace and as pastoral grace the word differs from the LDS tradition of a general adjective describing things that God has done throughout the plan of salvation. There remains one quandary about grace, however, and it emerges in connection with the idea of moral perfection. It would be relatively easy but misguided, for example, to argue a stage-theory of LDS attitudes to moral perfection and to say that earliest Mormonism was Protestant, knew that humanity was sinful and depended upon divine grace for salvation, and then that exaltation doctrine and temple endowments turned the meaning of perfection into pragmatic rites to be performed and duties to be done. Then, one could argue, as I have just done with regard to some contemporary Saints, that a sense of the impossibility of attaining such great performance prompted a return to a grasping of divine grace as the acceptance of the underperformer.

The potentially misguided reason for following that developmental scheme lies in the question of what 'perfection' and moral achievement meant to the Saints of, for example, Brigham Young's day. Here we encounter a problem when hearing early LDS sources speak of, on the one hand, degrees of glory combined with a sense of the mysteries now being revealed about the afterlife with, on the other, an expectation of certain behavioural goals, including plural marriage, that should be attained by dedicated believers.

In other words, great merit was possible through the very act of plural marriage. To engage in it was to obey a major divine command. In today's church, by contrast, this is neither commanded nor possible, so that any single sense of a major act of obedience gives way to the challenge of accomplishing innumerable smaller tasks, the cumulative load of which is hard to sustain in contemporary life. Since the LDS stress on monogamous families and extensive church involvement has, to many intents and purposes, replaced the enormous single commitment of plural marriage, it may have made life more complex and difficult. In other words 'perfection' is not what it was. If there is any truth in this hypothesis, it can be seen as the outcome of another internal change of church organization, albeit demanded by the pressure of a secularizing external Federal force that was compelling the end of plural marriage.

Still, monogamous marriage remains of paramount importance and, both in conclusion and as a preparation for the following chapter on temples, I introduce one doctrine and its allied temple practice that continue to express the LDS theology of the family and enshrine prime Mormon concepts within the home whilst also relating both home and temple to the eternal future. The doctrinal idea is called the patriarchal order of the priesthood and the rite is one in which husband and wife engage in special covenants with God.

Here, once more, we return to the significance of 'principles' by which all things are organized, in this case 'three principles' are said to 'underlie the patriarchal order' (McKinlay 1992: 1067): the belief that Adam and Eve were joined by eternal ties prior to the 'fall'; that the fallen world tends to estrange partners, parents and children; and that harmony can be restored in a relationship that will lead to the eternal capacity to procreate. So it is that husband and wife enter into a covenant with God and are, concurrently, bound to each other so that they come to share in the Melchizedek order of the priesthood, itself described as 'the organizing power and principle of celestial family life'. Here we see the necessity of marriage before individuals can gain the highest rewards of the celestial kingdom in which they will, for all eternity, become their own form of deity and monarch within an ever-expanding family. It is at this point in LDS life that the relationships between the home, temple and eternity come to play upon each other and to demonstrate the complex doctrinal scheme that underlies daily life for those who are core, committed, Latter-day Saints.

CHAPTER 8

Temples and ritual

Soteriology, as a technical theological term that describes theories of salvation, is particularly useful when discussing Mormonism precisely because 'salvation' applies to only part of the overall scheme of things in the LDS Church but it embraces the whole scheme in other churches. As we have seen in previous chapters, Mormonism uses 'salvation' to describe Christ's atonement and the resurrection it brings to all people and goes on to use 'exaltation' to account for the ultimate realms of glory in the celestial kingdom obtained through obedience and the fulfilment of the 'ordinances of the gospel'. It is in and through these ordinances that the 'principles' underlying LDS thought become powerfully apparent.

Exaltation is the ultimate word in Mormon soteriology. In order to grasp its import, this chapter will sketch the history not only of the doctrine but also of the temple as the arena of its implementation. 'Exaltation' is an instructive doctrine, in the sense that it cannot be explored simply as some abstract idea, but requires an understanding of the theological significance of temples and the way in which the emergence of temple ritual turned Mormonism into a distinctive form of western, Christianly sourced, religion. To document this development is to note the Church's transition from an intrinsically Protestant-like group that is focused on atonement to a movement that is characterized by 'temple-Mormonism' and is directed towards exaltation; this style becomes so distinctive that many scholars ponder whether it is Christian at all or whether, perhaps, it has become a religion all of its own. The shift from 'chapel' to 'temple' Mormonism can also be considered in terms of the two notions of 'relations' and 'principles', which I explained in chapter 1 and to which I return in the final chapter.

TEXT AND TEMPLE

Here, however, I begin with detailed consideration of some texts from the Book of Mormon, which is representative of the Church's early phase, and from the Doctrine and Covenants, which underlies the second. Text and temple are closely related in the emergence of Mormonism, albeit in a complex fashion. In strictly chronological terms text preceded temple, with the Book of Mormon being published years before places of special ritual action were built. In that strict sense, too, the text of the Book of Mormon preceded the text of the Doctrine and Covenants. During this period of change Mormonism experienced a shift in its approach to and engagement with ritual, making it the most ritual-focused of any Protestant-related Christian tradition. This movement into a ritualizing of salvation can better be understood against the wider ritual background of Christianity for, as with all religions, Christianity involves ritual actions through which ideas are expressed and distinctive goals achieved. Although social scientific disciplines were paramount in the study of ritual in the twentieth century, many religious traditions have also paid considerable theological and philosophical attention to their own ritual or liturgical activities, as they might call them. This is particularly true for Christianity which has been increasingly explicit about the theological meaning of ritual for much of its history. The Reformation, especially in the sixteenth century, caused Christians of increasingly differing persuasions to debate the meaning of the Eucharist as well as of baptism. But the biblical roots of similar issues extend back to the Old Testament prophets and their questioning of the sincerity of formal worship if its ethical outcome was insincere (Amos 5: 21–4). The teachings of Jesus stressed that same point (Matthew 12: 1–14). Then, in the formal documents of earliest Christianity, the role of circumcision was hotly debated in relation to membership of the new culturally eclectic community that was emerging from Judaism (Acts 15: 1–29).

Subsequent Christian history witnessed similar disputes concerning the outward performance of rites in relation to their inner sincerity or in relation to one's ultimate religious destiny. In the seventh and eighth centuries the Iconoclastic Controversy famously argued about the positive and negative worth of icons. In the twelfth and thirteenth centuries the ritual of the Mass assumed new significance and devotional consequences following the newly formulated doctrine of transubstantiation, in which the bread and wine were believed to become, in their inner essence, the very body and blood of Christ. From earliest Christianity baptism was regarded as the basis of Christian identity, even leading to the belief that those who die unbaptized lie beyond salvation. Then, as already suggested, the Reformation prompted widespread debate about ritual and the emergent Protestant tradition regularly linked many forms of ritual – which comes to gain a rather negative status of its own – with insincerity and untruth. What was heard in the preached word took precedence over what was seen by the ritual eye. So much was this the case that many Protestant churches came to regard the very word 'ritual' with deep suspicion. Even when, sociologically speaking, events are obviously ritual in form, members of Protestant churches would avoid the word 'ritual', sometimes preferring the more theological notion of liturgy. In Britain in the nineteenth century, for example, great energies were expended on proper and improper forms of ceremony, leading, for example, in 1867 to the establishment of a Royal Commission – the Ritual Commission – to decide on matters of what might be worn and done in Church of England ceremonies. Many similar examples could be given in different countries. The point is that Christians are often sensitive to the division between sincerity of heart and mere outward form of behaviour, and ritual is easily associated with the latter rather than with the former. In addition to this, there remains the fundamental question of religious authority in relation to salvation. Does salvation depend upon particular rituals performed by particular people? In Roman Catholic theology this question is directly grounded in the issue of ordination. Is salvation dependent upon or fostered through a person being baptized, absolved and given the Holy Eucharist by a properly ordained priest? Indeed, is the Catholic Church the only ark of salvation? In traditional terms the answer to these questions was in the affirmative and led Catholic theology to view other denominations and their ministries as invalid. Protestants have been much less exclusive as far as institutional membership of a church is concerned, preferring to root salvation in faith in Christ and in a personal knowledge of God rather than in the observance of formal rites governed by church institutions. Though much has changed since the Catholic Second Vatican Council of the 1960s, these attitudes have been and, in many places, remain influential.

It is against that background that the emergence of Mormon ritual from the 1830s is significant. The North American Christian world reflected many of these European Christian debates as manifested, for example, by the Founding Fathers and subsequent Puritan traditions. While 'simplicity' was often the watchword of church activity, as of life at large, many other cultural factors helped to forge the attitudes of different Christian denominations. These included values brought to the United States by European immigrants, so much so that some of the first major steps in the sociology of religion were taken by theologically motivated scholars, especially Richard Niebuhr (1929) and Ernst Troeltsch (1931). Earliest Mormonism, as reflected in the Book of Mormon, followed this Protestant spirituality of inner sincerity which found a doctrinal emphasis in repentance, faith and baptism, all grounded in group meetings for prayer, worship and teaching. Adult rather than infant baptism was the norm. But, unlike the great majority of Protestant groups, Mormonism very rapidly developed an interest in ritual practice alongside an emergent theology of ritual that became determinative for its future life. From a theology of organization, with divine revelations covering the format of the church and its leadership (e.g. D&C 53, 54, 55), there developed a theology of priesthood, covenant and endowment which promised the conquest of death and the inheritance of heavenly and eternal glory, status and identity. Underlying this ritual culture lay two fundamental points of theology, one affirming church exclusivity and the other the necessity of ritual itself.

First, this newly restored church was the exclusive means of attaining exaltation even though, in a qualified sense, it was practically universalist in doctrine. In most other churches this would have been, literally, paradoxical but Mormonism achieved a complementarity here by establishing a soteriological distinction between salvation and exaltation. It argued that all people would attain some degree of salvation in an appropriate lower level of heaven, depending upon their degree of achievement, whilst exaltation in the highest heaven was retained for committed Latter-day Saints. I have, elsewhere, explored this kind of 'super-salvation' in sociological terms, through the notion of 'super-plausibility', a process in which one religious tradition renders redundant the beliefs of others and replaces them with its own (Davies 2002: 152–5). The sociological genius of Mormonism lay in bringing that process about within its own fold.

Second, the Church argued that rituals conducted on earth, in specially designated places, were prerequisite for specific effects to be possible in heaven. Ritual was the prime soteriological medium. This was as true for baptism and confirmation in relation to 'salvation' as for temple rites of eternal marriage and endowments for 'exaltation'. Despite the fact that these 'ordinances of the gospel', a phrase that roughly equates to sacraments in Catholic Christianity, were necessary both for salvation and exaltation, Mormonism did not leave itself with the unanswered question of those who had lived and died ignorant of these necessities. By framing the doctrine of what we might call 'the necessity of ordinances' with the complementary doctrine that ritual can be vicariously performed, those long dead could now benefit from the ritual service of the living.

This kind of ritualized activity has also exerted a wider effect upon LDS cultural life in fostering a sense of the importance of formal acts. One historical example is that of Brigham H. Roberts (1857–1933) who, while on his missionary activities as a young man, was rather rudely repulsed and ejected from a particular farm. On leaving, he came across a stream and decided in a formal way to wash his feet in testimony against 'this man and his house for the rejection of me': It was the only time he 'felt at liberty to attend to this ordinance' (Roberts, B. H. 1990: 92). He did this after recalling a section of the Doctrine and Covenants (D&C 84: 92–3), a fact that illustrates both the importance of that book in the life of a young missionary in the 1870s and the power of ritual in framing his life.

FROM CHURCH TO TEMPLE

The doctrinal and ritual shift from the Protestantism inherent in these soteriological views can be traced in the architectural transition from the chapel form of meeting house to the temple form of site for sacred rites. Here some care is needed in using the phrase 'chapel' or 'chapel Mormonism' because, as Quinn has described, a great deal of Mormon religious activity from 1830 to 1846 'occurred in private residences and commercial buildings or in the assembly room of the Kirtland temple or in Nauvoo's open-air grove' (Quinn 2001: 142; cf. Bitton 1994: 24–30). Similarly, in Britain and other European countries, missionaries and early congregations hired halls or utilized public places for much of the nineteenth century, and it was only in the 1920s and 1930s that Welsh and Scottish Saints, for example, gave themselves to the building of permanent chapels, once they had finally accepted the message that emigration to the United States should give way to a building of Zion wherever people might live (Davies 1987: 65ff; Craig 2000: 73, 91–105). Still, 'chapel' Mormonism, is a useful way of distinguishing between general congregational meetings and the specific events associated with Mormonism's secret sacred rites. The distinction between chapel and temple is also, for example, one of the best expressions of the category distinction that Harold W. Turner established in his influential analysis of the difference between the *domus ecclesiae* – meeting house – and *domus dei* – the house of God, in the field of the history and theology of religions (Turner, H. W. 1979). With those cautions in mind, I explore the place of temples within LDS sacred texts, an exploration that will serve the additional purpose of exemplifying one stream of LDS doctrinal development to complement chapter 3 and its consideration of LDS doctrine.

Temples and temple ritual are of absolute theological importance for LDS life and, in textual terms, a basic doctrinal scheme emerges in the Standard Works and moves from the depiction of a 'church' to a 'temple' form of religious life. Here 'church' describes the meeting house and the standard practice of Protestant religion, in which people meet together in a particular building to worship God; this is often in the singing of hymns, through prayers, the practice of baptism and the Christian Holy Communion rite, and with sermons or educational talks. Meetings are almost always open to the general public. This pattern occurs in nearly all denominations, varying only in emphasis and with some inclusions and exclusions of practice. The Salvation Army, for example, does not use the Holy Communion rite and the Society of Friends largely employs silence. Early Mormons followed this general pattern of Christian association. 'Temple', by contrast, refers to buildings that are dedicated to be especially holy, in which rites are performed by specifically ordained levels of priests who effect contact between humanity and deity. While the Christian world was already attuned to the notion of a temple through the place of Jerusalem's temple in the Hebrew Bible, Mormonism transposed this picture from the imaginative world of the geography of faith, sermon and hymn to the concrete realm of architecture. It did so with all the energy that came from viewing itself as the new people of God, a new Israel that had moved to its own promised land under its own prophetic leadership. But the change was not immediate and by no means the inevitable outcome of a self-identification with Israel.

The Book of Mormon was published in 1830. Of its dozen or so references to 'temple' all are of the Old Testament type (see 2 Nephi 5: 16). The image painted of worship amongst the Nephites – who had believed in Christ on his appearance in America in AD 34 and for two hundred and one years after – is that they 'had all things in common', and were given to 'fasting and prayer, and in meeting together oft to pray and hear the word of the Lord' (4 Nephi 1: 12). Elsewhere, too, the picture is very much that of a Protestant-like community in which a 'church' is established as people repent and are baptized (Alma 19: 35). Then, due to growth in numbers and hardness of heart, the people began developing churches of their own, led by priests and false prophets (4 Nephi 1: 34). In all of this there is no notion of a temple or of any distinctive ritual. Whether the true church or the false churches, all are much of a muchness as far as their activities are concerned and differ only in sincerity and source of authority. In Moroni, the final book in the Book of Mormon, instructions are given on how the rites of the true church are to be performed, especially those for the laying on of hands to confer the gift of the Holy Ghost, for ordination and for the Sacrament Meeting as it came to be called (Moroni 3–5). At its outset, the LDS Church possessed explicit ritual formulae for baptism, ordination and for what other churches called the Holy Communion, Lord's Supper and such like. All this reinforces the idea of the early LDS movement as a Protestant-style group that 'did meet together oft, to fast and pray, and to speak with one another concerning the welfare of their souls', and 'to partake of bread and wine in remembrance of the Lord Jesus' (Moroni 6: 5, 6). Similarly, when King Benjamin gives a formal address to the people at the end of his life, his words are entirely consonant with much of the Protestant theology of Joseph Smith's day in an essential message of atonement, forgiveness and a subsequent life of obedience. So, too, when the language of covenant is employed (Mosiah 5: 5, 7) there is no sense of its being different from 'covenant' in a general Christian sense and no hint that it refers to LDS temple rites and to the increasingly complex significance of covenants in them, a significance that, over time, made 'covenant' a deeply powerful Mormon concept.

At the outset of the Doctrine and Covenants it is this essentially Protestant church that is still in evidence, just as it was such a church – restoration ideas apart – that was formally established in April 1830. The Restoration was expressed in the Book of Mormon both as a restored history of salvation and as a charter document validating and explaining the nature and authority of its prophetic leadership and hierarchy. The theme of mysteries and the gaining of knowledge of mysteries appears in the earlier parts of D&C to refer to the text and teachings of the Book of Mormon, to the discovery of the plates from which they were translated and to the process of translation itself (D&C 8: 11). Only later do mysteries come to apply to the more esoteric temple-related doctrines.

ENDOWMENT PREPARATION

The idea of temples, in the more specifically LDS sense, appears in a December 1832 revelation (D&C 88: 119), followed by a minor rebuke in June 1833 for those lax over the temple project. This reference is more concrete than the earlier one in that it refers to a place where God wishes to 'endow those' whom he has chosen (D&C 95: 8; cf. D&C 105: 33). This is a particularly interesting text, not simply because it gives the size of the 'house' that is to be built, 55 feet wide and 65 feet long, with a ground floor for the 'sacrament offering... preaching... fasting... praying, and the offering up of your most holy desires' but because the upstairs section is to become 'the school of mine apostles, saith Ahman: or, in other words. Omegus: even Jesus Christ your Lord' (D&C 95: 16–17). The descriptive titles of Jesus as 'Ahman' and 'Omegus' reflect the esoteric direction in which the ritual life of Mormons was about to accelerate. A slightly earlier revelation of March 1832 had also used Ahman for Jesus, in a text that had already used the place-name Adam-ondi-Ahman, a site in Missouri associated with Adam on his expulsion from Eden according to LDS mythical-history (D&C 78: 20, 15). A brief revelation, included in Doctrine and Covenants as Section 116, specifically refers to this name and extends the Adam reference to speak of the place 'where Adam shall come to visit his people, or the Ancient of Days shall sit' (D&C 116).

In moving towards the more developed form of LDS ritual and practice, a revelation of March 1835 provides a full account of the two priesthoods, their authoritative basis for conducting the rites of the Church, and the first formal statement in connection with temples (D&C 107). Then, Doctrine and Covenants Section 109 of March 1836 rehearses the dedication prayer given at Kirtland Temple's formal inauguration. The very next section, Section 110, relates to experiences in that temple only days later and is particularly distinctive in describing a theophany, a revelation of the divine, in the person of Jesus, who is clearly identified as 'the Lord standing upon the breastwork of the pulpit'. His eyes are as flames, his face shone and his own voice – 'even the voice of Jehovah' – describes himself as the 'first and the last', and as he 'who was slain', he is the 'advocate with the father' (D&C 110: 3–4). Among the words that Jesus the Lord speaks on this occasion is a reference to 'the endowment with which my servants have been endowed in this house' (D&C 110: 9). Brigham Young, for example, received 'a partial endowment in the Kirtland temple' in 1836 though he later received 'a more complete endowment from the Prophet on 4th May 1842' (Backman 1995: 111). Then, in October 1838, a revelation speaks of the necessity of a font for the baptism of the dead along with an entire list of innovative rites of 'anointings, washings' and other 'ordinances' (D&C 124: 29, 39). These innovations relate to 'things that have been kept hid from the foundation of the world' and which 'pertain to the dispensation of the fullness of times'. Within this account of rites that are basic to salvation God calls the Saints to build a new temple, this time at Nauvoo, telling them that their provisional use of more temporary buildings for the performance of what are, in effect, endowment rites will be acceptable only for a limited period. The call to temple building is urgent (D&C 124: 55). Further encouragement, this time to build cities as part of the gathering of the Saints, follows (D&C 125), as does an emphasis upon completing the temple for the rites of the baptism of the dead (D&C 127: 4, 9, 10). Baptism for the dead, along with other doctrines associated with the conquest of death (D&C 128), including that of plural marriage (D&C 132), are obviously becoming pressing issues for Joseph Smith.

As a reflection upon the evolution of theological ideas in the Doctrine and Covenants it is worth comparing Section 132, reckoned to be a revelation of 1843, and Section 133 dated in 1831, which was initially an appendix to the book before gaining full inclusion. The earlier revelation is fully occupied with the millennial ideal of gathering to Zion to prepare for the coming of the Lord and to avoid the negative outcome of divine judgement. The later text, by contrast, is entirely given to the special rites of blessing accomplished at the hands of properly ordained priests as they foster the spiritual development of devotees in becoming 'gods'. Here we can view the two manifestations of Mormonism: the Protestant millenarian and prophetic movement seeking a homeland and building churches, and the post-Protestant priestly mystery-religion preparing its members for apotheosis in their eternal post-mortal realms. Each possessed its own ethos and distinctive attitude to time.

THEOLOGY OF TEMPLES

While Latter-day Saints speak less of the theology of temples than of the doctrine related to their rites or ordinances, it is useful to think rather generally of the theology of temples, given their primacy of place in LDS life. Christian theology has seldom tied doctrine to places, whether geographical or architectural, and while Rome may be significant to Catholics, Canterbury to Anglicans and Geneva to Reformed Protestants, and while church buildings with their altars, pulpits and fonts are deeply significant to each of these traditions, as are many pilgrimage sites, all such locales and objects are not essential: prayer, worship, preaching and the Eucharist can take place anywhere. In earliest Mormonism this was also the case. In hired halls, public places and in the open air, as well as at a local river, Latter-day Saints preached, met together for the sacrament service and baptized converts. In the migration westward they certainly made use of these kinds of provision but they also sought to build temples. After abortive attempts at Kirtland and Nauvoo, and in the final settlement in Utah, they set out to build very permanent temples and, whilst awaiting their completion, they made use of an Endowment House for the key rites that became the focal means of enacting the Church's developing doctrine. In this way LDS theology came to be place-related in both a geographical and architectural sense.

The geographical State of Utah became established as the Mormon heartland in the later 1840s, albeit after the prophet's death in 1844. A concentration of Church leadership into what had been called a 'Head-quarters Culture' made Utah, and its cultural centre Salt Lake City, the dynamic generator of the Church (Quinn 2001: 135–64). Once it seemed as though Zion was not simply going to be in the hills of the Midwest; Latter-day Saint temples built in each major part of the world would ensure that Zion existed within an architectural context rather than in one specific geographical territory. In this limited sense, temples replaced territory as arenas of Zion. This involved a significant theological shift of emphasis from the Second Coming of Christ to the performance of salvation-focused temple ritual. Latter-day Saints would themselves become 'saviours in Zion' as their temple work was undertaken for the good of the dead and the living.

The shift from the religion expressed in the Book of Mormon to that revealed in the Doctrine and Covenants reflected a church moving from its Protestant cradle towards its own more distinctively mature identity. The beliefs and practices surrounding the emergent dominance of temple ideology within LDS culture focus on a crucial cluster of three prime elements, two ritual and one doctrinal: (i) baptism for the dead; (ii) endowments; (iii) 'turning hearts'. The first of these is well known beyond Mormonism, even if only vaguely apprehended; the second is hardly known and seldom discussed publicly in Mormonism outside temple circles; the third is somewhat cryptic as expressed here and would, quite often, not attract sustained attention, not even in LDS groups except in a well-known and even clichéd fashion. Yet this 'turning-hearts' motif, already alluded to in chapter 4 when discussing the spirit world, informs both vicarious baptism and endowments and will, therefore, be treated first.

TURNING HEARTS

If temple followed text, as intimated at the outset of this chapter, they were never more intimately linked in their overlap than in the passage telling how the Lord turns the hearts of fathers to children and children to fathers. This text, arguably the single most influential in Mormonism, closes the Old Testament in the final chapter of the Book of Malachi with a promised day of judgement and destruction of evil people. It recalls the devout to the laws of Moses and promises the coming again of the prophet Elijah, identified as he who will, purposefully, 'turn the hearts of fathers to their children, and the hearts of children to their fathers, lest I come and smite the land with a curse' (Malachi 4: 5).

Law and prophets combine to end the Old Testament with a promise and a curse. Together, these stamped a hallmark upon the entire Book of Mormon but not upon the combination of texts known as the Doctrine and Covenants and the Pearl of Great Price, even though obedience and disobedience would remain a strong undercurrent of LDS spirituality. The difference between the two sources lay in the Doctrine and Covenants' new doctrinal and practical nexus of vicarious baptism and endowment, which were framed by this text on the mutual 'turning of hearts'. Baptism for the dead and covenant-endowments for the conquest of death both found their ultimate validation in the power of the priesthood yet these three elements are absent from the Book of Mormon, whose emphasis upon baptism is always a baptism of repentance of the living for themselves. Indeed the Book of Mormon could almost be described as a manual of personal repentance; a manual for the baptism of the dead it is not. This negative appraisal must, however, be understood in relation to the point made in chapter 4 concerning the salvation of those who lived before Christ and who heard the gospel 'in advance' of its first-century proclamation, even though the explicit treatment of baptism for the dead emerges later. Endowments, by contrast, simply do not exist in the Book of Mormon. Though the word 'ordinance' does occur on some eight or so occasions, its reference is of a general nature and does not refer to such detailed ordinances as are disclosed in the Doctrine and Covenants. This is perfectly intelligible in terms of the Doctrine and Covenants that describes Elijah as holding the power – or 'keys' in the special LDS terminology of authoritative power – of turning hearts; keys that are then passed on to Joseph Smith (D&C 27: 9; 110: 14–16).

While church members in general are encouraged 'to seek diligently to turn' hearts (D&C 98: 16), it is to the central church leadership of Joseph Smith and Oliver Cowdery that the real transfer took place in one of the high-profile revelations that occurred at the Kirtland Temple on 3 April 1836: the Lord announces that 'the time has fully come' for the day of Malachi's prophecy to be fulfilled, when the hearts of fathers and children are turned to each other. Accordingly, Elijah, the ancient prophet who was translated to heaven without tasting death, appears to Joseph and to Oliver Cowdery and into their hands 'the keys of this dispensation are committed'. This itself is a sign 'that the great and dreadful day of the Lord is near, even at the door' (D&C 110: 14–16). It was an additionally significant day for Joseph, for the 'turning heart' text had been cited in his 1823 vision of Moroni. A great deal of opposition from outside the Church beset Joseph over the next few years and it was not until September 1842 that a revelation on baptism for the dead was given, a revelation that can be seen as the crucial fulfilment of the 'heart turning' prophecy.

BAPTISM FOR THE DEAD

As Joseph expressed it, it was precisely when he was 'pursued by his enemies' that the subject of baptism for the dead seemed 'to occupy my mind, and press itself upon my feelings the strongest' (D&C 128: 1). He is very particular in giving instructions on keeping records of those for whom the baptism is performed and of the witnesses to it. 'You may think this order of things to be very particular', he tells them, but it is in accord with divine command and also reflects the biblical text of the Book of Revelation in which the dead have details written of them. The power of biblical passages is both intense and subject to Joseph's distinctive interpretation. Just as the heavenly records are, in fact, the ultimate version of the records being kept on earth, so he takes the biblical notion of apostolic authority by which 'what is bound on earth is bound in heaven' and interprets it to mean 'whatsoever you record on earth is recorded in heaven' (D&C 128: 8, 10). He acknowledges that these commands to baptism and record-keeping of and for the dead 'may seem to some to be a very bold doctrine' and goes to some length to argue that it is the crucial focus of priesthood activity. He invokes St Matthew's record of Jesus telling Peter that he was the rock on which the church would be built and that he would be given the keys of the kingdom; he then brings things to sharpest focus in a verse that is, essentially, one of the foundation stones of Mormon theology.

Now the great and grand secret of the whole matter, and the *summum bonum* of the whole subject that is lying before us, consists in obtaining the power of the Holy Priesthood. For him to whom these keys are given there is no difficulty in obtaining a knowledge of facts in relation to salvation of the children of men, both as well for the dead as for the living. (D&C 128: 11)

The biblical 'keys' and their affinity with the rock-sure foundation of Peter as the basis of Christ's Church are extrapolated into the new Church of Jesus Christ in the latter-days. It is grounded in revealed knowledge and embodied in distinctive individuals. The combination of knowledge and embodiment is a characteristic feature of the developing LDS Church and of the Doctrine and Covenants; this text dramatically demonstrates the disjunction between the Book of Mormon – which is a unity within itself, grounded in ideas of obedience, disobedience, repentance, faith, grace and salvation – and the Doctrine and Covenants and Pearl of Great Price, with their revelation of the power of the priesthood, the conquest of death and the transformation of human nature by the possibility of its divine exaltation, all within the plan of salvation.

If we wished to establish any kind of parallel in Mormon scripture to the Old and New Testament division of the Bible, it would have to be between the Book of Mormon and the Doctrine and Covenants and not within the Book of Mormon itself. The distinctive feature separating the two parts would lie in the plan of salvation's power of the restored priesthood, which alone makes possible both baptism for the dead and the triumph over death in the endowment rite. The notion of the mutual turning of hearts lies precisely in this new capacity of bringing salvation to dead family members as far as the retrospective view is concerned, and in bringing the anticipation and possibility of apotheosis of family members as far as the future is concerned. Joseph leaves us in no uncertainty about the significance of the heart-turning and priesthood power. Indeed, 'the grand secret', the 'whole matter' and the 'whole subject' is nothing less than the 'powers of the Holy Priesthood'. It is worth noting the relatively rare Latin intrusion into the text when Smith refers to the *summum bonum*: it is his way of adding seriousness to 'glory and honor, and immortality and eternal life' (D&C 128: 12). Joseph immediately relates these high themes to the principle of opposition and balance, which have already been documented in chapter 6. Here the opposition is between death and resurrection, with the baptismal font that is symbolic of the grave and the font of resurrection: death is earthly while resurrection is heavenly, just as humanity is first of earth and then of heaven. 'The natural' nature of things is set against the heavenly nature of things. These parallels provide the rationale for the keeping of records on earth, for they, in turn, match the keeping of records in heaven (D&C 128: 14). Yet another balanced opposition is set up between the salvation of the dead and the salvation of the living; it is here that the turning-of-hearts motif finds a powerful expression in the fact that 'their salvation is necessary and essential to our salvation'. The biblical Epistle to the Hebrews is cited to the effect that those long dead of Israel should only be 'made perfect' along with the new believers in Christ, and is combined with the rhetorical text from 1 Corinthians 15 alluding to the baptism of the dead (Hebrews 11: 40; 1 Corinthians 15: 29). These New Testament references lead Joseph to the final citation from Malachi on the turning of hearts. In a starkly lucid fashion Joseph Smith adds that he 'might have rendered a plainer translation' of Malachi but did not do so because 'it is sufficiently plain to suit my purpose as it stands' (D&C 128: 18). That purpose is to explain the 'welding link of some kind or other' between the father and the children, and that link is nothing less than baptism for the dead.

This is a crucial expression of Mormonism's doctrinal creativity, distinguishing the movement both from the Protestant religiosity of Joseph's past and from the entire text of the Book of Mormon. To the practical details of baptism for the dead I will return later; for the moment I remain with this Doctrine and Covenants section, where further ideas are woven into a rich tapestry of Mormon theological belief. Almost all major features come together to display the wonder that is the Restoration in that 'whole and complete and perfect union, and welding together of dispensations, and keys, and powers, and glories', things that have been hidden for ages but now revealed, and revealed in North America (D&C 128: 18, 20). The rest of Section 128 is jubilant, expressing praise to God for these truths and calling on others to respond to them and to complete a temple in which records of this saving work can be presented. Successive chapters exhibit a boldness and sureness of touch, whether in describing the difference between angels and resurrected beings or in interpreting a verse from John's Gospel to the effect that the Father and the Son will make their home with the believer (John 14: 23). Instead of meaning that they will come and 'dwell in a man's heart', which is 'an old sectarian notion, and is false', Joseph is clear that the place of God's residence 'is a great Urim and Thummim', that the earth will itself become such a Urim and Thummim and that each believer will come to possess a Urim and Thummin, these objects being the means of insight and knowledge of truth. Those who gain the celestial kingdom will be given their Urim and Thummim in the form of a white stone, which will bear their secret and new name, a name that is itself a 'key word'.

Here the dynamic-mystical characteristic of Mormon religiosity is manifest. The Urim and Thummim, described in the Old Testament as part of the ceremonial vesture to be worn upon the breastplate by Aaron when approaching the Lord (Exodus 28: 30), had been taken by Joseph to refer to the spectacle-like objects granted to him as the means of translating the plates of the Book of Mormon and now, in his broader usage, it comes to serve as a symbol into which are condensed several kinds of meaning that unite the capacity to access knowledge through mystical power. While disclosing these technical features of the ultimate transformation of the world, he makes additional prophecies that are distinctly world-focused, including the fact that the bloodshed that will precede the Second Coming of Christ will 'be in South Carolina' and may involve 'the slave question'. Moreover, God has told him that the date of that coming will be related to his achieving the age of eighty-five, yet he is unsure if this means he will live to eighty-five to see it, or whether it would come after his death, or even if it did refer to 'the beginning of the millennium' at all (D&C 130: 15–16) Returning to more certain principles, he tells how the level of intelligence attained in this life will be retained in the resurrection, that obedience is crucial to the gaining of divine blessings and, finally, that 'the Father has a body of flesh and bones as tangible as man's; the Son also: but the Holy Ghost has not a body of flesh and bones, but is a personage of Spirit. Were it not so, the Holy Ghost could not dwell in us' (D&C 130: 19–22).

BAPTISING THE DEAD

Amongst Joseph's greatest certainties was the practice and purpose of baptism for the dead. A crucial revelation of January 1841, when the Saints were in Nauvoo, called them to build a house in which the 'Most High' might dwell and within which numerous lost truths might be restored through the activity of the 'fullness of the priesthood', not least through baptism for the dead (D&C 124: 27–34). God acknowledges that they would have to perform baptisms elsewhere until the special house was built but this should not lessen their haste in construction. A further revelation details the necessity of having a witness who is both an eye-witness and also what might be called an ear-witness, one who should 'hear with his ears, that he may testify of a truth'; once more, strict records must be kept and lodged in 'the archives of my holy temple' (D&C 127: 6–9). As we saw earlier, record-keeping was essential since, as with other actions conducted on earth, it possessed a heavenly echo. Earthly records are 'recorded in heaven' precisely so that what is 'bound' or 'loosed' on earth may also be so bound or loosed in heaven. The Doctrine and Covenants goes into considerable detail over record- and certificate-keeping, indeed, as I have already mentioned, the text recognizes this in saying, 'you may think this order of things to be very peculiar' before explaining it as necessary 'to answer the will of God' by firmly fixing 'the salvation of the dead who should die without a knowledge of the gospel' (D&C 128: 5). Here, in two ways, we find an extreme development of the practice of baptism in other Christian churches. First the absolute necessity of baptism for salvation – already present in some Christian sacramental traditions – but extended to the dead as well as the living. This approach clearly and unambiguously addresses itself to the question often ignored by Christianity at large, regarding 'those who die without ever hearing the gospel'. Second, the necessity of record-keeping as the basis of the link between earth and heaven. While most Christian traditions relate earth and heaven through a wide variety of means, including, prayer, worship and afterlife beliefs, LDS theology engages with the interlinking of earth and heaven in a far more extensive and explicit ritual fashion, framed by its doctrine of the spirit world, which was outlined in chapter 4.

As for vicarious baptismal rites, after an initial phase of river baptism they were moved into temples as soon as possible. The rites prompted the architectural feature of a large baptismal font carried upon the backs of twelve oxen, which symbolized the twelve tribes of Israel, and this was usually located in the temple basement. In modern temples these structures continue. Even though the oxen may not always be of bronze, they are large enough to accommodate two people and have a platform to one side of the circle that enables others to be present as well as the formal witness, who today has a visual display unit linked to computer facilities to ensure correct record-keeping. Here an individual is baptized for deceased ancestors. He or she takes the name of the deceased ancestor and may act for numerous such individuals in the course of one session. Such baptism provides the dead, if they wish to avail themselves of it, with the opportunity to accept the LDS message and to progress through the various processes of ordination, marriage and endowments that together bring them to exaltation.

In the earlier history of the Church, members might also be baptized for a wide variety of non-relatives in a way that throws a particular light on the way the Church saw itself as part of the grand scheme of history. It was one way in which the plan of salvation embraced world history. One example will suffice, namely that of Wilford Woodruff (1807–98), to whose part in the ending of polygamy I return in the final chapter. Here, however, we see him in 1877, some twelve years before he became prophet-president, and much in evidence at the dedication of the St George Temple in Utah, preparing the text for the rituals, dressing in white doe-skin temple clothing, and much affected by his experiences. Woodruff, whose own mother had died when he was an infant, suffered much bereavement himself, as when his two-year-old daughter died at home while he was in England. He longed for some sense of the salvation of his dead relatives and when the St George Temple was dedicated, he wrote of a revelation he received there that gave him a sense that his dead had been redeemed. 'I presided at the Temple to day [*sic*]. While praying at the Altar I received a Revelation Concerning the redemption of my dead'; it was like light bursting upon his understanding and he felt like 'shouting Glory Hallalulah to God and the Lamb' (Woodruff 1993: 313). He speaks of helping to conduct numerous endowments and of going through them as if in a dream. For him, religious experience linked his sense of earth and heaven, an important background feature for the one who, in August 1877, was baptized for a hundred persons, including 'the signers of the Declaration of Independence', thereby embracing American history within the plan of salvation. His vicarious baptisms also included, for example, Michael Faraday, Edward Gibbon, Sir Joshua Reynolds, Robert Burns, Goethe, Schiller, Lord Byron and Wordsworth, as well as Napoleon Bonapart and Lord Nelson, David Livingstone, Samuel Johnson and John Wesley. It is unlikely that any more eclectic company of eminent men had ever been brought together in any single religious ritual in the history of the world. His diary rather simply commented: 'it was a very interesting day' (Woodruff 1993: 318). Having been baptized for these and many more, Woodruff exhorted his fellow Saints to undertake other rites on their behalf, especially endowments.

ENDOWMENT

Endowments are crucial. Nowhere do LDS views of divine wonders, eternal states and ritual interconnect more than in endowment rites, rites that explain, prepare for, and confer upon select members both an identity as divine individuals set within eternal relationships and the capacity to conquer death. These rites are not publicized and, for individual Saints, are viewed as precious and sacred. This sacredness is a dominant idea and takes precedence over the element of their secrecy, which is the feature most often pinpointed and criticized in non-Mormon sources. The present concern, however, lies with their soteriological importance for believers. The endowment follows after temple marriage and presupposes it, just as it presupposes an earlier baptism outside the temple as a symbol of repentance. Accordingly, I begin my consideration of it with Doctrine and Covenants Section 131, where the prophet turns to the future life and asserts one of the absolutely distinctive aspects of Mormon theology in which marriage, priesthood and destiny are bound together in a dramatic way. There he reveals that, in the

celestial glory there are three heavens or degrees: And in order to obtain the highest, a man must enter into this order of the priesthood (meaning the new and everlasting covenant of marriage); And if he does not, he cannot obtain it. (D&C 131: 1–3)

Here, then, soteriology, gender and obedience become foundational. In terms of soteriology it takes the celestial realm, itself separate from the terrestrial and telestial realms of glory or heavenly reward (already described in chapter 3), and subdivides it into three. In order to ensure access to the highest of these a man must engage with a form of priesthood, which, together with a form of marriage, comprises what is described as a new and everlasting covenant. In this, gender factors predominate and, while the man is the prime actor, he is as dependent upon a woman as a woman is upon a man: for both, exaltation and marriage cohere and are grounded in obedience. Obedience is not only basic to LDS ethical life, as already intimated in chapter 6, but also to ritual and its eternal consequences.

This intimate alignment of marriage and priesthood is unique in Christian theology. In historical terms it completely inverts the ideal of priesthood and celibacy which Roman Catholicism developed into a binding ideal for all priests and which Greek Orthodoxy applies to its bishops. This demonstrates Mormonism's historical roots in Protestantism and marks another case in which it develops Protestant ideas well beyond any advanced by that source tradition. The Protestant Reformation of the sixteenth century firmly turned its face against celibacy just as it did against the Catholic scheme of sacramental priesthood; indeed, the Protestant doctrine of the priesthood of all believers radically undermined the significance of sacramental priesthood and, in so doing, reduced the significance of men as priests and as controllers of ultimate destiny. Henceforth, individuals would be responsible for themselves before God and in relation to God's grace. Still, churches remained vital for Protestants, and the congregation of the faithful furnished the arena within which the word was read, preached and received, where baptism and the Lord's Supper might be enjoyed as sacraments fostering the life of faith and where God was collectively worshipped. Still, the ministers of these churches were, essentially, like any other member of the congregation except that they had been selected and appointed to act as leaders, delegated to deploy for the common good that priesthood which all believers actually possessed individually.

Among the theological elements that bring distinctive power to the LDS theology of priesthood is the notion of agency. Agency, as the potential for decision and action, needs to become a willed desire of individuals to serve God and to seek exaltation through the restored priesthoods. The Melchizedek priesthood was derived from Peter, James and John, who visited Joseph Smith and Oliver Cowdery and ordained them, following an earlier ordination when John the Baptist ordained the pair into the Aaronic, or lower, priesthood. Ideally, the entire male membership of the Church is a membership of priests. This might, at first, seem a strange form of organization but it makes sense in view of the Protestant background of the priesthood of all believers on the one hand, and the LDS necessity for marriage on the other. Men cannot fully exercise their priesthood outside marriage and women cannot fully benefit from the power of the Melchizedek priesthood unless they are married to a member of it. Only in an everlasting covenanted union can both male and female benefit from the glorious power of the priesthood.

The very expression 'power of the priesthood' reflects within Mormonism something of the value invested in prime religious ideals in other religious groups as, for example, in the very word 'priesthood' in the sacramental traditions of Catholicism and Anglicanism. In Mormonism priesthood, directed by agency and combined with covenant, yields a core spirituality that adds up to more than the sum of its parts and underlies all church and family life. This is because priesthood is incomprehensible without marriage and priesthood-marriage is incomprehensible without temple rites.

TEMPLE MARRIAGE

Temple marriage has changed a great deal since the days of Joseph Smith especially through the cessation of plural marriage. From a relatively early period LDS marriage involved polygamy, or plural marriage or spiritual marriage as the Saints often called it. This lasted from the 1840s until its official ending at the close of the nineteenth century, though a few were contracted into the first decade of the twentieth century as far as the Church of Jesus Christ of Latter-day Saints was concerned; it is still practised by some other restoration groups, as I detail in chapter 9. Twentieth-century temple marriage focused on monogamy and the growing ideals of LDS family life described earlier. Here I begin with a brief discussion of the early period before passing to selected features of contemporary aspects of LDS family life, given that chapter 7 has already dealt with more mundane aspects.

SEALING

The essence of temple marriage is that a man and woman are joined together through the power and authority of an officiating Melchizedek priest. This 'sealing', as it is called, is not a simple union until death parts the pair, but is for eternity. Herein lies what ultimately distinguishes LDS temple marriage either from LDS marriage in local chapels or from non-LDS unions whether conducted by other Christian churches or by civic authority. Precisely because it takes place in that sacred place where time and eternity meet, and is conducted under the power of the officiating person who holds the necessary high-priesthood authority and power, what is done on earth will have heavenly consequences. People married in the local LDS meeting house, stakehouse or chapel, none of which carries the symbolic significance of a temple, will simply be married for time – 'till death us do part', as the popular phrase taken from the Anglican *Book of Common Prayer* expressed it – just as they would if they were married in any other church or at a civic ceremony. Children, too, experience the sealing rite, for children need to be sealed to their parents and parents to children in order that they be together as a family unit after this life.

Contemporary temples have special sealing-rooms that are dedicated to the purpose of marriage. Other rooms are also set aside for the bride to prepare her dress for the rite. The sealing room has at its centre an altar structure, usually with a padded surface and a kneeling platform on each side. The couple kneel facing each other and their hands meet across the top of the altar. The officiant seals the pair through a prayer-blessing, invoking the power of his priesthood to unite them for time and eternity. This is witnessed by other family members who are qualified to be in the temple.

TEXTUAL BACKGROUND

The revelation covering what would come to be called temple marriage was presented in language of considerable seriousness and set against examples drawn from the Bible. Joseph must prepare himself to receive it, and disobedience would come at the cost of damnation. Here, in Doctrine and Covenants Section 132, the Mormon religion of restoration announces itself through a complex rationale of divine commandments, given to ancient patriarchs, concerning polygamy and adultery, emphasizing the need for rites to be performed on earth if they are to have an effect in heaven. Amidst these most serious instructions come very direct words addressed to Joseph Smith's wife, Emma, to the effect that she should believe, accept and practise the newly revealed commands on plural marriage. The import of this text demands some detailed consideration.

At the outset of Section 132 comes one of the Doctrine and Covenants' 'question–revelation' items, as I called them in chapter 2. In this case the prompting issue is the polygamy of Abraham, Isaac, Jacob, Moses, David and Solomon. The revelation the Lord is about to give on this topic through the mouth of Joseph Smith is a dynamic and potentially dangerous one in that 'those who have this law revealed to them must obey the same' (D&C 132: 3). Once more, not to obey is to be damned and denied divine glory. The power to oversee the implementation of the truth enshrined in this new 'law' is vested in Joseph Smith. He it is who must implement this law and he must do it on earth because all covenants or contracts – and here the text lists no fewer than ten such agreements – must be established on earth if they are to be eternally effective. It will not be possible to contract them in the afterlife. Much as we have seen above, the effectiveness of all contracts in the afterlife depends upon their original earthly enactment. When conducted under this proper authority, they take effect for time and for eternity (D&C 132: 19).

Having been sealed for time and eternity, a married couple who meet the moral, doctrinal and economic demands of the Church may take their endowments. Joseph Smith first introduced the notion of endowment for men who had proved themselves in God's service and who, whilst yet living, could be sealed for exaltation, in other words their eternal destiny was ensured prior to their death. Preliminary to the actual endowment, individuals receive special washing with water and anointing with oil, accompanied by special prayers or blessings. Various parts of the body are set apart for their service to God prior to the individual being vested with the temple garment, a form of undergarment covering chest and lower body.

Vested with additional temple clothing, members set about the endowment proper. It is both an educative and dedicatory rite concerning the plan of salvation that extends from pre-existence through mortality to post-mortem existence, as already described in chapters 1 and 3. Historically, this occurred through dramatic representations, often in different rooms such as creation and world rooms with appropriate murals; in more recent times films have replaced actors but in either case the initiate is part of a sacred drama that comes to embrace and frame their own individual and family life. Vows are taken to bring the believer into a covenant with God. Hand shakes and arm movements are learned, and a new and secret name is given when the initiate moves through the symbolic veil of the temple from the terrestrial into the celestial room, the latter symbolizing the highest heavenly realms. This happens first to the male as husband and then to his partner. Just as someone plays the part of God to the male so the male comes to play the part of God to his wife. She receives a special name known only to her husband, the name by which she will be called to life in her resurrection. Basic to these endowments is the idea of the conquest of death. This cannot be underestimated, for the very purpose of endowment was to prepare believers for their new status as divine agents; it was part of the process of apotheosis, of the making of Gods, and intrinsic to that process was the conquest of death. Devotees were given signs and special formulae so that they could pass through the gates of death along with all the guardians of those mysterious paths. Invested with the powers of the priesthood, and holding the 'keys' of knowledge and the means of implementing them, the believer was more than equal to the perils that beset the deceased. The significance of endowments for the living was reinforced when endowments for the dead were introduced in 1877. Starting in a limited way, this involvement of the dead in the overall strategy of salvation and exaltation grew, so that, for example, the one hundred millionth was conducted in 1988 (Cowan 1992: 1455).

Another and higher-level rite has also been periodically available for dedicated LDS couples in the form of second anointings, which take place in the special temple room, the holy of holies, at the Salt Lake Temple. It is currently unclear whether other temples are to have similar rooms dedicated for this purpose or whether the rites themselves may be put on hold until the millennium itself arrives (Quinn 2001: 159). Still, typically, the husband is anointed with oil as 'a king and priest unto God to rule and reign in the House of Israel forever', and then the wife is anointed, 'as a queen and priestess to her husband, to rule and reign with him in his kingdom forever' (Buerger 1994: 66–7). Both husband and wife have special blessings conferred on them, with the details recorded for posterity. As part of that ritual process, there remains a further rite, a kind of continuation of this second blessing, but one taking place within the home and not at the temple. It is, essentially, a private rite between husband and wife. He dedicates the home in a special way and she washes his feet. This echoes the biblical event in which Mary Magdalene washes Jesus' feet as a symbolic act that indicates his forthcoming death. Buerger describes this rite not only in terms of the husband being prepared for burial but also as the wife laying 'claim upon him in the resurrection'. He even sees in this an echo of some early Mormon opinion that Jesus had been married to Mary and Martha (Buerger 1994: 67). In strictly LDS theological terms there would be no objection to Jesus having been married – indeed it would fit better with the ideal of consecrated unions entered into for eternity than would an unmarried and celibate individual. Mormonism does not carry with it the same negative view of sexuality and the body that underlay a considerable amount of earlier Christian theology, especially that of some Christian Church Fathers in the fourth and fifth centuries who so easily linked sex with sin, which was therefore unacceptable in the Saviour.

Rites of sealing grew in significance throughout early Mormonism and paralleled, to a degree, Joseph Smith's progressive revelations on the very nature of salvation and on the nature of the priesthood. The introduction of high priests in 1831 gave them the capacity to 'seal' people; further foot-washing rites to cleanse individuals from the moral pollution of their day followed in 1832 and further depth was added through the endowments at Kirtland in 1836. As Buerger has argued, the further revelation on heaven as an internally divided place was aligned with the 'higher ordinance, or second anointing' of 1843, making soteriological doctrines and practices quite different from what they had been at the time of the publication of the Book of Mormon in 1830. In fact he described this period of developing revelations and rites that offered new levels of spiritual opportunity as one of 'the fullness that was never full' (Buerger 1989: 166–7). These rites were administered to forty-four couples by Joseph prior to his death, but to some '5000 people in two months – from December 1845 to February 1846' by Brigham Young and other apostles (Quinn 2001: 140). Joseph's death in 1844 added a degree of urgency to the ongoing completion of temples as venues for gaining all these endowments and all entailed by them.

TEMPLE GARMENT

One feature of the endowments was, and is, the temple garment. This is particularly significant in LDS life because it is the mark of having obtained one's endowments and of both the individual commitment and formal act of covenanting with God involved in so doing. Because endowed Mormons continue to wear the temple garment under their ordinary clothes during daily life, it becomes part of their embodiment as temple Mormons. Theologically, it is as though the temple moves back out into the wider world in and through this garment: just as the inside of the temple is a sacred and secret place so is the garment. Saints are encouraged not to reveal it to non-Mormons. They are sold in special church-outlets and should be worn with modesty. As might be expected from such a sacred symbol that becomes part of everyday and intimate life, the temple garment has attracted a great deal of folk belief. Church leaders have sometimes had to restrain this, as in the case of the notion that the garment would prevent soldiers from being shot during active service. Similarly, some mothers might wish to retain contact with their garment while giving birth. In practical terms the physical style of the garment has changed several times with an ongoing trend of abbreviation in the length of arms and legs.

TIME AND ETERNITY

To wear the garment is to be set within a world-view that differs from that of Gentile neighbours and marks the ongoing differentiation of Mormonism from other forms of Christianity. In addition to clothing and, for example, food rules, Mormonism's transition from an Adventist, millenarian, sect to its own form of distinctive church aimed at worldwide evangelism and the transcendence of death is also marked by its attitude to time. Even though this transition would not fully emerge until after Joseph Smith's death and not, in effect, until the move from the nineteenth into the twentieth century, its classification of duration began with the prophet, largely in the early 1840s.

Millenarian Mormonism, classically represented in the epics and events of the Book of Mormon, speaks with urgency concerning immediate activities. All must repent and be forgiven and prepare for the coming of the Lord. There is urgency about the need to gather to Zion to achieve this. The major end-point involved the coming of Christ and the two resurrections. In this Mormons differed in relatively minor detail from other Adventist groups. It was in the new revelation on priesthood and celestial marriage that a conceptual change, a theological paradigm shift, took place as the decade-old group moved towards becoming what I described in chapter 2 as a post-Protestant priestly mystery-religion that prepares devotees for apotheosis in the afterlife. Just as its Protestant millenarian form possessed its attitude to time, one of urgent gathering for Christ's imminent return, so its mystery-religion form generated an attitude to eternity whose focus lay in post-mortem life. A new time-space element appears. While the millenarian locale of salvation would be on a transformed earth, the mystical arena would be somewhere beyond.

The linking feature that allowed this shift to take place was that of resurrection. The millenarian outlook saw the resurrection as the means by which people faced the coming Christ for judgement, whether in the first resurrection of the faithful or in the second and general resurrection of all humanity. In that perspective resurrection was the goal. While the mystical outlook also focused on the resurrection, it was on resurrection as a beginning, as the gateway to eternity. It was not so much resurrection and the day of judgement that were crucial for the Latter-day Saint but resurrection and the events that followed after it. Under the new order, those engaging in the new form of marriage that was introduced by Joseph Smith would come forth in the first resurrection – or perhaps in the second, for the text admits of that possibility – to inherit 'thrones, principalities, and converts to Mormonism, especially Heber C. Kimball, Newell K. Witney, John C. Bennett and Brigham Young, were all Masons and some were very close companions and advisors to the prophet (Buerger 1994: 44, 49–50). Buerger suggests that Smith's general sense of fear of enemies, along with the benefits to be gained from secrecy, might have fostered his interest in the movement, not to mention Smith's growing 'preoccupation with ancient mysteries'. Whatever the motivations might have been, Joseph Smith became a Freemason, going through the three grades of entered apprentice, fellow craft and master mason, on 15 and 16 March 1842. It was seven weeks later that Joseph introduced the endowment ritual at Nauvoo. As already intimated, these rites were conducted in a meeting room rather than a temple because the Nauvoo Temple was not completed until early in 1846, approximately a year and a half after Joseph Smith's death. This is a telling point as far as the future of the LDS movement was concerned because it underscores the dramatic importance of Smith's introduction of a cluster of practices before he died, practices that would flourish and provide a major ritual process for the future development of this religion. What is more, this innovation came in time to encourage the Saints in a task on which they could focus and that would help to carry them through the bitter period in 1844 when Joseph was killed. This deep dual theological challenge, to both the creative minds and the hands of leaders and members at large, was likely to have been a considerable stabilizing force during this most turbulent period of earlier Mormonism.

ARCHITECTURE AND THEOLOGICAL PURPOSE

When referring above to temple marriage, I alluded to the significance of particular rooms in LDS temples. Here I can develop that point because it marks a real difference between the LDS and other churches, which have far fewer purpose-built spaces within their buildings and certainly do not set aside special rooms in which to conduct marriages. In Catholic, and in Protestant churches of a more sacramental nature, the marriage rite is conducted in the main body of the church, as are all other rites. LDS temples, by contrast, are architecturally distinctive and must be theologically understood as possessing special spaces for particular tasks. In the Kirtland Temple, for example, one of the major spaces was so organized that special curtains could be lowered to divide it into sections when required for different groupings of the priesthood and women.

It is occasionally possible for people who are not Latter-day Saints to visit temples, usually for a limited period prior to the dedication or rededication

powers, dominions, all heights and depths' (D&C 132: 19). Having passed out of this world, and due to the benefits made possible through Joseph as God's servant, they would 'be full of force' and be able to 'pass by the angels, and the gods, which are set there' as they move into their own 'exaltation and glory' when 'they shall be as gods, because they have no end… because they have all power, and the angels are subject to them' (D&C 132: 19–20).

DIVINE JUDGEMENT

To set up these two descriptive types of Mormonism, millenarian and mystical, is to raise an enigmatic theological issue concerning the place of divine judgement. From today's perspective in the early twenty-first century it is doubtless the case that divine judgement plays a serious part in Mormon spirituality, where ethical performance and obedience to moral rules are related to the reward given and glories obtained in the afterlife. In the immediate context in which the revelations of the Doctrine and Covenants were given, however, the question of judgement and afterlife does not seem to be so simple. More to the point, it would not seem improper to see divine judgement as belonging less to the day of Christ's second advent than to the day when the devotee was presented with Joseph Smith's new revelation of the 'order of priesthood consisting in the new and everlasting covenant of marriage' (D&C 131: 2). When the text says that those who do not accept this law 'are damned', and that salvation depends upon entering into this law, it suggests that judgement has come into the present moment and depends upon a person's response to the divine command (D&C 132: 4, 6, 32). The power given to Joseph reinforces this view because the crucial Section 132 of Doctrine and Covenants sets firmly under his control the capacity to forgive sin and to seal benefits on earth, with a consequent divine acknowledgement that they will be forgiven and sealed in heaven. This again is a form of judgement that is vested in Joseph Smith (D&C 132: 46–50). Another of his powers was to give a suitably innocent and qualified woman to a man as wife 'by the power of my Holy Priesthood' specifically conferred upon him. In these closely related verses the capacity to judge and to seal in eternal marriage are aligned.

FROM ADVENT TO TEMPLES

In other words, judgement in early Mormonism involved obedience to the call of the prophet to gather to prepare for Christ's coming. Within decades of the founding of the Church, obedience also came to mean acceptance of polygamy. But polygamy as a special form of covenant went hand in hand with the emergence of special buildings for the covenant's enactment and these, in due time became temples. As Christ's Second Coming had not happened, these temples increasingly became the arena for rites involving formal levels of obedience for expected behaviour and commitment to the Church.

We have already seen how LDS sacred texts move on a theological continuum from a standard form of Christian millenarianism through to the conquest of death in an apotheosis gained through ethical achievement but, so far, I have mentioned only that ritual places evolved to match this development: this now needs to be demonstrated in more detail. It involves a dramatic movement from simplicity to complexity, both in theology and in a parallel architectural intent. The first Doctrine and Covenants reference to building is to the building of a house for Joseph in which to 'live and translate' (D&C 41: 7). This is rather pragmatic, as are references to 'houses of worship' (D&C 42: 35); similarly the reference to the Lord suddenly coming to his temple is an echo of a biblical text (D&C 42: 36). The broad command of earlier Mormonism is to 'build up churches unto me' (D&C 45: 64). And this is the general background to the Kirtland temple, Mormonism's first venture in temple building.

KIRTLAND TEMPLE

'For all practical purposes the temple functioned as a meeting-house' reflecting the 'relatively uncomplicated Mormon behavioural and theological tenets of the 1830s' and demonstrating established pattern books of building design that were then readily available (van Wagoner 1994: 169). Even the introduction of foot-washing, as a preparation for the religious blessings anticipated at the completion of the temple, was well known from the Bible and would have been familiar to Rigdon since the 1820s when he was part of the Sandemanians, a Protestant group that originated in Scotland and had a strong commitment to a reasoned faith; amongst their number was the eminent scientist Michael Faraday. In 1835 the leaders also practised, for the first time, a washing of their bodies along with an anointing with 'holy oil', apparently in the form of 'whiskey perfumed with cinnamon' (van Wagoner 1994: 170). As already discussed in chapter 3, this day of the first ordinance, 21 January 1836, was highly significant for Mormon doctrine, as for Joseph Smith's own emotional life, for it was during the ceremonies that he

received a vision of his dead brother Alvin as well as of 'all children who died before arriving at the age of accountability' (van Wagoner 1994: 170). The benefits of this temple were, however, short lived, for by 1838 most of the Saints had left Kirtland and abandoned their temple as they removed themselves from political and social hostility.

MASONIC INFLUENCE AND THE NAUVOO TEMPLE

We have already seen in chapter 1 how Freemasonry made an impact upon early Mormonism. This was particularly apparent as far as the emergence of LDS temples was concerned and became increasingly apparent in the activities of the Nauvoo Temple, the next raised by Mormons after Kirtland. This was a distinctly important venture because it was finally completed only after the death of Joseph Smith. Shortly before his death Joseph had, in a more ordinary building, introduced core leaders to the rites that would develop into major channels of LDS religiosity within the Nauvoo and subsequent temples. In one sense the dedication of many Saints to complete Nauvoo's temple carried the Church through its period of institutional bereavement and leadership change, fostered, no doubt, by Brigham Young's deep conviction of and adherence to the ideas Joseph had taught him. It did not matter that Nauvoo and its temple would also be abandoned as the Saints moved on yet again, for they had raised a temple to vindicate Joseph's life and teaching. It had also served as the arena of their own initiation into the rapidly evolving theology of the Latter-day movement.

While, at first glance, the entire realm of Mormon temples can appear so distinctively different from other Christian traditions, it is wise to note that many features already existed in other groups, not least in Masonry. Freemasonry had undergone a major transition in the later seventeenth and early eighteenth centuries in that guilds of actual, or operative, stonemasons were adopted by freethinking and intellectual individuals who came to call themselves speculative masons. This was particularly the case in Great Britain and elsewhere in Europe where major lodges and associations of Freemasons emerged before spreading to America in the later eighteenth century (Brooke 1994: 140–6). As Buerger demonstrated, 'Smith's official experience in Freemasonry began five months before the first Nauvoo endowment' (Buerger 1994: 50). His reference to 'official experience' is important because he also documents the more informal, yet none the less potentially significant, fact that Joseph Smith's brother Hyram and possibly his father, had become Masons prior to 1827. Similarly, several key of the founding of the Church, obedience also came to mean acceptance of polygamy. But polygamy as a special form of covenant went hand in hand with the emergence of special buildings for the covenant's enactment and these, in due time became temples. As Christ's Second Coming had not happened, these temples increasingly became the arena for rites involving formal levels of obedience for expected behaviour and commitment to the Church.

We have already seen how LDS sacred texts move on a theological continuum from a standard form of Christian millenarianism through to the conquest of death in an apotheosis gained through ethical achievement but, so far, I have mentioned only that ritual places evolved to match this development: this now needs to be demonstrated in more detail. It involves a dramatic movement from simplicity to complexity, both in theology and in a parallel architectural intent. The first Doctrine and Covenants reference to building is to the building of a house for Joseph in which to 'live and translate' (D&C 41: 7). This is rather pragmatic, as are references to 'houses of worship' (D&C 42: 35); similarly the reference to the Lord suddenly coming to his temple is an echo of a biblical text (D&C 42: 36). The broad command of earlier Mormonism is to 'build up churches unto me' (D&C 45: 64). And this is the general background to the Kirtland temple, Mormonism's first venture in temple building.

KIRTLAND TEMPLE

'For all practical purposes the temple functioned as a meeting-house' reflecting the 'relatively uncomplicated Mormon behavioural and theological tenets of the 1830s' and demonstrating established pattern books of building design that were then readily available (van Wagoner 1994: 169). Even the introduction of foot-washing, as a preparation for the religious blessings anticipated at the completion of the temple, was well known from the Bible and would have been familiar to Rigdon since the 1820s when he was part of the Sandemanians, a Protestant group that originated in Scotland and had a strong commitment to a reasoned faith; amongst their number was the eminent scientist Michael Faraday. In 1835 the leaders also practised, for the first time, a washing of their bodies along with an anointing with 'holy oil', apparently in the form of 'whiskey perfumed with cinnamon' (van Wagoner 1994: 170). As already discussed in chapter 3, this day of the first ordinance, 21 January 1836, was highly significant for Mormon doctrine, as for Joseph Smith's own emotional life, for it was during the ceremonies that he powers, dominions, all heights and depths' (D&C 132: 19). Having passed out of this world, and due to the benefits made possible through Joseph as God's servant, they would 'be full of force' and be able to 'pass by the angels, and the gods, which are set there' as they move into their own 'exaltation and glory' when 'they shall be as gods, because they have no end... because they have all power, and the angels are subject to them' (D&C 132: 19–20).

DIVINE JUDGEMENT

To set up these two descriptive types of Mormonism, millenarian and mystical, is to raise an enigmatic theological issue concerning the place of divine judgement. From today's perspective in the early twenty-first century it is doubtless the case that divine judgement plays a serious part in Mormon spirituality, where ethical performance and obedience to moral rules are related to the reward given and glories obtained in the afterlife. In the immediate context in which the revelations of the Doctrine and Covenants were given, however, the question of judgement and afterlife does not seem to be so simple. More to the point, it would not seem improper to see divine judgement as belonging less to the day of Christ's second advent than to the day when the devotee was presented with Joseph Smith's new revelation of the 'order of priesthood consisting in the new and everlasting covenant of marriage' (D&C 131: 2). When the text says that those who do not accept this law 'are damned', and that salvation depends upon entering into this law, it suggests that judgement has come into the present moment and depends upon a person's response to the divine command (D&C 132: 4, 6, 32). The power given to Joseph reinforces this view because the crucial Section 132 of Doctrine and Covenants sets firmly under his control the capacity to forgive sin and to seal benefits on earth, with a consequent divine acknowledgement that they will be forgiven and sealed in heaven. This again is a form of judgement that is vested in Joseph Smith (D&C 132: 46–50). Another of his powers was to give a suitably innocent and qualified woman to a man as wife 'by the power of my Holy Priesthood' specifically conferred upon him. In these closely related verses the capacity to judge and to seal in eternal marriage are aligned.

FROM ADVENT TO TEMPLES

In other words, judgement in early Mormonism involved obedience to the call of the prophet to gather to prepare for Christ's coming. Within decades received a vision of his dead brother Alvin as well as of 'all children who died before arriving at the age of accountability' (van Wagoner 1994. 170). The benefits of this temple were, however, short lived, for by 1838 most of the Saints had left Kirtland and abandoned their temple as they removed themselves from political and social hostility.

MASONIC INFLUENCE AND THE NAUVOO TEMPLE

We have already seen in chapter 1 how Freemasonry made an impact upon early Mormonism. This was particularly apparent as far as the emergence of LDS temples was concerned and became increasingly apparent in the activities of the Nauvoo Temple, the next raised by Mormons after Kirtland. This was a distinctly important venture because it was finally completed only after the death of Joseph Smith. Shortly before his death Joseph had, in a more ordinary building, introduced core leaders to the rites that would develop into major channels of LDS religiosity within the Nauvoo and subsequent temples. In one sense the dedication of many Saints to complete Nauvoo's temple carried the Church through its period of institutional bereavement and leadership change, fostered, no doubt, by Brigham Young's deep conviction of and adherence to the ideas Joseph had taught him. It did not matter that Nauvoo and its temple would also be abandoned as the Saints moved on yet again, for they had raised a temple to vindicate Joseph's life and teaching. It had also served as the arena of their own initiation into the rapidly evolving theology of the Latter-day movement.

While, at first glance, the entire realm of Mormon temples can appear so distinctively different from other Christian traditions, it is wise to note that many features already existed in other groups, not least in Masonry. Freemasonry had undergone a major transition in the later seventeenth and early eighteenth centuries in that guilds of actual, or operative, stonemasons were adopted by freethinking and intellectual individuals who came to call themselves speculative masons. This was particularly the case in Great Britain and elsewhere in Europe where major lodges and associations of Freemasons emerged before spreading to America in the later eighteenth century (Brooke 1994: 140–6). As Buerger demonstrated, 'Smith's official experience in Freemasonry began five months before the first Nauvoo endowment' (Buerger 1994: 50). His reference to 'official experience' is important because he also documents the more informal, yet none the less potentially significant, fact that Joseph Smith's brother Hyram and possibly his father, had become Masons prior to 1827. Similarly, several key converts to Mormonism, especially Heber C. Kimball, Newell K. Witney, John C. Bennett and Brigham Young, were all Masons and some were very close companions and advisors to the prophet (Buerger 1994: 44, 49–50). Buerger suggests that Smith's general sense of fear of enemies, along with the benefits to be gained from secrecy, might have fostered his interest in the movement, not to mention Smith's growing 'preoccupation with ancient mysteries'. Whatever the motivations might have been, Joseph Smith became a Freemason, going through the three grades of entered apprentice, fellow craft and master mason, on 15 and 16 March 1842. It was seven weeks later that Joseph introduced the endowment ritual at Nauvoo. As already intimated, these rites were conducted in a meeting room rather than a temple because the Nauvoo Temple was not completed until early in 1846, approximately a year and a half after Joseph Smith's death. This is a telling point as far as the future of the LDS movement was concerned because it underscores the dramatic importance of Smith's introduction of a cluster of practices before he died, practices that would flourish and provide a major ritual process for the future development of this religion. What is more, this innovation came in time to encourage the Saints in a task on which they could focus and that would help to carry them through the bitter period in 1844 when Joseph was killed. This deep dual theological challenge, to both the creative minds and the hands of leaders and members at large, was likely to have been a considerable stabilizing force during this most turbulent period of earlier Mormonism.

ARCHITECTURE AND THEOLOGICAL PURPOSE

When referring above to temple marriage, I alluded to the significance of particular rooms in LDS temples. Here I can develop that point because it marks a real difference between the LDS and other churches, which have far fewer purpose-built spaces within their buildings and certainly do not set aside special rooms in which to conduct marriages. In Catholic, and in Protestant churches of a more sacramental nature, the marriage rite is conducted in the main body of the church, as are all other rites. LDS temples, by contrast, are architecturally distinctive and must be theologically understood as possessing special spaces for particular tasks. In the Kirtland Temple, for example, one of the major spaces was so organized that special curtains could be lowered to divide it into sections when required for different groupings of the priesthood and women.

It is occasionally possible for people who are not Latter-day Saints to visit temples, usually for a limited period prior to the dedication or rededication of a temple, but at any other time only accredited Saints may attend. One feature that often strikes non-Mormons if they take this opportunity to visit what we might call the classic LDS temples – those built in the late nineteenth century and throughout the twentieth century- is that they contain very many rooms rather than a single and major central space. As they are rather large buildings, the cultural expectation is that temples will resemble the great cathedrals of Christendom, which are typified by a single central space for the gathering of large numbers of people for worship. Even when, as in Catholic Cathedrals, there may be many side altars, they too open into the central nave. Classic LDS temples, by contrast, are not places of collective worship in the same way; such worship belongs more to the local chapel or stakehouse or at local tabernacles, as some early local meeting houses were called, many of which still exist in established LDS communities in Utah.

The Mormon temple is a hive of activity – it is no accident that Saints speak of 'temple work', for work is precisely what is taking place within them. Here one might take Max Weber's long-established sociological notion of the Protestant work ethic and use it to model a notion of the Mormon work ethic (see pp. 159–62). There would be more to that simple borrowing than initially meets the eye, given the discussion in chapter 4 on the relationship between 'works', faith and grace in LDS and in broad Christian theology. The point is that the work undertaken in the temple becomes the vehicle for the potential salvation and exaltation of the dead and of the living. One of the reasons why Protestant Christians often find it difficult to understand the LDS view of such 'works' lies in the fact that Protestants have nothing like the temple as a space in which to engage in 'saving work', an issue to which I return in the final chapter.

Architecturally, classic LDS temples possess an internal division of space in which ordinary church members move from the basement, where the font is housed, through various floors with rooms representing the creation and the fall, and the world room representing the state of current affairs, before passing through the veil of the temple into the celestial room. This progression is both educative and performative. The rooms are educative as 'classrooms' in which initiates learn doctrinal aspects of the plan of salvation, by which families may develop together towards the celestial realms. Here knowledge is contextualized and often related to visual forms of teaching, whether through murals or film or, as in the earliest days, in enacted formal dramas with actors representing various heavenly personages and human individuals. These rooms are also contexts for performative activity as initiates make vows and learn special hand and arm movements.

It is through specific acts that, for example, husband and wife are finally accepted through the veil of the temple and, symbolically, become god and goddess together. Through learning and action, more passive and more active endeavours, Latter-day Saints enter into covenants with God and with each other that are believed to be the basis upon which death may be conquered and the life of eternity entered into through clear acts of personal and family commitment. Yet, the overall activist mood engendered by temple endeavour may be one factor contributing to the sense of failure that some Saints experience in their wider life. The attitude needed for temple work, as also for missionary work, as discussed in chapter 9, could militate against the more receptive state required for engagement with divine love. Whether that is the case or not, the Church is set on an extensive project for the building of many more temples, matching its earlier expansion and growth. In 1997 the President, Gordon B. Hinckley, set as his task the establishing of a hundred temples by the close of the year 2000. This included an increasing number of 'small, beautiful, serviceable temples' that would ensure that the essential nature of Mormonism would be present and distributed throughout the world (*Almanac* 2001–2002: 2). Not only does this building programme express the geographical extension of Zion but it also echoes the history of the Church, for it includes a new temple at Nauvoo to replace Mormonism's historic temple that was burned by fire in 1848 after the Saints departed for Utah.

CHAPTER 9

Identity, opposition and expansion

Salvation and exaltation are the two strands of Mormon soteriology that combine in the Church's single nature as a missionary movement. In this final chapter we see how these two messages reflect stages in the development of the group, and how their complex combination allowed it to flourish and expand, despite external and internal opposition. Mormonism was amongst the fullest manifestations of the new 'missionary' Christianity of the late eighteenth and early nineteenth centuries but, in taking up the dead as well as the unconverted living, it advanced beyond many of the others; this has prompted the question whether it is now becoming the next major world religion. This chapter's emphasis upon Mormonism's missionary nature, in terms of the salvation of converts and of the exaltation of both the living and the dead, finally brings together these two strands of soteriology that have run together throughout this book and highlight them as a key aspect of the movement's ongoing success. To ponder the growth and development of the Church of Jesus Christ of Latter-day Saints and the opposition it has engendered inevitably involves an account of polygamy and of that Mormon fundamentalism which takes LDS ideas in a distinctly conservative direction, just as it demands a description of the Reorganized movement which takes it closer to mainstream Christianity.

CHURCH IDENTITY

From the outset Mormonism grew and expanded, but not without suffering internal division and external opposition. Internal differences of doctrinal opinion and claims concerning leadership were exacerbated by Joseph's death in 1844, while subsequent events, especially government opposition over the issue of polygamy, redirected the political and religious path taken by the Church in the twentieth century. Although at the outset of the twenty-first century the Church is, in many theological respects, far removed from that of the 1830s, it still carries within its theology and practice clear doctrinal markers of its successive stages of growth. The success of Mormonism has consisted in a fortunate combination of these elements and the outcome amounts to more than the sum of the parts.

The changing identity of the Church is manifested in the names it has favoured for itself. 'The Church of Christ' was the first name given to Joseph Smith's movement in 1830. Soon afterwards, it was loosely called the Church of the Latter-day Saints and only arrived at the Church of Jesus Christ of Latter-day Saints in 1838 (D&C 115: 4). For much of its history outsiders have called it the Mormon Church, often using that name in a derogatory fashion whilst members have been content to refer to themselves in the simple abbreviation LDS. In 1995 the Church further adjusted its name, when appearing in logo form, to increase the font size of 'Jesus Christ' and to reduce that of 'The Church of. . . of Latter-day Saints'. This stress on 'Jesus Christ' by the Utah-based church was pressed further in 2001 when Elder Dallin H. Oaks, one of the Twelve Apostles, said that while the full name of the Church had been given by revelation, the leadership wished that secondary references should call it 'the Church of Jesus Christ' rather than the 'Mormon Church' (Niebuhr, G. 2001: 8). Even so, I have throughout this book retained 'Mormon', LDS, or the full title as the more familiar terms of reference.

This issue of name reflects a tension of considerable importance regarding the nature of the Church's Christian identity and relationship with other churches. At the simplest level, LDS leaders see the Church as Christian because Jesus Christ plays a considerable part in its theological plan of salvation. They see the Bible as important and, implicitly, identify the period of Christ's earthly ministry as foundational for the history of Christianity and as the basis for the Restoration through Joseph Smith. 'Christian' thus expresses a connection with the early and authoritative nature of a 'church' of God. 'Christian' also carries a highly positive significance in many parts of the world, not least in the United States, and leaders would wish to be seen as part of that religious heritage. This is a complex issue, however, because leaders also seek to avoid being thought of as 'not Christian'. Not to be viewed as Christian would be a fundamental problem for LDS leaders even though, in any fully developed discussion, they would want to clearly assert their difference from other 'Christian' churches, precisely because they consider themselves to be the one true church. So it is that the name 'Christian' comes with both benefits and costs: whether to be identified with those who do not have the fullness of truth but who carry a certain degree of authenticity in the public's mind or to stand quite clear of any confusing association and yet be perceived by many as more marginal, especially beyond the United States. The Church has chosen the path of public identification, knowing that greater clarification can always be pursued with people who wish to explore the movement for personal reasons.

Behind the issue of identity lies the numerical growth of this movement, from six individuals in 1830 to over 11 million members by 2002, and the power of a theology to help to forge a community of faith. While it is not easy to define in terms of sect, denomination or church, many have sought to describe Mormonism in ways that set it apart from ordinary branches of Protestant religion; there is much to be said for this, since both the theology and ritual practices of the Church of Jesus Christ of Latter-day Saints took their own path of development in the 1830s and 1840s. This path was not followed, for example, by the group that became the Reorganized Church of Jesus Christ of Latter Day Saints, which I describe below as very recognisably Protestant. The fact that the LDS and the RLDS Churches had a common origin but are now radically distinct reflects the fact that the LDS Church can almost be described as two churches in one. This is very easy to describe architecturally in terms of the distinction between local chapels and regional temples, as explained in chapter 8, but is less easily explained in terms of the intricate relationship between chapel and temple life. Still, the two kinds of building reflect Mormonism's double history and its dual theological perspectives. For LDS leaders, of course, the Church does not appear to be double, dual or divided in any way; for them the temple and its rites exist as a goal for all members and as a natural progression from family and local chapel life. This is not always the case for local chapel members, however, for whom the higher level of committed activity is not always achievable. As far as mission and expansion are concerned this double form is profoundly significant since new converts can be made, gathered into local meeting places and taught the faith very much in terms of repentance and faith within a widely shared Christian vocabulary and grammar of discourse. At the same time they can be integrated into a strong community whose ethical demands can often improve their way of life by bringing a clear structure and increased quality of behaviour to families especially when, for example, drunkenness and allied forms of unreliability are abandoned. Such changes enhance the chance of employment and increased income. If and when such converts are solidly made and soundly retained, they can then have the entire issue of temple marriage and related rites brought to their attention in preparing for what is, almost, a second level of LDS life. By this time the advantage in daily life of being a Latter-day Saint will serve as its own form of validation of the new doctrines and eternal possibilities that are presented.

I have explained how Mormon theology changed from the initial millenarian sect of mixed Protestant origin, grounded in repentance, baptism and salvation, into a church which was committed to temple rituals of endowment and whose covenants with God promised an eternal progression and exaltation of increasingly godlike family groups. As in many religious traditions, this involved one set of ideas being added to pre-existing ones in ways that could not guarantee complete consonance. Throughout this book, for example, we have seen how the earlier ideas of repentance, forgiveness and salvation and later notions of achievement and covenants that are aimed at exaltation can be difficult to integrate, not least when it comes to the notion of grace. Similarly, earlier and rather traditional notions of God as eternal and unchangeable do not find a clear echo in later notions of ever-progressing deities. While some of these changes came about from Joseph Smith's own prophetic activity, others were born of necessity and under external cultural constraint, such as when, at the close of the nineteenth century, the Church had to battle for survival with the Federal Government and formally abandon polygamy as a foundational element of earthly life and heavenly exaltation. By then, too, the Church no longer actively awaited Christ's Second Coming. Unlike that belief, which declined in emphasis though remained an 'official' church teaching, LDS views of the family become even more intensely focused as polygamy gave way to the dual emphasis upon the nuclear and extended family on earth, symbolized in the Family Home Evening, and the widest possible extended family in the afterlife, symbolized in genealogical research. With growth in numbers and growing success in the mid and especially the later twentieth century, the Church increasingly sought to establish Zion across the world and not simply in Utah or even in America; this was symbolized through the growth of temples, to which I return below.

From its birth in a culture of religious confusion, through its progress amidst political and cultural constraints in North America, the Church of Jesus Christ of Latter-day Saints expanded to its current strength. Just as its earliest theology affirmed this one Church as the truest amongst all churches and just as it was sustained by a policy of resistance and survival during political opposition, so now it is moving into a theology of success. One of the features of a successful theology associated with expansion is that church leaders experience considerable power as they take a strong hand in managing development. As far as doctrine is concerned, this involves a firm conservative attitude as central church leadership commits itself to a consolidation of a rapidly expanding membership. For some of its relatively few liberal-thinking members this control has been experienced as an authoritarian wielding of power, occasionally involving excommunication. For many of its leaders, however, such control appears to be a duty to protect revealed truth and to faithfully manage the clear and explicit growth of world membership. In terms of the history of religions and of religions' theologies there is nothing strange in this development. Earliest Christianity as a sect of Judaism also emerged amongst numerous other competing movements; it underwent periods of opposition and grew into a flourishing church with an increasingly strong leadership whose power was related to the control of the means of salvation through the developing sacramental system.

EARLY DISPUTES

As in Christianity, so in Mormonism, church development was not without internal fragmentation and the parallel emergence of differing groups. In the case of Mormonism dissent was more apparent in the earlier years than at present. In 1844, when the LDS community was still at Nauvoo, some of Joseph Smith's innovations were not agreeable to all, for example, the formation of the Council of Fifty, a group established to develop and manage a theocratic form of church government; so, too, Smith's revelation on plural marriage. Opposing the prophet, a small group established itself as a separate church and used the publication *The Nauvoo Expositor* to oppose these developments (Arrington 1986: 111). The group was, in turn, opposed by Joseph and other church members, and its press destroyed. This apparent attack upon the 'free press' provided just the occasion for many other opponents of Mormonism to engage in serious criticism and counter-attack: Joseph and some others were imprisoned for causing a riot and the immediate outcome included the mobbing of the prison and Joseph's death on 27 June 1844. This was a clear example of internal dissent about 'truth' triggering external aggression.

The question of the truth of beliefs is something that depends upon individuals and their judgement; the way people handle ideas believed by others to be true is quite a different issue. Mormonism presents numerous cases of individuals who have been Saints but who then, for many reasons, cease their membership. J. C. Bennett, for example, had been mayor of Nauvoo and general in its military group but when he was virtually excommunicated for seduction in relation to polygamy, he published an exposé of Mormonism which in 1842 prompted Joseph Smith to send several leading Saints to counteract Bennett's anti-Mormon lecture tour (Arrington 1986: 103). Another case was that of Sidney Rigdon, who had been extremely influential in Smith's life, as we have seen in chapter 5; his departure immediately after Joseph's murder and the competition for leadership that ensued has led to his being written out of Mormon history. Richard van Wagoner comments on the fact that Rigdon and Frederick G. Williams were partners in the inspiring visions associated with new rites introduced at the Kirtland Temple in 1836, yet both were later expelled from the Church and many of the Quorum of the Twelve of that day, who were also party to the revelations, also subsequently left (van Wagoner 1994: 170). Care is needed when evaluating information like this because of the implicit assumption that if someone leaves a movement its message must be untrue or its messengers insincere. While truth, as I have said, remains grounded in personal evaluation, as does the question of sincerity, there always remains the question of changing evaluation. Individuals may at one point in their life genuinely regard an idea as the truest of all ideas or may view an individual as the most sincere of all persons only to change these views at some later time. What often happens is that people view truth as some changeless entity in which one either believes or does not believe. But people change and come to see ideas in different ways over time. Sometimes the major emphasis upon change is philosophical, being related to ways of assessing information, and sometimes it is more personal and psychological. Major shifts in a basis of judgement can also occur, often related to changed circumstances of life and human relationships, while particular doctrinal schemes retain their form. Some religious groups tolerate much higher degrees of change than do others; Mormonism's tolerance has fluctuated at different periods of its existence, sometimes accepting a breadth of interpretation, as in the later nineteenth century, and sometimes being more authoritarian, as in the later twentieth century.

OPPOSITION

One unmistakable aspect of the history of the Restoration that had been initiated by Joseph Smith Jnr was that at his death not all members accepted the leadership of the Twelve Apostles headed by Brigham Young. Divisions occurred and, while these involved the inevitable likes and dislikes of individuals each with their claim for power, they also allowed theological ideas to gain or lose support, not least the intricately networked cluster of doctrines and practices that were focused on plural marriage and eternal exaltation: only about a half of Joseph Smith's followers joined Brigham Young's westward movement.

In Nauvoo on 4 May 1842 the Endowment Quorum, also called the Holy Order, was established to bring round certain core members to the idea of plural marriage and to the temple rites that bring about the union (van Wagoner 1994: 334). Plural marriage, or polygamy, was a serious problem in early Mormonism. William Law, who, along with Sidney Rigdon, was a counsellor to the prophet, was excommunicated in April 1844 for opposing polygamy and served as leader for some other separatists. Together they set about producing a newspaper, *The Nauvoo Expositor*, which, as just mentioned above, prompted a strong negative response from the LDS leadership and led to the press being smashed by a mob. It was largely for this that Smith was arrested and, while being held in custody before trial, was killed by another mob, 'a rabble of freemasons' (van Wagoner 1994: 335). With regard to the numerous consequences of Joseph's death and the topic of polygamy I will consider only the enduring outcome of the Reorganized Church of Jesus Christ of Latter Day Saints and the occasional publicity of what are called Fundamentalist Mormon groups, who are committed to continuing polygamy but lie apart from both the LDS and the RLDS traditions.

REORGANIZED CHURCH

Following Joseph's death one group saw the future leadership as lying in his son, Joseph Smith III (1832–1914), who assumed leadership of the Reorganized Church of Jesus Christ of Latter Day Saints and was succeeded by lineal descendants of Joseph Smith Jnr until W. Grant McMurray was appointed prophet-leader in 1996, aged only 51; this was a remarkably young age when compared with contemporary LDS prophets. Joseph III was absolutely opposed to polygamy, indeed would not accept that his father had practised it, and his group also rejected the later LDS beliefs of evolving gods. He also encouraged members not to gather to any one place but to build up Zion wherever they lived, a message that would still be a feature of LDS life decades later; it was even reaffirmed by the First Presidency in December 1999 when they gave counsel 'to members of the Church to remain in their homelands and help build up the Church in their native countries, rather than migrate to the United States' (*Almanac* 2000: 8). Even so the RLDS Church developed a sizeable population in Missouri, where, at Independence, they built a major auditorium in 1926 and dedicated and built a new temple in 1994. This temple symbolizes the crucial difference between the two major 'Mormon' churches in that the Reorganized Church possesses none of the covenant-making and death-transcending rites of the 'Utah' church and is open to anyone. The RLDS temple is essentially a meeting house, as was the first Mormon temple at Kirtland, which, as it happens, remains in the legal ownership of the RLDS Church. In all this it resembles much more the Book of Mormon period of the restoration movement than it does the ritual-mystical church of Joseph's Doctrine and Covenants.

The Reorganized Church has itself undergone several critical internal disputes over its own identity and mission but, in broad terms, it has moved more towards the Christian mainstream and away from the distinctive outlines of the developed doctrine of the Church of Jesus Christ of Latter-day Saints. It has, however, retained belief in revelation and possesses its own Doctrine and Covenants that includes many more later revelations than in the LDS version. For example, the RLDS Church ordained Negro males from 1865, and, with an eye to cultural appropriateness, polygamist converts in Asia and Africa were admitted to membership on the basis that they would take no further wives. This was a powerful move, given that the RLDS had taken an extremely strong stand against polygamy in the North American context of Joseph Smith's day. Again, in 1984, the RLDS decided to ordain women to the priesthood, a move that not all accepted and which caused some to abandon the Church. As to the name of the church, it decided in 1972 to use as an abbreviation of its longer name not the familiar RLDS but 'the Saints Church' and in 2001 decided to re-identify itself once more, this time as the 'Community of Christ'. Given its doctrinal and ritual practices, which are essentially Trinitarian and orthodox in the historical Christian sense, it is not easy for this church to give crisp reasons for its distinctiveness except insofar as it rehearses its historical footing in Joseph Smith's sense of vocation as a prophet. In some ways it resembles, for example, the African Christian denomination that emerged with the prophetic Simon Kimbangu (1889–1951), who died in prison for his convictions but whose movement grew and went on to gain affiliation with the World Council of Churches in 1969.

As with Kimbanguism, the Reorganized Church – Saints Church, or Community of Christ – is also a form of Christianity with a prophet, one that emerged from a most distinctive cultural context. Through the theological motif of Zion or Zionic Community the Church has come to foster the ideal of world community, issues of service, peace and Christian education and to encourage intercultural experience (Bolton 1986: 125). It is also a movement that possesses an ecumenical ethos so that, for example, it is not strange to find references in its literature to thinkers such as the Protestant theologian Dietrich Bonhoeffer; it also lays emphasis upon both the cross and grace, which is identifiably Protestant (Judd and Lindgren, 1976: 202–3, 49, 52). Its whole grammar of theological discourse is particularly interesting in terms of wider Protestant thinking because, while its doctrinal basis moves in an essentially orthodox direction, its historical framework demands some inclusion of Joseph Smith's early history and the history of the Mormon Church. In effect, the Community of Christ is a manifestation of the earliest millenarian Mormonism, pre-endowment, pre-polygamy and pre-exaltation, but a millenarianism that has been transformed into an ethical commitment to work for world transformation. Because the relatively small membership of under half a million or so is far from growing at the pace of the LDS Church, it offers no serious competition to Utah Mormonism; in the later decades of the twentieth century they tended to relate to each other in a polite mutual acknowledgement of a shared heritage, not least in the acknowledgement of prophetic leadership.

MORMON FUNDAMENTALISM

If the prophetic leadership of the Community of Christ produced a church that has taken its early Latter-day elements back towards mainstream Christianity, the other major prophetic strand to be considered here has taken the opposite route, emphasizing the radical break with orthodoxy in its polygamy-exaltation doctrines. This concerns what is often called Mormon fundamentalism, a term needing particular care in this context for two specific reasons, one technically academic and the other popular.

Technically speaking, in terms of the history and sociology of religion, fundamentalism is a term that was generated between approximately 1895 and 1915 to describe some conservative Christian believers in the United States who themselves produced a series of pamphlets – *The Fundamentals* – as a defensive response to liberal theology. Such fundamentalists were opposed to 'modernists'. In more popular terms 'fundamentalist' has come to be a pejorative term used by mainstream groups when accounting for the opinions of religious or political extremists. To speak of Mormon fundamentalism thus requires a careful use of words, not only to avoid this pejorative perspective but also, when appropriate, to avoid anachronism. When referring to Joseph Smith's day, for example, more is gained by speaking of religious primitivism than of fundamentalism. Primitivism denotes an attitude to the Christian past that involves a corresponding 'effort to return to a purer form of Christianity' (Givens 1997: 65). This is no new desire within Christianity, nor indeed within other religions. The longing for truth which drives so much creative religious experience and was, for example, a powerful tide in Joseph Smith's life is such that it wishes to experience anew what are perceived as past times of strong faith when the truth was purer than in a corrupted present. But – and this is an equally important point that is regularly ignored in more sociological studies – that backward look of longing is frequently aligned with an up-ward look of faith. Theologically speaking, it is often a sense of God as a contemporary experience that prompts the exploration of the past in a search for truths that were manifested at a time when God is thought to have been just as real to a previous generation. It is this conjunction of past and present in relation to God's revelation that adds an additional dynamic power to primitivism, as detailed by Terryl Givens (1997: 65). That view resonates strongly with Richard Bushman's very similar notion of a 'reunion with the deep past', which has already been discussed in chapter 1 (1984: 185).

The desires involved in that view of the past are profound and it is not surprising to find them recurring at times of trial. For example, Wilford Woodruff, when in hiding over the polygamy issue, tells of a dream in which he saw the Twelve Apostles and President Taylor all gathered together with the glory of God resting upon them whilst Taylor sealed all who wished it in 'the Church Plural marriages', when they were able to complete their work 'openly and the government had no power over us and we rejoiced together' (Woodruff 1993: 339). Yet that was not to be in Woodruff's day as far as the main stream of the Saints' tradition was concerned because it abandoned polygamy. Subsequent publications on Mormonism, especially those that are not anti-Mormon in intent, would come to use 'fundamentalism' to describe the increasingly 'deviant' groups within the broad restorationist class of religion that did espouse polygamy.

These small groups are led by individuals who claim prophetic status and they are rooted in an ongoing commitment to polygamy, even within contemporary North American society. One significant example can be seen in the story told of President John Taylor, just a year before his death in 1886 and whilst in flight from government officials over the polygamy issue. He is said to have been visited at night by Joseph Smith and Jesus Christ who affirmed the rightness of plural marriage, which led Taylor to ordain his hosts, Lorin and John Wooley, and to give them authority to conduct plural marriages; they subsequently did so in an ongoing tradition, albeit one deemed heretical by subsequent mainstream LDS Church authorities (Altman and Ginat, 1996). Although subsequent historical research has made the dating of that story and even its occurrence highly questionable, it offers one example of how conservative Mormonism identified itself with the ancient past in ways that made the past live again in the present in small polygamous groups of contemporary Mormons. These groups reflect very strongly the sociological account of those who seek the 'retrieval of fundamentals' as one hallmark of the fundamentalist approach to religion. 'Retrieved fundamentals' refers to doctrines and practices that a group takes from earlier periods of history and, after appropriate reordering, advances afresh as the prime answer to contemporary liberalism in belief or to decline in levels of religious life and commitment. Fundamentalists assume some former 'golden age' along with a nostalgia for that perfect period before the ravages of time took their toll of piety.

While in a most immediate sense Mormonism's self-description as a 'restoration' movement does exemplify the idea of retrieved fundamentals, its fundamentals refer as much to rites as to beliefs. Certainly this group did not emerge as a movement resembling, for example, twentieth-century fundamentalist groups. Its pre-fundamentalist nature gave it a degree of freedom over doctrine, not least in being able to develop revelation and scripture-like texts as its founding prophet and subsequent leaders saw fit. An interesting question concerns the degree to which Mormonism in the mid–later twentieth century did become more 'fundamentalist' within an American religious milieu framed by the fundamentalist-liberal dynamics of religious belief. In some respects the retrenchment described by Armand Mauss can be set within this responsive religious context. A degree of freedom was present in aspects of nineteenth-century Mormonism in pre-fundamentalist North America that was lost after the conservative-liberal engagement engendered new styles of religious encounter and defence. Certainly, the polygamous fundamentalists comprise a very small group in terms of world Mormonism and are no more than a minor embarrassment to the LDS Church but to themselves they stand as the true expression of prophetic leadership through practising the deeper covenants that confer the highest ultimate eternal rewards. They, like the earliest Latter-day Saints, stand against the mores of contemporary monogamous American society but they also have to stand against the LDS Church which has, in their view, capitulated to the world.

In sociological terms these are sect-like groups who express the distinctive sectarian spirit of protest that Troeltsch fully documented as one essential element of ongoing Christianity (Troeltsch 1931). By protesting against the way in which their parent church has capitulated to the world and accommodated to its demands, these fundamentalist Saints speak of a loss of pristine power. They draw attention to what they, at least, identify as crucial theological ideas. In this case it is the abandonment of plural marriage with its power as a vehicle for exaltation and as the vehicle through which the priesthood most fully manifests its power. For the main body of the Church of Jesus Christ of Latter-day Saints to turn its back on plural marriage was, for some Mormon fundamentalists, a turning of the back on its very essence. That it did so under pressure of a secular government was, in their opinion, to aggravate the error in so far as the Church was abandoning its stance of protest against error and witness to the truth. The real significance of fundamentalist LDS groups lies in their identification of crucial theological ideas as a form of inner-sectarian protest.

But the mainstream Latter-day movement sought survival and emerged from the period of hardship of conflict with Federal authorities between approximately the 1880s and 1920s with a commitment to doctrines and practices that could also absorb spiritual energies but, at the same time, did not engender Gentile hostility. Foremost amongst these was the LDS mission to the dead. In practical terms this mission was as important to twentieth-century Mormonism as its mission to the living had been in its formative decades of the nineteenth century.

MISSION TO THE DEAD

Section 138 of the Doctrine and Covenants is foundational. It consists of Joseph F. Smith's revelation, dated October 1918, prompted by his reading of the Bible on Christ's atoning sacrifice and on 'obedience to the principles of the gospel'. His pondering of both New Testament and distinctively LDS ideas brought him to the First Epistle of Peter, chapters 3 and 4, where he became greatly impressed by the text that refers to Christ, after his physical death by crucifixion, going 'by the Spirit' to preach to the 'spirits in prison'. Then, as he says, 'the eyes of my understanding were opened, and the Spirit of the Lord rested upon me, and I saw the hosts of the dead, both small and great'. These were in two distinct groups, one of the righteous and the other of the wicked. It was to the righteous that Christ came and they joyously welcomed him and his message both of their 'redemption from the bands of death' and of the knowledge that 'their sleeping dust was to be restored to its perfect frame... the spirit and the body to be

united never again to be divided, that they might receive a fullness of joy'
(D&C 138: 17).

A great deal was thus achieved in the short period after Christ's crucifixion and before his resurrection – but what of the wicked and rebellious
spirits to whom 'he did not go'? The answer to this brings in the second
and doctrinally innovative element of the revelation that tells how Christ
'organized his forces and appointed messengers' from amongst the righteous to take the message to the people of the darker side of the afterlife.
The description is highly reminiscent of earthly Mormon missionaries and
that, in effect, is what they were, for their teaching was of faith, repentance,
vicarious baptism, the laying on of hands for the conferring of the Holy
Ghost 'and all other principles of the gospel' (D&C 138: 34). There then
follows a list of those he saw in that afterworld; it begins with Adam and
'our glorious Mother, Eve', then Noah and a list of Old Testament figures,
with a crucial highlighting of Malachi and Elijah that draws attention to
the 'turning hearts' motif of LDS theology, which I have fully explored in
chapter 8.

Joseph also saw leading Mormons there including his uncle Joseph Smith
with Brigham Young, John Taylor and Wilford Woodruff. Each had, of
course, been the prophet-leader of the Church and this revelation, accepted
for publication as revelation by church authorities, provided a contemporary reaffirmation of their status. While this was hardly required for most
of them, it should be remembered that Wilford Woodruff had only died in
1898. He had been polygamous, with nine wives, and had assumed leadership of the Church as an eighty-year-old man at a time of great difficulty
as it came increasingly under Government pressure to abandon polygamy.
It was in 1890 that the Woodruff Manifesto finally removed polygamy or
plural marriage from the LDS style of life. This, as it happens, appears in
the Doctrine and Covenants as an Official Declaration along with some
other writings of Woodruff and comes immediately after Joseph F. Smith's
Section 138. The burden of Woodruff's work cited there falls upon the
redemption of the dead and the necessity of temples for the sacred work
involved, temples that would become impossible to retain if the Government stepped in as a result of the Saints continuing polygamous practices.
This was at a time when the Salt Lake City Temple was still being built.
At its dedication, made possible by the abolition of polygamy, Woodruff
spoke of the Lord's decree that 'the Devil should not thwart' the completion
and dedication of that most symbolic of all Mormon temples. He emphasized, 'If you can understand that, that is the key to it', for in Woodruff's

view any sacrifice was worth the goal that 'the salvation of the living and the dead should be given in these valleys of the mountains' (D&C 1981: 292).

Joseph F. Smith, as a prime LDS authority, had lived in hiding during part of the conflict between the Church and US authorities over polygamy; he had been counsellor to President Woodruff and involved in the promulgation of the Manifesto. In all this he was close to the profound issues of polygamous marriage as a dominant Mormon doctrine of the last years of Joseph Smith's work and the early Utah period of the Church, a doctrine explored at length in chapter 8. Plural marriage and baptism for the dead were fundamental complements within the LDS scheme of family salvation and exaltation and it would have seemed that they were inextricably bound together. In most respects they were, and for some Saints they continued to be, as Mormon fundamentalism and its adherence to the principle of plural marriage makes clear in the fundamentalist promotion 'from 1910 onward' of a 'polygamous counterculture' (Quinn 2001: 152).

It is no wonder that Joseph F. Smith should have pondered greatly on the future of his church and on the will of God in respect to it. What emerges in his revelation, when 'the eyes of his understanding were opened', is a renewed emphasis upon one of these foundational features of the faith. If plural marriage had ceased and the Saints could no longer have very large families, families that allowed many spirits to take a human body as part of their path of salvation, they need not be disappointed. Their work as saviours in Zion could continue and must continue through the temples and their saving ordinances. Instead of great emphasis falling upon the present and future generations it could, for the moment at least, fall upon past generations. For this temples were needed, and with this the secular authority could not interfere.

Here Mormonism steps into the twentieth century not only with its dynamic-mystical perspective intact but with a clear ongoing commitment, through revelation of its work for the dead. Here, too, is a renewed theological charter for the family and family life and, alongside it, a radically reinforced sense of the reality of the spirit world, for in the closing section of Doctrine and Covenants Section 138 Joseph F. Smith not only saw the spirits of people who had yet to be born and become church leaders on earth but, as described elsewhere, he also learned that LDS believers could continue in active service of their faith after death. Against this background of a highly personalized afterlife, Latter-day Saints could, and still do, speak of their sense of the presence of their dead kin, not least when engaged in genealogical research and, even more so, when undergoing vicarious baptism and other rites on their behalf. Within a month of this revelation Joseph F. Smith was himself part of that 'great world of the spirits of the dead'. He died on 19 November 1918

ANTI-MORMONISM

Joseph F. Smith helped the process of transition from polygamy to post-mortem commitments in LDS practical spirituality. In a minor way Mormon fundamentalists remain problematic for the LDS Church despite their small numbers and relative social irrelevance in that they fan the embers of 'polygamy', one of the most focused reasons for anti-Mormon literature in the nineteenth century and a practice that many non-Mormons still attribute to Latter-day Saints. Towards the end of a powerful essay on the nature of agnosticism and of religious faith the highly influential British Victorian philosopher Thomas Henry Huxley pinpointed the birth of 'two new sects' which, he thought, represented 'the most curious and instructive events in the religious history of the preceding [nineteenth] century' (1889: 192). The movements he found so instructive were Mormonism and positivism, the one the outcome of Joseph Smith's activity and the other of the French social philosopher and originator of sociology, Auguste Comte. Huxley held very negative views of Joseph Smith as a prophet, while he was moderately accepting of Comte. Two points emerged in his discussion that are appropriate here. The first touches on the fact that Comte sought to turn his positivist philosophy into a form of religion and failed in the event, and the second marks Mormonism's success and rapid growth in numbers: 'In spite of repeated outbursts of popular hatred and violence... the Mormon body steadily increased, and became a flourishing community', so much so that, for Huxley, there was 'in the whole history of religions... no more remarkable example of the power of faith' than in Mormonism (1889: 193). His point was to focus on the faith of ordinary Mormons and to do so despite his own opinion that their founder was a 'low-minded, ignorant scamp' who 'stole the "Scriptures" which he propounded; not being clever enough to forge even such contemptible stuff as they contain' (1889: 192). But he also saw in Joseph Smith 'a man of some force of character' able to gather a significant group of disciples around him. Huxley notes the oppression suffered by the early Saints, stresses the way they established themselves in 'the oasis of Utah', and favoured their life within the law until polygamy was outlawed. Indeed he compares the American Republic and its treatment of Mormons with the Roman Empire's treatment of early Christianity.

Huxley's essay ends, quite intentionally, unfinished. 'The history of these sects in the closing years of the century is highly instructive. Mormonism...' The sentence is incomplete, for, finally, he adds that he is not equal to the 'prophetical business, and ought not to have undertaken it' (Huxley 1889: 194). But what is obvious is that he entered this diversion to indicate that Mormonism was set on a path of growth and development despite, in his view, the incredible nature of its origin, prophet and scriptures; for, his concern is with the nature and significance of the faith of those within the Mormon Church. Though the positivists had much zeal for a philosophy, they possessed no faith; 'their love soon grew cold', as 'refined, estimable people, living in the midst of the worn-out civilisation of the old-world', where no one would ever think of persecuting them (Huxley 1889: 194). August Comte's Religion of Humanity simply would not do as a religion for humanity. More than a century later the intellectual 'prophetical business' remains just as great a challenge and even more of a temptation than it was for Huxley as one ponders the future. Since the Church looks set for continuity and growth, it is worth asking how it might maintain itself amongst other religious traditions, especially those of Christianity.

The anti-Mormon literature of the nineteenth century ensured that Mormonism would be known as intrinsically different from mainstream Christianity, and Terryl Givens has provided an excellent account of such material, in which, for example, early Mormonism was sometimes compared with exotic eastern groups such as Islam, and the question was raised about how best to protect good citizens and ordinary Christian believers from these *Viper(s) on the Hearth* as Givens entitles his study (Givens 1997). While anti-Mormon feeling has come from political, economic and religious sources, it is the last that occupies us now since it is the most significant in a world in which Protestant Evangelicalism is increasing in strength, not least in the South American contexts where Mormonism is also expanding quite considerably (Gooren 1998).

Generally speaking, Evangelical Christianity identifies itself as the purest and most sincere form of the faith. Evangelicals see themselves as heirs of the Protestant Reformation and, as such, freed from the encrustations of priestly practices and converted by the power of the Holy Spirit in the here and now to understand the Bible aright. They sense themselves to be close to God and God close to them. Because of this freedom from tradition and because of the immediacy of God, Evangelicals possess a self-identity of some considerable power. These dynamics of Evangelical spirituality guarantee a degree of hostility to Mormonism, given that both claim freedom from all false interpretations, the one through the Reformation and the immediacy of the Spirit and the other through the Restoration and the authority of the priesthood, and since both also stake a claim upon personal testimony of inner, individual, experience.

Ultimately the Protestant espousal of the priesthood of all believers, coupled with the idea of faith and grace, quite contradicts and challenges the LDS priesthoods and the achievement inherent in exaltation. I have shown throughout earlier chapters just how different the meaning of common theological terms can be between Mormons and mainstream Christians and this becomes particularly apparent with Evangelicals, for whom the very meaning of words is related to authentic belief and salvation. Mormons and Evangelicals see the world through quite different lenses and the shared use of common terms only confuses and sometimes frustrates relations between them in a way that is not simply theoretical or abstractly theological but emotional. Most religious and cultural traditions invest their prime doctrines and ideas with such significance that they can be denied only at the cost of being charged with heresy or serious betrayal. The theological idea of abomination is one description of this sense of revulsion at falsehood and it surrounds the way in which some believers in the one tradition view those in the other. Indeed this boundary of similarity–difference can itself breed a kind of theological revulsion when Evangelicals think that Mormons are twisting the great and wonderful words of the true gospel for their own ends. Even the very word 'gospel' carries a fundamentally different connotation in the usage of each tradition.

In chapter 1, for example, I discussed 'principles' as a basic category of LDS thought and said I would return to it here in relation to the theological notion of 'justification'. One telling example can be found in McConkie's account of 'justification', the foundational notion of the Protestant Reformation and essential to any discussion between LDS and Protestant Christianity, where he speaks of the necessity of 'compliance with this basic doctrine of the gospel, the law of justification' (McConkie, B. R. 1979: 408). To employ the very phrase 'law of justification' is to engage in a theological grammar of discourse that is fundamentally different from Protestant theology in which 'law' and 'justification' belong to different domains. McConkie defines the 'law of justification' as originating in Christ's atonement but becoming 'operative in the life of an individual only on conditions of personal righteousness'. The very notion of justification being conditional upon any human act involves a theological error as far as Protestant theology is concerned and indicates the radically different theological realms and domains of spirituality occupied by these two traditions. What is especially interesting is that McConkie describes justification in terms of ritual action, of the 'covenants, contracts, bonds, obligations, oaths, vows, performances, connections, associations, or expectations...in which men must abide to be saved and exalted'. Once more, ritual action is a negative feature in any Evangelical theology of salvation – even baptism would not be spoken of in such terms.

Another example can be found in one of the most influential of later twentieth-century anti-Mormon books, which has also been the topic of a film of the same name – *The God Makers* (Decker and Hunt 1984). This covers a wide variety of theological differences between Mormonism and Evangelical Christianity and, for example, notes how one LDS leader, Milton R. Hunter, defined 'the gospel' in terms of 'our heavenly parents' learning 'an untold number' of 'everlasting laws' and through employing them 'these laws became subject unto Elohim and henceforth were His laws – or, in other words, the Gospel of Jesus Christ' (Decker and Hunt 1984: 260). What essentially happens in such descriptions of LDS ideas is that a form of theological revulsion occurs. Truths and ideas that form the very core of someone's identity, in this case a religious identity, are held to be most precious to them and if they find those ideas abused or given a quite different meaning, their own response is deep, strong and negative. Here we are not simply in the realm of theological or philosophical ideas but of realms of meaning in which ideas penetrate the emotional lives of people. And in such contexts responses to ideas became part and parcel of gut-responses.

JESUS: MORMON AND EVANGELICAL

The fundamental theological issue of Evangelical Christianity is Christology: who Jesus is and what he has done for the salvation of humanity is of paramount importance. But theology alone does not explain the power of religious beliefs within an individual's life. It does not explain the psychological and sociological dynamics of one's sense of identity. For many Evangelical Christians the theological centrality of Christ takes root within a self-identity that often involves religious experiences interpreted as an experience of Jesus Christ. The precise nature of the church within which, or in relation to which, this experience takes place is, both theologically and psycho-sociologically, secondary to the inner event. And this is crucial for understanding the difference between an Evangelical-Christian and a Mormon understanding of Jesus. For, while Mormons would also say that Jesus is basic to their life, the church framework within which they 'know' him is of primary and not secondary importance. In theological terms, ecclesiology is foundational as the setting for Christology.

As the changed emphasis upon the name of the Church indicates, there is one crucial difference between the framework within which the Evangelical and the Mormon understands 'Jesus'. The Evangelical feels that Jesus is his or her intimate friend, close and personal. Religious conversion involves a personal sensation that sins are forgiven and that Jesus, somehow, has come into their life. Hence the well-known Evangelical expectation of being 'born-again' and of asking Jesus into the heart. A sense of freedom and newness is associated with this feeling. The Mormon may also gain a personal feeling of Christ, called a testimony, but the framework within which it works is much more formally that of the Church. Often, the testimony tells of coming to find that the Church is the true Church and that Joseph Smith was a true prophet. It is within that framework that Jesus takes his place as part of the overall plan of salvation. The Evangelical Christian can conceive of a relation with Jesus, of being saved from sin and of inheriting eternal life, without caring about any particular kind of church organization. Converts from Mormonism to Evangelicalism are so emphatic about the power of Christ precisely because they believe that they have gained a direct and personal relationship with him that transcends any particular church. The Latter-day Saint, by contrast, tends to find Jesus as part of a firm church organization that includes extensive temple activity. These two positions involve a quite different sense of self in relation to church, even though in practice the Evangelical may be just as subject to particular ecclesiastical interpretations of scripture or of leadership authority. Similarly, some converts to Mormonism speak of finding a church with clear and definite teachings, rites and leadership, which they saw as lacking in their early religious affiliation.

So it is that, in the inner world of experience of God, relationship to written scriptures and freedom from accumulated religious error mark the shared and strongly contested boundaries between Evangelicals and Mormons. Claims to church uniqueness, to divinely validated authority, to a salvation granting priesthood and rites are, by contrast, contested by Mormons and Roman Catholics. Mormons see themselves as owning an authentic form of apostolic succession in the line of ordination that each male holds back to Joseph Smith and to the purely restored priesthoods he received. Similarly they see the Church itself as a divinely willed and sanctioned institution. As already noted, some LDS leaders see the Catholic Church as an example of a universally present and large religious institution offering, perhaps, some cause for reflection on how the LDS Church might be if predictions of growth are fulfilled.

Ecclesiastical power blocks, just like the blockages within personal psychology, are often quite hidden under the theological arguments used between Catholics, Evangelicals and Mormons; nevertheless they often motivate the various critiques of Mormon history, of the contradictory utterances of leaders or between the Book of Mormon and later LDS doctrine. It is important to remember this when evaluating, for example, anachronisms pointed out in the Book of Mormon, such as when the internally dated sixth-century BC character Nephi finds his adversary Laban drunk and, taking Laban's sword kills him. The shaft of this sword was made of 'the finest steel' (1 Nephi 4: 9) and, as critics rejoice to make clear, there was no such thing as steel in the sixth century BC. Similarly Alma 18: 9 refers to Ammon as feeding horses at a date reckoned to be 90 BC, almost a thousand years before horses were introduced to America; again, when king Lamoni and his wife have fallen into a swoon on hearing God's word, as she recovers she speaks out, 'O blessed Jesus, who has saved me from an awful hell!', some ninety years before the birth of Christ and expressing feelings more reminiscent of an early twentieth-century revivalist meeting (Alma 19: 29).

It is easy for critics of the Book of Mormon to deride it for using as prophecy what is in fact history. In other words, they would say, for example, that when King Benjamin announces the birth of Jesus and identifies Mary as his mother at a date reckoned to be 124 BC (Mosiah 3: 8), this is simply Joseph Smith or some other author of the Book of Mormon writing up history after the event and presenting it as prophecy. That is one way of reading the situation, albeit a negative way grounded in what is likely to be an apologetic and critical attitude; another approach could be to see in it the prevailing Christological tendency of the Book of Mormon, as I argued in chapter 2. Many similar examples could be furnished and are especially advanced when Evangelical Christians wish to undermine the Book of Mormon. This is an exchange and encounter that is likely to grow considerably as the LDS Church itself grows in number and as some of its members leave, for whatever reason, and join other churches. Various groups of former Mormons exist who have been converted to Evangelical Christianity and now wish to see others join them. Not all who formally leave the LDS Church become Evangelicals or Catholics or some other denomination: some simply wish to live without formal religion, which is not always easy after being part of a strongly community-focused group. In order to cope with the transition some join various kinds of mutual support groups, often aided by contemporary forms of information technology as a means of learning about those groups. Expansion of the Church will almost inevitably foster the growth of such groups.

EXPANSION

The Church has, most certainly, expanded; so much so that one American sociologist, Rodney Stark, has argued that it is set to become the next new world religion (Stark 1984, 1998). Taking statistics of church membership and projecting them into the future, he presents both low and high estimates of membership, as represented here in millions for several decades into the future: 2020 (13, 23), 2030 (17, 35), 2040 (22, 53), 2050 (29, 79). So, by the year 2050, for example, his low projection is 29 million members and the high projection some 79 million members. Church leaders have themselves paid explicit attention to Stark's work and used these figures to reflect on possible developments (*Almanac* 2001–2002: 148–52). Still, they remain acutely aware of the problems involved in administering such a growing institution and are alert to, for example, the processes and strategies that other groups, not least the Roman Catholic Church, encounter as a worldwide and large-scale operation.

This growth is closely related to the dual Mormon theological message of building Zion throughout the world through converts and building up families for eternity through relatively large numbers of children. This is a powerful theological combination of ideas and comes to formal expression in the Church's programme of temple building that had reached over 100 by the year 2000. This compares, for example, with approximately 26,000 wards and branches of the Church. A new programme to match the rise in membership through a major increase in smaller and less elaborate temples heralds the twenty-first century.

New mission-religions

Developing an idea from the previous chapter on temple work, I turn now to comparing Mormonism with its Protestant parent with regard to the place of temples as 'places of mission', for Mormonism is as fundamentally concerned with 'converting' the 'dead' as with converting the living. In theological terms, Protestantism has, classically, viewed the 'mission field' as its arena for extending salvation and viewed its church buildings as places to nurture converts and foster the faithful. Mormonism fully adopted the same notion of the mission field and has organized its members, especially its youth, to engage with non-members to a greater degree than probably any other church. For example, in 1960 of approximately 1,700,000 members there were 4,700 missionaries, while in 1999 of roughly 10,800,000 members there were 34,600 missionaries worldwide, which represents a steady increase over the period. One feature of this remarkable missionary activity should not be ignored, for it concerns the nature of the relationship between Mormonism and one very particular aspect of Protestantism.

In order to make this point a distinction has to be made between Protestantism in its fifteenth- to seventeenth-century 'Reformation' mode of organization and intent and its late eighteenth- and nineteenth-century 'missionary' mode. As indicated in chapter 1, the Dutch scholar Peter van Rooden has persuasively argued that a new form or style of Christianity developed in the late eighteenth and early nineteenth centuries in both Europe and North America, typified by formally organised missionary societies (van Rooden 1996: 65ff.). His approach encourages a bifocal view of Protestantism rather than seeing in it a single and rather uniform integration of theology and action: the Reformers were not missionaries. In ordinary Christian thought, especially in everyday evangelical reflection, Reformation theology and missionary activity tend to coalesce; this is unfortunate if it obscures the rather different motivations of each era. It also blurs the focus when considering the nature of the LDS Restoration.

At several points in this book I have indicated areas in which Mormonism has taken aspects of Protestant religion and, by developing their theological logic or pressing the logic to its potential conclusion, has produced a different doctrine or practice. This is also the case here and I would suggest that the LDS Restoration participates far more in Protestantism's new 'mission mode' than in its Reformation mode. Van Rooden spoke of missions as expressing 'the originality of Western Christianity' and, if his basic thesis carries weight, then we might extend his view to say that Mormonism represents the most advanced form of such a western Christianity (van Rooden 1996: 73). When, then, we consider the issue of growth in membership and its potential for expansion and change of status as a religious movement, we should not too quickly forget the underlying theology and organization that makes it so.

If, as I have argued elsewhere on this very issue, Mormonism's birth was grounded in missionary activity, it is no accident that growth and expansion ensue (Davies 2000: 195). But neither should 'missionary work' be narrowly conceived. The single major difference between the LDS and other Protestant mission-minded churches concerns the dead. This is the point at which the LDS movement presses an element of theological logic far beyond any that was conceived of in mission-based Protestantism. For, while missionaries who were sponsored by Protestant missionary societies and churches sought to reach the benighted heathen and bring the saving gospel message within reach, the LDS Church set itself the task of also reaching the dead through vicarious temple work on their behalf. Over time, this not only had the effect of fostering genealogical research, which reinforced family identity, but also opened two different yet complementary 'mission fields' for its active members. The mutual effect of temple work and missionary work can, itself, be easily overlooked, yet its theological significance is as great as its sociological consequence is influential.

Theologically, mission field and temple become complementary in relating the processes of salvation and exaltation. These two dimensions of soteriology have run together throughout this book and have been used almost as symbols of the earlier 'Protestant' form of Joseph Smith's new church and of its more ritual-mystical form, which was developed shortly before his death and much developed afterwards. Now we can see how they succeeded in becoming complements within, rather than competing fragments of, a single church. And the two became more than the sum of thier parts. But so many factors are involved that it is slightly hazardous to make the point that when the restoration movement is left only with the missionary element of salvation and lacks the exaltation processes of temple, as does its RLDS stream, then it is dramatically less successful.

Sociologically, the missionary and temple activities are mutually reinforcing in two ways, one general and one specific. Generally, they foster a sense of activity – itself a highly prized LDS term – and ensure no discontinuity between different aspects of church life. Specifically, they also allow Latter-day Saints to be fully engaged in 'mission' work at different stages of life since it is generally, but not exclusively, the case that young adults serve as field missionaries while older people, often fairly old people, become engaged in what we might call 'temple-missionary' work, a phrase that – unlike its potential equivalent, 'saviours in Zion' – is not an LDS usage. Temple and mission field become partner soteriological arenas in a way that simply does not occur within any other church tradition, Catholic,

Protestant or Orthodox. The catalytic effect of this complementarity is one element that feeds into the LDS process of expansion.

WORLD RELIGION: GLOBAL RELIGION

Whether Mormonism will become a new world religion or not is, in many respects, a question of definition. There is no widely accepted definition of 'world religion' in the formal study of religion and much depends upon the emphasis of particular authors (Davies 2000: 213–66). For example, if a world religion is one that becomes established in many different cultures and adapts itself to local patterns of ritual and of thought as have Buddhism, Christianity and Islam, then Mormonism is unlikely to follow that path. Judaism, Hinduism, Sikhism and the faith of Parsees or Zoroastrians, by contrast, have come to be present in many parts of the world but largely as culturally distinct communities with very few or no converts from those cultures. It is highly unlikely that any subcultural area will become 'Mormon' in the way that Utah became 'Mormon' in the nineteenth century. It is far more likely that, with its strong central control from Utah, which will continue for some considerable time albeit with the incorporation of a few South Americans and Asians into the General Authorities, Mormonism will become a 'global' religion. By 'global' I refer to the process of globalization by which an institution makes its presence felt within hundreds of societies yet retains its distinctive identity. Indeed, it is the maintenance of that identity that is its reason for existence and the very basis for its theology and mission. It will appeal to and attract people in need of a distinctive identity and who are prepared to be different from their neighbours.

At the same time it is likely that Christianity itself will respond to the two world processes of globalization and localization and will witness a fragmentation of the great churches into increasingly local versions of Catholicism, Orthodoxy, Anglicanism and Lutheranism. Such growing independence will result from changing cultural conditions in different countries and, where that does not happen, the traditional forms of Catholicism, for example, will come increasingly to resemble global Mormonism, with a strong central authority maintained through committed local leaders.

Mormonism's early success depended upon the critical mass of converts who had commited their lives to following Joseph Smith and gathering to Zion. They were numerous enough to survive the fragmentation that followed the death of Joseph, while the Utah period allowed a degree of consolidation and growth of a strong network of families within a subculture. The increased growth in the twentieth century and the beginning of the twenty-first now ensures a religious tradition that will exist for a considerable period of time and which, by its very nature, is set for ongoing enlargement as much through inborn members as through converts.

Sign of difference

Demography, the practical science of populations, here encounters millenarian theology that still heralds a day when Jesus Christ will return and a millennial reign will be established. Jerusalem in the old world and Zion in America will both have their parts to play in this new world order. Jerusalem will be developed through the tribe of Judah and Zion through that of Ephraim, for it is an LDS view that most Mormons belong to the tribe of Ephraim (Mauss 2001: 103–34). So it is that the new world order is integrally rooted in Mormonism's grasp of the Bible complemented by its own Standard Works as Zion becomes the dominant location of Christ's reign.

But until that day how will the Church affirm its own identity? One way might be through the place and use of the Book of Mormon itself. Terryl Givens, for example, in an initially paradoxical suggestion indicates that 'there is something new in the modern infiltration of the Book of Mormon into Latter-day Saint culture'; indeed he sees the book as being 'poised to become increasingly central to Mormon worship, identity and culture' – this at the very same time as the Church encourages the use of the name the Church of Jesus Christ (Givens 2002: 244–5). Jan Shipps foresees a time when the Book of Mormon 'will be more significant for the faith than the Joseph Smith story' (Shipps 2000: 385). As Givens interprets events, it is precisely as the Church affirms its identity in relation to Christ and Christianity that it also affirms an 'irreducible sign of difference'. This pinpoints the central issue of Mormonism's identity from its first day of existence until today: how to be true to Christianity whilst being different from all other forms of Christianity?

While the Book of Mormon was a major sign of LDS difference in 1830 it rapidly took third or fourth place as the Doctrine and Covenants presented the new revelations on endowment and exaltation and as temples arose for the rites that made that super-plus form of salvation available. Polygamy had been the domestic form of organization that enshrined those doctrines and rites within the home, and when polygamy ceased under government pressure in the 1890s, the major 'symbol of difference', as Mark Leone argued, was the Church's opposition to the ordination of black males, which lasted until 1978 (Leone 1979: 223–6). He then wondered whether the Church would simply allow itself to become more like other Christian churches – as we have seen with the RLDS Church – or establish some new symbol of difference; he mentioned ethical issues on abortion, gay rights or traditionalist views on women and the family. The very last sentence of his book has, in retrospect, been the route adopted, even though Leone utters it almost as an impossibility as the way in which Mormonism could cease to be a 'colonial' religion producing 'people without memories': to alter this situation, he says, 'Mormonism would have to overcome its own internal weakness and dominate itself' (Leone 1979: 226). This it has, very largely, done through the process of correlation in which central authorities have become increasingly powerful, by addressing themselves to ethical and social issues and by controlling to a considerable degree more liberal and free-ranging intellectuals in their interpretation of Mormonism's history. Jan Shipps has argued that the growth in significance of correlation in the later twentieth century was a major factor in the transition of the Church from what she called a 'tribalized and auxiliarized church' to one that is centrally controlled, itself a shift demanded by the overall growth of the Church (Shipps 2000: 379). What is particularly significant here is the very fact of numbers. She is doubtless correct in describing a shift from a community ethos in which many members had some form of personal contact, however transient and brief, with major leaders to a much more distant and impersonal kind of knowledge. Quinn has, for example, sketched an entire history of the Church in terms of 'Headquarters Culture', tracing the way in which central leaders were personally known to many very early Mormons whilst, with time, even access to them has become increasingly difficult, so that today, 'the vast majority of Mormons living at headquarters have no closer association with the LDS president than Mormons in Boston, London, Tokyo, or Mexico City' (Quinn 2001: 157). Some other Saints have even spoken of 'the two churches of Mormonism', seeing the growth of managerialism in the Church as understandable in terms of coping with its growth in numbers but questioning whether the control involved has compromised Mormonism's vigorous and early commitment to free agency, 'with the view that the glory of God is intelligence, with the concept of eternal progress, and with the optimism of the ideal which counters Calvinism: "man is that he might have joy"' (Molen 1991: 26).

One consequence of this for LDS theology is that it is almost certain to become more conservative. If a person's place within the Church depends less upon a network of family relationships, as existed in the older Mormon heartlands, it is likely that acceptance will depend upon more formal kinds of agreement about doctrine and formal acceptance of leadership. Similarly, any who are thought to be dissident can be treated from a distance and can very easily sense the Church to be an impersonal bureaucracy that no longer truly reflects, for example, the teaching of Jesus, which, in its biblical expression, is distinctly individualistic and has an emphasis upon love and mercy rather than upon formal principles (see Toscano 1994: 133–184).

At the larger level, one sign of difference that Givens, Leone and Shipps largely ignore, which may yet prove to be of fundamental significance, is Mormonism's attitude to death and the afterlife. Superficially it might seem that a committed belief in the afterlife is no sign of difference between the LDS and other Christian churches, but this is deceptive. In chapter 4 I have already explored death in LDS culture; here I return to the topic precisely because most Christian traditions, especially at the beginning of the twenty-first century, say very little about death and the afterlife: they prefer to concentrate their theological and ethical efforts on this life. Latter-day Saints, by contrast, have intensified their commitment to eternity as an aspect of the plan of salvation. As Mormonism continues to expand in countries where Catholicism had deeply influenced popular culture, it is likely that its clear doctrinal position and its implementation through the ritual practice of temples will furnish a distinctive appeal. Christian theology at large has very little to say about death and the afterlife beyond a generalized affirmation of life after death, and in some denominations that is weak. Most formal theologies, including those of the greatest Catholic and Protestant theologians, present their briefest essays when it comes to death and heaven. Much of what they do say would have relatively little appeal to non-theologians.

Mormonism, by sharp contrast, is a church organized around temples that are organized around the transcendence of death. The biggest transition that was made in the theological evolution of this Church was the leap from millenarianism to exaltation – from the Second Coming of Christ to the future godhood of individual married couples and their families. The traditional theology of the kingdom of God was replaced by the divine kingdoms of innumerable husbands, wives and children. Of this the shift from chapel to temple is the architectural symbol. Mormon temple activism with its relational and covenantal foundation is opposed to the doctrinal silences of most other churches and the effort of many other churches to focus their concern on the care of the bereaved rather than the 'care' of the dead. Both the abandonment of earthly polygamy and the ordination of Negro males attracted more members for temple activities. Current world expansion will generate through the chapel system millions more candidates for the temple means of death-transcendence. Here Mormon theology pervades architecture, organization and homes, and the very power of ritual performance is likely to render marginal the critiques of intellectual dissidents.

Christian Mormonism

Still, there remains a final 'sign of difference': the very existence of the Church itself. Over and above distinctive beliefs or practices that signal one group's difference from another there comes a time when the very existence of a group becomes its own marker. The LDS Church has now arrived at that state. Its size and widespread presence quite simply places Mormonism, the Latter-day Saints or the Church of Jesus Christ, amongst the major players on the religious map. This is significantly reinforced by its acceptability within mainstream North American culture, which itself confers a cultural credibility upon it. How important that American core-control will be in the future is difficult to predict: just as the major European cultures held sway within their own empires only to crumble in the twentieth century, so the 'imperial' cultural influence of the United States in many parts of the world may also fade in as short a time. Further research should be devoted to the 'American culture' of Mormonism, not simply through the punishing detail that historians have exacted, but through theological methods. For example, it would be illuminating to ponder Mormonism's North American matrix in the light of the influential twentieth-century Protestant theologian Paul Tillich, whose study *The Courage to Be* has been described as 'the most penetrating theological analysis of American culture that has been written' (Heywood Thomas 1973: 291). To take but one example from it: Tillich relates mysticism and courage and asks how the mystic's 'power of self-affirmation' is drawn from 'the experience of the power of being-itself' (Tillich 1962: 154). Such an approach would set Joseph Smith in quite a different interpretative context from that of historical or doctrinal criticism. Such serious theological appreciation lies in the future.

Generally speaking, the prophet and his movement is seldom admitted into that arena of reflective seriousness. In terms of acceptibility, Mormonism will never be counted as Christian by Rome, given the very similar yet ideologically opposite parts played by authority and priesthood in the two traditions. Protestant and Evangelical streams of Christianity, themselves undergoing extensive growth in many parts of the world, will never accept Mormonism as Christian as long as exaltation-Mormonism devalues grace and decentralizes the cross of Christ. It has never been sufficient for one tradition of Christendom to accept others simply because they come from the same stock, as appealing as that genetic classification is to sociologists or historians. Christianity has known too much of heresy within itself for too long. Yet, within contemporary Mormonism there are at least two voices, not loud or much heard by outsiders, that raise conflicting hopes and fears for the future. The negative voice of some LDS thinkers decries an overbearing authoritarianism on the part of central church leaders: members who would have been thoroughly at home in Joseph Smith's and Brigham Young's more speculative days of theological inquiry, with its ethos of excitement (described in chapter 1), now find their critical reflections curbed. For scholars outside the Mormon Church, themselves often theological or intellectual liberals, there is a dislike of hearing church leaders speak of 'so-called' intellectuals. Still, all church history reflects something of St Augustine's pragmatism on the point that it is better for a few to perish than that all are led astray.

The positive voice, by contrast, pursues a personal religiosity amidst the bureacracy. Here the drive is towards a spirituality of love and acceptance rather than of control. It speaks of grace, neither in the LDS sense of atonement linked to resurrection nor in terms of the process of creation, but rather as the divine–human relationship that extends throughout life and which even pervades the covenants of endowment and the pursuit of exaltation. Armand Mauss describes contemporary Mormonism as, in part, 'returning to its roots in the Christian gospel of Jesus and Paul (Mauss 2001: 133). Here, in concluding, we are once more directly faced by the dialectical dynamic of 'relations and principles'. LDS theology was, at its outset, a creative and energetic venture in finding faith amidst a world of Christian faiths. It sought the Church amidst the churches. To itself it became that Church and, in the process, 'principles' developed apace, even at the expense of 'relations'. Once established and successful it will be interesting to see if 'principles' alone will sustain the faithful. In the overall history of Christendom it was no accident that the Reformation caused 'relations' in the form of 'grace' to reappear amidst the 'principles' of sacramentally controlled salvation. The Restoration, in its way, increasingly fostered 'principles' to the point where, perhaps, the 'relations' with God had become excessively circumscribed. This may, now, in its turn, be changing once more. And it may be changing at the same time as official LDS theology is itself moving from Mormonism's 'old time religion' of 'godmaking' to a more traditional Christian doctrinal view of a divine 'Trinity'. As for the entire temple ritual, it would not be impossible for this to assume something of the character of the sacramental system of some major Christian denominations. Its continuing appeal, however, would lie in the attractive combination of death conquest and family life. The Church, whatever particular name it adopts in each of its eras of existence, is still an extremely young institution that has many miles to travel, and many vestures to change, before its vision of Zion is realized.

Bibliography

Aberbach, David (1989) *Surviving Trauma, Loss, Literature and Psychoanalysis*, New Haven and London: Yale University Press.

Alexander, Thomas G. (1986) *Mormonism in Transition: a History of the Latter-day Saints 1890–1930*, Urbana and Chicago: University of Illinois Press.

—— (1989) 'The Reconstruction of Mormon Doctrine', in Gary James Bergera (ed.), *Line upon Line: Essays on Mormon Doctrine*, Salt Lake City, UT: Signature Books.

Allen, James B., Ronald K. Esplin and David J. Whittaker (1992) *Men with a Mission, 1837–1941: the Quorum of the Twelve Apostles in the British Isles*, Salt Lake City, UT: Deseret Book Company.

Almanac 2001–2002 The Church of Jesus Christ of Latter-day Saints, Salt Lake City, UT: Deseret News.

Altman, Irwin and Joseph Ginat (1996) *Polygamous Families in Contemporary Society*, Cambridge: Cambridge University Press.

Anderson, Lynn Matthews (1995) *Easy-to-Read Book of Mormon*, Apple Valley, MN: Estes Book Company.

—— (1996) 'Issues in Contemporary Mormon Feminism', in Douglas J. Davies (ed.), *Mormon Identities in Transition*, London: Cassell.

Anderson, Richard Lloyd (1983), *Understanding Paul*, Salt Lake City, UT: Deseret Book Company.

Anderson Cannon, Elaine (1992) 'Mother in Heaven', in Daniel H. Ludlow (ed.), *The Encyclopedia of Mormonism*, New York: Macmillan.

Arrington, Leonard J. (1986) *Brigham Young: American Moses*, Urbana and Chicago: University of Illinois Press.

—— (1995) 'Brigham Young and the Great Basin Economy', in Susan Easton Black and Larry C. Porter (eds.), *Lion of the Lord: Essays on the Life and Service of Brigham Young*, Salt Lake City: UT: Deseret Book Company.

Aulén, Gustav (1953 [1930]) *Christus Victor: an Historical Study of the Three Main Types of the Idea of the Atonement*, tr. A. G. Hebert, London: SPCK.

Backman, Milton V. Jr (1995) 'The Keys Are Right Here', in Susan Easton Black and Larry C. Porter (eds.), *Lion of the Lord*, Salt Lake City, UT: Deseret Book Company.

Barlow, Philip L. (1991) *Mormons and the Bible*, New York: Oxford University Press.

Benson, Ezra Taft (1983) *Come unto Christ*. Salt Lake City, UT.

Besterman, Theodore (1924) *Crystal-Gazing: a Study in the History, Distribution, Theory and Practice of Scrying*, New Hyde Park, New York: University Books.

Bitton, Davis (1994) *The Ritualization of Mormon History and Other Essays*, Urbana and Chicago: University of Illinois Press.

    (2000) *Historical Dictionary of Mormonism*, second edn, Lanham, MD, and London: The Scarecrow Press, Inc.

Bolton, J. Andrew (1986) *Restoring Persons in World Community*, Independence, MO: Herald Publishing House.

Bonhoeffer, Dietrich (1955) *Ethics*, ed. Eberhard Bethge, tr. Neville Horton Smith, London: SCM Press.

Boone, David F. (1992) 'Perpetual Emigration Fund', in Daniel H. Ludlow (ed.), *The Encyclopedia of Mormonism*, New York: Macmillan.

Brady, F. Neil (1992) 'Ethics', in Daniel H. Ludlow (ed.), *The Encyclopedia of Mormonism*, New York: Macmillan.

Brodie, Fawn M. (1995 [1945]) *No Man Knows My History: the Life of Joseph Smith*, New York: Vintage Books.

Brooke, John L. (1994) *The Refiner's Fire: the Making of Mormon Cosmology, 1644–1844*, Cambridge: Cambridge University Press.

Brown, S. Kent (1992) 'Gethsemane', in Daniel H. Ludlow (ed.), *The Encyclopedia of Mormonism*, New York: Macmillan.

Brunner, Emil (1934) *The Mediator*, London: Lutterworth.

Buerger, David John (1989) 'Salvation in the Theology of Joseph Smith', in Gary James Bergera (ed.), *Line upon Line: Essays on Mormon Doctrine*, Salt Lake City, UT: Signature Books.

    (1994) *The Mysteries of Godliness: a History of Mormon Temple Worship*, San Francisco: Smith Research Associates.

Bushman, Richard L. (1984) *Joseph Smith and the Beginnings of Mormonism*, Urbana and Chicago, University of Illinois Press.

Callister, Douglas L. (1992) 'Resurrection', in Daniel H. Ludlow (ed.), *The Encyclopedia of Mormonism*, New York: Macmillan.

Calvin, John. *Institutes of the Christian Religion* (many editions).

Cannon, Janath R. and Jill Mulvay-Derr (1992) 'Relief Society', in Daniel H. Ludlow (ed.), *The Encyclopedia of Mormonism*, New York: Macmillan.

Catechism of the Catholic Church (1994) London: Geoffrey Chapman.

Cherrington, David J. (1992) 'Work, Role of', in Daniel H. Ludlow (ed.), *The Encyclopedia of Mormonism*, New York: Macmillan.

Congar, Yves (1966) *Tradition and Traditions*, London: Burns and Oates and the Macmillan Company.

Cowan, Richard O. (1992) 'Temples', in Daniel H. Ludlow (ed.), *The Encyclopedia of Mormonism*, New York: Macmillan.

Craig, David (2000) *Saints and Spinners: the Church of Jesus Christ of Latter-day Saints in the Town of Paisley, 1839–2000*. No publisher named.

Dahl, P. E. (1992) 'Godhead', in Daniel H. Ludlow (ed.), *The Encyclopedia of Mormonism*, New York: Macmillan.

Davies, Douglas J. (1973) 'Aspects of Latter-day Saint Eschatology', in Michael Hill (ed.), *Sociological Yearbook of Religion*, London: SCM Press.

(1987) *Mormon Spirituality: Latter-day Saints in Wales and Zion*, Nottingham: University of Nottingham Series in Theology.

(2000) *The Mormon Culture of Salvation*, Aldershot: Ashgate.

(2002) *Anthropology and Theology*, Oxford: Berg.

Decker, Ed and Dave Hunt (1984) *The God Makers*, Eugene, OR: Harvest House Publishers.

Durrant, George D. (1992) 'Genealogical Society of Utah', in Daniel H. Ludlow (ed.), *The Encyclopedia of Mormonism*, New York: Macmillan.

Fiddes, Paul S. (1989) *Past Event and Present Salvation*, London: Darton, Longman and Todd.

Gardner, Martin R. (1979) 'Mormonism and Capital Punishment: a Doctrinal Perspective Past and Present', *Dialogue*, spring, 9–25.

Gaustad, Edwin S. (1984) 'Historical Theology and Theological History: Mormon Possibilities', *Journal of Mormon History* 11, 99–111.

Givens, Terryl L. (1997) *The Viper on the Hearth: Mormons, Myths and the Construction of Heresy*, New York: Oxford University Press.

(2002) *By the Hand of Mormon: the American Scripture that Launched a New World Religion*, New York: Oxford University Press.

Godfrey, Kenneth W. (1992) 'Freemasonry in Nauvoo', in Daniel H. Ludlow (ed.), *The Encyclopedia of Mormonism*, New York: Macmillan.

Gooren, Henri (1998) *Rich among the Poor: Church, Firm and Household among Small-Scale Entrepreneurs in Guatamala City*, Utrecht: Thela Latin America Series.

Hale, Van (1989) Defining the Contemporary Mormon Concept of God', in Gary James Bergera (ed.), *Line upon line: Essays on Mormon Doctrine*, Salt Lake City, UT: Signature Books.

Hansen, Klaus, J. (1984) 'Jan Shipps and the Mormon Tradition', *Journal of Mormon History* 11, 135–45.

Hartley, William G. (1992) 'Organization', in Daniel H. Ludlow (ed.), *The Encyclopedia of Mormonism*, New York: Macmillan.

Heelas, Paul (1996) *The New Age Movement*, Oxford: Berg.

Heywood Thomas, John (1973) 'Introduction', in Paul Tillich, *The Boundaries of Our Being*, London: Collins.

Hill, Marvin S. (1989) *Quest for Refuge: the Morman Flight from American Pluralism*, Salt Lake City, UT: Signature Books.

Hinckley, Gordon B. (1989) *Faith: the Essence of True Religion*, Salt Lake City, UT: Deseret Book Company.

(2001) 'The Family: A Proclamation to the World', in *Almanac 2001–2002 The Church of Jesus Christ of Latter-day Saints*, Salt Lake City, UT: Deseret News.

Huxley, T. H. (1889) 'Agnosticism', *The Nineteenth Century*, no. CXLIV, February.

Hyde, Paul Nolan (1992) 'Intelligences', in Daniel H. Ludlow (ed.), *The Encyclopedia of Mormonism*, New York: Macmillan.

Hymns (1978), Salt Lake City, UT: Deseret Book Company.

Jensen, J. Y. (1992) 'Spirit', in Daniel H. Ludlow (ed.), *The Encyclopedia of Mormonism*, New York: Macmillan.

Jessee, Dean C. (1992) 'Wilford Woodruff', in Daniel H. Ludlow (ed.), *The Encyclopedia of Mormonism*, New York: Macmillan.

Jordan, L. H. (1905) *Comparative Religion*, Edinburgh: T. & T. Clark.

Judd, Peter A. and A. Bruce Lindgren (1976) *An Introduction to the Saints Church*, Independence, MO: Herald Publishing House.

Kear, Warrick N. (2001) 'The LDS Sound World and Global Mormonism', *Dialogue* 34, fall–winter, 77–94.

Kildahl, J. P. (1972) *The Psychology of Speaking in Tongues*, London: Hodder and Stoughton.

Kirtland, Boyd (1989) 'The Development of the Mormon Doctrine of God', in Gary James Bergera (ed.), *Line upon Line: Essays on Mormon Doctrine*, Salt Lake City, UT: Signature Books.

Kraemer, David (2000) *The Meanings of Death in Rabbinic Judaism*, London and New York: Routledge.

Kraut, Ogden (1969) *Jesus Was Married*, Dugway, UT: Pioneer Books.

Lasseter, Courtney J. (1992) 'Dispensations of the Gospel', in Daniel H. Ludlow (ed.), *The Encyclopedia of Mormonism*, New York: Macmillan.

LeBaron, E. Dale (1996) 'Mormonism in Black Africa', in Douglas J. Davies (ed.), *Mormon Identities in Transition*, London: Cassell.

Leone, Mark P. (1979) *Roots of Modern Mormonism*, Cambridge, MA: Harvard University Press.

Lucas, James W. & Warner P. Woodworth (1996) *Working toward Zion: Principles of the United Order for the Modern World*, Salt Lake City, UT: Aspen Books.

Ludlow, Daniel H. (ed.) (1992) *The Encyclopedia of Mormonism*, New York: Macmillan.

Luther, Martin (1961) *Luther: Lectures on Romans*, tr. and ed. Wilhelm Pauck, Philadelphia, PA: Westminster Press.

Lyon, Joseph Lynn (1992a) 'Coffee', in Daniel H. Ludlow (ed.), *The Encyclopedia of Mormonism*, New York: Macmillan.

(1992b) 'Word of Wisdom' in Daniel H. Ludlow (ed.), *The Encyclopedia of Mormonism*, New York: Macmillan.

Malinowski, B. (1974) *Magic, Science and Religion and Other Essays*, London: Souvenir Press.

Mangum, Donald P. and Brenton G. Yorgason (1996) *Amazing Grace: the Tender Mercies of the Lord*, Salt Lake City, UT: Bookcraft.

Mangum, Garth L. (1992) 'Welfare Services', in Daniel H. Ludlow (ed.), *The Encyclopedia of Mormonism*, New York: Macmillan.

Marty, Martin E. and R. Scott Appleby (1993) *Fundamentalisms and Society*, Chicago and London: University of Chicago Press.

Matthews, Robert J. (1985a) *Joseph Smith's Translation of the Bible*, Provo, UT: Brigham Young University Press.

(1985b) 'Major Doctrinal Contributions of the JST', in Monte S. Nyman and Robert L. Millet (eds.), *The Joseph Smith Translation*, Provo, UT: Religious Studies Center, Brigham Young University.

(1992) 'Joseph Smith Translation of the Bible', in Daniel H. Ludlow (ed.), *The Encyclopedia of Mormonism*, New York: Macmillan.

Mauss, Armand L. (1994) *The Angel and the Beehive: the Mormon Struggle with Assimilation*, Urbana and Chicago. University of Illinois Press.

(2001) 'Mormonism's Worldwide Aspirations and Its Changing Conceptions', *Dialogue* 34, fall–winter, 103–34.

May, Frank O. (1992) 'Correlation of the Church', in Daniel H. Ludlow (ed.), *The Encyclopedia of Mormonism*, New York: Macmillan.

McConkie, Bruce R. (1979 [1966] revised edition) *Mormon Doctrine*, Salt Lake City, UT: Bookcraft.

McConkie, J. F. (1992) 'Holy Ghost', in Daniel H. Ludlow (ed.), *The Encyclopedia of Mormonism*, New York: Macmillan.

McConkie, Mark L. (1992) 'Translated Beings', in Daniel H. Ludlow (ed.), *The Encyclopedia of Mormonism*, New York: Macmillan.

McKinlay, Lynn A. (1992) 'Patriarchal Order of the Priesthood', in Daniel H. Ludlow (ed.), *The Encyclopedia of Mormonism*, New York: Macmillan.

McMurrin, Stirling M. (1959) *The Philosophical Foundations of Mormon Thought*, Salt Lake City, UT: University of Utah Press.

(1969) *The Theological Foundations of Mormon Theology*, Salt Lake City, UT: University of Utah Press.

(1994) 'Introduction: the Mormon Theology of B. H. Roberts', in B. H. Roberts, *The Truth, the way, the Life*, ed. Stan Larson, Salt Lake City, UT: Smith Research Associates.

Millet, Robert L. (1992) 'Jesus Christ', in Daniel H. Ludlow (ed.), *The Encyclopedia of Mormonism*, New York: Macmillan.

(1994) *Christ Centred Living*, Salt Lake City, UT: Bookcraft.

(1995) *Within Reach*, Salt Lake City, UT: Bookcraft.

Molen, Roy (1991) 'The Two Churches of Mormonism', in John Sillito (ed.), *The Wilderness of Faith*, Salt Lake City, UT: Signature Books.

Moltmann, Jürgen (1974) *The Crucified God: the Cross of Christ as the Foundation and Criticism of Christian Theology*, tr. R. Wilson and J. Bowden, London: SCM Press.

Müller, Max. (1880) *Chips from a German Workshop*, London: Longmans, Green & Co.

(1898) *Natural Religion*, London: Longmans, Green & Co.

Niebuhr, Gustav (2001) 'Adapting "Mormon" to Emphasize Christianity', *New York Times*, 17 February.

Niebuhr, H. Richard (1929) *The Social Sources of Denominationalism*, New York: Henry Holt and Company, Inc.

Nyman, Monte S. and Robert L. Millet (eds.) (1985) *The Joseph Smith Translation*, Provo, UT: Religious Studies Center, Brigham Young University.

O'dea, Thomas (1957) *The Mormons*, Chicago: Chicago University Press.

Parry, Donald W. (1992) *The Book of Mormon Text Reformatted according to Parallelistic Patterns*, Provo, UT: FARMS.

Paulsen, David L. (1996) 'Must God Be Incorporeal?', in Douglas J. Davies (ed.), *Mormon Identities in Transition*, London: Cassell.

Peterson, Paul H. (1989) ' "The Mormon Reformation of 1856–1857", The Rhetoric and the Reality', *Journal of Mormon History* 15, 59–88.

Poulain, A. (1921) *The Graces of Interior Prayer*, tr. L. L. Yorke Smith, London: Kegan Paul, Trench, Trubner and Co. Ltd.

Quinn, D. Michael (1994) *The Mormon Hierarchy: Origins of Power*, Salt Lake City, UT: Signature Books with Smith Research Associates.

(2001) 'LDS "Headquarters Culture"', *Dialogue* 34, fall–winter, 135–68.

Richards, A. L. (1992) 'High Priest', in Daniel H. Ludlow (ed.), *The Encyclopedia of Mormonism*, New York: Macmillan.

Richards, LeGrand (1969) *A Marvelous Work and a Wonder*, Salt Lake City, UT: Deseret Book Company.

Roberts, A. and J. Donaldson (eds.), (1869) *Origen against Celsus. Ante-Nicene Christian Library*, Edinburgh: T. & T. Clark.

Roberts, B. H. (1990) *The Autobiography of B. H. Roberts*, Salt Lake City, UT: Signature Books.

(1994) *The Truth, the Way, the Life*, ed. Stan Larson, Salt Lake City, UT: Smith Research Associates.

Robinson, Stephen E. (1992) *Believing Christ*, Salt Lake City, UT: Deseret Book Company.

Schillebeeckx, E. (1963) *Christ the Sacrament*, London: Sheed and Ward.

Shipps, Jan (2000) *Sojourner in the Promised Land*, Urbana and Chicago: University of Illinios Press.

Shoemaker, Thaddeus E. (1989) 'Speculative Theology: Key to a Dynamic Faith', in Gary James Bergera (ed.), *Line upon line: Essays on Mormon Doctrine*, Salt Lake City, UT: Signature Books.

Smith, Joseph (1985) *Lectures on Faith*, Salt Lake City, UT: Deseret Book Company.

Smith, Wilfred Cantwell (1963) *The Meaning and End of Religion*, New York: Macmillan.

Stark, Rodney (1984) 'The Rise of a New World Faith', *Review of Religious Research* 26, 18–27.

(1998) 'The Basis of Mormon Success: a Theoretical Application', in James T. Duke (ed.), *Latter-day Saint Social Life*, Salt Lake City, UT: Bookcraft.

Stroup, George W. (1981) *The Promise of Narrative Theology*, London: SCM Press.

Studdert Kennedy, Geoffrey A. (1983 [1927]) *The Unutterable Beauty*, London: Hodder and Stoughton.

Swainston, Howard D. (1992) 'Tithing', in Daniel H. Ludlow (ed.), *The Encyclopedia of Mormonism*, New York: Macmillan.

Swanson, Vern G. (1989) 'The Development of the Concept of a Holy Ghost in Mormon Theology', in Gary James Bergera (ed.), *Line upon Line: Essays on Mormon Doctrine*, Salt Lake City, UT: Signature Books.

Talmage, James E. (1962 [1915]) *Jesus the Christ*, Salt Lake City, UT: Deseret Book Club.

Taves, Ann (1999) *Fits, Trances and Visions*, Princeton, NJ: Princeton University Press.

Tillich, Paul (1962) *The Courage to Be*, London: Fontana.

Toscano, Paul James (1994) *The Sanctity of Dissent*, Salt Lake City, UT: Signature Books.

Troeltsch, Ernst (1931) *The Social Teachings of the Christian Churches*, tr. Olive Wyon, London: The Macmillan Company.

Turner, Harold W. (1979) *From Temple to Meeting House: the Phenomenology and Theology of Places of Worship*, The Hague: Mouton Publishers.

Turner, Rodney (1992) 'Sons of Perdition', in Daniel H. Ludlow (ed.), *The Encyclopedia of Mormonism*, New York: Macmillan.

Underwood, Grant (1993) *The Millenarian World of Early Mormonism*, Urbana and Chicago: University of Illinois Press.

Van Rooden, Peter (1996) 'Nineteenth-Century Representations of Missionary Conversion and the Transformation of Western Christianity', in Peter van der Veer (ed.), *Conversion to Modernities: the Globalization of Christianity*, New York and London: Routledge.

Van Wagoner, Richard (1994), *Sidney Rigdon: a Portrait of Religious Excess*, Salt Lake City, UT: Signature Books.

Vogel, Dan (1989) 'The Earliest Mormon Concept of God', in Gary James Bergera (ed.), *Line upon Line: Essays on Mormon Doctrine*, Salt Lake City, UT: Signature Books.

Weber, Max (1976) *The Protestant Ethic and the Spirit of Capitalism*, tr. Talcott Parsons, London: Allen & Unwin.

Welch, John W. (1990) *The Sermon at the Temple and the Sermon on the Mount*, Salt Lake City, UT: Foundation for Ancient Research and Mormon Studies.

Wesley, John (1831) *Explanatory Notes upon the New Testament*, London: John Mason.

Westcott, B. F. (1889) *The Epistle to the Hebrews*, London: Macmillan and Co.

White, O. Kendall (1987) *Mormon Neo-Orthodoxy: A Crisis Theology*, Salt Lake City, UT: Signature Books.

Whittaker, David J. 1992. 'Articles of Faith', in Daniel H. Ludlow (ed.), *The Encyclopedia of Mormonism*, New York: Macmillan.

Widmer, Kurt (2000) *Mormonism and the Nature of God: a Theological Evolution, 1833–1915*, Jefferson, NC and London: McFarland & Company.

Woodruff, Wilford (1993) *Waiting for World's End: the Diaries of Wilford Woodruff*, ed. Susan Staker, Salt Lake City, UT: Signature Books.

Young, Brigham (1854–86) *Journal of Discourses*, Liverpool: Church of Jesus Christ of Latter-day Saints.

(1992) *The Essential Brigham Young*, with a foreword by Eugene E. Campbell, Salt Lake City, UT: Signature Books.

Index of passages cited

PEARL OF GREAT PRICE

General index

LaVergne, TN USA
26 March 2010
177221LV00008B/1/P

THE
PERFECT
ASSASSIN

A list of titles by James Patterson appears at the back of this book

THE
PERFECT
ASSASSIN
JAMES
PATTERSON
& BRIAN SITTS

CENTURY

1 3 5 7 9 10 8 6 4 2

Century
20 Vauxhall Bridge Road
London SW1V 2SA

Century is part of the Penguin Random House group of companies whose
addresses can be found at global.penguinrandomhouse.com.

Penguin
Random House
UK

Copyright © James Patterson 2022
Excerpt from *The Girl in the Castle* © James Patterson 2022

In association with Condé Nast and Neil McGinness

James Patterson has asserted his right to be identified as the author of this
Work in accordance with the Copyright, Designs and Patents Act 1988.

First published in the UK by Century in 2022

www.penguin.co.uk

A CIP catalogue record for this book is available from the British Library.

ISBN: 978–1–529–13657–9
ISBN: 978–1–529–13658–6 (trade paperback edition)

Printed and bound in Great Britain by Clays Ltd, Elcograf S.p.A.

The authorised representative in the EEA is Penguin Random House Ireland,
Morrison Chambers, 32 Nassau Street, Dublin D02 YH68

MIX
Paper from
responsible sources
FSC® C018179

Penguin Random House is committed to a sustainable future
for our business, our readers and our planet. This book is made
from Forest Stewardship Council® certified paper.

ONE

Eastern Russia
30 Years Ago

A MOTHER CAN sense a disturbance in her world, even in her sleep.

Marisha did.

The late-night snowfall made the small village on the Kamchatka Peninsula look like a cozy Christmas painting, but the wind was harsh. It whistled around the cottage and seeped through the walls of the tiny nursery where the six-month-old twins slept in a single crib, spooned together for warmth. Like tiny dolls. They were just five minutes apart in age, with matching features and the same delicate, pale skin. But the similarities stopped at the top of their heads. One girl had her father's dark, straight hair. The other had lush copper-colored curls, like nobody else in the family.

Marisha was a physicist. Her husband, Mikhail, was a mathematician. In their courting days at the university, they had long talks about what extraordinary children they would have together. And that's exactly what happened. Two in one day. The babies were remarkable—so beautiful and loving. And now, at just half a year old, already advanced for their age. They were everything a parent could wish for, and more.

Mikhail had put the girls down just after seven. At 2 a.m., Marisha woke suddenly. Something was off. She could feel it. She pushed back the covers and slipped out of bed, not bothering to nudge her husband or find her slippers. She grabbed her robe from the wall hook and wrapped it hastily over her nightgown as she hurried down the short hallway, feeling the cold tile against her bare feet.

When she opened the door to the nursery, a waft of frosty air crossed her face. In the next second, she felt a matching chill in her gut. She took a step toward the center of the dark room and inhaled sharply. Snow dusted the floor under the half-open window. Marisha grabbed the side rail of the crib with both hands, then dropped to her knees and screamed for her husband. Mikhail stumbled into the doorway seconds later, his eyes bleary and half closed. He saw his wife on the floor and then—the empty crib. His eyes opened wide.

"They're gone!" Marisha wailed. "Both of them! *Gone!*"

TWO

A MILE AWAY, two thickset men in heavy wool coats were making their way up a rugged slope. The village lights were already fading behind the scrim of windblown snow. The footing was treacherous, and they were not familiar with the terrain.

Bortsov, the taller of the pair, used a heavy hiking pole to probe the path ahead. Gusev, the shorter partner, carried a high-powered hunting rifle. In their opposite arms, each man carried a tightly wrapped bundle. The men were killers by trade, and this was their first kidnapping. In fact, it was the first time either of them had held an infant. They clutched the sixteen-pound babies like rugby balls.

After twenty minutes of steady hiking, they were out of sight of the village. Still, Gusev kept looking over his shoulder.

"Stop worrying," said Bortsov gruffly, pointing at the trail behind them. "We were never here." He was right. Just a few yards back, the snow was already filling their tracks. The search would begin at dawn. By then, it would be no use.

Bortsov had scouted the campsite the day before. It was

a natural shelter beneath a rock overhang. He'd even taken the time to gather wood for a fire. By the time the kidnappers reached the spot, it was nearly 4 a.m. They were both exhausted from the climb and their arms were cramped from gripping the babies. Bortsov walked to a snowdrift about ten yards from the shelter. He bent forward and set the bundle he'd been carrying down in the snow. Gusev did the same with his.

They stepped back. The twins were about four feet apart, separated by a snow-covered log. They were both squirming under their tight wraps, their cries muffled by wool scarves around their heads. Bortsov pulled a handful of coins from his pocket and placed them on a rock in front of the baby on the left. Gusev placed a bunch of coins in front of the baby on the right. Then they shuffled back toward the shelter and started a fire.

When the wood caught, flames and sparks illuminated the small recess. The kidnappers tucked themselves under the rock and pulled their thick coats up around their necks. Gusev fished a flask of vodka out of his coat pocket, took a deep gulp, and passed it to his partner. A little extra warmth. Before long, their eyes were glazed. Soon after that, their stupor faded into sleep.

The babies, left in the open, were no longer crying.

THREE

MORNING. GUSEV WOKE first, stirred by an acrid waft of smoke from the smoldering fire. He brushed the snow off his coat and shook his flask. It was empty. Gusev's head throbbed and the inside of his mouth felt thick and pasty. He glanced across the small clearing to where the two babies lay silent in the snow. He elbowed Bortsov in the ribs. Bortsov stirred and rolled over. Gusev nodded toward the twins.

Both men rose slowly to their feet and walked on unsteady legs to the snowdrift. Over the past few hours, the wind had blown a fresh coating of white over both babies. Bortsov pulled the stiff scarves away from their faces. In the dawn light, their skin was bluish, their lips and nostrils coated with frost. Obviously dead. A total waste of a trip.

"Weak! *Both* of them!" said Gusev, spitting into the snow.

Bortsov turned away, snarling in frustration. "Food for the bears," he muttered.

As Gusev retrieved his rifle, he heard a small mewing sound. He turned. The baby on the left was stirring slightly.

Gusev hurried back and knelt down. He pushed the frozen scarf back off the baby's head, revealing coils of copper hair.

"We have one!" Gusev shouted. "She's alive!"

Bortsov tromped over. "Mine!" he called out with a victorious sneer. He scooped both sets of coins from under the snow and pocketed them. Then he lifted the copper-haired girl from the snowbank and tucked her roughly under his coat. Gusev gave the dark-haired baby one final shake, but there was no response. He kicked fresh snow over the tiny corpse, then followed his partner up the mountain, cursing all the way. He hated to lose a bet.

The walk down the other side of the mountain was even harder than last night's climb. Bortsov's knees ached with every step, and Gusev was coughing in the thin, cold air. But they knew the effort would be worth it. They had conducted the test with the babies, side by side, as they had been instructed. A survivor this strong meant a big payday, maybe even a bonus. An hour later, Bortsov and Gusev pushed through the last of the tree line into a rolling snow-covered valley.

Straight ahead was a campus of sturdy buildings made of thick stone. A few simple balconies protruded from the top floors, and most of the windows were striped with heavy metal grates. In the early morning, a light glowed from a corner room, where they knew the headmaster would be waiting for the new student. Bortsov pulled the copper-haired baby out from under his coat as they approached the imposing school gate. He knew the headmaster would be pleased. This child showed exceptional promise.

PART 1

CHAPTER 1

University of Chicago
Present Day

I'D FORGOTTEN HOW much I hated first-year students.

I'd just finished a solid fifty minutes of a cultural psych lecture, and I might as well have been talking to a roomful of tree stumps. I was already pissed at Barton for asking me to sub for him at the last minute—and a 9 a.m. class, no less. I hadn't taught this early since I was an anthropology TA. That was twelve long years ago.

Barton's lecture notes were good, but since I'd actually written my thesis on South Pacific cultures, I was able to ad lib some interesting insights and twists on tribal gender roles. At least *I* thought they were interesting. Judging by my audience, not nearly as interesting as TikTok.

After class, the students moved toward the door with their eyes still glued to their screens. I felt like I was forgetting something. *Shit. The reading assignment!* I scrolled through Barton's notes. *Jesus. Where is it? Right here. Got it.*

"Sorry!" I called out to the departing crowd. "Listen up, please! Reading for next class!" I held the textbook over my head like a banner. It was as heavy as a brick. "In Muckle and

Gonzalez! Chapters Five and Six, please!" Most of the students just ignored me. I tried to catch their eyes as they walked past, but up-close contact has never been my strength. Lecturing to a class of a hundred, no problem. Just a faceless mass. Close up, I tended to get clammy.

Sometimes I thought I might be on the spectrum. No shame in it. So was Albert Einstein. I definitely met some of the criteria. Preference for being alone? Check. Difficulty in relating to people? Check. Stuck in repetitive patterns? Check. On the other hand, maybe I was just your garden-variety misanthrope.

I plopped the textbook down on the lectern. Two female students were the last to leave. I'd noticed them in the back row—way more interested in each other than in my cogent analysis of the Solomon Islanders.

"Awesome class," said the first student. Right. As if she'd heard a word of it. She was small and pert, with purple-streaked hair and an earful of silver rings. "So interesting," said her blond friend. Were they trying to suck up? Maybe they were hoping I'd be back for good and that I'd grade easier than Barton, who I knew could be a real prick.

"Good, good, thanks," I mumbled. I stuffed Barton's iPad and textbook into my briefcase and snapped it shut. Enough higher education for one day. Out of the corner of my eye, I saw Purple Hair nudge her partner. They looked over their shoulders at the whiteboard, where I'd written my name in big capital letters at the start of class.

DR. BRANDT SAVAGE

Purple Hair leaned in close to the blonde and whispered in a low, seductive voice, "I'll *bet* he's a savage!" She gave her friend a suggestive little hip bump. Nothing like freshman sarcasm. Make a little fun of the gawky PhD. Got it. And not the first time somebody had made the point: I was about as far from a savage as a man could possibly get.

I headed down the hall to the department office to pick up my mail. As I pushed through the heavy oak door, I could hear Natalie, our department admin, helping a student sort out a snafu in his schedule. When she saw me, she held up her index finger, signifying "I need to talk to you."

I liked Natalie. She was all business, no drama. Quiet and efficient. Herding cats was a cinch compared to keeping a bunch of eccentric academics in line, and she did it well. The student jammed his new schedule into his backpack and headed out the door. Natalie leaned over the counter in my direction.

"So where will you be going?" she asked, flashing a knowing smile.

"What do you mean?" I asked. My only travel plans involved heading home and heating up some soup. Natalie leaned closer and looked both ways, as if she were revealing a state secret. She gave me an insider's wink and held up a slip of paper.

"Your sabbatical," she whispered. "It's been approved!"

CHAPTER 2

HOW THE HELL did *that* happen, I wondered? I headed down the corridor with the slip in my pocket, dodging students as I went. I'd put in the sabbatical request eight months ago and hadn't heard a thing. The university system was definitely not built for speed. Ulrich, my department head, was unearthing a crypt somewhere in the Middle East. I'd given up on an approval until he got back. Had somebody gotten to him? I guess miracles do happen.

My only problem was that I hadn't really given any thought to a destination. All I knew was I'd earned six months of peace and quiet. Now I just had to figure out where to spend it.

I pushed open the main door and stepped out through the Gothic stone front of Cobb Hall. My glasses were immediately speckled with falling snow, and the cold cut right through my overcoat. That Chicago wind everybody talked about was no joke. I put my head down and almost banged into two students rushing up the steps.

"Sorry," I said. "My bad."

Even on sub-zero days, I looked forward to the

twenty-minute walk to my apartment. Time to clear my head. A break from crowded classrooms and talky colleagues. As I headed toward East 59th, my shoes lost traction on the sidewalk and I had one of those real-life cartoon moments, where your arms flail in the air while you try to keep from falling on your ass and you hope to hell nobody is watching. Once I got my footing again, I walked the rest of the way across campus with short, careful steps. Like an old man with an invisible walker.

I dipped my head into the wind and headed up the city sidewalk, squinting to keep the snow out of my eyes. Most people who passed me from the opposite direction gave me a wide berth, probably because I looked half blind. The next time I looked up, I saw a young woman in a puffy parka headed toward me through the snow.

She was walking at a quick pace, staring straight ahead. As she passed, our elbows bumped.

"Sorry, sorry," I mumbled. I was a real menace to humanity today.

The woman stopped and turned abruptly. "Don't apologize!" she shouted.

The shock froze me in place. Before I could open my mouth again, she grabbed my upper arms and turned me to face the curb, like a cop getting ready to frisk a suspect.

Adrenaline shot through me. "Hey!" was all I could get out. I saw a green van with an open cargo door right in front of me. She shoved me forward, and I sprawled into the van head first. My face slapped hard against the rubber floor liner. When I flipped myself right side up, the door was sliding shut.

My heart was beating so hard I could hear my pulse in my ears. This had to be a prank, or some terrible mistake. I kicked against the inside of the door, but my rubber soles didn't even make a mark. A second later, I heard the passenger door open. There was a thick divider between the cargo section and the front seats. It was black metal at the bottom with thick, clear plastic across the top. I saw the woman slide into the driver's seat. I pounded on the plastic with my fists. She ignored me and turned the key in the ignition. She cranked the wheel and pulled out onto the street. Then she floored the accelerator. I fell backward against the rear door. I didn't bother trying to stand up. I crawled forward on my hands and knees.

"Hey! What are you doing??" I shouted. "Where are you taking me??"

My face was jammed right up against the plastic. The woman stared ahead, arms straight out on the steering wheel, weaving through the morning traffic like an Indy racer. We were heading north, out of Hyde Park. I turned to the side and started pounding on the sliding door. I twisted the door handle back and forth. It wasn't just locked. It was unscrewed. Totally useless. I tried the rear door. Same thing. I put my face against the cold metal of the truck wall. "Help!" I shouted. "I need *help*!"

"No whining!"

It was her. She was shouting at me from the front seat. Her voice cut right through the divider.

I kept on yelling. Every true-crime show I'd ever watched flashed through my brain. Rule Number One: Never get into a stranger's vehicle. Once you're taken, your chances of survival go way down. Why hadn't I put up a fight? Because it happened so fast, that's why. In real life, you don't get time to think about it. All I could do now was keep making noise and hope that we'd pull up next to a police car. *Any* car. But when

I looked out through the plastic, I could see that we were now on a deserted street, or maybe in an alley. There was nobody around.

I kept pounding and shouting for dear life anyway. Suddenly I felt the van pull over and skid to a stop. I flew forward and my shoulder banged hard against the partition. I was frantic, confused, terrified. My knuckles were bruised and bloody. As I got up from the floor, the cargo door slid open. The woman was outside, leaning in.

She had a no-bullshit look on her face. Her voice was low and even.

"I said, no whining."

The punch came so fast I barely saw it. There was a sharp pain in my jaw and I felt my head snap back. I was out cold before I hit the floor.

CHAPTER 3

WHEN I CAME back to life, I was lying on my back inside some kind of bag. I could feel thick rubber against my glasses and forehead. It was hard to breathe. I was on top of a narrow cushion, and I was rolling forward. I could feel the vibration of wheels on a hard surface. My jaw ached and my head throbbed.

Everything was hazy, like coming out of anesthesia. The rolling stopped, then started again. I heard a door slide closed and felt a thump. I was in an elevator, going up. I heard the rattle of chains in the shaft. The elevator stopped with a lurch. I started to thrash around inside the bag, but I realized my hands and ankles were wrapped tight. I felt a hard slap on the side of my head.

"Quit moving." It was her.

I was rolling forward again. A couple of turns. Then another stop. A series of beeps. The sound of a heavy door swinging open. Wheels rolling again. Different surface now. Stopped again. Boots on wood. I felt hands rustling the top of the bag. The sound of a zipper. Then a wide gap opened over my face.

The sudden light made me blink. I was looking up at an industrial ceiling—raw aluminum ductwork and beige pipes. The woman's face appeared in the opening, leaning over me. She yanked the zipper down to my knees. I saw the flash of a blade. I felt tugs at my hands and feet and then I realized that I was loose.

"End of the line, Doctor," the woman said. "Up you go."

She crooked her arm under my neck and lifted me to a sitting position. I pulled my feet out of the bottom of the bag. There was gray duct tape clinging to my ankles and wrists. I sat on the edge of the cushion and then slid off and stood up, dizzy and disoriented. I rubbed my jaw where she'd clocked me. She reached out, tilted my chin up, and appraised the damage.

"First lesson," she said. "When I tell you to stop doing something—stop doing it."

"Who the hell *are* you?" I asked. My brain was foggy and my jaw hurt when I talked.

"Wrong question," she said. She rezipped the body bag and folded it on the cushion, which I could now see was the top of a hospital gurney. I swiveled my head to look around, looking for accomplices. I didn't see anybody.

"It's just us," she said. "Go ahead. Take in the atmosphere."

You're a trained observer, I told myself. So *observe*. Like they say on a dig, everything is evidence. We were on a high floor. Brick walls. The wood planks had dark outlines and metal plates where heavy machinery had been bolted down. This was no modern high-rise. It was a high-priced renovation. I was pretty good at estimating spaces, and this place was big—over a thousand square feet, not counting whatever was behind the doors at the far end. My apartment would fit in here twice.

The space was wide open, with one area flowing into the other. Trendy. And expensive. There was an industrial-sized kitchen at one end. At the other end, I saw a classy seating area with a cushy leather sofa, a glass table, and a baby grand piano. In the middle of the space, on a black rubber surface, there was a bunch of high-tech workout machines with names like Precor and Cybex. Luxury loft meets CrossFit gym.

"This is yours?" I asked. "You live here?" Make a human connection, I was thinking. And maybe she won't kill you.

"Yes," she said, matter-of-factly. "And as of now, so do you."

My gut turned. She sounded like a psycho. She unbuttoned her parka, took off her cap and scarf, and tossed everything onto a bench. Underneath, she was wearing black tights and a long-sleeved athletic jersey. I tried not to be obvious, but I studied every inch of her. I wanted to be able to give a good description to the cops, if I ever got the chance. Late twenties or early thirties. Tall. Probably five foot ten. Athletic build. Blue eyes. Pale skin. No visible piercings. And one really distinctive feature: long curly hair, the color of a bright copper penny.

I suddenly felt woozy, like I was about to pass out. I leaned back against the gurney.

"Hold still," she said. "You need water."

She turned and walked toward the kitchen, her boot heels clicking on the hardwood. I glanced toward the elevator. It was about six feet away. I took a small side step in that direction. The woman took a glass from a cabinet and turned on the faucet. Her back was to me. I took a deep breath and lunged for the elevator button. I pounded it hard with my closed fist. Nothing happened. No light. No ding. No hum. I heard footsteps behind me. Shit! I whipped around. My glasses flew off and skittered across the floor. Everything went blurry. I panicked. I dropped to my hands and knees and reached for my frames. Her boot heel came down and smashed them to pieces.

"You don't need those anymore," she said. "I mean, you *won't.*"

CHAPTER 4

Eastern Russia
26 Years Ago

IT WAS MIDNIGHT. Headmaster Alexei Kamenev was still in his office at the school. The curriculum he had inherited was excellent, but he often worked on small tweaks late into the night, refining a technique or devising a new challenge. The wall facing his desk was covered with 5"x7" black-and-white photographs of his students, hundreds of them. So many that the faces practically filled the space from floor to ceiling. Kamenev felt a deep interest in every single one. Affection, even. He understood all their strengths and weaknesses—but most of all, their potential for greatness. After all, he had chosen each of them personally. By now, he knew them better than their parents ever had.

Kamenev looked up as a thin shadow passed across the frosted glass panel of his office door. He usually left bed check to his staff, but tonight he felt like stretching his legs. He closed his leather notebook and put down his pen.

When he reached the doorway to the preschool girls' dormitory, Matron Lyudmila Garin was already walking the room like a wraith. Maybe sixty years old, she looked ten years older, pale and sickly. She looked up at Kamenev with hollow eyes and gave him a respectful nod.

The narrow beds were arranged in neat rows a few feet apart. Garin glided easily between them, but Kamenev, with his extra bulk, had to be careful not to knock against the bedframes. The light from the full moon passed through the window bars and cast shadows across the room. It was a chilly night, and most of the girls were tucked under their wool blankets, but there was one, at the far end of the room, who was not. Curious, Kamenev walked over.

It was the copper-haired girl. She was lying on top of her blanket, curled around a ragged stuffed bear. Kamenev looked up as Garin approached. In the dim light, the matron looked even more frail and wasted. Kamenev tapped the bear lightly.

"What's this?" he asked, keeping his voice low.

Garin looked down at the skinny four-year-old, already tall for her age. She was holding the bear tight, spoon fashion, her arms around its soft belly.

"It's the only way she can sleep," said Garin softly. She stifled a cough.

"An indulgence," said Kamenev curtly. "Remove it." He turned and walked back down the row toward the door. Garin hesitated, then leaned over and pulled the bear gently from the girl's grasp. The girl's eyes popped open. Startled, she blinked and looked up. Seeing the bear in Garin's arms, she reached up with a whimper, tears pooling in her eyes. "No! *Please!*" she said softly. Garin leaned back down and brushed the copper curls away from the girl's forehead.

"You have only yourself," she whispered softly. "Nothing else."

Garin held the scruffy stuffed animal tight to her chest and walked toward the doorway, where Kamenev stood in silhouette. She glanced back and saw the copper-haired girl trembling as she curled herself around her thin white pillow.

CHAPTER 5

Chicago

I DON'T UNDERSTAND how I managed to sleep, but I guess I did. For all I know, the water she gave me was drugged. When I opened my eyes, I instinctively felt around for my glasses. Then I remembered. Right. Crushed. The whole world was fuzzy, which made it even more terrifying.

It took me a few seconds to realize where I was, which was in some kind of cell in a rear corner of the loft. Cot up against one side. Metal stool bolted to the middle of the floor. Metal toilet against the back wall. Clear shower stall. And transparent Plexiglass all around. Maximum security. Zero privacy.

My suit and shoes were gone. I was wearing gym shorts and a Nike T-shirt. Had she actually undressed me while I was unconscious?? Jesus! I didn't see or hear her anywhere. Was she gone? Did she leave me here to starve to death? Was she watching me right now on a camera? I squinted to make things a little sharper, but I couldn't make out any movement.

I slipped out from under the blanket. My bladder felt like a water balloon. I stared at the toilet. Normally, there's no way I could pee right out there in the open. But my body wasn't giving me a choice. It was either that or wet my pants. I walked the two steps to the toilet and tugged the leg hole of my shorts aside. As the stream hit the bowl, I heard footsteps.

"Morning, Doctor."

Shit! Her voice put a crimp in my flow. I hunched forward, doing my best to shelter my privates. I saw her shape pass by on the way to the kitchen.

"Don't mind me," she said. "Do what you need to do."

I did my best to finish up, then tucked myself back in and flushed. She was heating a kettle, putting a teabag into a cup. "Sorry about the Hannibal Lecter setup," she said. "Probably overkill. At least in your case."

I pounded on the clear wall facing her and shouted. No words, just a guttural scream—at the top of my lungs.

"Speak normally, Doctor," she said. "The cell is wired. I can hear you perfectly."

This was insane! Sociopathic. She was going about her business like she was talking with a house guest. On the other hand, if she really wanted me dead, she'd had plenty of chances. Or maybe she was just drawing it out. Making me suffer. A sociopath *and* a sadist. What had I done to deserve this?? Why *me*??

She poured her tea and carried her mug over to the front of my enclosure. She pulled up a rolling stool and sat down. She took a sip of her tea and tilted her head. Her face was blurry from where I stood, but I felt that she was looking at me like I was some kind of rare zoo specimen. She set her mug down on the floor and crossed her legs. She cleared her throat.

"Okay," she said calmly. "A few things you should know."

I stood with my hands pressed against the Plexiglass, my heart racing. I was all ears. I wanted any information I could get.

"The loft is totally sealed, soundproofed, and lead-lined,"

she said. "The elevator is locked, as you discovered. There are two staircase exits, also locked. Against fire codes, I know. But my house, my rules. In terms of the university, you've decided to take your sabbatical, effective immediately, on an island with no cell service. Your colleagues are annoyed by your sudden departure, but they'll get over it. For now, Professor Racine will be taking over your classes."

"Racine??" I said. "That moron wouldn't know an Aborigine from an Inuit."

"Not your first choice for a fill-in, I realize, but under the circumstances, he was the best option. He had some holes in his schedule."

I pounded on the Plexiglass. I was confused and furious. How had this woman managed to get control of my life??

"Who the hell *are* you??" I shouted.

"Wrong question," she said, and then pushed right on. "Your colleagues will be receiving occasional emails from you through a VPN. The IP address will be untraceable. Your snail mail is being forwarded to a post office box. Your rent has been paid in advance. Your landlord has a note from you that you'll be abroad and unreachable. Obviously, since you have no friends, nobody else will be looking for you."

That stung. But she wasn't wrong. I guessed that she knew that I also had no family, no girlfriends, no pets, no Facebook account. I realized that if you were looking for someone who could disappear without a trace, I was a great choice.

"In case you're holding out hope," she continued, "nobody witnessed your abduction. The street was clear and the surveillance camera at the intersection was disabled. The van will never be found. And according to the building plans, this floor does not exist."

"Tell me who you are!" I shouted.

"Wrong question," she said again.

"What do you want??" I asked. "Is it *money*?" I was getting frantic.

"Do you mean the five thousand, three hundred and sixty-two dollars in your PNC savings account?" she asked.

She stood up and walked right up to my enclosure. We were just two or three inches apart. I could see her face clearly, even without glasses. She was very attractive. Stunning, in fact. It felt weird to even be noticing that.

"What do you mean, 'wrong question'?" I asked.

She leaned in even closer, almost touching her side of the clear cell wall.

"I don't need money, Doctor," she said. "All I need is you. This may be hard to believe, but I'm actually going to turn you into somebody worth kidnapping."

CHAPTER 6

SHE TAPPED A combination on a keypad and let me out of my cage. Then she nodded toward a shoebox on a chair. "Put those on," she said, walking back to the kitchen.

I picked up the box and pulled off the lid. Inside was a pair of orange and turquoise running shoes with the Nike swoosh on the side and *ZoomX* stamped on the heel. I slid them on over my socks and laced them up. Perfect fit. Light as air.

"Nice, right?" she called out from the kitchen. "Carbon fiber sole plates."

I had no idea what that meant, but they were the most comfortable shoes I'd ever worn. I walked over to the kitchen counter and pulled up a metal stool. Morning light was streaming through the massive windows. It felt like a cozy little domestic scene, except for the fact that I'd recently been snatched off the street, punched in the jaw, and stuffed in a body bag—and the perp was fixing breakfast. I figured I had no choice but to play along until I found a way to escape. Unless she decided to kill me first.

I watched as she pulled ingredients off the shelves and out of the fridge. Fruit. Powder. Seeds. Olive oil. She started dumping everything into a huge industrial blender. She gave the blender a couple of quick pulses and then dumped in a load of plain yogurt and a bunch of spinach leaves. She put the machine on high until the ingredients turned into a thick green fluid.

I waited for the blender noise to stop, and then I spoke up. I was sure she would say "wrong question," but I had to give it a shot.

"Do you have a name?" I asked. "Or should I just call you Dear Leader?"

She gave the concoction a few more pulses and lifted the top to check the consistency. She looked up. "Call me Meed," she said.

"Is that your real name?" I asked.

"Not even close," she said.

She lifted the pitcher off its base and poured two glasses of the gross-looking drink. She slid one glass across to me and raised the other in front of her chin.

"Bottoms up," she said, and started gulping.

I stuck my nose into the top of the glass. It smelled like compost.

"*Now,* Doctor," she said. Her glass was already empty.

I could feel grit and chunks in my throat as the slime went down. I could see Meed—or whatever her name was—staring at me, hands on her hips. In a few seconds, it was over. I shoved the glass back across the counter.

"That's vile," I said, wiping my mouth with the back of my hand. I could feel the mess churning in my stomach, threatening to come back up.

"Get used to it," said Meed. She slapped her hands together. "Anyway, time to get started!"

"Started with what?" I asked. I was feeling weak and queasy. And her enthusiasm made me nervous.

"Training, Doctor," she said. She walked around to my side of the counter and poked me hard in the belly. "In case you hadn't noticed, you're not exactly in Wheaties-box shape."

That poke was all it took. I hunched over and vomited my entire green smoothie into the sink.

CHAPTER 7

Eastern Russia
25 Years Ago

FIVE A.M. A line of groggy, sullen five-year-old girls shuffled down the stone corridor from the dormitory toward the dining hall. Teenage hall monitors in blue uniforms were stationed along the way. At the back of the line, the copper-haired girl followed along, eyes down. Her mind was dull, but not from sleep. She had simply found a way to turn herself off. Every day, she ate her meals, learned her lessons, did her chores. But she wasn't really there. At least not in her head.

Suddenly, there was a new sound in the hall. Piano music. Complex and dramatic. It echoed off the stone walls and filled the corridor. The copper-haired girl looked up. It was like nothing she had ever heard. Something in her brain woke up. There were speakers everywhere in the school buildings, but the music was coming from somewhere else, close by. It didn't sound like a recording. Someone was playing it live, right now.

The girl turned her head from side to side, trying to figure out where the music was coming from. As she passed a doorway, she paused and stood on tiptoe to look through the thick glass pane. Inside the small room, a woman was hunched over an upright piano. It was Miss Garin, the matron. She looked lost in her own world, rocking slowly, her fingers flying back and forth across the keys. The girl stood, transfixed, as the line moved ahead without her. A moment later, she felt a knee in her back.

"Move it!" the monitor growled.

The girl doubled her pace to catch up to the others. Suddenly, a dark-haired girl darted away from the front of the line. She ran to the wall and pulled herself up onto a stone window ledge. The copper-haired girl recognized her right away. Her name was Irina. She slept in the next cot but never spoke to anybody. She had dark, flashing eyes and a face that looked angry even when she was sleeping.

One of the male monitors lunged for her. Irina already had one leg out of the window bars, and she looked skinny enough to slide the rest of her body through. The boy grabbed her trailing leg and wrapped his thick arm around her waist. He pulled her down and slammed her onto the floor like a slab of meat. The other girls winced at the sound of it. Irina stood up slowly, rubbing her side. The monitor slapped her on the cheek, sending her back down to her knees. Irina didn't cry. She barely flinched. She just stared back at him and slowly stood up again.

"To the back!" the monitor shouted into Irina's face, spittle flying.

Irina wiped his saliva off her chin and walked slowly past the long row of stunned, silent girls until she was next to the copper-haired girl, the last in line. Instinctively, without thinking, the girl reached out to hold Irina's hand. She squeezed it tight. Irina squeezed back—so hard it hurt.

CHAPTER 8

Chicago

I WAS BEGINNING to feel like a science experiment. Meed had me standing in the workout area in just my shorts and new training shoes, with electrodes connected to my bare chest and a blood-pressure cuff around my left biceps. She reached into a metal instrument drawer and pulled out a pair of creepy-looking black pincers. My heart started speeding until I realized that they were skin calipers. She pinched the loose folds on my chest, belly, and right thigh. She checked the gauge and shook her head.

"Twenty-two percent," she said. "I need you under ten."

Besides exercise equipment, the workout area was filled with high-tech medical gear. The university clinic would have been jealous. After my body-fat shaming, Meed did a pulmonary function test and a flexibility assessment. Both results were disappointing. She wasn't surprised.

"That's what happens when you spend ninety percent of your existence sitting on your ass," she said. "That's about to change. Big time."

She sat me down on the weight bench, then tied an elastic band around my biceps. She reached into a drawer and pulled out a plastic packet with a small syringe inside. I twisted away. She yanked me back.

"Quit moving," she said, in that low, even voice. I didn't want to get punched again, but I really hated needles.

"What are you *doing*?" I asked. I was squirming. She tightened her grip and tore open the packet with her teeth. She curled my fingers into a fist.

"What do you *think* I'm doing?" she said. "I'm turning you into a heroin addict."

I tried to jerk my arm loose. She held it tight.

"Kidding, Doctor," she said. "I just need a blood sample."

She tapped the inner hollow of my elbow and jabbed the needle into a vein.

"Don't faint on me," she said.

I watched my blood trickle through a narrow tube into a small glass vial. When the vial was full, Meed pulled out the needle and swiped a small Band-Aid over the hole it had left. She set the sample on a chrome tray next to a machine. "We'll run a CBC later," she said, "and then we'll tune up your supplement mix."

"Are you licensed for this??" I asked.

"This—and bartending," she replied. "Stand up."

The wires from the electrodes dangled from my chest. She connected them one by one to a white plastic machine with an LED screen and a bunch of colored buttons.

She wheeled the device, with me attached, over to a serious-looking treadmill.

"Hop on, Doctor," she said.

I was still weak from tossing up my breakfast. My arm was sore from the needle stick. And I was tired of being led around like a lab monkey. Enough.

"No way," I said, planting my feet. "These things make me dizzy."

She reached back into the instrument drawer and pulled out a slim black metal rod. "Okay," she said. "Let's try this." She poked the tip of the rod under the bottom edge of my shorts. I felt a hot shock on my ass cheek.

"Fuck!" I shouted at the top of my lungs.

"That's the spirit," she said, shoving me onto the machine. She punched the touchscreen, and I felt the belt start to move under my feet. I took a couple of quick steps to get up to walking speed. She started cranking the control higher—and higher. I was jogging. Then running. Then sprinting. I grabbed for the handrail. The wires on my chest were bouncing up and down. I had no idea how to stop the damned thing, and if I tried to jump off at this speed, I'd probably break an ankle. I felt sweat seeping from my scalp and armpits. I was already panting so hard it hurt.

"Are you trying to kill me?" I gasped.

"What fun would that be?" Meed replied.

She tapped another button. Music started blasting from speakers hidden in the ceiling. I heard Eminem's voice. The song was Dr. Dre's "I Need a Doctor."

"Not funny," I wheezed. My legs ached. My lungs ached. And my butt was still tingling. Meed dialed the incline up to twenty degrees.

"While we're at it," she said, "we also need to work on your sense of humor."

CHAPTER 9

Eastern Russia
20 Years Ago

THE TEN-YEAR-OLD STUDENTS were high on a snowy mountain far above the school. The air temperature was below freezing, and the wind took it down another fifteen degrees. The atmosphere was thin, and the students were struggling to breathe. They had been hiking for five hours.

Annika, the blond sixteen-year-old instructor, was at the front of the line, with the students linked behind her by lengths of climbing rope. She had led this hike three times since first completing it herself. It never got any easier. As the students pressed forward, thigh-deep in snow, Annika peppered them with questions. The exercise was designed as an intellectual challenge, not just a physical one. Annika had started with simple questions. Now it was time to push. Her trainees needed to be able to think under stress.

"Square root of ninety-eight!" she shouted over her shoulder.

"Nine point eight nine nine," the class called back in near unison, their voices weak and almost lost in the wind. Irina and Meed were near the end of the line, separated by a five-foot length of rope. Meed stared ahead at the tips of Irina's dark hair, almost frozen solid.

Annika called out the next question. "Six major tributaries of the Amazon!"

One by one, from various students in the line, the names came back. "Japurá!" "Juruá!" "Negro!" "Madeira!" Then, a pause.

"Purus!" shouted Irina.

Annika waited, then stopped. That was only five. She turned and stared down the line. "Meed!" she shouted. "What's missing?"

Meed was so cold she could hardly feel her fingers. Every breath burned her lungs. She closed her eyes and let her mind flow. She imagined herself as a bird over the rainforest. She was being carried on a warm breeze. The geography appeared below her like a map on a table. And the answer came. "Xingu!" she called back.

Annika turned forward and led on, her long braids stiff from the cold. She had been in charge of this group since she was just thirteen. Kamenev had chosen her personally. At first, it was hard for her to keep her charges straight, so she had given the students Russian nicknames, based on their attributes. She called the speedy Asian girl Bystro. The kid who bulged out of his uniform was Zhir. The dark-skinned boy was Chernit. *"Fast." "Chubby." "Black."*

As for the girl with the unforgettable hair, nobody had ever called her anything but Meed, a nickname derived from the word for copper. Annika had tried out a few nicknames for the sullen dark-haired girl. But she only received glares in return. Irina would only respond to "Irina."

"Zhir!" Annika called out over the sound of the wind.

"Name the most celebrated Roman legions!" Silence. Meed looked back. The boy with short legs at the rear of the line was sunk into the snow almost to his waist. His eyes were glazed. Meed knew the signs. The boy's brain had stopped working on higher-level problems. It was in triage mode, redirecting resources, calculating how to survive another minute.

"Zhir!" Annika shouted again. "Answer!"

Zhir did not reply. He didn't even hear the question. His lips were blue, and his breath was coming out in short bursts. His head tipped forward like a deadweight. His knees buckled. He groaned once and fell facedown into the snow.

Meed was just a few steps ahead of him. She turned around and tugged on the rope attached to the boy's waist, struggling to turn him over.

"Zhir!" she shouted. The boy was heavy and half buried in the snow. Meed leaned back with all her strength, but he wouldn't budge.

"Stop!" Annika's voice. She was walking back down the ridge, her pale cheeks reddened by the cold. She pulled a hunting knife from her belt and sliced through the green rope connecting Meed to the unconscious boy.

"Leave him," said Annika. Then she turned and headed back to the front of the group. Meed stood still for a moment, looking back.

Irina grabbed her arm and pulled her forward.

"Stop being weak," she whispered.

Meed stared straight ahead, cold and numb. The class moved on. They had another five hours to go. On Annika's orders, they all smiled the whole way.

CHAPTER 10

THAT NIGHT, IN Kamenev's fire-lit office, Garin and the headmaster stood in front of the wall of photographs. Garin was bent forward, her right palm pressed against her abdomen. Her pain was worse at night. Kamenev reached up and pulled down the photo of a round-faced boy. Garin had heard about the incident during the mountain exercise. Now the victim had a face.

"Zhir?" asked Garin. "He was the one?" She had been fond of the boy. Not as fit as the others, but a hard worker.

Kamenev nodded. The death had been regrettable, but not totally unexpected. The training was demanding, and not every child lived up to expectations. He slid the photo into a folder and placed the folder inside an open safe. He closed the heavy steel door with a thud. Outside the office, music filled the hallway. Rachmaninoff. The Piano Concerto no. 3 in D Minor. Garin knew it well. A very challenging piece. Kamenev tilted his head to listen.

"She's advancing," he said.

"The best student I've ever had," Garin replied.

In the small practice room down the corridor, Meed sat at the piano, head down.

The feeling had finally returned to her fingers, and she played her lesson with fierce intensity, blocking out everything else.

Even the body on the mountain.

CHAPTER 11

Chicago

"STICK THIS IN your mouth."

I was moving from the Pilates reformer to the mini-trampoline when Meed shoved a small round plastic device between my lips.

"Bite down," she said.

I was drained and panting after a ninety-minute workout. And I knew I still had another thirty minutes to go. Just like every morning. "Whasthis??" I mumbled through clenched teeth. It felt like a mouthguard attached to a whistle, and it tasted like melted plastic.

"It's an exhalation resister," said Meed. "Stimulates deep diaphragmatic breathing. Which you need. Because your respiration stats suck."

In the two weeks since I'd been taken, I'd pretty much stopped arguing. Every time I even made a sour face, Meed waved her little shock wand at me and I'd fall right into line. I'd gotten used to my see-through cell and my daily smoothie. I'd even gotten used to needles. I had no choice. Every day started out with an injection of Cerebrolysin, taurine, glycine, and B6. At least, those were the ingredients Meed was willing to tell me about. For all I knew, I might have been getting steroids and hallucinogens, too. It was obvious that I was being biohacked. I just couldn't figure out why. Every time I asked, I got the same answer: "Wrong question."

After twenty minutes on the trampoline, the exhalation resister had me feeling light-headed. I spit it out onto the floor. Meed glared at me.

"Time for some capillary stimulation," she said.

I had no idea what she was talking about. But I got a twinge in my gut. When she brought up something new, it usually involved pain.

"This way," she said.

All I knew about the layout of the loft was what I could see from my cell or from the kitchen and workout area. And without my glasses, I couldn't see much. We never went into the living room on the far side of the space. Every night, Meed disappeared behind a door next to the kitchen. Now she was leading me to an alcove I'd never seen, tucked on the far side of the elevator shaft. As we rounded the corner, I saw a semicircular ribbed wooden door. She pulled it open.

"Step into my chamber, Doctor," she said.

I didn't like the sound of that. I got nervous in tight spaces. A dim light behind the door showed a small room, no bigger than a closet. The sweat was cooling on my back and shoulders. I felt clammy and sick to my stomach. It was getting to be a familiar feeling.

Meed nudged me inside the tiny space and stepped in beside me. She closed the door and pressed a button on the wall. A motor hummed. Two large panels in the floor moved apart, revealing a tank of water below, lit from underneath. I could feel freezing cold wafting against my ankles. It was ice water.

"Hop in, Doctor," she said. "Does wonders for the circulation."

I tried to back away. She raised her shock wand. The message was clear. I could either jump in on my own, or get prodded like a cow in a slaughterhouse. I inhaled once and jumped in, feetfirst. The instant the water covered my head, I felt my blood vessels constrict. My brain felt like it was about to explode. I could see the blur of an eerie blue light illuminating the tank from underneath. When the ringing in my ears stopped, I heard another sound, so loud it actually pulsed the water against my body. Underwater speakers were playing Kanye West. The song was "Stronger."

CHAPTER 12

AFTER I'D SPENT ten minutes in the ice bath, my lips were turning blue. Meed was sitting in a lotus position a couple feet back from the edge of the tank. She didn't take her eyes off me the whole time.

"How much longer?" I asked. My teeth were chattering.

"I'll let you know," she said.

I knew this was some kind of endurance test. I just didn't know how much more I could endure. But she did. She knew *exactly* how much. At the point where I stopped feeling my limbs, she stood up.

"Out you go," she said. I put one numb foot on a narrow ledge inside the tank and pushed myself out and onto the small deck. I was trembling all over. Meed reached into a wooden bin and tossed me a towel.

I was still shaking as I shuffled across the floor to my cell. I dropped my wet clothes on the floor and stepped into the shower. The hot water felt like it was searing my skin, and my numbed hands and feet ached as blood and oxygen flowed back into them. I closed my eyes, breathed in the steam, and eventually began to feel human again.

Then I heard tapping on the shower wall. I reached over and wiped a small patch of condensation off the enclosure. Meed's face was peering through from the other side. Jesus! This woman had absolutely no sense of personal space.

"Enough," she called out. "I don't want you pruning up on me."

I turned off the tap. When I opened the shower door, she was gone. I reached for a towel and patted myself dry. I got dressed. My cell door was open. I stepped outside and immediately smelled something wonderful.

Meed reappeared. She was holding two bowls of freshly made popcorn. Was this a reward for good behavior, or some kind of trick? Popcorn did not seem like something Meed would allow on a strict training diet. She handed me a bowl.

"Organic, gluten-free, and non-GMO," she said. "Also excellent roughage." She headed across the loft toward the living room area. "Follow me, Doctor," she said. "We're going to the movies."

I followed and sat down next to her on the thick leather sofa across from a massive flat-screen TV. I started to relax a little. I took a handful of popcorn. It tasted amazing. I thought maybe she was actually giving me a break. I thought maybe, for once, we were actually about to do something normal.

"What are we watching?" I asked.

"You," she said.

Meed clicked Play on the remote, and the screen lit up. Sure enough, there I was. The footage was a little shaky, like it was taken with an iPhone. The first scene zoomed in on me walking across campus in the middle of winter. I looked gawky and awkward. I could tell I was trying not to slip on the sidewalk. The first scene dissolved into a shot of me in the aisle of Shop & Save. I was wheeling a mini-cart down the cereal aisle, picking out oatmeal.

Next came a long scene of me sitting at Starbucks before class. Then a shot of me buying a magazine and a pack of gum at a newsstand. There was a hard cut and then I was sitting at a long table in the university library. I had a thick comparative cultures text in front of me. The shot was so close I could read the title on the spine of the book. She must have been shooting from the next table. About ten feet away.

"You were following me?" I asked.

"*Surveilling* you," she said. "Every minute. For months."

"What the hell...?"

"Keep watching, it gets better," she said. "Actually, it gets worse."

I put down my popcorn. I'd suddenly lost my appetite. The next few scenes came in quick succession: A long shot of me buying an umbrella during a rain shower. Me walking through Lincoln Park Zoo. Then a grainy scene of me sitting in my recliner in my living room. *My living room!* I looked over at Meed.

"Needed my extra-long lens for that one," she said, tossing a handful of popcorn into her mouth. By now, I was used to feeling violated. But this was something else. And it made me mad.

"What was the fucking *point*?" I asked. "Tell me! You obviously knew who I was. Why didn't you just grab me the first day you saw me? Why all this Peeping-Tom bullshit??"

Meed nodded toward the screen. "Pay attention. I don't want you to miss the theme here."

I looked back to see myself opening my door for a pizza delivery guy. Then riding a rental bike on the Lakefront Trail. Then tossing bread to a family of ducks in a pond.

"See what I mean?" said Meed. "Boring, boring, boring. Also repetitive, dull, and monotonous. That's what your life was. Same Caffè Americano every morning. Same tuna sandwich for lunch. Same miso dressing on your salad. Your favorite cable channel is Nat Geo. You subscribe to *Scientific American* and *Anthropology Today*. You watch YouTube videos of Margaret Mead, for God's sake! In four months, you went to three museums and not a single rock concert."

Yep. There I was, walking into the Chicago History Museum. Then the Museum of Science and Industry. Then a night shot of me walking out of the Adler Planetarium. I felt my face getting red. I was starting to feel embarrassed and defensive.

"I live a quiet life, so what? We can't all be spies and kidnappers."

Meed leaned in close. I could smell the popcorn on her breath. "Correction," she said. "You don't live a quiet life. You live a *nothing* life. But don't worry, that's all about to change. Believe me, you'll *want* it to change." She turned back to the screen. "After you watch this a few hundred more times."

CHAPTER 13

Eastern Russia
18 Years Ago

MEED, AGE TWELVE, stood on a frozen lake wearing a blue one-piece swimsuit and rubber sandals. Nothing else. She hunched and trembled along with her classmates as they stood in a ragged line about a hundred yards from shore. In front of them were two large circular holes in the ice, exactly thirty yards apart. The holes had been cut before dawn by supervisors with chainsaws. Meed had heard the sound from her bed. The shivering had started then. For weeks, she'd known this test was coming.

Annika was wearing a fur jacket over black leggings and boots. She walked to the edge of the closer hole. Bluish-green water lapped against the opening. The ice that rimmed the hole was three inches thick. Annika turned to the class.

"Keep your wits," she said. "Swim in a straight line. Block out the fear. Block out the cold. Block out failure." She looked over the class. "Who's first?"

Meed glanced sideways as Irina stepped forward.

"Good, Irina," said Annika. "Show them the way."

Irina stepped up to the hole. She kicked off her sandals.

She knelt on the ice, her knees at the edge of the opening. She raised her arms over her head, leaned forward, and tipped herself into the water. The soles of her feet flashed for a second at the surface, and then she was gone, leaving a swirl of bubbles behind. Annika pressed the Start button on a stopwatch. Desperate and scared, some of the students began to huddle together for warmth, pressing their bodies against one another. Until Annika noticed.

"No clusters!" she shouted. "This is a solitary exercise. You have only yourself." The girls stepped back, restoring the gaps between them. Annika looked toward the distant hole and checked her stopwatch. Fifteen seconds. Then twenty.

Meed stamped her feet on the ice and stared through the mist. From where she stood, the far hole looked like a small, dark wafer. Suddenly the water in the hole frothed. Two arms shot out. Irina! Wriggling like a fish, she worked her way onto the surface and jumped to her feet. She trotted with small steps toward the class, doing her best to stay balanced. When she got close to the group, Annika reached into a plastic tub and tossed her a thin blanket. Then she turned toward the rest of the line.

"Next!"

One by one, the students made the dive. One by one, they emerged shaking and stunned, grateful to be alive. Meed was second to last, just before Bystro, the Asian girl. When it was her turn, Meed did not hesitate. She jumped in feetfirst.

The freezing water hit her like a hammer, forcing the breath out of her. She surfaced again for a second to take a fresh gulp of air, then started scissor-kicking her way under the ice. Below her, the water was pitch-black. She stayed close to the surface, letting her shoulders and heels bump against the ice roof as she swam. Her lungs burned. Her heart pounded. White bubbles trickled from her nose and mouth.

Just as her air was about to give out, she sensed a slight shift in the light above her. She stretched one arm up and felt cold air. As soon as her head cleared the water, she looked back to see Bystro plunging into the first hole. The terrified girl had waited until she had no choice.

Meed walked quickly back toward the rest of the class. Annika tossed her a blanket as she checked her stopwatch for Bystro's time. Twenty seconds. Then thirty. She began to walk toward the distant hole. Forty seconds. The students walked forward, too, a few steps at a time, staring down at the ice.

Meed spotted her first. "Bystro!" she shouted.

The slender girl was just a faint shape beneath the ice, yards off course, flailing and twisting. Meed dropped to her knees, pounding on the hard surface. But there was no way to break through. The ice was too thick. Annika was standing over her now. The white of Bystro's palms showed through the ice, pressing desperately from the other side. Then, one at a time, her hands pulled away. Her pale figure faded. A few seconds later, she dropped completely out of sight. Meed screamed with rage.

Annika stopped her watch.

CHAPTER 14

Chicago

DAMN! I WAS impressed. She never missed.

The target was a male silhouette made of plywood. Meed's knife hit the upper left chest, right where the heart would be. It was my job to retrieve the knife after every throw. When I handed the knife back, Meed threw again. And again. Overhand. Underhand. Over the shoulder. A kill shot every time.

The next time I returned the blade, she wrapped my fingers around the grip. "Your turn," she said.

I looked across the room at the target. I squinted. From a distance, it was nothing but a dark blur to me. I felt the weight of the blade in my hand. I did my best to imitate Meed's stance. I whipped my hand forward and heard the blade clink off the brick wall.

"Can you hit the side of a barn?" said Meed.

Now I was pissed. I was tired of being a joke. I lost it.

"You're the one who stomped on my glasses!" I yelled. "How the hell do you expect me to see anything??"

Meed pulled herself up next to me and waved a finger in

front of my eyes. She lifted my eyelids one at a time and peered into my irises.

"You have convergence insufficiency," she said.

"No," I corrected her. "I have congenital corneal astigmatism."

She took another look, deeper this time, waving her finger back and forth.

"That, too," she said. "Your adjustment might take a little more time."

She flipped the blade over her shoulder. Another kill shot. I could tell without looking.

"Visual training starts tomorrow," she said. "I need you to be able to hit a target."

I knew better than to ask why.

By then, it was almost time for lights out. She was very strict about that. I needed my REM sleep, she kept saying. Good for tissue repair and muscle growth. I knew the drill. I walked over to my cell and let myself in, like a trained dog. I pulled the door shut and heard the click of the electronic lock.

I sat down on my cot and watched Meed walk up the two steps to the door of her bedroom. At least, I assumed it was her bedroom. For all I knew, it could have been a passage to another apartment or another whole building. Maybe there were other rooms with other prisoners. Maybe she was assembling an army of mind slaves. Why should I be the only one? Or maybe she had a night job as a dominatrix. I'd gone from a world where everything was predictable to a world where *nothing* was.

From my cot, I could see one of the big flat-screen TVs that hung from brackets all over the loft. Some were tuned to CNN, some to the local news channel. Usually, the volume was down and the caption setting on, but sometimes during my workouts Meed turned up the sound. I always kept my ears open for news about a missing anthropology professor.

But Meed was right. There was nobody looking for me. I was starting to believe what she kept telling me, over and over. "You have only yourself."

CHAPTER 15

Eastern Russia
17 Years Ago

MEED, NOW THIRTEEN, felt the blood rushing to her head and with it, the sickening feeling of defeat. She was upside down, bound with thick rope, hanging from a long wooden beam ten feet off the ground. She was wriggling and red in the face, trying her best to get free. But nothing was working. The situation was even more humiliating because she was the last to finish. All the other students had already completed the assignment. She could see their inverted faces below her in the school courtyard. They were looking up at her with eerie smiles.

She saw Annika's face most clearly, just inches away. Annika reached up and tapped Meed's forehead with her index finger.

"Time's up, Meed," she said. "Do what you need to do."

Meed sucked in a breath and clenched her teeth. Of course, she knew the last-resort procedure, but her brain was telling her not to do it. Would not allow it. So she simply overruled the warning, pushing past logic and fear and reason, as she'd been trained to do. There was no other way.

She hung limp and then, with a violent twist and flex of her torso, she wrenched the ball of her humerus from its socket. The pain was like an electric shock, stunning her into semi-consciousness. The muscles in her arm spasmed and tingled. Her vision dimmed. But through it all, Meed focused on the next step. As her upper arm dislocated forward, the ropes slackened around her chest—just by millimeters. But enough.

She pushed through the agony and flexed her body upward. She grabbed the middle coil of rope in her teeth and jerked her head back, pulling the rope with it. The other coils loosened. More wriggling and struggle. More excruciating pain. A second later, Meed felt herself slipping down. Then, suddenly, she dropped from the beam, landing on her back on the hard dirt. She was writhing and grimacing, but refused to scream. Her classmates crowded around her. Through a haze, she saw Annika nod to Irina.

Meed felt Irina grab her limp arm and extend it out to ninety degrees. It felt like the limb was being torn from her body. She felt Irina's foot against her upper rib cage and then a steady, strong pull on her wrist. There was another blast of stunning pain and then a loud click as the joint reassembled. Meed felt her head spin as she fought to stay conscious. A sheen of cold sweat coated her face. She rolled to her opposite side and struggled to her knees, and then to her feet. She set her legs to keep from dropping again and clutched her relocated shoulder.

She heard the sound of distant clapping—but not from a crowd. Just from one person. As she looked up, she saw the headmaster observing from the stone balcony outside his office. Standing next to him was a guest, a tall man in a well-cut suit, with blindingly white teeth. Meed could tell that the guest was impressed. He was the one applauding.

CHAPTER 16

KAMENEV PLACED HIS hand on his guest's elbow and guided him back into the oak-paneled office. The visitor had a thick mane of black hair to go with his impressive teeth. He spoke in an accent that could have been Middle Eastern or Central European or a blend of both. Or it could have all been an act. Kamenev knew the type well. The guest gave his name as Mazen. But, of course, that could have been made up, too.

"My contacts did not exaggerate," Mazen said. "Your students are highly..." He searched for the right compliment, then found it: "motivated."

"They do what is necessary to succeed," said Kamenev. "As do you, I'm told."

Mazen shrugged off the transparent flattery. "I sell weapons of mass destruction to self-destructive people. It's a lucrative business. I never run out of customers." He cocked his head at his host.

"And what, exactly, is *your* business, Headmaster Kamenev? Help me understand. What degree does your institution confer?" There was a touch of playful sarcasm in his voice. He knew the school had never handed out an actual diploma.

Kamenev pressed his hands together. In conversations like these, he always picked his words carefully. His guest had been fully vetted, but no need to reveal more than necessary. Just enough to make the sale.

"Thousands of our graduates are already at work in every country," he said. "Every government. Every agency. Every organization. Every multinational company. We handle intelligence, operational assistance, special assignments." He was sure that Mazen could translate the euphemisms. "For fair compensation," Kamenev continued, "we support the right people, and they support us." Kamenev smiled. "As you say, it's lucrative."

"And the price?" asked the guest, with his brows raised.

"Numbers are not the point," said Kamenev. "Whatever we charge, you can afford."

The guest leaned back in his chair. He knew it was true.

"As you've seen," Kamenev continued, "our students are highly skilled, with no messy political or religious preconceptions. Raw clay, to be molded to the needs of the assignment. They have been raised here since infancy. They are infinitely adaptable. They live only for the mission."

The guest appeared to be thinking something over, then revealed the full glory of his brilliant smile. He stood to shake Kamenev's hand.

"Very well," he said. "Arrangements will be made." He rebuttoned his suit jacket and picked up his slim attaché case. "To start with," he said, "I will require an attractive female."

As it turned out, he already had one in mind.

CHAPTER 17

Chicago

THE RACKET WAS so loud I could hear it through my cell walls. The treadmill was whining at top speed, and Meed's feet were pounding hard on the belt. She'd unlocked my cell door and left it open a crack so I could get out on my own. It was one of the few tiny ways she'd eased up on security recently, but I knew cameras were on me the whole time. I still couldn't even use the toilet in private.

She'd installed a small TV hanging from a bracket near the ceiling of my cell. She ran the movie of my solitary life on a loop, 24/7. Her idea of motivation, I guess. At night, I tossed a towel over the screen.

When I walked out into the kitchen, my smoothie was waiting on the counter. I picked up the glass and guzzled the slime like always, then walked over to a bench near the workout area. I glanced up at the flat screen overhead, where a CNN correspondent was reporting on a mudslide in Ecuador. Out of the corner of my eye, I watched Meed. In her black workout outfit, she looked like an Olympic athlete or some kind of superhero.

Her hair was pulled into a bun on top of her head. After a minute, she reached up and pulled out a hairpin and let her curls fly. She was wearing a short-sleeved top, which was a different style for her. I'd never seen her in anything but long sleeves. As her arms pumped, I could see marks on both of her forearms—small red welts, like cigarette burns.

For a split second, I considered asking about them. But I knew better. Wrong question, no doubt. Since she seemed to be a stickler for physical perfection, it felt strange to discover that she was a little less than perfect—which somehow made her even more of a mystery.

It was all very confusing. I still hated her for keeping me a prisoner and not telling me why. And for working me to exhaustion every single day in her private boot camp. But that didn't change the fact that she was the most gorgeous woman I'd ever seen, scars and all.

I saw her punch a button on the console. The treadmill slowed down. She grabbed the handrails and vaulted off to the side like a gymnast. Sweat was dripping from her nose and chin. Her hair was soaked and matted around her neck.

She grabbed a towel from a cabinet and pressed it against her face. Then she tossed the towel aside and took a step toward me. She set herself on the balls of her feet and bounced from side to side. She shook her head, sending sweat droplets flying from her hair. The adrenaline started to shoot through me.

"Front!" she shouted.

I knew the drill. By this time, I was like one of Pavlov's pups. I jumped up and lowered my head. I set my feet, then charged full out across the room. I launched myself toward her waist, already thinking through the move, just like I'd practiced—how my shoulder would slam into her gut, bringing her down hard onto her back. But that's not what happened. That's not what *ever* happened. This time, she whipped her right leg around and caught me in midair. Her foot hit my ribs like a baseball bat. I landed on the mat so hard I saw sparks. I hadn't laid a finger on her. Not once. But I'd swear this time I got close.

When I rolled over, I felt her heel in my diaphragm. With one hard shove, she could have turned my liver to mush. I knew, because she'd drawn me a diagram.

Then I felt the pressure ease off. I crunched myself up to a sitting position as she walked away with her copper curls bouncing. She turned to look at me over her shoulder.

"Better, Doctor." she said, as she headed toward the door to her room. "Not great. But better."

I thought it was the nicest compliment I'd ever heard.

CHAPTER 18

Eastern Russia
16 Years Ago

SOME SCHOOL DAYS, like this one, stretched long into the night. The classroom on the top floor was totally dark, windows blocked with heavy shades. Meed and her classmates stood on one side of the room wearing night-vision goggles. Gunich, the owlish instructor, walked to the opposite side of the room, which was shrouded by a black curtain. He tugged a cord. The curtain dropped, revealing a row of iron safes—all types and sizes, from compact office models to bank-sized vaults, sealed with the most ingenious locks the industry had ever devised.

Meed had studied hard for this drill. Her mind was a maze of mechanical diagrams, electronic circuits, and metallurgy formulas. It was a maze she needed to solve, under challenging conditions and extreme time pressure. But that was her specialty.

"Execute!" said Gunich. He stepped to the side and put on his own goggles to observe.

The students rushed to the safes, reaching for the lock dials and electronic keypads. Working alone or in teams, they fished in their pockets for listening devices and electronic readers—all permitted during the exam. One team produced a compact acetylene torch. Gunich was impressed. Points for ingenuity.

Meed ran to the largest safe in the row, claiming it for her own. Through her goggles, the whole scene had a bizarre glow. In the greenish image, her classmates looked like bug-eyed reptiles. Gunich, in his long lab coat, looked like some kind of spectacled Druid.

Meed pressed her ear against the safe door and rested her fingers lightly on the dial of the combination lock. She rotated the dial with the lightest touch, letting the sensation flow through her fingertips. She pictured the tumblers, the wheel pack, the lever nose, the whole internal mechanism concealed behind four inches of tempered steel. But it wasn't the image that mattered. It was the sound. She had trained for months using a physician's stethoscope, but now she had sharpened her senses even further.

She pressed her ear tight against the metal and slowly turned the dial. There were three metal wheels buried inside. Meed was listening for the distinctive clicks the wheels made as they lined up. Her first try, at the start of the semester, had taken her five hours. But that was then. This was now. She heard the first click.

She turned the dial again and sensed another. She heard the beeping of a digital code reader from two stations down. She could tell that Irina was getting close to solving her challenge on one of the electronic locks. Meed concentrated on the safe in front of her. No distractions. One more twitch of her fingers. She felt something give inside the door, almost imperceptible—the feel of a small metal arm dropping. She leaned on the heavy handle. The massive door swung open. Twenty-five seconds.

Gunich's eyes opened wide behind his goggles. The lock-whisperer had done it again.

Meed moved on to the next safe and nudged a classmate aside. In twelve seconds, that safe was open, too. One station away, Irina gave Meed a small nod and fussed with her own quirky lock. She wanted to succeed on her own. Meed stepped past her, working her way down the rest of the row. Five minutes later, Irina yanked open the door to her safe. She looked up. Meed had opened all the rest.

The other students set their tools down on the floor. They were stunned and embarrassed. And they knew the consequences. Gunich stepped out of his corner.

"Meed and Irina pass," he said. "The rest of you will repeat the class."

The students yanked the goggles off their heads. A few of them glared at Meed. She glared right back.

"Dismissed," said Gunich. He opened the classroom door, letting the dim light from the hallway spill in. "I suggest you review your manuals. Section 5 in particular."

The students shuffled out the door past him, handing him their goggles as they went. Meed hung back until she was the only student left. Gunich walked over and plucked the night-vision goggles from her head.

"Time to go," he said. "You did well."

Meed leaned back against one of the open safes and brushed her fingertips against her shirt, as if honing them.

"I think I'll do some extra practice," she said. "Please. Just a few minutes more."

Gunich had never seen a student like her. A savant. Who

was he to interfere with genius? He shrugged and headed out the door. Meed called after him.

"I'll lock up when I leave," she said.

She knew Gunich would not appreciate the joke, much less her true plans, and the real reason she needed to be alone. Safe-cracking (technically, "Barriers & Intrusions") was the only class held on the administrative floor. Meed knew this was where the school's deepest secrets were kept. And there was one secret in particular she intended to uncover. It was her own personal extra-credit project.

For Meed, passing the exam had been the simplest part of her night. The real challenge was about to begin.

CHAPTER 19

THE PLAN HAD taken months of careful preparation. Meed hadn't told anybody about what she was up to. Not even Irina. Walking to class day after day, she had mentally mapped the entire floor and watched the comings and goings of every administrator. Especially Kamenev.

As it turned out, the headmaster's schedule was as predictable as the menu in the dining hall. He paid no attention to the students as he walked back and forth from his office. But Meed had certainly been paying attention to him.

An hour after Gunich left the classroom, all footsteps in the corridor had stopped. The last doors had been closed. The only sound was the rattle and hiss from the metal radiators.

Meed slipped through the classroom door and tiptoed down the paneled hallway. The walls were white plaster with dark oak wainscoting. The floor was covered with lush Persian rugs. The rest of the school buildings were stark and utilitarian, but this was a showpiece, built to impress. The hallway was dark except for the dim security lights along the corridor. There was a large antique clock hanging on the wall at the far

end of the hall. Thirty minutes until bed check. More than
enough time.

The security camera at the end of the hall was static. An
easy target, especially with the low ceiling. Meed pulled a
laser from her pocket, stolen during a morning lab. It was a
Class 3B model, not strong enough to blind the camera, just
enough to cause a little distortion. Two or three seconds was
all she needed.

The sensor was right below the lens, similar to a device
she'd dissected that morning. Meed gave the sensor a quick
blast with the laser, then moved along the edge of its coverage
field. If anybody in the security office was paying attention
to that specific feed, it would have looked like a minor glitch.
Nothing to get alarmed about.

The heavy oak door to Kamenev's office was set into an
alcove, out of sight of the camera, but secured with an electronic lock. This part was easy. Meed had watched Kamenev
open the door three times and memorized his finger positions
on the keypad. One. Zero. Four. Six. Child's play.

Meed turned the knob and pushed the door open. The air
inside smelled of stale smoke and wood polish. The office
was spacious, lined with heavy bookshelves. With her eyes
adjusted to the darkness, Meed could make out the shape of a
large sofa, a massive desk, and a wall filled with photographs.
She recognized the faces, including her own.

In a corner near the desk sat a huge safe. It was a model she
hadn't seen before, but no matter. Her senses were tuned, and
her confidence level was high. She rested her fingers lightly on
the lock dial and pressed her ear against the cold metal door. She
heard a rustle from the darkest corner of the room. Then a voice.

"I can save you the trouble."

CHAPTER 20

MEED FROZE. SHE let her hand drop slowly from the safe dial, then turned her head to face the corner. A lamp clicked on. Lyudmila Garin sat slumped in a leather chair, her hands clawed tight around the wooden armrests. She was thin and wasted. Almost a ghost. In her lap was a thick manila folder.

"I knew it was just a matter of time," she said. "I thought this might be the night."

Meed thought carefully about what to say. Or not say. Obviously, she'd been caught in the act. No denying it. But if there was anyone she could trust not to turn her in, it was her devoted piano teacher.

Meed stood and stepped forward into the lamplight. "I'm sorry," she said. "All I want..."

"I know what you want," said Garin. "I have it right here."

With a shaking hand, she lifted the folder from her lap and held it out. Meed took it. The spine of the folder was soft from handling, and the edges were frayed. The label tab contained what looked like a random combination of numbers and letters.

"What's this?" Meed asked, pointing at the code.

"It's you," replied Garin.

Meed opened the folder and rifled through the contents. The records went back fourteen years. It was her entire history at the school, starting at the age of six months. In meticulous detail. Height and weight charts. Academic grades and reports. Records and transcripts. Athletic ratings. Intelligence and aptitude tests. At the very back of the folder was a page labeled "Entrance Assessment." Attached to it was a small color photo of a baby in an institutional bassinet. A baby with bright copper curls. Meed felt the breath go out of her. She unclipped the picture and turned it to the light. She stared at it for a long time.

"You were distinctive from the start," said Garin, managing a thin smile.

Clipped to the inside cover of the folder was another photo—a picture of a young man. The image was yellowed, like a picture from a history lecture. The man was posing proudly in front of a building under construction, with stones and lumber all around. Meed recognized the building. It was the one they were in right now. But she had never seen the man before.

"Who is this?" she asked. She held the photo out toward Garin.

"Your great-grandfather," said Garin, her voice thin and hoarse. "A genius, in his own dark way. The school's cofounder."

Meed looked up, stunned and confused. The whole idea of relatives was foreign to her. The subject was never discussed, or even mentioned. None of the students knew anything about their families. And they had learned not to ask. "Wrong question," was the rote response. Meed stared at the picture again, straining to make sense of the connection.

"The founder?" she asked, bewildered. "I don't understand…"

"That's why you're here," said Garin. "That's why you were chosen. Your parents were not considered worthy of his heritage. You are. *You* are the legacy."

"What kind of legacy is that?" Meed asked. She didn't know how much Garin knew. Or how much she would say. But she had years of questions boiling up in her brain, and she realized that she might not get another chance to ask them. Trembling, Meed closed the folder and clutched it tight with both hands.

"*Tell* me!" she said. "What's all this all about? What are we doing here? What are we being trained for? When students leave, where do they go?"

Garin took in a raspy breath. "They go wherever they're needed," she replied. "They go to help others gain power, steal power, stay in power. Eventually, the graduates of this school will control everything, everywhere in the world." She jabbed a thin finger at Meed. "And you could be the best ever. You have the gift. It's in your blood."

Garin straightened herself in the chair. The shift made her wince. Meed reached out, but Garin waved her hand away. "You have only one weakness," she said softly.

"You seek comfort in others." Garin lowered her head to cough, then looked up again. "Always remember—you have only yourself."

Meed heard footsteps from far down the corridor. Maybe the camera glitch hadn't gone unnoticed after all. Garin waved her hand.

"Go," she said. "Disappear. I'll make sure my prints are on everything." A wet rattle rose from her throat. "There's nothing they can do to me now."

As Meed handed the file back to the matron, a small card

fell to the floor. She picked it up. It was a torn sheet with two words printed in pen. Meed stared at the paper and then looked up at Garin. The matron nodded.

"That's your name," she said. "Your true name. That is who you really are."

CHAPTER 21

AFTER MEED WAS safely away, Garin slipped out of the building through a secret exit, one not even security knew about. She found the well-worn path that led west, away from the school. She had made this same walk many times before over the past five decades—as a student, as a teacher, as a supervisor. But never at 3 a.m. And never alone. She kept her scarf wrapped around her face to muffle the sound of her coughs. Behind her was the glow of lights on the school walls. Ahead, there was only darkness.

The path wound through fir trees until it reached the edge of the lake, flat and frozen. Snowy mountain peaks rose in the distance. Lyudmila took a few tentative steps onto the ice and extended her arms out to her sides for balance, like a tightrope walker. She was so slight that, from a distance, she might have been mistaken for a young girl. But nobody was looking. In a few minutes, she reached the large hole in the ice, its surface lightly crusted over.

Lyudmila looked up at the stars one last time, then closed her eyes. A Rachmaninoff concerto swirled in her head. Her fingers twitched as if touching piano keys. She took one final step forward and dropped through the hole. The dark water closed over her. Compared to the cancer, the brutal cold was a lesser pain—and a much kinder death.

CHAPTER 22

Chicago

MEED CALLED IT a titanium posture brace. I called it a torture device. It went around my waist and pressed into my back like a plate of armor. But I can't deny that it worked. It kept my core firm and tight while I did another dead lift.

"Watch your form," Meed called out from her chair. "Don't get sloppy."

My max was now up to 300 pounds, which I realized would be like lifting my office desk. I wouldn't have thought it was possible. But I never could have imagined I'd be at nine percent body fat either. Or that I could blow through the Marine Corps Physical Fitness Test like it was nothing.

Thanks to Meed's bizarre retinal focus drills, my eyesight was sharp and clear. For the first time since I got my learner's permit, I wouldn't need corrective lenses to drive. Not that Meed ever let me anywhere near a vehicle. Or even a street. I'd been trapped in the loft for four months straight. I did one last lift and dropped the barbell on the mat like a load of cement.

As I shifted to free weights, I decided to quiz Meed again. I'd given up on getting anything meaningful out of her, but we'd made a little game out of personal trivia. I grabbed a twenty-pounder in each hand and squeezed in my questions between reps.

"Ever been to Disneyland?" I asked.

"Twice," she said. "Hated it both times."

"Favorite color?"

"Black."

"Best pizza in Chicago?"

"Dante's."

"Where were you born?"

"Wrong question."

Typical conversation. Three steps forward, one total roadblock.

"Stand up straight," said Meed. I looked over. She was aiming a handheld laser at me.

"I *am* standing up straight," I said, tapping the brace. "How could I not?"

"Good news," she said, checking the readout. "You're now officially six foot two."

Amazing. That was up a quarter-inch in the last month. Plus another three inches around my chest. Another two inches around each biceps. And two inches *less* around my waist. My gym shorts were actually starting to bag a bit. And for the first time in my life, I had something approaching a six-pack. I was being turned into somebody else—somebody I didn't even recognize—and I still didn't know why. I was bigger, stronger, smarter. But for what?

I put the weights back in the rack and wiped my face with a towel. When I looked up again, Meed was tapping a syringe. She definitely had a needle fetish.

"For Christ's sake, what now?" I asked.

"Assume the position," she said. No sense in arguing. I peeled down the waistband of my shorts. She jabbed me in the right upper glute.

"Just a little extra vitamin B," she said. "We've got a training run tonight."

Training run? That was the last thing I wanted to hear. I pulled my shorts back up and slumped against the weight rack. My head sagged. Since my kidnapping, I estimated that I'd run over a thousand miles—going absolutely nowhere.

"I'm so sick of that goddamn treadmill," I muttered.

"Not on the treadmill," said Meed. She nodded toward the window. "Outside."

My heart started fluttering like I'd just gotten a puppy for Christmas.

"Outside??" I asked. "You're serious?"

"Why not?" said Meed. "Let's get some fresh Chicago air into those lungs."

I looked out the window. Rain was sheeting against the glass. I wouldn't have cared if it was hot lava. I realized that this was my chance. Outside, I might be able to flag down a cop or jump into a cab. Or lose Meed in a crowd. Or maybe just shove her down an open manhole and run for help. Anything to get away and get my life back again.

Meed picked up the shock wand and waved it back and forth. Sometimes it felt like she could actually read my mind.

"Don't even think about it," she said.

CHAPTER 23

Eastern Russia
15 Years Ago

OF ALL THE weapons on the firing range, Meed found the .50 BMG machine gun the hardest to handle. It could vaporize a watermelon at a hundred yards, but the recoil was enough to bruise her collarbone. Her scores on long guns overall were solid, but she preferred pistols. After firing five brain-shaking rounds, she set the big gun back in the rack and picked up a Glock 9mm. Much better.

Irina was standing on the next platform with a Beretta .22, punching hole after hole into the center of a target downrange. Meed slid a clip into the Glock and started firing at the next target over. Compared to the heavy .50, the Glock felt like a popgun.

Meed was matching Irina shot for shot. Within twenty seconds, both target centers were shredded.

All the way down the firing line came the cracks and bangs of every kind of firearm, from MIL-SPEC models to expertly hacked hybrids. Only the instructors wore ear protection. For the students, the noise was an important part of the lesson—how to think with your head pounding and your ears ringing.

In the middle of it all, one student was even more solid and unflappable than the others. His name was Rishi. He was slightly built, with a caramel complexion and thick black hair. He was also younger than everybody else on the range by a couple of years. He'd recently been moved up from a lower class, where he had no real competition.

Between clips, Meed glanced his way. Rishi was lying flat on his belly, cradling a Barrett M82, his sniper rifle of choice. His target was a small circle on a brick wall 150 yards away. Meed could see Rishi's ribs through his T-shirt as he sent another round. There was a small kick of brick dust from the center of the circle. Another direct hit.

Meed glanced at Irina. Neither of them liked being shown up, especially by a runt like Rishi. Irina squinted down the barrel of her pistol and kept firing. But Meed was annoyed enough to take action. She flicked the safety on the Glock and set it down on the shooting stand. Then she walked over to the weapon vault anchored in cement behind the firing line. The vault was the size of a coffin. The heavy steel lid was open. Meed ran her hands over the assortment of armaments inside and found just what she was looking for.

Rishi loaded another round into his rifle. He set the cross-hairs on the target again. His finger moved slowly from the trigger guard to the trigger. Suddenly there was a huge blast downrange. Rishi jerked his head up from his scope. The target was gone. Not just the circle on the bricks. The entire brick wall.

All sound on the firing line stopped. Students and instructors were frozen in place by the violence of the blast. All that was left in the distance was a cloud of dust. Meed lowered the RPG launcher from her shoulder and wiped a streak of soot off her cheek. She leaned down and patted Rishi on the head.

"Don't worry," she said. "They'll give you something new to shoot at."

CHAPTER 24

Chicago

IT WAS 10 p.m. when we stepped into the elevator for our run. Meed pressed the Down button. I heard the chains rattle and felt the car lurch into motion. I thought back to my ride up in that same elevator four months back. The day my life had disappeared.

My new red running suit was a little tight in the crotch, but otherwise it felt pretty sleek. Meed was wearing the female version. In black, of course. We both had our nylon hoodies up, ready for the rain.

The elevator door opened onto a narrow basement corridor with cinderblock walls. Meed led the way up a set of cement stairs with a narrow metal railing. We took a turn on a narrow landing and then up a few more steps to a heavy swinging metal door, the kind you'd find on a loading dock. Meed shouldered her way through, and we stepped out onto the sidewalk. My first taste of freedom. But not really. I was out in the world, but I was still a prisoner. I figured Meed had waited for weather like this so we'd be the only two people on the street. The rain was coming down so hard it sounded like white noise. She looked both ways then headed west, starting off at a quick jog.

In spite of the chilly March rain, I was already starting to sweat inside my tracksuit. I rolled back my hood and let the water roll down my neck. It felt good. For most of the way, I ran behind Meed, just far enough to avoid getting her shoe splatter in my face. I came up next to her while she marked time at a stoplight. My lungs hurt already.

"Where are we headed?" I asked.

"Wrong question," said Meed. She wasn't even breathing hard.

We turned south. After about forty-five minutes, the surroundings started to get sketchy. Most of the streetlights were out and there was a lot of chain-link fencing. I could tell from street signs that we were near Fuller Park. It was a neighborhood I wouldn't even drive through during the day, let alone run through in the dark. On the plus side, the rain had let up. Now it was just a light mist.

Here and there along the street, a few beat-up cars sat at the curb, but this wasn't a place you'd ever want to park overnight. Not if you planned to see your vehicle in the morning.

On the right, a low wooden fence blocked off a site with a half-demolished building. The store next door looked like it was next for the wrecking ball. Meed took a right and turned down the alley just past the store. It took me a few seconds to catch up. When I rounded the corner, I felt a prickle at the back of my neck. The alley was narrow and the far end disappeared into darkness. Meed was nowhere in sight.

I heard a rustle. I picked up my pace. Suddenly, somebody grabbed me hard from behind, lifting my feet off the ground and pinning my hands against my sides. I felt the bristle of stubble against my neck. A raspy voice mumbled into my ear.

"Slow down there, Usain Bolt."

CHAPTER 25

I BENT FORWARD hard and twisted my shoulders, but it was no use. The guy was a brute. With one hand, he grabbed me by the chin and pulled my head back up again. That's when the other guy stepped out of the shadows.

I could see his pale shaved dome glistening in the light of a streetlight near the alley entrance. He had a ripped T-shirt under a greasy denim vest. A cobra tattoo twisted up his neck. He had a jerky, dangerous energy, jacked up and ready for trouble. My heart was already thumping from the run, but now I could feel my pulse pound even harder in my head. I got a bitter taste in my mouth. I suddenly went cold and clammy all over.

I looked down the alley past the thug in front of me. Where the hell was Meed??

She would have missed me by now. Was she knocked out somewhere back in the dark—or dead? Was I next? I started to shake.

"Whaddaya got for me tonight?" said Cobra Neck. The guy behind me tightened his grip, his forearms locked around my rib cage.

"We *know* you got somethin'," he said, shaking me from side to side.

"I don't!" I said. "I don't have anything!" That was the truth. Meed had my wallet and phone locked up somewhere in the loft. I hadn't touched cash in four months. Cobra Neck flicked the collar of my tracksuit.

"Definitely not bargain bin," he said, leaning in. "C'mon. I know you got somethin' for me."

I felt an arm slide up to my throat. That was the trigger, the second when something kicked in. I rolled hard to the right and reached my leg back. I shoved the guy's elbow up and slipped my head out of his grip. I got my first look at his face—pale, bristled, dead-eyed. I twisted his arm behind his back and kicked him hard behind his knees. He dropped to the wet pavement. I spun back around with my hands up— and froze. There was a gun two inches from my forehead. Cobra Neck waved the barrel. He was pissed off and out of patience. I could hear the guy behind me groaning and cursing under his breath.

"Let's try again, asshole," said Cobra Neck. "Empty your goddamn…"

The shock wand caught him right under the chin. The gun dropped and clattered on the pavement. I saw the flash of Meed's hand as she chopped the guy hard across his carotid artery. He spasmed and crumpled, out cold. I heard feet scrambling behind me and turned around. The other guy was already rounding the corner onto the street. Gone. When I turned back, Meed was in my face, glaring at me.

"I thought I told you to keep up," she said.

The adrenaline was flooding through me, making me dizzy. I'd never felt anything close to this in my life. I bent forward at the waist, trying to catch my breath. I replayed the last minute like a movie in my head. It didn't seem real.

"I broke a choke hold," I said. "I dropped that jerk." I could hear myself trying to sound tough.

"I noticed," said Meed. "Just before you almost got your head shot off. You were too slow on the second target."

She noticed? "You were *watching*??" I asked.

"I was," she said. "Until I saw you failing."

I thought I might get some compliments on my martial arts skills. Instead, I had to eat crow. Nothing new in this relationship. I felt my shoulders slump as I looked up at her. She was tucking the shock wand back into her sleeve.

"Sorry," I said. I couldn't explain it, but letting her down felt even worse than almost dying.

"I won't always be there," she said. "You have only yourself."

CHAPTER 26

THE NEXT MORNING was brutal. Whatever mission Meed was preparing me for, I clearly wasn't ready, and she let me know it. Again and again, she made me come at her, full out. Front. Back. Side. And every time, she put me on the floor. Over and over, she drilled me on the right way to knock away a gun and leave the guy with a shattered wrist. She showed me the death points on the back of the neck, the belly, the chest.

I learned that the clavicle is an easy bone to break and that it takes about 130 pounds of force to crack somebody's jaw.

What was strange was how normal it was all starting to feel. I'd spent my whole life studying people—their cultures, traditions, religions. Now I was learning how to maim them. And I was okay with it. Meed had done something to change my head, not just my body. I didn't know who I was anymore, or what I was turning into.

After an hour, Meed let me stop to catch my breath. I was aching all over and dripping with sweat. I saw her reach into a plastic bin and pull out a large brown paper sack. It was leaking a watery red fluid. When the bag dropped away, I rocked back. She was holding up a huge severed pig's head, with a long pink snout and its mouth set in a sickly grin. She jammed the head down on top of a metal stand so the pig was looking right at me. Meed shoved me into position in front of the gross, dripping head.

"Set your hands for a punch," she said, "then rip out the left eye."

What the hell?? This was a whole new level of insanity. The smell of the pig head was bad enough—sharp and rancid. The thought of touching it made my stomach turn.

Meed pointed to the outside corner of the pig's eye, which looked disturbingly human. "Right here," she said. "Jam your thumb in hard and hook it."

"You've done this?" I asked, raising my hands to the ready position.

"Wrong question," she replied. "Do it. Hard and fast."

I took a few quick breaths to psych myself up. I re-ran my mental movie of the night before, with a gun barrel pointed at my head. I let out a loud shout. Then I did it. I stabbed my right thumb into the outside edge of the pig's left eye and drove it behind the rear curve of the eyeball. I crooked my thumb and jerked it forward. The eyeball jutted out of its socket like a soft marble, still attached by nerves and small muscles, but now staring wildly to the side.

I gagged and turned away, shaking sticky pink goo off my fingers. I wanted to wash my hands. I wanted to take a shower. I wanted to vomit. I waited for Meed to say something. Like "good job." Or "poke out the other one." But when I looked over, her back was turned. She was suddenly more interested in something on the TV screen overhead.

The TV was tuned to a local Chicago station. A young

female reporter with bobbed hair was doing a remote from a downtown street. At the bottom of the screen was a crawl that read, "AFRICAN PEACEMAKER WILL SPEAK IN CHICAGO TODAY." Behind the reporter was a temporary speaking platform with some of the scaffolding still showing. She was already talking when Meed turned up the volume.

. . . and if there is any hope of bringing peace to the warring factions in the splinter nation of Gudugwi, it lies with former Ghanaian minister Abrafo Asare. If he succeeds in his mission, a number of African warlords and arms dealers are expected to be brought before the International Court of Justice in The Hague. Which, in some dark quarters, makes Abrafo Asare a very unpopular man. Asare will speak to human rights activists and supporters here in Chicago this afternoon before heading to the United Nations in New York. City Hall will be closed, and expect street closures in that area, because security will be tight. This is Sinola Byne, Channel 7, Eyewitness News, Chicago.

Without a word, Meed turned and headed for her room behind the kitchen. Apparently, the lesson in eye-gouging was over. It wasn't unusual for Meed to disappear into her private space with no explanation—in the middle of a meal, in the middle of a workout, in the middle of a sentence. I was used to it by now. When she closed the door behind her, I looked back up at the TV. I was staring at a commercial for Jimmy Dean breakfast sausage.

Just me and the dead stinking pig.

CHAPTER 27

BY THE TIME the commercial break was over, Meed was out of her room and moving with purpose through the kitchen. She had quick-changed out of her workout gear into street clothes—skinny jeans, a sweater, and a burgundy leather jacket. Her hair was tucked under a floppy beret. She looked like she was heading for a brunch date.

"I'll be out for a while," she said.

Out? This was a first. She had never left me alone in the open part of the loft.

Was it possible she trusted me enough to let me roam the whole space on my own?

"Come here," she said. She led me to the weight bench and sat me down. I thought maybe she was about to explain where she was going or what kind of workout she expected me to do while she was gone. Instead, she pulled a length of heavy chain from the floor and wrapped it around my chest in three tight loops, trapping my arms above the elbows. She wrapped the other end around the base of the weight machine. So much for trust.

"What are you *doing*??" I asked. "If you think I'm a flight risk, just stick me back in my cell!"

"Too easy," she said. "I need to expand your horizons."

She reached into the tool drawer and pulled out a padlock with a long shackle. She hooked it through a few links of the chain across my chest and clicked it shut. I was now bound to the Precor trainer, which was loaded with about 400 pounds of weights. My arms were bound tight, with my forearms wriggling out underneath. But she wasn't done yet.

She reached into the drawer again and pulled out a small beige rectangle. Five months ago, I would have thought it was modeling clay. Now I knew better. It was C-4 explosive.

"Jesus!" I said, struggling against the chains.

"Praying won't help," Meed replied.

She jammed a fuse into one side of the rectangle and then dropped it down the back of my gym shorts. I could feel the cool brick against my lower spine. I squirmed and shouted, "Why are you doing this??" She pretended not to hear me. The rest of the fuse was in a thick coil. Meed unwound it quickly as she backed across the living room area to the far wall of the loft.

"What the hell are you *thinking*??" I yelled. She pulled a lighter out of her pocket and touched off the fuse. It lit up like a sparkler as she dropped it onto the hardwood floor. I bounced up and down on the bench, trying to jar the chains loose, but it wasn't working.

"Is this a joke?" I asked. She was heading for the elevator.

"Figure it out," she said, staring at my shorts. "Or there will be consequences."

She pressed the Down button. The door opened.

"Are you *insane*??" I shouted. I really thought she might

be. Or maybe she'd seen some kind of secret code in the TV report? Something that set her off. A reason to get rid of me for good. Maybe I'd washed out as a trainee. Maybe I knew too much. At this point, anything was possible. Including getting blown to pieces, ass first.

As the elevator door slid shut, Meed gave me a little wave.

"Bye-bye, Doctor."

CHAPTER 28

MEED STEPPED OUT of the cab at the corner of Clark and Madison, near St. Peter's.

It was as close as the driver could get. She handed him the fare and started walking up North LaSalle. Police barriers blocked traffic in every direction, and cops strolled around on both sides of the barricades, scanning the crowd and talking into their shoulder mics. Here and there, state police in camo stood in small clusters with semi-automatic rifles slung across their chests. A K-9 sergeant led an eager German shepherd on a bomb-sniffing patrol from one manhole cover to another.

On paper, the perimeter was tight. To Meed's trained eye, it was a sieve. Loose surveillance. Too many access corridors. Plenty of escape routes. Security seemed to improve as she strolled closer to the speaker's platform, but even there, she saw gaps and lapses. Listening to the radio chatter, she wondered if the local and state police were even using the same frequency.

The platform, now draped in colorful bunting, was placed directly across from City Hall, with its majestic columns.

Police guarded the entrances. Some of the media had set up in front of the iconic facade so the background would lend gravitas to their standups.

There was a controlled space for a small audience directly in front of the platform. Plainclothes agents funneled visitors through a portable metal-detection gate into an area of pavement filled with plastic folding chairs. The metal detector was a solid choke point, which Meed had no intention of testing. Because she was definitely carrying metal.

CHAPTER 29

ELEVEN STORIES UP on the other side of the street, the sprawling City Hall rooftop garden was already starting to burst into life. The crabapple and hawthorn trees were beginning to bud, and the perennials and thick grasses were getting more lush with each warm spring day. "An urban oasis and an environmental masterpiece," just like the guidebooks said. Also, excellent cover.

At the edge of the roof, just outside the border of the vegetation, a lone sniper took his position overlooking the street, extending the barrel of his rifle over the low parapet. From there, he had a direct line of sight to the speaker's platform and the crowd surrounding it. The distance was around 250 feet. The scope was hardly necessary. He shifted his arms to get comfortable. The bulky CPD uniform was a loose fit on his lean frame, but he hadn't exactly had a choice of sizes. He had taken the first one he could get.

The uniform's original owner was lying just twenty feet away, concealed in a stand of tall grass, his bare limbs turning bluish-gray as his blood oozed into the fertile black garden soil.

CHAPTER 30

CHRIST! THE SPARK on the fuse was snaking its way across the living room. I pulled and strained against the chains, as if that would make a difference. I was a lot stronger than I used to be, but I wasn't the Incredible Hulk. I tried tugging against the weight machine, thinking that if I could rock it, I might be able to flip it over. Then I remembered that it was bolted to the floor through iron plates. Solid as a rock.

I twisted to the side as far as I could and braced my feet against the edge of the treadmill, but I couldn't get any leverage. The treadmill wasn't bolted down, so it skidded when I pressed against it.

I looked back across the room. The spark was just ten feet away and starting to wind around behind me. I stared down at the padlock dangling in front of my chest. I could reach it with my hands, but there was no way I could budge it. Then something flickered in my brain. There must have been a reason Meed hooked the padlock in front instead of in back, out of reach. She wasn't that sloppy. She must have been giving me some kind of hint. Or some kind of hope.

I ran through the endless series of mantras she'd planted in my brain over the past five months. A lot of them sounded like they were translated from a different language. For some reason, the saying that came to me now was, "Become a master or be gone." I could hear the fuse fizzing around the base of the weight machine. I scanned the floor around me. That's when I saw it.

I kicked off my shoes and used my left foot to push down my right sock. When it was halfway down my foot, I shook it off. I stretched out my leg and rolled my bare heel over a tiny black object lying on the side of the treadmill. When it was close enough, I started to work it up between my toes, gripping like a chimpanzee. It was a thin piece of black metal, about two inches long. If I could manage to get it from my feet to my hands in time, I might have a chance.

CHAPTER 31

MEED MOVED THROUGH the crowd, acting like a curious tourist, watching the cops and soldiers and security people, but trying not to make eye contact. She kept her hands out of her pockets and wore a pleasant expression. When other civilians looked at her, she smiled politely, like a true Midwesterner.

As she passed a thickset CPD officer, she heard his shoulder mic crackle with a two-number code. The officer quickly turned to face south and pounded a few junior officers on their shoulders and pointed.

"One minute!" he said, his voice gruff and tight. "One minute!"

Meed looked in the direction the officer was pointing and saw a stir in the crowd one block down. A CPD motorcycle cop rounded the corner from Washington onto LaSalle. A trio of black Suburbans followed right behind.

As she moved toward the inner perimeter, Meed saw a tall SWAT commander with his walkie-talkie pressed to his mouth. "Station 5, check," he muttered. There was no response. "Station 5, check," he repeated. Still nothing. He looked up to the roof of City Hall and saw his man in position, barrel protruding just as it should be. "Learn to use your radio, asshole," he muttered. Then he gave up and started to move his ground people into position. Meed stopped. She looked up, too. In an instant, she sensed why the sniper hadn't responded. And she knew what she needed to do.

The SWAT squad moved into position as the caravan rolled up. The motorcycle cop pulled to the side and let the three SUVs move slowly into a line alongside the speaker's platform.

In the center compartment of the middle vehicle, behind two inches of bulletproof glass, an assistant handed Abrafo Asare a neatly typed page with the day's remarks. He glanced over the five short paragraphs and slipped the paper into his jacket pocket. He looked through the window at the speaker's stand. Podium in place. Cordon of security. Local officials taking their seats. A Ghanaian flag had been placed to the left of the Stars and Stripes, as requested. A nod to his homeland.

Asare turned to admire City Hall, a solid granite rectangle that looks sturdy enough to withstand a hurricane. The building's massive columns cast deep shadows. It's no wonder Asare didn't notice the flicker of movement along the side of one of those columns. Nobody else did either.

There was a tap on the car window. Asare looked out to see his chief security officer reaching for the door handle. The massive car door swung open and the previously muffled sound of the crowd was suddenly full volume. Asare glanced at his assistant and turned on his full-wattage diplomat's smile.

"Let's do some good," he said. "Showtime."

CHAPTER 32

MEED WAS OUT of practice. In her prime—maybe age 14—
she could have made the free climb up the building in two
minutes. Now it was taking her twice as long. She kept to the
shadows on the dark side of the column in order to stay hidden from spectators below. Her arms ached. Her legs burned.
Her fingers were raw from finding handholds on the stone.
But the last stretch was a snap. The elaborate carving on the
eleventh-floor corner offered an easy foothold for her final
move. As Meed swung herself over the granite top rail, she
found herself facing a disorienting maze of plants and grass—
a foreign landscape for a city rooftop. She stayed low, skirting
around the perimeter of the roof to the west-facing side. From
below, she could hear the echo of the PA system from the
speaker's platform, where a man was speaking in a smooth,
friendly baritone.

"So, thank you, my friends," the man was saying, "for this
very warm Chicago welcome, and for the support you've given
to the pursuit of peace...."

As she reached the corner, Meed saw the sniper in a crouch

below the wall, his cheek nestled against the stock of his flat-black rifle. He was totally focused—too focused to notice Meed moving quietly behind the vegetation. She saw him tighten his grip and adjust his eye against the scope. She saw his finger slide from the trigger guard to the trigger. *Now!*

Meed covered the short stretch between them in a split second. She kicked the long barrel into the air as the shot rang out, echoing against the opposite building. Shrill screams rose from the street below. Meed dropped hard onto the sniper's back, her elbow in his ribs. He rolled hard to the opposite side and pulled free, then sprang to his feet. When he lifted his head, Meed took a step back, stunned. In an instant, she recognized the sniper's face—still smooth and boyish. It had hardly changed in sixteen years.

Rishi.

He stared back at her, his expression quickly morphing from shock to recognition to fury. He unbuttoned the bulky police jacket and stripped down to his black T-shirt.

"Meed! Goddamn you!" he said. "This is not your business!"

Meed stayed cool, watching for his next move, knowing just how dangerous he was. "Does it pay well, Rishi?" she asked. "Is it worth it?"

Rishi moved back from the edge of the wall. "You should know they only pay for a body," he said with a sneer. Suddenly, there was a blade in his hand. "Maybe I can still provide one."

Meed slipped her hand into her jacket pocket and pulled out a knife of her own. The two former classmates circled each other slowly at the edge of a large rectangle of greenery, blocking out the shouts and sirens from below. Rishi lunged. The blade sliced the shoulder of Meed's jacket. She followed his momentum and kicked his right leg out from underneath him. Rishi landed hard on the stone roof as his knife flew into the greenery. In a flash, Meed was on top of him, knife raised, but in the next second, Rishi hooked her legs and flipped her over. His right hand grabbed her wrist, pinning her knife hand against the roof, while his left hand hooked around her throat. Meed gasped as her windpipe was crushed flat. She tried to twist her head and punch with her free hand, but Rishi's grip got tighter. Meed's vision started to cloud. Jagged flares appeared in her periphery. Her chest heaved. Her back arched violently. She could feel herself fading.

Losing. Dying. Rishi leaned forward, applying more force. Feeling Rishi's weight shift, Meed slipped one knee out from under his leg and brought it up hard into his crotch. For a split second, his grip on her throat relaxed. That was enough.

Meed shoved Rishi's head hard to the side and rolled with him until she was on top again, her knee in his solar plexus, her knife blade poking the skin over his jugular.

"You were always better with a gun than a knife," she gasped, her voice tight and pained.

"We all have our talents," Rishi replied in a harsh whisper. In spite of the knife at his throat and the knee in his gut, his face suddenly relaxed. He almost looked like a kid again.

"They've never stopped looking for you, Meed," he said. "Kamenev won't stop until you're dead."

"Then he should have made me the target," said Meed.

There was a loud bang as a metal door flew open on the other side of the roof, followed by heavy boot steps. Meed rolled to the side and crawled behind a stand of grass, leaving Rishi in the open as the cops rounded the corner. He sat up slowly as the officers shouted their commands: "Don't move! Lie flat! Arms out!"

From where she was hidden, Meed could see the section of wall where Rishi's rifle was still leaning. It was just five feet away. Suddenly Rishi jumped up and dashed toward the edge. He paused there and turned back toward Meed. Then he gave her an eerie smile.

"Stop! Freeze!" the lead officer shouted. Meed crouched back down, expecting to hear a volley of gunfire. Death by SWAT. But no shots came. The next sound she heard was the sickening crack of a body striking the street far below. As boot-steps rushed forward from the other side of the roof, Meed faded into the garden. In seconds, she was gone.

CHAPTER 33

HOURS LATER, MEED'S thighs were trembling and the muscles in her lower back were threatening to spasm. She had spent the long afternoon braced in a shadow of one of the building's side columns, waiting for the excitement to fade. It was after dark when she made her final descent, a few inches at a time. By the time she dropped the last few feet to the sidewalk, pedestrians hardly noticed. The security cordons were gone. The only remaining flashing lights reflected from the messy suicide scene at the front of the building.

As she walked back through the city, Meed kept her eyes down, her head low.

She knew Rishi had told her the truth. A save like this had been a huge risk. What if it had all been a lure? What if there were other assassins on other rooftops, aiming down at her? She tugged her beret tight over her hair and walked west, then south again. Twenty minutes later, when she was certain she wasn't being tailed, she headed for home.

The moment she walked out of the elevator into the loft, she saw a pile of chains lying loose across the workout bench.

She looked to the right. The professor was enjoying a protein shake in the kitchen, his feet up on the counter. As soon as he saw Meed, he lifted his hand triumphantly.

He was holding a hairpin.

"Lose something?" he asked with a self-satisfied grin. So proud of himself.

"I shouldn't have made it so obvious," said Meed. The professor's cheer faded a little. He held up the small cake of clay, with a hole where the fuse had been pulled out.

"And this..." he said, "this isn't really C-4, is it?"

"Silly Putty," said Meed. "The color should have been a give-away." She pulled off her beret and let her copper curls loose. "What did they teach you at those Mensa meetings anyway?"

Meed was exhausted. But the events of the day had reminded her that she could not relax. Especially not now. And neither could Doctor Savage. She could see that he was learning, getting more resourceful and creative every day. More independent. But there were bigger challenges ahead. She had to stop going easy on him.

CHAPTER 34

Eastern Russia
14 Years Ago

THE THIN COPPER coin was no match for concentrated nitric acid.

As soon as Irina let the disk drop into the beaker, the solution started to foam and bubble. Within seconds, all that was left of the metal was a cloudy green mist. At the next lab station over, Meed was working with magnesium, causing a bubbling hiss and a burst of orange vapor.

All along the rows of black-topped tables, the students tested their caustic mixtures on an assortment of materials—cloth, metal, plastic, wood—and watched with fascination as the powerful corrosives did their work. Ilya Lunik, the bearded instructor, paced along the tables, mentally scoring the teams on accuracy and laboratory technique.

Lunik, a fastidious man in his late sixties, was a master chemist, one of the most brilliant of his generation. His coursework included formulas he had perfected years ago for the Russian government. He still kept those formulas in his head. During the Cold War, he had also dabbled in sedatives and poisons.

But acids were his specialty, and his research had been widely respected in the darkest corners of the Soviet Union.

There had been no patents for his work, of course. No inventor's royalties or prestigious medals. Only personal pride. And the satisfaction of passing his knowledge on to those who could put it to productive use. He walked to the chalkboard and started scrawling a complex chemical diagram.

For once, Irina and Meed were not the first team to finish their assignments.

While the other students recorded their observations diligently in lab notebooks, the dark-haired girl and her partner were deviously searching for other items to destroy. A pencil eraser in hydrochloric acid. A strand of hair in sulfuric acid. A fingernail clipping in hydrobromic acid. Lunik had just finished his work on the chalkboard when he heard the room erupt in excitement. One of Irina's solutions had produced a thick white cloud, and the other students had abandoned their stations to observe the spectacle.

"Irina!" shouted Lunik from the front of the room. "Stick to the protocol!"

As soon as Lunik turned back toward the chalkboard, Irina thrust her hand at him in a rude gesture. The thick vapor blocked her view of a beaker on a tall stand. As she pulled her hand back, she accidentally knocked against the support. The beaker fell and crashed onto the lab table. The contents spattered on a bare patch of Irina's right arm just above her rubber glove. Instantly, her flesh reddened and bubbled. Irina fell to the floor, slapping her other gloved hand over the wound. She gritted her teeth, trying not to scream.

Lunik whipped around, his chalk crumbling against the board. He rushed to Irina's side, bent over her—and did nothing. As she writhed and twitched on the linoleum floor, Lunik looked down and said just three words to the class.

"Don't move. Observe."

This would be an object lesson, and a powerful one. The students were frozen in place. All except one. Meed lunged toward a side table and grabbed a gallon of distilled water. Lunik held a hand up to block her.

"No!" he said firmly.

Meed pushed past him. She uncapped the container and dropped to her knees at Irina's side, then poured the clear water in a torrent over Irina's forearm, which was now bright scarlet with ugly white patches. Irina arched and moaned with pain. The other students jumped back as the water splashed and seeped across the floor, afraid that the mixture might dissolve the soles of their shoes.

"Meed!" shouted Lunik, furious and red-faced. "Mistakes must be paid for!"

Meed set the water jug down and stood up. She grabbed a flask of hydrochloric acid from the lab table. She grabbed Lunik's collar and held the flask over his head.

"Are you willing to pay for yours?" she asked.

Lunik stepped backward, shocked into silence. In his career, he had dealt with Kremlin bosses, the KGB, and professional torturers. All of them paled beside this copper-haired girl.

She was barely sixteen. But she was truly terrifying.

CHAPTER 35

Chicago

"FIVE MORE! RIGHT now! Don't quit!" I was doing hundred-pound leg presses with Meed shouting into my ear. Her heavy metal playlist blasted from the ceiling speakers. Top volume. It was hard-core, so loud that it felt like it was actually penetrating my organs. Screams. Aggression. Raw fury. That's what it took to get me through my two-a-day workouts, which had gotten more and more intense. I gritted my teeth and kept working the weight machine. I felt like a machine myself. My muscles were burning, almost exhausted. But Meed would not let up. She punched my shoulder—hard.

"That last rep was half-assed!" she shouted. "Give me an extra!"

I was into the fifth superset of my morning session. With my last rep, I was finished with legs, moving on to arms and back. I was panting, sweating, aching. I used to think a set of tennis was a solid workout. I had no idea. "Toy exercise," Meed called it. "Wimpy and soft." My soft life was definitely over. I'd almost forgotten what that life was like.

Now my world was a blur of preacher curls, lying triceps

extensions, cable pulls, dead lifts, and hang power snatches. I jumped rope like a maniac and swung fifty-pound kettle-bells. I balanced on a tilt board while holding sandbags in each hand. I was burning 400 calories an hour and replacing them with mass-gain supplements. I weighed myself religiously every morning, like a fighter in training. I was now up to 195. A twenty-pound gain in six months. All muscle. A whole new me.

"Let's go, Doctor!" Meed yelled. "Let out your inner savage!" I knew she liked that joke. But it wasn't a joke, not really. She was bringing out a side of me I'd never seen. Never *wanted* to see. She was turning me into her own personal monster. And I still didn't know why. No point in asking. Always the wrong question.

As I rested for a moment on the seat of the universal, I saw Meed glance up at the screen over the workout space. The TV was set to CNN, as usual. With Meed, it was all news, all the time. I looked up to see what was catching her eye.

At the start of a new report, a photo of a blue-eyed baby had popped up on a panel to the left of the anchor's head. Meed cut the music. The sudden silence left my ears ringing.

"Turn up the TV," she said.

I found the remote and clicked off the Mute button just as the anchor got into the meat of the story. His eyebrows were furrowed. His tone was concerned.

. . . Evan Grey, eight months old, the only son of MacArthur Fellow Devon Grey and his wife, research physicist Anna Grey, has disappeared from his parents' remote campsite near Bend, Oregon. According to park rangers, the infant was napping in a portable playpen at the edge of a clearing in broad daylight yesterday, with

his parents nearby. The couple noticed him missing at approximately 2 p.m. and immediately contacted the local ranger station. Other campers and local residents of the remote mountain community have joined the search, while the parents are begging the public for any information about their missing child.

The screen cut to a shot of the two young parents. They looked drained and scared. The mom spoke up, looking into the camera. Her voice was shaking. Her eyes were red.

If you know anything about where our baby is . . . if you have our baby . . . we just, we just want him back. We need him back. We'll do anything. Please! Please contact us.

Her voice trailed off at the end, and her husband wrapped his arms around her. When the report cut back to the anchor desk, there was an 800 number in bright red across the bottom of the screen. The anchor wrapped up the story:

Anybody with information on the whereabouts of young Evan Grey, please call this anonymous toll-free tip line. For now, authorities are looking into all possibilities, including the chance that the baby may have been the victim of a rogue bear.

And then it was over. The next story was about a flood in Missouri. Meed grabbed the remote and muted the TV.

"Bear, my ass," she said.

"It's possible, right?" I replied.

Meed pounded her fist on the weight rack. "Do you have any idea how many kids are taken in the world every year?"

"Thousands?" I guessed. I thought that might be too high.

"Eight *million*," said Meed. Her jaw was tense. It seemed like she was trying to keep herself under control. "In most countries, nothing happens without payoffs to the right people. No money, no investigation. After a year or so, the leads dry up, the case goes cold, the family moves on. The kid is just gone. Some of them pop up on sex-trafficking sites. Some of them get traded or sold. Many just vanish into thin air."

"Okay," I said. "But Oregon isn't some backwater country. Seems like they're on it, full force. They'll find him."

As usual, I could tell that Meed knew more than she was telling.

"Don't get your hopes up," she said. "That's a very valuable child."

CHAPTER 36

IT WAS 3 a.m. But Meed wasn't even aware of the time. She sat alone in front of a crowded desk, scanning the screens in front of her. From her secure room behind the kitchen, she had a complete view of the entire loft. Cameras captured every angle with overlapping fields of coverage. No blind spots. With one click, she could shift to views of the elevator interior, the entrance hallway below, or the exit to the street.

One full screen was dedicated to the professor's cell, with a shot from a wide-angle lens mounted in the ceiling. Dr. Savage was asleep now under a thin blanket, exhausted from the day's workouts. He'd been down since 10 p.m. The professor's schedule called for a solid eight hours of rest. Not Meed's. Even after a hard day, her mind buzzed with activity. She'd always been a poor sleeper.

Meed leaned forward in her Aeron chair, focused now on a large computer screen in the center of the console. This was the heart of the system, with multiple windows displaying a constant flow of reports from every region of the globe. Custom software scanned for designated keywords and images, and elegant hacks opened the most secure government files. Meed hadn't cracked everything—not yet—but her reach was wide and deep. And the whole picture was becoming clearer.

Her fingers danced over the computer keyboard, bringing up image after image on the screen in front of her—scrapes from news sites, police investigations, Amber Alerts, and the darkest corners of the dark web. The reports and data scrolled by in dozens of languages. Meed tapped from one window to the next with a flick of her right middle finger, translating in her head as she went, report after report, headline after headline.

INFANT MISSING FROM NEW DELHI SCIENCE COMPOUND

YEAR-OLD SON OF FRENCH TECH MOGUL DISAPPEARS DURING CRUISE

NORTH KOREAN CELLIST HOLDS OUT HOPE FOR LOST BABY

The reports and stories were spread over years and continents, too isolated and random to be connected. Some incidents, especially those from China and the Arabian Peninsula, had never been made public. The files started with blurry microfiche images, decades old, and accelerated through the turn of the millennium, with a spike over the past ten years. Babies with superior genes. Taken without a trace before fourteen months. All resulting in dead-end investigations.

The flickers on the screen reflected on Meed's face. She froze on a recent picture—the blue-eyed baby stolen from the Oregon campsite just thirty-six hours earlier. No blood. No body. No leads. No trail. Same pattern. Law enforcement had no clue how a baby could simply evaporate without leaving a shred of evidence. It seemed impossible. But it wasn't. It happened all the time.

After an hour in front of the screens, Meed pushed away from the console and flopped down onto the neat single bed against the opposite wall. Her gaze settled on the surveillance screen showing Dr. Savage in his cot. In fact, his cell was just a few feet away. If it weren't for five layers of cement, soundproofing foam, and tempered steel, she could have reached out and touched him.

Meed stared at the professor as he shifted and turned under his blanket. His physical progress had been impressive. His genes were even stronger than she'd hoped. But mentally, he still needed toughening. He wasn't nearly ready for what needed to be done.

Meed still didn't feel like sleeping, but she was determined to try. She wrapped herself around her pillow and forced herself to close her eyes.

CHAPTER 37

Eastern Russia
13 Years Ago

THE STUDENTS STOOD in a circle, arms at their sides, eyeing each other nervously. The entire faculty sat on an elevated platform on the far side of the classroom, talking among themselves in a low murmur. Headmaster Kamenev sat at the center in a high-backed chair, saying nothing. Meed had heard that he always took a special interest in this particular final. His presence added a whole new layer of tension.

Like everybody else, Meed needed to pass this test to move on to the next level of training. And this was one course nobody wanted to repeat. It was mental agony. The preparation had consumed days and nights for weeks. The drills had been exhausting, and Meed's brain felt close to a meltdown. But in ten minutes, one way or the other, it would be over. Kamenev shifted in his chair. The conversation from the faculty trailed off. Then the headmaster waved his hand toward the circle of students.

"Begin," he called out. "And watch your words!" A few chuckles from the teachers, but not from the students. For them, this was dead serious.

Meed had drawn first position. She stepped to the center of the circle, chin up, projecting confidence, as if daring her classmates to do their worst. As her eyes moved around the circle, a tall Hispanic girl took a step forward to face her.

"Nepovjerenje je majka sigurnosti!" the girl said.

The language was Croatian. Not Meed's strongest. She knew that she had to replicate the phrase exactly. No hesitation. No flaws. No hints that she had not spoken the language from birth. That was the only way to pass.

"Nepovjerenje je majka sigurnosti," Meed repeated. Out of the corner of her eye, she could see the language teachers nodding. Her pronunciation was impeccable.

She knew it. And so did they.

"Translation," the Hispanic girl said. Part two of the challenge. This was harder. Several Croat nouns sounded very close to Serbian. Meed cleared her throat and spoke out clearly, praying that she was making the right choice.

"Distrust is the mother of safety," she said.

Meed got it right. She knew it the moment the Hispanic girl lowered her eyes. As she stepped back into the circle, a boy with fair skin and blond hair stepped forward.

"Ferī bewīha wisīti'īnikuwanī labī yiḫonalī," he called out.

The boy's Scandinavian looks were a distraction, but Meed wasn't fooled. The language was Amharic, from the horn of Africa.

"Ferī bewīha wisīti'īnikuwanī labī yiḫonalī," Meed parroted back.

"Translation," the blond boy said.

"A coward will sweat even in water," said Meed.

With that answer, her confidence grew. One after another, her classmates stepped up to challenge her, faster and faster.

Time after time, she took in the phrase, then adjusted her jaw, her tongue, her lips, her throat, to deliver it perfectly, like a native speaker. After Croatian and Amharic, there was Urdu. Then German. The final challenge was from Irina.

"Ek veit einn at aldrei deyr domur um dauoan hvern."

It was Norwegian. Obscure and lyrical. To the rest of the room, the pronunciation sounded impossible. But Meed was fond of ancient poems. *The Aeneid. Beowulf.* And even the Old Norse *Hávamál,* where Irina had found the quote. Meed repeated the phrase syllable for syllable, careful to distinguish her Norwegian inflection from Swedish.

"Translation," said Irina.

Meed looked at her with a triumphant expression.

"I know one thing that never dies—the dead man's reputation."

Irina stepped back. That made five. All that was required. Meed was sure she had passed. She turned to take her place again in the circle. Then Kamenev stood up. Meed froze in place. The headmaster looked directly at her.

"One more, if you don't mind," he said.

Meed turned to face him. She straightened her back and took a deep breath. She nodded once.

Kamenev puffed out his chest, clearly relishing the moment. He rubbed his chin, considering his options. Meed clenched and unclenched her fists as the seconds ticked by. Kamenev cleared his throat, then spoke out, his diction crisp and precise.

"Tantum est fortis superesse!"

The phrase was Latin. That much was obvious. But Latin was a dead language, rarely spoken outside the walls of Roman churches. The pronunciation could be studied only by listening to recordings of Papal letters. Not many students went to that length. But not many students were as thorough as Meed.

"Tantum est fortis superesse!" she repeated forcefully. Kamenev turned to his language faculty. Heads nodded. Meed's pronunciation would impress a Vatican cardinal.

"Translation!" Kamenev called out.

Meed knew the phrase was a message to the class—and to her especially. She stared straight at the headmaster and delivered the answer in a calm, clear voice.

"Only the strong survive."

CHAPTER 38

Chicago

"PROTECT YOUR DAMNED queen!"

Meed was right. I was getting careless. Maybe because we had been playing for five hours. Until I became a kidnapping victim, I had thought three-dimensional chess existed only in old *Star Trek* episodes, but it turned out it was a real thing. And Meed was a master.

Night after night, she brought out the chess set. It looked expensive—three teak playing boards mounted one above the other on a wrought-iron stand, with hand-carved playing pieces. Keeping track of three levels simultaneously took some getting used to.

"Focus," Meed told me. "You can do it."

And it turned out I could. Even though I'd never played chess before. I still didn't know if Meed was sneaking brain-altering chemicals into my protein shakes and injections, but I was starting to notice that my logic skills were sharper—sometimes almost magical. I could now solve a Rubik's Cube in four seconds. I could memorize playing cards so easily that I'd be banned from a casino. But all that added brain power couldn't help me figure out what was really going on, or what I was being trained for. In a lot of ways, I was still totally in the dark.

Chess was Meed's obsession. She loved the planning, the strategy, the practice of thinking two or three moves ahead. She was a fierce player and a demanding teacher. She made me more aggressive. Made me concentrate harder. She said it was good for my fluid reasoning and processing speed. Also, it was the only time when she actually answered anything I asked. As long as the topic was chess.

"Best player?" I asked.

"Carlsen."

"Better to give up a bishop or a knight?"

"Knight."

"Who taught you the game?"

"I learned at school."

"Where was that?"

Meed didn't even look up. Nice try.

"Your move, Doctor."

I'd started that game with the French Defense. It was a beginner's ploy, and Meed saw right through it. She'd anticipated every move and had embarrassed me up and down the boards.

But now that I'd managed to shield my queen on the top level, I could actually see an opening. In two more moves, I could make it happen. But only if Meed blinked. I shifted my knight and held my breath. Meed stared at the board for a full minute, then countered with her bishop. My heart started racing. I slid my rook forward two squares and looked up. "Check," I said.

I could hardly believe the word was coming out of my

mouth. Meed tilted her head and looked across all three boards, as if she couldn't believe it either. Then she tipped her king onto its side and reached across the table to shake my hand.

"Nicely done, Doctor," she said. I could see that she was annoyed—but also impressed. Part of her liked that I beat her. I could tell. So I decided to push my luck.

As our hands met, I slid two fingers under the cuff of her right sleeve. When she pulled back, I slid out the throwing knife she had hidden there. Before she could react, I held the knife up and whipped it at the man-shaped target across the room. It stuck hard in the left upper chest. Kill shot. My first.

I could tell that Meed liked that even better.

CHAPTER 39

THE NEXT MORNING, I woke up with a strange voice in my head. Female. Chirpy. A bit nasal.

As I came out of my sleep fog, I realized that I had headphones over my ears. I didn't remember putting them on. What I was hearing was a series of repeated phrases about Chinese etiquette. When I blinked my eyes open, Meed was standing over me. She lifted the earphones away from my ears and asked me a question. In Mandarin. Without thinking, I gave her the answer. Also in Mandarin. My voice was doing things I didn't know it could do, making sounds I didn't know it could make.

I'd never studied Mandarin in my life, partly because everybody said it was the hardest language on earth to learn. But now, somehow, I could not only understand it, but *speak* it. How was that possible? I'd always been a quick learner, but now my brain was doing things that seemed way beyond reality. Freakish. I was absorbing information as I never had before, sometimes without even knowing it.

I pulled the headphones off. They were connected to an old-school disc player lying on my blanket. It looked like something Radio Shack might have sold thirty years ago.

"What the hell is this?" I asked. "What am I listening to?"

"I don't have time to explain everything," said Meed. "Some things I can teach you. Other things you need to learn for yourself, just like I did." She held up a pile of worn discs with handwritten labels. "You can absorb a lot during the REM stage. Why waste it?"

I tossed the headphones onto the blanket. I rubbed my eyes and swung my legs out from under the covers. This was crazy. Now she was even invading my dreams.

"What *else* have I learned in my sleep?" I asked.

"Wouldn't you like to know," said Meed.

I reached for my workout clothes at the end of the bed. "Don't bother with those," she said. "Just leave your shorts on."

"What? Why?" I asked. Wake. Health shake. Workout. That was the morning routine. I hated it, but I'd gotten used to it. I got nervous whenever she broke the pattern.

"Follow me," she said.

I pushed the blanket aside and put my feet on the floor. I got a tingle in my belly and I started to sweat. Meed opened my cell door.

"You know I hate surprises," I said.

"You really need to be more flexible," she replied.

She led the way through the kitchen, past the utility closet, and around a corner to a door that led to a back staircase. At least that's what I always assumed. The door had a heavy-duty alarm bar across the center. A small window with wire mesh showed a dim hallway on the other side. But when Meed disarmed the alarm and pushed the door open, I realized that the view of the hallway went along for the ride. It was simply an image set into the window frame. A trompe l'oeil. An illusion. What was behind the door wasn't a hallway at all.

It was a gigantic swimming pool.

CHAPTER 40

"YOU HAVE *GOT* to be shitting me," I mumbled. The door closed behind us. We were standing in a sealed room with no windows. Just white brick walls and a narrow tile ledge around the edge of the pool. It was competition length, with three lanes. The bottom and sides were painted deep blue. A huge TV screen hung from a metal beam across the ceiling. I could hear the patter from a morning news team echoing off the walls.

As I took it all in, my stomach churned. It wasn't just the scent of the chlorine. It was pure, primal fear. Taking a dip in an ice bath was bad enough, but this was something else. I was absolutely terrified of pools. And lakes. And oceans. Because I'd never learned how to swim. While other kids were at summer camp, I was digging up artifacts in New Mexico. I didn't know what Meed had in mind, but it was going to take a shock wand to get me into that water.

"Have a seat," she said. She pointed to a narrow wood bench along the wall. Underneath was a plastic bin.

"What are we doing here?" I asked. I was trying not to

sound scared, but my voice was pinched and thin. The air in the room was warm and thick, almost tropical. But now I was shivering all over.

"We're testing your resolve," said Meed. "Among other things."

When we reached the bench, she pushed me down by the shoulders. Then she reached under and lifted the lid on the bin. I felt something being wrapped around my ankles. When I looked down, my feet were strapped together with thick nylon straps connected to lead weights.

"No!" I shouted. "Don't do this! I'll *sink*!"

Meed looked me right in the eyes. "That's correct," she said. "What happens after that depends on you."

My head was spinning. My mouth went dry. I pressed my back up against the tile, as if I thought I could push myself through it.

"Up we go, Doctor," said Meed, tugging on my wrists. When she pulled me to my feet, I was hobbled and off balance. She nudged me toward the pool. I tried to pull back.

"Meed!" I shouted. "Please! I can't swim!"

"I know," she said. "That's a serious gap in your education."

She wrapped her arms around my chest and swung me hard. I felt my feet fly out from under me. The next second I was in the water, dropping to the bottom. Ten feet down.

I thrashed my arms and tried to move my legs, but it felt like my feet were tied to a bowling ball. I started to panic. I flexed my knees and managed to press off the bottom, kicking like a wounded porpoise. I muscled my way to the surface and gasped for air. Meed was standing at the edge of the pool.

"Ten laps, Doctor!" she called out.

What was she *talking* about?? I threw my head back and screamed.

"I'm going to *die* in here!"

"After all I've done for you?" Meed called back. "That would be really inconsiderate."

The lead weight was pulling me down again. My head went under. My toes touched the bottom. My cheeks puffed out. My lungs burned. I could feel my brain starting to blur. For a split second, I wondered what it would be like to just open my mouth, breathe in, and end this insanity once and for all. How long would it take to drown? Would it hurt? Could it be any worse than this?

Then my body took over. I pushed off against the bottom again and shot back to the surface. I leveled my chest in the water and started to kick my legs out behind me. My feet were like a single unit, so I had to generate all the torque from my hips and knees, until I felt myself moving forward through the water. My vision narrowed and my brain went numb. I was conscious of the splashes behind me, the rhythm of my arms in front, and my head turning to breathe after each stroke. The weight on my ankles was still there, but now it felt like part of me. I stopped treating it like an obstacle and started using it as a lever to propel myself. Faster and faster.

I looked up and saw the end of the pool. Four yards away. Now *three*! I could have grabbed the ledge, held on, and hauled myself out. That's what any normal human being would have done. But I wasn't normal. Not anymore. I swung my feet against the pool wall and pushed off in the other direction.

One lap down. Nine to go.

CHAPTER 41

MEED PACED CASUALLY along the edge of the pool. She was ready to make a rescue dive if necessary. She was even ready to perform CPR if it came to that. She was fully certified. But so far, she was impressed with the professor's adaptability. It looked like she wouldn't even have to get wet.

On the TV overhead, the hard-news block was over, and a young, doe-eyed culture reporter was talking about a gallery opening. Meed looked up.

The event of the week is tonight's opening of the Armis Gallery in Pilsen, one of the city's trendiest creative centers. The exhibits include paintings and sculpture from American and European artists. Part of the admission for tonight's benefit opening will go to support arts programs in Chicago schools.

As the reporter spoke, prerecorded footage showed the stylish gallery owner giving her a tour of the artwork on display in the sun-flooded space. The collection was first-rate. But it was the owner who caught Meed's attention. Handsome.

Impeccably groomed. Expensively tailored. With shockingly white teeth.

Meed felt a jolt deep in her gut. She never forgot a face. And certainly not this one. The gallery owner rested one hand lightly on the young reporter's shoulder as she delivered her wrap-up to the camera.

"Join us tonight for great art, and a great cause." The camera moved in for her close-up. *"For Chicago's Art Beat, this is Amy-Anne Roberts."* With that, the show cut back to the studio for a cooking demo.

Meed walked to the far end of the pool and knelt down to meet the professor after his last lap. He had done well. Even better than she expected. It occurred to her that she might have gone too light on the ankle weights. Dr. Savage thrashed his way to the edge. He was breathing heavily, too exhausted to speak. But Meed saw fierce pride and determination in his eyes. Which is exactly what she was looking for.

"Not bad, Doctor," she said. "Now climb out before you grow gills."

CHAPTER 42

MEED HAD CHECKED her computer a dozen times during the day, waiting for the gallery segment to be posted on the Channel 7 website. Now, at 6 p.m., the link had finally appeared. She sat down at her console and got to work. Better late than never.

She stopped on a two shot of the reporter and the owner. She zoomed in on the face with the impossible smile and froze the frame. He might have had a lift or two since she saw him last, but it was first-rate work. Probably Mexico or Brazil.

With another click, she started running her facial recognition program. The software scanned through hundreds of documents and images a second, until it locked onto a series of matches. Over the past twenty years, that smile had been all over the world—anywhere death was profitable.

The man was a consummate chameleon, sometimes appearing in a business suit, sometimes a tunic or a Pashtun robe. He was frequently standing or sitting in the background of grainy group photos taken with telephoto lenses. In most of those pictures, weapons were in the foreground. Rifle crates, missile launchers, chemical cannisters. Some of the reports linked to images of carnage—bomb craters, leveled buildings, burned-out vehicles, charred corpses.

In more recent shots, the same bright smile stood out at a restaurant opening in Morocco and a ribbon cutting at a bank in Belize. Meed realized that both were convenient fronts for arms dealing. But nothing as highbrow as a big-city art gallery. Maybe the smiling man had taste. Or maybe he was just looking for a more elegant place to launder his blood money.

Meed took a deep breath. She had choices to make.

She pulled a small drawer out from under her console. She ran her fingers over the shiny cylinders inside and made an important selection.

Flamingo Pink would be perfect.

CHAPTER 43

I WAS JUST finishing up my final bench-press routine when I saw Meed's door open. My arms still ached from the pool torture that morning, but I knew I'd catch hell if I didn't stick with the program. There was no time off. Even though Meed had been in and out of her room all day long, I could always feel her eyes on me.

When she stepped down into the kitchen, I wasn't even sure it was her. For one thing, the curls were gone. Now she had wavy black hair, parted in the middle. She was wearing a tight dress and a blue velvet jacket. And high heels. That was a first. I'd never seen her in anything but crew socks and sneakers. But the biggest change was her face. It looked like the face of a *Vogue* model. Her eyelids were blue and her lips were bright pink. Her cheeks and forehead sparkled with some kind of glitter. She looked spectacular, in a whole new way.

"Wow!" I said. "Is it prom night??"

Meed unlocked one of the kitchen drawers and put a small container in her purse.

"Something like that," she said. "And sorry, I already have a date."

"You look...like somebody else," I said.

"How do you know this isn't the real me?" she replied.

She had a point. Every time I thought I had something figured out in Meed World, something else happened to turn it upside down. I already knew her name was made up. Maybe the copper curls were fake, too. I wondered what else she wasn't telling me—or just plain lying about?

"I'll be out for a few hours," she said.

I suddenly got a sting in my gut. For a second, I was afraid she was going to chain me up again. Instead, she opened a cabinet and pulled out a bunch of audio discs. She put them in a little stack on the counter. Then she tapped them with her fingernail.

"Learn something new while I'm gone," she said.

"Like what?" I asked.

She walked to the elevator and pressed the button.

"Your choice," she said. "Surprise me."

CHAPTER 44

THE CROWD ON the sidewalk outside the gallery was a mix of rich patrons and local bohemians, heavy on the under-thirty side. More vapers than smokers. Several sleek town cars idled at the curb. The exterior of the gallery was laced with thousands of tiny white lights. A well-curated music mix flowed out from the open door, along with the clink of glassware and the hum of lively conversation.

It had been a while since Meed had worn heels this tall or a dress this fitted.

But after a quick scan of the other guests, she saw that she'd blend right in. There was a small bottleneck at the entrance as a young hostess took entry donations with her iPhone card reader. When it was Meed's turn, she reached into her small evening purse and pulled out ten crisp hundred-dollar bills.

"I hope you don't mind a donation in cash," she said with a smile.

The hostess blinked as if she'd been handed wampum. But she recovered graciously and slid the money into a drawer under her hostess podium. "Would you like a name tag?" she asked.

"I think I'll stay anonymous," said Meed. She added a charming wink.

The main hall of the gallery was broken up by curved white partitions. The floor was some kind of exotic hardwood. The paintings and sculptures were illuminated with pin spotlights, while the rest of the space was bathed in amber light, the kind of glow that made everybody look their best. Beautiful people, beautifully lit.

The first person Meed recognized was Amy-Anne Roberts, the peppy arts reporter from TV. She was stick-thin, wearing a shimmery silver dress and a quirky tiara. She looked even younger than she did on TV, and her eyes looked even bigger. Meed turned to the right and saw another woman heading her way. She was carrying a neat stack of paper at waist level.

"Welcome to Armis," she said. "Would you like a guide sheet?"

She was a tall blonde in an elegant blue suit, as formal as a uniform. Meed looked up, started to smile, and instantly froze.

It was Annika.

Meed hadn't seen her school instructor for almost twenty years. One day, Annika had been leading the class—the next day she was gone. No explanation. And now, here she was.

"Descriptions and prices," said Annika, holding out an elegantly printed sheet. "Let me know what interests you, and I'll introduce you to the artist."

Meed held her breath and looked down as she took the cream-colored paper. She nodded, but said nothing. Annika moved on casually to the next guest. Meed turned and walked off in the opposite direction, trying not to flinch. Work the wardrobe, she told herself. Trust the illusion. Be the new you.

"Champagne?"

A young man paused in front of her, his tray filled with crystal flutes. "Thank you so much," said Meed, picking up a glass. It was exactly what she needed. The server smiled and moved away. Meed took a small sip and surveyed the room.

In a far corner of the gallery, the man with perfect teeth was chatting with an elegantly dressed couple in front of a huge canvas. He was about the same distance from her now that he had been when she first saw him on Kamenev's balcony. Even then, her intuition had told her that he had a dark soul. Now she knew just how dark.

The artwork the owner was showing off was bare white, except for a few oddly placed orange triangles near the center. To Meed, it appeared that he might have misjudged the couple's interest, because they quickly excused themselves and moved toward a grouping of more conservative works. For an awkward moment, the owner was left alone, sipping his red wine. Meed moved in quickly, placing her shoulder just inches from his as she faced the spare abstract on the wall.

"Derivative of Malevich, don't you think?" said Meed.

The owner turned and took a moment to appraise Meed's profile. Then he glanced from side to side and leaned toward her in a playful whisper, his lips almost touching her ear.

"I thought the same," he said. "But the artist draws a crowd."

"Well," said Meed, staring at the canvas, "it's too big for my apartment anyway."

"You live in Chicago?" asked the owner.

Not a pickup line, exactly. Just an opening move. Smooth, thought Meed. She expected nothing less. She took another slow sip from her glass.

"New York," she said. "Just visiting."

"Gregor Mason," said the owner, turning to extend his hand.

Meed turned toward him and returned his grip with a delicate squeeze of her fingers. When she looked into his face, her mind flashed on a review of his handiwork around the world. Terror. Destruction. Death.

"Belinda," said Meed. "Belinda Carlisle."

The owner's eyes crinkled. "Wait," he said. "Belinda Carlisle? As in . . . ?"

"The Go-Go's," said Meed with a wry smile, as if she'd made this explanation a thousand times before. "Yes. Blame my parents. Big fans." Meed leaned in toward him, taking in a whiff of his smokey cologne. "But trust me—I can't sing a note."

Mason smiled. Those teeth. Almost blinding. Meed let the guide sheet slip from her hand. It floated to the floor near her host's feet.

"Oh, *no*!" said Meed, looking down in playful alarm. "Now I won't know what anything costs!"

"Allow me," said the owner with a gracious smile. Meed knew he was charmed.

And that made him careless.

As he bent forward, Meed slipped her hand into her pocket. She put the toe of her shoe on the paper so that it took her host an extra half second to tug it free. In that interval, Meed dropped a tiny tablet into his wineglass, where it instantly dissolved.

"We need to get you a new one," he said as he straightened up, frowning at the scuff mark in the corner of his pricey matte paper. "Annika!" he called out. She was standing near a metal sculpture on the other side of the room. At the sound of her name, she turned and headed over.

"Sorry," said Meed. "Would you mind?" She handed her host her glass and pointed toward the ladies' room. "Too much bubbly."

"Of course," he said with a slight bow. Meed headed for the restroom, waited for the crowd to obscure the owner's view, then detoured into the back hallway that led to the kitchen. A catering van was backed up to the open door. Meed slipped out into the loading zone and headed through a narrow alley to a side street. In minutes, she was too far away to hear the screams. She knew that by now, the gallery owner would be vomiting blood all over his expensive floor.

She only wished she could have been there to see it.

CHAPTER 45

"HEY THERE! *YOU! *You . . . are *stunning*!"

As Meed crossed the street a few blocks from the gallery, a frat boy in a Bulls T-shirt was hanging out the window of an Uber. She could hear the slurring in his voice. He was a harmless mess, just cocky and drunk and acting out for his buddies in the back seat. Meed stared straight ahead and kept up her pace as she reached the curb and headed down a side street.

She wanted to avoid crowds, but she needed the fresh air. And time to think. Her heart was still racing. She knew that her gallery mission had been dangerous, that it might attract attention in all the wrong places. Just like her encounter with Rishi. But she was tired of being afraid, tired of doing nothing. She'd spent more than ten years in hiding, pretending to be somebody she wasn't. More than a decade on her own, just watching the evil in the world grow, knowing where a lot of it was being sown. Mostly she felt helpless against it. But now she had to take action—just *had* to. No matter how risky it was for her. If they were coming for her, she had decided, let them come.

Meed tried to focus her mind on Dr. Savage. Her work with him was nearly done, she told herself. And then everything would change. At least that's what she was counting on. He was her secret weapon. He just didn't know it yet.

She rounded the last corner toward home and looked both ways before slipping through the back entrance. As soon as she stepped into the elevator, she pulled off her wig and unpinned her hair, shaking her copper curls loose. Then she kicked off her heels and stood in stockinged feet on the bare metal floor, wriggling her aching toes for the first time in hours. She couldn't wait to wipe her face clean—to wipe the whole evening off. The makeup felt sticky on her skin and the glitter was starting to itch. She pressed the Up button.

When the door to the loft slid open, Meed stepped out—then stopped. The loft echoed with music. *Live* music. It was coming from the living area. From Dr. Savage. He was sitting at the piano, his back to her, working the Steinway with so much concentration that he hadn't even heard her arrive. He was playing Rachmaninoff, and his technique was brilliant. Meed felt a pang in her stomach, and then a blind rage rose up inside her.

She dropped her heels and wig on the floor and walked over to the piano. The professor was on the second movement of the 3rd Concerto, executing a very difficult passage. Meed reached for the key lid and slammed it down hard. If the professor's reaction time hadn't been so sharp, she might have crushed his fingers. He jolted back on the bench and looked up.

"What the hell . . . !!" he shouted.

"Why are you playing that?" Meed demanded. "How do you know that?"

Dr. Savage pointed to the audio player and headphones lying on the piano top.

"You told me to surprise you," he said.

Meed reached for the player and ejected the disc. She held it in both hands and bent it until it shattered into bright shards. When she looked down, she realized that one of the sharp edges had sliced a finger. She let the blood run down her hand until it dripped onto the floor. The professor sat, stunned, not moving from the bench.

"Never that piece," said Meed coldly. "Never that composer. Not *ever*."

CHAPTER 46

Eastern Russia
12 Years Ago

IT WAS RACE Day—one of the most anticipated events of the school year, and one of the most dangerous. Meed's leather gloves rested on the throttle of her growling black ATV. She tested the brakes, but she wasn't planning to use them much. Speed was everything. The engine vibration rattled her hips on the leather seat. Standard racewear was a nylon jumpsuit with a single zipper from neck to crotch, plus a pair of goggles. Meed had added a red bandanna for style. As always, helmets were optional, and it was a school tradition to refuse them. Some students also considered safety harnesses a sign of weakness. But not Meed. She had hers buckled tightly, intending to stay one with her machine.

To reach the day's competition, every student had already survived a course in evasive and tactical driving in high-powered sedans, pickups, and SUVs. Brutal and demanding. But the ATV race was the crucible—a no-holds-barred competition among the senior students. Rule number one: Last machine moving was the winner. There were no other rules.

The oval dirt track was rugged and uneven. It had been

carved by bulldozers and left rough on purpose. The quarter-mile circuit route was interrupted by dirt mounds and wooden ramps at random intervals, adding to the perils. The infield was dotted with a few equipment hangars and an open-sided white medical tent. Spectators—younger students and school instructors—watched from a set of crude bleachers.

The outer edges of the track were ringed with bundles of hay staked to the ground with metal bars. All around the perimeter, flaming torches had been jammed into the bales. The torches gave off streams of oily black soot, which mixed with the bluish ATV exhaust fumes. The effect was hellish.

Meed had spent weeks working on her ATV, tuning the carburetor for the optimal mix and swapping out the clutch for a heavy-duty design. Her wheels were extra-fat, with high-performance treads, and the chassis was low and stubby. The machine looked lethal just sitting still.

Sitting at the starting post, riders revved their engines aggressively, sending fresh plumes of exhaust into the air. At one end of the track, the head mechanics instructor stood on a high platform with a pistol in his right hand. With his eyes on the pack, he raised his arm and fired a bright green flare into the sky. The engine noise rose to a thunderous din as tires bit into the dirt. Within seconds, all twenty-four ATVs were careening around the track, and drivers were picking their targets.

As Meed cranked her throttle, Irina slid her blue ATV into position just behind her on the right—the wingman slot. Irina's job was defense, keeping attackers at bay while Meed concentrated on the action in front. They planned to switch positions after two circuits.

Meed had studied the videos of the previous year's competition and calculated the most effective strategies. She was determined to strike early, while her machine was in peak condition. She crouched low in her seat, leaning forward, copper curls blowing behind her. Just ahead, one of the senior boys was already showing off, standing on the floorboards of his ATV as he drove, harness-free, stupidly raising his center of gravity. First victim.

Meed goosed the throttle and whipped her machine to the left in order to get a better angle, then turned hard right, cutting through the crowd. The show-off didn't even see her coming. She banged into his left front tire with her thick steel bumper. The impact knocked the boy sideways. As he clung desperately to the steering wheel, his ATV spun wildly and tipped onto its side, sending him flying hard into a hay bale. One down. Meed swerved back to the center of the track as Irina held her position six feet to the rear.

Suddenly, Irina heard a fresh roar behind her. She glanced back. A boy with a blond crew cut had zoomed up from the rear in a dark green machine. He was making a move to pass. Irina swung left to block him. The pack was now moving at fifty miles per hour on the straightaways. The track was a blur. The intruder yanked his steering wheel to the right. Irina leaned forward to check her distance from Meed. In that split second, the pursuer banged hard into Irina's rear bumper. A few yards ahead, Meed dodged a two-foot mound in the middle of the track. Irina swerved a split second later. Too late. She hit the hump hard with her right front tire and went airborne. Meed glanced into her rearview just in time to see Irina's ATV crashing onto the infield. Irina flew from her machine, bounced, and rolled across the grass. Meed was another hundred yards around the track when she saw a team of white-jacketed medics rush out of their tent.

Meed had two choices. She could pull off onto the infield and help her partner. Or she could keep going and avenge her. Her foot inched toward the brake. Then, above the roar of the engines, she imagined Irina's voice, low and even. Just like on the mountain.

"Stop being weak," the voice said.

Meed hit the throttle.

CHAPTER 47

FIVE MINUTES LATER, the track was Armageddon. Students were ramming each other from every direction, causing spectacular spinouts and flips. Engines sputtered, transmissions whined, tires squealed. A few wounded ATVs limped to the side on bent rims. Others were left as smoking wrecks in the middle of the track, creating a fresh set of deadly obstacles. Out of two dozen starters, only a handful were still running. Meed was one of them. So was the crew-cut boy in the green machine.

He had vaulted past Meed to weave through what was left of the pack, so far evading every hit. Meed dodged a pair of ramps and accelerated toward him. A bright orange ATV knocked into her from the right, but only managed to bat her slightly off center. Meed straightened out and rocketed forward with just a minor dent. Her engine was still solid, her transmission tight and responsive. Her mind flashed to Irina, picturing her broken—or dead. But she shook it off and concentrated on the task at hand. *I have only myself,* she kept thinking.

About fifty yards ahead, two other drivers were working as a team to close in on the green machine from both sides. The boy with the crew cut waited until his pursuers were parallel to his rear wheels, then slammed on his brakes. As he dropped back, he knocked into the ATV on the right, causing it to career into the machine on the left. A two-for-one hit. But costly, because now the two damaged machines had him blocked on the track.

Meed dropped her head low as she rounded the corner, sighting the center of the green ATV as it tried to maneuver around the wreck in front. She feathered the throttle, adjusting her speed to inflict maximum damage on the other machine without demolishing her own—a critical balance. Just as she made her final attack run, a mound of dirt obscured her view of the target. She leaned right in her seat, straining to see around it. Suddenly, she felt a violent shock on her left rear bumper. Her machine went spinning out of control. As she crashed hard into the side barrier, she caught a flash of orange. Her attacker sped by and hit the mound ahead at high speed, launching into the air.

The boy in the green ATV put his machine in reverse, but his wheels locked up. He unstrapped his harness and started to lift out of his seat. The orange ATV had become a 500-pound missile. It landed hard and bounced once, turning on its side as it flew forward. In less time than it took the crew-cut boy to blink, the roll bar caught him in the chest, knocking him fifteen yards down the track. He landed like a heavy sack, blood pouring from his mouth. The green and orange machines crumpled together in a single, smoking heap.

Meed glanced around the oval. In every direction, ATVs littered the track, but none of them were moving. She tested her throttle to see if her machine had anything left. It lurched forward, shaky and sputtering. There was a loud scraping noise from underneath, metal on metal. Meed worked the clutch and the shift lever. The whole transmission felt balky. It felt like she had only one gear left. But that was one more than anybody else had. She knew that all she needed to do to secure the win was to thread through the smoke and the wrecks and cross a white line fifty yards ahead.

Mead revved her engine. The sound reverberated around the track like a wounded animal. Every spectator and driver turned in her direction, expecting her to roll forward. The instructor on his platform readied the blue flare to signal victory.

Instead, Meed swerved directly across the track and bounced onto the infield. It was twenty yards to the medical tent. When she got there, she jumped out of her seat and ran to the open side—just as Irina burst out.

Irina's driving suit was torn and stained with grass and blood. Her eyes were wild. Meed leaned forward, exhaling a sigh of relief. Irina grabbed her by the shoulders, pulled her up, and shook her hard.

"Why didn't you *finish*?!" Irina shouted into Meed's face. *"Why??"*

Meed stared back in stunned silence. She realized that she had no answer—at least not an answer that Irina would ever accept.

CHAPTER 48

IN THE SMOKEY aftermath of the race, Meed and Irina headed across the rutted track toward the school. They walked side by side, but not speaking. Irina could barely *look* at her partner. All around the dirt oval, students stood on top of their wrecks or tried to rock them upright. One boy kicked his dead machine with his boot, again and again. Two boys with huge wrenches had already started to cannibalize parts.

Several students sat on the grass while medics tended to bloody gashes and twisted limbs. Meed looked to the left, where the boy from the green machine lay still on the grass, a blanket pulled over his face, his crew cut showing at the top. His hands, now bluish-white, were clawed at his sides.

Meed yanked off her gloves and wiped the mud from her face with the back of her hand. Irina pulled a few stray strands of grass from her jet-black hair. She was limping slightly, but Meed knew better than to offer help, even when they reached the rise that separated the track complex from the main campus. She slowed down to match Irina's pace.

When they crested the hill and looked down the other side,

they saw Kamenev standing at the edge of the main school-yard, hands behind his back. It was not unusual to see the headmaster outside, especially on the day of a major event. The girls nodded respectfully as they approached. Then it became clear that Kamenev was not just out for a stroll. He was waiting for them. Meed and Irina stopped, suddenly nervous.

"I see you both survived," said Kamenev.

"We both failed," said Irina—brutally honest, as always.

Meed looked down, not wanting to make things worse. No use in trying to explain her motivation at the end of the race—why concern for her partner was more important to her than winning. That was a conversation she could never have, not with anybody at school. And definitely not with Kamenev. But the headmaster did not seem concerned with the outcome of the race. He pulled a folder from behind his back.

"This is your final test," he said.

Meed and Irina looked at each other, hearts pounding. From the age of five, they had been told this moment would come. They just didn't know exactly when or how it would happen. But they instantly knew what it meant.

With those five simple words from the headmaster, they understood that their classwork was over, competitions done, a lifetime of training complete. There was only one more thing to accomplish. The last assignment. The final test.

Over the years, Meed had managed to tease out a few details about finals from Lyudmila Garin during her piano lessons. She knew that every final was different, meant to reveal each student's strengths and weaknesses. Some finals were solos, others paired. Meed glanced over at Irina and felt a sense of relief. In spite of their conflict over the race, there was nobody alive that she trusted more. Nobody had more determination.

If they'd been assigned to their final as a team, Meed had no doubt that they would both succeed, no matter how impossible the task appeared.

"There's a village six miles to the east, over the mountain," said Kamenev. "A matter there has been festering for years. It needs to be cleaned up once and for all."

A village? To Meed, it felt odd to realize that there was any other kind of civilization nearby. For as long as she could remember, all she had known of the world was what she experienced at school and what she'd seen in videos and photographs. There had been nothing else. No other contact. The final was a huge step from theory to reality. Meed knew that it was meant to be disruptive, even shocking. Students never spoke about a final test after it was completed. That was an ironclad law. But she knew that they came back changed— and that, soon after, they usually left the school for good.

Kamenev held out the dossier. Irina took it and opened it. Meed leaned in to see the contents. She had expected a complex file, filled with data and background information. It was nothing like that. The file was bare bones. A simple hand-drawn map was clipped to the inside cover. A single sheet of paper showed an address and photo scans of two people. Just faces. A man and a woman. Total strangers. There were no names on the paper, just four digits and a letter, repeated twice. The assignment codes. Meed knew the codes. They were death warrants.

Meed felt her adrenaline start to pump as her mind shifted. She *forced* it to shift. Because whoever these people were, they were not human to her anymore. They couldn't be. They were simply targets.

"Final test accepted?" asked Kamenev.

Both girls nodded.

"I need to hear it," Kamenev said.

"Final test accepted," said Irina, closing the folder.

"Final test accepted," said Meed softly.

Meed understood that there would be no further clarifications or explanations. They had the assignment. The rest was theirs to decide. She knew that from this point on, anything they asked would receive the same reply: "Wrong question."

CHAPTER 49

IT WAS ONE o'clock the next morning when Meed and Irina first saw the village. They were still half a mile up the mountain. The whole place looked smaller than the school grounds. In fact, from this height, the buildings looked like a set of toys.

"Wait," said Irina, tugging Meed down behind a fallen tree. Irina pulled out a set of binoculars and scanned the streets below. They were too far up to see address numbers, but the map left no doubt that they were headed for the right place. It was the only human settlement for miles around. Irina stood up and started angling her way down the slope. Meed followed close behind, placing her feet in Irina's footprints.

They both knew how far sound could carry in the mountains. From here on, there would be no talking. Meed was grateful for that. She was afraid that her voice would reveal her shakiness about the assignment—the fact that she was about to graduate from student to killer. If Irina had any concerns like that, she wasn't showing them.

As they got closer, a winding trail spilled onto a small field at the far edge of the village. Now the girls could see the actual scale of the place. It looked cozy, with neat two-story frame houses and tree-lined streets—like a place that hadn't changed in decades.

The streets were empty, but the main route was well lit. On the side streets, the street lamps were placed only on the corners, spaced far enough apart to create shadows at the center. Irina led the way, glancing at the map, picking her way block by block. Meed followed at her elbow, so close that anybody looking might have seen one shape, not two. After scouting for a few minutes, they huddled by the side of a dark drugstore and peeked out across the side street. Irina pointed to the brown house directly opposite. Meed squinted at the porch and saw three numerals lit by a small bulb above the door. 4-6-6. That was it.

The girls wound their way all the way down the block through backyards and alleys before crossing to the other side. Meed tried to tamp down her emotions and focus on the task. Her brain was pulling her two different ways. Part of her hoped that something would happen to force them to abort the mission. The other part just wanted to get it over with.

As the girls passed behind a corner house, the door to the rear porch opened, slamming hard against the outside wall. They crouched down and held perfectly still. Two men came through the door holding beer bottles. They were laughing loudly and almost tripping as they stepped. One man rested his bottle awkwardly on the porch rail and lit a cigarette. The other man tucked his bottle under his chin, unzipped his fly, and urinated off the porch. Irina tugged Meed's sleeve. They melted back into the shadows, picking their way toward the brown house farther down the row.

When they arrived, they sat on the soft ground behind a

low wood fence and watched for a full ten minutes, looking for any movement. On Irina's signal, they moved forward. The fence had a simple latch gate. Irina opened it and slipped through. As they walked softly across the small backyard, Meed suddenly stopped. Her stomach roiled and her mouth felt sour. She bent over a bush and vomited. Irina quickly scanned the house and the neighbors for any reaction. Meed wiped the spittle from her lips. Irina leaned in close.

"What's wrong with you?" she asked. She didn't speak it. She mouthed it.

Meed made one final cleansing spit into the bush and looked up. "I'm fine," she mouthed back. Even though she knew she wasn't.

The porch looked old and likely to creak. Irina climbed the steps on all fours, distributing her weight. Meed followed her up the same way. When they reached the back door, they found it secured with two sturdy locks. Top quality. Professionally installed.

It took Meed a full twenty seconds to get them open.

CHAPTER 50

THE INSIDE OF the house was as modest as the outside. Neat and well organized.

No children's toys on the floor to avoid. No sign of a dog. No security cameras. A lingering aroma of vegetables and herbs hung in the air. Potatoes. Onions. Garlic. Rosemary. Meed felt the bile rising in her throat again. She swallowed it.

The girls moved through the kitchen and into a hallway intersection. One path led to the front of the house. They could see a small living room to the left and a dining room to the right. The other path led lengthwise across the back of the house. The bedroom corridor. The door to the left was open to a small empty room with bare wood floors and a solitary window. The door in the middle of the hallway was ajar, revealing the corner of a porcelain sink. The door at the other end of the hall was closed. Meed jabbed her finger toward it. It was the master bedroom. She felt it.

They moved slowly down the hall, hugging the sides, where the floorboards were less inclined to squeak. When they reached the door, Irina turned the knob slowly and pushed it open. It gave a tiny groan near the end position. By then, Meed and Irina were both inside. Meed held her breath. Her heart was pounding so hard she was afraid Irina could hear it.

The room was simply furnished. Dresser. Dressing table. Double bed. End tables on each side, with matching picture frames. Two people asleep in the bed. Male on the left, female on the right. A shaft of moonlight came through the small window over the headboard. Irina stood on tiptoe to get a better angle on the faces. She nodded and held up two fingers, close together, then dipped them forward. Confirmation.

Meed's head felt spacey and light. She fought to keep her focus. All her training told her not to hesitate, not to judge, not to worry, not to think. But she couldn't help it. Who were these people? Why were they chosen? Why did they deserve what was about to happen to them? And could she really do it? She thought back through all the death she had seen. She understood that it had all been meant to harden her for this exact moment. Now. Or never.

On the street in front of the house, a truck banged over a pothole, causing a loud metallic shudder. The girls shrunk back. The man in bed stirred and rolled over onto his side. Then, suddenly, he sat up. Early fifties. Bearded. Slightly built, wearing a light-blue T-shirt. For a split second he froze in place, peering at the two shapes against the wall. He settled back down, facing the outside of the bed, as if he thought he'd been dreaming.

Irina was not fooled. As she took a step forward, she saw the man's hand snake into the open drawer of his side table. Suddenly, he was upright again, wide awake, his upper body thrust forward, a black pistol in his hand. The barrel was pointed at Irina's head.

"Don't move!" he shouted. "What do you want?"

At the sound of his shouts, the woman jolted awake. She stared toward the foot of the bed and grasped her husband's shoulders. The woman had dark hair and a lined face. She looked older than her picture.

Meed instinctively stepped to the side to split the man's attention. Give him two targets instead of one. Make him choose. As she moved, the barrel of the pistol followed her. She heard the hammer cock, then a quick swish and a thud. The man fell back against the headboard, eyes wide and frozen. Irina's throwing knife was buried in his heart. Meed jumped back in shock. The woman screamed and reached for the gun as it fell onto the blanket. She picked it up. Her finger found the trigger. Meed pulled a knife from her sleeve. For a split second, she hesitated, her hand trembling. She felt Irina grab the knife out of her hand. All she could hear was the woman's voice.

"Stop!" she was yelling. "Whoever you are, just..."

Another swish. Another thud. Another kill shot. The woman's gun hand dropped limply onto the bed. The other hand flailed out and knocked into an end table. A framed photograph flew off the table and landed at Meed's feet as the glass shattered.

Meed looked down. In the pale light from the window, she could see the picture clearly. It showed an infant girl sitting against a white pillow. Meed gasped. Her mind reeled. Kamenev's office. Garin. The file. The photograph. The infant girl in the bassinet. Same age. Same copper-colored curls.

Oh, dear God!

Meed looked up from the picture to the bleeding shapes on the bed. That was the instant it all clicked. Irina stepped forward to pull the knives from the bodies. Meed put her hands over her mouth, suddenly feeling sick again.

"My *parents*!" she screamed. "Those were my *parents*!"

CHAPTER 51

MEED LURCHED TOWARD the bed, reaching out with both arms. Irina grabbed her hard and wrestled her toward the door, whispering harshly into her ear.

"It's over!" she said. "There's nothing to be done."

Meed shook free and staggered down the corridor. Disoriented, she turned right past the living room and jerked the front door open. She ran down the front steps and into the middle of the street. Not thinking about exposure. Not caring. She dropped to her knees and started retching onto the dark pavement. Irina was at her side, tugging her to her feet. Meed swung wildly with her fists, her blows glancing off Irina's shoulders, mostly striking empty air. She started screaming again.

"No!" she wailed. *"No, no, no!!"*

Up and down the street, lights began to pop on. Silhouettes appeared in second-floor windows. Halfway down the block, a front door cracked open. Meed couldn't walk, couldn't move. She felt Irina's arms tight around her shoulders, supporting her, holding her up. And then she felt the sharp sting of a needle in the side of her neck.

In two seconds, Meed was limp and unconscious, unaware that for the second time in her life, she was about to be carried up a dark mountain.

CHAPTER 52

MEED'S EYES DIDN'T flicker open again until 4 a.m. She was in her bed. Her lids were heavy and her vision was slightly blurred. The sedative had not fully worn off. But as her mind flashed to what had happened just hours earlier, the fury burned off the fog. In her rage, Meed was clear about what she had to do. The events in that bloody bedroom would not be her final test.

This would be.

Meed turned her head from side to side to check around the dormitory. The other girls were sleeping soundly. She slipped out from under her blanket and rested her feet lightly on the wood floor. She slowly slipped on socks and boots. Then she reached under her thin mattress and pulled out a three-foot strand of knotted rags. It had taken her weeks to collect and prepare them. They had been hidden under her mattress for months. She never knew exactly when she would need them.

It was now.

Two beds over, Irina lay curled under her blanket, her head facing the opposite wall. Meed walked quietly to the sink, turned on the tap, and let a slow trickle of water soak the cloth. She twisted the excess water from the whole length and snapped it tight. It could have been a noose or a garotte. But it was neither. It was a science experiment.

Meed tiptoed to the window, an arched opening with a hinged frame of thick glass. Meed flicked the latch and slowly pulled the window open. Behind the frame were sets of vertical metal bars set into the stone, top and bottom. The water was starting to activate the acid mixture with which she'd infused the cloth, giving off wisps of white vapor.

Meed knew she had to work quickly. She wrapped the rag strip around the two center bars, close to where they were set into the granite sill. The iron began to steam and sizzle. As the reaction intensified, Meed pressed her body up against the window. Sparks from the melting metal sprayed onto her forearms, leaving small searing marks on her skin. She winced. Her eyes teared with pain. But she did not make a sound.

In just a few seconds, the cloth had dissolved. The bases of both bars were now withered and shaky. Meed pried the loose bars out of the bottom sill and pushed them out as far as she could, creating a gap barely ten inches wide. It would have to be enough.

She looked back at her sleeping classmates, and then wormed her way through the opening. The rough stone scraped her thighs through her thin cotton pajama pants. Her arms burned with pain. She clung to the two remaining bars as she slid her shoulders and head through, and then hung dangling against the outside of the building. She was twenty feet off the ground. If she fell the wrong way, she would break an ankle or a leg. Her training had made her both an athlete and an acrobat, and she would need both skills now.

The grass at the bottom of the wall sloped slightly away from the building. Meed braced her feet against the stone and kicked away as she let go with her hands. As she landed, she tucked in her arms and rolled to the bottom of the slope, coming to rest on her belly on level ground. The coarse grass scraped against her burns, now a pattern of swollen red welts on each arm. As she lay flat, breathing hard, Meed dug into the ground with her fingers, then rubbed cool dirt onto the wounds. It was all she could do. It was a pain she could deal with.

The dawn light was just beginning to stripe the horizon to the east, toward the village. Meed rose to her feet and started to run in the exact opposite direction—slowly at first, then full-out, feet pounding, hair flying. She had no map, no weapons, no tools. She was leaving the only place she had ever known, and there was nobody in the outside world that she could trust. Nobody she even knew. Not a single human being.

She had only herself.

CHAPTER 53

Chicago

"READY TO BE dazzled?" asked Meed.

"I'm not sure," I said.

That was the truth. I was nervous. I didn't know what to expect. For six months, I hadn't once looked in a mirror. Meed hadn't allowed it. One of her many rules. Since the day I'd been kidnapped, I'd never seen a single picture or video of my new self. I'd learned to shave my face by touch.

Of course, I knew how I looked in bits and pieces. I could see the changes when I checked out my arms, my chest, my legs, my abs. I knew that I was bigger and stronger than I had ever imagined. I could recite my new measurements to the centimeter. But I didn't have the whole picture. I had no clue how I looked to anybody else. Only Meed did. So she'd decided that tonight was the big reveal. Tonight, I was being introduced to myself.

She was holding a full-length mirror turned backward against her torso. I was standing in my gym shorts and bare feet. I was still pumped and sweating from my workout. For some reason, I guess she thought this was my best look.

"On the count of three," said Meed. She wiggled the mirror in a little tease. "One . . . two . . . *three*!" Then she flipped it.

When I saw the man looking back at me, it was like looking at a stranger.

"Holy shit," I said softly.

"Mr. Universe competition, here we come," said Meed.

This was crazy. Over the past couple months, I'd felt my development accelerating. It wasn't just the extra training or the protein shakes or the mass-gain powder or the endless brain exercises. Something had fundamentally shifted in me, physically and mentally. I felt myself progressing in leaps, not just steps.

"Look," said Meed, tipping the mirror, "even your hair is better."

I leaned forward and ran my fingers over my scalp. She was right. I still had my widow's peak, but the hair on top was now thick and full. The little bald patch on the crown of my head had completely filled in. The last time I had hair like this, I was in high school.

"Go ahead," said Meed, twirling her index finger in the air. "Take in the rear view."

Now I was really self-conscious. But also kind of curious. I did a three-quarter turn and looked over my shoulder into the mirror. Jesus! My traps and lats were carved like marble. My waist was narrow and tight. My external obliques looked like thick straps. My glutes bulged like two solid rocks under my shorts.

"Work of art, right?" said Meed. She turned the mirror around and leaned it against the wall. "Hold on. I have another treat for you."

I never knew when to take her literally. She always kept me

off balance. Usually, when Meed said she had something special for me, it turned out to be pure misery. But sometimes, she actually came through with something great. Like Kobe steak for dinner instead of tofu. Or letting me choose the playlist.

She bent down and reached into a cooler. I stepped back.

"That better not be another pig head," I said.

"Give me some credit, Doctor," she said. "We're celebrating."

Sure enough. When her hand came out of the cooler, she was holding two frosty bottles of Blue Moon Belgian White beer. I almost started panting. I hadn't tasted any liquid besides protein shakes and bottled water since last November. Just the thought of that cold beer hitting my throat made me tremble.

She knocked off both caps on a corner of the weight machine. Little dribbles of foam spilled out of the necks. She handed me one of the bottles and tipped the other to her lips. I felt the frosty sensation in my hand then took my first delicious sip. Sweet Lord. Heaven.

I heard Meed shout. It was earsplitting. I saw a flash in front of my face as she knocked the bottle out of my hand and into the side of the treadmill. I heard it crash and shatter.

"What the *fuck*!!" I shouted.

She rammed her elbow into my gut with enough force to rock me. Instinct took over. I put my arms up and lunged at her. She stepped back, then moved in for another punch, this time to my mouth. I felt the flesh split and tasted blood. She came at me with a chop toward my neck. I knocked her hand aside with my forearm. She used the momentum to spin on the ball of her foot and whip her leg around. The instant before her heel was about to hit my temple, I grabbed her ankle and twisted it hard. She screamed and went face-down onto the mat. When she flipped face up, I was on her. Her hand whipped up and I saw the flash of a blade coming straight at me. I knocked it away with one hand and pinned her wrists to the side. I had one knee across her thighs and the other knee jammed into her solar plexus. For the first time—the very first time—I realized that I had her. She was done, and she knew it. In that instant, I felt all the fight go out of her. I let go of her wrists and backed off. I sat back, breathing hard.

"What the hell was *that*?" I asked, dabbing blood from my lip.

She winced as she sat up.

"That was your final test," she said. "You passed."

"I could have killed you just then," I said. "You know that, right?"

She actually smiled a little. "That's all I've ever wanted."

I shook my head. I was starting to feel like a trained monkey again—totally manipulated. Was I supposed to feel great about being able to murder a woman with my bare hands? Meed reached over and tapped my arm. She leaned closer.

"Ask me something," she said.

"What do you mean?" I replied.

"Anything you want," she said. "No wrong questions."

"Bullshit," I said.

"Try me," she said.

I was fed up. But if this was another mind game, I was going to swing for the fences. I didn't go for anything new. I went straight to two questions I'd asked her a hundred times—questions she'd never come close to answering.

"Okay, Meed," I said. "What's your real name? And why am I here?"

She tipped her head back and took a deep breath. Then she

looked me straight in the eye. Over the past six months, I'd seen this woman mislead me, trick me, and lie to my face over and over again. But we had just crossed some kind of border. I could feel it. And somehow, in that moment, I knew she was about to tell me the truth.

"My name is Kira Sunlight," she said. "And I need you to save my life."

PART 2

CHAPTER 54

SUNLIGHT?! MY GOD!

That was the last name I expected to hear—or *wanted* to hear. But in that instant, at least I knew I wasn't some random kidnapping victim. And my kidnapper wasn't some local psycho. This woman and I were deeply connected. I suddenly realized that this whole setup had been decades in the making. Maybe a century.

"Sunlight?" I repeated. "You're related to . . ." I stopped and let her finish the sentence, just to be sure I was right.

"John Sunlight," she said. "Yes. He was my great-grandfather."

I'd known about John Sunlight my whole life. And not in a good way. He was a part of my family's past that I'd tucked away, further than the rest of it, thinking it would never surface again. But here it was, staring me in the face, three generations later.

I was amazed that this woman and I would ever be in the same room. Stunned, in fact.

Because her ancestor and mine had been determined to kill

each other. Now I had to wonder about her intentions all over again. The change in her name changed everything. She was a Sunlight. I was a Savage. It was a bad combination.

"You realize that if John Sunlight had had his way," I said, "I would never have been born."

"Think how *I* feel," she said. "It's kind of like being related to Hitler."

From what I knew, it was a fair comparison. Because back in the 1930s, John Sunlight had also wanted to rule the world. And, like Hitler, he almost succeeded. He built his own private army and tried to corner the market on the world's most devastating weapons. The only thing standing in his way was *my* great-grandfather, Doc Savage. Which is why John Sunlight tried to wipe him off the face of the earth. But all that was in the distant past, done and buried long ago. Ancient history. I'd heard about the battle between Doc Savage and John Sunlight from my parents before they passed. But it wasn't something I ever thought about. As far as I was concerned, it had nothing to do with me.

"Your great-grandfather has been dead for decades," I said. "So has mine. I need to save your life?? Who the hell wants to kill you?"

She didn't seem scared. But she did seem nervous. I'd never seen that before.

"Let's just say my past is catching up with me," she said. "So is yours."

CHAPTER 55

Gaborone, Botswana

EIGHT THOUSAND MILES and eight time zones away, in a small neighborhood bistro, sprinter Jamelle Maina was on her first wine spritzer of the evening. The cool chardonnay was easing her guilt—slightly.

She was really enjoying the company of her fellow runners, but she had a definite twinge about leaving her infant daughter with a new sitter. Jamelle was so in love with that baby— the baby the trainers had told her she should never have. She hated to be away from her, even for a minute. But this evening was special. Her *friends* were special. And her apartment was just down the street.

She had *earned* this evening, she kept telling herself. After all, how often does a single mom from the African bush get to compete in the Olympics?

"Jamelle! Where is your *mind*??" It was her teammate Luanna, the tall runner. She reached across the table and snapped her fingers in Jamelle's face.

"Sorry!" said Jamelle, coming back to the moment. "I'm here!"

* * *

Half a block away, in Jamelle's tidy apartment, Irina was busy wiping down everything she had touched since she arrived. Light switches, refrigerator, toilet handle. It was an unnecessary precaution, since her fingerprints were not on file anywhere in the world. But she had been trained to be thorough. And it was her nature.

She could hear the music from the bistro down the block as she walked softly into the nursery and lifted the tiny black baby from her crib. The doctored formula had done its work. The baby would not stir for hours. Irina just hoped the diaper would hold out.

As she picked up the limp infant, she wondered if she would feel anything this time. She didn't. Not really. No more than she would feel about any other piece of valuable merchandise. It was just another assignment. Get in. Get out. Deliver the goods. It did occur to Irina that the baby would not remember anything of this room, or this apartment, or her mother. That was probably a mercy, Irina thought. From now on, this little girl would have only herself. And someday, she would serve a bigger purpose.

Irina wrapped the baby in the blanket from the crib, then found another to add an extra layer of cushioning. She folded the top of the second blanket lightly over the baby's face. She checked the Mother Goose clock on the nursery wall. Time to go.

The transfer team would be waiting.

As Irina stepped into the stairwell leading down to ground level, a couple passed her heading up. They were young and tipsy, interested only in each other. When the police interviewed them the next morning, along with all the other residents of the small apartment complex, the couple would only remember seeing a young woman with a duffel bag, looking as if she were leaving for a weekend trip. The surveillance video would be no help. For a few critical intervals, it would show nothing but static.

CHAPTER 56

Chicago

I WAS ON my own again. After telling me the truth about who she was that afternoon, Kira had disappeared into her room. I just kept on with my training routine. What else could I do? Whatever had gone on in Kira's past, she wasn't ready to get into details. Not yet. So I just kept pumping iron and thinking about all the other questions I needed answers to. What was the threat? Who was coming for her? Would it ever be over? Was I ever going to get my life back again?

I finished my last workout at about 8:00 p.m. and took a shower. I was getting ready to lock myself in for the night, following the rules. I put on some old sweats to sleep in and sat down on my bed. That's when I saw Kira standing outside my cell, holding a bottle.

"Join me in the kitchen," she said. So I did.

In six months, my kidnapper had never poured a glass of wine without quizzing me about tannin levels, complexity, and region of origin. She never let me drink. Just taste and spit. But tonight was different. Maybe because she wasn't pouring wine. She was pouring mezcal.

"Sip it. Don't shoot it," she said. Good advice. The taste was smokey and fierce. I almost coughed it back up. My eyes were watering.

"How long has this stuff been aging?" I asked.

"About a hundred years," she said. "That's why it's so mellow."

I picked up the bottle. The glass was thick and heavy, and the label was all in Spanish. The vintage year was handwritten. Sure enough. *1922.*

"Did you steal this from a museum?" I asked. She shook her head.

"From a private collection."

I took another sip. This one went down easier. I started to feel warm all over. Anybody looking at the two of us would have thought that we were just a regular couple enjoying a quiet evening together. Not quite. For one thing, I was still adjusting to my companion's name. Her *real* name. As I looked at her across the counter, I pictured a giant *K* on her forehead so I wouldn't slip up and call her Meed. There were so many blanks I needed to fill in that I didn't know where to start. But she beat me to it.

"How much do you know about Doc Savage?" she asked.

It was a loaded question. I'd basically spent my life trying to pretend the guy never existed. It was a pain in the ass to be descended from a legend as big as my great-grandfather. Genius. War hero. Crime fighter. Soldier of fortune. You name it, he did it. Hard to live up to. Even harder to live down.

"I know he was brilliant," I said, "and a great inventor. But I think he depended on brawn over brains too much. From what I've heard, he was a pretty violent guy. After my folks died, I thought about changing my last name to get rid of the connection once and for all. Fresh start."

"So why didn't you?" Kira asked.

The reason was pretty embarrassing.

"Because *Savage* was already on all my diplomas," I said.

Kira gave a quick laugh. "Right," she said. "I guess all that calligraphy would be a bitch to redo." I realized that I'd never heard her laugh before. Maybe it was just the mezcal, but it sounded terrific.

"Look," I said, "I know there's probably a ton of exaggeration in the old Doc Savage stories. Pirates? Ghosts? Phantom cities? Evil hunchbacks? That stuff can't be true. It sounds like pure fantasy."

Kira took a slow sip and raised her eyebrows, like she was holding back another secret. I leaned toward her over the counter.

"Wait," I said. "How much do *you* know?"

Kira put her glass down on the counter.

"Follow me," she said.

By this time, the rest of the loft was mostly dark, except for a dim glow from inside my cell and a few under-counter lights in the kitchen. And with all that mezcal on board, my vision wasn't super-sharp. Kira led the way through the kitchen and stopped at the metal door that said UTILITY. I'd never paid much attention to it. Why would I?

Nothing but circuit breakers and HVAC equipment inside, I figured. Besides, it had a pretty sophisticated electronic lock. Kira tapped the lock with her finger.

"Open it," she said.

Open it? I could barely *see* it. "I have no idea how to do that," I said.

"Sure you do," said Kira. "You learned it in your sleep two nights ago."

I didn't remember the session, but I suddenly recalled the content, every single detail. Even with the Mexican buzz in my brain. I ran my finger over the lock face, then reached into a kitchen drawer and pulled out a butter knife. I pried off the small screen that was meant for displaying the pin code. Underneath was a set of very small circuit boards.

At that point, I was as focused as a surgeon. I pried off the top board to get at the one underneath. I pulled two small wires loose from the second board and pressed the bare ends against two metal leads, one on the board itself, the other on the inside of the lock casing. I heard a small click.

"Told you," said Kira.

I grabbed the thick metal handle and gave it a tug. Sure enough, the door was loose. But I almost didn't want to open it. Something told me that whatever was behind that door was going to change my life in a major way. Probably more pain. I looked at Kira.

"This isn't really a utility closet, is it?" I said.

"It was mislabeled," she replied.

CHAPTER 57

I OPENED THE door. An automatic sensor turned on a bank of industrial lights overhead. As my eyes adjusted, I suddenly felt totally sober again. I couldn't believe what I was looking at.

We were in a huge room with a high ceiling and no windows. It was filled with metal shelves in long, neat rows. It looked like a natural history archive. It had the smell of old paper, old chemicals, old leather.

"Welcome home, Doctor," said Kira.

She stood by the door as I started walking through the room. At first, there was too much to take in. Stacks of journals. Jars of sand and soil and dried plants, all neatly labeled. Topographical maps with notes and arrows drawn all over them. Files with TOP SECRET government stamps. And that was just the first row. It was overwhelming.

"What the hell *is* all this?" I asked.

Kira walked down the other side of the shelf and looked at me through the gap. She ran her hand over a pile of thick dossiers tied with twine.

"This whole floor belonged to Doc Savage, your great-grandfather," said Kira. "Everything in here was his."

"I thought Doc Savage lived in New York," I said. I remembered some lore about a hideout on the eighty-sixth floor of some Manhattan skyscraper.

"That's true," said Kira. "He had an apartment there. But after a while, too many of his enemies knew about it, so he just kept it as a decoy." She looked around the room. "*This* is where he did his experiments, and perfected his training, and worked on his inventions. Right here."

At the back of the space, there was a long lab table with gas outlets and cartons of unused test tubes and petri dishes. One end was filled with dark brown chemical jars. The other end was piled high with lab notebooks.

Another corner of the room was filled with electronic devices, some finished, some half assembled. There were coils of wire and bins filled with parts—knobs, switches, dials, and a lot of stuff I didn't recognize.

It looked like the secret lair of some mad scientist, but there were some personal items, too. A watercolor painting of a small boat with *Orion* on the stern. A theatrical makeup kit. A pair of boxing gloves. And leaning up against the wall, a battered violin case. Along with everything else, I'd heard that my great-grandfather was a musical prodigy. Maybe it was true.

On the floor was an old wooden liquor crate, top ripped off, with one bottle missing. Now I knew where the mezcal came from. I squeezed past the memorabilia and peered into the far corner.

"Jesus!"

I was staring at an antique arsenal. Shotguns. Pistols. Hunting knives. Military rifles. Bayonets. Hand grenades. Just about every possible way to kill another human was sitting right there. It felt weird. I turned to Kira.

"Don't tell me this was all for self-defense," I said.

Kira shrugged. "Dangerous times. Dangerous tools."

I turned away from the weaponry to a small table. There was a black and white photograph sitting on top. It was Doc Savage himself, no doubt about it. I'd seen the illustrations from the pulp stories, but this was the first actual photo of him that I'd ever laid eyes on. I spotted the family resemblance right away. Same widow's peak, for one thing. In the picture, my ancestor looked strong and fit. Totally buff. In fact, he looked a lot like me.

There was another picture underneath. Another man. Same era. Same features. Except this guy was no great physical specimen. He was stooped and awkward-looking. Kind of like I looked before I was taken.

"Who's this?" I asked.

Kira walked over to meet me at the table. She ran her finger across the picture.

She hesitated for a second before she answered, like she wasn't sure how to break the news.

"That's Doc Savage's brother, Cal," she said.

I shook my head. Wrong. That made no sense.

"You don't know what you're talking about," I said. "Doc Savage was an only child."

"No," said Kira, looking straight at me. "Doc Savage was a twin."

CHAPTER 58

I STARED AT the two pictures side by side. Out of nowhere, a new branch of my family tree had just been added. Suddenly, I had a great-uncle.

"Why didn't I know about this guy?" I asked.

"Because your family was really messed up," said Kira. She took the pictures and put them down on the table. She pulled out a ledger and opened it to a middle page. It was filled with anatomical stats—heights, weights, muscle measurements— along with nutritional data and athletic performance records. Running, swimming, hiking, boxing, marksmanship. All noted in painstaking detail, like lab notes.

"Doc Savage was a human science project," Kira said. "He was part of a twenty-year experiment conducted by his father. The goal was to create the perfect physical and mental specimen—a man who was the best at everything. The twin brother was the control. Their father turned one brother into a superman and let the other brother fend for himself. That's why you've never heard the name Calvin Savage. Nobody has."

She walked over to another row of shelves and came back

with a thick leather binder. The title stenciled on the cover was "Sunlight." She handed the binder to me. I opened it. Stuck between the cover and the first page was a photo of a man in a lab coat. Bursting out of it, actually. Because his build was almost as big as Doc Savage's.

"John Sunlight," I said. Who else could it be? I looked for any similarity to Kira. Definitely not the hair. Her great-grandfather was totally bald.

"Let's sit," said Kira. She cleared off two leather armchairs against the wall. The chairs looked like they belonged in a men's club. They even smelled like cigars. I sat down. The leather was soft and worn. Pretty comfortable, actually. I felt like I should be wearing a smoking jacket. Kira tugged her chair around to face mine. Our knees were almost touching.

"Listen," she said. "My great-grandfather was a genius. Close to Doc Savage's level. But he was twisted. Delusional. Probably a sociopath. He had all these insane theories about how to reorder the world. He even managed to steal some of Doc's technology and weapons. But he realized that to get *all* the secrets, he needed an inside man. So he reached out to Cal, who didn't have much going for him. He and Cal made a pact. That's how John Sunlight got his hands on the manual for Doc Savage's training."

"There was a *manual*?"

"Absolutely," said Kira. "The full regimen, from fourteen months of age to twenty-one. It was all written down. Physical training. Mental challenges. Martial arts. Languages. Science. History. Music."

"So after Sunlight stole the manual," I asked, "what did he do with it? Use it to train his mercenaries?"

"No," said Kira. "He used it to start a school. With himself and Cal in charge."

"A school?" I asked. "Like what? A college?"

"A secret academy," said Kira, "based on the Doc Savage methods. Strict discipline from infancy on, every minute programmed, no outside influences. My great-grandfather took the Doc Savage training and corrupted it, turned it into something else."

"Turned it into *what*?" I asked.

"Into something that would help him extend his influence and take over the world," said Kira. "Espionage. Infiltration. Psyops. Murder."

"How do you know all this?" I asked. "How can you possibly...?"

Her look stopped me in mid-sentence.

"Because I was raised there," said Kira. "I was trained there. In eighty years, I'm the only student to leave without authorization. I escaped when I was a teenager."

I leaned back against the wall. Suddenly a lot of things were adding up. But not everything.

"Wait," I said. "So you mean you put up with that evil shit for all those years and then decided to run away? Why? What changed? Did you suddenly grow a conscience?"

Kira's eyes dropped. Her voice got soft and low.

"I can't talk about that," she said.

Something in the way she said it told me to leave it alone.

"Okay," I said. "But where did you go? You're not a teenager anymore. Where have you been all this time? What were you doing—kidnapping innocent college professors?"

"I promise," she said, "you're my first. I've been all over the world. Made plenty of money. I've been lots of different people, and I've covered my tracks pretty well. But the school is still operating, still pumping out graduates. They're getting better, and smarter, and more dangerous. You cannot believe the amount of evil they are responsible for. It's everywhere."

"And that's why you needed my help?" I asked.

She nodded. "I knew you had the right genes," she said, "but I had to bring out your full potential. I couldn't tell you the truth until you were ready. Until I knew I could trust you." She leaned toward me in her chair. "I'm sorry." That was the first time she'd ever uttered those two words. And somehow, in that moment, I felt sorry for *her*. I reached over and put my hand on top of hers. I expected her to pull away, but she didn't.

The effects of the mezcal had mostly worn off, but now there was something else. I felt like I'd stepped into a different time and place—a world where only one other person knew what was going on. Over the past six months, I'd been afraid of her, I'd hated her, I'd admired her. And now I was having *other* feelings. Maybe stuff I'd been suppressing. I wondered if maybe she was feeling the same thing. Kira stood up.

"I think we need to release some tension," she said.

Finally, it sounded like maybe we were on the same page.

CHAPTER 59

"STOP BEING SUCH a baby!"

I'd never been touched like this in my life. The pain was intense. But Kira said it was all for my own good.

I was lying on a massage table behind a set of linen curtains in a corner of the loft. My face was poking through an oval in the table cushion and all I could see through it were floorboards. I was naked except for a towel across my backside. That part didn't bother me. I'd gotten over my self-consciousness around her a long time ago. But my body was definitely going through some new experiences. Kira's elbow was buried in the muscles that ran along my spine. I could feel her leaning in with the full weight of her upper body. She slid her elbow up and down, from the base of my neck to the top of my sacrum. I flinched from the pressure.

"What are you *doing* to me?" I asked.

"I told you," she said. "Deep-tissue massage and myofascial release. Just breathe through it."

"I'm trying." More of a groan than actual words.

I felt her applying more warm oil to my back, spreading it

in a diamond pattern, her palms moving across my shoulders, down my back, and over the top of my hips, then back up again. When she stood at the head of the table, I could see her black tights and bare feet through the opening. Then she was gone again, moving around to another part of my anatomy. Neck. Arms. Hips. Calves. Feet. She used her knuckles, thumbs, and knees. She pressed deep into my muscles and tendons, probing for every knot.

"Don't fight me, Doctor," she said. "Let go."

Slowly, bit by bit, my body stopped resisting and gave in. At some point, I crossed the boundary between pain and relief. By the end of an hour, I felt warm and loose from head to toe. More relaxed than I'd felt in a very long time. *Years,* maybe. Maybe my whole damned life. I could hardly speak.

"Where the hell did you learn *that*?" I mumbled.

"Like I said," replied Kira, "I've been lots of people."

Her last big move was a rolling motion with her forearms up and down my back. Like she was ironing me out. Then I saw her feet through the hole again. I felt her hands resting lightly on my head. She curled her fingers through my hair and massaged my scalp. I could feel the skin moving over my skull. It was heaven. After a minute of that, she gently lifted her hands away.

"We're done, Doctor," she said softly. "How do you feel?"

"Amazing," I sighed.

I gripped the towel around my waist and slowly turned face up on the table. I raised myself up on my elbows. Kira was closing the top of her oil bottle and slipping back into her shoes. She looked down at the same instant I did—and saw my erection poking up under the towel. Kira put the oil bottle down on the side table.

"Autonomic reflex," she said. "Totally normal." Then she disappeared behind the curtain. I flopped back down onto the table. I felt flushed and embarrassed.

Autonomic reflex. It sounded so clinical. So scientific. Maybe that was all there was to it, I thought.

Maybe.

CHAPTER 60

THE NEXT MORNING, breakfast was a little awkward. One reason was the menu. I'd gotten used to Kira's weird nutrition repertoire. Goji berries, chia seeds, flax, maca, and the rest of it. Some of it I'd learned to like. Some of it I'd learned to tolerate. Some of it I still had to choke down. But now I was staring at a plateful of wet green weeds.

"What in God's name is *this*?" I asked. "And don't say 'wrong question.'"

"It's kelp. You're low on antioxidants."

Now that she said it, it looked exactly like stuff I'd seen in nature documentaries, waving around underwater. It was seaweed, pure and simple. I pushed the plate away.

"Thanks," I said, "but I draw the line at algae."

I was a little surprised when she didn't push back or try to force feed me. She downed the last of her smoothie and wiped her lips with a napkin. She looked serious. She put her elbows on the butcher block.

"Doctor," she said, "we need to have...the talk."

More awkwardness. I figured this was about my display the night before. Had to be. I cleared my throat.

"Right," I said. "I'm sorry about the…" I glanced down at my lap. Kira shook her head.

"It's not about that," she said. She leaned toward me over the kitchen island. "I have a confession to make, Doctor. It's about me. About you and me. *Our* history."

"Our history?" I said. "I've seen our history, remember? Our history is you stalking me, stealing my mail, hacking my router, and spying on me from the bushes."

"You're absolutely right," she said. "And that's what I can't really explain. I think I **liked** watching you from a distance. I could see how awkward you were. The way you kept to yourself, lost in your own little universe. No friends. No relationships. No adventure."

She was right, of course. Her little film had proven the point in spades.

"I'm a loner," I said. "Always have been."

"To be honest," said Kira, "I found the whole package kind of irresistible."

I sat up in my chair. Was she playing another game? I'd never felt the least bit irresistible. To *anybody*. I never expected to have a stalker with some strange long-distance crush. Especially one who looked like Kira.

"And what *about* now?" I asked. "Now that you've turned me into this…this physical masterpiece."

She shrugged. "That's the weird part," she said. "Now you're just another guy."

I guess I should have been hurt. Or insulted. Or disappointed. But mostly I was confused. What Kira seemed to be saying was that back when I thought I would *never* have a chance with a woman like her, I actually *did*. And now that I looked like somebody who might *actually* have a chance with her, I *didn't*. It was a head-spinner. Over the years, I'd been attracted to plenty of women who had stuck me permanently in the friend zone. But this was a whole *new* zone. The Kira zone. And I was totally lost.

"Don't feel bad," said Kira. "I'm no prize, believe me. I have baggage. I'm not easy to be with."

At that point, all I could do was laugh. "Tell me something I don't know," I said.

And that was it. No meaningful looks. No hugs. She'd said what she needed to say, and then she shifted gears. She took the plate and scraped the seaweed into the garbage, where it belonged. At least *that* was a relief.

"Come with me, Doctor," she said. She headed back toward the door that said UTILITY. "I've got something else to show you." I got up from my chair as she pulled the door open. She had a strange smile on her face. "You probably shouldn't have too much in your stomach for this anyway."

CHAPTER 61

A FEW MINUTES later, we were standing on a narrow ledge that projected from the side of the building and I was preparing to die. We were about sixty stories up, wearing silver overalls over our clothes and helmets on our heads. Kira said the overalls were fireproof. But fire was the least of my worries. I was way more afraid of ending up as a bloody speck on the sidewalk.

"Adjust your straps, Doctor," said Kira. "Like this."

The straps were attached to big chrome canisters on our backs. They looked kind of like old vacuum cleaners. I looked over as Kira pulled the loose ends of her front straps down tight across her chest. I did the same. Then I tightened the belt around my waist. I felt the canister press even harder against my back.

I looked over at Kira like she was nuts, because I truly thought she was. This whole project seemed suicidal. But she wouldn't back off.

"Don't worry," said Kira. "I've bench tested these things a dozen times. Doc Savage knew what he was doing. The thrust and aerodynamics all add up."

I'd read about some of my great-grandfather's inventions. Fluoroscopes for night vision. The first hi-def TV. Ejection seats for airplanes. But I never knew how much of it was real. And I definitely never expected to be standing on a ledge wearing one of his 1930s-vintage jetpacks. That part felt absolutely *insane*.

Kira took a step forward. She was standing right next to me, just one foot from the edge.

"Trust me," she said. "Trust your great-grandfather."

I didn't. Not for a second. Not when it came to a 600-foot drop. I felt like throwing up. Kira reached over and made a small adjustment to a dial on the side of my jet canister.

"What are you doing??" I asked.

"Giving you a richer mixture," she said. "More power."

"Is this another one of your manhood tests?" I asked. "I thought I'd already passed!" My voice was shaky. I sounded desperate, and I was.

"I no longer doubt your manhood," she said.

"I can't do this!" I said. I backed up against the wall. "This is *crazy*!"

Kira pulled me forward again and stood right behind me. Her hands were on my shoulders. She spoke right into my ear. Her voice was calm and reassuring. I thought maybe I could still talk her out of it.

"Wait! I just need a little more time!" I could feel my palms sweating.

Her voice was calm and reassuring. "No rush, Doctor. I know you're nervous. Totally understandable. We'll go when you're ready."

I took a deep breath. She shoved me off the ledge.

CHAPTER 62

I MIGHT HAVE screamed. I don't really remember. What I *do* remember is the feeling of my heart thudding and the air rushing up against my face. I was falling straight down, head first. I could see the street and all the traffic zooming closer in a blur. Then I heard a loud bang and a roar behind me. I felt a tremendous jolt. And suddenly I wasn't falling anymore. I was shooting up into the sky like a rocket, so fast it felt like my stomach was being pressed down toward my feet.

I looked over. Kira was right alongside me. I saw a bright tear-shaped flame blasting out of the bottom of her jetpack. Her hair was whipping out from under her helmet in little copper-colored waves.

She flexed her legs and leveled out until she was flying parallel to the ground. I copied her exactly. Got the same result. I was a bad judge of heights, but it looked like we were a couple thousand feet up. We were soaring over the center of Chicago, with skyscrapers stabbing up and all the other buildings laid out like a giant puzzle. The streets were a neat crosshatch pattern. The Chicago River was like a blue ribbon winding through the city.

It probably took me a half minute to adjust to the reality of what was happening—the fact that we were flying with machines built sixty years before I was born. And that they actually worked. There was no use trying to talk, or even shout to each other. The wind was too loud. But I could read Kira's body language in the air.

She was having a ball. And once I realized that I wasn't going to drop out of the sky like a stone, I started to have a ball, too.

At first, Kira took the lead, and I followed what she did. She was like a ballet dancer in the air. A total natural. I wasn't quite as smooth, but I was getting the hang of it. I realized that I could control my position in the air by dipping my head and adjusting my arms. When I tucked my arms tight against my sides, I swooped down. When I lifted my arms out to the sides, I rose back up. After I got a little confidence, I straightened out and shot out in front. The sensation was unbelievable. It was a mix of lightness and speed and amazing power. I had to hand it to my ancestor. I'd never felt anything like it.

Lake Michigan was off to the east, looking like a big green carpet. I banked to the left and headed out over the water. Kira was right behind me. I tucked myself into a dive and plummeted down until I was about thirty feet above the surface. When I passed over a lake freighter, I was close enough to see the crew looking up and pointing. The lower I got, the faster it felt like I was going. It was a total rush, and I was loving it. I lost all sense of time. I wanted it to last forever.

Suddenly I felt a lurch from my rocket pack. Instantly I dropped about ten feet. I looked over at Kira, who was flying right next to me. The flame from her rocket was coming out in short bursts, with little belches of smoke in between. I felt another lurch, then a loud pop. Then I started to spin like a pinwheel, end over end. My vision flipped between sky and water. Sky and water. And then only water. I hit feet first.

I sucked in one last breath, and then I went under, sinking fast. I saw Kira plunge in a few yards away. She sank down in a cloud of bubbles until she was out of sight in the murky lake. I couldn't see the bottom. But I knew that's where I was headed. With fifty pounds of metal strapped to my back, it's not like I had a choice.

CHAPTER 63

I STARTED TO panic. The light was fading above my head and the water under my feet was getting blacker. My lungs were on fire. I wrestled with the straps around my chest and middle but they wouldn't budge. I lost all sense of space. There was nothing but murk all around me. I tried to swim up, but it was no use. With my jetpack attached, I was dead weight.

About five seconds later, my boot landed on a long piece of metal. I had reached the lake bottom. I spun hard to the left. Something caught on the strap behind my back. I felt around with my bare hands and realized that I had fallen onto a pile of cement and rebar. Pure terror shot through me. After everything, that's where I was going to end up—wrapped around a pile of construction debris at the bottom of Lake Michigan.

I saw a blast of white in the distance. Then I saw Kira swimming toward me out of the dark. Her jetpack was gone. So was her helmet. Bubbles were blowing out of a device attached to her face.

When she got close, she went blurry. I was starting to pass out. She grabbed at my strap fasteners and yanked them open.

I felt the weight of the jetpack drop away. I was loose. But still drowning.

Then Kira was in my face, holding up a set of nose plugs attached to something that looked like a toothpaste tube. She yanked off my helmet. She jammed the plugs into my nostrils and twisted the top of the tube. I felt a rush of air into my lungs. I clamped my mouth shut and inhaled through my nostrils. My head instantly cleared. I was breathing again. Kira gave me a thumbs-up. I think I nodded. I wasn't sure what was happening. I only knew that I was alive.

Kira started kicking her way through the water. I followed right behind, trying to keep her in sight in the murk. After a few minutes, the water started turning green again.

Suddenly there was a ripple of light above. A few strokes later, my head broke water. I opened my mouth and took in the fresh air. Deep, long breaths of it.

"Pretty ingenious, right?" Kira's voice, yelling from a distance. I twisted around in the water. She was about twenty feet away, holding up her breathing apparatus.

"Thank your great-grandfather for these!" she shouted.

All I could do was shake my head and spit out some lake water. I was starting to wonder how many lives I had left. We were still about fifty yards from the shoreline. I could see a modern building with white pillars overlooking the lake. The Oceanarium of the Shedd Aquarium. We started swimming toward it.

As we approached the shoreline, I could see crowds of families on the curved sidewalk in front of the building. There was some kind of water festival going on. I saw kids and balloons and costumed characters dancing around. The outdoor sound system was blaring Disney music.

We climbed over the ribbed cement wall between the lake and the sidewalk. Water drained out of our fireproof suits. I still had my breathing tube dangling from my face. The whole crowd turned in our direction. A little girl holding a toy lobster started bouncing on her toes and laughing. She poked her younger brother and pointed at us. Then they both started clapping. Their parents joined in. So did the rest of the crowd. They thought we were part of the show. I looked at Kira and pulled the apparatus out of my nose. I was exhausted and mad.

"You planned that whole disaster, didn't you?" I said.

Kira wasn't looking at me. She was looking at the crowd. She had a big smile on her face.

"Wave to the nice people," she said.

CHAPTER 64

Gaborone, Botswana

THE OFFICE OF private investigator Jaco Devos was small and cluttered. It was also sweltering. The only moving air came from an anemic desk fan pointed mostly in his direction. Jamelle Maina sat across from the sweaty PI, an Afrikaner with a grayish complexion. The smoke from his cigarette spun in the vortex created by the fan blades. Jamelle's thin cotton dress stuck to the back of her metal chair. Devos flipped through the thin file in front of him on his desk, pretending to study it intently.

"Can you help me?" Jamelle asked, her voice soft and pleading.

"I have the police report right here," said Devos, cigarette ashes dropping onto the papers. "Your babysitter's credentials were impressive forgeries. No surveillance footage. No forensics. Not a single hair. In terms of a conventional investigation, this woman does not exist."

"She took my *baby*!" said Jamelle, tears brimming in her eyes.

Devos closed the file and squinted at his prospective client. "There are no reliable witnesses, other than yourself. Nothing else to go on." He paused and looked up, as if searching the heavens for a solution. "But . . ."

Jamelle leaned forward. "Yes? *What?*"

"Remind me," said Devos. "Who referred you?"

"My friend Luanna. Luanna Phiri."

Davos reflected for a second.

"Yes! The other runner," he said. "I remember. Boyfriend issue. Nasty man."

"Can you help me?" Jamelle asked again, her hands stretched out toward him on the desk.

"Miss Maina," said Devos. "Let me be clear. The authorities have done all they can. They will keep your case open and say reassuring things. But frankly, after a month or two, they will lose interest and move on. I will not. I have connections in places they don't. The people I talk to are people who will not talk to the police. That is my value to you."

"Yes!" said Jamelle. "Anything you think might work! *Anything!*"

Here Devos took another pause. Another salesman's trick. He sighed. "I'll have expenses, of course," he said. His voice conveyed resignation, even regret.

Jamelle nodded quickly. "I understand. I do."

Luanna had told her to bring cash. She reached under her chair and pulled up a nylon gym bag. She unzipped it and dumped a pile of money on the desk. It was all the money she had in the world. She would pay anything—*do* anything—to get her baby back.

Devos began stacking the bills and gave Jamelle a tight smile through a haze of smoke.

"Right," he said. "Good for a start."

CHAPTER 65

Chicago

I WAS STILL pissed off at Kira for almost killing us. Putting me in mortal danger was getting to be a pattern with her. I didn't appreciate being treated like a guinea pig—or like some kind of new-and-improved version of my ancestor. But our near miss didn't seem to bother Kira in the least. As soon as we got back to the loft and dried off, she took me back into the Doc Savage archive for more research. I held my tongue. I was afraid of what I might say if I let loose.

"All right," said Kira, clapping her hands together. "Time to get serious."

That did it. Was she kidding? I grabbed her by the shoulder and spun her around. I shook her.

"Serious??" I said. "A flameout over Lake Michigan wasn't serious enough?? Kira, we almost *died* out there!"

"Those were toys," she replied calmly. "We need protection."

I felt myself getting red in the face. I was getting tired of the runaround and the cryptic hints. "I thought *I* was your protection," I said. "For Christ's sake, you've turned me into Captain America! You've made me a mental marvel! Isn't that *enough*??"

Kira pulled away. "No, Doctor," she said, "you're *not* enough. Neither am I. Not with what we're up against. We're not ready yet. We need to pick Doc Savage's brain a little more. And this is where we do it."

She walked off and started rummaging through the shelves, sorting through parts and devices, pulling things aside and piling them on the lab table. I had no intention of helping. Not today.

"Pick away," I said. "Be my guest." I was feeling surly, and this room was starting to give me the creeps.

I wandered off into the corner and found myself staring at the Doc Savage arsenal. I ran my finger over the blade of a long cutlass. It still felt sharp enough to slice a man in half. I reached into a corner and picked up a rifle with a huge barrel. It was as heavy as a ten-pound weight. I realized that I'd never held a gun before in my life. I lifted the rifle up to my shoulder and pointed it at the brick wall across the room, aiming at a small stripe of mortar. Kira looked over.

"That's an elephant gun," she said. "Five-seventy-seven. Too heavy to carry. Forget it."

"I wasn't planning to put it in my pocket," I said.

I squinted down the barrel and tried to picture an actual human being in the sights. If it came right down to it, I wondered, would I actually be able to pull the trigger? Even if my life depended on it—or Kira's? I put the gun back in its place.

"Try a pistol," said Kira, nodding at the handguns. "Much more practical." There were about twenty of them, all shapes and sizes, hanging from wooden pegs. Some looked like they came straight from the O.K. Corral. Others looked like World War I vintage. I wondered if any of them still worked. I didn't really care. Just looking at them made me queasy.

"No thanks," I said.

Kira was dumping items out of containers and sorting them out on a small table. I could see her flipping through journals and reference books, trying to put the pieces together. I wondered how many days she'd spent in this room by herself. How many nights. How many *years*.

As I moved through the rows of firearms and ammunition, I picked up a sharp odor. I stopped and looked down. I realized that I was actually smelling the gunpowder from inside the cartridge casings. Was that even possible? My head started throbbing. I was sweating all over. The ceiling lights flared. I squeezed my eyes shut. That only made it worse. I suddenly felt weak and sick. I fell backward against a metal shelf.

The next second, an image flashed into my head. I was standing next to my great-grandfather in a jungle. It felt as if I could reach out and touch him. I could feel the heat radiating off his body. He had a gun in each hand and a wild look in his eyes, like he was facing down some kind of danger. Suddenly, he went into a crouch and started firing away through the thick foliage. I couldn't tell what he was shooting at. Animals? Humans? Ghosts? Flames shot out of the gun barrels. Shredded leaves and branches flew into the air like confetti.

Each shot was like a hammer hitting my skull. The smell of gunpowder was overpowering. Smoke was everywhere. My knees buckled. Everything went dark. I felt my body hitting the ground.

Was I shot? Was I dead? Was it over?

CHAPTER 66

"HEY! HELLO? YOU in there, Doctor?"

I felt my eyes being pulled open. It was Kira. She was pressing my lids up and staring deep into my pupils. I was sitting on the floor with my back against the kitchen wall. It felt like my brain was coming out of a fog. I pushed her away.

"What the hell was *that*?" I asked. "What happened?"

"Not sure," said Kira. "Migraine maybe?"

"I've had migraines," I said. "That was no migraine. It was that goddamn *room*!"

"You might be right," said Kira. "There's some strange energy in there."

"No shit," I said.

I wondered about a Doc Savage curse. It sounded like something out of the old stories. Too crazy to be true. But what I felt was definitely real.

"Don't move," said Kira. "I'll be right back."

She stood up and walked into the kitchen. I squeezed my eyes shut and opened them wide to bring my vision back into focus. I heard the blender whirring, which was the last thing my throbbing head needed. When Kira came back, she was carrying a thick green smoothie.

"Let's get your blood sugar up," she said. "You didn't eat enough today."

She had a point. I was hungry. Starving, actually. But Kira's high-fiber slurry was not the answer. The sight of it turned my stomach.

"Pass," I said.

"You need protein," she said.

"I don't need it *that* bad," I replied.

She put the glass down. I could see her turning things over in her mind. I knew she was reading my mood, trying to figure out a way to get me back into the game.

"I have an idea," she said.

Naturally, I was suspicious. "What *kind* of idea?"

"What if we went out for dinner?"

I rubbed my temples and looked up. Was this some kind of trick? I sat forward.

"*Out* out?" I asked. It sounded too good to be true. "You mean to an actual restaurant—with normal food?"

"Why not?" said Kira. "My treat."

"Tonight?" I asked, still not believing it. "We can go out *tonight*?"

"If you're up for it," she said.

Maybe she was feeling sorry for me. Maybe she was manipulating me. I didn't care. Suddenly, my head was clearing. I could breathe again. The queasiness was gone. In fact, I was already thinking about a fat, juicy cheeseburger. I could almost taste it.

"You're on," I replied. "It's a date!"

Kira gave me a slight smile and patted my arm.

"Let's not use that word," she said.

CHAPTER 67

Lake Trasimeno, Italy

AS PREDICTED, CLOUDS covered the moon by 10 p.m. The water in the cove was still and inky black, with no reflections. The two people in the small boat looked like a high-school couple out for a romantic rendezvous.

The boy cut the engine and turned off the running lights as the girl readied herself in the prow. Silent and nearly invisible, the skiff drifted toward the dock below a small hillside villa. The home was modestly impressive and slightly run down, the kind of lake estate that stayed in families for generations. The boy and the girl exchanged strange smiles. They were on time and on target.

Inside the dimly lit villa, chemist Angelo Chinelli was toking away his disappointment at missing out on the prestigious Antonio Feltrinelli Prize. Short-listed, but no win. Second year in a row. "Goddamn politics!" he muttered bitterly. But the bitterness was quickly fading. The weed he was smoking was top-notch, cultivated by one of his lab assistants. After just three hits, he was already feeling relaxed and drowsy. The two goblets of Barolo he had downed earlier contributed to the stupor.

As he eased back into the large worn sofa, his wife, Lucia, came down the hall from the nursery. She was wearing a cotton robe and her dark brown hair fell loose around her shoulders.

"She good?" Angelo asked, his lips barely moving.

"Sleeping like a baby," Lucia reported with a soft smile.

Angelo smiled back. His daughter, Carmella, was the true prize of the year, he told himself. Just eleven months old and as beautiful as her mother. Brilliant, too. He could tell already.

"I'm heading in the same direction," said Angelo, eyelids fluttering. Lucia flopped down next to him on the huge soft cushions and plucked the joint from his lips. She took a deep drag, held it, then exhaled a purple plume into the candle-light. She nuzzled up against him and gave him a warm smile.

"Next year, the Nobel," she said, stroking his cheek.

"Next year," Angelo replied with a soft laugh and a touch of pride. He knew that it might actually happen.

Lucia dropped the roach into a ceramic ashtray. She swung her leg over Angelo's lap, then pressed forward to deliver a warm, lingering kiss. She tasted of smoke and red wine. Angelo gently tugged the top of her robe open.

The next twenty minutes went by in a haze, but a very pleasant one. When it was over, Lucia rolled to the side and curled up. Angelo slid a pillow under her neck and gave her a soft kiss on the forehead. She was asleep already. Angelo looked at his watch, then slid off the sofa and walked back toward the nursery for one last check.

In the semi-darkness, it looked like little Carmella had burrowed under her blanket again. But when Angelo stepped closer, his dulled senses suddenly blasted back to life.

The blanket was there. The baby was not.

CHAPTER 68

Chicago

I WAS FEELING almost normal, which felt totally amazing. The sidewalk café was trendy and hopping. The street traffic was a little noisy, but nobody cared. It was exciting to be out in the middle of the city. We were sitting in a small grouping of tables on the wide patio just outside the front door. By 8 p.m., every table was filled. It seemed like the kind of place people went to kick off an evening.

I remembered going to places like this after work by myself, with my nose buried in a research paper. But tonight was different. Tonight, I actually had female company. It felt nice. Even if the female was my kidnapper. Even if she was totally not attracted to me.

Kira was wearing skinny jeans and a flower-print blouse. Her hair was tucked under a black cap. She looked like an art history grad student. She looked great. I saw a few guys checking her out as they passed, but they lowered their eyes as soon as they noticed me. I realized that I now looked like the kind of boyfriend who might punch their lights out just for looking.

I was wearing the new white shirt and khaki pants Kira

had ordered to fit my new physique. Larger neck size. Smaller waist size. In addition to everything else, Kira was now my personal shopper. It had been a long time since I made any real decisions for myself. She picked up the little card that listed the evening's wine specials.

"Are we drinking tonight?" I asked.

"We certainly are," said Kira. "And I won't even drill you on the vintage."

She ran her finger down the choices. I looked over the appetizer options. I realized that, for the first time, I could read a menu without my glasses. New eyes. New body. New clothes. New everything. Mostly, it felt good to just pretend that I had an actual life again, even if it was only for a few hours. I tried to put Doc Savage and his blazing guns out of my mind.

Kira was still reviewing the wines when a blond waitress walked over and set a red votive candle down in the center of the table. The flame wobbled slightly and then settled. Kira looked up to order the wine, but the waitress was already gone.

Kira shrugged. "I guess she's just the official candle placer." I went back to the appetizer list. But only for a second. Something was off. A smell. Like bleach from a table cleaner. No. Stronger. Sodium hypochlorite. I jumped out of my seat.

"Bomb!" I shouted.

I grabbed the votive off the table. I glanced toward the street and saw a stake-bed truck passing by. I hurled the votive into the back of the truck, then dove across the table and threw Kira to the ground. I heard a huge blast and felt the shock wave pass through me, shaking my insides. The café windows shattered. Tables flipped, and people were blown out of their seats onto the patio.

I turned my head back toward the street. It was filled with smoke and ash. The truck bed had absorbed most of the blast. The wooden frame had exploded into a thousand chunks and splinters. The driver staggered out of his cab, blood pouring from his nose. All over the patio, people were crawling and reaching for one another, covered in blood and debris. My ears were numb. All I could hear was a high-pitched hum.

I grabbed Kira under one arm and pulled her to her feet. There was a rip in the back of her blouse and she had a scrape on one cheek. But other than that, she seemed okay. As I tried to recover my balance, she patted me down for damage. All I was missing were a few shirt buttons.

Kira turned toward the restaurant and looked down the alley that ran beside it. The hum in my ears was still too loud to hear what she was saying. But I could read her lips.

"The waitress!"

CHAPTER 69

WE HEADED DOWN the alley at a dead run, dodging dumpsters and wooden pallets. Halfway down, I saw a blond wig sticking out of an open trash can. The noise in my ears had dissolved into a mild buzz. I could hear shouts and screams and sirens behind us.

A block ahead, I saw a female figure running away. She was slender and agile. When we reached the end of the alley, she was gone. Kira looked left and right down the busy street. Then she looked back and saw a fire escape ladder hanging off the side of the building we had just passed. She grabbed onto the rungs with both hands and started climbing.

"Up here!" she said.

"How do you know?" I asked.

"I know," she said, scrambling higher.

As soon as she cleared the first floor level, I followed. In about twenty seconds, we were both crawling over a low wall onto the roof. The sunset was casting long shadows over the whole city. We were in a strange landscape of massive AC units and satellite dishes. We ran across the rooftop to the other side of the building. I caught a flash of movement from the roof on the other side of the street.

"There!" I shouted.

Kira spun around and ran halfway back across the roof. Before I could react, she bounced on the balls of her feet and then headed toward the edge at top speed. When she was about four feet away, she launched herself across the gap, four stories up. She landed in a somersault on the other side and jumped to her feet. She looked back at me.

"Let's *go!*" she shouted.

I wasn't sure I had it in me, but there was no way I was letting her go on alone. I gave myself plenty of room for a head start and then jumped off from the same spot she did. But I misjudged my bulk or the distance, or both. As soon as I was in the air, I knew I was coming up short.

As I fell, I grabbed for the bars of a window guard on the top floor. The rusty metal cut into my hands and my knees banged into the bricks below. I gritted my teeth through the pain and pulled myself up. When I rolled over the low wall onto the other roof, Kira was already on the move.

The rooftop was a maze of bubble-shaped skylights and old water tanks. We threaded our way through until we could see across to the next building. A woman with dark hair was hanging from a stone parapet just twenty feet away. As she muscled herself up, her right sleeve fell back to her elbow. Her forearm was red and scarred. Kira immediately dropped down behind the low wall on our side.

"Oh my God," she muttered to herself. She looked pale and stunned. I watched as the woman flipped herself over the parapet like a gymnast. She crouched low for a second, staring right back at me. Then she ran off and disappeared behind a mass of metal ductwork.

"C'mon!" I said. "We can catch her." I started to psych myself up for another jump. But Kira didn't move.

"No," she said. "That's exactly what she wants."

I looked down. Kira had her fists balled against her forehead and she was rocking back and forth, muttering to herself over and over again. "Not her, not her, not her..." She looked scared. I'd never seen that in her before. *Never.*

"Wait," I said. "You *know* her?"

Kira nodded slowly. She sounded numb. "Her name is Irina," she said. "We were classmates. I haven't seen her for more than a decade."

"What does it mean that she's here?" I said.

"It means we don't have any more time," said Kira. Her voice was strong again, and when she looked up, her expression had changed. There was no more fear in her eyes. Just rage.

CHAPTER 70

WHEN WE GOT back to the loft, Kira was quiet and focused. All I saw was cold determination.

"Hang on a minute," she said, then disappeared into her room. Actually, it was less than a minute. When she came out, her casual clothes were gone. She was back in athletic gear. All black. Her hair was pulled back tight. She looked like a commando.

I was watching the news report on the TV over the workout area. Explosion outside a Lakeview restaurant. Twenty injuries. Three people in critical condition. So far, no motive, no suspects, no leads. Terrorism could not be ruled out.

Kira glanced up at the screen. "I was careless and stupid," she muttered. "I felt sorry for you, and look what happened."

"So this is my fault now?" I asked. "This is on *me*??"

She opened the door marked UTILITY. "We don't have time to argue."

Inside the vault, Kira moved quickly. She grabbed a small backpack and tossed me another one. She started throwing in canisters, packets, and tools off shelves and tables. She grabbed a pistol from the rack and handed one to me. As soon as my hand touched the grip, I started to twitch. Kira grabbed my arm—hard.

"Hold it together, Doctor," said Kira. "Now is when I need you."

I stuffed the pistol into my backpack. She tossed me an extra box of ammunition, then took one last look around the vault.

"That's it," she said. "Let's go."

"Where are we going?" I asked.

Kira slung her backpack over her shoulder and walked straight out toward the elevator. She glanced at me over her shoulder.

"Back to school," she said.

CHAPTER 71

WHEN WE GOT to the street, Kira scoped out the traffic and speed-walked to the nearest intersection. I saw a cab idling at a stoplight. Kira ran in front of the car and slapped the hood. The cabbie shook his head. She moved around and rapped her knuckles against the driver's window. The glass slid down two inches. I heard the cabbie say, "Off duty." The light turned green. The cab started to move. Kira moved right along with it. She pulled out a hundred-dollar bill and slapped it flat against the window.

"How about now?" she shouted.

The cabbie stopped and unlocked the doors. Horns were blaring from the cars behind. Kira yanked the rear door open and we slid into the back seat.

"Where to?" asked the cabbie. He accelerated before the door was even shut.

"O'Hare," said Kira. She pulled out another bill. "And here's another hundred to ignore the speed limit."

"You got it," said the cabbie, glancing down at his dashboard clock. "What time is your flight?"

"As soon as we get there," she said.

I didn't think we had a flight booked. I didn't even know where this mysterious school was located. I also didn't know how Kira planned to get us on a plane carrying a bunch of metal devices and two loaded pistols. But at the moment, I was more worried about dying in a car crash.

The cabbie shot through River North traffic, running two yellow lights and one red before turning onto I-90. The car rattled and roared as he pushed it up past seventy on the highway. Kira twisted herself backward to look out the rear window, her hands gripping the headrest. Suddenly, she whipped back around.

"Damnit!" she shouted. "Get *down*!"

"Get down where?" the cabbie shouted back. "I'm fucking *driving*!"

"Lower your head! *Now!*" shouted Kira. She looked at me. "She's back," she said.

The cabbie slid down in his seat until his eyes were barely at the level of the steering wheel. A second later, the rear window exploded into a million pieces. I dropped down in my seat as hard pebbles of safety glass rained through the cab.

I turned and looked up—just far enough to see a black sedan weaving through traffic behind us, approaching fast. A dark-haired woman was leaning out the driver's window, arm extended. Irina! I saw the muzzle blast and heard two loud metallic bangs inside the cab.

"Son of a *bitch*!" shouted the cabbie. "Who *are* you people??"

"Do not stop!" Kira yelled back. "Do not slow down!"

Kira shoved me down on the seat. She reached into her backpack and pulled out a small metal oval. It looked like an egg. She leaned out the rear window and tossed it onto the roadway. I heard a huge bang and screeching tires. I jerked my head up again to look. The black sedan was spinning off to the side of the highway. The front end smashed into the guardrail, and I saw the airbags deploy. Cars careened around the wreck. A truck slammed into a Prius, and they both ended up cross-wise on the interstate as cars piled up behind them.

We were way ahead of the wreckage, coming up on the Canfield exit.

"I'm getting off here!" shouted the cabbie. "I gotta find a cop!"

Kira pulled the pistol out of her backpack and pointed it at the rearview mirror.

"You're going to the airport," said Kira. "You're not stopping anywhere."

"Okay, okay," said the cabbie, raising one hand. "No more shooting!"

He crouched as low as he could behind the wheel and sped up again. I looked out the window and saw signs for the departure terminal. Kira stuffed the gun in her backpack and braced herself on the edge of the seat, ready to move. The driver sped up the ramp, cutting in line. He swerved toward the curb and jammed on the brakes.

"Out!" he screamed. "Get out now!"

I shoved the door open and scrambled to the curb, brushing bits of glass off my clothes. Kira followed right behind. She leaned through the front window and tossed a wad of bills at the cabbie.

"For your back window," she said. She looked up at the two holes punched through the cab's roof. She pulled out a few more bills and tossed them in. "And the rest of it." The cabbie didn't even reach for the money. He just let it flutter onto the floor mat as he pulled away. I watched him dodge a traffic guard and bounce hard over a speedbump. Then he sped off toward the airport exit. He didn't look back.

"Let's go," said Kira.

She was heading toward the bank of sliding doors at the terminal entrance. Suddenly she stopped and pulled me down behind a low cement divider. All around us, people were moving through the doors with their carry-on bags and rolling suitcases.

"Don't move," she said.

"What?" I asked. "Irina's gone. You bombed her off the road."

Kira jerked her head in the direction of an entrance door about twenty yards down the row. I poked my head over the barrier. I didn't see anything strange—just a bunch of neatly dressed teenagers near the door, ten or twelve of them. They looked like an international youth group. Maybe a choir.

As I watched, one of the guys pulled out his cell phone. He glanced at the screen, then gave a hand signal. The other kids gathered around him and looked at one another with weird robotic smiles. Kira pulled me back down and leaned in close to my ear.

"Irina didn't come alone," she whispered. "She brought a whole damned class."

CHAPTER 72

"JESUS!" I WHISPERED back. "Somebody must really want you dead."

"You and me both," said Kira.

She pointed toward the entrance door closest to us. Then she glanced toward the curb and gestured for me to wait. An Uber had just pulled up and a whole family was spilling out—mom, dad, and four young kids, all chatty and excited, hauling color-coordinated luggage. As they walked past us, we stood up and blended in with them, like a friendly aunt and uncle.

The automatic doors parted and then we were all inside. I looked back. The students had passed through the door on their end of the terminal. They were glancing in our direction, trying not to be obvious. The happy family headed toward the ground-floor elevator, leaving us alone and exposed. Then the students started to move. Not like a youth group. More like a military squad, or killer robots. They fanned out, slow and deliberate. No rush. I got a sick feeling.

"Damnit!" I said. "How many of them *are* there??"

"Look around, Doctor," said Kira. "Or do you need your glasses back?"

She tugged me toward the escalator that led to the upper level. We walked quickly, weaving through the crowd. One team of students followed us, matching our pace. Another group suddenly emerged near the escalator at the other end of the terminal. Kira was right. They were *everywhere*. We stepped onto the metal stairs and jostled past the other passengers as we headed up. When I looked back, I could see the pursuit team right behind us.

We stepped off onto the second level and started speed walking, trying to open the gap. The team was about ten yards back. Three male, two female. They looked eighteen, maybe twenty. They moved as a unit, slipping between other travelers, excusing themselves with strange smiles. I started looking for places to duck into, but this part of the terminal was wide open. Like a target range.

"They won't shoot in here," said Kira. "They don't want the attention."

"Are they planning to *smile* us to death?" I asked.

"They'll try to separate us," said Kira, "then get close enough for a needle stick—make it look like a heart attack."

I nodded toward her backpack. "Don't you have any escape tricks in there?"

"Nothing that's any good in the open," she said. "We don't want any attention either." She glanced back. "We need to get out of here. *Now!* Keep moving."

The second team of students stepped off the other escalator, moving along the right side of the corridor in a neat line, just waiting to pick us off. Kira headed toward a young attendant in a United Airlines uniform.

"Hang back," said Kira. "When this guy starts talking to me, bump my elbow. Make sure I feel it."

Kira sped up. I slowed down. She stepped up square in front of the airline attendant and waved her hand in his face.

"Sorry," she said. "I'm all turned around. Which way is Terminal C?"

The attendant gestured toward the TSA checkpoints to his left. "That way," he said. "There's a moving sidewalk once you get through security."

That's when I bumped Kira, knocking her forward into the attendant. She whipped around and glared at me.

"Watch where you're going, idiot!" she said.

"Sorry!" I said, looking back. The attendant recovered quickly. He was already turning to answer another traveler's question. Kira caught up to me.

"What was *that* for?" I asked.

"For this," said Kira.

She opened her hand. I looked down. The attendant's plastic key card was in her palm. I looked back. The class was closing in.

Kira headed toward a nondescript metal door in the right-hand wall. It had a square Plexiglass panel at eye level and a metal alarm bar across the middle. The students to our right were moving past the TSA podiums. If we didn't speed up, they'd get to the door first.

"Go!" said Kira.

We started running. So did the students. They got tangled up with a tour group and started pushing their way through. That bought us a few seconds. When we got to the door, Kira waved the key card over a plastic panel on the wall. She pushed the alarm bar. The door opened with a loud beep.

I heard a rush of footsteps behind us. We slipped through the door. I rammed it shut with my shoulder—just as a bunch of faces mashed up against it from the other side. They looked agitated and fierce. Kira looked back at them and lifted her middle finger.

"Hey, kids!" she said. "Who's smiling *now*??"

CHAPTER 73

WE DUCKED OUT of sight behind the door and moved down a short hallway. Kira keyed us through another exit door and we stepped outside into the night air. It smelled like jet fuel. There was another long terminal building glowing brightly a few hundred yards to the right. I looked back over my shoulder.

"Did we lose them?" I asked.

"No," said Kira. "We just pissed them off. They'll find a way out."

"Should we get help?" I asked.

"Help?" Kira just stared at me. "You still don't get it, do you? There's only one person in the world that I can trust right now. And that's you."

She led the way across a grass border onto a large section of asphalt. I looked past the end of the other terminal and saw the outlines of three sleek executive jets.

"Don't tell me you have a plane," I said.

She stared straight ahead. "Not yet."

It was another few hundred yards from the corner of the far

terminal to the edge of the runway. We hung tight against the terminal building as airport workers buzzed back and forth on their little carts with their warning lights blinking.

The jet closest to us had its boarding stairs down, and the interior lights were on.

The pilot was walking underneath doing his preflight check. As he moved toward the tail section, a white stretch limo approached from the rear. The pilot straightened his jacket and walked toward the car.

"Now!" whispered Kira.

It was a thirty-yard dash. We ducked underneath the fuselage and hung there in the shadows for a few seconds. Twenty yards behind the tail, the limo doors were opening. The pilot shook hands with a man in an expensive suit. Two stylish young women slid out of the back seat.

Kira yanked the chocks away from the jet's front wheel. We came out on the other side of the fuselage and raced up the six steps to the main door. We stepped inside and looked left and right. Empty. The cabin looked like a luxury lounge. There were six huge passenger seats and a sofa in the passenger section. Lots of leather and expensive wood trim. No economy class here.

Kira ducked into the cockpit and slipped into the left-hand seat. It took me a second to realize what was happening.

"We're stealing a *jet*??" I asked.

"Fastest way out of town," Kira replied. She was already flipping switches. I heard a loud hum and saw the stairway being pulled up into the fuselage.

"Lock it!" Kira called out.

I cranked the locking lever hard in the direction of the big red arrow. There was a satisfying *thunk*. Two seconds later, we started rolling forward.

I peeked out one of the cabin windows to where the pilot and limo passengers were sorting baggage on the tarmac. They looked up. The pilot blinked in disbelief and then started chasing after us, waving his arms like crazy. Kira made a hard turn to the left. I fell against one of the leather seats.

"Get up here and strap in!" she shouted.

I scrambled forward and dropped into the copilot seat. I pulled the harness over my shoulders and fastened it. Kira was already turning onto the runway. I could see the long stretch of asphalt reaching into the distance. Back near the terminal, red lights started flashing. Workers in coveralls were climbing into emergency trucks. Guys in white shirts ran out of the terminal with walkie-talkies. I saw a couple of security guards with their guns out.

"No way we're getting away with this," I muttered.

Kira looked over at me. "Hold my beer," she said.

She had her hands on two large white handles on the divider between us. She pushed the handles forward. There was a strong vibration and a roar from the back of the jet. We started rolling down the runway. In a few seconds, we were at highway speed. The ground started to blur.

"Let's go, let's go!" Kira muttered, low and intense, as we ate up the runway. At that moment, the nose lifted and suddenly the windshield filled with sky. I looked back to my right and saw a cluster of red lights circling the end of the runway like angry fireflies. I let out a huge breath and looked for something to hold onto. This was *nuts*!

"Aren't we supposed to talk to the tower or something?" I asked.

"Don't be such a goody-goody," said Kira.

She put the jet into a steep climb. I felt myself being pressed back against the seat. I looked down at Cook County disappearing below. My heart rate started to settle, but my brain was still buzzing. Kira was cool and calm, like she was taking a drive to the mall.

"You should have told me you knew how to fly," I said.

Kira tapped a few buttons on the console. We started to level out.

"Don't look surprised," she said. "So do you."

She nodded toward the screen in front of my seat. "Set a course 330 degrees northwest," she said.

I had no clue how to make that happen. For a few seconds, I just sat there, staring at the console.

"I'm not kidding, Doctor," said Kira. "*Do* it."

I reached out and put my fingers on the screen. Suddenly, the whole navigation protocol popped into my head. Every single step.

I must have learned it in my sleep.

CHAPTER 74

"KAMCHATKA," I SAID. "Never heard of it." That was the destination readout that popped up on the screen as we got closer. "That's where we're going?"

We'd already been flying for five hours.

Kira nodded. "It's a tiny piece of Russia, like a finger poking down along the Bering Sea." I looked at the map on the screen. That's exactly what it looked like.

"Why would anybody put a school there?" I asked.

"My great-grandfather was Russian," said Kira, "or *said* he was. Nobody really knows. But that's where he built his little empire. Up where he knew nobody would ever find it."

"What happens when we get there?" I asked.

Kira stared out through the windshield. "We save the world," she said, "starting with a few hundred kids."

Okay, I thought to myself. One step at a time. First step—land in one piece. I looked out my side again. We'd crossed over western Canada and the lower edge of Alaska. Now we were cruising over open water.

"Are you sure we've got enough fuel?" I asked. The gauges looked low to me.

"We're cutting it close," said Kira. "But we're not stopping at a Shell station."

I stared out through the windshield. At this point, there was nowhere to land anyway. There was nothing outside but dark sky and even darker water.

Suddenly, a bright orange streak shot past my window like a comet. Before I could even register what I was seeing, I heard Kira shout.

"Damnit! Missile! Air-to-air!"

I whipped around in my seat.

"Are you *shitting* me??" I yelled. I'd actually started to feel cozy in our luxury ride. Now somebody was trying to blast us out of the sky.

"Who the hell is shooting at us??" I yelled.

"Does it matter??" Kira yelled back.

She banked hard to the left. My head banged against the side of the cockpit. A second streak passed by her side, close enough to shake the whole body of the jet.

I felt trapped, terrified, helpless. My mind flashed to ejection seats and parachutes. But I knew better. We were in a cushy executive jet, not an F-16.

I heard a loud bang and felt a huge jolt on my side. The fuselage rocked. I saw another orange flame going by, but this one was fragmented into separate flares. The nose started to drop, and the horizon disappeared.

"Sonavabitch!" Kira shouted. "It clipped the wing!" The jet wobbled and started doing crazy corkscrews. Kira kept punching controls and pushing forward on the throttle handles. The

engines whined and rattled behind us. Everything through the windshield was black. I felt a sick drop in my belly. I was losing all sense of direction.

Down was up. Up was down. I braced my arms against the top of the console. I looked over at Kira. I couldn't believe this was happening.

"Is this another one of your goddam *tests*??" I shouted. The sound of the engines was so loud I could barely hear myself.

"This time you might be on your own," Kira shouted back. She was doing everything she could to regain control. But none of it was working. I stared at the altimeter. 1,000 feet. 500 feet. Blood rushed to my head. My vision clouded over. Then another woman's voice filled the cockpit, sounding like a very stern Siri.

"Pull up!" she kept saying, "Pull up!"

That's the last thing I remember.

CHAPTER 75

THE FREEZING COLD brought me back. Or maybe the pain in my head. I woke up floating in black water with a sharp stabbing sensation over my left eye. When I touched my forehead, I felt a long gash. My fingers came away covered in watery blood. My legs were numb, but I could move them. They were all that was keeping me from going under. I had no memory of the crash, no idea how long I'd been out.

I twisted around, looking for Kira. Or wreckage. Or land. But there was nothing. The night was so dark that the sky blended with the water.

"Kira!"

I shouted her name, over and over. It felt like hours. Until my voice gave out and I couldn't shout anymore. My body was getting stiff. My brain was starting to shut down. As I stared into the darkness, small waves started to look like fins. I just hung there, trying not to thrash around. I knew there was blood in the water. It was mine.

I squinted to sharpen my vision. My heart started to pound, and I got a jolt in my gut. There was a small lump floating in the distance, maybe fifty yards away. Was it human?? *Please, God!*

"Kira!" I shouted again. By now, my voice was barely a squawk. I started swimming as hard as I could. The lump, whatever it was, kept disappearing behind the waves and popping up again.

When I was about twenty yards off, I took a deep breath and did a surface dive. I knew I could move faster underwater. Just as my breath ran out, I stretched my arms forward and grabbed. I was praying that it was Kira, and that she was alive. Instead, I felt a small bundle of leather and cloth.

My heart dropped. It was my backpack.

It was floating because of a small inflated sack in the lining. A Doc Savage invention, no doubt. I opened the flap and looked inside.

I saw some rope. A coil of thin wire. A pair of goggles. A bunch of loose buttons. A small water bottle. One energy bar in a foil wrapper. But no life vest. No signal flares. And no mini underwater breathing device. I should have known we'd used up the last two in existence.

I reached into the bottom of the bag and felt hard metal. The pistol.

I pulled the gun out and pointed it into the sky. Three shots meant SOS. Kira didn't teach me that. I learned it in the Boy Scouts. I squeezed the trigger. There was nothing but a loud click. The shell casings were soaked and useless. At that point, the gun was just deadweight. And it felt like the worst kind of bad luck. I dropped it into the water and watched it sink.

I was shivering all over. My lips were trembling. I tried to blink the salt out of my eyes. Then I saw something new in the distance. At first, I thought it was just another line of whitecaps. But it wasn't moving. It just sat there. I couldn't tell how far away it was. I had no reference point. A mile maybe?

I wasn't sure I could make it that far. Then I thought about the ice bath. The swimming pool. The plunge into Lake Michigan. In my head, I could hear Kira yelling at me, pushing me, *shaming* me. I felt fresh energy flowing into my limbs, and my mind started to clear. I realized that the old Doctor Brandt Savage would have been dead already—broken to pieces or drowned. But somehow, I was still here.

I wrapped the backpack strap around my shoulder and started kicking like a porpoise toward the white something in the distance. I thought it might be a mirage, just my mind giving me false hope. But I kept going. What else could I do?

It was the only hope I had.

CHAPTER 76

Eastern Russia

AT THAT HOUR, the school was mostly dark. But underground, the warm nursery ward still glowed. A long row of rocking chairs lined one whole wall. Seated in each rocker was a stone-faced woman with a baby at her breast. The wet nurses were stout, red-faced Slavs, but the babies were of every race and complexion. It was a multinational feeding station.

The woman at the end of the row sat alone, rocking more slowly than the others. The door from the corridor opened. The nurse looked up. A female attendant walked in, carrying an infant wrapped in two blankets.

"Two-day trip from Africa," said the attendant. "She's weak."

The nurse reached up and took the small bundle into her arms. She peeled back the blanket to expose the baby's face. Dark brown skin. Huge brown eyes. Tiny puckered mouth. The baby mewed softly, not enough strength to cry. The nurse looked up at the hovering attendant.

"Get out," she said bluntly. "Let her feed."

The attendant turned and walked back into the corridor. The nurse opened one side of her blouse to expose a large, elongated breast. She teased her nipple around the baby's lips until the little girl latched on.

As the infant suckled, the wet nurse started to rock in sync with the rest of the row. When she looked up again, there was another figure in the doorway.

It was the headmaster.

Kamenev caught the nurse's eye and nodded approvingly. Odd, thought the nurse. It was unusual for Kamenev to check on a new arrival. He obviously had high hopes for this one.

CHAPTER 77

THE WATER WAS getting choppier. It took me twenty minutes to get close enough to realize what I'd been swimming toward. It wasn't some hallucination after all.

It was an iceberg.

The part I could see was about fifty feet long, with a couple of jagged peaks jutting up toward the sky. I felt a sudden surge of relief. I figured if I could get there and climb on, at least I wouldn't have to die from drowning. I could just die from hypothermia. I'd read that it was like going to sleep.

I breast-stroked the final fifty yards or so, then used my elbows to haul myself onto a low ledge just above the waterline. I rolled onto my side and lay there for a few minutes, catching my breath. I flexed my fingers to get the feeling back in the tips. I stared up at the sky and watched the vapor clouds blow out of my mouth.

I realized that my wet clothes were starting to freeze in the open air. Before long, I'd be covered in an icy shell. Part of me just wanted to close my eyes and let go. That would be the easy way out. No pain. No fear. But I couldn't do it. Something inside made me start moving.

I rolled over and pressed against the ice to push myself up. It felt strange. I pounded on the surface. I scraped at it with my fingernails. I leaned closer. I scraped again. I realized that what I was feeling wasn't ice at all. There was nothing natural about it. It was some kind of manufactured material, made to look like ice from a distance—like a gigantic Hollywood prop.

What the hell was going on? I looked up and saw a series of indentations in the white surface, leading up the side of one of the peaks. From out in the water, they'd looked like natural formations. From where I stood now, they looked like steps. I started to make my way up.

Even though the ice was artificial, it was covered with a layer of actual frost, slick and dangerous. One wrong move and I'd be back in the water. I felt for handholds as I moved up the steps. Just ahead was a large overhang, dripping with icicles. I reached up and touched one. A convincing fake.

I peeked under the overhang and saw a hard vertical edge—some kind of hatch. It looked rusted shut. I scraped through the thin coating of frost until I found an indented metal handle. It wasn't much of a grip. I hooked my fingers in and pulled. The hatch groaned slightly and the gap widened a few millimeters. I tried again. My fingers slipped off. They were stinging from the cold and scraped raw from the rough metal.

I was getting nowhere.

I pulled the backpack off my shoulder. I unfastened one of the straps and slid the metal buckle into the small gap between the hatch door and the frame. Then I pulled the strap up until the buckle caught underneath. I gripped the strap with both hands and tugged. The hatch groaned some more. The gap got wider. Now I had enough space to jam my hands underneath. I strained and pulled until the hatch door gave way.

I leaned over and peeked inside. I saw the top edge of a rusted ladder. There was light coming from below. I flipped onto my belly and put my foot on the top rung, then slowly backed through the opening. I pulled the hatch closed behind me.

I was inside a translucent tube. The ladder stretched down about twenty feet. My feet were still so numb I could barely feel the rungs. When I got to the bottom, I was below sea level, in a room about half the size of a football field.

I couldn't believe what I was seeing.

Of all the stories I'd heard about my ancestor, this was the one I thought had *zero* chance of being true. Even the name I'd heard for this place seemed overblown. But it was obviously real.

I was standing in the Fortress of Solitude.

CHAPTER 78

I LOOKED AROUND for a minute, barely moving. It took that long to absorb the scale of the place. The whole interior was supported by a framework of wooden beams, running up, down, and crossways. The ceiling was nearly as high as the peaks outside, maybe thirty feet up. The floor was made of thick planks, like a boardwalk or dock.

When I started walking around, the planks creaked and groaned. There were cracks in the walls where seawater had leaked in, and I saw big puddles and salt stains on the floor. If this place had actually been around since the 1930s, it was amazing that it hadn't sunk. Even more impressive, some of the lights still worked. They looked like primitive fluorescent tubes, dim but still glowing. They gave the whole place a tunnel-of-doom look. Which reflected exactly how I felt.

In the center of the space, there were long wooden tables covered with all kinds of electronic devices and tools. Most of the stuff looked corroded and useless. I walked over to a row of rusted metal bins against one wall, each one as big as a washing machine. I lifted one of the lids and got hit with a horrible odor. I held my breath and peeked inside. There was a layer of black sludge lining the bottom. I figured it used to be food. Now there was nothing but stench.

At the far end, there was a kitchen with a propane stove and an open cupboard with pots, dishes, and coffee mugs. Against one wall, there were long shelves filled with books—an impressive private library.

A lot of the bindings were falling apart, but I could still read some of the titles, mostly science textbooks and literary classics. *The Complete Works of William Shakespeare,* the *Iliad, The History of the Decline and Fall of the Roman Empire.* I picked up a couple leather-bound books from the end of the row. The first one was *Twenty Thousand Leagues Under the Sea,* by Jules Verne. The second one was by Robert Louis Stevenson. *Kidnapped.*

I winced—and thought about Kira.

CHAPTER 79

I SLID THE two books back onto the shelf. My head felt light. I was achy and exhausted. I leaned against the wall and tried to organize my thoughts. They were scattered, and pretty dark.

I was alive, but I wasn't so sure that was a positive. I'd been trained for a mission, and the mission had failed. It was my job to protect Kira, and I hadn't done it. And somewhere on the Kamchatka Peninsula, her school was still pumping out smiling killers. It felt strange to think about it, but after all these years, John Sunlight's vision was actually taking over the world. And there was nothing I could do to stop it. *Nothing!*

All of a sudden, the anger and helplessness boiled over. I started screaming at the top of my lungs. I grabbed a hammer off a workbench and threw it into a glass cabinet. It shattered with a loud crash. I ran my arm along a crowded benchtop and knocked everything onto the floor—machine parts, chemical bottles, piles of loose papers.

A book tipped off the edge of the bench and landed with a heavy thud. I don't know why, but something made me reach down and pick it up. It was as thick as a Bible, with brown leather binding. I brushed off the dust and saw a name embossed on the cover. It took me a second to understand what I was looking at.

Dr. Clark Savage, Jr., the lettering read.

Doc Savage's full name.

My hands actually started trembling. I set the book on the workbench and started leafing through the pages. The paper was yellowed, but the contents were totally readable. I realized that I was looking at my great-grandfather's journal. The famous Doc Savage genius was right there in front of my eyes. There were plans for X-ray cameras, fluoroscopes, and desalinization units. There were sketches for gyroscopes and flying wings and crazy pneumatic tube systems. It was like paging through one of da Vinci's notebooks.

One page near the end stood out from all the scientific scrawls. It was some kind of personal manifesto, handwritten in bold lettering. I ripped the page out and put it on the bench. Then I flipped to the last page of the journal. Glued to the inside back cover was a small sepia photograph. It showed two infant boys, no more than a couple months old. They were lying side by side on a thick blanket. At the bottom of the picture were two names written in bold script: *Clark & Cal.*

I stared at the picture. Kira had been right. The twin story was true. I carefully pulled the photo loose and put it on top of the ripped-out page. In that instant, I felt a weird sensation come over me. My whole body started shuddering. It was as if everything I'd gone through was catching up with me at once. My legs buckled and my head started spinning. I staggered down the length of the workbench, holding on to the thick wooden top for dear life. I managed to reach a wooden bulwark a few feet from the end. I looked around the corner and saw a row of military cots, each one with a small pillow and a folded blanket. As I eased myself around a support post, I caught a glimpse of myself in a shaving mirror. It was not pretty.

I had a day's growth of beard. My eyes looked hollow, and my skin was pale. The gash on my head was red and angry looking. I'd have a scar there for sure. Not that anybody would ever see it. Nobody was going to find me. Not here. Not *ever*.

I stripped off my clothes and lay down on the nearest cot. I pulled the wool blanket over me. I realized that I'd never felt so alone. I thought back over the last six months—about how Kira had changed my body, and my brain, and my life.

For what?

Maybe I should have hated her for leaving me in this position, but I didn't. Somehow, I felt that I'd let her down, and I couldn't believe I'd never see her again.

It wasn't possible. It wasn't fair. After all we'd been through together, how could she go and die without me?

"Wrong question," I could hear her saying. And then, "You have only yourself."

I turned my face to the pillow and started sobbing like a baby.

CHAPTER 80

Eastern Russia

THE MAIN GROUNDS OF the school compound were dark, except for the glow of security lights from the main building. After his stop in the nursery to admire the new enrollee, Kamenev walked across the yard toward the far edge of the property, beyond the firing range and the oval dirt track. There, at the end of an asphalt strip nearly half a mile long, he waited. Before long, he heard a low whistle in the sky and saw a set of navigation lights beaming through the cloud cover in the distance. Kamenev reached into a metal junction box and flipped a switch. Rows of bright blue lights came to life on both sides of the asphalt, forming bright stripes.

The compact fighter jet touched down at the far end of the runway at 150 miles per hour. By the time it reached the apron where Kamenev was standing, it was rolling to a gentle stop. The engine shut down. The cockpit hood folded back. Irina unfastened her harness and pushed herself out of the pilot's seat.

Her face was bruised and she favored her left leg as she walked across the tarmac. Kamenev stepped forward, expecting his usual thorough debrief, but Irina brushed past him without even looking up.

"Target destroyed," she said numbly. "No survivors."

CHAPTER 81

Gaborone, Botswana

IT WAS JUST past noon when Jamelle Maina finally opened her eyes. She rolled to the side and tossed back her top sheet. Her body was covered in sweat. Since her baby had been taken, she'd had an impossible time getting to sleep. But last night's pills and wine had finally knocked her out. Now the midday heat was bringing her around.

She swung her long, muscular legs out of bed and walked over to the boxy air conditioner in the window of her tiny bedroom. The machine was rumbling, but the fan wasn't blowing. With her bare feet, Jamelle could feel a small puddle of warm water on the floor underneath. She banged the unit with her fist, but that just made the rumbling louder.

She walked to the bathroom, turned on the sink tap, and wiped her forehead and neck with a wet towel. She stared into the mirror. Her face was drawn, and her eyes were red. She felt like she looked a decade older than her twenty-three years.

Another week had passed without word from the police—and without contact of any kind from the private investigator.

In the beginning, Devos had returned her calls and texts, but now all she got was his voice-mail greeting.

Jamelle flopped back onto the bed and turned toward the wall, staring at a photo she kept taped at eye level, so close she could touch it. Her little girl. Jamelle ran her finger over the picture and imagined the feel of her baby's skin, the smell of her hair, the sound of her laugh. As tears dripped down her cheeks, Jamelle called her daughter's name softly, over and over again. Like a prayer.

CHAPTER 82

Eastern Russia

ON THE REMOTE peninsula two continents west, dawn was still several hours away. In a small room buried beneath the school's main building, security officers Balakin and Petrov were eight hours into their shift, their eyes bleary from staring at screens all night long. It was boring work. The only activity had been a solitary fox crossing the perimeter, its eyes glowing yellow on the night-vision camera. Everything else was quiet and secure, as usual.

Balakin pulled a cigarette from his pack and lit it. He leaned back in his chair, took a deep drag, and exhaled toward the ceiling. A forbidden pleasure. This was the one place on the property he could smoke with impunity, in violation of Kamenev's strict prohibition. The room's powerful vent filters removed every trace of smoke and odor. Petrov used the soundproof room to indulge in a vice of his own—one that drove Balakin to distraction.

"How can you *stand* it?" Balakin shouted. He was referring to the German techno music blaring from Petrov's Bluetooth speaker.

"Keeps me awake," Petrov called back, bobbing his head in time to the pounding beat.

"Hey!" Balakin shouted.

"All right, all right!" said Petrov. "I'll turn it down . . ."

"No!" said Balakin. *"Look!"*

He was leaning over the console, his nose just inches from one of the monitors—the one showing the outside of the explosives shed on the far side of the property. "Shed" was a misnomer. It was a pillbox-shaped building with walls two feet thick and six feet of solid steel descending into the ground to prevent burrowing, animal or otherwise.

Balakin dropped his cigarette through a metal floor grate and rolled his chair forward. The shed was just a blocky outline in the darkness, but there was a bright flare around one side of the heavy metal door, so strong it almost whited out the camera lens. Petrov shot his partner a look. Balakin nodded.

Petrov reached to the far side of the console and pounded a red alarm button. They both stood and tightened their gun belts. Balakin turned the handle to open the vacuum-sealed door. Outside, they jumped into matching black ATVs and raced toward the location.

By the time they arrived, the whole scene was swarming with a dozen other ATVs, their headlights shining across all sides of the shed. The student squad on call had responded to the alarm in record time. They seemed excited that, for once, it was apparently not just a drill. When Balakin pulled up, the students greeted him with unsettling wide-eyed smiles. He nodded back. He avoided the students whenever possible. They made his skin crawl.

Petrov pulled up right behind. He jumped out of his vehicle and walked to the building. He placed his hand on the seam of the metal door. It was blackened and pitted, but otherwise intact. No intrusion. No structural damage. All around the building, ATV engines revved and roared, blocking out any other sounds. Balakin rolled his ATV forward and swiveled the powerful spotlight beam across the thick woods in the distance.

He saw nothing but trees.

CHAPTER 83

The Bering Sea

I THOUGHT THE banging noises were part of a dream, but when I woke up, they were still there. I didn't know how long I'd slept. Maybe hours. Maybe days. The only light came from the fluorescent tubes overhead. No clue about the world outside. My whole body felt bruised and sore. My skin was still crusty from the salt water, and my throat felt like sandpaper.

I reached into my backpack and pulled out my lone bottle of water. As I guzzled it down, I heard the sounds again. They were coming from the other side of the fortress.

I rolled my aching body off the cot and walked around to the other side of the partition into the main space. I started following the sounds. They had more definition now. Rhythmic. Hollow. Metallic. I looked up and down for something that might have come loose, maybe something knocking into a beam. Nothing. I looked for pumps or heating units. Again nothing. Except for the sleeping area, the fortress was wide open.

The sounds reverberated through the space. I froze in place and tried to triangulate the source. Then I took a few steps forward. The sounds were louder now. Closer.

I was almost at the other end of the vast room when I felt a vibration under my feet. The planks I was standing on trembled in sync with the noise. A few steps farther, I saw a metal hatch set flush with the floor. There was a handle near the top. I pulled on it, but the hatch door was rusted to the frame. I braced my legs and pulled again. The handle ripped off in my hand. I leaned down. No question now. The banging was coming from underneath the hatch. Like somebody or something was trying to get in.

I was out of patience. I grabbed a crowbar and jammed the edge under the floorboards on one side of the hatch. I worked the bar back and forth, splintering the wood until I'd exposed the edge of the metal. I took a deep breath, hooked my hands underneath, and ripped out the entire hatch, frame and all. It fell back onto the planks with a huge bang, leaving a gaping hole in the floor.

I looked down through the opening. I was staring at a black metal object floating in a large chamber of seawater right below the level of the floor. It was about twice the size of an oil drum. One side was banging against an underwater support post. That was the noise.

I dropped to my knees for a closer look. It wasn't a drum— more like a stubby tube, with tapered ends and a round lid in the center.

A submarine.

CHAPTER 84

Eastern Russia

"I SHOULD HAVE been called sooner," said Irina, her voice steely.

She stared straight ahead as Petrov and Balakin led her to the front of the explosives shed. Irina was running on two hours of sleep and she was in a dark mood. As she approached the building, students were still circling it in their ATVs. When they recognized Irina, they cut their engines and stiffened in their seats.

Dawn was just rising over the mountains, and the west-facing half of the structure was still in shadow. Irina stared at the damaged door. She leaned in and stroked her index finger over the sooty residue on the metal. She sniffed it.

"Old-school thermite," she said. "*Very* old."

Thermite was no match for titanium. Even the weakest students would know that. The intrusion attempt had been amateurish. Almost like somebody was playing games, or trying to attract attention. She turned to Petrov.

"You have video?" she asked. He nodded.

Back in the basement security center, Balakin watched

nervously as Petrov cued up the segment from the early hours. Irina had her chair rolled up tight against the console. The image was dark, the outlines of the shed barely visible. Suddenly, the explosive flare illuminated one side of the building, blowing out the picture for a few seconds before fading back into darkness.

"Stop it there!" said Irina.

Petrov hit the Pause button. Irina leaned in.

"Toggle the last two frames."

Petrov switched back and forth. Irina's jaw clenched. At the far-left edge of the second frame, a figure was partially silhouetted by the dying flare. It was a woman's figure. The head was surrounded by a halo of copper-colored curls.

Irina's fists clenched the console in disbelief. Her jaw tightened. She wasn't just angry. She was humiliated. And that was worse. She realized that for the first time in her entire life, she had failed to complete an assignment.

As Irina shoved her chair back, the wheels hit the metal grate in the floor. She glanced down and spotted a flake of ash hanging on the edge. She looked over at Petrov, then at Balakin.

"Somebody's been smoking in here," she said evenly.

Both guards blanched, but Irina noticed that Balakin's eyes blinked faster. She stood up and walked to his chair. She crouched behind him, hands on his shoulders. She could feel him trembling. She leaned in close to his ear and whispered.

"Smoking will kill you," she said.

Balakin released a nervous laugh.

"Don't worry," said Irina. "I won't say a word."

Balakin exhaled in a heavy rush. Irina felt his whole upper body relax under her touch. She cupped her forearm around his chin and yanked violently, breaking his neck in an instant. The pop of his vertebrae sounded like a whip crack.

Petrov flew out of his chair and stood shaking against the wall. Irina released her grip and let Balakin's body slide onto the floor. She advanced slowly toward Petrov.

He reached down and fingered his gun holster. Irina rested her hand lightly on top of his. She was smiling now, strangely polite and composed.

"Plant him in the woods," she said, "or sink him in the lake. Your choice."

CHAPTER 85

The Bering Sea

FOR A SOLID hour, I went back and forth in my mind. I was so hungry I couldn't think straight. I was getting weaker by the minute, and my mind was getting foggy. I knew I had to make the most of my body and my brain cells while they were still functioning.

The way I saw it, I had two choices, both of them bad. I could resign myself to dying a slow death inside my ancestor's artificial iceberg. Or I could take a chance on getting out—in a machine that might kill me. I paced around the gaping hole in the floor, looking down into the chamber of seawater, watching the submarine bobbing in its berth. The more I stared at it, the more I felt like Doc Savage was taunting me—or daring me.

Then I thought about Kira again, and about the battle we were supposed to face together. She'd never told me her plan. Maybe she didn't have one. Maybe she assumed that we'd figure it out as a team. I definitely didn't feel up to saving the world on my own, but I realized that if I had a chance to complete the mission, I had to try. For her.

In other words, I didn't really have a choice.

I grabbed my backpack. I tossed in a hammer, a screwdriver, and a pair of pliers. I grabbed a butcher knife from the kitchen and the wool blanket from the cot. I rustled through the rusty devices on the worktables, but nothing else looked useful.

I stood for a minute at the edge of the hole in the floor, then stepped onto the top of the sub. The metal shell was curved and slippery, and the whole thing shifted under my weight. I grabbed the edge of the lid. I figured that opening it was going to take all my strength. But it flipped up with no effort, as easy as popping a beer can. There was a thick steel wheel on the inside of the lid. I used it to steady myself as I lowered myself into the cabin.

Once I was inside, I could barely move. Even with my old physique, it would have been a tight fit. The only light came through the hatch from the space above. I took a chance and flipped a row of switches on the inside curve of the submarine wall. A row of light bars popped on along the sides, casting a weird bluish glow. I felt a sick wave of claustrophobia. The whole idea seemed suicidal. *Suck it up, Doctor,* I told myself.

I reached up and pulled the hatch shut. I cranked the wheel to the right and heard the opening seal tight. I felt like I had just locked myself in a tomb. The sub was still banging against the support post, but now I was hearing it from the inside—a metallic echo. Like a bell tolling.

I wedged myself into the single seat and looked around. For all I knew, I was sitting in an unfinished model or a decoy. I wasn't even sure it had a working engine. I looked around, trying to read Doc Savage's mind from the distance of a century. Some of the controls seemed obvious. I assumed the metal stick in front of me was the speed control, and that the foot pedals turned the rudder.

I ran my fingers over the maze of buttons and switches on the small console in front of me. A few of them actually had labels. One said *PWR*. I hovered my finger over it, then pressed. I heard a low whine behind me, then loud thumping. The thumping got faster and faster until it turned into a throbbing hum. The whole sub vibrated and I could see white bubbles blasting up from underneath.

I took a guess that *RLS* meant "Release." I pressed the button. I heard metal parts grinding and felt something give way. Suddenly the sub dropped a few feet lower in the water and rolled to the left. I pushed forward on the stick between my knees. The engine hum turned into a growl. The sub righted itself and began to glide forward out of the chamber.

All I could see through the small porthole in front was greenish-blue water filled with whitish fragments, like dandruff falling from the underside of the fortress. In a few seconds, I could see that I was emerging from under the far edge of the structure into the open sea. The water turned a lighter shade of green. I exhaled slowly.

If this was my tomb, at least it was moving.

CHAPTER 86

Eastern Russia

ON THE FIRST floor of the school's main building, an austere lecture hall now doubled as a ready-room. It was crowded with students, the school's most senior and seasoned, the ultimate survivors, male and female. They were all dressed in tactical gear. Nobody sat. They were all too nervous and eager. The news of the attempted intrusion had spread through the student body, but only the elite—these twenty—had been chosen for primary pursuit. The room hummed with anticipation.

The side door to the classroom flew open and Irina walked in, her face grim. The room instantly fell silent. Irina walked to the front and looked over the class. She had trained most of these students herself, and she knew they were ready. She clicked a controller and brought up an image on the monitor at the front of the room. It showed a close-up of the blackened metal door.

"You all know we had an attempted breach early this morning," she said. "Unusual. And unacceptable. But we also happen to know who's responsible." She paused. "It was somebody who lived here and trained here."

The students eyed one another nervously. Was this a setup? A test? Was there a traitor in the room?

Irina clicked to the next image—the grainy frame of the woman's silhouette. The students leaned forward, trying to digest every pixel of information. Irina let them stew for a few seconds, then clicked again. The next image was sharp and clear. It was an enhancement of a surveillance photo taken in Chicago. It showed Kira alone on a city street. Her copper curls glowed in the light.

"Her name is Meed," said Irina. "She's brilliant and she's dangerous. She is a danger to this school's existence, and to our power throughout the world. She is a threat to me and to Headmaster Kamenev and to each and every one of you."

She zoomed in on the image until Kira's face filled the screen.

"This is your target," said Irina firmly. "This is your final test."

CHAPTER 87

The Bering Sea

ACCORDING TO THE dials on the console, I was moving at about ten knots. I'd found the switch for the forward-facing spotlight, and the beam cut through the water for a distance of about twenty feet. Beyond that, it was all haze.

My depth was twelve meters. And if I could believe the compass, I was headed due west—directly toward the Kamchatka Peninsula, ten kilometers away. The hull was making terrifying noises, creaks and thuds that were even louder than the hum of the engine. Heat blasted through the cabin. I could smell motor oil and fuel and my own sweat. Every muscle in my body was tense. I was taking quick shallow breaths and keeping my movements to a minimum. I felt like I was in a very fragile egg, and I prayed that it would go the distance.

Suddenly a loud squawk filled the cabin. My adrenaline shot through the roof. A red light on the panel was blinking. A second later, I knew why. I looked down and saw water seeping through a seam on the floor. I pulled the ballast lever to lift the nose angle, but the sub wasn't responding. There was no way to surface. I felt a sudden rush of ice water over my feet, then my ankles.

I scanned the controls and flipped the switch marked *PUMP*. Somewhere behind me another motor fired up, and I could hear water being sucked out through a vent. But not fast enough. The flood was rising up my calves. The nose of the sub was tilting down. I was descending fast. Twenty meters. Now thirty.

The creaking got louder. I heard a rivet pop, then another. Like gunshots. I looked around the cabin. I started pressing every button, hoping something might seal the leak. I looked behind me. The only thing I saw was a hand-cranked radio mounted to the rear of the cabin, like something out of a museum. The sub tipped almost vertical and picked up speed. I knew I didn't have much time. I was riding a rocket to the bottom of the sea.

CHAPTER 88

Eastern Russia

THE ATVS WERE even louder than Kira remembered.

She covered her ears and held perfectly still as the search party bounced over a ridge and down a rocky slope at the bottom of a steep 200-foot cliff. Kira knew the riders would be jostling for position, each one hoping to spot the target first. She knew they'd be pumped with energy and bent on speed. Her hope was that they'd scan the trail ahead but ignore the perimeter.

Huddled under a pile of brush, covered with a thin mesh net that make her look like part of the landscape, Kira lowered her head and held her breath. The riders passed so close to her that the tires threw sharp bits of stone against her head and back. She did not flinch.

Her body was already bruised and aching from the night before. She had no memory of the crash, and no idea how long she'd been unconscious in the water, only that her backpack had somehow kept her afloat until she'd washed ashore. She'd spent a desperate hour in the dark searching for the professor, hoping he'd been carried in on the same current. But there was no trace of him. She'd lost the one person on earth who could help her, the one person she could depend on. No matter how unlikely, the professor had become her partner. Now she was on her own again.

Kira was furious with herself for her clumsy attempt on the shed early that morning. She should have known that the thermite had been degraded by age and by the salt water. She realized that she might as well have left a fingerprint. But she was desperate for weapons, something to even the odds—something beyond the meager supplies in her backpack. She'd hoped that she'd retreated far enough to avoid the dragnet. But she now realized that they were looking everywhere.

As the roar of the ATVs faded into the distance, Kira shrugged off the camo net and stuffed it into the backpack. She needed to move, improvise another plan, accomplish the mission, no matter what. The mission was everything. She stood up, legs aching, and started to head back in the direction of the school.

She'd gone just a few yards when a single ATV crested the hill in front of her.

The rider was slender, with black hair and a bruised face.

Irina.

Kira gasped. She felt bile rise in her throat. She froze in place, but she was no longer camouflaged. She was trapped in plain sight.

Irina froze, too, but only for a second. Then her mouth curled into a strange smile. She revved her engine.

Kira made a dash across the trail for the cliff, about twenty yards away. She saw Irina begin to roll down the hill on her ATV. She was in no rush. She was enjoying this.

The cliff face was nearly vertical, but it was laced with

narrow cracks. Kira reached into her backpack and pulled out a handful of steel climbing pegs. She jammed them into small cracks and began to pull herself up the rocks. She looked back as Irina rolled to a stop at the base of the cliff. As Kira found another handhold, an incendiary bullet spattered flames and stone fragments inches from her head. She swung herself around a ledge and nearly lost her grip. Another shot exploded just below her feet. Kira knew that Irina was an expert sniper. She wasn't going for a kill shot. She was just playing with her. For now.

Thirty feet up, Kira plunged her hand into her backpack again and pulled out a large button. She slammed it against the rock face. In a second, she was enveloped in a thick gray cloud. For the moment, she was invisible again. She ducked behind a protruding section of rock and hung there motionless. When the cloud cleared, she looked down. Her heart was pounding.

Irina was nowhere in sight.

CHAPTER 89

The Bering Sea

THE SUB WAS resting on a ledge forty meters down. I heard the engine sputter and die. The water in the cabin was up to my chest. The pump was no match for the surge. The electronics under the console crackled and sparked like underwater fireworks. I was about to be drowned or electrocuted, maybe both.

My heart was thumping and my mind was racing. I flailed around and grabbed the wheel on the inside of the hatch lid. I turned it to the left as hard as I could. I managed to loosen it, but I couldn't push the hatch open. The water pressure from above was too much. I heard more rivets popping. It was like the entire Bering Sea was out to crush me. My lungs burned. I was floating inside the cabin now, kicking off the back of the seat to keep my head above water. The water bubbled up to fill the last air pocket. This was it. I tilted my chin back and took one final gulp of air.

As my head went under, I heard a series of muffled beeps, about one second apart. Like a countdown. My only thought was that the sub had been programmed to self-destruct.

Which meant I was about to be blown to pieces. I closed my eyes tight and waited for the blast. I wondered if I'd feel it, or if it would just be over. In that moment, I wasn't afraid anymore, just frustrated and mad. I let out one last scream as I went under.

Suddenly, the hatch blew off. The impact rocked me back against the inside of the hull. In less than a second, the pressure equalized. There was a hole above me—and open water. I grabbed my backpack, pushed myself through the hatch, and started kicking toward daylight.

CHAPTER 90

Eastern Russia

EXHAUSTED, KIRA PULLED herself over the top of the cliff. She lay flat on the rock ledge, breathing hard. When she turned her head, she was staring across a narrow plateau covered with dirt and grassy stubble. The tree line was about twenty yards away. That was the cover she needed. She got to her knees and steadied herself.

Suddenly, a violent kick to the ribs knocked her backward, almost over the edge.

"Welcome home, Meed," said Irina.

Kira looked up. This close, Irina's face showed the years. But the voice was the same—and it took Kira back. For a second, she flashed back to that bedroom fifteen years ago. The terror in her parents' eyes. The blood on the bedsheets.

"This is not home," she said.

Kira got back onto her knees and took another kick, this one to the head. As she went down again, her backpack slipped off her shoulder onto the dirt. She reached for it, fingers stretched out. Irina booted the bag off the cliff.

"No toys," said Irina. "Just us." She bent down and lifted

Kira's head roughly by the hair. Kira spit a string of saliva and blood and wrenched herself free. She rolled hard to the left and struggled to her feet.

Irina was circling, knees bent, arms flexed and ready. Kira aimed a kick at her knee and heard cartilage pop. Irina didn't even react. She stepped forward and swung her leg at Kira's midsection. It connected—hard. Kira crumpled as the breath was knocked out of her. She raised her arms to block the next blow, but Irina blasted through her defense, throwing her onto her back. In a blink, she had her hands around Kira's throat.

With her last surge of strength, Kira hooked her leg under Irina's left knee. Irina grunted as Kira flipped her and pinned her wrists to the ground. As Irina struggled to lift her head, her eyes shifted. Kira turned and saw a tall boy in tac gear emerging from the edge of the tree line. His right arm was raised in a throwing position, a knife in his hand.

Kira waited for his release, then rolled hard to the side, carrying Irina along with her. The knife buried itself in Irina's thigh. Irina's lips tightened, but she didn't make a sound. She pulled the blade out and slashed it toward Kira's throat. Kira knocked it away. They rolled again. With a powerful shove, Irina pushed herself loose. Her momentum carried her over the edge of the cliff. At the last second, she grabbed tight onto Kira's wrists, dragging her across the rocky ledge.

Kira lay flat and dug her shoes into the dirt, but Irina's weight pulled her forward, until they were face to face, with Irina dangling in the air. Irina's sleeve was ripped open, exposing her angry scar. She stared up at Kira, eyes bright with fury.

"Your parents were weak," said Irina, spitting out the words. "And the weak need to be weeded out."

Kira felt her arms and back straining from Irina's weight.

"Their blood is my blood," said Kira. "Does that make me weak, too?"

Irina glanced down the cliff at the boulders below. She looked at Kira.

"Not weak," said Irina. "Just needy. We could be stronger as a team, Meed. We could be unbeatable."

"Sorry," said Kira. "I have only myself, remember?"

She wrenched her wrists free and let Irina drop.

Kira rolled onto her back, gasping. In an instant, she saw the glint of a knife swinging down toward her chest.

CHAPTER 91

THE BOY SMILED as he went for the kill.

Kira batted the knife away with one arm and brought her knee up hard against his temple. The kid dropped onto his side, stunned and groaning. Kira picked up the knife and wiped Irina's blood off it. She took a step toward the boy and instinctively visualized his carotid artery. One quick stroke was all it would take. He looked about sixteen. She hesitated, then slipped the knife into her belt and headed for the woods. The trail she'd taken from the school last night would be too dangerous now. She'd have to make her way back cross-country. As soon as she moved through the tree line, the forest closed in around her. The tall firs formed a canopy. White birches shot up everywhere in vertical stripes, and the undergrowth was daunting. After just a few hundred yards, Kira's hands were scraped and bloodied from pushing through the tangled brush. As she tugged aside another prickly branch, she froze. Then she tilted her head slightly and listened. She was not alone.

A twig cracked in the distance, then another. Fifty yards

ahead, a line of students appeared through the trees. It was a foot patrol, moving slowly and deliberately. Younger students, Kira figured. Not yet worthy of ATVs. The automatic rifles looked incongruous against their narrow shoulders. But she had no doubt that they were deadly shooters. That skill was taught early.

Kira was in a thicket of birches. She realized that her black outfit was a poor disguise against the white trunks. She kicked herself mentally for not putting her camo net in her pocket, instead of in her backpack, which was lying somewhere at the bottom of the cliff. She ducked down as the patrol moved toward her. Suddenly, she heard footsteps coming from the opposite direction. Then, a shout.

"She's here! I saw her!"

It was a boy's voice, calling out from a few yards behind her. Kira pressed her face into the brush, thorns stabbing her cheek.

"*Evanoff??*" A voice called back from the approaching patrol. "Where the hell have you been?"

Kira heard steps behind her, coming closer. Her hand tightened around the handle of the knife. The boy passed within ten feet of her as he hurried to reunite with his squad. It was the boy from the cliff. Kira gritted her teeth. This is what I get for showing mercy, she thought.

Kira held still as the boy joined the other students. She could hear their voices, but the sentences weren't clear. The boy pointed in the direction he came from, then turned to lead the way back. The entire squad moved with fresh intensity, spreading out in formation, with students a few yards apart.

Kira rolled slowly to the side, trying to stay low. Her hip

bumped the trunk of a thick birch. She crouched behind it, searching for a path out. In every direction, she saw ground cover that would rustle and crack if she made a run for it. The patrol was getting closer.

She reached slowly into a pile of deadfall and picked up a thick branch about two feet long. She pressed herself against the backside of the birch then swung her arm in a high arc and let the branch fly. It sailed end over end and landed in the brush with a loud crunch about twenty yards away.

"Target left!" a voice called out sharply. She heard steps moving quickly in that direction. Kira grabbed the birch trunk with both hands, braced her feet against it and climbed. Fifteen feet up, she reached a section where the white bark was mottled with gray. It was the best she could do. She rested one toe on a knotty stub, hugged the trunk, and held on tight.

A half minute later, the near wing of the squad swept by underneath her. Kira's foot was starting to slip off the tiny protrusion. The coarse bark was scraping the inside of her wrists. She adjusted her grip and tried to ignore the fire in her biceps and thighs.

Through the light scrim of birch leaves, Kira watched the patrol moving off in the direction of the cliff. When the last figure disappeared, she began to ease herself down the birch, a few inches at a time. Suddenly, she felt herself slipping down the slick bark. She scraped her left shoe wildly against the trunk, feeling for a new foothold. Her toe hit a slick patch of moss. Her weight shifted, too far to recover. She clawed at the tree with both hands, but too late.

She landed hard. Her right shoulder separated with a loud pop and she felt a blinding stab of agony—even more painful than she remembered. She jammed her mouth into the crook of her elbow and bit down on the fabric of her sleeve. She did not scream. After the initial shock passed through her, the pain came in nauseating waves. Kira folded her bad arm across her chest and rose to her knees. Then she stood up. Each shift brought a fresh blast of agony.

She staggered over to a twin birch, with two trunks that split about four feet off the ground. She slid her wrist into the V and made a fist to wedge it tight. She rotated her torso to face the tree. She took a deep breath and jerked her body backward with all her strength. She heard the snap of the ball popping back into the socket. She saw bright sparks. She fell to her knees again and pulled her hand out of the wedge. Tears of pain streamed down her cheeks. Her body was telling her to stay still and conserve her energy. But she wouldn't listen.

As soon as the flashes in her eyes eased, Kira backed away from the thicket, found a small gap in the underbrush, and headed west.

CHAPTER 92

The Bering Sea

I SWAM FOR an hour through cold, choppy water. Even while I was doing it, I couldn't believe my own strength. It was more than adrenaline. More than Kira's training. I felt like I had left my old body behind, almost like I had turned into a different species.

When my feet finally touched bottom, I was still about twenty yards off the peninsula. I could see waves curling around huge rocks at the shoreline. A steep hill rose just beyond, covered in brownish grass and stubby bushes.

I sank calf-deep into cold muck as I half-walked, half-swam toward the beach.

For the last few yards, I was tripping over jagged rocks. I fell on my face in the water and crawled the rest of the way. When I finally got to shore, I crawled behind a craggy boulder and pulled my backpack under my shoulder for a cushion against the hard rocks.

The beach was just a narrow strip. It was littered with boulders, blasted from some ancient volcano. Back in the years when I was doing my doctoral research, I would have been scouring the site for signs of life, traces of lost civilizations. Now I was looking for a school of killers. And my only advantage was that they probably thought I was dead.

I heard a roar in the distance, coming from the south end of the peninsula. At first, I thought it was a chainsaw. But it kept getting louder. Then I spotted movement. It was a pack of ATVs, moving single file in the narrow space between the hillside and the beach. Four of them.

For a second, I thought about backing out into the water and waiting until they passed by. But I was tired of running. In the past two days, I'd been firebombed, shot at, and blasted out of the sky. I'd almost drowned. Twice. But Kira had taught me to survive, no matter what. She'd given me the power to fight. I decided it was time to start using it.

I reached into my soggy backpack and pulled out a roll of wire. I unspooled a few feet of it between my hands and tugged on it. It felt as strong as piano wire, but as flexible as fishing line. The ATVs were still just specks in the distance, bouncing over rises, kicking up dust. The sound of the engines rolled up the steep hill and echoed back down.

I darted from boulder to boulder until I was at the edge of the trail. I wrapped one end of the wire around a rock the size of a dumpster. Then I made a quick dash across the trail and wrapped the other end around a thick tree stump. I lay down on my belly in the low grass and waited. The sound of the machines got louder and louder. They were moving fast, and I could hear the riders yelling back and forth above the engine noise.

I ducked low as the first ATV flew by. As it passed the stump, the wire caught the front of the chassis and the whole thing flipped end over end. The rider flew out and landed hard about fifteen yards away. The other three riders jammed on their brakes, but they couldn't stop in time. One after the other, they spun out and piled up. I heard yelps of pain and crunching metal.

I knew I had to move fast, while the riders were still in shock. I got up and made a dash for the last ATV in the pile. It was the only one still running. The kid behind the wheel had a bloody lip and his eyes were glassy. He looked startled and confused as I grabbed him.

"Who the fuck are *you*?" he mumbled.

"Nobody you know," I said.

I yanked him out of the driver's seat and hopped in.

By now the kid from the flipped ATV up front was struggling to his feet, and the other two drivers were sliding out of their seats. They both looked banged up and dazed. I put the ATV in reverse and cranked the throttle. The tires spun in the rocky sand, then bit. I shifted into low gear and did a full 360. The water was at my back. I had no idea who else might be coming down the trail. So I headed in the only direction I had left—straight up the hill.

In a few seconds, I was bouncing up the slope at a forty-five-degree angle. I heard a rattle behind me. I turned and saw a rifle fly off a rack on the ATV and slide down the hill. No way I could stop to pick it up. If I lost my momentum, I'd stall or flip over backward.

Suddenly, a bullet ricocheted off my front fender. The kids below had recovered enough to shoot. I ducked forward to make myself a smaller target. I hit a patch of loose rock. My rear tires started to spin. I cranked the wheel left and picked up traction again on the grass.

Another shot blasted into the metal frame. I felt hot

fragments dig into my leg. The engine was whining and smoke was pouring out from underneath. The summit was just a few yards farther. But now the slope was even steeper. I gave the machine more gas.

Another shot grazed my roll bar just as I flew over the top of the hill. I landed hard on the other side, and started swerving down the slope, weaving through bushes and boulders.

I'd never driven an ATV before in my life. Turns out, I was damned good at it.

CHAPTER 93

KIRA DIPPED HER face into the clear mountain stream and wiped the sweat from her face and neck. She held her bad arm across her torso. The pain radiated from her shoulder to her collarbone and across her ribs. The fingers on her right hand were tingling, mostly numb.

She lifted her head, took a few deep breaths, and then bent down again to take a few short sips of the cold water. She sat back on the bank and looked around. The setting felt strangely familiar. The bend of the stream. The angle of the hill. Then it came to her. She realized that she'd crossed this stream before, close to the same spot, fifteen years ago, heading in the other direction.

She closed her eyes and thought back to that desperate morning. Her plan had been simple. Find the shore. Then find a port. Then find a ship. The destination didn't matter. All she wanted was to forget everything she'd seen, and everything she'd learned, everything she'd turned into. It took her more than a decade to realize that she *couldn't* forget, couldn't leave the past alone. She had to go back. The evil had to be stopped at its source. Even if she had to do it by herself.

Now that she'd figured out exactly where she was, the rest of the route unfolded in her head, as clear as a line on a GPS screen. She wiped the water off her face and waded through the stream to the other side.

An hour later, she huddled at the edge of the tree line and looked across the grass at the main wall of the school compound. She'd scaled that same wall the night before to reach the explosives shed. But now it was broad daylight, and she had only three working limbs.

She ran to the outside of the wall and crouched against it, then started moving around the perimeter, hugging the stone as she went. She still needed weapons. And she knew one more place to find them.

Moving a few feet at a time, it took her another ten long minutes to reach the firing range. It was located at the bottom of a wide depression, about twenty feet below the level of the school buildings. The range was empty and quiet. Nobody there. Probably because by now the whole school was out looking for her.

Kira slid down the slope on her back, cradling her bad arm. She crept toward the long metal weapons bin near the firing stations. The lock was new. Electronic. Kira plucked a spent cartridge clip from the ground and pulled the spring out. She used the sharp end of the thick wire to pry off the small LED screen. She cracked the lock in seconds and flipped the metal clasp. Then she used her left arm to raise the heavy metal lid. She looked inside.

The box was empty.

Then she heard the sound of metal clicking above her. Rifle bolts.

CHAPTER 94

KIRA LOOKED UP. The rim of the hill was lined with students in tac gear. All with high-powered weapons. All aiming directly at her. Another squad was rounding a wall on her right flank.

Kira dropped the lid on the weapons box. She turned and sprinted toward the closest mound on the target range. Shots rang out as she dove behind the huge earthen barrier. Dirt splattered up beside her.

Kira could hear the squad advancing toward her from two directions. She knew the students were angling for position, looking for the honor of blowing her head off. She wondered if being hit by a bullet could be any worse than the pain in her shoulder.

Suddenly, there was a crackle from the PA speakers mounted on poles overhead. A voice boomed out.

"All students! Weapons down! I repeat, weapons down!"

Kira hadn't heard that voice in a very long time. Her whole body tightened at the sound. Kamenev! She squeezed her eyes shut and clenched her fists. Her mind flashed again to the bodies of her parents in their bloody bed, and pure fury swelled inside her.

"The target is isolated!" the headmaster called out, his voice echoing across the range. "Your new assignment is to take her alive!"

Kira took a quick look around the side of the dirt mound. The students had lowered their rifles and pulled out their truncheons. They were advancing like machines, smiling as they came.

Kira braced herself against the back of the dirt pile, then made a run for the next mound, about ten yards away. Then the next. Her chest was heaving. Her arm was throbbing. She thought maybe—*maybe*—she could reach the trees beyond the perimeter. She had to try. As she ran, she spotted a horizontal ridge about twenty yards in front of her. Kira thought she knew every inch of the grounds. But this was new.

As she ran, the ridge seemed to get longer and higher. When she reached it, she stopped short and gasped. The ridge was the top edge of a deep ditch, filled with broken glass, rusted metal, and coils of razor wire. Too wide to jump and impossible to crawl across.

Kira looked back. The students were closing in from two sides. A slow, deliberate pincer action. She realized that she was out of time and out of tricks. She had tried and failed.

She had only herself. And that was not enough.

CHAPTER 95

THE STUDENTS MOVED slowly toward her, scores of them now.

Kira looked down into the ditch and thought about diving in. With luck, a sharp scrap of metal would slice an artery and she'd bleed out before they could get to her. At least she'd be spared whatever Kamenev had in mind. He'd have to make an example of her—the school's one and only dropout. Even if he didn't kill her right away, he'd make sure that she never escaped again. One way or another, Kira knew, she was going to die at this school.

The speakers were silent now, except for a low crackle of static. But there was a quiet buzz from somewhere in the distance—getting louder by the second.

Kira looked to her right. Her line of sight was blocked by a huge target mound, tall enough to absorb a grenade blast. Suddenly an ATV vaulted over the mound, twenty feet in the air. It looked like a giant insect. The roar was deafening now.

The machine landed hard on the packed dirt. The driver

bounced in the seat, then stood up as he cranked the wheel, kicking up a cloud of dust, riding the machine like a bronco.

Impossible! Kira couldn't believe what she was seeing. *Who* she was seeing. The professor's shirt was ripped open to his waist and his pants were torn. He vaulted out of the ATV and pushed Kira behind him, placing his body between her and the menacing crowd. For a second, she couldn't move, couldn't speak. Then she threw her good arm around his chest and leaned into his ear.

"You're *alive*??" she said. "I thought . . ."

"I know," the professor replied. "Me, too."

All around them, the students were massing for the final push, pounding their truncheons against their palms in unison. And smiling. Always smiling.

"Why aren't they shooting?" asked the professor.

"They want me alive."

"No problem. So do I."

In another second, the first wave of students was on them. Doctor Savage took them as they came, tossing them aside in bunches, blocking punches and the blows from the long, black clubs. Kira stood back-to-back with the professor. She still had two good legs. Her roundhouse kicks connected time after time, slamming students to the ground.

But they kept coming. They just wouldn't stop. A truncheon came down hard on Kira's bad shoulder. She grimaced in pain as she kicked the attacker away. They were surrounded now, about to be overrun and pounded into the ground.

Doctor Savage grabbed the ATV by the upper frame and lifted it into the air. He threw it into the next assault wave, knocking a dozen students onto their backs.

Kira had her knife out. She slashed the air, daring the closest attackers to move in again. She knew that she was just delaying the inevitable, but she wasn't about to go down without a fight. And at least she wouldn't go down alone.

Suddenly, the air was filled with a tremendous vibration and a stinging blast of wind-blown dirt. The students were blown back, blinded by the swirling cloud. The professor turned toward Kira and pushed her to the ground. Her shoulder bent the wrong way. She grimaced in pain and nearly passed out. What happened next felt like a dream. She felt a strange calm come over her. The deafening noise became a gentle hum. The professor's arms were wrapped around her. She realized that she had never felt safer.

Kira lifted her head and looked into the sky. Directly above, two massive Black Hawk helicopters were blocking the sun. Black-clad men with rifles were dropping out of the doors on ropes. When they hit the ground, they formed a solid cordon around Kira and the professor.

"Face down! Arms out!" a tall officer shouted toward the mass of students. Other commandos spread out through the crowd, kicking weapons away. The officer bent down until his helmet touched the professor's head. Kira could read the insignia on the officer's chest: INTERPOL.

"Sir!" he shouted. "Are you the one who called?"

Kira looked at the professor, stunned.

"Called??" she said. "Called from *where*?"

Doc Savage looked stunned, too. The submarine radio hadn't been useless after all.

"Holy shit," he said. "Somebody actually *heard* me!"

CHAPTER 96

THE HEADMASTER'S DEMEANOR was calm, but his mood was dark. He was angry and disappointed. He had thought that this day would never come. In fact, he had taken extensive steps to prevent it. He believed he had placed people and money where it mattered, but somewhere there was a gap in his coverage, or a failure of loyalty. The defect needed to be corrected. But now he had more urgent things to take care of. Starting with his own survival.

From the window in his office, he could see the helicopters hovering over the firing range. Black-clad commandos were already moving across the main compound.

Kamenev walked to his massive safe and dialed the combination. He pulled the heavy door open and pulled out a thick leather binder, worn with age. It was the school's sacred text. The fundamental principles. The original Doc Savage training methods.

The data and techniques had never been copied or transferred to digital form. Kamenev was too smart for that. Everything was either in the book or in his head. That was all he needed to start over—that and the billions resting in anonymous accounts across the globe.

The headmaster closed the door to his office and walked briskly down the back staircase to the first floor. The whole building was in chaos. Young students and their instructors crowded around windows as another Black Hawk roared overhead at rooftop level. Kamenev ignored it all. This establishment was no longer his concern.

When he reached a room off the middle of the hall, he opened the door and locked it behind him. He drew a shade down over the window in the door. He was standing in a small, utilitarian room with a linoleum floor and bare walls. A worn upright piano sat against one wall. Kamenev opened the piano lid and pressed a lever inside. He stood back. The left side of the piano swung forward two feet, revealing a hatch set neatly into the wall behind it.

Kamenev angled himself behind the piano and pushed the hatch open. Behind it was an opening just wide enough for a grown man. Kamenev dropped to his knees and backed through. His feet found the steps of the staircase inside. He pressed a lever and leaned back as the hatch slid closed. Then he waited for the sound of the piano settling back into place against the wall. He looked down. A row of small amber bulbs lit a winding staircase leading down into a chamber carved out of solid rock.

When he reached the bottom, Kamenev headed down a narrow stone corridor. He was now two stories below the building. In his practice runs, he had never gone beyond the top of the stairs. Waste of time, he'd thought. Now he regretted being so cavalier.

He remembered from the plans that the main corridor

branched off into a maze of passageways, leading to various storerooms and exits. But he couldn't recall which was which. He moved quickly down the main route until he reached an intersection, with tunnels leading off in three directions. Kamenev hesitated. He turned left, then right. Then he froze. There was somebody behind him.

"Looking for a way out, Headmaster?"

CHAPTER 97

KIRA STEPPED OUT of the shadows and into the dim glow of an overhead light. She could tell that Kamenev was rattled, but he was doing his best to maintain his command presence.

"You're trying hard not to act surprised," she said.

"Meed," said Kamenev, his voice low and calm. "Our master of escapes."

"Meed is not my name," Kira said softly. "But you always knew that."

"It suited you," said Kamenev. He angled his head to get a better look at her. "It still does."

"Do you remember the last time you saw me?" asked Kira.

Kamenev looked past her, down the corridor. Kira shifted her head to block his view.

"There's nobody coming. It's just us," she said, taking a step toward him. "I asked you a question."

Kamenev took one step back, his hand clasped tight around the binder. "Of course," he said. "It was . . ."

"Let me help you," said Kira. "It was fifteen years ago. The day you assigned my final test. *Our* final test. Me and Irina."

Kamenev stiffened his spine and looked Kira straight in the eye.

"It was a necessary mission," he said.

Kira's throat tightened. Her fists clenched at her sides. She wanted nothing more than to choke the life out of this man. But first she needed some answers.

"Why?" she asked. "Why them?"

Kamenev took another step back. The stone wall stopped him. Kira saw his expression curl into a bitter sneer. His old arrogance resurfaced.

"Because my brother was weak," he said.

"Your brother?" asked Kira. "What does your brother...?"

"My brother," said Kamenev firmly. "Your father."

Kira felt the breath go out of her. She struggled to maintain her composure, but she couldn't hide her shock from Kamenev. He knew her too well.

"All your research didn't turn up that fact, did it?" said Kamenev. "From early on, your father and I took very different paths. He was a pacifist. A dreamer. Same with your mother. No concept of how the world really works. When I left and changed my name, I was erased from the family history. I had to make my own way—just like you."

Kira shook her head. Her research had been painstaking. Impeccable. No way she could have missed this.

"My father didn't have a brother," said Kira.

"May 1st, 1955," said Kamenev.

Kira blinked. She recognized the date.

"Our birthday," said Kamenev. "Your father's and mine."

Kira's head was spinning.

"Don't look so shocked," Kamenev went on. "Twins run in the family. But you know that."

The last sentence hit Kira like a club. She blinked and rocked back. Her mind flashed to a small room with a tiny crib, in a time before her conscious memory. But there was something she felt clearly, as if it was happening to her right now. It was the sense that she had her arms wrapped around another body, breaths and heartbeats in perfect sync, like two halves of a whole.

Then the other heartbeat stopped.

Kira felt the blood drain from her cheeks. And in that instant, she knew who she had been missing for her whole life. Kamenev could read it on her face.

"You were better off without her," he said. "*Tantum est fortis superesse*. Only the strong survive."

CHAPTER 98

KIRA LUNGED AND grabbed Kamenev's jacket with both hands. She winced as the pain from her right shoulder shot down her arm. Kamenev twisted away and turned toward the wall. Kira saw his hand go to his chest. The binder fell to the floor. When he turned back, she saw a flash of metal in his hand. Kamenev fired as he turned, without aiming. The blast echoed through the corridor as the bullet struck the stone arch behind Kira's head. And now, the gun was in her face.

"You froze," said Kamenev. "That night. You couldn't do it. That's what Irina reported. You can imagine how disappointed I was. I thought we'd trained you better than that."

Kamenev brought his fist down hard on Kira's right shoulder. She grimaced in agony and fell to her knees.

"I can sense your weak spots, Meed," said Kamenev. "I have a gift for it."

Kira felt the cold barrel of the gun pressing through her curls onto the crown of her head. She closed her eyes. Then she drew a deep breath and let it out. She had one more question to ask before she died.

"Tell me," she said numbly. "Did you kill her? Was it you? Did you kill my sister?"

Kamenev pressed the barrel harder against her skull.

His voice was almost soothing. "Let's just call it natural selection," he said.

Kira went blind with rage. She reached into her belt and brought her hand up hard. Kamenev rocked back against the wall and slid to the floor, his eyes glazed and still. Kira's knife protruded from his chest, between his third and fourth ribs. The gun dropped from his hand.

Kira knelt on the cold stone floor, breathing hard, cradling her aching arm across her torso. She stared at Kamenev's still body as blood oozed from around the edge of the knife blade. Kira knew it wasn't just his blood. It was *family* blood. The same blood that ran in her. After generations of good and evil, she was now the last of her line.

She had only herself.

Kira rose to her feet, leaned over, and picked up the tattered binder. She tucked it under her right arm. Suddenly, the tunnel was pierced by thin, distant cries. In the eerie echoes created by the tunnels, it sounded like cats howling.

Kira grabbed the pistol and gripped it in her left hand. She walked in the direction of the sound. The corridor curved for about twenty yards until it ended at a stone staircase. The sound was coming from behind a door at the top of the stairs.

Kira raised the pistol. She inched her way up the steps and eyed the door. Above the handle was a clasp sealed with a simple padlock. Kira blasted it apart with one shot. She pressed herself against the frame and pushed the door open. She stepped into the room and swept the pistol from side to side. There were no threats.

The room was huge. Maybe fifty yards long. Both sides were lined with bassinets—filled with crying babies.

CHAPTER 99

THE HEADMASTER'S BODY was lying on a plastic sheet at the edge of the schoolyard. Kira and I watched as a couple of soldiers loaded him into a body bag. She had told me about the fight in the tunnel, but I knew she wasn't telling me everything. She was quiet and numb, off in her own world.

Another Red Cross helicopter set down in the center of the compound. The first had arrived twenty minutes earlier. Medics and volunteers were already setting up white tents and tables. Nurses in blue scrubs were wheeling bassinets from the underground nursery and carrying wailing infants toward the tents.

In the past half hour, the place had turned into a refugee camp. Kira had finally gotten some medical attention, too. Her right arm was in a sling, but she'd turned down the pain meds. I'd started to ask one of the medics to check the gash in my forehead, but then I realized that it had totally healed. That brought up a question I was dying to get answered. It had been stuck in my head for a long time. Maybe it was a way to get Kira talking.

I looked over at her. "Can I ask you something?"

She nodded.

"What can I *do*?"

She stayed quiet for a moment, then looked at me with an annoyed expression. "What can you *do*?? There's *plenty* to do," she said, looking at the chaos across the compound. "For one thing, we need to figure out where all these babies belong."

She wasn't understanding my question.

"No," I said. "I mean, what can I *do*? What are my powers?"

"Your *powers*?"

"I mean, obviously, I can survive plane crashes. I can learn languages overnight, swim for miles in freezing water, repair my body, lift an ATV with my bare hands. What else??"

"This is really what's on your mind right now?" Kira asked.

"Just curious."

Kira got quiet again and looked away. She was giving me nothing. I'd obviously picked the wrong time. And the wrong topic.

"Never mind," I said. "Forget it."

She let out a slow breath and turned back toward me.

"Okay," she said, "if you really need to know, start with this: your reaction time is three times faster than normal. Your muscle strength and endurance have quadrupled. You can run a quarter mile in under forty seconds. Your vision is 20/10 in both eyes. Your skin is thicker, more resilient . . ."

"Like Superman??"

She grabbed my arm.

"Look at me," she said. "You're *not* Superman. You're just the best version of yourself. New and improved. We've maxed out your natural potential. That's what the original Doc Savage experiment was all about—seeing how far native ability could be pushed. Not by coming from another planet. Just by starting with what you already have."

"And how did you know what I already had?" I asked.

"I studied your ancestors," she said. "I knew the techniques. I *lived* the techniques. I gambled that you were a diamond in the rough. And I was right."

She went back to staring into the distance. I couldn't leave it alone.

"So could I stop a bullet with my body?" I asked.

"Don't push your luck, Doctor."

CHAPTER 100

LATER THAT MORNING, another INTERPOL chopper settled down in the main yard and a dozen more commandos poured out. Kira had wandered off. I had no idea where to. I knew I'd pissed her off with my questions about superpowers. Probably good to give her some space, I thought. As the chopper blades wound down, a new squad leader walked up to me, goggles on his face, rifle across his chest. I must have looked like somebody who knew something.

"What the hell *is* this place?" he asked.

"It's a school," I said.

The commando looked around at the crowd of kids sitting on the grass, sullen and quiet. Some of them were picking at the ground or mumbling to themselves.

"So where are the shooters?" he asked.

"You're looking at them," I said.

"Jesus!" the soldier said, lifting his goggles. "They're *kids*!"

"Do yourself a favor," I said. "Don't turn your back."

We'd already sorted through the students from the main attack force, separating them by age. The oldest were about nineteen, and some looked as young as fifteen. They were divided into groups of ten, with one or two commandos watching over each bunch. Other commandos had set up a perimeter outside the compound to snare ATV riders as they returned.

Confiscated weapons were being collected in a huge bin. Rifles and clubs were just the start. A lot of the kids had pistols strapped to their ankles or tucked into their waistbands. Some of the older kids had grenades and stun guns clipped to their belts. They all had knives up their sleeves.

As I walked across the yard looking for Kira, I spotted a slight girl with braids inching backward on the grass at the edge of her group. The next second, she jumped up and started sprinting toward the outside wall. One of the soldiers who'd been minding the group turned and started after her.

"Stay there!" I shouted. "I got her."

The girl was fast. She was almost at the wall when I caught up. When she realized she had no way out, she whipped around to face me. There was a razor blade in her hand. She held the blade across her wrist. I inched closer. Her lips curled into an eerie smile. She slid the blade across her skin, drawing blood.

"Stay back," she said.

"You must've skipped a class," I said, tracing a line up my forearm. "Vertical cuts work much better." She blinked. That's all the time I needed. I snapped my arm forward, grabbed her hand, and squeezed it until the blade dropped into the dirt. Then I scooped her up sideways with my hand wrapped tight around her waist. She started kicking and clawing like a wildcat in a trap. Then she started screaming at the top of her lungs.

"Run, you assholes!" she shouted at her schoolmates. "Fight back! They're going to kill us all!"

I'd had enough. I flipped her right side up and sat her down hard on the dirt. "Knock it off!" I yelled, right into her face. She was so stunned that she quieted down. I did, too. "Nobody's killing anybody," I said softly. "Not anymore. That's done. You're all going home."

She stared back at me, eyes blazing.

"Fuck you, Paul Bunyan!" she said. "This *is* home!"

Two soldiers ran over with a set of zip cuffs and hauled her away.

"Careful," I said. "She's stronger than she looks. And get a medic to check her wrist."

I realized I didn't have any answers for the girl. For *any* of them. They'd never known any life but this. These kids had been raised here since they were babies, the same as Kira. No wonder they were out of their minds. In the last hour, their whole world had exploded.

I saw a group of soldiers heading into the main building and jogged over to join them. The first team through the door stopped to check for booby traps. When they gave us the all clear, we moved in. As we swept through the first floor, we found young kids hiding in closets and under desks. One by one, the commandos dragged them out.

Some of the instructors and security guards tried to make a run for it, but we rounded them up pretty easily. They were all worn down and scared. From the looks on their faces, I think they all expected to be executed, too.

While the soldiers marched the students and teachers outside, I walked up a curved staircase to the second floor by myself. One of the commandos was on his way down, guiding a line of toddlers—*Sesame Street* age. Some of the kids looked terrified. Others just looked stunned.

When I got upstairs, everything was quiet. I walked down the long empty corridor. It was littered with clothes and other belongings. Some of the rooms had been barricaded with chairs and desks. When I got to the end of the hall, I stopped and looked into the last room.

And there she was.

She didn't even look up when I walked in. The room was filled with metal cots arranged in neat rows. There was a sink against one wall. Kira was staring out a window. It was blocked with heavy metal bars. As I got closer, I could see scorch marks on the sill, like old cigarette burns.

"Is this where you slept?" I asked.

"Tried to," she said softly.

She ran her fingers over the windowsill.

"This was my way out," she said. "This is where I jumped. I was eighteen."

I looked at the bars. Not even a skinny teenager could have slipped through. "How?" I asked.

"I burned through the bars and bent them," she said. "These bars are new. Stronger. They made sure nobody else escaped."

"You burned through a set of metal bars?" I asked. "With what?"

"Acid," she said.

Kira pulled up her left sleeve. I bent forward to look. The scars on her forearm matched the scorch marks on the stone. "Nothing was going to stop me," she said. "Nothing."

I could see tears brimming in her eyes. I didn't know how to react, or what to say.

All I knew was that I was sad for her. Angry for her. Angry

for *me*. After all, one of my ancestors had helped build this place. My family. My blood. In a twisted way, I felt partly responsible. I wrapped my hands tight around the bars and ripped them out of the stone one by one.

When I was done, the view was clear all the way to the mountains.

"You're okay now," I said. "It's over."

Kira stared off into the distance.

"I wish," she said softly. "I wish."

CHAPTER 101

THAT AFTERNOON, I asked the commando in charge to gather all the kids together in the gym. It was bigger than any class I'd ever taught. I stood in front of a massive wooden table and looked out over the crowd. Some of the students looked back at me with cold, dull eyes. But most of them just stared at the floor.

The older kids were in orange jumpsuits and cuffs. A lot of them were still bandaged up from the battle. The younger students were in oversized Red Cross T-shirts, like kids at a sleepaway camp.

A sturdy sergeant stood at my right side, legs apart, rifle at the ready. My personal bodyguard. Kira was standing on the other side. She'd found a microphone and connected it to the gym's PA system. When I brought the mic up to my face, there was a short whistle of feedback. The noise got everybody's attention.

"I want to read you all something," I said. My voice boomed across the gym, loud and clear.

It was a tough audience. Zero interest. Zero expression.

Even the creepy smiles were gone. I unfolded the sheet of paper I'd torn out of my great-grandfather's journal back in the Fortress. I cleared my throat.

"An ancestor of mine wrote this a long time ago," I said. "It was hidden away for almost a hundred years. But I believe somehow he meant for me to find it. It's something I think you should hear. Maybe these words will help you as you move on and start over. Believe me, there is a better world than this place. There is a better life than the one you've all been living."

I realized that my hands were shaking a bit. I looked over at Kira. She gave me a little nod. I started reading what my great-grandfather had written to inspire himself. Doc Savage's personal code.

Let me strive, every moment of my life, to make myself better and better, to the best of my ability, so that all may profit by it. Let me think of the right, and lend all my assistance to those who need it, with no regard for anything but justice. Let me take what comes with a smile, without loss of courage. Let me be considerate of my country, of my fellow citizens and my associates in everything I say and do. Let me do right to all, and wrong to no man.

When I finished, the room was silent, except for some awkward coughs. I held the paper over my head. Like Moses with the Ten Commandments.

"Bullshit!" a female voice called out.

I heard a loud crack. A bullet punched a hole in the paper.

Everybody in the audience ducked or scattered, except for one person. A woman in an orange jumpsuit stepped forward from the middle of the crowd. Her dark hair was matted, and her face was swollen on one side. She had a pistol—and it was pointed at Kira.

"My God," Kira gasped. "Irina!"

"Did you think I'd go that easily, Meed?" Irina shouted. "Do you think you're the only one who knows how to survive?? How to come back??"

The sergeant had his rifle up.

"Drop the weapon!" he shouted.

Irina flicked her aim left and shot him through the forehead. He spun backward and landed with a heavy thud, his rifle underneath him. I crouched down, my heart racing. I felt Kira beside me. Irina stepped forward, picking her way through the students hugging the floor. She fired again. The bullet splintered the desk leg right over Kira's head. There was nowhere to go, no way to move.

I glanced to my left. I saw the butt of a Glock in the dead soldier's holster. I reached out and grabbed it. With my other hand, I shoved Kira down behind me. I heard another crack and felt the impact—like I'd been punched in the chest by a prizefighter. I whipped the gun up and squeezed the trigger. Irina flew backward and landed hard on the wood floor. There was a neat purple hole in her chest.

A squad of commandos burst in from outside, rifles raised. Two of them rushed forward to the dead sergeant. One of them stopped and checked for Irina's pulse. I knew he wouldn't find one. He looked up at me and saw the pistol.

"Dead, sir," he said. "Perfect shot."

I dropped the gun onto the floor. I winced and put a hand over my sore chest. Kira reached over and yanked my shirt open. I looked down. There was a circular red welt above my left pec, with a flattened piece of metal in the center. I pried the bullet out of my skin and dropped it onto the floor. Kira didn't say anything. She just held my arm and stared at me. I pushed her away and stood up. I walked past Irina's body and headed for the door.

The crowd parted like the Red Sea.

CHAPTER 102

I SHOVED THE door open and walked outside, past the huge Black Hawks and all the men with guns. I felt sick. I felt angry. I felt relieved. I felt guilty. What the hell are you supposed to feel when you end somebody's life—even if it's somebody who was trying to end yours?

I walked across the yard to the stone wall that surrounded the compound. I stretched out and leaned both arms against it. I felt burning in my chest, but it wasn't from the bullet. It was from somewhere a lot deeper. I squeezed my eyes shut and felt tears streaming out. Then I felt a hand on my shoulder.

"Thank you," said Kira.

I felt sick to my stomach. I pushed off the wall and turned on her.

"*Thanks??*" I said. "I don't want to be thanked. Do you want me to be proud of that??"

"I'm not asking you to be proud," said Kira. "Would you rather see *me* dead? And you? Because that was the choice. Her or us."

She was right. But it didn't help. I still felt sick and twisted inside.

"I just made a big, noble speech about being human," I said. "Now I'm a killer. And a good one. That's what you made me."

Kira cocked her head. She wasn't joining my pity party. Something about seeing me breaking down made her toughen up. She was right in my face.

"So maybe I should have left you alone," she said. "All by yourself in your one-bedroom apartment with your books and your research papers and your microwave dinners. Maybe I should have let you be nervous and afraid for the rest of your life. Would that have been better for you?"

I looked right at her.

"Everything I've learned over the last six months," I said, "it was for you, not for me."

She knew it was true. I was a tool for saving her life. And I'd done my job. She'd been raised to be a killer, and she'd turned me into one. A miserable piece of role switching. She turned and walked away. But I wasn't done.

"You missed your calling, Kira," I called after her. "You should have been a teacher."

CHAPTER 103

KIRA SAT AT a long folding table in the Red Cross tent, making the last of her hundred calls for the day. She rubbed her right shoulder. The sling was gone. The pain was not.

After a week of DNA matching and searching missing-children files from all over the world, they'd made progress. The younger children were being sent home to their families or to temporary foster care, the older kids to deprogramming centers. The teachers and security guards had been processed, too. A high percentage had outstanding international warrants, some decades old. A team had been flown in from The Hague to deal with the extradition paperwork.

There were still hundreds of connections to be made, especially for the babies. One whole tent had been set up as a temporary nursery, with the military nurses in charge. From where she sat, Kira could hear squeals and cries all day long.

Something else had changed, too. As she looked out across the compound, Kira saw that the whole dynamic of power in the operation had shifted. Now it was Doctor Savage who was in control. She watched him striding back and forth across the compound like a giant, looming over volunteers, medical staff, and military alike. As he ushered groups of kids onto helicopters, commandos and pilots responded crisply to his orders. Some had even started saluting him.

Kira knew that the only person he wasn't talking to was her. They hadn't exchanged a single word since the day he'd taken a bullet for her. She still wondered if he'd regretted doing it.

One of the newly arrived military staffers dropped a new stack of papers onto Kira's table. He looked out at the powerfully built man in the torn shirt—the one ordering everybody around like a general. He looked bigger than life. Superhuman.

"Who the hell is *that*?" the staffer asked. "Is he from Delta Force?"

"Actually," said Kira, "he's a college professor."

The tent flaps billowed as another loaded chopper lifted off. A minute later, a new Black Hawk settled down in its place. The side door slid open.

Kira saw the professor duck under the spinning blades and yell something up to the pilot. He put one foot on the skid. It looked like his ride had arrived. He paused for a second and looked toward the open tent. It wasn't exactly an invitation, but Kira figured it was the closest she was going to get. Her last chance to say good-bye.

She stood up and walked outside. The chopper was idling now, the propeller in slow rotation, beating a rhythmic pulse. It was still enough to blow back her copper curls as she walked up. Doctor Savage had one hand on the grip inside the chopper door.

"No luggage?" asked Kira.

The professor looked up into the hold of the helicopter, then back at her.

"All I brought was a backpack," he said. "You keep it."

Kira nodded toward the chopper. "This is it?" she said. "You're leaving?"

"You've got all the help you need here," he said. "I'm going home. I'm done. I've got classes to teach."

Kira fought the urge to step closer. *Let it go,* she thought. *Let him go.*

"Okay then," she said. "So long, Doctor."

The professor hesitated, then took his foot off the skid. He took a few steps toward her. "You're allowed to call me Brandt, you know. That's my name."

Kira shook her head. "Nope. Sorry. You never seemed like a Brandt to me."

A commando hustled over and slapped the professor on the shoulder. The chopper engine kicked into gear. "Let's go, Doc!" he said.

Kira smiled. "Doc." That sounded about right.

CHAPTER 104

Gaborone, Botswana

JAMELLE MAINA WAS on her forty-first circuit around the quarter-mile track. Her only competition was a pair of middle-aged joggers. She had lapped them several times.

Jamelle knew that if she ran long enough and hard enough, she could sometimes press the image of her missing daughter to the back of her mind. Otherwise, that was pretty much all she thought about. She slowed for a cool-down lap—as if it was possible to cool down in 91-degree heat.

Jamelle felt the vibration of the phone ringing in her arm strap. She mopped her forehead and put the phone to her ear. The voice on the other end was thin and scratchy. A bad connection. Jamelle could only pick up scraps of what was being said. "Report...match...international..." Her pulse rate was at 150 BPM from the workout. Now it shot up even higher.

"What?? Hello??" Jamelle screamed into the phone.

She spun around on the track, straining for better reception. "What did you say??" It wasn't the PI calling. She hadn't heard from him in months. Besides, this was a woman's voice.

She jogged to the edge of the track and jumped onto a

bench, as if the two feet of elevation would help. Amazingly, it did. The caller's voice was still distant, but a bit clearer.

"Is this Jamelle Maina?" the woman asked.

"Yes!" Jamelle shouted into the phone. "Who are you? What do you *want*??"

"My name is Kira," the voice said. "I have some very good news."

CHAPTER 105

Eastern Russia

THE OPEN AREA of the compound was empty now. The relief organizations had finished their work. The huge tents were folded in neat piles on the grass. The students were gone. After intensive interrogations, some of the teachers and staff had been released to restart their lives; others were in custody, awaiting trial on outstanding charges from human trafficking to manslaughter.

Kira was standing next to the INTERPOL commander at the far end of the compound. As they looked toward the complex of buildings, a small squad of commandos ran toward them from that direction.

The squad leader stopped directly in front of the commander.

"Charges set, sir," he reported crisply.

"Copy that," the commander replied.

The commander turned to Kira and handed her a device that looked like a heavy-duty flip phone. "Whenever you're ready, Ms. Sunlight, just press Send."

Kira took a deep breath. She stared at the buildings at the

other side of the huge yard. Administration building. Gym. Classrooms. Eighteen years of her life. And almost a hundred years of pain for the world. Enough.

"Fire in the hole!" the squad leader called out.

Kira placed her thumb lightly on the Send button. She closed her eyes. A Rachmaninoff piano concerto swirled in her head. She pressed down hard.

A series of muffled bangs echoed across the compound. Puffs of white smoke burst from the pillars and windows. One by one, the buildings imploded, walls collapsing inward and downward.

Within seconds, all that remained of the school was metal, stone, and dust.

CHAPTER 106

Sir Seretse Khama International Airport, Botswana

JAMELLE STOOD NEAR the arrival area, bouncing nervously on the balls of her feet. As passengers from Flight 3043 started to emerge, her heart started to pound even harder. Her eyes were wide and her breath came in shallow bursts. She tilted her head back and forth, trying to peer around the passengers as they surged forward to greet friends, relatives, and drivers.

The last traveler to emerge was a tall woman with copper-colored curls. She looked exactly like the picture she'd sent. Her arms were cradled across her chest. She held a small bundle in a baby blanket.

Jamelle ran past the barrier, laughing and crying at the same time, jostling other passengers as she went. When she got closer, she locked eyes with the woman.

"Kira??" she asked. As if there were any doubt.

"Jamelle," said Kira, "it's so good to meet you."

Kira bent forward and slipped the sleeping baby into her mother's arms. Jamelle looked down at her beautiful daughter, then back up at Kira. Tears streamed down her face. Her throat was so tight that she could no longer form words, but Kira understood.

Kira brushed her hand over the baby's plump cheek one last time.

"Keep her safe," she said. "Raise her well."

CHAPTER 107

Chicago
One Year Later

DONE.

It was a relief to have the first class of the semester behind me. It felt good to shake the cobwebs off my delivery and get back into the rhythm of a lecture. I'd stayed a few minutes after class to answer the usual assortment of inane student questions. *"Will this material be on the final?" "Will you be posting your lecture notes?" "Is class attendance required for a grade?"* Christ. Some things never change.

As the lecture hall cleared out, I gathered my notebooks and laptop and tossed my water bottle into the recycling bin. At the last minute, I grabbed the eraser and wiped my name off the whiteboard. Clean slate for the next instructor using the room.

Behind me, a few rows back, I could hear two girls whispering as they headed for their next class. Before my transformation, their conversation would have just blended into the general buzz of the room. Now I could make out every word. My hearing was as sharp as my eyesight. Sometimes it could be a distraction.

"Think this class will be tough?" the first girl asked.

"Who cares?" her friend said, low and confidential. "The professor is really *hot!*"

I felt an odd flush and a flutter in my stomach, and it wasn't from the backhanded compliment. It was something else. I put down the eraser and turned around. The room was empty now, but there was a figure silhouetted in the doorway. I caught a flash of color—and a halo of curls.

Dear God. It was her.

I felt the breath go out of me. I did my best to stay aloof and professorial, even though my heart was just about thumping through my chest. I hadn't seen or heard from Kira since the day I climbed aboard that helicopter in Russia. I didn't think I'd ever see her again. I walked over.

"Am I too late to audit this class?" she asked. Still a wiseass.

I tried not to react. Tried not to reveal all the conflicting feelings running through my head. Tried to play it cool and match her flip attitude.

"Are you enrolled as an undergraduate?" I asked.

"Not really," she said. "I'm a high-school dropout."

"In that case, you're trespassing."

I'd forgotten what it was like to spar with her. I'd forgotten a lot of things. She moved into the room and leaned against the wall.

"Why are you here?" I asked.

"I'm looking to improve myself," she said. "How about you? Anything new in your life? Anybody special?"

"You mean you're not surveilling me?"

"I lost my camera."

"Well," I said, "to quote somebody I used to know—I have only myself."

She smiled. Just a little. "Coffee?" she asked.

There was no way I could say no, and she knew it.

"Okay," I said. "Let's go off campus."

"Agreed," she said. "To be honest, school gives me the creeps."

CHAPTER 108

THE CHILLY AIR hit us as we exited Cobb Hall. It was only September, but the Chicago wind was already kicking up.

We headed up East 59th. The coffee shop was a few blocks away. The sidewalk was crowded with college folk hurrying to and from campus. We weren't talking. Just walking. I didn't quite know what to say, and I don't think she did either. But it felt good just to be near her again. In the middle of the next block, I slowed down, then stopped. Kira went on for a few steps then turned around. I just stood there. I wondered if she'd remember.

"Why are we stopping?" she asked. "Don't tell me you're out of breath already."

"This is it," I said. "This is the exact spot."

"*What* exact spot?"

"The exact spot where you kidnapped me."

Kira looked around.

"Damn," she said, "you're right. I staked out this street for a solid week."

Suddenly, all the feelings from that day came rushing back.

Confusion. Terror. Panic. Along with my first impressions of Kira—her face, her hair, her voice, her power. That day was the first of many times I thought she was about to kill me. We stood there for a long, awkward moment as pedestrians moved past us.

"Are you sorry it happened?" she said finally. She was dead serious now. "Are you sorry I took you?"

I glanced over at the curb where her van had been parked. I'd asked myself the same questions for a year, every time I'd walked up this block. I'd thought about everything I'd been through, and tried like hell to get past it.

But being with her again, just *seeing* her again, made it all crystal clear. Even after having my whole world ripped apart—I realized that I would do it all again. *All* of it. I'd do it for her. And I couldn't hide it.

"No," I said. "I'm not sorry."

"Good," she replied. "Me neither."

Then she grabbed my arm, pulled me close, and kissed me on the mouth. It was like an electric shock shooting through me. For a second, I was so stunned I couldn't move. Then I wrapped my arms around her and kissed her right back. I couldn't believe it was happening.

It was a serious kiss. When it was over, she leaned her head against my chest and just held it there, syncing her breathing with mine. We stayed like that for a long time, just breathing. Then she spoke up again.

"They're still out there, you know—*thousands* of them. Everywhere."

I knew who she meant. And I knew *what* it meant. I hugged her tighter. And I realized that I didn't want to lose her again. Ever.

"Exactly how many times do I need to save your life?" I asked.

Kira took a small step back and pushed her curls away from her face.

"Probably not as many times as I'll need to save yours," she said.

Suddenly, something shifted. Her eyes widened. Her whole body tensed. She was staring past me, over my shoulder.

"Starting right now," she said.

I turned around and saw the pack heading toward us. Mid-20s. Athletic. Clean-cut. With strange, unnatural smiles.

I turned back toward Kira. I gave her a little smile of my own. We planted our feet and got ready, side by side.

Savage and Sunlight versus the world.

ABOUT THE AUTHORS

James Patterson is one of the best-known and biggest-selling writers of all time. His books have sold in excess of 400 million copies worldwide. He is the author of some of the most popular series of the past two decades – the Alex Cross, Women's Murder Club, Detective Michael Bennett and Private novels – and he has written many other number one bestsellers including stand-alone thrillers and non-fiction.

James is passionate about encouraging children to read. Inspired by his own son who was a reluctant reader, he also writes a range of books for young readers including the Middle School, Dog Diaries, Treasure Hunters and Max Einstein series. James has donated millions in grants to independent bookshops and has been the most borrowed author in UK libraries for the past thirteen years in a row. He lives in Florida with his family.

Brian Sitts is an award-winning advertising creative director and television writer. He has collaborated with James Patterson on books for adults and children. He and his wife, Jody, live in Peekskill, New York.

Discover the next psychological thriller
by James Patterson . . .

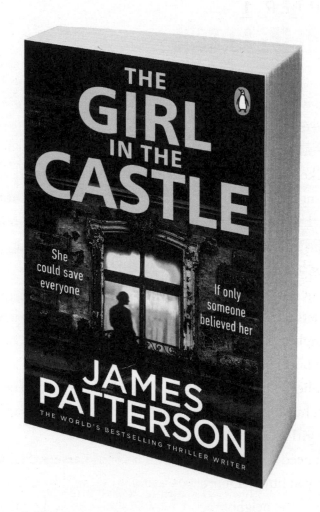

Read on for an exclusive extract

CHAPTER 1

It starts with a girl, half naked and screaming.

Even though it's midtown Manhattan, in January, the girl is wearing only a thin white T-shirt over a black lace bra. She slaps at the air like she's fighting an enemy only she can see.

A gangly teen, halfway through his first-ever shift at the Gap, watches her nervously through the window. Every other New Yorker just clutches their phone or their Starbucks cup and pretends not to see her.

Maybe they really don't.

She lets out a tortured cry that strangles in her throat, and then she crumples to her knees. "How do we get out of the castle?" she wails. "They're going to kill us all!"

A police car speeds up to the curb and two officers step out. "Are you hurt?" the first asks. DUNTHORPE, his name tag reads.

The girl's answer is more wordless screaming.

"We need you to calm down, miss," his partner, Haines, says.

"Are you hurt?" Dunthorpe asks again. He thinks he's seen this girl around the neighborhood. Maybe she's one of the shoplifters or the dopeheads—or maybe she's just some scared, crazy kid. Either way, he can't just let her stand here and scream bloody murder.

When Dunthorpe moves toward her, she drops to her hands

and knees and starts crawling away. Haines tries to grab her, but the minute he touches her back, she spins around at the same time her right foot flies out, smashing into his chest. Haines loses his balance and falls backward, cursing. The girl stands up and tries to run, but she stumbles over her backpack and goes down on all fours again.

"Help me!" she screams. "Don't let them take me! Call off the guards! They'll kill me!"

As Dunthorpe moves toward her with one hand on his Taser, she launches herself forward and hits him in the face with a closed fist. He reels backward, roaring in surprise, as Haines springs into action and gets her into a headlock.

Dunthorpe rubs his cheekbone and says, "Call the ambulance."

"But the little bitch hit you."

Dunthorpe's cheek smarts. "That'll be our secret."

"You sure you don't want to book her?" Haines's arm tightens around the girl's neck and her knees buckle. Quick as a snake, Haines gets behind her, grabs her hands, and cuffs them behind her back.

"I'm sure," Dunthorpe says.

The girl keeps quiet until the ambulance comes, and then she starts screaming again. "Don't let them take me!" she yells to the passersby as the two cops and an EMT wrestle her onto the gurney. "I have to save Mary. Oh, my sweet Mary!"

Strapped down, the girl wails over the sound of the ambulance siren.

"You can't take me! I need to save Mary! No, no, you can't take me!"

But of course, they can take her wherever they want to.

Half an hour later, the ambulance pulls up to the hospital, where a small but powerfully built nurse stands with her hands on her hips, waiting.

Arriving at the exact same time—but on foot, and voluntarily—is a handsome young man of nineteen or so. "Excuse me," he says, peering at the nurse's badge, "are you Amy Navarre? My name's Jordan Hassan, and I think I'm supposed to shadow you—"

"You'll have to wait," Nurse Amy says curtly as the ambulance doors open.

Jordan Hassan shuts his mouth quick. He takes a step to the side as the EMTs slide a metal gurney out of the back. Strapped onto it is a girl, probably right about his age, with a dirty, tear-streaked face. She's wearing a T-shirt and pair of boots but little else.

The nurse, who he's pretty sure is supposed to be his supervisor for his class-credit internship this semester, walks toward the girl. "You can take the straps away," she says to the EMT.

"I wouldn't—" he begins.

The nurse looks at the girl. "It's okay," she says.

Jordan's not sure if she's reassuring the EMT or the girl. In any case, the EMT removes the restraints, and the nurse gently helps the girl off the stretcher. Jordan watches as the girl shuffles toward the entrance.

As the doors slide open automatically, she feints left and bolts right.

She's coming straight for him.

Acting on reflex, Jordan catches her around the waist. She strains against his arms, surprisingly strong. Then she twists her head around and pleads, "Please—please—let me go! My sister needs me!"

"Keep hold of her!" Nurse Amy shouts.

Jordan has no idea what to do or who to listen to.

"I'm *begging* you," the girl says, even as Amy advances, radioing security. Even as one of the girl's sharp elbows jams into his solar plexus. Jordan gasps as air shoots out of his lungs.

"Just let me go," the girl says, quieter now. "*Please*. I need your help."

Jordan's grip loosens—he can't hold her much longer, and he doesn't want to, either. But then two uniformed men come running outside, and they grab the girl's arms and drag her into the hospital, and all the while she's fighting.

Nurse Amy and Jordan follow them into a small room off the lobby. The guards get the girl into a geri chair and strap her down, and Jordan watches as Nurse Amy prepares a syringe.

"Your first day, huh?" she says to Jordan, her face looking suddenly worn. "Well, welcome to Belman Psych. We call this a B-52. It's five milligrams of Haldol and two milligrams of Ativan, and we don't use it unless it's necessary for the safety of patient and staff." She injects it intramuscularly, then follows it up with an injection of diphenhydramine. "Don't worry. It'll quiet her down."

But it's not like in the movies, when the patient just slumps forward, drooling and unconscious. The girl's still yelling and pulling against her restraints. It looks like she's being tortured.

"Give it a few minutes," Amy says to Jordan.

Then she touches the patient's hair, carefully brushing it away from her gnashing teeth. "You're home, sweet Hannah. You're home."

DELIA F. BELMAN MEMORIAL PSYCHIATRIC HOSPITAL
INTAKE & EVALUATION

PATIENT INFORMATION

Name: Hannah Doe

Date of Birth: 1/14/2005

Date Service Provided: 1/17/23

FUNCTIONING ON ADMISSION

ORIENTATION: Confusion w/r/t to time, place, identity; pt believes herself to be in a castle, possibly as a captive

APPEARANCE/PERSONAL HYGIENE: Pt presents disheveled, dirty, with clothing missing. Underweight. Superficial contusions and excoriations on legs and arms

PSYCHOSIS: Pt experiencing auditory and visual hallucinations

MOOD: Angry, upset, incoherent,
    uncooperative

LABORATORY RESULTS: Lab evaluation within
    normal limits. Toxicology report
    negative, and pt does not have history
    of substance abuse.

NOTES: After a breakdown on 44th St.,
    pt was brought by ambulance at 9:34
    a.m., mildly hypothermic from cold
    exposure. She attempted escape before
    being admitted. She was unable to
    answer orienting questions and insisted
    security staff wanted to kill her and
    her sister. Tried to attack security
    guard. We were unable to complete intake
    interview due to her delusional state;
    we will conduct further evaluation
    tomorrow if she is coherent.

Chapter 2

My name is Hannah Dory. I am eighteen in the year of our Lord 1347, and God forgive me, I am about to do something extraordinarily stupid.

I crossed myself, stood up, and threw a heavy cape over my shoulders.

"Hannah!" cried my sister, Mary. "Where are you going? Mother won't like—"

I didn't wait to hear the rest of the sentence. I marched down the narrow, frozen lane toward the village square, my jaw clenched and my hands balled into fists.

It was deepest winter, and there was misery everywhere I looked. A boy with hollow cheeks sat crying in a doorway of a thatch-roofed hovel, while a thin, mangy dog nosed in a nearby refuse heap for scraps. Another child—a filthy little girl—watched the dog with desperate eyes, waiting to steal whatever it scavenged.

I had nothing to give them. Our own food was all but gone. We'd killed and cooked our last hen weeks ago, eating every bit of her but the feathers.

My hands clutched over my stomach. There was nothing in it now—nothing, that is, but grief and rage. Just last night, I'd watched my little brother Belin die.

Mother hadn't known I was awake, but I was. I saw him take his last awful, gasping breath in her arms. He'd been only seven, and now his tiny, emaciated body lay under a moth-eaten blanket in the back of a gravedigger's cart. Soon he'd be put in the ground next to his twin, Borin, the first of them to come into the world and the first one to leave it.

My name is Hannah Dory. I have lost two brothers to hunger, and I will not lose anyone else. I am going to fight.

Have you ever felt a beloved hand grow cold in yours? If not, then I don't expect you to understand.

"Blackbird, Blackbird," crazy old Zenna said as she saw me hurrying by. She winked her one remaining eye at me. "Stop and give us a song."

She called me Blackbird for my midnight hair and my habit of singing through a day's work. She didn't know that my brothers had died—that I'd rather scream than sing. I bowed to her quickly, then hastened on.

"Another day, then," she called after me.

If we live another one, I thought bitterly.

Mary caught up with me a moment later, breathless and flushed. "Mother wants you at the spindle—I keep over-twisting the yarn."

"What use is spinning when we're starving?" I practically hissed. "We'd do better to *eat* the bloody wool."

Mary's face crumpled, and I instantly regretted my harsh tone. "I'm sorry, my sweet," I said, pulling her against my chest in a quick embrace. "I know Mother wants us to keep our hands busy. But I have...an errand."

"Can I come?" Her bright blue eyes were suddenly hopeful.

My Mary, my shadow: she was four years younger than me and four times as sweet, and I loved her more than anyone else in the world.

"Not today. Go back home," I said gently. "And take care of Mother and little Conn." *The last brother we have.*

I could tell she didn't want to. But unlike me, Mary was a good girl, and she did what she was told.

Down the hill, past the cobbler's and the bakehouse and the weaver's hut I went. I didn't stop until I came to the heavy wooden doors of the village church. They were shut tight, but I yanked them open and stumbled inside. It was no warmer in the nave, but at least there was no wind to run its cold fingers down my neck. A rat skittered into the corner of the bell tower as I grabbed the frayed rope and pulled.

The church bell rang out across our village, once, twice—ten times. I pulled until my arms screamed with effort, and then I turned and went back outside.

Summoned by the sound of the bell, the people of my village stood shivering in the churchyard.

"Only the priest rings the bell, Hannah," scolded Maraulf, the weaver.

"Father Alderton's been dead a week now," I said. "So I don't think he'll be complaining."

"God rest his soul," said pretty Ryia, bowing her head and folding her hands over her large belly. She'd have a baby in her arms soon, God willing.

Father Alderton had been a good man, and at my father's

request, he'd even given me a bit of schooling and taught me to read. He'd never beaten me or told me I was going to hell for my stubbornness, the way the priest before him had.

Now I just hoped God was taking better care of Father Alderton's soul than He had the priest's earthly remains. Wolves had dug up the old man's body from the graveyard and dragged it into the woods. Thomas the swineherd, searching the forest floor for kindling, had found the old man's bloody, severed foot.

Do you see what I mean? This winter, even the predators are starving.

"What's the ringing for?" said Merrick, Maraulf's red-cheeked, oafish grown son. "Why did you call us here?"

I brushed my tangled hair from my forehead and stood up as tall as I could.

My name is Hannah Dory, and I am about to save us—or get us all killed.

Also by James Patterson

ALEX CROSS NOVELS

Along Came a Spider • Kiss the Girls • Jack and Jill • Cat and Mouse •
Pop Goes the Weasel • Roses are Red • Violets are Blue • Four Blind
Mice • The Big Bad Wolf • London Bridges • Mary, Mary • Cross •
Double Cross • Cross Country • Alex Cross's Trial (*with Richard DiLallo*) •
I, Alex Cross • Cross Fire • Kill Alex Cross • Merry Christmas, Alex
Cross • Alex Cross, Run • Cross My Heart • Hope to Die • Cross Justice •
Cross the Line • The People vs. Alex Cross • Target: Alex Cross • Criss
Cross • Deadly Cross • Fear No Evil • Triple Cross

THE WOMEN'S MURDER CLUB SERIES

1st to Die (*with Andrew Gross*) • 2nd Chance (*with Andrew Gross*) •
3rd Degree (*with Andrew Gross*) • 4th of July (*with Maxine Paetro*) •
The 5th Horseman (*with Maxine Paetro*) • The 6th Target (*with Maxine
Paetro*) • 7th Heaven (*with Maxine Paetro*) • 8th Confession (*with Maxine
Paetro*) • 9th Judgement (*with Maxine Paetro*) • 10th Anniversary (*with
Maxine Paetro*) • 11th Hour (*with Maxine Paetro*) • 12th of Never (*with
Maxine Paetro*) • Unlucky 13 (*with Maxine Paetro*) • 14th Deadly
Sin (*with Maxine Paetro*) • 15th Affair (*with Maxine Paetro*) •
16th Seduction (*with Maxine Paetro*) • 17th Suspect (*with Maxine Paetro*) •
18th Abduction (*with Maxine Paetro*) • 19th Christmas (*with Maxine
Paetro*) • 20th Victim (*with Maxine Paetro*) • 21st Birthday (*with Maxine
Paetro*) • 22 Seconds (*with Maxine Paetro*)

DETECTIVE MICHAEL BENNETT SERIES

Step on a Crack (*with Michael Ledwidge*) • Run for Your Life (*with
Michael Ledwidge*) • Worst Case (*with Michael Ledwidge*) • Tick Tock
(*with Michael Ledwidge*) • I, Michael Bennett (*with Michael Ledwidge*) •
Gone (*with Michael Ledwidge*) • Burn (*with Michael Ledwidge*) • Alert (*with
Michael Ledwidge*) • Bullseye (*with Michael Ledwidge*) • Haunted (*with James
O. Born*) • Ambush (*with James O. Born*) • Blindside (*with James O. Born*) •
The Russian (*with James O. Born*) • Shattered (*with James O. Born*)

PRIVATE NOVELS

Private (*with Maxine Paetro*) • Private London (*with Mark Pearson*) •
Private Games (*with Mark Sullivan*) • Private: No. 1 Suspect (*with Maxine
Paetro*) • Private Berlin (*with Mark Sullivan*) • Private Down Under
(*with Michael White*) • Private L.A. (*with Mark Sullivan*) • Private India
(*with Ashwin Sanghi*) • Private Vegas (*with Maxine Paetro*) • Private Sydney
(*with Kathryn Fox*) • Private Paris (*with Mark Sullivan*) • The Games
(*with Mark Sullivan*) • Private Delhi (*with Ashwin Sanghi*) • Private
Princess (*with Rees Jones*) • Private Moscow (*with Adam Hamdy*) •
Private Rogue (*with Adam Hamdy*)

NYPD RED SERIES

NYPD Red (*with Marshall Karp*) • NYPD Red 2 (*with Marshall Karp*) •
NYPD Red 3 (*with Marshall Karp*) • NYPD Red 4 (*with Marshall Karp*) •
NYPD Red 5 (*with Marshall Karp*) • NYPD Red 6 (*with Marshall Karp*)

DETECTIVE HARRIET BLUE SERIES

Never Never (*with Candice Fox*) • Fifty Fifty (*with Candice Fox*) • Liar Liar
(*with Candice Fox*) • Hush Hush (*with Candice Fox*)

INSTINCT SERIES

Instinct (*with Howard Roughan, previously published as* Murder Games) •
Killer Instinct (*with Howard Roughan*) • Steal (*with Howard Roughan*)

THE BLACK BOOK SERIES

The Black Book (*with David Ellis*) • The Red Book (*with David Ellis*) •
Escape (*with David Ellis*)

STAND-ALONE THRILLERS

The Thomas Berryman Number • Hide and Seek • Black Market • The
Midnight Club • Sail (*with Howard Roughan*) • Swimsuit (*with Maxine
Paetro*) • Don't Blink (*with Howard Roughan*) • Postcard Killers (*with Liza
Marklund*) • Toys (*with Neil McMahon*) • Now You See Her (*with Michael
Ledwidge*) • Kill Me If You Can (*with Marshall Karp*) • Guilty Wives (*with
David Ellis*) • Zoo (*with Michael Ledwidge*) • Second Honeymoon

(with Howard Roughan) • Mistress (with David Ellis) • Invisible (with David Ellis) • Truth or Die (with Howard Roughan) • Murder House (with David Ellis) • The Store (with Richard DiLallo) • Texas Ranger (with Andrew Bourelle) • The President is Missing (with Bill Clinton) • Revenge (with Andrew Holmes) • Juror No. 3 (with Nancy Allen) • The First Lady (with Brendan DuBois) • The Chef (with Max DiLallo) • Out of Sight (with Brendan DuBois) • Unsolved (with David Ellis) • The Inn (with Candice Fox) • Lost (with James O. Born) • Texas Outlaw (with Andrew Bourelle) • The Summer House (with Brendan DuBois) • 1st Case (with Chris Tebbetts) • Cajun Justice (with Tucker Axum)• The Midwife Murders (with Richard DiLallo) • The Coast-to-Coast Murders (with J.D. Barker) • Three Women Disappear (with Shan Serafin) • The President's Daughter (with Bill Clinton) • The Shadow (with Brian Sitts) • The Noise (with J.D. Barker) • 2 Sisters Detective Agency (with Candice Fox) • Jailhouse Lawyer (with Nancy Allen) • The Horsewoman (with Mike Lupica) • Run Rose Run (with Dolly Parton) • Death of the Black Widow (with J.D. Barker) • The Ninth Month (with Richard DiLallo) • Blowback (with Brendan DuBois) • The Girl in the Castle (with Emily Raymond) • The Twelve Topsy-Turvy, Very Messy Days of Christmas (with Tad Safran)

NON-FICTION

Torn Apart (with Hal and Cory Friedman) • The Murder of King Tut (with Martin Dugard) • All-American Murder (with Alex Abramovich and Mike Harvkey) • The Kennedy Curse (with Cynthia Fagen) • The Last Days of John Lennon (with Casey Sherman and Dave Wedge) • Walk in My Combat Boots (with Matt Eversmann and Chris Mooney) • ER Nurses (with Matt Eversmann) • James Patterson by James Patterson: The Stories of My Life • Diana, William and Harry (with Chris Mooney)

MURDER IS FOREVER TRUE CRIME

Murder, Interrupted (with Alex Abramovich and Christopher Charles) • Home Sweet Murder (with Andrew Bourelle and Scott Slaven) • Murder Beyond the Grave (with Andrew Bourelle and Christopher Charles) • Murder Thy Neighbour (with Andrew Bourelle and Max DiLallo) • Murder of Innocence (with Max DiLallo and Andrew Bourelle) • Till Murder Do Us Part (with Andrew Bourelle and Max DiLallo)

COLLECTIONS

Triple Threat (*with Max DiLallo and Andrew Bourelle*) • Kill or Be Killed (*with Maxine Paetro, Rees Jones, Shan Serafin and Emily Raymond*) • The Moores are Missing (*with Loren D. Estleman, Sam Hawken and Ed Chatterton*) • The Family Lawyer (*with Robert Rotstein, Christopher Charles and Rachel Howzell Hall*) • Murder in Paradise (*with Doug Allyn, Connor Hyde and Duane Swierczynski*) • The House Next Door (*with Susan DiLallo, Max DiLallo and Brendan DuBois*) • 13-Minute Murder (*with Shan Serafin, Christopher Farnsworth and Scott Slaven*) • The River Murders (*with James O. Born*) • The Palm Beach Murders (*with James O. Born, Duane Swierczynski and Tim Arnold*) • Paris Detective

For more information about James Patterson's novels,
visit www.penguin.co.uk.

Double Bill

Double Bill

80 YEARS OF ENTERTAINMENT

Bill Cotton

FOURTH ESTATE • *London*

First published in Great Britain in 2000 by
Fourth Estate Limited
6 Salem Road
London W2 4BU
www.4thestate.co.uk

Copyright © Bill Cotton 2000

10 9 8 7 6 5 4 3 2 1

Picture Credits: BBC © BBC Picture Archives: p.6, p.8, p.11, p.12, p.13 (bottom), p.14, p.15 (top), p.16 (top), p.17, p.18, p.19 (bottom), p.21. *Daily Mirror* © MSI: p.20 (top). *Daily Express* © courtesy of the *Daily Express*: p.6 (bottom right). Pearson Television © courtesy of Pearson Television: p.22 (bottom). All other pictures author's personal collection.

The right of Bill Cotton to be identified as the author of this work has been asserted by him in accordance with the Copyright, Designs and Patents Act 1988

A catalogue record of this book is available from the British Library

ISBN 1-84115-327-3

All rights reserved. No part of this publication may be reproduced, transmitted, or stored in a retrieval system, in any form or by any means, without permission in writing from Fourth Estate Limited.

Typeset in Plantin Light by MATS, Southend-on-Sea, Essex
Printed in Great Britain by Clays Ltd, St Ives plc

:20041952

MORAY COUNCIL
LIBRARIES &
INFORMATION SERVICES
791. 40922

This book is dedicated to my wife, Kate, for things too numerous to mention, but above all for her love.

ACKNOWLEDGEMENTS

Anyone embarking on writing their first, and probably their last, book needs help. I have been well served by many people. First and foremost my good friend Colin Morris. In 1997 over lunch he suggested we should do a series of programmes for Radio 2 about my father and myself; I agreed. The title for the series was suggested one evening when my wife Kate and I were having a drink with Dave Allen and Karen Stark. Karen said out of the blue, 'You must call it *Double Bill*,' and so we did.

Two years later Colin insisted that I should write a book with the same title. He promised to help me and certainly has. I also thank the many friends and colleagues who refreshed my memory of the events and anecdotes that make up this story. However the stories and opinions here show how I saw things at the time, and I have tried to make it as entertaining as possible. I've always believed a little about the politics of broadcasting, in particular of the BBC, goes a very long way. It's the people and the programmes that matter.

I would like to thank my wife who typed 'what I wrote', Hilary Carrigan who was more than helpful, Pat Coward who checked facts; and Bobbie Mitchell who helped with the photographs.

Finally thanks to the staff at Fourth Estate, and in particular Christopher Potter, their Publishing Director, to whom I can only express my gratitude for his confidence and support throughout.

To my children and grandchildren, I am only sorry we didn't see much of each other while I was trying to become a literary giant – I feel much better now.

PROLOGUE

On a crisp spring afternoon in 1969 I sat in St Margaret's, Westminster, which is next door to the Abbey. It was my father's funeral and, because he had been what one newspaper obituary called 'one of the greatest entertainers of modern times', the church was packed. My father was as usual playing to a full house, but this was the very last time he would do so. Celebrities like the great band-leader Henry Hall rubbed shoulders with hundreds of ordinary folk for whom Billy Cotton and his band had become over the years a valued part of their lives, on radio, television and in the theatre.

St Margaret's is one of the most fashionable and beautiful churches in the land; MPs in particular cherish the privilege of being married or having their children baptised there. But it was the location for my father's funeral not because he was famous or important but because he was born in the parish. When I went along to ask the rector if the service could take place there, he seemed dubious: Lent was a busy time; there were lots of services planned; the choir would be at full stretch; and so on. Beneath his expressions of regret, though, I detected just a tinge of scepticism at my claim that Dad had grown up in the parish and sung in St Margaret's choir. Then a verger appeared and the rector explained to him what I was doing there and the difficulty of fitting in the funeral. 'That's a pity,' said the verger. 'He really loved this place. I often chatted with him when he slipped in to listen to the choir.' That settled it. It was agreed that Dad should be laid to rest in his own parish church.

In fact, Dad had been born at what is now an exclusive address, No. 1 Smith Square, adjacent to the Conservative Party central offices. In 1899 it was a two up, two down terrace

1

house (rent: seven and sixpence a week) and Dad shared a bedroom with three brothers while six sisters squashed into an attic room. Westminster was then a self-contained village within London. Like the other kids in the area, my father played in the streets around the Parliament buildings, hitched lifts on the cow-catchers of trams and swam in the Thames off Lambeth Bridge when the police weren't looking. (If they *were* looking, Dad would often end up running home, naked and dripping wet, his boots tied by their laces round his neck.)

Dad's father was a ganger in charge of a section of the Metropolitan Water Board, and looked splendid in a top hat with a badge on it. He was a huge man who could with one hand pick up his wife, Sukey, who was only four feet tall, and tuck her under his arm. He was once invited onto the stage of the Aquarium in Tothill Street to try his luck against George Hackenschmidt, the Russian world-champion wrestler. In a flash he was on his back, but went away with the ten shillings promised to anyone brave enough to go into the ring against the world's strongest man.

I still use my grandfather's malacca walking-stick which has a gold band around the top inscribed, 'To Joseph Cotton: from X Division, Metropolitan Police in appreciation of help with violent prisoners. May 1925.' He must have been sixty-five years of age when he came to the rescue of a couple of police constables trying to arrest a gang of thugs. So he knew how to take care of himself.

Grandad was mad on clocks. However complicated they were, he could take them to pieces and put them together again. He had three or four clocks in every room of the house – cuckoo clocks, chiming clocks, water clocks. It was bedlam to walk through the house on the hour or half-hour.

In the deep silence before the funeral service began, I gazed around the church to keep my mind occupied and my eyes off Dad's coffin. As a choir boy, under the eagle eye of St Margaret's legendary organist and choirmaster, Dr Goss-Custard, Dad had sat in one of those stalls practising every weekday at noon between morning and afternoon school-lessons. Apparently he had a beautiful voice, and besides enjoying the singing earned a few precious shillings for special services such as weddings and funerals. And so began a life dedicated to music. To the end of his life he could sing arias such as 'I Know That My Redeemer Liveth' from *Messiah*, though since that was composed for a soprano voice it sounded strange in his husky bass-tones. According to my grandmother he was a typical choirboy: cherubic in surplice and ruff collar but a tough, vigorous lad elsewhere, especially on the football field. His school played all their matches on Clapham Common, and they'd have to march the three miles there and back carrying the goalposts.

Tattered regimental banners, worn with age and damaged in battle, hung down from the nave of St Margaret's, and I wondered whether the standard of the Second Battalion, the London Regiment, was among them. Popularly known as the Two-and-tuppences, this was the regiment my father joined in 1915. He'd volunteered as soon as the Great War broke out the previous year, but as a spotty fifteen-year-old couldn't convince the red-sashed recruiting sergeant that he was 'sixteen, coming on seventeen'. Twelve months later he enlisted as a boy bugler and was posted to Malta, where he was introduced to the seamier side of life in the quarter of Valletta the troops called the 'Gut'. There were peep shows where for a penny you could see a naked lady, but Dad was perpetually hungry and preferred to go instead to the Salvation Army. They gave him a cup of tea and a fairy-cake in return for him standing on the roof of the building, bashing a tambourine and pointing at the red-light district. 'That's the way to the Devil,' he'd shout, 'and this is the way to the Lord. Come on in!' And whenever one of the lads followed his advice Dad would get another fairy-cake.

From Malta he sailed to the Dardanelles, where a desperate engagement against the Turks was being fought. He later recalled that as he clambered down the troopship's side to wade ashore off Cape Hellas, a huge Marine asked where his rifle was. Touching the musician's badge on his arm, Dad replied, 'I don't carry a rifle. I'm a bugler.' The Marine snorted, 'There's only one bugler around here – that's Gabriel. He's in heaven and

3

you'll soon bleeding well be joining him without one of these. Catch!' With that, the Marine threw him a rifle and Dad became a serious soldier. Unable to move inland from the beaches, under constant Turkish shelling and German aerial bombardment from Taube biplanes that dropped steel darts to skewer you to the ground, Dad spent weeks sleeping in the freezing rain amid the bodies of his comrades and scurrying rats. He grew up during that doomed and brutal campaign. There was precious little chivalry around; the Turks mutilated prisoners and the Allied soldiers sometimes retaliated by hurling hand grenades into the POW cages where the Turkish prisoners were held.

Dad's mother didn't know he'd been posted abroad until she got a home-made Christmas card from him. He'd drawn a soldier holding a Christmas pudding with a bubble coming out of his head that read, 'With thoughts of home from your loving son, Will.' It was postmarked the Dardanelles. She nearly had a fit and started proceedings to buy him out of the army, an option open for boy soldiers. It cost thirty pounds, a king's ransom, but somehow she scraped the money together. However, by the time the army's bureaucracy creaked into action the Dardanelles expedition had ended in disaster and Dad was evacuated with everybody else. On the way home he helped stoke the boilers on the old three-funnelled battleship *Mars,* which was on its last voyage to the breaker's yard via Southampton. When the *Mars* docked Dad queued up with the rest of the complement, clutching his pay-book. His turn came and the paymaster smiled sardonically, 'Run along, son, I've got no chocolate.'

He had to find his own way home from Southampton. By this time the family had moved from Westminster to Kilburn, so he caught a train to Victoria then a bus up the Harrow Road, where he met a postman doing his rounds at ten o'clock at night. He asked the man if he knew where the Cotton family lived. The postman looked at this boy with a pack and rifle, obviously exhausted, and immediately said, 'Yes, I know Joe Cotton's house; it's a bit of a walk but I'm going that way.' While this wasn't entirely true, he nonetheless picked up Dad's kit and helped him home.

Dad was given a hero's welcome but found a huge gap in the family he'd left. His elder brother Frederick had been in a reserved occupation as a draughtsman at Vickers. When he saw Dad leave for the army he couldn't bear not being in uniform, and told his mother he too was going to enlist. He was killed in France within a fortnight.

Being a returned juvenile hero held no attraction for my father, so at the age of seventeen he again volunteered, this time for the Royal Flying Corps (later to become the Royal Air Force). When it was suggested during the interview by one of the board that Dad was too young to be commissioned in the RFC, the presiding officer said, 'As far as I'm concerned, if he's old enough to fight in the Dardanelles, he's old enough to fight in the RFC.' So Dad began a lifelong love-affair with flying and became a pilot, though because of a crash in training he never fought in the air – which probably saved his life: on the Western front, the life-expectancy of RFC aircrew was measured in weeks.

He left the RAF with a gratuity of two hundred and fifty pounds, spent ninety of it on a belt-driven Norton motor cycle and started looking for work. He tried motor-cycle racing in Ireland; then tried being a mill-wright's assistant; and finally got a steady job as a bus conductor. Throughout this time he was playing football regularly. He played in the Middlesex Senior League and eventually got a trial for Brentford, whose manager with gritty realism told him, 'Remember one thing. Brentford can't play football so we make bloody sure nobody else does!' Dad was not a professional and whenever Brentford didn't pick him he got a game for Wimbledon, which at that time was an amateur side in the Athenian League.

Army buglers were also trained drummers, and Dad decided to cash in on his experience by joining a part-time band called the Fifth Avenue Orchestra – not Fifth Avenue, *New York* but Fifth Avenue, *Queen's Park*. He played the drums badly until the best musician in the band, the pianist Clem Bernard, suggested the sound would improve if Dad quit the drums, stood in front and waved his arms about in time to the music – which he did brilliantly for the rest of his life.

5

In 1921 he married my mother, Mabel Hope Gregory. She too had a brother killed in the war and her mother was an invalid, so she played a vital part in her father's business (he owned a chain of butcher's shops in which my father worked for a time). He was less than entranced about his Mabel marrying a penniless musician-cum-amateur footballer, but eventually accepted the inevitable. Dad and Mum took a couple of rooms behind a barber's shop in Kilburn Lane, where they were poor but happy. Sometimes of an evening, coming home from a gig at a dance hall, they would toss a coin to decide whether they should eat or ride home on the bus – it didn't matter which way the coin fell, they always chose to buy something to eat and then walked home, lugging a set of drums between them.

Then Dad and the band were offered an engagement at the Regent, Brighton which was part cinema and part dance-hall. He decided that the Fifth Avenue Orchestra needed a more sophisticated name now they had hit the big time, so they became the London Savannah Band. After Brighton came Southport, then the Astoria on Charing Cross Road, London, and finally Ciro's Club. By now, instead of playing for dancing they had become a stage band, putting on a show including vocalists and much clowning around. Billy Cotton had emerged as a showbiz personality in his own right; he was no longer just the leader of the band, he was its chief attraction.

Dad was now able to indulge his favourite pastimes. He gave up football but played cricket for Wembley when his engagements allowed, and he'd take me and my brother Ted with him. The whole family was there the day he scored a century, and my mother said it meant more to him than when he appeared in his first Royal Command Performance.

But he couldn't wait for the day when he would be able to afford to race motor cars at Brooklands. When the time came he bought a clapped-out Riley Nine and got it tuned by an Italian mechanic called Charlie Querico. Being a professional, Charlie had a healthy contempt for all amateurs – especially showbiz types – so Dad decided to teach him a lesson. Just as all the cars were on the grid with their engines warming up, Dad raised his hand and beckoned to Charlie, who had a limp and hobbled over in a panic.

'What's the trouble?' he yelled over the roar of gunning engines.

'Which gear do I start this thing in? I've forgotten,' Dad roared back.

'First, of course!' shrieked Charlie. Then, seeing the old man grinning at him, added, 'You're bloody mad,' and got quickly out of the way.

Memories . . . Dad's had been a boisterous, generally happy life. He swept us all up – family, friends and fans – in his warm, jolly embrace. Wherever he was there was noise and activity – I'd never known him as quiet as he was that afternoon in St Margaret's. For an instant I was tempted to shatter the solemn silence by shouting out his famous slogan 'Wakey! Wakey!' with which he had begun a thousand performances. But I knew that this time it was no use. He had dominated my life, now I was on my own. No more amusing incidents where people mistook me for my Dad or got our names mixed up. An extraordinary Double Bill had come to an end.

But that afternoon, as one does when reluctant to face a tragic present, I dwelled on happier days . . .

ONE

My father had two sons and each of us inherited different parts of his nature – which just shows what a larger-than-life personality he was. My brother, Ted, who was five years older than me, shared my father's love of flying – just as Dad had piloted Bristol fighters in the First World War, Ted flew Mosquito fighter bombers in the Second. As Dad's younger son and named after him, I was fairly good at sports such as football and cricket, but chiefly I inherited my father's love of show business and some of his flair for popular musical entertainment – though neither of us could read a note of music.

I think my earliest memory of my father was of him being very upset. When I was about four years old we lived on a new housing development in Kingsbury, north London. There was still plenty of building work going on and a constant stream of lorries passed our front gate. Apparently, one day someone left our gate open; I ran out into the road and got pinned to the ground by the front wheels of a truck. Miraculously I wasn't seriously hurt but a doctor was called and, so the story goes, I remained utterly silent while he used a fork to dig out the stones that had been imprinted on my back by the lorry's wheels. When he'd done he gave me a couple of sharp slaps on the backside and I screamed the place down. My silence had not been bravery but shock.

Meanwhile, in the road outside, my father was lambasting the poor lorry driver who'd really done nothing wrong. When my father was aroused he could be frightening; he had a Cockney's ripe turn of phrase and was a trained boxer – I once saw him knock a motorist who picked a fight with him right across Denmark Street. He wasn't particularly proud of the bellicose

8

side of his nature but he had learned as a boy in the backstreets of Westminster that you either stood up for yourself or went under.

In a way, it's poignant that my earliest memory should be of him being fiercely defensive of me. I recall him as an unfailingly loving father; I remained secure in that knowledge even when he did things I found puzzling or even upsetting. When I was small I didn't realise that he was a famous band leader. I didn't know what he did for a living, he just seemed to live life the wrong way round. He would set off for work as Ted started his homework and I was being put to bed, and it's a miracle we didn't become chronic insomniacs for he had a habit of bawling up the stairs, 'Anyone awake?' at whatever time he got home. If he got any answer, he would carry us both down to share his supper. We were a tightly knit family, and always if it was humanly possible Dad came home. Even when the band had played miles away he would drive through the night to get back to his own bed.

Though Dad was my hero, throughout my childhood my favourite band-leader was in fact Henry Hall, whose BBC Dance Band broadcast every weekday evening from Savoy Hill. After I'd had my bath, brushed my teeth and hair and put on my pyjamas, I was allowed into the front room to listen to the programme. I loved his music, especially 'The Teddy Bears' Picnic', which he made a hit. Years later, when I was running BBC TV Entertainment we did a programme celebrating fifty years of broadcast music. We got Henry Hall to conduct a band made up of all the top session-musicians, and they played a medley of the famous signature tunes of big bands of the thirties, which included amongst others Jack Hylton's 'Oh, Listen to the Band', Jack Payne's 'Say It With Music', Henry's own signature tune, 'Here's to the Next Time', and of course Billy Cotton's 'Somebody Stole My Gal'. It was a magical, nostalgic occasion. At the end the band gave Henry, by then in his eighties, a standing ovation, and he said afterwards that he'd never officially retired as a band-leader until that moment. There wasn't a dry eye in the house, including mine.

It was at the Holborn Empire that I heard Dad's band for the first time. My mother, my brother and I caught a bus from Kingsbury which dropped us off in Oxford Street, from where we took a cab for the rest of the journey so we could arrive in style. For me the star of that evening wasn't my father but my Uncle Bill, who happened to be the senior commissionaire at the theatre. There he was, dressed in a magnificent green uniform with gold piping, war medals clanking on his chest. He opened the taxi door, saluted and called me 'Young sir'. I was speechless with pride. A page-boy took us up to a luxuriously upholstered box in the circle. I was about to see my first variety show; it included dancers, jugglers, comedians, a ventriloquist and a magician. Then the melody of 'Somebody Stole My Gal' rang out, the curtain went up and there was my father in white tie and tails conducting his band. When the signature tune ended he turned to the audience to do his opening patter and I couldn't contain myself. I jumped up and shouted out in a loud voice, 'Hello, Dad!' Quick as a flash he called back, 'Now, don't give me away, son,' and there was a sympathetic chuckle from the audience. I sat back proudly and clutched my mother's hand.

A few years later when my brother went away to boarding school, Dad would take me on my own to any nearby theatre he was playing at. I would stand in the wings and when he took his curtain call run onto the stage and solemnly bow to the audience with him – the old girls in the front stalls loved it, but not half as much as I did. It was on trips like this that I met face to face some of the great stars of the day, especially at the Palladium. There would be American superstars like Joe E. Brown and Laurel and Hardy whom I had seen only on the screen of the local cinema at Saturday matinées. There was also home-grown talent such as Will Hay, Max Miller, the Crazy Gang and Bud Flanagan.

Bud was a great joker. I remember Dad treating me and some school pals to lunch at the Moulin d'Or. You'd see all the big stars there – it was *the* place to eat, and to be seen. Bud was at another table, and when we got up to leave and our coats were handed to us he jumped up and started shrieking, 'Stop! Call the police!' I was embarrassed beyond belief as he proceeded to tip out of our coat pockets knives, forks and spoons he'd bribed the waiters to plant in them.

I loved going with the band when they did cine variety, playing between film-showings at two cinemas such as the Dominion, Tottenham Court Road and the Trocadero, Elephant and Castle. They started at two in the afternoon and by the time they finished at ten p.m., they'd done seven shows. Though I was allowed to travel with the band, I don't think they were all that keen on having me aboard because my father didn't tolerate bad language in front of his family. When I appeared the band members would pass the word along: 'Ham sandwich' was their warning they'd better watch their tongues. Why 'ham sandwich' I don't really know; perhaps it was rhyming slang for 'bad language'. Another code word was 'Tom', their private name for Dad so they could discuss him without outsiders realising who they were talking about.

It was around this time that Dad adopted 'Somebody Stole My Gal' as his signature tune. When asked why he said the idea had been put into his head by his nephew Laurie Johnson who was in the orchestra. On one occasion Laurie had observed Dad standing on the edge of the dance-hall floor, turning every dance into an excuse-me whenever a pretty girl whirled past him, and said to him, 'You're always stealing somebody's girl!' Dad responded by singing him a verse of 'Somebody Stole My Gal', and one thing led to another.

Dad was constantly on the move and the family didn't see as much of him as we would have liked. He had become involved in what were known as Blue Star Flying Visits to the various Mecca dance-halls all over the country. The proposal had come from a Dutchman called C.L.H. Heimann who had heard Dad's band in one or two theatres and been very impressed. He had just bought a chain of Mecca cafés and proposed to turn them into dance-halls. He engaged Dad and supplied a state-of-the-art motor coach to take the band on one-night visits to every Mecca venue. Thus was born what later became an institution of British popular culture before, during and immediately after the war – Mecca Dancing.

Dad soon began to take the idea of flying visits literally and bought himself a second-hand Puss Moth, a wooden aircraft, very reliable and simple to fly. In it he flew to the nearest aerodromes to the towns where the band was performing – I was thrilled by the drama and excitement of it. I recall my cousin Laurie telling me of an occasion when he flew with Dad to a booking at Great Yarmouth Pier. They flew to the Boulton and Paul aerodrome at Norwich where a car collected them and took them on to the coast. The next day they drove back to the aerodrome, and while they were sitting in the club house an official came in and told them they ought not to fly because the weather was deteriorating. The misty rain and murk for which the Fenlands are notorious was closing in.

Dad chose to ignore the weather warning and fly on to Leicester, where the band was performing that evening at the Palais de Dance. Visibility was nil and in those days the only available navigational aid was a bubble and compass. In such conditions the single course open to aircraft was to 'Bradshaw' – follow the railway lines. But railway lines to where? Dad was hopelessly lost and realised that he was also low on fuel. He decided to hedge-hop in the hope of spotting a familiar landmark. He pushed down the stick, and the aircraft was swooping towards the ground when Laurie screamed through the voice tube, 'Look out!', whereupon Dad hauled back the stick and just missed a place in the history books as the man who demolished Peterborough Cathedral.

He had just enough fuel left for a quarter of an hour's flying, so decided to land at the first flat field he saw. It turned out to be the jumping arena of a stables, complete with fences he had to sail over one by one until he came to a halt. Plenty of horses had taken the jumps but this was the first time an aeroplane completed the course. The owner came out to greet them and Dad introduced himself; they had a drink together then pushed the Puss Moth, wings folded, into a shed. The owner's driver took Dad and Laurie to Melton Mowbray station, from where they caught a train to Leicester. The next day Dad returned, collected the aircraft and flew it back to Croydon. The joys of flying in those carefree early days! Little wonder that Dad was my childhood hero when his life was punctuated by escapades like these.

It was much to our delight that for one period in the 1930s Dad spent much more time at home. This was while he and the band were the resident orchestra at Ciro's Club in London's Park Lane. It was a very upmarket, even exclusive, establishment, quite different from the general run of variety theatres in which Dad spent much of his professional life. Entertainment correspondents of various newspapers were astounded at the appointment and predicted that it would be a very brief engagement – just long enough for Dad to open his mouth, as one unkindly put it. Because Ciro's was a very select place the band had to play very quietly, muffling the brass by stuffing scarves and handkerchiefs down the bells of their instruments. The clientele didn't want to hear the band so much as feel it; it was an accessory, like the vastly expensive flock wallpaper or the periwigged flunkeys in knee-breeches who manned the cloakroom and served the drinks.

When Dad returned home from nights at Ciro's he would tell us about some of the more exotic or distinguished people he'd met. For a while the Prince of Wales, later Edward VIII, was an *habitué*. He was fond of night-life and partial to the club's dark, romantic atmosphere. Though flattered by HRH's presence, the owners of the club found him a bit of a pain because he would arrive with an entourage and insist on being treated like royalty, killing an evening stone dead. All the other guests sat in respectful silence as the Duke chuntered his way through the wine list, ate his meal and eventually left (which he'd do after requesting the Billy Cotton Band to play his favourite tune, the Waltz Intermezzo from *Cavalleria Rusticana* – not a theme calculated to set feet tapping or bring the crowds onto the dance-floor).

The third time the Prince requested the same piece Dad, exasperated, said to the club manager who'd brought the message, 'Go and ask the silly so-and-so if he knows any other tune.' The following day Dad was summoned to the presence of the chairman of the board, Lord Tennyson, who told him that although he and the band were popular with members, they did expect a little more courtesy. 'You mean "servility",' replied Dad. 'That's not my style. I certainly believe in greeting people in a proper manner, but they'll get no bowing and scraping from me.' Lord Tennyson then broached the subject of HRH, pointing out that even among club staff the heir to the throne was not to be referred to as a silly so-and-so. 'The problem is, Cotton,' said the noble lord, 'that you are too outspoken. You'll be calling him that to his face next.'

The upshot was that Dad and his band were banished to Ciro's in Paris for three months, in a role-exchange with the club's resident band, the Noble Cecil Orchestra, and he found the clientele there much more responsive and uninhibited than their London counterparts. Cecil's band was initially greeted with shock at the London Ciro's, because every one of its players was black – though nothing unusual these days, the fact was considered scandalous at that time among the club's many ex-colonial members.

However, whereas at home Dad was 'one of us' and expected to behave as such, Noble Cecil and his orchestra got away with murder. As Dad himself acknowledged, all the noisy, catchy tunes he had been barred from playing, the Cecil band blasted out – and the clients, including the Prince of Wales, came to love them. When the two bands swapped venues again, Dad found he was able to play his own kind of music, the Billy Cotton sound, trombones blaring, saxes wailing and drums thumping out the rhythm. He also enticed one of Noble Cecil's band to stay and work for him: trombonist Ellis Jackson was still playing in the Billy Cotton Band and doing a credible tap dance well into his eighties.

I was absorbing the ethos of show business through my skin when I was still a boy. I learned a lot; things like the significance of the running order on a variety bill. In those days the Billy Cotton Band would be one of perhaps three or four star attractions whose names were emblazoned in huge letters across the posters, but I also watched from the wings as the names in little letters the supporting acts, especially comedians – performed. With desperation lurking behind the laughter in their eyes, they worked frantically to get some response from audiences who were waiting impatiently for the big stars and daring these lower-order comedians to make them laugh. Their act done, they'd leave the stage to the hollow sound of their own footsteps, head for the bar and demolish half a bottle of whisky while they waited to die the death again in the second house. Comics suffered this ritual humiliation year in and year out in the hope that one day there might be a talent spotter in the audience who would pluck them from obscurity. It amazed me how few stand-up comedians gave up in despair; they all seemed to be incorrigible optimists.

A boyhood spent standing in theatre wings watching the contrasting scenes before me – stars excited by roaring crowds and also-rans withering at the sparse applause of bored audiences – bred in me an empathy I have never lost towards showbiz performers. When eventually I became a BBC Television executive and had the power to employ musicians and entertainers, though I couldn't let my professional judgement be distorted by sentimentality, every time I auditioned a TV hopeful I willed him or her to succeed. In my mind's eye I could see some miserable comedian gloomily staring into an empty whisky glass waiting for the call of destiny that would never come.

In the late nineteen-thirties we were living in a family house in Willesden which had a large garden, stables and a proper snooker room. There Dad entertained an eclectic mix of the kinds of personality who occupied the gossip- and feature-columns of the day's newspapers. There was the motor-racing set, many of them the younger sons of the aristocracy; flying aces like Amy Johnson; show business stars; music publishers; and the sporting mob – footballers, cricketers and boxers. One regular visitor was the world snooker champion Joe Davis, who would play a dozen of us at once and we'd get just one shot each before he cleared the table. The only person who could beat him was the comedian Tommy Trinder, who reduced him to such helpless laughter that he fluffed his shots. In fact, Tommy had everyone present in stitches except for his wife, Vi, who never laughed at anything he said – ever. Tommy had a lifelong ambition to get a smile out of Vi but he never realised it; my father, on the other hand, had only to make a mildly amusing remark and she'd explode with mirth.

Vi was an extraordinary character. She put the kibosh on a tour Tommy made of Australia when they were both inter-viewed by the press on the airport tarmac before they flew home. Tommy rhapsodised about Australia, its wonderful climate, its beautiful scenery, its marvellous audiences . . . Eventually, a reporter asked Vi what was the best thing she'd seen in Australia. She said, 'This aeroplane that's going to take me back to my bulldog in Brighton.' She hated the razzmatazz of show business, and I think she warmed to my dad because he was totally without any overweening self-regard. Fame left him totally unaffected. To the end, he remained a big-hearted, down-to-earth Cockney, noisy and affectionate.

My mother ran our family effortlessly. She'd inherited her father's head for business and had the only bank account in the family, from which she doled out cheques to my father as he needed them. And she wasn't dealing in loose change either – Dad made big money in his time, but since one of his famous sayings was 'Money is for spending', it was up to Mabel to keep the ship afloat. She was the still centre of a hurricane. There was noise and frantic activity all around her, and she went on calmly holding the family together while my father dashed about playing the theatres, driving racing cars, flying aeroplanes and sailing boats. She graciously entertained the big show-business names who blew in and out of our house, but she wasn't overly impressed. All that was another world; what mattered to her was giving her sons as normal and loving an upbringing as possible, and looking after the old man.

That in itself was a full-time job. One day when I was quite small, Dad complained of pains in his arms and legs and developed a high temperature. Rheumatic fever was diagnosed, he became seriously ill and was looked after round the clock at home by two nurses. The house was darkened and Ted and myself were sternly enjoined to keep quiet. I was given the job of keeping guard at the entrance to our drive and waving down passing vehicles if they were going too fast or making a lot of noise – even the Walls ice-cream man was asked not to ring the bell of his tricycle or call out his wares until he was beyond earshot. For a couple of weeks it was touch and go as to whether or not Dad would make it, but he was as strong as an ox and once he turned the corner he quickly recovered. Whilst Dad was ill, though, the entire brass section of his orchestra, which included some of the finest trumpet and trombone players of the time, the best-known being Nat Gonella, was enticed away by a rival band-leader called Roy Fox. Dad screamed 'Theft!' and never forgave those who deserted him; the rest he rewarded with inscribed silver cigarette boxes which became known as 'loyalty boxes'.

When I was nine years old I joined Ted at Ardingly College. As a new boy I wasn't allowed to have any contact with him – we travelled there together, but as we approached the school Ted warned me that tradition decreed juniors mustn't socialise with seniors during term-time. As is often the case with younger siblings, my elder brother had excited in me both admiration and envy, so I had been desperately keen to follow him to public school. But on that day, as Ted left me behind and strolled away chatting and joking with his contemporaries, I stood there alone, clutching my suitcase, gazing at this gloomy Victorian building which made Bleak House look like a holiday camp looming ahead in the dark winter afternoon, and I just wanted to be back with Mum and Dad. I lived for their visits and pursued a curiously schizoid existence. For one third of the year I mixed at home with the stars who made a great fuss of me, the other two thirds were spent in this miserable barracks of a place where the masters beat any cockiness out of me.

It was only when I had settled down at school and got to know my school-mates that I realised how famous my dad was, and I did quite a brisk trade in enrolling them as members of his fan club for two-pence each. I remember one weekend he visited Ted and myself in his state-of-the-art car, a Lagonda which boasted a car radio – a real novelty in those days. Every Sunday, Radio Luxembourg transmitted a programme – recorded in advance – called the *Kraft Hour,* which featured Dad and his band. On this occasion showing off the car, Dad turned the radio on, and hey presto! there he was on the air. Since these were the early days of radio, when pre-recorded programmes were rare, some of my astonished school-mates didn't understand how Dad could be in two places at once.

I confess I swelled with smug pride whenever my father visited Ardingly College on open days. He would sign up for the Boys versus Parents cricket match, knock out a quick half-century, bowl some unplayable balls and then dash off to Croydon where he kept his aeroplane, fly back and, to the delight of the boys, buzz the school. No doubt some sniffy parents thought it was all outrageous exhibitionism, but Dad was so artless in his desire to give people pleasure it would never occur to him that anyone could think he was doing it to stroke his own ego. In spite of his great fame, there was an engaging innocence about him; he had no pretensions about his importance. He was, for example, terrified of Ardingly's headmaster, Canon Ernest Crosse – of course, we all were in our early days in the school. Even when I became a sixth-form prefect and counted Canon Crosse more as a friend than a teacher (he later conducted my marriage service and baptised my children) Dad never lost his apprehensiveness about having to make conversation with him. 'He's your headmaster,' he used to say. 'You talk to him.'

After I'd been at boarding school for a couple of years, World War II broke out and Dad, who was on the Reserve of Air Force Officers, was called to a board at Uxbridge which tried to decide the best use to make of him. Obviously *he* wanted to fly in combat; *they* on the other hand decided that although he was a very fit forty-year-old, he should become adjutant to an RAF squadron at Northolt. Dad was outraged – Billy Cotton a pen pusher? The Air Marshal who presided asked him why he was wearing glasses. 'Is it true that you have a defect in your left eye?' Dad had to agree that he had sight problems, and that was that. They spared him an office job and recommended that he and his band should be loaned to ENSA to entertain the troops in France during that first cold winter of the war. Then, after Dunkirk, he was seconded to the Air Training Corps and spent the rest of the war trying to keep up morale on the home front as well as doing his bit to ginger up the teenagers who enlisted in the ATC as the first step to service in the RAF. It was my brother, Ted, who did the family's stint in the RAF.

When I came home for school holidays, my Dad often took me touring with him. People needed something to take their minds off the war, so the theatres were packed. The band played patriotic songs like 'We're Gonna Hang Out the Washing on the Siegfried Line', 'Wish Me Luck as You Wave Me Goodbye' and 'The White Cliffs of Dover' over and over again. Petrol was rationed and we had to travel everywhere by slow train. The hotels were unheated and the food was pretty basic but I still enjoyed myself. Many of the younger stage performers were in the forces, so the old stars came out of retirement to do their bit. I got the chance to see the likes of G.H. Elliott, who was truly a show-business legend. He was known as the 'Chocolate Coloured Coon' because he wore black face make-up. I heard him sing 'Lily of Laguna' and watched his soft shoe shuffle; it was an education in stage technique. Even in old age he was a song and dance virtuoso.

A great friend of my father's was Jack Hylton, probably the most famous of the pre-war band-leaders. By the time the war began, he'd become an impresario and got the rights to do stage versions of two hit radio shows, Tommy Handley's *ITMA* and *Garrison Theatre* which was set in an army base and fronted by the actor Jack Warner, later famous for his lead in *Dixon of Dock Green*. Jack introduced variety acts and kept lighthearted banter running through the show. On radio these two shows were great successes but good theatre demands action and spectacle – the eye as well as the ear has to be entertained – and Jack Hylton realised he needed to add an extra dimension, so he engaged the Billy Cotton Band to bolster the stage show.

Thanks to Tommy Handley's genius, *ITMA* did well in the wartime theatre. *Garrison Theatre*, though, was a real turkey, so when it transferred to Blackpool, Hylton persuaded Tommy Trinder, one of the biggest comedians of the time, to join the show for a limited season. Then began the great dressing-room saga. Contractually, my father was entitled to the No.1 dressing room and Jack Warner to No.2. These pecking-order squabbles might seem trivial to outsiders, but they mattered a great deal to stars whose self-worth as well as bankability could depend on a detail such as the number on a dressing-room door. Where was Tommy Trinder to be accommodated? As he was a great pal of my father's, it was suggested that Tommy should move in with him. (Jack Warner had no intention of moving out, and who could blame him?) Instead, Tommy insisted on having a special dressing-room built out of scenery on the side of the stage.

During one performance, Jack Warner was on stage doing an impression of Maurice Chevalier, which had a certain poignancy because France had just fallen. The band played the French national anthem, the Marseillaise, quietly in the background while in ringing Shakespearean tones Jack Warner declaimed that France would rise from the ashes again. At this point Tommy's voice rang out from the makeshift dressing-room, 'A drop of hot water in No.9 please' – a well-known catch phrase in public bathhouses at the time. Jack was beside himself with fury, Tommy assumed an air of innocence and couldn't understand what the fuss was about, and my father as usual tried to be the peace-maker. Then a stray German bomb dropped near the theatre, which besides playing havoc with bookings put these silly artistic tantrums in perspective.

Dad may not have achieved his dearest wish and flown in combat, but he and the band were subject to the dangers of travelling around Britain during the war, playing as they did in towns and cities that got a pasting from the German air force. In Plymouth, both the theatre where they were appearing and the hotel where they were staying went up in flames. The band got out just in time and spent the night on the moors overlooking the city. Dad was having supper at the Adelphi Hotel in Liverpool when it was hit by a bomb. He escaped injury and for the rest of the night travelled backwards and forwards on the Mersey ferry, on the principle that it was harder to hit a moving target.

During the blitz, a bomb dropped in the garden of our Willesden house and blew the front off, so we had to move out. We stayed at Farnham Common for a while with a good friend of my father's, Jimmy Philips, who was a music publisher. We eventually found a house nearby and we'd frequent the local pub, the Dog and Pot. It was there that my father and Jimmy first heard a German song which was a favourite of Rommel's Afrika Korps in the desert. The Eighth Army lads had adopted and adapted it, adding some pretty ribald words. Both Jimmy and my father were struck by the tune and got a song writer called Tommy Connor to put some lyrics to it. It was called 'Lili Marlene' and became immortal.

At about this time Leslie Grade, who had become my father's agent, went into the RAF. His brother Lew took over the agency and with his other brother, Bernard Delfont, created one of the greatest show-business dynasties of the century. The Grade organisation represented Dad until he died. There were plenty of heated discussions between client and agent over the years. Leslie used to tell the story of my dad pitching up in his office and demanding more work in London. When he was told that there weren't any more theatres left, that they were either booked up or bombed out, Dad hit the roof and shouted that he'd had enough, their partnership was forthwith dissolved. As Dad stormed out of the door Leslie shouted, 'You'll be back!' – and sure enough, he was. He'd left his hat behind.

In spite of having in Leslie Grade one of the best agents in the business, my father's career took a dip in the immediate post-war period and he seriously considered giving up the entertainment business and buying a garage. The problem was that the Billy Cotton Band seemed to have been around for ever; there was a dated feel to their music compared with that of orchestras such as the Ted Heath Band and the Squadronaires who had first formed ad hoc as groups of musicians serving together in the forces, then decided to stick together when they were demobbed. To the millions who had served in the forces these were the exciting and evocative sounds of the hectic war years, whereas Dad's band, having been playing since the twenties, seemed to belong to a sedate era that had vanished for ever.

I remember going with him to the Streatham Empire where he was playing to a half-empty theatre and worrying whether his share of the box-office takings would pay the musicians' wages. The truth was that live variety was dying – though ironically television was responsible for its resurrection and my father, having suffered through its declining years, was one of the chief beneficiaries when a bright new age dawned.

To add to the family's problems, my brother while in the RAF had been posted to Burma where he contracted first malaria and then TB. After a long convalescence at the famous Baragwanath Hospital in South Africa, Ted came home, was demobbed and got a job in the film industry. Then TB broke out in his other lung, at which point my father flew him out to Switzerland, which as a result of its crystal-clear and unpolluted mountain air had become a leading centre for the treatment of the disease. Following intensive care, Ted went back to work again, but the family always had some anxiety about his health – as it turned out, with good reason.

In desperate need of work, Dad went to the BBC to see an Australian called Jim Davidson who was at that time Assistant Head of Light Entertainment. Jim proposed some radio work on different days of each week. This was no good to Dad because he played all round the country, often in towns a long distance from the nearest radio studio. On the other hand, he couldn't afford to abandon live variety and keep the band in existence just for one broadcast a week. Jim Davidson thought for a moment and then said, 'How about a show on Sunday mornings?' This was a startling proposal. The BBC was still shrouded in Reithian gloom on Sundays, the founder of the BBC having decreed that no programmes should be broadcast which might distract churchgoing listeners from holy things. And the Billy Cotton Band with its raucous leader hardly qualified as a suitable religious offering. But Jim Davidson decided to take the risk and booked the band to do half a dozen shows at ten-thirty on Sunday mornings.

The show was an immediate success, though the strain on Dad and the band was immense. After a hard week on the road, they often had to travel through the night to get to the BBC studio by seven o'clock on Sunday morning for rehearsals. My father was to claim later that his famous catch phrase 'Wakey! Wakey!' was born when he arrived at the studio one Sunday morning to find the members of the band nodding with weariness in their chairs. 'Oi, come on,' he roared. 'Wakey! Wakey!' Noting its tonic effect on everyone in the studio, the producer suggested that that's how the show should begin. Far from being outraged by *The Billy Cotton Band Show*, the representatives of the churches on the BBC's religious advisory committee felt that the programme sent people off to church in an upbeat, cheerful mood. There was, though, the odd Puritan who believed that broadcast dance music on the Sabbath was the work of the devil. One Lancashire vicar was reported in the press as telling his congregation, 'The choice is yours, Billy Cotton or the Almighty!' Dad was flattered by the comparison. The Church's only concern was the programme's timing, which clashed with most church services which began somewhere between ten and eleven. The BBC then proposed that the programme should be moved to one-thirty, Sunday lunchtime, when families traditionally all gathered round their tables in convivial mood. It was this decision which transformed my father from being a fading band-leader into a national institution. Whole generations grew up and grew old associating the sound of *The Billy Cotton Band Show* with the smell of roast beef and Yorkshire pudding.

One unexpected side-effect of the radio show's success was that Dad's theatre bookings perked up again. Leslie Grade booked the band for a four-week tour with Two-Ton Tessie O'Shea. The show was called *Tess and Bill*, and ran for more than two years. Both Dad and Tessie were larger than life personalities – hugely so in Tessie's case – and they got on well together. They toured all round the country to packed theatres and were at one about everything but money. Tessie had a much shrewder appreciation of Dad's radio popularity than he had himself, and decided she'd take a percentage of the box office, whereas he preferred a fixed fee. Tessie's instinct paid off and the tour made her very rich, until she made a fatal miscalculation. They had worked all the London suburban theatres, from Edgware to Hackney and New Cross to Lewisham, then Tessie proposed a final visit to the Victoria Palace – a West End theatre with an enormous coach trade. Dad felt that Londoners who'd paid four and sixpence to see them in the suburbs wouldn't shell out twelve and sixpence for a repeat performance at the Victoria Palace, and he was right. Tessie lost a lot of money and *Tess and Bill* eventually split up.

Dad was soon drawing big crowds on the strength of the huge popularity his radio show had given him. Initially he had no interest in television, which began developing into a mass medium once the war was over. With the exception of a couple of Royal galas – celebrating the Coronation, and then the Queen's return from Australia – he refused invitations to appear. His reasons for doing so were strictly commercial: so long as the BBC had monopoly of television, their fees would remain unrealistically low – too low, Dad decided, to make it worth his while to put together elaborate programmes which could be used on only one occasion. Once the public had seen a show, that was that, he thought. Radio was different: the listeners were curious to see in the flesh the performers they had come to love. It was the arrival of ITV which changed his mind.

Meanwhile I had left school and toured the country with Dad while I waited to be called up for National Service. For Ted's twenty-first birthday, Dad bought him a brand-new MG Midget, in those days virtually the only mass-produced sports car on the market. A few months later, Dad and I were driving through Coventry and stopped off at a garage for petrol. There in the garage's showroom was a brand-new fire-engine-red

MG. I was gazing at it longingly when Dad came up and said, 'By the way, that's your car. Look after it.'

Later he told me that Ted had felt uncomfortable about having a state-of-the-art sports car while I was driving a clapped-out pre-war Fiat Topolino. He lobbied Father to get me one for my eighteenth birthday. What a way to get your first car, and how typical of both Ted and my father's generosity of spirit! I was a very lucky lad, and knew it.

My father loved cars, every type of car, from Rolls Bentley through Aston Martin to Jaguars and Mercedes and the latest line in runabouts. He had a Morris Minor which we called 'Leaping Leaner': it leaned when he got in and it leaped when he got out! One day I was in his office when he received a phone call from Jack Barclay, the distributor for Rolls Royce and Bentley in Hanover Square. Jack invited him for a sherry. When we arrived at the showroom there was a magnificent Rolls Bentley gleaming in its newness and with the number-plate BC 1. Dad took one look and said, 'I'll have it.' The sherry was swapped for champagne and joy was unconfined – until they produced the invoice. 'What's this?' he asked. 'It's the number-plate I want – I've got a Bentley and you sold it to me!' Jack Barclay took it very well and gave the old man the number-plate. BC 1 was on many a car until Dad died.

I was eventually called up, and joined the Royal Sussex Regiment in late 1946 when the world was comparatively peaceful. On the basis that I preferred to ride than walk – especially with full equipment on my back – I was commissioned into the Royal Army Service Corps as a transport officer.

The only truly terrifying thing that happened to me during my military service was my encounter with the legendary Regimental Sergeant-Major Brittain on the parade ground at Mons Barracks, Aldershot. He was a fearsome sight and had a voice that could shatter glass at half a mile. One exchange with him when I was dozy on parade still lingers in my memory.

RSM: 'Are you a spiritualist, sir?'

Me: 'No, sir.'

RSM: 'Well, you've got your head on an ethereal plane, your body in the West End, and your feet are just about in Aldershot. Put him in the guard room.'

Long after I left the army, I met the RSM again. I was producing a record show for television and a girl singer known as Billie Anthony had a new record out called 'Fall in for Love', on which Brittain, long since retired from the army, appeared at the beginning of the song bellowing the command, 'Fall in for love!' So we booked Billie Anthony and also Mr Brittain to perform the song live in the studio. When Britten arrived I went up to him and said, 'I have waited a long time to say this, *sir*. Stand there and don't move till I tell you.'

The only time I fired a shot and hit a live target was not during my army career but shortly afterwards. We were staying at Sandbanks for Christmas, and there was quite a big house party that included the composer and impresario Noel Gay. We used to go sailing every day, and on this occasion I took with me a four-ten shotgun to shoot shag, the voracious green cormorant. Fifty yards off our port bow, a beautiful swan gave us a disdainful glance and then lazily spread its wings to take off. Jokingly, I said, 'I'll ginger him up,' and fired quite casually into the air in the general direction of the bird. To my horror, this freak shot killed the swan outright. My father said, 'That's illegal. All swans belong to the Queen. You could go to gaol for that.' Someone else suggested that 'we'd better suppress the evidence', so we pulled the body into the boat and cruised around until dusk fell. Then we went ashore and marched in single file up to the house, the swan over Dad's back while the rest of us chanted the Seven Dwarfs' 'Heigh-ho' song from *Snow White and the Seven Dwarfs*.

We found Noel Gay dozing on a settee in the sitting-room. 'Look, Noel,' someone shouted, 'a Christmas goose.' Noel opened one eye. 'I never eat goose,' he confided and went back to sleep. Just so he wouldn't feel left out of the fun, we decided to stow the swan in the boot of his car, until Christmas night, when we all dressed in dinner jackets and boarded a dinghy to bury the swan at sea. The corpse was tied to a trawler drag and heaved overboard. We underestimated its weight: all that happened was the swan's neck went under and its bottom bobbed up. I doubt whoever found it with an iron bar round its neck would think it had died a natural death.

Dad was at his most exuberant on holiday at Sandbanks, when laughter, joking and frenzied activity surrounded him. Next door to our house was the Royal Motor Yacht Club whose Commodore was an ex-naval officer called Bersey, a splendid man but a stickler for protocol. Every morning at eight o'clock a saluting gun would be fired and a Blue Ensign run to the masthead. It so happened that in the garage of his Sandbanks house Dad kept a whole load of old stage-props, including the Soviet flag, the Hammer and Sickle, which had been used for a stage song called 'Comrades'. This was in the early days of the Cold War when the former camaraderie between Russia and the West had evaporated.

One morning the steward came out of the club house, checked his watch, fired the saluting gun, tied the furled Ensign to the halyard and looked up to see the Hammer and Sickle already flying proudly from the masthead. He dashed inside and brought out the apoplectic Commodore in his dressing-gown. The local constabulary was called in just in case the Russians were planning an invasion of the Bournemouth area and had landed an advance raiding party. About a year later, the Commodore came up to my father who was drinking in the Club verandah. 'Don't think I don't know who put that Russian flag up,' he spluttered.

I was demobbed in the latter part of 1948. I had a place at Clare College, Cambridge but I didn't fancy taking it up; the world of academia wasn't for me. So I became slightly unfocused and, having nothing better to do, went on tour with Dad, protesting all the time that I really must set about getting a career. He couldn't see the problem. He'd say, 'You're enjoying yourself, aren't you?' and point out that we enjoyed each other's company; he was doing very well financially and I was very useful to him. That was debatable. I had two main tasks: one was to act as his chauffeur; the other to reconnoitre every town the band was visiting to find out which cinemas might be showing cowboy Western films in the afternoons.

I went to enormous trouble to locate these local flea pits where Dad would sit down assuring me we were in for a treat. Before the opening titles had finished running, his head would drop onto his chest and he'd snore his way through the entire film. Having woken up, he'd take off in search of a cup of tea, murmuring appreciation of a film he'd never seen. That happened again and again.

During this period, my father took a week off which happened to coincide with the British Grand Prix for Formula One racing cars. He suggested we drive up to Silverstone to watch the practice laps for the great event. Since pre-war days, he had been a member of the prestigious British Racing Drivers' Club, so he knew most of the personalities in the motor racing game. He also displayed proudly on his radiator the Brooklands 120 mph badge commemorating the occasion he clocked a lap at 123.89 mph in an MG and became one of a very select group.

We waved goodbye to my mother who fondly imagined that Dad was going to the Grand Prix as an interested spectator. When we arrived at Silverstone, Dad sought out Wilkie Wilkinson who used to prepare his racing cars before the war and had joined forces with a couple of wealthy up and coming drivers to form an ERA (English Racing Automobile) team. It soon became clear that Dad had arranged beforehand to drive one of Wilkie's cars.

I was dumbfounded. Dad was forty-nine years of age and suffered from high blood pressure. I watched in amazement as he got his crash hat and visor out of the boot of our car, put them on, and drove off round the circuit. He clocked up a respectable if not spectacular lap time and on returning to the pits said that since there were still four days of practice before the big race he'd plenty of time to sharpen up. On the drive back home he said nonchalantly, 'Best not to tell your mother about this, she'll only worry.'

And so this charade went on throughout the rest of the week. Each morning at breakfast he'd spin some yarn about his plans for the day and Mother would nod, apparently understandingly

until Saturday, the day of the race, when she cut short Dad's fanciful musings. She said, 'I don't mind you not telling me you're driving in a motor race today, it's the insinuation that I can't read that upsets me. The story's in every newspaper, including the fact that I'm not supposed to know about it. So off you go and if you kill yourself I'll never talk to you again. *And* don't come home stinking of petrol as you've done every day this week.'

In the actual race he did remarkably well. He was due to take the car over at the halfway point when it stopped to refuel. Just before the car arrived at the pit, the petrol bowser drew up and through some fault starting spewing fuel under pressure all over the place. Dad was crouched on the pit counter ready to jump into the car as soon as it arrived and so got a face-wash of high-octane petrol. His goggles were soaked and he obviously couldn't see clearly. I begged him not to get into the car, but he said, 'If you think I'm missing this, you're out of your mind,' and off he went. He started slowly but the wind soon blew away the petrol film on his goggles and he finished the race a creditable fourth. Some of the legendary pre-war drivers, George Easton, John Cobb and Earl Howe, came up to congratulate him and they all agreed that he'd taught the youngsters a thing or two and shown there was still life in old dogs. However, the strain had obviously taken its toll on him and on the way home he confided in me regretfully that he was hanging up his helmet and goggles. His part-time career as a racing driver was over.

TWO

When I came out of the army, the Cotton family had a house on the Thames, at Old Windsor. There was a whole colony of showbiz people living on Ham Island, and one of them, Reginald Armitage, better known as Noel Gay, was a great friend of my father and mother. He was a successful music publisher who also wrote best-selling songs: 'The Lambeth Walk', 'Round the Marble Arch', 'There's Something about a Soldier', 'The Fleet's in Port Again', 'Hey! Little Hen' and 'Run Rabbit Run' – just the kind of music my father's band played best. One day Noel Gay invited me for a trip up river on his launch. I set out unemployed and I came back with a job as a song-plugger for the Noel Gay Music Company based in Denmark Street, better known as Tin Pan Alley.

In these jargon-ridden days, song-pluggers would be known as exploitation men. This was a time when many people still had pianos in their front-rooms and made their own music. They'd go along to a Littlewoods store and there in the music department would be a song-plugger sitting at a piano inviting them to buy the song he was playing. If you strolled down Denmark Street in the summer when office windows were open, you'd hear a piano in every room bashing out the publisher's latest song for the benefit of singers, band-leaders and anyone else who might perform or broadcast it. The song-plugger spent his life trying to bribe, cajole and persuade performers to include his songs in their programmes, which in turn created a market for the sheet music.

We paid special attention to bands and artists who had spots on radio. Record programmes were becoming a big thing in the broadcasting schedules – there was *Jack Jackson's Record*

Round-up on a Saturday night, for example, which played many records and helped to create some hits. The ultimate goal was to get your song played in programmes like his or *Two-Way Family Favourites, Housewives' Choice* or *The Billy Cotton Band Show.* We'd even shell out a fiver, which was a lot of money in those days, to get hold of an advance copy of the *Radio Times* to find out which stars and bands were scheduled to appear on air a couple of weeks later. Then we could badger them to play our music. The band-leader Geraldo was a very big star at that time; he was always on the air, so if you could get him to add one of your songs to his repertoire you were quids in. Another target of the song-pluggers was a vocal group called the Keynotes who had a weekly spot on a radio show called *Take it from Here.* And at that time every self-respecting cinema had a resident organist. There was a regular spot on the BBC's Light Programme at around ten o'clock two or three times a week, which was dedicated to cinema organ music, so organists like Reginald Dixon and Robinson Cleaver were among the song-pluggers' favourite prey.

The seamy side of the industry was the payment of 'plug-money' to bribe artists to sing or play particular songs. A popular singer called Issy Bonn used to start at the top of Denmark Street and call on the music publishers one by one, telling them he had a number of radio engagements coming up and asking if they would they like him to sing one of their songs. He invited them to put their responses in a plain brown envelope. Eventually the BBC, which was still the only domestic broadcaster around, put a stop to plug-money by warning performers they would be banned from the airwaves if they were caught taking bribes. But there was an atmosphere of desperation about the whole business as records became more and more popular and the sales of sheet music plummeted.

When I first joined Noel Gay, I had business cards printed with my name, William F. Cotton, inscribed on them. One day I tried to get to see the band-leader Oscar Rabin to sell him a song. I gave my card to his secretary who returned it to me smartish saying that Mr Rabin was far too busy to see me. Oscar was a good friend of my father's but I took his refusal philosophically and was just leaving when he came out of his office.

'Hello, Bill,' he said, 'what are you doing here?'

'I'm a song-plugger for Noel and I popped in on the off chance you might be interested in our latest number, but you were too busy to see me,' I said.

He looked puzzled and then said, 'So *you're* William F. Cotton! For heaven's sake, don't embarrass your dad's friends by not letting on who you are. You're not William F. Cotton, you're Billy Cotton Junior. That's what your card should say.'

Thus was my identity in show business fixed by my relationship to my father, and though he's been dead for more than thirty years, I'm still conscious of being the junior member of a wonderful though sometimes stormy partnership.

I didn't work for Noel Gay for very long. Noel had brought his son Richard Armitage into the firm at the same time as I joined, and although Richard and I got on very well – indeed, he was among my dearest friends to the day he died – there wasn't really room for two apprentices in the business and I wasn't learning much, so I moved over to Chappell's in Bond Street, which was run by two American brothers, Max and Louis Dreyfus. They were probably the biggest music publishers in the world at that time, so song-plugging was a serious part of their operation. A chap called Teddy Holmes was the boss of a whole army of song-pluggers and he kept us on the hop; we must have made three or four visits every night to theatres and broadcasting and television studios.

One of the great things about working for Chappell's was that they controlled the music for most of the big American musicals around at that time. *Oklahoma!*, *Annie Get Your Gun*, *Carousel* . . . name any Broadway show, Chappell's would probably have the rights to it. I put some of these American songs my father's way. The very first, I recall, was 'Bewitched, Bothered and Bewildered'. Played by a pianist called Bill Snyder, it had gone to the top of the Hit Parade in the States and the Billy Cotton Band was among the first to play it in Britain. At that time Chappell's had an office in St George's Street above which there was a flat where a very young and gorgeous Joan Collins lived with her lover at the time. It was a volatile relationship; they clearly didn't always see eye to eye. We in Chappell's office could tell this was the case because it wasn't only sparks that used to fly above our heads – I remember hearing plenty of furniture and crockery being smashed. That's perhaps how the delectable Joan trained for some of her later roles.

It wasn't all hard grinding labour – we started a show-business football team. One of our numbers was a big strong Scots lad who was in the chorus of *South Pacific*. He wasn't all that good a footballer but he made a super special agent. His name was Sean Connery. Eventually the showbiz football team became famous and had a star-studded line-up: Tommy Steele, Kenny Lynch, Glen Mason and Ronnie Carroll all played for us regularly. Ronnie had been in the Northern Ireland youth team but by the time he joined us his footballing brain was having ideas his body couldn't cope with.

I was sharing a flat in London with Gerry Kunz, a childhood friend whom I'd met again in the Army. Gerry's father Charlie was the famous pianist, and *he* was a great friend of my father's. We lived in London during the week and spent the weekends at our respective parents' homes. One day Gerry said to me, 'Can you lend me a fiver?' I asked him why he needed it. Solemnly, he replied, 'Because I want to take out the girl I'd love to marry.' Until that moment I didn't know of her existence. I hadn't a spare fiver but I did offer to get him a couple of free tickets to my father's show at the Victoria Palace. I was off to play football but I said casually that I'd pop round to the theatre after the game and perhaps we could persuade my father to take us all out to supper. My offer may have *sounded* offhand but I was consumed with curiosity about this girl. Unfortunately, during the game someone kicked me in the ribs and afterwards I was in too much pain to pay much attention to her.

That Christmas, Gerry spent Christmas with the Cottons and then in my red MG we drove down together to his family in Middleton for New Year. On New Year's Day we were invited

33

to a party at the home of Gerry's girlfriend. Her name was Bernadine Maud Sinclair but she was universally known as Boo – a nursery pet name derived from her Norfolk nanny's insistence she was a 'booty'. This party was the climax of a highly alcoholic festive season – I vaguely recall at some point drinking gin from a tea pot. I was already fairly merry when I got to the party. I was chatting to the girl I had taken there, looked up and saw Boo standing on the other side of the room in a grey dress with a rope belt round it. It was a moment of revelation; it was as though I was seeing her for the first time, and I was bowled over. I went over to her and said, 'Excuse me, would you like to marry me?' She grinned and said, 'I think you've had too much to drink.' 'All right,' I replied, 'I'll ask you again when I'm sober.'

As these parties do, we moved on to someone else's house and eventually staggered home to bed, but at eight-thirty a.m. sharp I was up and in my right mind and presented myself at Boo's house again. Her mother's housekeeper opened the door, obviously not amused that I was disturbing the family at such an hour. She closed the door in my face and left me standing on the doorstep while she went to fetch Boo, who said, 'Hello, what do you want?' I replied, 'Well, I've just come to say that I'm now stone-cold sober and will you marry me?' She laughed and said, 'No, but I'll give you a cup of tea.' The family was at breakfast, and her stepfather, who harboured the deepest suspicions about the motives of any young man courting his stepdaughter, was less than cordial. But I'd learned a thing or two as a song-plugger about the art of ingratiating myself with people I needed a favour from, so I behaved towards Boo's parents in a most deferential manner, calling her stepfather 'sir' and charming her mother with my sunny smile.

Boo had a *pied-à-terre* in London, a flat over the family's undertaking business in Kentish Town, and every day I contrived somehow to propose to her either by letter or phone or face to face in the romantic setting of stacked coffins and blank tombstones. First I had to establish that my pal Gerry was not a contender for her affections. She quickly reassured me:

she'd grown up with Gerry and it was one of those relationships that could never move beyond the stage of close friendship. A year or two older than me, Boo had served in the WRNS during the war and been engaged to an RAF officer, but the relationship didn't survive the anti-climax of peacetime and they split up. She insisted she wasn't looking to marry *anyone* at the moment, but that didn't put me off my daily proposal ritual, and after my laying siege to her for about six months she finally surrendered.

I was ecstatic but slightly apprehensive about telling my parents. I knew my mother would be a pushover – Boo's genuine charm was bound to win her over – but my father was a different matter. He had a very curious attitude to his sons' girlfriends; it was almost as though he resented them for taking our attention away from him. So I summoned up my courage, picked up the phone and told him that I had got engaged and I'd like him to meet the girl. 'Engaged?' he growled. 'What do you want to do that for?' I'd no intention of getting into a pointless argument with him so I asked him if I could bring her along to the Brixton Empress where he was performing. 'Fine,' he said casually. I persisted. 'Is there any chance you might take us out for a meal afterwards?' No, he already had an arrangement. 'Fine,' I said casually, put the phone down and waited. Sure enough, he phoned back and said, 'Your mother says I should take you out.'

I introduced Boo to Dad in his dressing-room. He was barely polite, though in mitigation it should be said he was always extremely nervous before a show, pacing the floor, clicking his fingers and wiping the sweat from his brow. Boo was quite unfazed by his cold manner. When we left him and went for a quick drink in the bar, she didn't ask anxiously, 'Do you think he liked me, and if not, why not?' She was one of those poised, self-possessed personalities who are at peace with themselves. If Dad took against her, that was his problem, not hers.

After the show, we waited in a corridor while he changed. Then my mother turned up, obviously anxious things should go well. Dad decided to impress Boo with his importance by taking

35

us to the exclusive Albany Club in Savile Row, which was run by a man called Bill Little who knew everyone who was anyone. As Billy Cotton, Britain's most famous band-leader, friend of the stars, confidant of royalty, strutted in, Bill Little came hurrying up, but then to Dad's astonishment and chagrin he swept right past him and greeted Boo like a long-lost friend, kissing her on both cheeks and enquiring how she and the family were. Dad couldn't believe he was being upstaged by my girlfriend whose name he could barely remember. Later, in a heavy attempt at humour, he surveyed the menu and said gruffly, 'Make the most of it, it's the last time we're coming here.' Quick as a flash, Boo said sweetly, 'If you can't afford it, I'll pay.' It took time, but in the end they became close friends because Dad had to admire her independence of spirit and honesty.

To celebrate our engagement, I took Boo to see Frank Sinatra at the Palladium, Dad having fixed a box for us. Frank was then at the peak of his career as a singer before he became better known as a movie star. He was sensational. When we left the theatre, Boo was very quiet, and when I pressed her she said, 'Do you think we are being a bit hasty, getting married?' I went cold. In a clumsy attempt at a joke, I protested, 'But I've already bought the ring.' She laughed it off and I delivered her to her flat and went home to mine, only to spend the whole night staring at the ceiling, convinced that my life was about to disintegrate. Years later, after Sinatra had been performing at the Royal Festival Hall, I had breakfast with him. I said, 'Do you realise you nearly buggered up my life?' I told him the story of Boo's strange turn and he howled with laughter. 'In the end it came out all right,' I said, 'but how many other people are walking around cursing you for breaking up their love affairs by doing nothing more than singing to them?'

We fixed the wedding for 21 October 1950. Predictably, Dad decided to be difficult. He said he couldn't make it; 'In October, I'm working in Newcastle.' I knew he'd plucked the excuse out of thin air; he never knew his dates off the top of his head that far in advance. I rang my mother and told her what Dad had said and added, 'Tell him, will you, that I recall a time when he changed his performance dates to fit in with a motor race, and if he doesn't want to do the same for my wedding, ask him to send along a cheque and I'll let him know how things went next time we meet.' I saw him a few days later. He cleared his throat and said, 'Oh, by the way, I managed to change those dates in October.' When I recounted the saga to my brother, he said, 'You're lucky! When I told him about the date of my wedding, he actually altered his programme to make sure he was so far away he couldn't possibly get to the ceremony. But when the great day came, he duly appeared in top hat and morning suit, having switched his dates around yet again.' Neither Ted nor I doubted that the old man loved us dearly; he just had this very strange quirk.

Chappell's recognised my married state by raising my salary to twelve quid a week and Dad let us have the bungalow at Ham Island as our first home – he bought a more spacious house in Farnham Common. The bungalow may have been too small for him but to us it was a palace and we knew most of the bohemian set who lived on that part of the island. As well as Noel Gay there was Lupino Lane, the star of the original pre-war Victoria Palace production of *Me and My Girl*, Bill Weston Drury, one of the original casting directors in the British film industry, and his son Budge, who did the same job at Pinewood. Budge's wife, Jean Capra, had been Poppy Poo Pah, the sexy female character in Tommy Hanley's *ITMA*. Then there was Jack Swinburne, the production manager for Alexander Korda, and his wife, Mamie Souter, an old music-hall star who had a habit of going on an alcoholic bender every now and again. There was also Russell Lloyd, a film editor, who had once been married to Rosamund John, a star of the silver screen, but had then married a gorgeous model called Valerie. My brother Ted and his wife Beryl also had a bungalow on the island, and he and Russell Lloyd worked together at the Shepperton Studios. The odd ones out were the Clarkes. He was a typical banker who worked at Hambros and went native every weekend. All in all we were a very happy community.

One day I called into the BBC studios when Dad was recording a programme and I ran into Johnny Johnston who had done well for himself master-minding the singing groups who provided the musical backing to radio comedies – he ran the Keynotes for *Take it from Here*, the Beaux and the Belles for *Ray's a Laugh* and the Soupstains for *Ignorance is Bliss*. They were more or less the same singers, Johnny just changed the name for each show – he sang in the group, composed some of the music, arranged the rest and acted as manager. He was a multi-talented musician who, like my father, had come up the hard way, so they were soulmates.

Johnny had founded a company with a woman called Micky Michaels. It was called The Michael Reine Music Company, a combination of the surname of Micky Michaels and the maiden name of Nona, Johnny's wife. Apparently, Micky Michaels wanted out, and Johnny asked me whether I would be interested in buying her share. I talked to my father and he lent me the money, which was fifteen hundred pounds. So I gave in my notice at Chappell's and went off to make my fortune at Michael Reine's.

The first project I was involved in was a song based on the old Irish folk ballad called 'The Bard of Armagh', whose traditional tune had also been used for a couple of Western songs, 'Streets of Laredo' and 'The Dying Cowboy'. Johnny Johnston adapted the tune, Tommy Connor wrote lyrics for it and they created a hit called 'The Homing Waltz'. Because the original tune was out of copyright, we were able to register our song and as a bonus got a percentage when any of the other versions were played. Johnny took the song along to Vera Lynn who had just enjoyed a huge success with 'Auf Wiedersehen, Sweetheart'. She sang it, Decca recorded it and the very first effort of Michael Reine reached the top of the pops.

Vera also recorded our next big hit, which was called 'Forget Me Not'. This time, Johnny had written it with Bunny Lewis who was a successful agent. But on the way to the studio they still hadn't managed to put lyrics to the middle four bars of the song. In a slightly inebriated state I burst out into poetry and suggested the six words: 'Parting brings sorrow; hope for tomorrow'. 'That's it!' they cried. It didn't win me an entry in the *Oxford Book of Poetry* but I ended up securing for myself the royalty on a third of the song, which proved to be a nice little earner.

We published 'Forget Me Not' in the run-up to Christmas and put in a lot of graft publicising it. One morning I read in the newspaper that the children in a spina bifida ward at Carshalton Hospital intended to sing it on Christmas Day in a programme presented by Wilfred Pickles who was a big radio star at the time. I showed the article to Johnny Johnston and we agreed that we've have to spend a fortune entertaining any singer we were trying to persuade to plug it, hence we ought to offer the same amount in kind to the children in hospital. We set off for Carshalton loaded down with toys, sweets and books.

When we arrived, the ward sister was fulsome in her gratitude. She explained that the children were from very poor homes and would probably be in hospital for a very long time. Johnny noticed a piano near the ward and was soon belting out popular songs, including, of course, 'Forget Me Not'. All the children joined in except for one little girl who was lying on a kind of board to keep her spine straight. She just looked on wistfully, and the sister told us that she never spoke; she had been virtually abandoned by her parents. After we'd done our round of the wards, we went up to the little girl and told her we'd be back again after Christmas and we'd expect her to join in the singing. We duly went back and she did join in. The presents were piled up round the Christmas tree and I was glad I wasn't there to see them opened – I'd have cried my eyes out.

At Christmas, the BBC often asked the old man to present a week of *Housewives' Choice*, the enormously popular record programme on what in those days was the Light Programme. He passed on to me the job of picking the records and writing his script in return for my being able to keep the fee as a Christmas present.

On one occasion, I included a Sophie Tucker record in the show and with eight million other listeners heard him announce,

'And now for all Sophie Fucker tans . . .' 'Do you think anyone noticed?' he asked me anxiously after the transmission. Dad was no mumbler, he spoke always at a near shout. 'Naw,' I said, 'I only just caught it and I was listening very carefully.' The listeners obviously realised it was a slip of the tongue and didn't hold it against him.

When he was invited to appear as a guest on Roy Plomley's *Desert Island Discs*, Dad asked me to sort out the records he should choose. When I showed him the list he was indignant. He'd assumed all eight would feature the Billy Cotton Band. He obviously had never listened to the programme.

Johnny and I imported a novelty song from America called 'Bell Bottom Blues' which brought me for the first time into contact with a lovely girl, Alma Cogan, who was to remain a firm friend of mine for the rest of her tragically short life. She recorded three of our songs – 'Bell Bottom Blues', 'I Can't Tell a Waltz from a Tango' and 'Never Do a Tango with an Eskimo' – all of which did very well at the sales counter. One day I met Alma in the street and invited her up for a cup of tea with Johnny and myself in our office, which was a pretty tatty back room in Denmark Street. I asked our factotum, Ronnie, to go out and get some tea. Meanwhile, Alma looked round the office and somewhat sniffily commented on the state of our sofa. I pointed out that it was actually very useful and doubled as a put-you-up bed, which I demonstrated by pulling it apart – whereupon a rat the size of a small cat jumped out and vanished into the back room. All three of us fought to be the first to get up on the desk. We were all standing on the desk when Ronnie came back. He looked up at us and said, 'I didn't realise you wanted *high* tea.' We moved out of the office very soon after that and got better premises on Denmark Street.

Our next stroke of luck had to do with a television series called *Friends and Neighbours*. Its theme tune was written by an excellent musician called Malcolm Lockyer. He'd been under contract to one of our competitors, David Platt of Southern Music, whose reaction to the song was, 'Don't bring me this sort of rubbish. Write me something decent.' Upset, Malcolm withdrew the song and offered it to us. It was perfect for *The Billy Cotton Band Show*, and shot into the Top Ten. We hit on a novel idea to plug it. There was a busking group called *The Happy Wanderers* who used to perform in Oxford Street, so we paid them a fiver to march up and down Denmark Street playing 'Friends and Neighbours'. It drove the other publishers crazy, though our visiting celebrities thought it a hoot. This wheeze got the Happy Wanderers an appearance on television, and it also got one of their number into plenty of trouble when his wife saw him on the box. When he went back home, she threw his supper at him: she'd never told the neighbours he was a busker; they thought he had a job in the city.

As well as my song-plugging, I had a sideline as a journalist writing a gossip column, 'The Alley Cat', for the *New Musical Express*. I enjoyed being the Nigel Dempster of Denmark Street and it confirmed my opinion that nearly everyone loves to see his or her name in print even if the story isn't particularly complimentary, just so long as the name isn't misspelled. My journalism helped our business along because a steady flow of performers came into the office with tidbits of gossip about show business in general and themselves in particular, and this mine of information produced all kinds of good business contacts.

One afternoon I took my weekly copy round to the *New Musical Express* offices and the editor asked me if I'd like to buy the paper. I thought he was being funny, but apparently the proprietor felt he was getting too old for all the worry of running a newspaper and he wanted to sell up. At the time our business, Michael Reine, was flourishing and quite cash-rich, so the more I thought about the idea of being a newspaper proprietor the better I liked it. At the asking price the *NME* was undoubtedly a bargain and its circulation was rising to the point where it was becoming a threat to the *Melody Maker*, the leading paper of the business. There was one catch. Another potential buyer was coming round to see the editor at seven o'clock that evening and he had instructions to do a deal with whoever came up with the asking price first.

When I got back, bursting to tell Johnny we were onto a

fortune, he was out of the office and despite all my frantic efforts I couldn't contact him. At eight o'clock that evening the *NME* editor phoned me at home to tell me that Maurice Kinn, agent of Joe Loss and Cyril Stapleton, two of the leading band-leaders in the country, had made an offer and he was now the new proprietor of the paper. I was quite sad. What made it worse was that Johnny chewed me off for not assuming he would have gone along with my decision. And to add insult to injury Kinn sacked me and took over my column himself. I would probably have done the same thing if I were him, so we remained friends. He went on to make the paper an extremely valuable property and became a very wealthy man when he eventually sold out.

During this period, political argument had been raging about whether or not there should be a rival television channel funded by advertising to break BBC TV's monopoly, and eventually the legislation was put in place to set up the commercial companies. This prospect sparked off a frenzy of activity in advertising agencies. They realised they'd need musical jingles to punctuate their commercials, so they began to look closely at the BBC's radio programmes and were impressed by their catchy theme tunes, the best of which had invariably been composed by Johnny Johnston. Soon a procession of bowler-hatted, grey-suited advertising executives were beating a path to our door. Johnny knew exactly what was required. To order, he could hammer out on the piano a catchy piece, both music and words; then he'd arrange it for one of his groups, sing the lyric himself and record it in his own studio. He made a lot of money, and deservedly so, because he had a genius for this highly specialised form of music and rhyme.

Nona, Johnny's wife, had a good head for business and was running the office very efficiently, and Johnny himself was on a creative roll as TV commercials took up more and more of his time. It was clear to me that the sheet-music industry was sinking into irreversible decline, and there wasn't much place for me in the business – though Johnny never even hinted that I was becoming virtually a passenger. I began to look around, and the larger than life figure of my dad again loomed into view. By now, independent television had been established and Lew Grade, who ran ATV, one of the biggest companies, contracted Dad to do half a dozen variety shows. Though popular, they lacked a distinctive format and so presented Dad with a problem. He couldn't afford to use material people were paying good money to see in the live theatre, and a radio show didn't usually adapt well to a visual medium. Hence, he wasn't a very happy man.

Dad shared his worries with me and I suggested to him that though the ITV shows didn't satisfy his high standards, the independent companies were trouncing the BBC in the ratings, which must be worrying the corporation no end – they might welcome an approach from him. I encouraged him to go and see Ronnie Waldman, who was the BBC's Head of Entertainment, to talk about a combined radio-television deal. In April 1955, Ronnie took Dad out for a meal and was most enthusiastic about the whole idea until they got down to talking about money. Quite simply, the BBC did not pay realistic fees. Although *The Billy Cotton Band Show* on radio gave my father priceless publicity, financially he was actually out of pocket because he only got the statutory fee for a half hour's broadcast, out of which he had to pay the wages of eighteen musicians.

The BBC's founder, Lord Reith, saw the BBC as a public service corporation for whom it is a privilege to work; vulgar questions of monetary reward ought to be of no consequence. Ronnie asked Dad outright how much he wanted. Without much hope that a deal was possible, Dad wrote down a figure on a paper napkin, folded it in two and handed it to Ronnie, asking him not to open it until he got back to his office in case it spoiled his lunch. Ronnie couldn't resist opening it on the spot and immediately agreed to meet Dad's price, though, as he told me afterwards, he had no idea how he could persuade the BBC to pay such a figure for one television act. Most of the BBC's top managers were still bogged down in the radio era. The show-business mentality, which ITV adopted from the beginning, had not yet permeated the corridors of Broadcasting House.

Somehow Ronnie managed to persuade the BBC to meet Dad's figure, pointing out to his bosses that quite apart from Billy Cotton's star quality and drawing power, he would become a reliable fixed point in the schedules. While most big stars tended to get bored, develop itchy feet and move on, the Billy Cotton Band constituted a built-in stabiliser – BBC work paid the band's wages bill for a significant part of the year, and that guaranteed Dad's loyalty to the corporation. So Dad signed up and became a BBC man for the rest of his life, simply on the strength of a figure scrawled in ink on a crumpled paper napkin which he and Ronnie accepted as a binding contract. It specified a three-year contract and ran for twelve.

If money was one problem Ronnie had to solve, the other was the creation of a distinctive production style with which Dad would be happy. Here Ronnie knew exactly what he wanted to do. In his department, there was a young producer called Brian Tesler who had a most unusual pedigree, having arrived in the television service by way of a first-class honours degree at Oxford. 'Trust me,' Ronnie said. 'He's a protégé of mine and I don't get paid to make mistakes.' He went on to point out that television was a much more complicated medium than radio, one which used expensive equipment and large production teams. He believed producers should be highly organised and possess brain power as well as creative flair. 'And Brian's got it all,' he added. Well, Dad went through the motions of huffing and puffing at all this highfalutin' Oxford stuff, but one good professional always recognises another and Brian soon won him over with a combination of genuine charm and great efficiency. Little wonder Brian ended up as Managing Director of London Weekend Television. After working with Dad, the rest of his television career must have been a doddle.

Brian recalls going to introduce himself to the old man who was working in Manchester, and hanging about waiting for the show to end. He and Dad went off for a late meal, during which Brian explained his ideas for the television series. As they parted, Dad patted him on the back and said, 'Sleep well, son. Don't worry. I'm much too good for you to be able to bugger up.' When Dad pitched up in the studio to meet Brian for a first rehearsal, he was confronted by a line of dancing girls called the Silhouettes He was appalled. The main attraction of every *Cotton Show* was Dad prancing around on the stage, but professional dancing was different. 'I'm no Anton Dolin,' he snarled, referring to one of the leading male ballet dancers of the time. 'I can't dance, and I'm much too old to learn now.' 'Nonsense,' said Brian cheerfully. 'You are going to like these girls so much the urge to join in with them will be irresistible.' And it was, though only after Dad went to the studio week after week and practised with the head girl and the choreographer, who commented that playing football and moving around a boxing ring must have given Dad a natural sense of balance. Eventually, he was to cherish a report in the *Dancing Times* which said, 'It takes a band-leader of sixty to show the British dancing public what a *pas de deux* should be.'

Dad's career might have been flourishing, but on the domestic front there was pain and strife. I don't know whether it was because my brother and I had both got married and set up our own homes or that Dad was going through some sort of male menopause, but he drifted into an affair with Doreen Stephens, the female vocalist in his band. He was quite open about it – indeed, he flaunted it, almost as though a relationship with a much younger woman was an affirmation of his virility. At first, my mother ignored what was going on, but it all became so embarrassing that she could stand it no longer. She moved permanently into the Sandbanks house and Dad bought a flat in London. All his friends tried to warn him that he was making a fool of himself, but the more people tried to dissuade him, the more stubborn he became and the whole thing reached the proportions of a public scandal. It was sordid beyond belief – at one point, Dad and a very close friend demeaned themselves by vying for Doreen's affections. To those of us who cared for him, the spectacle of two middle-aged men trying to out-macho each other in the pursuit of a young woman was utterly gruesome.

My mother behaved with great dignity throughout the whole business, which lasted for about four years. We none of us knew what was going to happen; Dad could be mulish in his single-mindedness. The extraordinary thing was that though he was a national figure, the press did not expose this affair; there was none of that intrusiveness into public personalities' private lives masquerading as investigative journalism to which we've since become accustomed.

All this took its toll on Dad's health. He was by now a man in his mid-fifties, and having to behave with the ardour of an ageing Lothario as well as working seven days a week put intolerable pressure on his system. He would work all week in some theatre or other, dash down to London for his weekly radio show and then travel to another town for the start of the following week's engagements. I think that deep down he hated himself for the way he was behaving towards my mother; he loved her deeply but couldn't resist the flattery implied by the attentions of a younger woman. Eventually, in 1955, he performed one time too many, did a show, took his bow, came off stage and collapsed. He was rushed to hospital with a suspected heart attack; in fact, he'd had a nervous breakdown. The doctors insisted that he needed three months' complete rest. We were relieved his condition was not more serious but the problem was what would happen to his band. Dad cared for them and worried about them. In fact, my cousin Laurie, a member of the band, took over as temporary leader so they were able to meet their immediate touring engagements.

The Sunday broadcast was a different matter. I phoned Jim Davidson at the BBC to discuss the crisis. To my astonishment he said, 'Why don't you do the broadcast? In fact, do the lot. There are only three left before the summer break.' When I recovered my equilibrium, I realised his proposal made sense. l often went to the broadcasts and indeed contributed to the scripts. I knew the band, they knew me, and I could rely on them absolutely to see me through. And this solution would put my father's mind at rest. He had been worrying about his radio show and loathed the prospect of the BBC's own house band taking over the slot. There was also the fact that I would be no threat to him. He behaved towards the band like a benevolent headmaster and he would see me not as a successor but as just the head prefect filling in while the beak was away.

Aided by an excellent scriptwriter who made jokes about Dad's absence and my ineptitude, and bolstered by the good-natured badinage of the band, I made a modest success of the three broadcasts. So much so that Dad's agent, Leslie Grade, rang me and said that Moss Empires, who had booked the band for the summer, would be happy to stick to the original schedule if I would carry on waving my arms around in time to the music. I agreed because this meant the band would be paid and Dad could enjoy a worry-free break in the south of France.

My first engagement with the band was at the Theatre Royal, Portsmouth on a Saturday evening, an easy start because at the weekend the place was sure to be packed. I made a deal with the leading saxophonist that he would beat time discreetly with his instrument while I gave the audience the impression that I was in charge. After a fairly chaotic rehearsal, I left the theatre and walked across the road to a café opposite. As I was tucking into a meal, I happened to look up and saw people queuing to get into the theatre. God Almighty! It suddenly struck me that what I was about to do was sheer lunacy. I'd never even been on the stage before, let alone faced an audience who had the highest expectations of a Billy Cotton Band show. 'What *are* you doing?' I asked myself desperately, barely avoiding the urge to bang my head on the table top.

I remember virtually nothing about the show that followed, so it must have gone well. Indeed, I went home to Boo with a feeling of euphoria which lasted all of twenty-four hours until I drove up to the band's next engagement in Peterborough. As I was to discover, a rainy Monday night in middle England is an entirely different proposition from Saturday by the sea. The place was only a third full, and in the front were the serried ranks of local landladies who'd been given complimentary tickets in the hope they would recommend the show to their guests. These dragons sat there glowering, arms folded, daring us to entertain them. If you want a really super-critical audience, hand out free tickets. When punters have to pay for their tickets, they are on your side because they have a vested interest in enjoying themselves, otherwise their money's been wasted. So I waved my arms around like crazy and babbled away, desperate to get *some* reaction from the audience. The band members, meanwhile, smiled cynically – they'd seen it all before. It certainly made me realise what my father had gone through in the lean years before he became famous.

To discomfort me even more, in a box surrounded by her acolytes there was Cissie Williams, the chief booker for Moss Empires. She was an awesome figure in the entertainment industry, able to make and break the career of performers by giving or withholding work or by placing them either in big London theatres or remote regional flea-pits. At the interval, she appeared in my dressing-room and I preened myself, fully expecting her to utter some words of congratulation or encouragement – after all, I'd taken over the band at short notice and, in all modesty, I thought I was doing rather well. Instead she snapped, 'You are contracted to do fifty minutes and you only did forty-five' – which was true, simply because we couldn't include the number Dad always sang at the end of the show. I thought quickly and said, 'I'll ask Alan Breeze to sing "Unchained Melody",' a big hit at the time. She nodded, said, 'Give my regards to your father,' and swept out.

Alan Breeze, the band's male vocalist, had been with my Dad for years and was the on-stage butt of his humour. He had a pronounced stutter which became worse in moments of stress. I told him the form and ensured the band had the music of 'Unchained Melody' on their stands. The following evening as the act came to its climax, we struck up the opening chords of the song and on came Alan Breeze, who looked at me desperately and muttered something I didn't quite catch. We waited for him to take his cue and nothing happened; Alan just stared at me like a startled rabbit. We reached the end of the introductory chords. Dead silence. Having learned a thing or two from watching my father exchanging badinage with Alan, I turned to the audience and said jocularly, 'I think we've got a problem here.' Then with a great melodramatic gesture I picked up Alan by his collar and with a big smile on my face for the benefit of the audience, hissed at him, 'What the hell's going on?' Spluttering and stuttering, he whispered, 'I . . . I . . . I've f-f-forgotten the w-w-words!' I could have killed him with my bare hands. *Everybody* knew the lyrics of 'Unchained Melody' – for a time they were more familiar than the words of 'God Save the Queen'. By enlisting the audience to sing along with Alan, I got us through the show and aged twenty-five years in five minutes.

Then we moved on to Brighton, where to my utter delight our takings for the week were up on the same period in the previous year when Dad was in charge of the band. I couldn't wait to give him the good news: I thought it would aid his recovery if he knew how well things were going. Fat chance. He hated being upstaged, even by his own son.

One evening during the interval between houses at the Hippodrome Theatre, I went down to the bar and saw there a famous Brighton resident, the comedian Max Miller. Miller had done a memorable season with my Dad at the London Palladium which I attended virtually every evening because I admired his stand-up so much. Whether he was the greatest comedian of his day was a matter of argument, but he was indisputably the meanest. He had never been known to put his hand in his pocket and buy a drink, so I was not surprised to see him sitting staring glumly into an empty glass. We exchanged pleasantries and then I offered to buy him a drink. He was very grateful. We talked some more. 'Can I refill your glass?' I asked. He was beside himself with gratitude. Later: 'Another one?' I enquired. He overwhelmed me with thanks. Eventually I had to get back to business, but as I left, the barman called me over and he said, 'Thanks very much for standing Max those rounds. If you hadn't, I'd have had to do it. Every night he comes in here and just stands silently at the bar until I offer him a drink.' Mean he might have been, but when he died Max left his entire estate to a home for unmarried mothers.

We ended our run with a week in Dublin. The Thursday happened to be St Patrick's Day, which meant there were only two bars open in the entire city: one was at the Dog Show and the other at the Theatre Royal, where we were playing. Though the Billy Cotton Band was the star attraction, the theatre also had its own pit orchestra which accompanied the other turns. Since we were the final act on the bill, with an expansive gesture of the kind Billy Cotton Senior was noted for I handed a tenner to the stage manager and told him to send the pit orchestra out for a drink on me. I assured him my band would close the show with the national anthem. He was very grateful, and off went the pit orchestra for a drink while I warned our band how the show would end.

Half way through our act, I was happily waving my arms around when I had a sudden premonition of doom. I left the stage, got hold of the manager and said, 'Where's the pit orchestra?' He told me they were in the pub where I'd sent them.

'For Christ's sake, get them back, quick!'

'Why?' he asked.

'Because my band doesn't know "The Soldier's Song",' I shrieked. 'They only know one national anthem, "God Save the Queen"!'

'Oh, my Gawd!' he said, and dashed off. I spent the rest of the show with one eye glued to the orchestra pit, praying that the players would get back before we finished our act. By the time we reached the final curtain, there were just enough of them to strike up 'The Soldier's Song'. The Billy Cotton Band stood respectfully, blissfully unaware of the narrow escape they'd had. 'God Save the Queen' in Dublin on St Patrick's Day in a house packed with drunken Irishmen!

'You weren't going to play what I think you were?' the stage manager asked, scandalised. 'What are you, a bloody kamikaze pilot?' Speechless, I headed for the nearest bottle of whisky.

In spite of my success with Dad's band, the experience did cure me of any idea of going on the stage permanently, though it was invaluable in later years when I had to deal with performers. I understood first hand the pressure they were under.

I had also come to believe that my future in show business lay in television, so I went to see Ronnie Waldman to ask if he would arrange for me to go on a BBC Television production course. I wanted no favours. I'd start at the bottom on a temporary contract, and if I didn't make the grade he could get rid of me with no hard feelings. I'd got to know Ronnie well enough to work out his thought processes. To take me on as a trainee would only cost him the standard BBC rate of fifteen quid a week for six months, which would earn him the gratitude of his biggest stars and be another silken thread binding my Dad to the BBC. There can't have been any other reason; I doubt Ronnie thought I was God's gift to television.

Shortly before I left the music business to join the BBC, I was coming out of the office in Denmark Street when I ran into Dick James, the singer who had recorded the original title song to the TV series *Robin Hood*. He'd just finished a spell with the BBC Dance Orchestra and told me he was thinking of setting up a music publishing business. 'You're wasting your time,' I said. 'I'm getting out. It's a dying industry. The record companies have it all sewn up; there's nothing left for independent publishers.' Like an idiot, he ignored my good advice, became the publisher of the Beatles and Elton John and made millions.

THREE

The first day I reported to the new half-built Television Centre at White City in January 1956 is indelibly imprinted on my memory. A young red-haired secretary who worked for Tom Sloan, the Assistant Head of Light Entertainment, greeted me. Her name was Queenie Lipyeat, and thirty years later she retired as my personal assistant because I was by then Managing Director of BBC TV. But on this particular day I was a trainee producer.

I knew Broadcasting House, the home of BBC Radio, very well. It had long, dark corridors and people worked behind closed doors. It had the hushed atmosphere of a museum or a library; John Reith called it (in Latin of course) 'A Temple of the Arts'. It didn't exactly buzz with excitement. Most of the actual broadcasting came from the Aeolian Hall in Bond Street and other studios around London. The Television Centre was quite different. It was noisy and bursting with life. Everyone seemed to be in a great hurry; the place echoed with shouting and laughter, and as you walked down a corridor you had to flatten yourself against the wall as technicians pushed past you trundling heavy camera equipment or pieces of scenery.

Since the BBC had begun as a radio service, all the big corporate decisions were made at Broadcasting House by a management who had originally been by and large lukewarm about television because they thought it was too expensive an operation to be paid for by the licence fee. However, against the BBC's bitter opposition, the government passed the legislation which produced an Independent Television system, and in no time these companies were beating the BBC for audiences in the geographical regions where they operated. This created a certain amount of concern, even panic, at Broadcasting House as those who ran the BBC saw their position as the main purveyors of broadcasting being threatened. Hence, from being viewed somewhat superciliously, television was moved much higher up the governors' agenda.

So in the very year I joined the BBC, it was decided that someone be appointed Director of Television. Gerald Beadle had no prior television experience and made no secret of the fact that up to the day of his appointment he didn't even own a television set. He had been controller in charge of the Western Region of BBC Radio, was fifty-five years of age, and was looking for a gentle canter down the finishing straight to retirement.

Shortly after he arrived, Beadle summoned the entire production staff of the television service to a meeting. They all fitted comfortably into the Television Theatre at Shepherd's Bush – by the time I left, it would have taken a football ground to contain them. I was present when Beadle asked what could be done about the mounting competition from ITV, and saw the legendary Grace Wyndham Goldie rise to her feet. She was a major figure in the Talks Department, then considered the serious side of the business, so her one-line intervention had a tremendous impact. She declared, 'The trouble with the BBC is that it is considered vulgar to be popular.' The roar of agreement from all the staff present shook Gerald Beadle and became something of a battle cry. He got the firm impression that the staff of the television service were a feisty lot, frustrated by lack of investment and the lukewarm endorsement of BBC management at Broadcasting House. Slowly the message got through to the powers that be and a new, exciting era dawned. I was fortunate to be there when it began.

I started work on the producers' course. There were lectures on such things as the theory of camera direction and lighting, the importance of design and the organisation required to run a producer's office. Clips of film illustrated many of these subjects. The problem was that every time they turned the lights down, I dozed off. But I'd learned a trick or two in the army and when the lights came up again I immediately asked the first question – which disarmed the suspicions of those who hadn't realised that my eyes were closed in deep contemplation. In spite of this foible I had the privilege of learning from dedicated and talented instructors who, being the first generation in BBC TV, had virtually invented the techniques of television production.

After the course, we were sent back to our departments for the remainder of the six months to learn the practical side of the job under the supervision of senior producers. I was attached to a young lion, Francis Essex, who had built a great reputation as a programme director. He was later to become a major figure in ATV, and when he retired he created musicals, of which *Jolson* was probably his most successful. His production assistant was Yvonne Littlewood, who forty years later in 1999 earned a richly deserved place in the Royal Television Society's Hall of Fame for her work in television.

There was also a production secretary, Hermione Doutre, and the four of us shared an office the size of a normal box room. Francis was a busy producer and for much of the time I just sat there and watched, very much a spare part. I sat at a small typist's desk in the corner of the room, and at lunchtime I often used to pop down to Tin Pan Alley to my other office where I could luxuriate at a big walnut desk in a room with a carpet, armchairs, pictures on the wall and full cocktail cabinet and ponder whether I was doing the right thing by joining television.

But before long I was given some nursery-slope programmes. Going out under the generic title of *Starlight*, these were fifteen minutes long and used either a pop group or a solo performer. I did one with the Ray Ellington Quartet and Marion Ryan and another with the pianist Semprini. He was very popular with trainee producers, partly because he was so co-operative and partly because his piano was a useful prop – a director could shoot it from every possible angle. If the director was a beginner, he or she invariably got the camera cables crossed and ended up in a complete tangle. But it was all valuable experience.

★

By 1956 Boo and I had lived at Ham Island for six years. We arrived there as newlyweds and soon became a family – Jane was born on 26 September 1951 and Kate on exactly the same day two years later. I did myself no favours with Boo when in one of my more jocular moods I explained the identical birth-date of two of my children at a dinner-party: 'If you work it back, it's Boxing Day,' I said. 'After all, Christmas Eve, you drink, Christmas Day, you eat, so what's left for Boxing Day?' My wife's laughter was dutiful but mirthless. I used to remind Dad every year as 26 September approached that it was the children's birthday. Every year he would ask, 'Which one?' and every year I would say, 'Both.' And every year he would say accusingly, 'You never told me that!'

We had thoroughly enjoyed living on the Island but now the children were getting near school age and Boo thought it was time to move nearer to town so that I wouldn't have as far to drive to work. Our chance came when an old friend of my brother, Bob Snell, told us of a new development called Parkleys his firm had built at Ham Common near Richmond. Bob and Ted had been at school together and served in the RAF as pilots at the same time. Bob's parents lived abroad, he spent his leaves with us and had become one of the family. He had moved into one of the new flats and there was another one on sale at £3500, which he assured me was a good investment. Boo and I went to see it. It had an open-plan living- and dining-room, two doubles and a small single room. There was, alas, no river at the bottom of the garden, but there were shops within walking distance. Boo was all for buying it, and I agreed, though I feared we might not get our money back if we wanted to sell it. Nevertheless her enthusiasm was irresistible.

The day we moved house, our bulldog, Bessie, had puppies. We'd always had dogs, starting with a Pekinese who was king of all he surveyed till one day he picked a fight with a boxer and a sheepdog and lost. So we decided to get a bigger dog; hence Bessie. Boo had arranged to make the actual house-move with the help of a friend, Patsy, while I was at work – in the morning I would leave from Ham Island and later come home to a new flat in Ham Common. It was a plan that suited a male chauvinist like myself down to the ground – or it would have done if Bessie hadn't interfered with it. The bungalows on Ham Island were built on stilts against the possibility of flooding and Bessie chose to deliver her litter underneath the bungalow. I had to crawl around in the mud, passing one puppy after another up to Patsy. At last we got all the puppies out, eight of them. We couldn't keep eight puppies in a flat, so we held on to two and the vet took the others. I left Ham Island for the last time feeling like a mass murderer.

Meanwhile, as part of Dad's contract while he was waiting to get the *Band Show* on air, he was asked to present a musical programme produced by Francis Essex called *The Tin Pan Alley Show*. It was not a happy experience, though we had a few laughs along the way – *wherever* Dad was there was jollity. The problem in this instance was that he didn't much like the show's format and wanted out, and by God, he could be mulish when he wasn't getting his own way. I swore at the time I'd never work with him again because it would obviously end in tears and I told Ronnie Waldman so.

Eventually I graduated as a full-blown producer and director on *Off the Record,* a show in which we put television pictures to records of current musical hits. We weren't allowed to play the actual records because the BBC had an agreement with the Musicians' Union who, naturally enough, wanted us to use live musicians rather than recordings. The show's presenter, Jack Payne, was, like my father, a band-leader of pre-war vintage. He could be very awkward and difficult to handle, but coping with temperamental band-leaders was a skill I'd absorbed with my mother's milk, so after a few preliminary skirmishes we got along fine.

It was on this show I was introduced to the world of special effects. Nowadays, they are an integral part of most shows, though all the fancy technical stuff is usually done after the programme has been recorded. But back in the fifties, when all shows were live, we had to put in the special effects during transmission as we went along. I remember Frankie Vaughan

Dad as a child sailor in 1903.

As a boy soldier in 1915.

As an airman in 1917.

My mother when my parents were
married, on Boxing Day in 1921 –
the only day they could get off.

The band my father made his reputation with in the Southport Palais and the Rialto, Liverpool, in the 1920s. Clem Bernard is on his right and Sidney Lipton, later to become a well-known band-leader, is standing between them.

The plane Dad bought for his flying visits to dance-halls. It was a Puss Moth and he kept it at Croydon Airport. In the summer when he finished at clubs very late, he often took it up to watch the dawn break.

The band in the thirties when it had become a stage band. This was the band I saw at the Holborn Empire. This picture is a still from the film *The First Mrs Frazier*.

A photograph sent to me recently, taken by a member of the public in Hastings where Dad was doing a Sunday concert. They were exciting days for a young chap.

A family group at Phoenix Park in 1936. In the race Dad came third – but the trophy he won stayed in Ireland. They wouldn't let it out of the country.

Ted and I with Dad admiring a silver trophy won by 'Max', a greyhound he bought. Behind us a clock and a radiogram he also won, a state-of-the-art piece of equipment at the time.

Ted, Beryl and Mother at the hospital in Switzerland he went to during his second bout of TB. Ted and Beryl married as soon as he was cured.

Dad driving round the banking at Brooklands in his MG K3 Magnette, with which he had a lot of success.

The nearest I got to driving a racing car. Following Eric Sykes practising for a charity Lord's Taverners race at Brands Hatch as a curtain-raiser for the British Grand Prix.

This was even worse than my meeting with 'Burma' the elephant. Stubby Kaye and Dad make substantial book-ends.

Kathie Kay and Dad giving out presents on a TV show at Christmas.

A portrait of Dad taken by Karsch for the *Daily Express* in the 1960s.

Bob Hope

Adam Faith

Stubby Kaye

Tommy Cooper

Alma Cogan

Russ Conway and Cliff Richard

Some of the guests who appeared on the show over the years.

The first management weekend I attended as Head of Variety. Huw Wheldon is seated in the centre of the settee with Sydney Newman on his right. David Attenborough is standing behind them. Paul Fox is top row right. Tom Sloan and Frank Muir are seated on the right (and I'm standing far right).

The last management weekend I attended. I was at this time Managing Director but Michael Grade chaired the meeting. There's a lot of talent in that picture.

apparently walking through a series of doors while singing 'Green Door' – not an easy effect to create when all television was black and white. Frankie just lifted and put down his feet on the spot and the illusion was created that he was moving through space from one door to another. These days it would be laughably simple to get that effect but at that time it seemed like magic.

I recall in my early days in the department producing a show featuring the singer Carole Carr. Basically, we had three types of shot: long, mid-shot and close up. At that time, there was no such thing as a zoom lens – the camera had to be moved physically nearer or further away from the star. I started on a long shot and Carole looked so lovely I decided to track in closer as she sang her heart out. I called for the cameraman to move nearer. Nothing happened. I added what I thought was more authority to my voice and ordered the cameraman to *move in*. Still nothing happened. I was beside myself with fury until someone in the gallery said in a quiet voice, 'If he does track in, there'll be a terrible mess in the stalls. His camera's at the front of the circle.' Another lesson learned.

I had my first success as a television talent-spotter when I was working on *Off the Record*. I had a friend called Hugh Mendl who worked for Decca Records and whom I'd known since my days as a song-plugger. He asked me to go and see a young rock and roll star who was appearing in Soho. We found ourselves in a reclaimed public toilet that posed as a club in the heart of Frith Street. We ordered a drink and settled down to wait for the boy to come on stage. Suddenly at our table appeared a bouncer the size of a house who said the manager was aware we were auditioning in his club and he'd like to see us in his office. I refused his invitation – the reason being that he terrified the life out of me. We found ourselves on the street and called it a day. Hugh, however, was nothing if not tenacious and pestered me until I went along to another club where the boy was appearing. He was a sensation. I asked Hugh what recordings he'd made. 'None,' he replied, 'but if you'll give him a spot on your show I'll record him tomorrow.' We shook hands on it and Tommy

Steele had his first recording, 'Rock with the Caveman', on the show the following week. I knew this was a big star in the making.

Discovering Tommy Steele presented me with an ethical dilemma. The man who wrote Tommy Steele's hit was Lionel Bart, who when I came on the scene hadn't found a publisher for the song. I had not divested myself of my interest in music publisher Michael Reine, but I had promised the Head of TV Entertainment, Ronnie Waldman, that I would not take advantage of my position in the BBC to advance the interests of my private company. I felt it right that I should not tell my partner at Michael Reine, Johnny Johnston, about the existence of Lionel Bart or the brilliant song Tommy Steele was turning into a hit. And that's why we didn't sign up Lionel Bart, who of course went on to write 'Fings Ain't Wot They Used To Be' and *Oliver*. Johnny was not best pleased.

By now, my dad's show was nearing its transmission date. The combination of Billy Cotton as presenter and the Silhouettes worked a treat. Jimmy Grafton wrote the comedy script; there were some instrumental numbers and a guest spot. Brian Tesler had got an ideal television format, infinitely flexible, and Dad was smart enough to stick with it for his entire television career. He may not have been the best song and dance man in the business but when the audience saw the sweat on his forehead they knew he was giving everything he had to entertain them, and they loved him for it.

Because office space was at a premium at the unfinished Television Centre, I worked from a caravan behind the scenery block in the carpark. It was a little like a holiday camp, and the occupant of the next caravan along was a brilliant young producer called Jack Good who was busy working on an idea that was to revolutionise pop programmes. He named it *Six-Five Special* and proposed employing a quite original production technique. The perceived wisdom at the time was that none of the technology which transmitted the programme

– cameras, lighting, microphones – should be visible to the viewer, who was supposed to assume the event was taking place in a corner of the living-room. It was a hanging offence to allow the tip of a microphone to appear in shot, and if one of the technicians was inadvertently picked up by the camera, the standard sarcastic quip was 'I hope he's a member of Equity', the actors' union.

Jack Good came up with the idea of letting the viewers see all the inner workings of television: cameras moving around, lighting rigs being adjusted, scenery pushed into place. It was an unheard-of innovation and some members of the department found it hard to swallow. Josephine Douglas, who was the co-producer and presenter of the show, came into my caravan in tears one day. She felt that Jack was taking all the magic out of television and blowing away its mystery. She pleaded with me to talk to Jack to persuade him to revert to the old formula. I did talk to him and thank God I wasn't able to change his mind, because he had hit upon a way of revitalising television. He stayed with the BBC for a while and then left to join ITV to produce *Oh Boy!* which launched Cliff Richard's television career.

After Jack Good had gone, we took turns in producing *Six-Five Special*, and it fell to me to produce the first show from outside London. We transmitted it from the town hall in Barry in South Wales. The guest presenter was Lonnie Donegan who had very pronounced ideas about what he wanted to do, which included doing without the other presenter, Pete Murray. Lonnie insisted he could handle it on his own. In the end we reached a creative compromise: Lonnie would do a little of what he wanted and a lot of what I wanted. This is what being a producer is all about; he carries the can and in the end what he says goes, however big the star with whom he's working. Compared to the Television Centre, the makeshift studio in the town hall was relatively small so I told the local BBC man that in order to allow as many people as possible to enjoy the show, we'd let in one audience to watch the run-through and another to attend the actual transmission.

There was only a thirty-minute gap between the run-through and transmission which meant we required a slick and orderly audience turn-round. At the due time, the red light went on and we were live on air. As we'd planned, I cued the number one cameraman to track in on Lonnie. He didn't move. I was bawling down the intercom at the floor manager until another cameraman turned his camera round and showed me his colleague's predicament. The first audience were so keen to see the show they refused to leave after the run-through, but the second audience had been allowed in and the camera was pinned against the studio's rear wall by a mass of screaming teenagers. For the first five minutes of the show, the pictures were all over the place, but we eventually sorted it out and the viewers assumed the chaos was the style of the show.

In 1957 Brian Tesler, having produced sixteen of Dad's shows, announced that he was leaving the BBC to join Lew Grade at ATV. The BBC therefore needed another producer to do the *Cotton Show*. Unbeknown to me, Dad had spoken to Ronnie Waldman to ask if I could take the show over, but Ronnie told him he and I had an agreement that I would not be asked to do shows with my father. Ronnie promised Dad he'd look around for a suitable replacement. I got home that evening to find my father sitting comfortably on the settee entertaining my wife with some of his numerous stories. Just a little suspicious, I asked him whether there was anything particular on his mind. He replied that he'd just come for supper – indeed, he'd brought it with him: smoked salmon and a good bottle of wine. So we had a very enjoyable evening.

At eleven o'clock he stood up, glanced at his watch and uttered one of his ritual phrases: 'Time a decent man was akip in his bed.' Then as he reached the door, he turned, looked me in the eye and said, 'Why won't you produce my show?' I was completely unprepared for that question and it took me a few moments to realise I'd been bushwhacked. Eventually I said, 'Dad, the producer of a show is in charge of it, and that often leads to arguments with the performers. I wouldn't want to argue with you and even if I did, I wouldn't want to win.'

'OK,' he replied, 'you have my word that I will never argue with you in public; we'll have all our discussions in private. Is it a deal?'

Of course it was. It was an offer I couldn't refuse and I realised I didn't want to. So 'Produced by Bill Cotton Junior' was the credit at the end of *The Billy Cotton Band Show* from April 1957 and for the next four years.

Thus ended my first year in television. I still went back to the office in Denmark Street occasionally and kept an eye on what was going on. Johnny was by then the uncrowned king of the TV jingle, though the music business generally was on the back burner. But every now and again, someone would record a song from our catalogue which ended up on the B-side of a hit, and then the royalties would roll in. It might be the A-side of a record the public wanted, but the B-side got the same royalties.

Back at the Television Centre, having completed a series of *Off the Record*, *The Show Band Show* and some music specials under the generic title of *Summer Serenade* with Geraldo and Frank Chacksfield, I was accepted as a full-blown producer/director. Around the department there were some mutterings about nepotism, but nothing serious. If anybody hinted at it, I would be quite brazen and unapologetic. In all walks of life, from the professions to the trade unions, being the child of an established father has its advantages. Sure, doors open and you get to walk through them, but the important thing is what you do with the chances you've been given.

Our boss, Ronnie Waldman, was a great talent-spotter and he laid the foundations of a department which in the 1960s and 1970s regularly out-performed ITV, the channel supposedly set up in order to be the nation's main entertainment outlet. Elitists both inside and outside the BBC who had greeted the arrival of ITV with relief because they thought it meant the BBC could concentrate on education and information, leaving entertainment to the commercial sector, were forced to eat their words.

Some of my colleagues had come over from radio: Duncan Wood, who produced *Hancock* and *Steptoe and Son*; Johnny Ammonds, who was responsible for shows featuring Val

Doonican, Morecambe and Wise and Harry Worth; and Dennis Main-Wilson, who was the glue that held together *Till Death Do Us Part* and *The Rag Trade*. Dennis was an extraordinary character; he'd been blooded on *The Goon Show* and became inured to the good-natured ridicule of Spike Milligan, Harry Secombe and Peter Sellers. Dad christened him Dame May Whitty which fitted perfectly his rather fussy and punctilious manner – but no one doubted that he was a great producer.

Some of that first generation of television producers were imports from the theatre: Jimmy Gilbert, for example, who had written the successful West End show *Grab Me a Gondola*. He became one of the most distinguished television producers of situation and sketch comedy, and later whenever I had a risky new show to launch I entrusted it to him in the absolute confidence that if it was workable at all, Jimmy would bring it off. There was also the occasional producer who had started his career as an engineer or floor manager and moved up through the ranks. Outstanding among them was T. Leslie Jackson, who master-minded *This Is Your Life* and *What's My Line?* Ronnie Waldman used to hold a producers' meeting every Monday morning during which we discussed and critically analysed the previous week's output. One of the most vocal contributors was George Inns, who had produced Jewel and Warriss's 1950s radio hit *Up the Pole*. He suggested a solution to what had become an intractable programme problem and in the process launched one of the great television and theatre shows. Every year there was a Radio Show at Earls Court or Olympia which was set up along the lines of the Motor Show and exhibited the latest models of radio and television sets. For a couple of years, we had built a makeshift studio at the show from which we broadcast some of our television programmes. Our producers hated it because the audience kept invading rehearsals and there were numerous technical breakdowns. Frankly, it was a mess, an embarrassment to the department, yet it was unthinkable that the BBC's Television Service should ignore an exhibition dedicated to selling television sets.

For ages, dear George had been plugging his pet idea of a

black-and-white minstrel show, and yet again on this occasion he went through his usual routine, insisting that the Radio Show would be an ideal setting for his great project. We all groaned, but nobody could come up with a better notion, so George was given the go-ahead. *The Black and White Minstrel Show* was born, and as is often the case in television, everybody in the business hated it except the audience. It became and remained a huge success. It was the BBC's first entry for the Montreux Television Festival and swept the board. In the end, political correctness decreed that the idea of blacked-up performers was racist, so the show died and has never been replaced.

Meanwhile I had turned my attention to the upcoming series of my father's show. It was to go out fortnightly on BBC1, alternating with *The Vera Lynn Show*. Once I became Dad's TV producer, the dynamics of our relationship changed. Throughout my childhood and schooldays, I had hero-worshipped him. During my time in the army and my career as a music publisher I had been quite dependent on his patronage, support and influence. Now the balance of power had shifted and to a marked degree *he* depended on *me*. Radio was still his great love but the proceeds didn't pay the rent. His main source of income was the variety theatre. Television paid good money, provided the band with regular work and gave him huge publicity – so he just had to knuckle down and accept that I was now in the driving seat.

For my part, I was simply happy to be able to repay Dad for all he had done for me. He knew he could trust me; I would never put him in a situation on television where he was asked to do something he couldn't do well. I was determined to exploit his strengths and build on the solid foundations his producer Brian Tesler had laid down. Our biggest problem was the one facing all general entertainment shows: how to find an adequate supply of interesting and talented guests. I looked around for a pianist, preferably someone who played the piano like the bloke down the pub. I mentioned this one day to Richard Armitage, who had taken over the Noel Gay agency. He told me about a young man EMI had just recorded and fixed it for me to hear him in Richard's office. He was actually called Trevor Stanford but was renamed Russ Conway by EMI. The name stuck and I was glad to sign him because he played just the sort of music I was looking for. And he was to become a big star.

I was due to produce the *Six-Five Special* show from Barry in South Wales, so I booked Russ to appear on it. I wanted to see how he looked on camera. It was a disaster. The studio was filled with fans of the reigning king of skiffle, Lonnie Donegan. That's what they'd come for, skiffle music, not honky-tonk piano-playing, so the applause was underwhelming. His confidence shattered, Russ dashed off the set and headed for the railway station. When I caught up with him in town, I managed to convince him that life on *The Billy Cotton Band Show* was going to be better than that. And it was, thanks partly to a song he'd composed called 'Side Saddle' which sold well and fitted the show like a glove. So Russ went from strength to strength, for quite apart from his good looks and pianistic virtuosity he got on well with my father. Jimmy Grafton wrote a duet for them called 'What Will They Do Without Us?' with flexible lyrics that could be adapted for different occasions: the chemistry between them was magical. Some of this magic must have affected me, for I seemed to have a capacity to communicate with Russ from a distance without benefit of wires. On the studio floor, he could look quite solemn while he was playing, so I'd mutter to myself, 'Smile, you bastard!' and at that instant, uncannily, he would look up at the camera and break into a broad grin.

The demands my father made on his orchestra were very heavy. They were committed to a season fifty weeks long on radio, television and in the theatre; they had to cope with a wide range of music thrust onto their stands at very short notice; and in addition they were expected to fool around as foils during my Dad's comic routines. Some critics sniffily claimed that music-ally they weren't outstanding. For my money, their work-rate, versatility and sheer discipline made them unique.

We also needed a new female vocalist, because Doreen Stephens had left to seek her fortune elsewhere. Johnny Johnston recommended a singer called Kathie Kay who had first appeared on the stage at the age of four and within ten years had appeared in every London theatre, including the Palladium. Then at the age of seventeen she retired, married a Scotsman and had three sons. She still did a certain amount of recording, and one day someone influential in the BBC overheard one of her records, so she started a second career in television and on radio. But her children took priority over her career, so she refused to make her home in London and instead travelled many thousands of miles every year between there and Glasgow. She wasn't prepared to go on the road with the band, either, so Dad agreed that while her children were growing up she should confine herself to radio and television engagements. As the years went by, Kathie grew ever closer to Dad and became his main pillar of support until he died.

Dad, of course, had been in the entertainment business for so long that he knew *everybody,* so getting star guests for the show wasn't too great a hassle. Max Bygraves was always good value. On one occasion we had two enormous puppet-heads made of the porcine stars of *Pinky and Perky,* a very popular show at the time. The sight of Max and Dad wearing these heads and performing a dance routine was hilarious, and we resurrected the routine later on for a Royal Variety Performance. Dad was absolutely dependent for his patter on cue cards scattered around the studio, and Max used to read out Dad's words in a different order to produce utter chaos. On one awful occasion, the teleprompter roller stuck, and Dad was reduced to reading the same cue again and again until the contraption freed itself. But the public loved it; he could have done *anything* and they would have roared in appreciation.

Coping with the script for a fifty-minute show made great demands on my Dad's memory – he was, after all, a band-leader not an actor. On one occasion, he kept muffing his lines and our rehearsal time was fast running out. I pressed the button on the production desk which enabled the studio to hear me and announced with a sigh that we would have just one more run-through of the routine. Unfortunately I forgot to take my finger off the button as I turned to the people in the control room: 'If he'd learned the bloody script we could get on.' Back came the unmistakable voice of the star: 'If you are so clever, why don't you come down here and do it?' I immediately went down to the studio floor where the band members who were used to the rough edge of my Dad's tongue looked expectantly at my getting some of the same treatment in a flaming row. But I was so appalled at my tactlessness that I immediately apologised: 'I am sorry, Dad, I shouldn't have said that.' A broad grin spread across his face: 'If I'd learned the bloody thing, you wouldn't have had to, would you?' I turned to the band, most of whom I'd known since I was a little boy, and in a spirit of camaraderie gave them the two-finger salute. In all the years I worked with my father, that was the one and only time we got near to a row.

Dad was a man's man who was very much at home with the ladies. Alma Cogan was one of his favourites – and mine. I'd known her since my days as a song-plugger and I could always rely on her to help out if we were stuck for a star guest, even though she was under contract to commercial television at the time. She was utterly without any sense of her own importance. I recall visiting her home one evening and finding Cary Grant sitting chatting to Sammy Davis Jr while in another room Alma was saying encouraging words to a penniless songwriter. She treated everybody the same.

On the eve of one show, our main guest dropped out and I was really desperate – I rang everyone I could think of, except Alma, who had appeared just a few weeks before. In the end I called round to the flat where she lived with her mother and sister. It was very late and she had been out working, but within minutes she volunteered to fill the gap. We sat up into the early hours working out a routine based on the song 'He's Funny That Way'. It worked very well and we put it on an LP for Columbia records.

While Alma came from the world of pop music and variety halls, Vanessa Lee was a theatre and musical comedy star. She had had the lead role in Ivor Novello's musical *King's Rhapsody* and *The Dancing Years*, and on the basis that she could only say no I offered her a spot on the show. We fixed it up on the phone and she agreed to do a number on her own, but also insisted on performing a duet with the old man as well. When I told Dad about the booking, he was not at all keen – he thought that coming from light operetta Vanessa might take herself too seriously. His reservations were swept away when she walked into the rehearsal room, took one look at him and said: 'Hello, I gather you can be a proper bastard.' For a second there was silence, quickly followed by peals of laughter. She was in. From then on, whenever there was a blank in the show Dad would say, 'What about Vanessa Lee?' It got quite boring.

One Friday lunchtime, there was great excitement when Dad took delivery of a new E-type Jaguar, the first to be seen in the London area. He was beside himself with delight and had a photo-session with showgirls clambering all over the bonnet. Eventually we all set off in convoy from the rehearsal room to the theatre, Dad leading the way in his latest toy. He left the car in a carpark round the back of the theatre and we started rehearsals, but I could see his mind wasn't on his work. So I told him we still had Saturday morning to get everything ship-shape and suggested he go for a spin in his new car. He was off like a shot, only to return ten minutes later.

'Some bastard's pinched it,' he wailed. The police were called and Dad was asked if he was willing to offer a reward to get the car back – a euphemism for paying an informer. Sure enough they found the car within hours in a lock-up in Earls Court. The policeman in charge came to the show that night and had a bite of supper with us afterwards, during which I asked him what could possess a thief to steal a car so distinctive as a brand-new E-type Jaguar, probably the only one in London, with the unique registration number BC 1. It seemed it was the beginning of a trend, which has since become common: a gang was stealing classic cars, driving them to a remote airstrip and flying them to some country where no questions would be asked.

Back at the factory, big changes were afoot. The BBC's Head of Light Entertainment, Ronnie Waldman, was promoted to run the commercial wing of the BBC, leaving behind as his legacy a department which was producing a stream of programmes of a range and quality unsurpassed anywhere on television. Ronnie was fundamentally a serious man, and had first made his name in radio producing and presenting a programme called *Monday Night at Eight* which included a section, 'Puzzle Corner', that became hugely popular on its own account. He was succeeded by Eric Maschwitz, who as a composer had written two of the most popular songs this century, 'A Nightingale Sang in Berkeley Square' and 'These Foolish Things', as well as a highly successful musical called *Goodnight, Vienna!* Eric was a bit of a wag, much less formal than Ronnie, and highly convivial; with Eric we did much of our business round the bar in the BBC Club.

Eric often told the story against himself of how he was driving through Lewisham one cold, rainy evening and noticed that at the local theatre a touring company was doing a production of his *Goodnight, Vienna!* He decided to encourage local enterprise by taking a personal interest, so walked into the theatre, saw the manager in the foyer and introduced himself with the words, 'I'm Eric Maschwitz. I wrote the book of *Goodnight, Vienna!* How's business?' The manager looked at him dolefully and said, '*Goodnight, Vienna!* is doing as well in Lewisham as *Goodnight, Lewisham!* would do in Vienna.'

Shortly after he took over the department, Eric sent for me and told me he'd just returned from Paris where he'd done a deal with the owners of a new nightclub, a Nouvelle Eve, to transmit their floor show using an outside broadcast unit loaned by RTF, the French national broadcasting authority. Politely I congratulated him on his coup. 'I'm glad you like the idea,' he chortled, 'because you're doing it as our big show on the evening of the August Bank Holiday. Come and see me to-morrow morning with some ideas for an English presenter.' My heart sank. Boo and I had planned to be on Dad's boat for Cowes Week, which in those days began on August Bank Holiday Monday. Then I hit on a brilliant wheeze. The old man could present the show – all he had to do was read a few links.

Meanwhile, his skipper, Sandy Wills, could take the boat with Mother and Boo on board over to Trouville; Dad and I would join them after the show and then we'd all head off to Cowes.

Eric thought this was a great idea, and so did Dad – after he'd convinced himself it was his idea in the first place. A few days before the Bank Holiday, off I went to Paris with a skeleton crew to meet the show's cast and sort out any technical matters. The show's resident stars were Robert Lamouret, a brilliant ventriloquist, Tonia Bern, a very good, sophisticated cabaret singer who was married to the racing driver Donald Campbell, and Aleta Morrison, a gorgeous and talented dancer with legs up to her armpits. After meeting the club's management, I settled down to see the show. On came a line of girls doing a short dance routine, which was fine, except that some of them were topless. This, after all, was Paris. I suppose it was incredibly naïve of me to expect anything else, but I realised I had a whale of a problem. Way back in the sixties there was no possibility of BBC television – or ITV, for that matter – transmitting pictures of topless girls.

I suspected that Eric, well lubricated with excellent French wine, had bought the show sight unseen. I reached him on the telephone and explained the problem. 'Just put tops on them all,' was his suggestion. 'But some of the girls don't dance,' I protested. 'They just walk around provocatively so it looks like a strip show.' To work up some dance steps for them would take ages, and anyway, the choreographer was away. 'I know you'll do your best,' said Eric encouragingly and put the phone down. What had seemed like a dream booking was turning into a nightmare. Fortunately the musical director of the show spoke English and was very helpful, so we were able to make some strategic cuts in the routine to curtail the topless parade.

Much of the ventriloquist's routine was also unacceptable; his assistant was a beautiful blonde German girl who cavorted around virtually nude, and some of his funniest material involved the reaction of his dummy to her superstructure. Luckily Robert Lamouret was a real pro who had cut his teeth in the variety halls, and we were able to get a comedy routine out

69

of him which wasn't quite so revealing. I also sent back to London for a musical arrangement of a duet called 'Voulez-vous Promenade Avec Moi?' which Dad had performed in one or two Sunday broadcasts and which Tonia had agreed to sing with him.

Then Monsieur Guillaume Cotton turned up. I hadn't been able to explain my problems to him before he settled down to watch the early show, which since it wasn't to be televised was uncensored. His eyes lit up. 'We're doing this?' he asked eagerly. 'No we are not,' I exclaimed. 'Pity,' was his comment.

We were still not out of the woods. French cameramen were not like their British counterparts – they had their own ideas about what pictures they should take, and though I was supposed to direct the show, I knew that my schoolboy grasp of the French language could only create even more confusion. Luckily the BBC's man in Paris, Robin Scott, was on hand; he spoke French like a native and was a very experienced TV producer, so I breathed a sigh of relief and let him get on with it. Robin had to employ some real gutter French to get the cameramen to give him the shots he had planned but, as often happens, a show which seemed doomed to failure miraculously turned out fine.

After the show there was a celebration during which champagne flowed freely, then off we went to Ciro's where Bob had booked a table. It was a touching gesture on his part; he'd learned that Dad's orchestra had played at Ciro's in the early thirties. So this was an occasion full of nostalgia, which was heightened when the doorman, who'd been a pageboy when my Dad was last there, recognised him and with loud protestations of respect kissed him on both cheeks. With a start like that, the night could only go from good to better. The service was attentive, the food and drink superb, the *maître d'* hovered respectfully, and to cap everything a troop of violinists appeared to serenade us. By now we'd partnered off: Dad was with Tonia, Bob Lamouret with Aleta, the show's main dancer, and I had become the escort of Bob's beautiful German assistant. She spoke no English and since I knew no German either we had to find inventive ways of communicating. Still, with lots to drink, plenty of dancing and general chitchat, the time flew until my companion managed to intimate to me that she would like to go home as it was four a.m. Dad's face was a picture as the two of us excused ourselves. He gave me an elephantine wink as I reminded him to keep an eye on the time because we were due to catch the train to Trouville at eight-thirty. 'Don't worry about me, my son, I'll be ready,' he said with a broad grin.

I hailed a cab, saw my companion to her digs, kissed her chastely on the cheek and headed back to our hotel, where I then ordered a wake-up call. A couple of hours later I knocked on Dad's door. He was sitting on an obviously unmade bed, looking slightly the worse for wear. I managed to get him bathed, dressed and packed and we caught our train with time to spare. When we were comfortably seated I said to him, 'Now, Dad, listen very carefully, we'd better get our stories straight before Ma and Boo start asking questions. My story is that we did the show, had a few drinks and dinner and then we went to bed – which in my case is the sober truth. I would appreciate it if you didn't go into any more detail than that. Don't start embroidering the story. Let's just have a nice friendly trip across the Channel with the family, OK?' He just grinned.

When we reached the harbour at Trouville, there was nobody to greet us or help us carry our luggage despite the fact there were two crew on the boat. We huffed and puffed up the gangplank and were greeted by my mother and Boo, whereupon the first words Dad uttered were, 'It only goes to show – last night I was being serenaded by violins, this morning I have to carry my own bags.' My mother smiled. 'Well, you must have had some women with you last night because no violinist would serenade *you*.' 'What women?' queried my wife sharply, and I knew Dad had dropped me in it and was going to enjoy every moment.

Once the atmosphere on board lightened a little and I managed to persuade Boo I'd behaved like a perfect gentleman the night before at Ciro's, the trip from Trouville to Cowes was great fun. Dad's boat was a sixty-eight-foot twin-engine

71

converted RAF rescue boat he'd bought from Max Aitken, Lord Beaverbrook's war hero son who had exchanged racing cars for Spitfires during the Battle of Britain. Predictably, Dad re-christened the boat *Wakey Wakey* and from time to time employed Sandy Wills, a mountain of a man who had served in the navy during the war and ran a business from Poole harbour skippering pleasure trips and delivering boats around the world. Since his youth he had been part of the Cotton family's seafaring life and was always prepared to drop everything when the old man needed him.

As always, we enjoyed soaking up the unique atmosphere of Cowes. Even wearing a yachting cap Dad, by now one of the best known faces on television, was instantly recognisable – to a point where it could become embarrassing. One day he was standing chatting on the balcony of the Royal London Yacht Club, a somewhat pukka establishment, when a crowd gathered beneath him and started shouting in unison 'Wakey! Wakey!' Dad was embarrassed and offered to leave, though he said he had no intention of apologising for his supporters: 'Without them, I wouldn't be up here in the first place.' He was persuaded to stay.

The summer break had ended and we needed to give some thought to the upcoming series of the *Band Show*. The traditional format was looking tired, so after much brain-storming and discussion we decided to set the show in an Edwardian hostelry which we'd call the Wakey Wakey Tavern. Dad was to be Mine Host complete with bowler hat, fancy waistcoat and cravat.

One of the advantages of the tavern format was that we could seat celebrities at the tables round the stage, where Dad would engage them in good-natured badinage. An early guest was Mike Hawthorn, who had just become the Formula One world motor racing champion. He and I had been at Ardingly College together and played in the Training Corps Band, so I knew him very well. Because of my father's interest in motor racing, it was easy for us to work out a comedy routine the climax of which was Dad admitting that Mike was probably a better driver, but saying that he was the better musician – whereupon Mike produced a bugle and, to tremendous applause, played a very creditable bugle-call.

After the show I made a date to talk to Mike about a programme idea I'd devised called *This Takes Nerve*. I wanted Mike as the presenter to talk to steeplejacks, deep-sea divers and test pilots, indeed anyone with a job that required nerve as well as skill. The day before we were due to have our planning meeting, I happened to pass an *Evening Standard* billboard which read: 'MIKE IS DEAD!' He was so popular, everyone knew him simply as Mike. The world champion had died not on a racing circuit but on a public road just outside Guildford.

On the first show of the run, I had a potentially disastrous contretemps with one of the stars, Richard Hearne (known as Mr Pastry), whom I had booked on the understanding he would produce different material from that which he'd used in a previous appearance on the *Band Show*. When he turned up at rehearsal with a routine I'd seen before, we had words and he stormed out of the studio. Dad overheard the row and nodded with approval at my firm stand, then added artlessly, 'So how do we fill the hole in tomorrow's show?'

Back at the office I ploughed desperately through our list of artists and their availability. Nothing there. Then I noticed a copy of the *New Musical Express* on my desk. At number five in that week's Hit Parade was Ted Heath's band playing 'Hot Toddy'. On an impulse, I rang Ted's office and was put through to him. I asked him if he and his band were working the next day; if not, would they fancy a guest slot on the *Band Show*? He was puzzled. 'You've already got a band, what do you want with another one?' 'Let me worry about that,' I replied. 'Will you do it?' He agreed and I asked him to bring along his arrangement of 'South Rampart Street Parade'.

Dad exploited the situation a treat. He innocently announced that in line with his policy of giving promising beginners a try, he wished to introduce this new young singer, Ted Heath. Ted came on and pointed out that he wasn't a singer but a band-leader. 'Do you mean to tell me there is *another* band-leader?'

Dad asked contemptuously, as onto the stage processed the Ted Heath orchestra to boos and hisses from the Cotton Band. They played their hit 'Hot Toddy' to the audience's delight and my father's feigned amazement. Finally the two bands joined forces in a rousing version of 'South Rampart Street Parade'. The theatre exploded in applause.

During that series, Dad walked into the office and announced that he had seen and heard a really sensational singer the night before at the Stork Club. She was an American, and after the show he'd had a drink with her, and from what he said it was clear that somewhere in the conversation the words 'Would you like to appear on my show?' had been uttered. I proposed that we should go along that evening to the Stork Club to hear her, and then we would make up our mind. 'Well,' said Dad sheepishly, 'I've already booked her.' The girl looked sensational and oozed star quality – until she opened her mouth. To say she caterwauled would be an insult to cats. She was terrible. After her first number I just stared at Dad. After a while he said, 'I must have had a few drinks last night.' So ended the first and only booking he ever made without consulting me. We got through her number by surrounding the poor girl with a vocal quartet who drowned out her unusual voice.

The actress Jayne Mansfield was a different proposition. She was a genuine Hollywood blonde bombshell who agreed to appear on the show providing we could fit the rehearsals around her filming schedule at Shepperton Studios. As often happens, on the day of the *Band Show*, her film schedule overran. She took off her film costume and, wrapped only in a mink coat, arrived at the Television Theatre near the end of the rehearsal, when we were just one hour away from transmission time. She walked onto the set and Dad appeared to rehearse their duet, which involved a little dance during which she would twirl around. As she did, her mink coat flew open, revealing all to the cameraman and myself. The old man was busy circling her so he didn't see the view, but realising what he had missed suggested we should repeat the routine – only this time he would watch, just to get the camera angles right, you understand. Jayne

Mansfield was a good sport, but not that good. After the show, Dad went up to her with a piece of paper in his hand. 'Autograph?' she said brightly. 'No, telephone number,' whispered Dad. The old goat.

About this time I was given a really plum assignment. One of the most popular American programmes was *The Perry Como Show*, the producers of which, having decided they wanted to make an edition in Britain, approached the BBC. Their own production staff would do the show using our facilities, and in return the BBC could transmit the show for nothing – a common enough arrangement these days, but at that time a ground-breaking proposal. Ronnie Waldman, who was by then running BBC Enterprises, was to handle the deal and he asked me to go with him to America to see how the show was made. I was excited at the prospect.

We arrived in New York where Ronnie had booked rooms at the Algonquin Hotel, where literary wits Dorothy Parker and Robert Benchley used to have their legendary lunches. We weren't due to meet *The Perry Como Show* producers until the next morning, so we had supper, did a little window shopping and then settled down to watch television. The television highlight of the evening was *The Jack Paar Show*, one of the very first chat-shows on television. I admired the improvised nature of the format: Jack talked to a guest just so long as he or she had something interesting to say then, if conversation lagged, would break off and introduce a commercial.

To my astonishment, on this night, after a commercial break, Jack suddenly addressed the viewers directly, pointing out that the previous evening NBC, who ran the channel, had without any prior discussion cut from his show a piece of recorded material which was considered vulgar – something to do with lavatories. Jack got very emotional and cried that he loved the American people and would never do anything to demean or insult them. In these circumstances, he'd decided to quit the show. And off the set he walked, creating consternation among the studio audience. It was a dramatic demonstration of both the power and the dangers of live television. Had this been the BBC,

75

we'd already have gone to a blank screen, but what followed was a free-for-all on air. Hugh Downs, the programme's master of ceremonies, appeared and asked one of the guests on the programme, the comedian Orson Bean, what he thought. Bean obligingly blew his top, asking rhetorically, 'Who are these faceless people in NBC who think they know better than Jack Paar?' He had never been so disgusted in his life. Like a rabbit paralysed in the headlights of a car, I watched as Downs sought the views of the musical director and a cameraman and then went down onto the studio floor and canvassed the audience's opinions. Meanwhile, the cameras rolled on and on.

I couldn't believe what I'd seen, and at our scheduled meeting the next morning, I asked the executive producer of *The Perry Como Show* what he made of it. He smiled. 'Jack probably wanted a couple of weeks off. He'll go off to his house in Florida and after a couple of days the bosses of RCA who own NBC will take a suite in the Hilton, there'll be some sweet talking and in no time the show'll be back on the air with an even bigger audience.' 'Do you mean to say,' I asked incredulously, 'that the whole thing was staged?' He didn't answer.

We watched the rehearsal for Como's show, a run-through with the star sitting in the stalls and a stand-in, usually his musical associate, Ray Charles, singing his songs and interviewing the guests. Then they brought in an audience and Como did a full dress rehearsal, and if any section went particularly well they would record it and play the tape into the live show. Finally, they brought in yet another audience and the show went out on air. It had the slickness and organisational skill of a military operation.

We then got down to planning the show Perry was to make in Britain. The two performers they had set their heart on were Ralph Richardson and Margot Fonteyn. We discussed locations and agreed on Westminster Square, the Tower of London, the Bull and Bush and Woburn Abbey. Harry Secombe, Russ Conway and Fenella Fielding would appear in the sequence at the Bull and Bush, and we decided to ask the Duke of Bedford to show Perry and the viewers round Woburn Abbey. I bearded

Ralph Richardson in his dressing-room at the Queen's Theatre and he was decidedly prickly. When I told him he would be required to rehearse with Perry's understudy, he snorted and asked what time Perry Como would make an appearance at the studio because that's when he would arrive too. 'I never work with understudies,' he sniffed, and swept out of the dressing-room. However, the standard fee for a guest on the *Como Show* was ten thousand dollars. 'For that he'll work with anybody,' said his agent with a grin. The only other hitch was a technical breakdown at Woburn Abbey. As I said smugly to Perry while we sat drinking on the Abbey's terrace, 'When the BBC breaks down, it does it in the best of surroundings.'

The day after the show was transmitted, Perry invited me to his hotel and there presented me with the latest type of camera, a Polaroid. Ruefully he told me that the man who invented it had begged him to invest in the invention; he had declined and now found that Polaroid could afford to spend a fortune advertising on his show. The instant photography of the Polaroid camera was still virtually unknown in Britain so I had great fun with it. At some function or other, I'd take a picture of a pretty girl and then go up to her and say, 'Good to see you here again this year.' She'd insist she hadn't been present last year, whereupon I would insist that not only had she been present but she was also wearing the same outfit, and with a flourish I'd produce the Polaroid picture. It was a great party trick while it lasted.

FOUR

I don't know about the 'Swinging Sixties' in general, but 1960 was certainly the start of a decade of swings between triumph and tragedy in my work and home. By then, I had been producing the *Band Show* for four years – a total of about fifty programmes – and it was a huge success. Dad was as popular on Saturday night television as he had been for years on radio at Sunday lunchtime. All this exposure in turn attracted packed houses in the variety theatres. He'd never had it so good.

I'd got to the stage of doing the shows on auto-pilot. Technically, I could produce *The Billy Cotton Band Show* in my sleep, but still I wasn't bored, chiefly because I got enormous fun out of some of our guests. Sadly, we lost Russ Conway. The *Band Show* had turned him into a big star, and he soon had his own television series and was doing exceptionally well around the theatres. His departure had left a big hole in our format, which was filled when by a stroke of luck I ran into an agent who, in the course of general chat, told me about this jolly twenty-stone woman who worked for the Post Office and did some semi-pro work at pubs as a pianist. 'If ever you lose Russ Conway,' he said, 'she's worth a look.' 'I need to look now. Russ has gone,' I replied.

He arranged for Mrs Mills to turn up at the Television Centre for an audition. She arrived an utter bundle of nerves, but it was soon clear that while she didn't have Russ's musicianship she certainly played the sort of music I was looking for. As it happened, Dad was in the building and I asked him to look her over. He came down to the music room, listened for a few minutes and said, 'Book her.' I don't think her prospects were harmed by the fact that she was the spitting image of Auntie Phoebe, one of my dad's sisters.

So Mrs Mills joined the show, and was a joy to work with. At first we had to arrange rehearsals around her shifts at the Post Office, because with typical Cockney shrewdness she refused to give up the day job when she was just ten years off her pension.

She was a huge bundle of fun and quickly became the butt of some diabolical practical jokes. At the start of one dress rehearsal we told her that Arthur Askey was to be the guest star and that he would be using her piano as a prop. The idea was that the piano's middle C key would be wired to a thunder flash, so when he hit the note there would be an enormous explosion. Therefore, Mrs Mills must under no circumstance touch that key during her medley, either at the rehearsal or in the show proper. Bursting as always with goodwill, she agreed, and then it struck her what it meant. Most of her tunes included middle C at some point, and without the note the din she made at the rehearsal was horrendous. We put her out of her misery before the actual transmission began and she took her discomfiture in good part.

This too was the decade in which Tommy Cooper began his rise to stardom, and I booked him as often as I could. The first time he appeared on the show he did a guillotine routine during which he put two carrots in the machine, dropped the blade and the carrots were cut in half. He then looked around for a volunteer, and the intention was that it should be the old man. At this time, Dad didn't know Tommy well enough to trust him absolutely so he wasn't ecstatic about putting his head on the block. He knew the whole point of Tommy's act was the tricks going spectacularly wrong, and it was with increasing apprehension that he watched the rehearsal. 'Don't worry, Dad,' I assured him. 'It's just a magic trick.' 'Yeah, and he's no magician!' he replied. Dad duly put his head on the block that once, but never again.

On another occasion Tommy put Dad in a wardrobe, closed the doors and when he opened them again, *hey presto!*, Billy Cotton had gone and couldn't be brought back. We agreed that as a trick it was passable but very unoriginal. Tommy obviously thought so too, for when the rehearsal was over he said he wanted to try out on me a better idea. Being hungry and tired, I very reluctantly agreed and sat on a stool on the stage while Tommy did a routine with a lot of different hats. It was pretty rough, and when he had finished I said, 'Tommy, let's do what we've already rehearsed.'

I took him off to an Italian restaurant for supper. The place was empty and after we'd eaten he proceeded to do an impersonation of me sitting on the stage looking bored stiff and giving the thumbs down to his bright idea with impatient comments like 'Yeah, fine, what's next?' We started to laugh and at one o'clock in the morning we were still laughing. I remember at one point lying helpless on the floor, begging him to stop before I died. The next day on the show he did the wardrobe joke we had rehearsed, but as he left he said, 'You missed being in on the start of a great piece of comedy.' He was right: the hats routine became a much-loved part of his repertoire.

Tommy became a great national institution, but there were one or two truly international comedians whom we couldn't afford, and I was surprised and delighted when the agent Leslie Grade phoned me to say he could fix it for Bob Hope to come on the show. Like the sharp agent he was, Leslie usually steered his stars exclusively towards Independent Television because they paid big money, but it transpired that Bob was making a film in Britain and some of the technicians on the set had said he ought to appear on the *Band Show*. He talked to Leslie who warned him that the BBC were not good payers, but still Bob was keen, so it was arranged.

This was a real coup for the show and we were all thrilled except for our star, Dad, who couldn't have been more offhand and unimpressed. He insisted on calling Bob 'Bing' and when it came to the duet he and Bob were to perform – the climax of the act – he was embarrassingly casual. The rehearsal dragged on and on until during one break Bob pulled me to one side and said, 'We have a saying in America: don't fight City Hall. We don't need to rehearse any more. He'll perform his can off on the night, believe me.' They both did, and Dad and Bob parted the best of friends, swearing undying love. Bob gave me a signed photo on which he had written 'We must do this again sometime'. I later tackled my father, asking him why he had been so difficult. His reply was classic: 'I saw your eyes light up when you were told about Bob Hope, and I wondered whose show it was going to be. I think he is a nice fellow, but he is worth ten minutes on this show and we'll probably never see him again.' He wasn't going to let me forget there was only one real star of *The Billy Cotton Band Show*.

After that, when Bob came over to Britain he'd occasionally phone me to find out what was going on at the BBC and to rib me about the fact we weren't buying *The Bob Hope Show* from American TV. Years later I attended an event at the American Embassy where the US ambassador was entertaining President Ford and Bob Hope. I joined a group around Bob, and heard him mention this pal of his at the BBC. Then he told a version of his one and only appearance on Billy Cotton's show. He didn't recognise *me* and *I* didn't recognise *his* story, but I remain a devoted fan.

It was around the middle of 1960 that I began to feel very lethargic and generally out of sorts. I thought at first it was just sheer tiredness. The pace of life in television was unremitting and I was wrung out. I assured myself that all I needed was a good holiday, so Boo and I booked a fortnight at the Hotel Aqua Brava on the Costa Brava in Spain. I wasn't sure I'd even last out until holiday time, though, so I went to see Bob Meyer, my father's doctor in Harley Street, who to my astonishment diagnosed me as having an attack of anxiety depression and put me on some medication. I couldn't understand it – why on earth should I be depressed? I had a lovely wife, two marvellous children, a nice home, a good job doing what I most wanted to do and, so far as I knew, doing it very successfully. The pills helped a little, but when we finally went on holiday my depression deepened and, despite the wonderful hotel, the beautiful weather, excellent food, swimming and general atmosphere, I just couldn't shake it off. We'd gone away with four friends among whom I was usually the life and soul of the party, and I just moped around and added guilt to my misery because I knew I was ruining everybody else's holiday. Everything was made infinitely worse by the fact that Boo was pregnant. She had enough to cope with without a miserable husband at a time when we ought to be looking forward with joy to another child.

At the end of the holiday I was due to go to a meeting with officials of Spanish television in Madrid. At the last moment I phoned my boss, Tom Sloan, and said I really couldn't face it. He tried to talk me into it but eventually agreed to send out another senior producer to support me. When we got to the meeting I had a panic attack and sat in complete silence throughout the whole discussion, much to the puzzlement of the Spanish officials. I felt I had let down the BBC and shamed myself, and as soon as I got home I went to see Bob Meyer again. He called in a psychiatrist.

Eventually it was proposed that I should have a course of ECT – electric shock treatment. I was enveloped in a mental cloud so black I would have done anything or undergone anything to relieve the torment and despair I felt. I went into a Harley Street nursing home, and looking back I can't be sure how many treatments I had. ECT treatment was then a fairly new method of treating depression, and was still very much at its hit-or-miss experimental stage. Someone described it as a kind of electric hammer that punched holes in the memory to break the chain of dark thoughts leading to depression. It certainly knocked holes in my memory, and for all the trauma and distress it entailed there didn't seem to be any obvious results.

Boo visited me every day, and finally she decided that enough was enough. She told the doctors that she thought the treatment, far from doing me good, was adding to my confusion and distress so she was going to take me home. She then sat me down and with sympathetic firmness talked to me like a Dutch uncle. She told me she was sure I'd get better if we worked on my problem together, and thought I ought to try to get back to work rather than spend my days pacing back and forth at home in a highly agitated state. If I agreed to go back, she promised she'd stay by the phone in case I got a panic attack. She managed to get it through to me that she and the children were completely dependent on me; she was happy and proud about that and confident I would not let the family down. As she pointed out, there was nothing to be ashamed of in my condition – it was an illness like any other and we had to fight it. After that conversation, my confidence slowly began to return.

I returned to work and was deeply moved by the amount of support and sympathy I got from the department. A new series of *The Billy Cotton Band Show* was coming up and it was decided that my colleague Duncan Wood would take re-sponsibility for producing it while I had merely to direct it on the night. I was still on medication and went through some pretty black periods, but they didn't last as long as they used to. A month after I went back to work I felt well enough to take over again as producer. And on 6 January 1961 Boo did her own producing: a gorgeous baby girl we christened Lisa and nick-named Lulu.

A few months later I was at a dinner with some friends and found myself chatting to a doctor whose specialism was psychiatry. I'm never bashful about telling doctors about my symptoms – after all, they aren't slow to give me their views on television. He encouraged me to talk about my depression, and after I'd described my lifestyle and feelings he said he thought the root of my problem was to be found in my professional relationship with my father. I was a very ambitious man tied to a show which though immensely successful was slowly running out of steam. I was building up my career just at the time my father was slowly but surely coming to the end of his, and my affection for him was so great that I couldn't cut myself loose and let him down. I was in a bind: the longer I stayed with him the greater my frustration would grow, but if I deserted him I would be riddled with guilt. Hence, I couldn't win; in that state of tension, psychological problems were inevitable. At the time I thought the doctor's theory was a bit far-fetched; in retrospect I have come to realise he was right. No doubt a good modern therapist would have been able to show me this downside of my relationship with my father.

My recovery was helped by another exciting challenge presented to me by my head of department, Eric Maschwitz. The famous comedy writers Frank Muir and Denis Norden had joined the BBC in 1960 as advisors and consultants. They wrote their own shows but also did some brainstorming about new comedy formats. Taking a close look at US television, they had been greatly impressed by a group of comedians who would now be described as 'alternative'. There was Lenny Bruce, whose obscenities put him out of bounds in polite circles, Shelley Berman and Bob Newhart, who had developed their stand-up acts in nightclubs, and Mort Sahl, who specialised in hard-edged political humour. Their reputations outside America were largely based on long-playing records of their acts. Mort Sahl in particular had gained a cult following in Britain because of his very funny attacks on American politicians and politics.

Frank and Denis pushed the idea of getting Mort Sahl to perform in Britain in order to shatter the aura of overweening respect with which the media surrounded our political leaders. Mort agreed to do a special show for the BBC provided he could bring with him his own producer, Helen Winston. I was to be the BBC's in-house producer working in co-operation with her. I learned later that booking Mort Sahl had been enthusiastically welcomed by the BBC's Director-General, Hugh Carleton Greene. He had been the Berlin correspondent of the *Daily Telegraph* in the 1930s and noted the effectiveness of the political satire which flourished in Berlin nightclubs as the last gasp of political freedom during the rise of Nazism.

I read everything I could find about Sahl and listened to all his records to get a feel for his talent. I also met Helen Winston who turned out to be a very feisty and wilful lady. If her considerable feminine wiles didn't do the trick, one felt the force of a tongue lashing, and my first meeting with Sahl precipitated such an outburst. Having read that Mort loved fast cars, I had arranged with Lofty England, the boss of Jaguar, that he should have the use of an E-type, which Jaguar had not yet marketed in

America. Lofty brought the car along to the Dorchester where Mort was staying. When I was shown into his presence, I told him about the car and suggested that Lofty might be invited up for a drink. I expected him to be both delighted and grateful, but he just shrugged and said, 'I don't want to meet him. Just tell him to leave the keys of the car at reception.' I wasn't standing for that, so I said, 'Forget it!' and left the room to thank Lofty for his trouble and call the whole thing off. Helen followed me out and went ballistic – how dare I offer Mort a car without her permission, how dare I speak to him dismissively because he didn't want to meet some car salesman? I pointed out to her that Lofty England was a director of Jaguar Cars and a major figure in the car industry, and that I had no intention of allowing him to be treated in such a dismissive way by anyone – even by Mort Sahl. In retrospect, he may well have thought the whole thing was a sales pitch. She warned me I'd better shape up or I'd be off the show. I told her to talk to my boss, Eric, and left. Within hours, she reappeared, her persona completely transformed, all sweetness and light. I suspected she hadn't got a sympathetic hearing from Eric.

Meanwhile Frank Muir and Denis Norden had done everything they could to help Mort to create some strong material about British political life, but he seemed reluctant to discuss ideas with them; a plentiful supply of newspapers was all he needed. So we shrugged and got on with the business of producing a set for Georgia Brown, who was to sing on the show. The set designer was a very clever Eastern European called George Djurkovick. He put together a simple set which when lit looked like a hacienda-type building on a beach in the Caribbean. Organising the lighting for this took quite some time, during which Helen, who was sitting behind me in the gallery, kept saying, 'I can't see anything, it is so dark – can't we have some more light?' Finally my patience ran out. I told the lighting engineer to turn on everything, including the house-lights, then I said, '*Now* can you see?' This pretty childish tantrum turned into a comedy routine when George burst in asking what was happening – I explained that Helen had demanded more light, whereupon in a thick European accent he muttered, 'How dare these foreigners come here and try to teach us our business?'

The day of the show, 19 July 1961, arrived and I asked Mort if he had anything he particularly wanted in the way of camera work. I got a blank look. Frank and Denis were to do the pre-show warm-up and we had a wonderful audience organised. Mort Sahl had become the darling of the politically aware intellectuals, so personalities such as Professor Bronowski and Jonathan Miller begged us for tickets. Alas, the show was a damp squib. He did not make enough references to the political issues or personalities in Britain, which left us wondering exactly what he'd been doing in his suite in the Dorchester for a whole week.

But the Mort Sahl fiasco had an important sequel. The BBC's Director-General decided that the Light Entertainment department didn't know how to handle political satire. However, he was determined to get some onto the BBC television screen, so he gave the green light to Donald Baverstock and Alasdair Milne of the TV Talks Department, together with Ned Sherrin, to develop a new satirical format. The result was *That Was The Week That Was,* the first series in which the BBC was to mix politics with hard-hitting comedy.

Early in 1962 there were changes to the management structure of BBC Television. Eric Maschwitz moved on to become a consultant to the Director of Television and Tom Sloan took his place, which created a vacancy for an Assistant Head of Light Entertainment. The job was duly advertised and attracted a number of applicants, including many of the senior producers in our department, a few from other departments and one or two from right outside the BBC. Appointment boards were set up which Tom chaired, accompanied by an appointments officer to ensure fair-play and a personnel officer to check the candidates were fit and proper people to do the job. But though everything had been done by the book, the board felt unable to appoint any of the candidates.

I hadn't applied for the job. I wasn't particularly senior in the department and I was quite happy producing programmes. When Tom asked me why I hadn't applied, I told him I would never appear before a board; I would be too upset if they turned me down. After all, the powers that be knew what my work was worth, and if I was needed in management they would have to make me an offer. Tom then took me aback by saying that if he were a free agent and not bound by the BBC's procedures, he would give me the job on the spot. I was flattered but not sure I wanted to take a staff appointment even if it were offered. I had a three-year contract which meant that every so often the BBC had to make up its mind whether it wanted to continue employing me and I in turn had to make up my mind if I wanted to be employed. Tom persevered. Would I have a drink with Oliver Whiteley, chief assistant to the DG, and see if something could be worked out? I agreed and an appointment was fixed for the next day.

I went home and told Boo about the meeting with Tom and his proposal. We argued the ins and outs of the matter until the small hours of the morning, and finally agreed that if the conditions were right and I was made an offer, I should accept it. Although I was very happy doing my current job, that might change if the assistant head's job was given to someone whom I couldn't get along with.

Oliver Whiteley was a marvellous man, the nearest thing to a resident saint the BBC possessed. He had a wonderful mind and a kindly disposition; he was easy to talk to and saw my point of view completely but thought that the best interests of the BBC came first. So within half an hour I had allowed myself to be persuaded. I could stay on contract and an announcement would be made directly the appointment had been rubber-stamped by the appropriate people. A couple of days later Tom called a meeting of the department so everyone could be told before the official promulgation was made. My appointment got a mixed reception, some of the old hands making it clear they weren't going to be ordered about by the youngest producer in the department. I saw their point and was determined to tread very carefully for a while.

The reaction from the department was as nothing compared to that of my father. I went to see him in his office in Soho. He was in his shirt-sleeves standing behind his desk with his trilby on the back of his head and a load of papers spread out in front of him. He was obviously sorting out a few problems. After we had exchanged the usual pleasantries, I broke the good news. His first question was: 'Does that mean you won't be producing my show?' I replied that it did but said I would make sure we found someone he approved of. His next statement completely scuppered me. 'Well, if I were you I would dig a hole six foot by six foot by two foot and put me in it.' He then returned to his papers. I was dismissed. Dazed, I left his office, walked round to the Michael Reine office in Denmark Street and from there phoned my mother to give her the good news. Or was it? In the light of Dad's reaction, I wasn't so sure. Her immediate response was predictable. 'Wonderful! Boo must be very proud of you and so am I.' I then told her what my father had said. She chuckled. 'I'll tell you something about your father. He didn't get where he's got by worrying about *his* father. He'll come round.' She knew her man and by the time I got back to my office after lunch, Dad had bought and delivered a desk set with a card that I still have to this day – 'Good luck Bill! I thought *I'd* get the DG's job, but some have what it takes and others haven't. Love Dad.'

Having cleared up the work I had outstanding, I moved into my new office complete with furniture which in the best civil service tradition was graded according to rank. I wasn't quite elevated enough to rate a fully fitted carpet, though its edges were only inches from the wall. I also had a carpark pass to the forecourt of Television Centre and was invited by the Assistant Controller of Administration, who doubled as president of the senior dining-room, to join that august body. He suggested that we should meet for a sherry in his office the next day and then proceed to the dining-room to be formally introduced. I paraded at twelve-forty-five sharp in his office, dressed in my best suit with shirt and tie to match. We drank our sherry and on our arrival at the dining-room I was introduced to my fellow managers, most of whom I knew pretty well anyway. When it came to ordering my meal I thought I would start as I meant to go on, so I asked for a steak with chips and made a point of requesting some HP sauce. I detected a few raised eyebrows but I kept my nerve. When my food came I picked up the sauce bottle and with a flourish shook it. Unfortunately the person who had used it before me had not replaced the cap properly and the contents shot all over my suit, tie and shirt. The raised eyebrows turned to knowing looks and smiles, and I retired to the loo to clean myself up. I smelled like an Oxo cube for the rest of the day.

My new job carried with it a salary increase and since our family was growing, it seemed the right time to look for a larger house. My friend Bob Snell who'd first encouraged our move to Ham Common had built twelve town houses on a plot that led directly to the Common itself. So we moved to a semi-detached house in Beech Row where Bob and his wife Jackie were our neighbours. Another neighbour was Dick Lester the comedy producer who had graduated to feature films and produced the Beatles' extravaganza *A Hard Day's Night*. When that film was finished, he had the Beatles to dinner and for security reasons went to great lengths to smuggle them into his home. A few days later, when the news got out, the adults in Beech Row understood and approved of Dick's circumspection but their children never forgave him. To think, the Beatles were actually *there* in the flesh a few yards away and they never knew!

One of the most urgent jobs I faced was to find a replacement for myself as producer of *The Billy Cotton Band Show*. There was a suggestion that I should keep producing it as well as doing my day job. I was absolutely sure this was wrong. You can't be available to and supportive of other producers if you are busy worrying about your own programme. And one of my responsibilities was to allocate staff and resources between the various departmental projects. The danger was not that I might favour Dad's show but rather give it *less* than its fair share so as not to appear biased. Anyway, that conversation with the doctor following my nasty turn still lingered. The person most qualified to do the show was Michael Hurll, whom I knew would have my father's confidence. Michael had been an assistant on the show since I started producing it and I trusted him completely. The problem was that he was not a fully fledged producer and could hardly be promoted for just one series. So we decided to put Johnnie Stewart in as producer with Michael backing him up. Johnnie had brought with him a high reputation from radio where he produced shows like *Sing it Again* and *The Show Band Show*. It was one of my better decisions: he went on to launch *Top of the Pops* and other musical shows of high quality. Michael Hurll after one series as Johnnie's back up became the producer of the *Band Show*, then later he took on *Cilla*, Cilla Black's original series, which started in 1968 and proved very success-ful. To my great relief, by the middle of 1962 Dad had been sorted out and there was no noticeable drop-off in the popularity of the series as a result of the change of producers. I wasn't indispensable to the old man after all – a realisation that consolidated my recovery from depression.

I had done an audit of the department's output. We had a number of classic programmes which provided us with a strong foundation of popular entertainment: *The Black and White Minstrel Show*, *This is Your Life*, *The Rag Trade*, Michael Bentine's *It's a Square World*, *Harry Worth*, *Juke Box Jury*, *Sykes* and *Steptoe and Son*. It was our Variety department which gave me cause for worry. When the BBC discontinued *Six-Five Special*, ITV stepped in smartly and took top place in the pop category with *Thank Your Lucky Stars* followed by *Ready, Steady, Go!*. The situation wasn't disastrous by any means but we urgently needed some fresh ideas and new programme formats, so I decided to do a trawl round the agents.

In the 1960s there were a few big agencies, like the Grade Organisation, Fosters, Richard Stone and Bernard Delfont, all of whom had large stables of performers. Some, such as the Grade Organisation, favoured working with ITV; others, such as Richard Stone, had a traditional relationship with the BBC, and one or two just played the field. The big stars were by and large already bound to the BBC or ITV with long-term contracts, so it was tomorrow's bill-toppers I was on the look-out for. This meant that I spent night after night in theatres and nightclubs – which sounds a highly desirable way to make a living, but it was a little like prospecting for gold: you had to plough through a mountain of sludge to find the odd nugget. Week in and week out, I had to sit through endless per-formances by no-hopers, my spirits only occasionally raised when someone with a glimmer of talent came on stage. I had one or two advantages. The majority of agents knew me and felt that although I was now firmly a BBC man, my heart was still in show business – in this sense I was one of them. They also liked doing business with the BBC. We couldn't match ITV's deep pockets but our production standards were higher and there was still at that time a certain mystique attached to those magic letters 'BBC'.

Because of my promotion I was introduced to the Wednesday TV Programme Review Board. All heads and assistant heads of output departments, together with the top brass, sat round a table and dissected the previous week's output, programme by programme. It was a privilege to be part of the process because all around me were some of the best programme brains in the business – legendary names in sport, current affairs, drama, science and light entertainment. They were merciless in their judgement of everyone else's output and more than a little defensive about their own. When I first attended the Light Entertainment contingent sat at the far end of the table leaving the journalists, who were said always to be willing to 'bob for a job', to grab the seats right under the eye of the bosses. We and the Outside Broadcast brigade were happy down at the far end, and would make subversive remarks there that could not quite be heard at the top table. When he became Controller of programmes, Huw Wheldon put a stop to our heckling by insisting we sit near the top of the table. 'Now we'll have just one meeting,' he said.

Quick-wittedness was a quality much appreciated among this highly sophisticated group of talents. I recall one occasion vividly. It was well known that Sydney Newman, the Canadian-born Head of Drama, had long wanted to take over opera which had been in the domain of the music department. Over the dead body of the Head of Music he succeeded, and proceeded to do a lavish production of Kurt Weill's *Mahagonny*. Besides much else, it involved three days in the studio. By the end of the third day the director still wasn't finished, and with the pressure on facilities it was unlikely he could get another free studio for weeks, not to mention that the extra cost would be enormous. After much wringing of hands it was decided that the project be abandoned altogether. When the fiasco was discussed among the Programme Review Board, one by one its members tore into the absent opera director and then waited for Sydney Newman's response. He looked up and with a smile on his face said, 'The trouble is, the man's a talented prick.' There was a brief silence then everyone started to laugh. Sydney was off the hook; he had defused a heated issue with a typical North American response.

The pop culture phenomenon of the sixties was Beatlemania, and I got swept up in it. One day I was having a drink with Cliff Richard and his agent, Peter Gormley, in the BBC Club after discussing Cliff's new show. We were gossiping about general matters when Cliff suddenly asked if he could go back to my office and watch the BBC's *625 Show* (a new talent show produced in Bristol) on television. Naturally I agreed, and when Cliff had left, I asked Peter Gormley what the interest was. He said casually, 'Apparently, there's some new group appearing on it that Cliff's interested in. They're called the Beatles, or some name like that.' 'Are they any good?' I asked. 'Good Lord, no,' he replied. There spoke the Shadows' agent.

Within a matter of months the Beatles had become the sensation of the century and their manager, Brian Epstein, was a man much in demand. They duly appeared on ITV's flagship programme, *Sunday Night at the London Palladium*, and a couple of other shows, so I was desperate to come up with an idea that might attract Epstein to the BBC. In the end we put to him a proposal that we should do a special *Juke Box Jury* with the boys as the panel, followed two hours later by a programme called *Here Come the Beatles*. To clinch it, I suggested we do the whole thing from Liverpool, the Beatles' home territory. This greatly appealed to Brian and he in turn suggested we use the Odeon cinema. He gave me a Saturday date for about three weeks later and the deal was sealed.

I set about booking the Odeon through the cinema chain's head office, and terms were agreed, subject to contract and approval from the Odeon board. Meanwhile I booked an outside broadcast unit from the BBC in Manchester together with their top producer Barney Colehan, whose name had gained the status of legend when he was doing the Wilfred Pickles show, *Have a Go*. Since then he had developed *The Good Old Days* for TV, so he had a lot of experience in television presentation from a theatre.

The day before the *Radio Time*s went to press I contacted the Odeon management to ask when the contract would arrive, as I wanted to put the venue in the programme billing. They asked me to go to their office, and when I got there, informed me that the board, fearing that a Saturday television schedule including Beatles appearances would seriously damage attendance at their cinemas, had decided to pull out of the deal. I was beside myself with fury. One of the great attractions of the whole concept was that the Beatles would perform on their own doorstep. I recall saying I intended to go ahead with a Liverpool venue even if it meant doing the show from a public lavatory. The Odeon management shrugged: they knew there was virtually no chance of my getting a suitable location in Liverpool at that late stage.

Still fuming and utterly distraught, I made my way back to the office. Casting about for something to do rather than just sit around in a rage, I decided to do the obvious and phone around other public halls in Liverpool. I started with the redoubtable Cissie Williams at Moss Empire. She was a great admirer of the Old Man, which meant that at least she would take my call. I explained my predicament and my treatment at the hands of the Odeon management. There wasn't the slightest chance the Liverpool Empire might be available, was there? The Empire was one of the biggest variety theatres in the country and the chances of it being dark were minimal. There was a pause and then, suddenly, it was miracle time! Cissie told me that the Empire was in rehearsal for pantomime and she thought they could make enough space for us to do the two programmes, but she would just check and phone me back. Within minutes we had the go-ahead. 'What about money, Cissie?' I asked anxiously, all too conscious that we were under the hammer and she could name her own price. 'The same as you were going to pay at the Odeon. And good luck,' she replied.

The shows, on 7 December 1963, were an experience I never forgot and I learned much from them. Liverpool was *en fête*. The city's most famous sons were to appear on television and its entire population was determined to be in the audience. The police organised orderly queues outside the theatre and more than two thousand teenagers packed the place. They began screaming the moment they sat down and didn't stop until they left the theatre hours later. David Jacobs, who chaired *Juke Box Jury*, managed to make himself heard from time to time, but the moment the Beatles said anything remotely funny or provocative the roof came off.

I had taken Boo and her friend Patsy up to Liverpool with me and initially sat them in the circle, but I fancied I saw the whole structure swaying so I quickly got them out and put them in a box. Throughout the performance, Brian Epstein leaned against the back wall of the stalls, stoned out of his mind. For hours the screaming went on, and when *Here Come the Beatles* began the noise reached such a pitch that the cameramen couldn't hear the director's instructions, so God knows where the cameras were pointing. The sound operator turned down all the audience mikes but it didn't make any difference. It was sheer bedlam, but it was also a mega-television happening, and that's what television lives by – the drama of epic events. We got a huge audience and punctured eardrums.

I was about thirty-five at the time and remember saying to David Jacobs as we made our way back to our hotel after the show, with screaming kids still milling all round us, 'I feel as old as God.' 'Me too,' said David, with feeling.

In my roller-coaster of a job, I went from the high excitement of a Beatles concert to the hushed surroundings of a management course run by Oliver Whiteley at Uplands, a conference centre near High Wycombe. The climax of the fortnight's course was the final Friday, when there was to be a talk by the DG, Hugh Carleton Green, in the morning and a visit from the BBC's founder, Lord Reith, in the afternoon. *That Was The Week That Was* was running at the time, and it had split the country in two. Some viewers thought it a breath of fresh air bordering on a wind of change while the more conservative considered it a disgrace and concluded that the BBC had completely lost its marbles. Sketches such as the one in which a vicar addressing the camera knocked out his pipe on a crucifix had them in a state of apoplexy. Still, it got an amazing number of viewers for the time of night at which it was shown and made its real impact through political satire. Some commentators said that the then Prime Minister, Alec Douglas-Home, lost the 1964 election because of the treatment meted out to him by *TW3*.

During his session, the DG gave a robust defence of the programme, mentioning in passing that satire was an area in which Light Entertainment had failed. He was talking about the Mort Sahl fiasco, but I don't think he remembered that I was the ill-fated show's producer.

Lord Reith was by now a gaunt, stooped figure but still a formidable personality, and he arrived bang on time – punctuality being in his eyes a supreme virtue. After receiving a fulsome introduction from Oliver he said words to the effect that he had only decided to come in order to keep his word as a gentleman to Mr Whiteley, but the disgust he felt at the direction the BBC had taken and some of the programmes it was transmitting was such that he could not bring himself to talk about them. Instead he would answer any questions, but before he did so he wished to say one thing. This one thing went on for over an hour without a pause for breath. At the end of the tirade he asked for questions. Anyone who tried to defend BBC policy in dispute of what the DG had said in the morning was swatted like a fly.

Eventually, I summoned up my courage and stood up. I said

I was desperately sad that the man who had created arguably the greatest broadcasting organisation in the world now seemed to take no joy in his creation. Of course some of the programmes now being produced were controversial, that was inevitably going to happen, but the majority of the output fairly reflected the brief Reith himself had given when the BBC was first created: the best of everything for everyone. He fixed me with a withering look then asked Oliver who I was and which department I worked for. On being told I came from Light Entertainment, he snorted and said, 'I thought so! I see the *Radio Times* put a variety performer on its front page recently . . .' He spat out the term 'variety performer' as though it was a species of child molester. 'I would never have allowed that to happen in my day,' he concluded. End of subject.

The course ended the next morning and Boo came to pick me up. On the way home she asked me my impressions of the fortnight. I found myself talking about the BBC in a different way. I realised I had caught the bug. The BBC was not just another broadcasting organisation, it was special. It had been developed by people who really cared and was one of the great bulwarks of British cultural life. Most of its thousands of programmes were made with love and aimed at increasing the viewers' and listeners' store of worthwhile experience. The Corporation had its faults, but I was prepared to nail my colours to its mast. And until I retired in 1988, though I was to receive a number of tempting offers, I never thought seriously of working for anyone else.

FIVE

Throughout 1963, the BBC was gearing up to launch its second television channel, BBC2. I suppose in retrospect this was an event of great significance, but for me at the time it was one completely overshadowed by the fact that in February Boo had discovered a lump in her breast. Unlike me, she never made a fuss about her health and I had great difficulty in persuading her to see Bob Meyer in Harley Street. He thought the swelling was mastitis and would go away in its own time; nevertheless he told us to keep an eye on it and come back if it persisted. It did persist, and to my shame I confess we did nothing about it.

Eventually our local doctor sent Boo to see a consultant surgeon, Mr Franklin, at Hammersmith Hospital who suggested she should have a biopsy straight away. He was a very gentle man and, when I went to see him on my own to ask what the likely outcome might be, he was cautious and suggested we wait until the biopsy results were known before drawing any conclusions. Boo, as always, was serene and I tried desperately to exude confidence. Mr Franklin said he would like the biopsy done at St Anthony's Hospital, Cheam. Though I suggested that Hammersmith would be more convenient, he insisted St Anthony's was the right place, so within forty-eight hours we found ourselves outside a forbidding-looking brick building in the Victorian style. Boo looked up at the place and said, 'I don't think I'm going to like this.' It was then that I realised for the first time how worried she was beneath her apparent air of confidence. I assured her that if she wasn't happy with the hospital I would phone Franklin and insist on our going somewhere else, but suggested we ought at least to go inside and see how we got on.

In those days, St Anthony's was supported by the NHS and run by a nursing order of nuns called the Daughters of the Cross. During the day, the sisters on the wards were all nuns; at night they returned to the adjoining convent and their duties were carried out by civilian nurses. There was also a nursing training school for women mostly recruited from Ireland. The Mother Superior, Sister Mary Perpetua, met us and explained the form for the next day's biopsy and then introduced us to Sister Ann Celine, the nun who would be looking after Boo. Apart from being a wonderful nurse, Ann Celine both looked and was angelic, and although this first meeting was a bit fraught (Boo had forgotten to bring something and Ann Celine was a bit short with her) in no time these two wonderful women had developed a close relationship. I was allowed to stay with Boo until way past visiting hours. We talked about the children, about my mother coming up from Sandbanks to look after them and how they all adored her and called her Nina, and we talked about work and I kept up a barrage of stories about the showbiz types with whom I dealt – we talked about *anything* to avoid the conversation turning to what might lie ahead. Eventually the night sister suggested I should go home and let my wife get some rest.

Boo had the biopsy mid-morning, and nowadays would probably have come home to wait for the results, but Franklin wanted her to stay at St Anthony's until the results came through. I'm sure he suspected she was going to have a major operation and wanted her to get used to the hospital. The next three days lasted a lifetime, but in a strange way as the time for the results drew nearer I felt more and more confident that everything would be fine. It was that old, old illusion that the worst couldn't happen to us because we'd done nothing to deserve it.

A few days later, on my way to work I decided to call on Mr Franklin at Hammersmith Hospital to see if he had heard anything. I breezed into his office full of cheer, had a joke with his secretary and then got rocked back on my heels. The news was not good. The biopsy showed that Boo had breast cancer, and Mr Franklin would operate the next morning. I remember asking him the usual fatuous questions, such as: 'She won't die, will she?' He was very patient and told me he would be talking to Boo at four o'clock that afternoon, and I arranged to meet him at St Anthony's.

I went off to my office in a daze. My secretary, Queenie, and Tom, my boss, knew as soon as I walked in what the form was. I said that I was going home and I would let them know how the operation went. At home I told my mother, then phoned Boo's mother; I spoke to my brother, Ted, and asked him to tell Dad, who I knew would take it quite badly. Also with Mother I discussed how and what we should tell the children. Jane was twelve, Kate was ten and Lulu was three; we had a Spanish au pair living in, so physically they would be well cared for, but we had no idea how long Boo might be in hospital, or how well she would cope when she got back home.

In the afternoon I drove to St Anthony's and went up to Boo's room. Mr Franklin thought it best that he talk to Boo on his own. When he came out I went in to find Boo smiling. 'How do you feel about having a wife who is one wing low?' she said. I wanted to cry my eyes out but felt I had to try to match her courage. We talked about the operation. I told her about the arrangements my mother and I had discussed concerning the children, and she approved. We didn't talk about cancer. I am now a vice-president of Marie Curie Cancer Care, and if I'd known then what I know now I might have been a greater help to her and to my children.

Boo's operation was successful but the cancer had spread to the lymph gland in her armpit, which was not a good sign. However, Franklin assured me he had got it all out; now we had to wait and see. There was a conservatory-like extension attached to Boo's room and the nuns let me sleep in there. I am forever indebted to those nuns. They nursed Boo with tender devotion and were exquisitely sensitive to the needs and fears of our family. On the night of the operation, Boo was still under the effects of the anaesthetic when the nurses came in to dress her wound. They asked me to leave; I pleaded with them to let me stay. 'I'll be looking at her for the rest of my life; please let me see the wound at its worst then I'll have the pleasure of seeing it get better.' They agreed.

A few days later Boo was talking about this and that, and happened to mention that the nurses were going to change the dressing before the next meal. 'I keep my eyes shut,' she said. 'I can't bear to look at it yet.'

I smiled. 'Don't worry, it looks great. Mr Franklin's done well.'

'How do you know?' she asked, puzzled.

'Because I watched them dress it the first night, and if ever you turn your back on me I'll divorce you on the spot.'

Although Boo made great strides, she was told she'd be in hospital for about eight weeks. We soon had a system going. If I had stayed the night at the hospital I would go to work via home, and if I spent the night at home I'd go to work via the hospital.

I'd been away from the BBC for a couple of weeks and work was piling up at the office. The imminent arrival of BBC2 meant that we needed extra staff to produce its entertainment programmes, so I was given the job of supervising their training. Among the new recruits was Jim Moir, who went on to become Head of Light Entertainment for BBC TV and then Controller of Radio 2, and Terry Hughes, who after producing shows with Ronnie Corbett and Ronnie Barker, Val Doonican, Harry Secombe and many others, went off to make his fortune on American TV. I confidently predicted he'd be back within a year, but I was wrong. He became director of *The Golden Girls,* which was an enormous hit in the States and later had a cult following in Britain.

Dick Clement was another student in the class of '63. I asked each trainee to put together and direct three fifteen-minute programmes. One involved matching pictures to gramophone records; another, directing a situation comedy script which I supplied; and for the third part, I asked them to do a production of their own choice. For Dick's third exercise he teamed up with a pal called Ian Le Frenais, and they wrote and produced an extended sketch about two feisty lads from Geordieland. I was so impressed with what I saw that I asked Michael Peacock, then the Controller of BBC2, if he'd look at it. If BBC2 was to be in the business of nurturing new talent, these two had to be sure-fire winners.

Michael liked what he saw and commissioned the series which became *The Likely Lads,* starring James Bolam and Rodney Bewes. It ran for three years and dealt with the manners and morals of the Swinging Sixties. In 1973 I got Dick and Ian to write a sequel, *Whatever Happened to the Likely Lads?,* about the more sober seventies. The introduction of Brigit Forsyth as Rodney Bewes's wife made the initial twosome a triangle. It isn't often that a sequel is an improvement on the original – this one was, and it won the BAFTA award for best situation comedy of the year.

Boo had been in hospital for about four weeks when we held a meeting in my office with Dad, George Inns, Tom Sloan and Michael Hurll to discuss the forthcoming series of the *Band Show*. The meeting was very relaxed and everybody was putting in their twopenny-worth when I noticed that my father's voice had started to shake a little. I asked him if he was OK and he replied that he was, but something seemed wrong. I said, 'Are you sure you're all right?' 'Of course I'm all right,' he replied aggressively. 'Well, stand up then,' I challenged. He growled. 'I can stand up if I want to.' 'All right, do it then,' I said. He tried to get up and literally fell into George's arms. I asked Queenie to get the duty sister to pop up and look him over. She wasn't sure – it might just have been a dizzy spell, or it could have been a minor stroke. Dad refused to believe there was anything wrong with him and asked me to call a taxi. I wanted to get an ambulance and haul him off to the nearest hospital, but he wouldn't hear of it.

It was by now fairly late in the afternoon, so I decided to call at his flat in St James before going on to see Boo. I arrived to find his doctor, Bob Meyer, already there. He thought it was likely that Dad had suffered a small stroke and said that he should just rest up. Kathie Kay, who was by now close to Dad, was due in town to do the Sunday broadcast, and said she would keep an eye on him. My brother Ted was also on his way so, feeling all was under control, I went off to see Boo at St Anthony's. We were chatting away when the phone went. It was Ted to say that the Old Man had had a major stroke and been taken to the Harley Street Nursing Home. There a neurologist had seen him, in whose expert opinion Dad had a thirty per cent chance of lasting the night – even if he did, he would be paralysed for life. I desperately loved my father but I would rather he died than end up paralysed.

I told Ted he would have to cope because I couldn't leave Boo. She sensed something awful had happened, took the phone from me and talked to Ted herself. When she'd put the phone down, she said gently, 'Well, are you going to see your father or am I?' I arrived in Dad's room at the nursing home to find him in bed, his right side trembling and his left side frozen in paralysis. Outside his room, Kathie was waiting with a woman I'd never met before. She explained that the woman, Mrs Finch, was a faith healer and would we mind if she went in to be with Father for a brief while? I was desperate enough to try anything and it seemed that orthodox medical science had done all it could, so I agreed. She was in with Dad for about ten minutes and when she came out she said, 'He'll sleep now and then start to get better.' Ted and I went in and found Dad sleeping like a baby, all the agitation and thrashing around gone. The next morning he slowly regained consciousness and I remember him saying, 'God's kind. I don't know what's happened but it doesn't hurt.' His gratitude to Mrs Finch was unbounded and afterwards he invited her regularly to his shows.

Meanwhile, we had the press to consider. What were we going to tell them? Back with us in the land of the living, Dad insisted that the press be told he had flu. We could never have got away with such a story these days – the press pack would have been all over the place – but life was different then. The BBC agreed to release me so that I could front the radio broadcasts. In fact there were only a few and then the band had a week off before they were due in Blackpool for a summer season. Dad's agent, Leslie Grade, contacted Jimmy Edwards and fixed it for him to front the band at the seaside.

On Sundays, I would do the show, visit Dad and then go on to see Boo, an arrangement which lasted about three weeks until the day I arrived at Harley Street to find Dad's room empty and his bed stripped. For a moment I feared the worst and rushed downstairs to ask the sister in charge where Dad was. Apparently, that morning he'd got up, dressed, called a taxi and discharged himself. 'What's more,' she said, 'he's taken one of our nurses with him.' 'Good God!' I thought. 'He's back to his old self.' I don't know whether I was more relieved or angry. I rushed round to his flat and sure enough, there he was with a male nurse in attendance. I closed the door behind me and burst out, 'Dad, this isn't fair!' He looked at me sadly and said, 'Don't worry, son. I'd rather do what I want to do and die than live doing what the medics want me to do.'

The Sunday after he went back to the flat, I did the show on radio and then decided to call in on him. I went into the vestibule of the block of flats and there, hanging on to the door of the lift to keep himself upright, was Dad, his shirt halfway out of his trousers and the knot of his tie askew. 'What on earth are you doing here?' I demanded. He looked at me and said, 'I heard your broadcast tonight – it was marvellous, so I'm on my way out to get you a bottle of champagne.' I told him he was in no condition to leave the flats and that he must go back upstairs. He insisted he was going to go out and buy some champagne, and that was that. So I lied. 'The street outside is full of reporters and photographers. They'd love to get a picture of you looking like this.' Reluctantly, he took the lift back to his flat where I tackled the male nurse. While I was belabouring him I noticed that he had a livid red mark, the beginnings of a bruise, on his cheek. 'I tried to hold him back and he hit me,' he said ruefully. Dad nodded. 'I reckon as long as I have my right hook there's not much wrong with me.' A week later, the male nurse suddenly vanished with a Dunhill cigar box in which Dad kept all his jewellery.

Dad set himself the task of getting fit again. His willpower was awesome. He would battle away fastening his collar button and doing up his studs, and then stagger backwards and forwards across the room. A couple of weeks later, he got himself to an airport, hired an aeroplane and flew up to Blackpool. Every night, he'd sit at the side of the stage, watch the band and then go off to the bar. He was still partially paralysed and could only walk with the help of a stick. One evening he was sitting in the bar when someone came up to him and said, 'I paid good money to see you tonight. They said you were ill, and I find you in here drinking.' Dad replied, 'You're right, lad.' He reached into his pocket and said, 'Here's your money back,' then turned to limp out. When the man saw Dad's condition he was full of apologies. 'No, you're right,' said Dad. 'I shouldn't be in here. Thanks for the tip.' And with that, he left.

The summer of 1963 was now upon us, and Boo was coming to the end of her treatment in St Anthony's. We thought it best to send Jane and Kate to a weekly boarding school and, with the help of Frank Muir's sister-in-law who was a teaching nun at St Mary's, Ascot, we managed to get them enrolled at the Marist Convent in Sunningdale. Jane loved it and Kate hated it. Looking back, there are a lot of things we would have done differently if we'd known what the future held. But some things we only learn the hard way. I was trying to protect them; what I should have been doing was gently involving them.

I found a means of beginning to repay the staff of St Anthony's for all they had done for Boo. They held an annual fete which was opened by a showbiz personality supplied by an agent, so I did the agent out of his commission by providing fete-openers for a number of years. Most stars are incredibly generous with their time for worthy causes: they are conscious of their own good fortune and so rally to help those less fortunate. Besides the fete we did a midnight matinee and a Sunday show at the Granada, Tooting by courtesy of Sydney Bernstein, the chairman of Granada. The Bachelors, Petula Clark, the Silhouettes and Harry Secombe performed in the midnight matinee and Morecambe and Wise topped the bill at the Sunday show.

They were all great troupers and good friends, but perhaps the most extraordinary fete opener was Jimmy Savile. He insisted on driving around Cheam with his head sticking out of the roof of his Rolls, bellowing at passers-by to tell them about the fete. He blasted through the wards like a hurricane, meeting every patient, frightening the life out of the nuns and setting the nurses squealing.

He was also to appear in a show which had started with an exchange between me and Donald Baverstock at one programme review board meeting. Baverstock ran BBC1 and was casting an eye over the previous weeks' programmes when he noticed that ITV's *Ready, Steady, Go!* was obviously the most popular pop show on television. He taunted me that I couldn't match it. Over the weekend, I gave the matter some deep thought. In the past, most of the pop hits were American so we hadn't been able to mount a Top Twenty TV show in Britain, but times were changing. This was the 1960s. Thanks largely to the Beatles, there had been an amazing renaissance in pop culture and by now most of the Top Twenty records sold in Britain were made by British acts. How about a weekly television programme featuring the Top Twenty? I went back to Donald with an idea for a short series and my enthusiasm won him over.

However, there was a real problem: the only studio we could get was in a converted church in Dickenson Road in Manchester. I took it in spite of the wails of woe from doubters in the department, who assured me I'd never get artists to go all the way up to Manchester to do a single number. I decided to trust my instincts – after all, show business is a profession made up of itinerants used to travelling to whichever venues promise good audiences. They'll go where the work is.

We got the go-ahead and I gave Johnnie Stewart the job of producing a show in which the performers were chosen on the sole criterion that they had a record in the Top Twenty. I remember saying to him, 'It'll either be off in six weeks or it'll run for ever.' Johnnie wanted to call the show *Pick of the Pops;* I believed we should be bolder and call it *Top of the Pops* because that told the audience what it was. Thus one of the most popular and durable of all television programmes was launched, alternating four presenters: David Jacobs, Alan Freeman, Pete Murray and Jimmy Savile.

The show started quite well, and I knew we were on our way when after the second show I got a phone call from the Beatles' manager, Brian Epstein. He offered his congratulations and asked if we would play the Beatles' new record, which had gone straight into the Hit Parade. 'Only if they'll perform from the studio in Dickenson Road,' I said. 'That's the rule, the performers must appear live.' 'Listen, Bill,' he replied, 'if they appear at Dickenson Road there'll be a riot.' Johnny and I chewed it over and decided on a compromise. The Beatles must do the number from Dickenson Road but we would pre-record it before the crowds arrived.

My personal interest in *Top of the Pop*s was described in the 1970s by a reporter from the American pop magazine *Rolling Stone*. He talked to the record companies, the current chart-toppers, and the two producers of the day, Stanley Dorfman and Mel Cornish. At that time underground music was the flavour of the month and a lot of people thought *Top of the Pops* should reflect it. After interviewing me the reporter wrote, 'If you want to know who controls *Top of the Pops*, he is a balding, bespectacled man sitting on the fourth floor of Television Centre who, when asked if he would let a producer take *Top of the Pops* underground, with the finality of a closing coffin lid said, "Not for long!"'

We had a good Christmas that year, 1963. Dad made a remarkable recovery from his stroke, apart from a minimal restriction of movement, and had gone back to work. He did the Sunday broadcasts, a few theatres and some of the bigger clubs. Because his activities were curtailed the band were not working full-time, though he paid them as though they were – at crippling cost in those days of very high taxation. One day I suggested that he should do what most other band-leaders did:

formally dissolve the orchestra and just employ them as individuals on a session basis. He wouldn't hear of it. 'If I disband the orchestra, I won't be a band-leader any more. In the good days I didn't share all my good luck with them – why should I share my bad luck with them now? Anyway, my son, would you like to discuss your proposition with their wives and children?' Deflated, I realised, and not for the first time, that the band were Dad's extended family; they depended on him and he wouldn't let them down.

Boo was also doing well. She had been through a course of radiotherapy without complaint, following which a check-up gave her the all-clear. As a way of expressing my gratitude to Mr Franklin, I asked him if he would like to see a television show being made. He took up my offer, and I presumed he would opt for *Panorama* or some other serious programme, but he chose *The Black and White Minstrel Show*. So on the Saturday before Christmas we sat in a box in the Television Theatre to see the Christmas edition. Boo looked radiant. I was chatting to Franklin and he suddenly said, 'I don't usually say this, but she looks so wonderful I really believe we've won. It's early days yet but I think the signs are excellent.'

We spent the Christmas holidays *en famille*. The band were doing a television show on New Year's Eve, so we all went along to watch the transmission and stayed on to see in the New Year. We kissed and cried when the New Year chimes rang out and held each other very tight.

At Easter we went down to Sandbanks to join Mother. I went back to town on Easter Monday, leaving Boo and the children to enjoy a further week. A couple of days later, Mother phoned to say that Boo had had a bad bilious attack and she needed to see her doctor. I drove down to the coast and was taken aback by the change in Boo's appearance in such a short space of time. Directly we got home I called in our GP. He examined her, gave her some medication, and then called me into another room and put it to me bluntly: he thought the cancer had spread to her liver.

BBC2 was due to go on air on 21 April 1964. Though the

channel was designed for minority viewing, its controller, Michael Peacock, decided he wanted to start with a bang with a feast of light entertainment. The main offering of the evening was to be the musical *Kiss Me Kate!* starring Howard Keel and Patricia Morrison, produced by Jimmy Gilbert, followed by a Duke Ellington concert for which Yvonne Littlewood, one of the best directors of musical shows in the business, would be responsible.

Michael had arranged for a small party of the executives involved, together with their wives and families, to watch and celebrate the opening. It was the opening of a new era, not just because the channel would be dedicated to experimental programmes and a forum for new talent but also because it was to be transmitted on the 625-line system as opposed to the old 405 lines. This meant that once the technology was in place BBC2 would be the first channel in colour.

History will record that BBC2's opening night was a disaster. The power lines between the Television Centre and Battersea Power Station failed and the expectant viewers were presented with blank screens. The lights also failed, so all the guests, including Boo and my mother in their glad rags, ate and drank by candlelight. In different circumstances it would have been a romantic evening. The indefatigable Michael Peacock decided to try again the following evening, so we were all summoned for a second time and everything went according to plan.

Just before the Duke Ellington show started, Boo asked me if I would call a taxi to take her home as she wasn't feeling too well. I stupidly persuaded her to stay and watch a little of the Ellington programme so that we could then leave together – an act of crass insensitivity I have often regretted.

Then the supreme nightmare of my life began. Boo went back to St Anthony's and, although we could not bring ourselves to admit it, we knew she would never come out. Her room was a riot of flowers and a constant hive of activity, as family and a steady stream of visitors came and went. She played her part brilliantly; no one left without feeling better for having seen her.

On the morning of 15 May, I arrived in her room to find her

asleep. I sat beside her bed reading for about an hour. Then she stirred, opened her eyes and said, 'Haven't I seen you before today?' I replied, 'No, you've been entertaining that secret lover of yours again.' She smiled, closed her eyes and died.

She rested in the hospital chapel until the funeral. It's a sad fact of life that we rarely realise how much people mean to us until we lose them. It isn't possible to over-estimate what Boo did for me during the fourteen years we were married. I was the son of a rich, famous man and had no particular ambition but to enjoy myself. Then I met her and quickly developed two ambitions: first to marry her and then to make her proud of me. I did the first and, I hope, accomplished a little of the second. When I joined the BBC for fifteen pounds a week, leaving a job where I'd been paid twice that, Boo's mother asked her, 'Why the BBC?' She replied without hesitation, 'Because he'll end up running it.' I didn't quite, but when in 1984 I was appointed Managing Director of BBC Television I stood outside Broadcasting House, looked up heavenward and said, 'What took you so long?'

Boo's influence on me has lasted all my working life. Together we had three happy homes. One was on Ham Island where she joined a showbiz crowd and fitted in like a glove. The second was at Ham Common, near Richmond, which she chose because it was that bit nearer the Television Centre and therefore meant a shorter journey for me to come home every night. From there we went to a house on Ham Common in another development, which was once again a warm, welcoming home. Boo was the perfect wife and mother; that's what she wanted to be, and that's what she was.

Boo was the light of my life for fourteen short years. Even so, I bitterly regret the hours I lavished on my job, which really belonged to her and the children. I hope they've forgiven me.

In those black days after her death I thought of happier times, especially our holidays. I remember our driving to a small fishing village on the Adriatic coast of Italy. I had taken with me all the AA recommended spare parts and a two-gallon jerrycan of petrol. While we were climbing the San Gothard Pass, the car radiator boiled over. Quick as a flash I poured the petrol from the jerrycan out onto the grass, filled the can with water from a nearby stream, and once the car cooled down poured the water into the radiator. We were soon on our way again. I was thinking smugly how impressed Boo must have been by my speed and efficiency in dealing with an emergency when she said quietly, 'I'm sure there's a good reason for it, but why did you pour the petrol from the can onto the grass and not into the petrol tank?' 'Because I'm a pillock!' was the only possible reply, and we laughed all the way to Italy.

I knew I had to get back to work or my grief would drive me crazy. I wanted to keep faith with Boo, which meant not parading my misery and avoiding the temptation to drown my sorrows in alcohol. I was by nature a man who liked his drink, but one way or the other I had seen its effects on people who relied on the stuff, so I was on my guard.

Back at the Television Centre the launch of BBC2 had gone very well, and the channel was rapidly becoming a familiar part of the landscape of British broadcasting. Nevertheless the increased number of staff for the department required more management supervision than Tom as head and myself as his deputy could give them, so we became a group with two parts: Variety and Comedy. I officially became Assistant Head in charge of Variety, and we began to look around for someone to be my opposite number and take over Comedy.

While we were talent-spotting for the job, I happened to be invited to spend a weekend with Nona, the wife of my old mate Johnny Johnston. Nona had said that she wouldn't be around until after nine p.m. on the Friday, so I decided to eat at the Pickwick Club in London before driving down to the Johnstons' house in Boxmoor. I was joined in the bar by Frank Muir, who was at a loose end because his wife, Polly, was in Corsica. We had dinner together, during which I told him that I was going to stay with Nona and added as an afterthought, 'Why don't you come too?' Frank was a great friend of Johnny and Nona's so I knew it was safe to invite him. The idea appealed to him, and we drove down to Hertfordshire together. Nona greeted us with open arms and allocated each of us a room, and after a couple of large 'whatever you fancies' we went to bed. The next day dawned and after a leisurely breakfast and an inspection of the Johnston estate we strolled down to the local hostelry for a pint. We stayed until about one-thirty, then at two sat down to a lunch that became a twelve-hour marathon conversation. Our common interest, if not obsession, was television entertainment and I found myself explaining to Frank the new structure we were proposing at the BBC – the separating of Variety from Comedy. I suddenly heard myself say, 'Why don't you come back to run Comedy?' To my delight he was interested because he and his mate Denis Norden had just decided to suspend their partnership and do their own things. Frank ultimately became a much valued colleague.

Meanwhile Dad had gone with the band for a summer season in Jersey. He was able to do the stage-show, the only problem being that he was a little forgetful. But the band were so well trained it didn't matter what Dad told the audience – the band would play the piece he ought to have announced. At first, it was a little confusing for the punters but they took it as part of the general jollity and nobody walked out.

Dad settled himself in for the season at one of the best hotels on the island, and got his skipper, Sandy Wills, to bring the boat over. He was looking forward to a nice relaxing summer, then I turned up with the children, and after a bout of his legendary moaning and groaning he did his share of looking after them. The producer of his television show, Michael Hurll, also came over to fix up some five-minute film inserts for the next series. The idea was to reproduce the black-and-white melodramas common in the days of the silent movies. One involved an exploding piano. The BBC's armourer duly arrived with the explosives and primed the piano to explode on cue. Unfortunately, things didn't go according to plan: there was one hell of an explosion which injured one of the dancers. Dad had been seated uncomfortably close to the piano, but fortunately he was wearing a large cloak which took most of the blast. However, his socks were blown off and it was a miracle he didn't suffer any sort of injury. On the other hand, the band's vocalist, Alan Breeze, heard the explosion, ran onto the stage, tripped and fell on his backside. He happened to have a bottle of brandy in his back pocket, and it shattered, lacerating his posterior rather badly. There wasn't much sympathy for him in the band. They thought it was typical of Breezy to do anything for a laugh.

The fact that I was utterly lost without Boo still showed itself in periods when I just dripped around the office, listlessly staring into space. Tom Sloan, ever sensitive to my feelings, suggested that I should join the BBC team at the 1964 Tokyo Olympics as a spare pair of hands. I could come back by way of America and make some contacts with the major agencies and television companies. Peter Dimmock, who was in charge of the operation, was agreeable, so it was arranged. I greatly appreciated Tom's concern, but wasn't sure I wanted to go. There was no problem about the children – they would be well cared for by my mother who had moved in with us. It was just that the idea of going round the world, which most people would think of as a treat or a prize, seemed inappropriate in the circumstances.

Nonetheless, when the time came I flew off, trying hard to look forward to the experience. I stopped off in Hong Kong and got myself a couple of lightweight suits made overnight, both of which shrank and became unwearable on their first outing in the heat. Not a propitious omen. I flew on to Tokyo the next day.

The hotel at which we stayed was old-fashioned, but the technology the Japanese had deployed to cover the Games was awesome – way ahead of anything we had in Europe. Each of the commentators had a small colour monitor which gave wonderful pictures. When his monitor went on the blink David Coleman, never one to be intimidated, noticed a technician standing looking on and said, 'Don't stand there admiring it, change it!' The Games were a great success and there was plenty to see, but I wasn't central to the operation and I was getting restless; I'd too much time to think. If you hold a five-penny piece close enough to your eye, it will blot out the sun.

My personal misery overshadowed everything else. Around me were taking place these dramatic and exciting events, world records were being broken (and I had always thought of myself as a sports fanatic), but it could all have been happening on another planet. One evening in desperation I phoned Tom Sloan and asked him if I could come home. He told me sternly that the best interests of the BBC required me to stay. But after a week, I caught a flight to America.

I had never been on the West Coast before and I was looking forward to seeing as much as I could of current US television production. It is said of the Beverly Hilton's Polo Bar that you always meet someone you know there. Sure enough, I ran into Terry Thomas, who swept me off to the theatre to see an American production of a West End hit. Terry and I had gone to the same school, although at different times. He was making his mark in Hollywood and invented a very ingenious way of solving the billings battle. Stars fight like mad to ensure that their names appear first on film titles. Terry told his agent he was happy for his name to appear last, provided the little word 'and' preceded it – a device much used since to give actors a special mention.

I swam every day before breakfast, and one morning I was holding onto the side of the pool when a female in tennis clothes dived in over my head. When she surfaced and apologised for not having noticed I was there, I heard the unmistakable drawl of Katharine Hepburn. I opened my mouth to reply and nothing came out. That's what comes of being starstruck.

I had a great time but was glad to get home again. You can't escape your grief by changing your geographical location, you carry it around with you like a great leaden weight. When Boo had been alive, my work had sometimes been a robber, stealing hours that belonged to my family. Now she was gone, work was to be my lifeline.

With Frank Muir looking after comedy, I had time to concentrate on developing more and better variety shows. In the

United States I had been much impressed with *The Perry Como Show*, so I was looking for a star who could do a Perry Como on a British television audience. When I saw Val Doonican in *Sunday Night at the London Palladium* I was pretty sure we'd got our man. He'd appeared on a couple of the Old Man's radio shows and been well received. After years as part of a singing group, he'd recently decided to go solo. His agent was a feisty woman by the name of Eve Taylor, who also handled Sandie Shaw and Adam Faith, so one way or the other we saw quite a lot of each other over the years. I agreed with Eve that Val should start by doing a series with BBC Manchester to be produced by Johnny Ammonds. It was small budget and not even a pale imitation of *The Perry Como Show*, but I liked it enough to bring it down to London where we put it out live on Thursday evenings.

I needed a stand-up comedian to act as a foil to Val Doonican, and since we were launching a new show with a new star I wanted to find some fresh talent, someone who was still making his way. The agent Richard Stone, whose clients included Benny Hill and Terry Scott, both of whom were doing shows for the BBC at the time, asked me to go and see a comedian who was appearing in a roadhouse outside Maidstone. On the way down, Richard explained to me that Dave Allen had been working in Australia where he had his own television show. Apparently, there had been a slight disagreement with the broadcasting company over the content of the programme, and the discussion culminated in Dave suggesting that the producer might like to go away for ten minutes and play with himself while the rest of them got on with the show. Dave left – in fact, he was banned for a year in Australia – and was now trying to establish himself in Britain.

The roadhouse was empty. Without an audience to respond to, a stand-up comedian is like a musician without an instrument; all the same I detected real talent in Allen and arranged to see him at work the following week at the Blue Angel, a club in Berkeley Street. I asked Tom Sloan along and he happened to arrive late. Tom was a classic blue-suited executive with a

Ronald Colman moustache and a rather formal manner, not at all the typical client of this racy kind of club. Dave had never met Tom, and was standing at the bar when he arrived. Since Tom *did* know Dave by sight, he offered to buy him a drink. For some reason Dave thought he was being picked up and started trying to lose Tom in the crowd. The harder he tried, the more determined Tom became – after all, he was auditioning him for a job. I arrived on the scene just in time to prevent the whole thing becoming either a farce or a fight, and introduced them to each other: embarrassed laughs all round.

We booked Dave for *The Val Doonican Show,* which began as a twenty-five-minute programme and was eventually expanded to fill fifty minutes on Saturday evenings – but without Dave.

Dave and I had become good friends and we discussed his future. He was keen to try a show similar to the one he had done in Australia, which involved him in meeting and working with 'unusual' people whom the uncharitable might call nutcases. We did a pilot. One of Dave's guests was a man who held the world record for eating the largest number of eggs in a minute. He put them in a glass tankard, opened his mouth and poured them down his throat. The idea was that having taken his bow, he would then hurriedly adjourn to the nearest men's room to regurgitate the eggs. On this occasion he lost his way and didn't quite make it. Word got round that the show wasn't quite the sort of thing the BBC ought to be doing, so the Controller of BBC1 turned it down. Dave took it to ITV, who snapped it up, and *Tonight with Dave Allen* became a real Saturday evening ratings-grabber.

One show doesn't make a schedule, so while I was grooming Val Doonican for stardom I also gave some attention to Cilla Black. I had long been an admirer of Cilla since her days with Brian Epstein, when she always struck me as being more focused than the average teenage star. I saw Cilla as the natural successor to Gracie Fields, who was reaching the end of her amazing career. Cilla's voice wasn't universally liked, but she had an ear for good songs and knew how to put them across. And she could talk! Unlike some pop singers, she wasn't tongue-tied when she had to talk to people, and she enjoyed doing it. When Brian Epstein died, her husband Bobby Willis became responsible for the nuts and bolts of her career. This he did brilliantly until his untimely death in 1999. It was during her time with the BBC that her producer, Michael Hurll, thought up the idea of filming Cilla on location, knocking on house doors and surprising the occupants – the forerunner of the shows such as *Surprise, Surprise!* she later did for ITV.

Cilla never lost her Liverpudlian canniness. In the days when Green Shield stamps were handed out with purchases, she was driving to Liverpool with her husband in her huge Rolls Royce. They stopped for petrol, filled up and drove off. When they were quite some way up the motorway she turned to Bobby and said, 'We forgot our stamps, we must go back!' and no amount of argument would change her mind.

Cilla has been very generous in public about the part I played in her career. But there is no doubt that Cilla Black is the reason for Cilla Black's success. She has remained a star through very hard work and a 'lorra talent'.

If Cilla oozed personality, Kathy Kirby's stock in trade was glamour. I first met her in prison, though I'd seen her on television as top of the bill on *Stars and Garters*. She was managed by Bert Ambrose, one of the major band-leaders of the thirties. I ran into him one day because my father had agreed to do a show for prisoners serving life-sentences in Wormwood Scrubs. Unfortunately Dad's vocalist, Kathie Kay, couldn't make the date, and as Bert had been trying to get me to see Miss Kirby I suggested she might like to do the show at the Scrubs. They immediately agreed. I knew prisons were not meant to be holiday camps, but I wasn't prepared for the grim reality of my first visit. I think it was the stench in the place that struck me so forcibly.

The show was being done in the prison theatre, and the stagehands and electricians were all prisoners, and very efficient they all were too. The prisoners were obviously enjoying the show, and eventually the Old Man introduced Kathy. Kathy was a platinum blonde in the Monroe style with a lovely face and a gorgeous figure. When she walked on the stage she got a terrific reception which went on for a couple of minutes, and when silence finally fell a voice from the back shouted, 'Is that yours, Bill?' The Old Man shook his head. 'Well, chuck it down here!' was the immediate request. Kathy thoroughly enjoyed it all, and with a literally captive audience went through her repertoire. When she finished the roof nearly came off, and I was more than impressed.

We fixed up for Kathy to do a series produced by Ernest Maxin. It went well, and Kathy became a considerable success but then it all ended in tears. At the end of one series I was chatting to the crew in the studio and a cameraman said how sorry he was that Kathy was leaving us. I asked him where he'd got such an extraordinary idea from, and he said one of his mates who worked for ITV had told him. I couldn't believe it. Bert Ambrose had said nothing to me. I stormed down to Kathy's dressing-room and confronted both her and her agent, Sydney Grace, who was with her. Kathy immediately burst into tears and I knew the rumour was true. The tragedy was that in the end the ITV series didn't go ahead because they could not agree on Kathy's role. We filled the vacant slot with another show and Kathy never worked for the BBC again.

1964 had truly been a roller-coaster of a year. Professionally, things were going well, but personally there was a huge void at the centre of my life. The truth was I needed someone to fill it.

SIX

In the months after Boo's death, everyone showed me enormous sympathy, understanding and affection, but my fourteen years with her had been so fulfilling that it would not be too much to say that she had made me a whole person – and now I was incomplete. Having to revert to being a loner left me prey to all my old psychological demons. I was effectively a married man without a wife; and I couldn't function without that depth of relationship. Some months after Boo's death, I found myself having a drink in the BBC bar with a group of people that included the supervisor in charge of make-up training. Her name was Ann Henderson; her father and mine were fellow members of the Yacht Club at Sandbanks. I vaguely recalled meeting her at the Club on one occasion when Boo and I were there for a drink.

I felt very comfortable with Ann and I remember hoping I would meet her again. She was different in looks and personality from Boo, but she had a good sense of humour and we found plenty to talk about. It turned out she'd been married to an Ulsterman, but the marriage had broken up leaving her to bring up alone a daughter who was of a similar age to Jane and Kate. Her life had its problems, and in a way we were in the same boat. While I had no wish to avoid women, equally I had no wish to play the field and by the spring of 1965 my relationship with Ann had blossomed enough for us to decide to get married. Out of concern for me, one or two friends felt it was all too soon. My mother, though, who knew me well, encouraged me with her assurance that Boo would have wished me to find a fulfilling relationship. Mother had been looking after the family since Boo's death but she handed over the running of my house to Ann with good grace.

Ann and I went to Corsica for our honeymoon, where among the other guests at the hotel were Peter Cook and his wife, Wendy, together with *Private Eye* columnist Christopher Logue. Peter told me that his old mate Dudley Moore was due to arrive at any moment with his girlfriend, Shirley Anne Field; in fact, he pitched up with his future wife, Tuesday Weld. As always, the cocktail of one part Cook and one part Moore provided to be highly explosive. The goings-on were frantic and very funny. In particular, Dudley's antics with his companion on a lilo twenty-five yards off the beach came under the heading of adult viewing. We all got to know each other very well, which was fortuitous because some weeks later one of our producers, Joe McGrath, who was working on a comedy show with Dudley Moore, approached Peter Cook to do a celebrity spot. So many good ideas were tossed around in their meeting that he proposed that both should star in it – *Not Only* [Dudley Moore] *But Also* [Peter Cook] was conceived. I was enthusiastic; David Attenborough, the Controller of BBC2, was also keen, so we went ahead.

The show itself worked like a dream, and from it emerged those two immortal characters, the raincoat-wearing, cloth-capped philosophers Pete and Dud, ruminating idiotically about the deep things of life. The show was so successful we immediately offered them a series. Peter Sellers, Spike Milligan, Barry Humphries and John Lennon were guest stars and usually ended up being ducked in a tank full of gung.

1966 saw the development of a new dimension of light entertainment. The trail-blazing political satire show *That Was The Week That Was* had been taken off the air by the BBC Director-General because of an imminent General Election, so *TW3*'s producers, Alasdair Milne and Ned Sherrin, launched a successor which was called *Not So Much a Programme, More a Way of Life*. Floated in the shadow of *TW3*'s gigantic success, it was inevitably something of an anti-climax and only ran for six months. That left the show's star, David Frost, at a loose end.

I am not sure how David and I ran into each other, but in conversation I mooted the idea of his doing a show under the

Light Entertainment banner, not a political satire but a sketch-type show with the highly talented Jimmy Gilbert as producer. David was interested so I said I would put the proposal to Tom Sloan. Tom was less than ecstatic. He *hated TW3,* which he believed was damaging to the BBC's reputation. I had great respect for Tom's judgement, but felt that on this one he was wrong. In my opinion, it would be tragic if the talents and enthusiasm of David Frost were lost to the Corporation. In the end, he agreed we should go ahead, though adding, more or less, 'On your own head be it!'

David Frost's agent was my very good friend Richard Armitage, and he arranged for Jimmy and myself to watch David do a stand-up spot at Quaglino's, which in those days had two venues, the main restaurant and a nightclub called the Allegro. David was booked to perform in both, so we decided to see him in action in the restaurant. David came on and died the death. It was perfectly obvious that the kind of people dining at Quaglino's were not his natural audience and that they were underwhelmed by his sophisticated wit. I was busy phrasing suitable words of commiseration in my head when David came bounding up. 'Weren't they wonderful?' he enthused. 'You must stay and catch my act at the Allegro, they're even better there!' That is one of the qualities I've always admired in David. His personal philosophy is well summarised by the poster many people pinned on their walls during the lowest ebb of the First World War: 'There is no depression in this house, we do not contemplate the possibility of defeat.' His other admirable quality is magnanimity; I've never heard him say a bad word about anybody and that is a rare attribute in the bitchy world of showbiz.

The show became known as *The Frost Report,* and the idea was that it should have a different area of investigation each week. Jimmy commissioned Tony Jay (later to become Sir Anthony, the co-writer with Jonathan Lynn of *Yes, Minister*) to write an essay on that week's theme. Somewhat pompously, this became known as the CDM – the Continuous Developing Monologue. It was used at the writers' meetings to stimulate

120

ideas for sketches and for David's monologues to camera. Some of these essays were works of art and were later published, but they frightened the life out of some of the jobbing writers who'd never thought of comedy as an intellectual assault-course.

Marty Feldman, who also appeared in the show, was paid an extra fifty quid a week to be script-editor. David Frost himself was keen to recruit Ronnie Corbett, who was doing a regular turn at Danny La Rue's club in the West End, and quite separately Jimmy suggested Ronnie Barker. At this time, we had not yet thought of the pairing which was to become immortal as the Two Ronnies. John Cleese and Sheila Steafel with American folk-singer Julie Felix made up the cast.

The show was due to run for thirteen weeks and after two or three programmes had established itself as compulsory watching on Thursday evenings. Its success was such that Tom and I decided we should enter it at the 1967 Festival of Entertainment for the Golden Rose of Montreux. To this end, we put together a special compilation called *Frost over England*, which included some of the best bits out of the series together with new material. It went out on BBC1 to a great reception, so we went off to Switzerland in a mood of quiet confidence.

The present-day Montreux Festival is a market place in which the main activity is selling and making deals, but in 1967 it was all about programmes and the Festival was attended not by money-men but by programme-makers. There were five awards to compete for: the Golden Rose, the Silver Rose and the Bronze Rose plus the City of Montreux Comedy Award and the International Press Prize. Entries came from Europe, America and the Iron Curtain countries and anywhere else that had a national broadcaster doing television. Each competing country could enter one programme for the competition and another programme, usually of an experimental nature, which was shown merely to demonstrate what pioneering and often daring work was being done in the industry. To put it kindly, these experimental programmes gave other producers ideas. Thus, in 1970 I made the mistake of showing *Monty Python's Flying Circus* in this section, only to find that the following year, when we entered it for the main competition, it was up against two or three very similar shows – one of which won the Golden Rose, leaving us with the Silver.

Each competing country was asked to nominate a member of the jury – which always included the president and two vice-presidents nominated by Swiss television, the Festival's hosts. I was a member of the jury in 1967 and it was hard graft. No matter how late you went to bed – and there were plenty of receptions and parties to keep you up all night – you were obliged to watch all the entries; it was a real challenge staying awake for some of them. Dark glasses became an essential fashion-accessory for jurors, partly to hide the bags under our eyes and partly to ensure no one could see our eyelids drooping.

On voting day, we were taken for a steamer trip on Lake Geneva, thus isolating us from everyone at the Festival and especially the press. Such an extreme measure had become necessary because the previous year a juror had gone to the lavatory and on the way telephoned the results to a paper in Geneva. This had the effect of killing the official announcement stone dead. We voted by a process of elimination, and the final run-off for the Golden Rose was between *Frost over England* and a Dutch show. Though the Dutch jury-member and myself were barred from casting a vote, when the Russian juror handed in his vote he smiled at me and winked. Since these were the days when the Eastern Bloc countries followed Russia's lead I knew we must be in a strong position. In fact, we won, whereupon the boat was sailed close to the shore and the result announced by loud-speaker.

The next morning we received a hero's welcome and front-page press coverage when we flew into London. With typical generosity, David Frost had three copies of the Golden Rose statuette made at Asprey's. He kept one himself and gave the others to Jimmy Gilbert and myself. *The Frost Report* became the template for a number of successful shows, an innovation which owed everything to Jimmy Gilbert, who in my opinion proved to be the best all-round entertainment producer in the business. His authority was matched only by his modesty, which allowed people like me to claim some of the credit.

The department may have been on a winning streak, but the Cotton family wasn't. In March 1966, my brother was taken to hospital for observation, and Dad suggested we drive down to Poole to see him. I phoned the hospital to find out what time would be convenient, only to be told that he had just died. It seemed unbelievable that within two years six Cotton children had become members of a one-parent family. Ted, his wife Beryl and their three children, Sue, Tim and Sally, lived in Camford Cliffs, ten minutes' drive from my mother's house in Sandbanks. She and Beryl had actually been sitting with Ted in hospital when he suddenly sat up and said, 'This is serious,' and fell back unconscious, having suffered an aneurysm. Later, the only words of consolation I could give to Mother were that if it had to happen at all, at least he was with the two women he loved most. It wasn't much to soften the blow but it helped a little.

While I had been making the phone call to the hospital from the Television Centre, Dad had set off from his flat to join me and was due at any moment. I flunked it. I simply couldn't face telling him that Ted was dead. Tom Sloan did it for me.

The funeral was held at the Bournemouth crematorium. I noticed at the back of the chapel Sandy Wills, Dad's skipper, who'd been a particular mate of Ted's. He was dressed in his sea-going gear, which I thought was a nice touch, but he was reluctant to come back to the hotel where we had arranged to have refreshments because he felt he wasn't dressed for a solemn function. I assured him his dress was the last thing he should worry about and I knew that Dad, Mum and Beryl would want him to be there. It was a large reception, and as often used to be the case the men and women congregated separately. Sandy joined my Dad and a few friends from the Yacht Club where Ted had been known as the 'Leader of the Opposition' because of his independence of spirit and irreverent sense of humour. The conversation was stilted and awkward until Sandy suddenly said, 'Well, old Ted was a right scallywag!' and told the story of a time he'd taken the boat with Ted and Dad to Weymouth. When they entered the harbour Ted, standing on the bow of the boat, asked the fishermen on the quay the way to The Hoe, which is of course a well-known Plymouth landmark. The fishermen looked disbelieving, whereupon Ted shouted to Dad, 'Sandy's lost his way again! This isn't Plymouth, it's Weymouth!' Sandy, who was well known to the fishing community in the area, was furious: his professional reputation was being challenged and his attempt to explain that it was all a bad joke on Ted's part was drowned out by general laughter.

The human mind is very selective in the way it deals with grief. Sandy's anecdote, told in a gentle Dorset accent, was in one sense inconsequential; nevertheless it is my most vivid memory of the funeral because Ted's sense of humour remains uppermost in my mind. Losing an elder brother who had stood by me through thick and thin was like having a supporting limb removed.

To Dad, Ted's death had the impact of a thunderbolt. His eldest son had survived the war in spite of contracting TB in the Far East, an illness which recurred after he was demobbed. Dad had worried about Ted being posted to the Far East because of his very fair skin and susceptibility to all kinds of bugs, but he decided against using his influence in the Air Ministry to get Ted's posting changed to Europe. Apart from the fact that Ted would have hated any kind of behind-the-scenes pressure being applied, RAF air crews were dying in large numbers over Europe. Suppose Dad's string-pulling had been successful and then Ted had been killed?

Dad was desolated. I recall driving him up and down between London and Sandbanks to see Mother at the time. Grief and bitterness were etched on his face. We made one journey in complete silence, and at the end of it he said, 'You drove very well, my son' – just what he used to say when I first got behind the wheel at the age of seventeen. We couldn't understand let alone discuss what had happened to Ted.

Although they were now living separate lives, Mother and Dad were still firm friends, and at this moment he wanted to be with her and share his loss with the only person who felt as he did. By now he had virtually thrown off most of the effects of his stroke, though he was much slower and tired easily. He also had financial worries. There was a huge family to support – if he wasn't working, there were still twenty-odd musicians at a loose end who had to be paid. Apart from his Sunday radio and television broadcasts, he worked the clubs rather than theatres because he was only required to do a single show each night.

The clubs were enjoying a great boom, especially Caesar's Palace at Luton which was the town in which his sister, my Aunty Vi, lived. The third-eldest of the ten Cotton children, she had more or less brought Dad up. In temperament she and my father were very similar; they even looked alike which is, I fear, really paying her no compliment.

Whenever I could, I went to see Dad when he was appearing near London. On one evening I pitched up at Caesar's Palace and there, sitting in the front lobby of the club, were Aunty Vi and her daughter, Daphne. I greeted her warmly and asked her if she was going in to watch the show. She replied, 'If your father wants me to go in I'm sure he'll come out and ask me.' 'But does he know you're here?' I enquired. 'I don't know, but I'm sure he'll find out.' 'I'll tell him,' I said and hurried through to Dad's dressing-room, where he was putting on his dinner jacket ready to go on stage. 'Aunty Vi's sitting in the vestibule,' I said. 'Well, tell her to come in,' he replied. 'No, she wants you to ask her.' 'That figures,' he said and went round to the front, where he and Vi confronted each other like a couple of gladiators.

'Are you coming in, Vi?'

'Are you inviting me, Will?'

'Of course I'm inviting you!'

'Well, we'd like that, wouldn't we, Daphne?' and with honour satisfied, she and Daphne steamed into the club.

Dad by this time was a lonely man. He spent much of his time hanging around waiting for Kathie Kay to come down from Glasgow. Occasionally, when I was going along Jermyn Street

125

in a taxi with people I'd been entertaining, I would see him ambling down the road, window-shopping on his way back to the flat, probably after eating alone at one of his favourite restaurants. In one sense he wasn't alone because everyone knew him and chatted to him, but the breakdown of his marriage and the loss of Ted and Boo had left him isolated and miserable.

My sympathy for him wasn't unqualified because, as always, he had chosen to do things his way and people got hurt as a result – chiefly, of course, my mother. I quite liked Kathie Kay – she came on the scene after Dad and my mother separated and she helped to ease his loneliness – but for Doreen Stephens, whom I considered to have been the cause of the break-up, I had no time at all.

Life had to go on. One weekend in 1967 I was visiting my mother in Sandbanks and she mentioned a young disc jockey she'd seen on Southern TV. He'd obviously made a big impression on her and she suggested I should have a look at him. At first I was quite dismissive in a patronising sort of way, but during the drive back I had second thoughts. After all, Ma had been in the front row of the stalls throughout Dad's long career and she must have developed an eye for talent. When I got back to town I made some enquiries. His name was Simon Dee and he had started his showbiz career as a DJ on a pirate-radio ship. We arranged to meet and I was very taken with him. He was a typical product of the sixties – good-looking, a snappy dresser who wore his clothes well, very articulate with a good broadcasting personality. I was keen to get a talkshow going and he seemed to fit the bill. I went through all the hoops at the BBC, signed him up and arranged to do two shows a week from Dickenson Road in Manchester, the studio having become free a short time before because we moved *Top of the Pops* to London.

The show was called *Dee Time* and it quickly established itself in an early slot on Tuesdays and Thursdays. Simon soon learned the ropes and became a confident performer. Not only was he becoming a star but he was also behaving as though he had been one all his life. He was acting the part before he had mastered the trade. However, he conducted interviews in such a way that viewers learned more about his views than those of his guests. The balance was wrong. We also had a free and frank discussion about the need for him not only to ask questions but to be seen to listen to the answers. This was one of the problems of trying to produce a show in a studio two hundred miles away from the office. In spite of these teething troubles, I felt sufficient confidence in *Dee Time* to transfer it to London and put it out on a Saturday.

By the second year of Simon's contract, the show was a major element in BBC1's Saturday early-evening schedule and he had become a polished interviewer. Because he had style and embodied the spirit of the times, Simon appealed to young people as well as their elders. Unfortunately he also had an irresponsible streak in him that worried me.

Simon and I had a stormy relationship throughout his contract with one row following another. One day he called in at my office to say that, since we used his name in the title of the show, he should have the sole right to choose the guests. I said I thought he had a very good point so we would change the show's title from *Dee Time* to *The Early Show (Introduced by Simon Dee)*, which would solve his problem. That idea didn't appeal to him at all and the rebellion subsided.

When Simon's contract was nearing its end, he and his agent, Bunny Lewis, came to see me and said they'd had an offer from London Weekend Television for a thousand pounds a show. Would I like to make a counter-offer? I couldn't have matched that figure – I think we were paying him £250 a show – and even if it had been possible I wouldn't have done it. I had come to feel that Simon needed to be cut loose to do his own thing for a while. So we parted company.

Sadly, his bright new career with ITV turned out badly for him. I last saw him when I was a magistrate in Richmond and he came before the bench for some minor misdemeanour. As soon he appeared, I told my colleagues I couldn't try the case as I knew the defendant. When Simon was asked why he had not paid some fine or other, he delivered an oration to the effect that in his profession certain people had the power of life and death – they could decide who worked and who starved. Apparently I was one of these god-like figures and had made decisions that meant he was out of work, hence, he couldn't pay the fine.

My colleagues delivered their judgement and Simon was told to stand down. He walked to the back of the court, turned, waved a hand and said, 'Bye, Bill!' My colleagues were outraged. One said, 'What a terrible man!' I replied, 'Not really. Once upon a time he earned me quite a slice of my wages.'

In marked contrast, Rolf Harris had reached stardom the hard way and never lost his Australian earthiness. One can use all kinds of complimentary terms to describe him – talented, versatile, homely, funny – but glamorous isn't one of them. And that was the element we needed to introduce into a new show we were planning for him. The show's producer, Stewart Morris, recalled that he had seen an Italian production in which a young star, Rita Pavaroni, got a lot of teenagers from the audience to dance to the music of the film *Zorba the Greek*. The result was electric. The problem was that *Zorba the Greek* had a dance routine built into it – if we wished to use a group of teenagers they would have to be professionals whose dances had been carefully choreographed; amateurs, however enthusiastic, wouldn't do. And we couldn't get away with less than thirty dancers – that was the magic number – but the effect on our budget would be horrendous.

After much agonising we decided to go ahead, and Stewart Morris and Dougie Squires created a dance team called The Young Generation. They proved to be the Factor X which helped to make *The Rolf Harris Show* a huge success. They were quite distinctive as a dance group – not as sexy as Pan's People on *Top of the Pops*, not as disciplined as the Toppers or the Silhouettes, the two popular lines of girls on *The Black and White Minstrel Show* and *The Billy Cotton Band Show*, nor as classical as Gillian Lynne's groups, who often danced in musical shows on television. The secret of the Young Generation's success was their enormous vitality. They were dressed like teenagers of the day, and Dougie choreographed them to dance in the uninhibited way that was characteristic of the sixties. They were a perfect foil for Rolf's homespun personality and performance, and well worth the arm and a leg they cost us.

We also booked Sandie Shaw to sing a song each week specially written for a spot in the show we called 'A Song for Europe'. The public were then invited to vote for the song they thought would make the best entry for the Eurovision Song Contest. From the first series, the viewers chose a little ditty called 'Puppet on a String' which Sandie took to Vienna and won the competition. One consequence of her success was that we would have to mount the Eurovision Song Contest the following year in 1968, which was simultaneously an honour and a burden.

Another famous troupe of dancers were the Bluebells from the Lido, Paris. Ken Dodd's agent, Dave Forester, managed to book them to appear on his show for a summer season at the Blackpool Opera House, and invited the BBC to televise the event. I rate Ken Dodd as highly as any stand-up comic I've seen, with the possible exception of Max Miller, but he could be a handful to deal with. He wasn't very punctual, which on live television can be a nightmare, so I asked Duncan Wood, one of my most senior producers, to be responsible for the transmission.

I decided to go up to Blackpool in the middle of the series with the family and spend a couple of weeks by the seaside. On the first Sunday morning I was sitting reading the newspapers when the show's production assistant, Tony James, burst into the room to tell me that Duncan had got the dreaded Blackpool flu and the doctor had said he must not leave his bed. Tony had no sooner delivered these tidings of doom than he too collapsed and had to be hauled to his bedroom. That left me the last man standing. I would have to produce and direct the shows myself, something I hadn't done for five years. I found it to be a bit like riding a bicycle, and in the end started to enjoy myself. I did two shows, at which the children thoroughly enjoyed themselves though Ann was not best pleased that yet again work had intruded into the family's private time.

That same year, BBC2 started transmitting in colour, and Light Entertainment's contribution to its first weekend was two fifty-minute shows with Sammy Davis Jr from the Talk of the Town, both to be recorded on the same night. Sammy was no stranger to us as we had done a special show with him in 1963, to the considerable embarrassment of Tom Sloan who negotiated the contract. The asking fee was $10,000, the going-rate at the time for a star of his distinction. Unfortunately Tom, who was in some respects a very unworldly man, had got it into his head that the exchange-rate must be something around four dollars to the pound – and that two and a half thousand quid was a fee the BBC's accountants would wear. In fact, the exchange-rate was nearer one and a half dollars to the pound and Tom had to do some nifty financial juggling with budgets. I thought Sammy was wonderful and worth every penny we paid him. After that amazing performance, Sammy was in tears. Why, he wailed, did he have to come to Britain to be allowed to do his own show? Because he was black, in the States he could only be a guest on someone else's show for fear advertising revenue would suffer. By 1967, though, everything had changed.

Thanks to Sammy Light Entertainment's first two shows in colour on BBC2 were triumphs. Sammy's performance was superlative. Because they were transmitted live, Sammy asked if he could see a play-back. This was in the days before VCR had been invented, so I asked Kenneth Adam, then Director of Television, if we could use his suite on the sixth floor of Television Centre to hold a party for Sammy and his friends during which we'd run the tape of the two programmes. Kenneth agreed and said that he would like to host the party himself. When we arrived at the appointed time we were met by a Director of Television whom *Private Eye* would probably have described as tired and emotional. Among the guests were

Jeremy Lloyd, who was beginning to make a reputation as an actor, and on his arm the absolutely fabulous Joanna Lumley. Kenneth rather fancied himself with the ladies and made a bee-line for Joanna; before I could introduce them, he started an animated conversation which was stopped in its tracks by Joanna asking to whom she had the pleasure of talking. For some reason, Kenneth assumed that he ought to have been universally recognised and was very put out. He pulled himself to his full height and announced, 'I am the Director of Television. You are in *my* Television Centre being entertained in *my* suite.' Joanna smiled sweetly, said, 'Good for you!' and walked away with Jeremy.

After the showing, Kenneth proceeded to conduct a seminar on the advantages of our colour system over its American equivalent. Eventually he asked Sammy which system he thought gave the better picture, and Sammy said he never answered questions like that sober, could he therefore have a drink? After the drinks and buffet, we sat down to watch the second tape, at the end of which, in an attempt to avoid another harangue from Kenneth, I got to my feet only to hear him say, 'Sit down, Cotton. You're not Director of Television yet.' Sammy fixed me with his good eye and mouthed, 'Shall I kill him now?'

Some time afterwards, Sammy was due to appear for a season at the London Palladium so we came up with the idea of laying on a week of late-night chat-shows after the curtain came down at the theatre, which was around ten-thirty p.m. Using a convoy of fast cars we could get Sammy and his backing group to the Television Centre for an eleven o'clock start. Everything was on course when the Musicians' Union put their oar in. They were not prepared to extend the work-permits of Sammy's musicians to enable them to do the television shows. Even my offer that we would pay an equivalent number of British musicians to sit in the audience and watch the show was turned down. While Sammy had no desire to take work away from Musicians' Union members, he did need to use his own backing group who knew his work backwards and would require no rehearsal.

I was deeply embarrassed by the whole affair, not least because the *Radio Times* had cleared the decks and splashed Sammy's face over the front cover. We got round that by buying in a *Sammy Davis Jr Special* from the States and putting it out on the first night of the proposed shows.

1968 saw the arrival of Morecambe and Wise at the BBC. They'd made a disastrous start on television in the early fifties with a series called *Running Wild*, after which they'd picked themselves up and resumed their career in variety. They'd been steadily gaining experience until Lew Grade signed them up for his company, ATV, where their television shows rapidly gained in popularity, and they became big stars. Their contract was due for renewal in 1968 and they fell out with Lew, partly about money but also about technology. ATV still made programmes in black and white, whereas Morecambe and Wise were convinced that the future of television lay with colour, and that meant BBC2, which was the only channel with the new system. Their agent, Michael Grade, who was also Lew's nephew, had failed to get his uncle to budge and so risked a family breach by phoning me. Hardly believing my luck, I got in a taxi and went straight round to Michael's office and offered a three-year contract based on a figure that was over the top for the first year but, if my judgement about their drawing power was sound, would prove to be a bargain by the third.

Once the contract was signed, I put Johnny Ammonds in charge of producing the show. He was a superb professional who could get the best out of Eric and Ernie and also win the respect of Sid Hills and Dick Green, Morecambe and Wise's scriptwriters and therefore a crucial part of the deal. The idea was that the show would go out on BBC2, which then had a small audience, with a guaranteed repeat on BBC1 for the big ratings. This second showing would help immensely with the overall contract money.

The programmes in the first series were thirty minutes in length, though my long-term plan was to extend them to fill fifty minutes. I wanted to use Morecambe and Wise to inject some comedy into a BBC1 Saturday evening schedule which was dominated by musical shows, one of which was my father's – I felt it had lost its sharp edge, and this worried me greatly.

The first Morecambe and Wise series was a great success, and they were on their way to becoming a national institution. Once the run was finished, Eric and Ernie went off to fulfil a bookful of engagements. I was sitting in my office one afternoon discussing the next series with Johnny Ammonds when we got word that Eric, who had been playing a club in Batley, Yorkshire, had suffered a major heart-attack. He hadn't been feeling well for some days and while driving back to his hotel after the show had experienced terrible pains in his chest and down his arm. He knew he was in trouble so he drew up alongside a passer-by in the street and asked him the way to the hospital. By now the pain was crippling, so he also asked the man if he would drive him there. The man said that the only vehicle he'd ever driven was a tank in the Territorial Army, but agreed to give it a try. Eric was in no condition to be fussy, and eventually they reached the hospital where Eric was given an injection which started to send him to sleep. Just before he dropped off he heard his erstwhile chauffeur asking for his autograph 'before you go'!

It would obviously be months before Eric was fit enough to start a new series, and while we were waiting for news about his condition Roger Hancock, scriptwriters Hills and Green's agent, asked for a meeting. We went for a meal together and Hancock dropped a bombshell: Hills and Green would only write the next series provided they were made its executive producers; if I didn't accept that condition they intended to sign a contract with ATV the following day to write, produce and appear in their own show. It didn't take me a moment to reject this ultimatum – I had no intention of allowing the lunatics to run the asylum. After that, there wasn't an awful lot to talk about throughout the rest of the meal. But in spite of my air of serene confidence I knew we were in deep trouble.

By this time Eric had made great strides, and with Ernie being away it was him with whom I got in touch. I told him that the whole contract was in jeopardy because of the unreasonable demands of Hills and Green. Eric felt able to speak for Ernie and assured me that they would do the next series for us. But who would write it? When Ernie got back we had a meeting and commissioned a number of ad hoc scripts to get us by until we found a permanent writer.

Then came a phone call from Michael Hurll to tell me that he'd just been told Eddie Braben, who'd been Ken Dodd's scriptwriter for years, had parted company with the comedian and was in the market for work. I knew something of Eddie's work, and although Ken was a stand-up comedian, Eddie wasn't a conventional gag writer; he had a surreal streak in him that might be ideal for Eric and Ernie's visual humour.

At first, Eddie's reaction was completely negative. He didn't think he could write the sort of material Morecambe and Wise needed. I asked him to come to London to discuss it further. A typical Liverpudlian, he asked whether I would pay the fare. 'I'll even pay for you to stay at a hotel overnight,' I said. Eddie was indignant. 'I'm not staying in London. I'll travel back on the milk train if I need to.' Having established the terms for the meeting, I then phoned Eric and Ernie. Though they were great admirers of Ken Dodd and therefore thought highly of his scriptwriter, they weren't enthusiastic. All the same I fixed up a meeting, which went well. They all spoke the same language of north country club-humour and had the same comedy heroes, such as Jimmy James and Dave Morris – both virtually unknown south of Watford but lions further north.

The meeting ended with Eddie promising to write a sample script. He came up with a very funny sketch set in a flat, but it was very different from Eric and Ernie's usual material so they were uneasy. I ended up making them an offer they couldn't refuse: we'd commission Eddie to write a whole show and put it out on BBC2, but it wouldn't be exposed to BBC1's huge audience unless everyone was happy. That's how one of the best teams in television was created – Eric Morecambe, Ernie Wise, Johnny Ammonds and Eddie Braben – each superlative in his own line of country as performers, producer and script-writer. There was nothing accidental about the supremacy of

The Morecambe and Wise Show, nothing was left to chance – immense brain-power, talent, money and technical skill went into the operation.

Certainly some of their success was due to the luck of timing. Eric and Ernie started young in show business and had a good grounding in variety, then their failure in television happened when it didn't matter too much. They returned to variety, topping the bill just before variety theatres went into terminal decline, and finally came back to television at the very moment the square-eyed monster in the sitting-room was becoming an essential piece of household furniture. They'd joined the BBC when the Corporation was at its most powerful; then their original writers chose to leave them and still their luck held, for an even better writer turned up. They were indeed lucky, but part of their genius was the capacity to take advantage of the cards fate had dealt them.

I was in the throes of being midwife to *The Morecambe and Wise Show* when the consequences of Sandie Shaw winning the Eurovision Song Contest the previous year put additional strain on an overstretched department. As the victorious country it was our privilege and duty to host the next one. Tom Sloan decided to take the project on personally as executive producer and chose the Royal Albert Hall as the venue. We asked Cliff Richard to sing our entry – he was an international star and any record he made immediately went into the charts not only in the UK but also throughout much of the world. The song we chose, 'Congratulations', was written by Bill Martin and Phil Coulter, who had done the honours for Sandie Shaw with 'Puppet on a String'. By the time the competition drew near, 'Congratulations' was already high in hit parades all over Europe. The only unanswered question seemed to be who would come second.

The production purred like well-oiled clockwork. Tom had picked the vastly talented and hugely experienced Stewart Morris to produce and direct the show, and his PA, Queenie

Lipyeat, was in complete control of the administration. There was an air of near complacency around the department, and this worried me somewhat. At lunch in the canteen with a group of variety producers, I was saying that things were going too well; there needed to be a salutary shock to put our team on their mettle. 'Such as what?' asked one. 'Well,' I said, feeling around desperately, 'suppose a delegation from behind the Iron Curtain turned up uninvited and unexpected and demanded admission to the contest?' What would Tom as the chief television official of the host country do? Such a challenge would ginger him up!

We broke up and a little later I had a visitation from three of the producers: Terry Henebery, Roger Ordish and Brian Whitehouse. They invited me to join them as they transformed themselves into the unannounced Albanian delegation, aided by one of Roger's girlfriends, a journalist who spoke Russian. I decided that as there was no disguise I could put on that Tom wouldn't penetrate, I would be the in-house mole.

The Albanian delegation arrived while Tom was having a drink with some visitors in his office. I'd already told him that a group of strange Europeans had pitched up at the Television Centre asking where the Eurovision Song Contest was being held as they wished to participate. I'd sent them on to the Albert Hall. 'Thank God for that,' said Tom. 'I really couldn't cope with anything else.' The sentence was barely out of his mouth when Jim Moir knocked, entered and announced that there was a delegation from Albania downstairs and what should he do with them? Jim was totally convincing; I'd no idea whether he was in on the joke or not. Before Tom could decide what to do, in burst the group. The girl rushed up to Tom, started pumping his hand vigorously and let loose a flow of fluent Russian. She then introduced him to the Albanian team, who were cleverly disguised, though Tom was so taken aback that he didn't look at them closely as he tried to point out that Albania wasn't a member of Eurovision, which meant they couldn't take part. Roger Ordish, who spoke a little Russian, then started to protest, and his interpreter pointed out to Tom that they had only been allowed out from behind the Iron Curtain because they would be participating in this great contest. Had Tom any idea what would happen to them if they were to return not having done so?

Tom tried to be firm, but the girl persisted and begged Tom to let them sing their song, because she was sure that once he heard it, he would change his mind and let them take part in the contest. Over Tom's demurrals, they started to sing in gibberish a song that sounded remarkably like 'Congratulations'. I found it almost impossible to keep a straight face throughout this pantomime. Jim Moir, who was out of Tom's eye-line, was shaking helplessly with laughter. They got halfway through the rendition when Queenie peered closely at one of the delegation and then shrieked, 'That's Terry Henebery!' The game was up.

As we expected Tom, like the good sport he was, took it wonderfully. He couldn't believe he had been confronted by three of his staff and hadn't recognised them. In the actual contest, the British entry fared little better than the pseudo-Albanian one. Despite Cliff giving a great performance of the song, Spain pipped us at the post with 'La La La' and the whole country went into mourning.

In 1972 the contest was held in Edinburgh, where we came second to Luxembourg who then went on to win it again the following year. Because they couldn't afford to host it two years running, we stepped into the breach and it was held in Brighton. There, Abba had the biggest hit the contest has ever produced with 'Waterloo'. Not only that, but the Italian runner-up and the song from Holland, which came third, also reached the Top Ten in the charts, and our entry, 'Long Live Love', sung by Olivia Newton-John, came fourth and missed the Top Ten by just a whisker.

These were years of intense IRA activity and security was a nightmare. Despite all our precautions, ten minutes before the show started, the police informed me that they had received a telephone warning that a bomb had been planted in the building and were inclined to take it seriously. I asked them what they wanted me to do and they replied, 'It's not what we want, it's what you want. It's your event.' I gave the matter some grave thought. I didn't see how anyone could have got round the security measures we had taken. There had only been one entrance, constantly manned; everyone entering and leaving the building was checked and sniffer-dogs swept through the place morning and night. Added to which I thought the IRA were sufficiently publicity-conscious to realise that it wouldn't do their cause any good if representatives of the European countries at the contest were killed or injured.

I decided to go ahead with the show. Ten years later, the IRA blew up Brighton's Grand Hotel just down the road. I still go cold when I think about it.

SEVEN

I was sitting in my office on 25 March 1969 when the phone rang. It was my father. He sounded in excellent spirits and told me that he had two tickets for the Billy Walker fight at Wembley that evening. We often went to fights together and were never short of tickets for good ringside seats because the two top promoters of the day, Harry Levene and Jack Solomons, were great pals of Dad's. He also had a financial interest in two fighters, Dave Charnley and Ron Barton. They were both handy boxers, though Dad suspected that Ron had secret aspirations to be a film star and so tended to keep out of real scraps in case his handsome face was damaged. It was great fun accompanying the Old Man to a boxing match because the crowds always recognised him, and shouts of 'Wakey! Wakey!' would ring round the arena. He would bounce about in his seat, joining in the funny and often cruel badinage the spectators directed at the contestants.

I couldn't accept his invitation that night because I was due at the Talk of the Town with Paul Fox, the Controller of BBC1, to watch a fashion show we were planning to transmit. I remember saying, 'Have a good night, Dad,' as I rang off, which wasn't something I usually said to him – though perhaps when looking back we do read more significance into details than was meant at the time.

The show at the Talk of the Town was rather boring and time dragged. Near the end I noticed a waiter weaving his way through the tables obviously looking for someone. I just had an uncanny feeling I was the one he was after, and sure enough he came up and said I was wanted on the telephone in the lobby. It was Myra, the wife of Eric Miller who had been at Wembley with Dad. Before she could say anything, I asked, 'Is he dead?' Tearfully she replied that he was and asked me to come to their house at the Little Boltons, by which time Eric would be back from Wembley and could tell me what had happened. Paul volunteered to go with me.

Apparently, Eric and a mutual friend, Cyril Castle – my father's tailor – had joined the Old Man in the restaurant at Wembley Stadium where you could have a meal and watch the fight at the same time. Dad had been in great spirits. The food was good, the wine flowed freely and the Old Man was on his best anecdotal form. They settled down to watch the Billy Walker fight and in the interval between the sixth and seventh rounds, Dad asked the waitress for a second peach melba, though he'd already had one with his meal. Eric Miller knew Dad was supposed to watch his diet and remonstrated with him, but it was no use. Dad tucked into his ice-cream and they turned to watch the next round. A minute later, Eric happened to glance at Dad, to find him with his head resting on his chest, deeply unconscious. The Boxing Board's medical officer was called and tried desperately to revive him. Then he was taken to Wembley Hospital where he was pronounced dead.

When I'd gathered myself, I phoned my mother at Sandbanks. I suppose the word which describes her reaction is 'resigned'. She said she'd been talking to him on the phone that afternoon and had asked whether he was still taking his pills. He had snorted and said that he hadn't taken them that day and didn't intend to in the future. Mother and I then had to talk business, and she agreed to come up to London to help deal with Dad's affairs and advise on the funeral arrangements.

My reaction to Dad's death was interesting. In one sense I was devastated – he had been the greatest influence in my life – and yet I couldn't feel his death was a tragedy, unlike those of Boo and Ted who'd gone before their time. Though Dad was only sixty-nine when he died, he'd packed an enormous amount of living into those years and in the words of Frank Sinatra's theme-song, he'd done it his way. He behaved exactly how he chose, brushing aside the warnings of doctors, refusing to moderate his great appetite not just for food and drink but for all experience. I heard him say more than once that he'd rather die doing what he wanted to do than go on living doing what his doctors told him to do. And he did.

Truth to tell, Dad faced what for him was a bleak future. His stroke had reduced his mobility and slowed down his thought-processes. His energy was strictly limited so he had to cut down his public appearances, and this in turn meant that he didn't get that adrenaline surge which exhilarates all true public performers and puts them on top of the world. The bookings were beginning to dry up, with severe financial consequences – he'd always lived to the limit of his bank-balance. Though still one of the best-known faces in Britain and dubbed by the Variety Club of Great Britain 'Mr Show Business', he knew that in his line, fame may be a bright flame but it quickly fades if it isn't constantly replenished.

His personal life, too, was frankly a mess. He had to keep two homes going: Sandbanks, where my mother, from whom he was separated, lived, and his London flat, where he spent much of his time just hanging about, waiting for Kathie Kay to come down from Scotland. But her visits depended on the work they did together. If the band wasn't operating, she had no reason to be in London. Looming ahead of him he saw an emotional problem which seemed insoluble.

Dad's funeral was of course held in St Margaret's, Westminster, and after the service he was cremated at Golders Green Crematorium. Through a misunderstanding between my mother and I, neither of us collected his ashes. By the time we realised what had happened it was too late – they had been scattered in the crematorium's rose garden. Our intention was that they be spread across Poole harbour, where the whole family had enjoyed such happy times on Dad's various boats and at his home by the sea. But as it turned out, he was laid to rest among thousands of ordinary people, the great British public whom he truly loved and by whom he was venerated in return.

Some weeks later, the BBC transmitted a documentary made

by Michael Mills, a producer of great taste and talent who knew my father well. It was presented by Cliff Michelmore. One of the guests on the programme was the man who had taught Dad to fly during the First World War. 'Daddy' Probyn DSO MC was my father's true hero. He described how Dad had broken the first rule of flying: don't show off near the ground. He was buzzing a squad of cadets standing between two hangars as he came in to land, and looked away for an instant only to find when he looked back that the mechanics had wheeled an RE8 into the gap. Dad wrote off two aircraft and ended up on the ground with bits of his Bristol fighter sticking into him, two broken legs and sundry other injuries. Apparently Daddy Probyn walked across as Dad was being put onto a stretcher and totally without sympathy snarled, 'You bloody Hun! We can spare you but not a Bristol fighter!' Dad would have been very proud that Air Commodore Probyn, by then in retirement in Kenya, had travelled all that way to pay tribute to him.

I was glad to see the end of the sixties. Though professionally it was a highly successful decade, there were too many family tragedies for me to think of it without pain. And disaster always seemed to strike in the spring. Shortly after the turn of 1970, Tom Sloan developed cancer and died in May. He had taught me an immense amount about television and light entertainment. He could be formal, even prickly in manner, but he embodied BBC management at its very best. He was efficient, forthright and highly respected for his professionalism and integrity.

A few months before Tom died, we went on a business trip together to the West Coast of America. We did various bits of business, but the highlight of the trip was a visit to the Californian home of the legendary silent-film star Harold Lloyd, who before his retirement in 1945 had made more than 500 films, some of which, like *Safety Last* – with that breathtaking scene where he hangs from the hands of a clock a long way from the ground – were absolute classics. Lloyd had been one of the few stars of the silent screen who had made a successful transposition to talkies. He was a contemporary and friend of Laurel and Hardy, but unlike them he had a shrewd business brain and bought up the rights to all his films once the distributors had finished with them. It turned out to be an immensely valuable archive.

Our visit to Harold Lloyd was not simply a pilgrimage, it was also a fishing trip. The dawn of the era of television had sparked renewed interest in the early cinema, and in a way television is a monster with a huge appetite, eating up a vast amount of material and always hungry for more. Laurel and Hardy films were shown on television all over the world, though because they didn't own the rights neither the two stars nor their estates benefited from this renaissance of their work. Lloyd, who stood to make a fortune if he released his library, sat tight. Not a single Lloyd comedy had reached American television screens.

More in hope than confidence, Tom and I put to him the proposition that we should have a festival of Harold Lloyd films on BBC2, guaranteeing they would be shown only once at prime time in a prestigious slot. Harold would have none of it. The vehemence with which he swept aside our request made us realise how much he hated television. In his view, it had destroyed the traditional movie industry.

Once we'd got business out of the way, he showed us round his house. It was a typical Hollywood mansion of the twenties, set in a large estate with a swimming pool and tennis courts and surrounded by an electrified wire fence interspersed with sentry posts for security men. A long line of garages contained every car he had ever owned, from the beat-up jalopies of his early days to the Rollers and Cadillacs of his time of affluence. He had a pathological horror of anyone owning anything that once had belonged to him, so he hoarded all the paraphernalia of his life around his estate. Curiously, he never talked about 'I' or 'me' – he spoke of himself constantly in the third person.

He showed us the centrepiece of his house. It was a boudoir with a sunken seating area and a huge silver screen covering the whole of one wall. Pointing to a settee, he informed us dramatically that in that very spot Harold Lloyd had slept with Mary Pickford. Then he confessed that while he and Mary were sitting together watching a very boring movie, they had both nodded off. That was the nearest to a joke the great comedian cracked the whole of the time we were there.

In the centre of another sitting-room was a tall fir tree with dozens of exquisite jewelled Fabergé eggs hanging from the branches. 'What should Harold Lloyd do with this?' he asked, pointing at the tree. 'Give it to the poor and needy?' I suggested, pointing to Tom, 'He's poor and I'm needy!' Not the merest suspicion of a smile crossed his lips. He looked and talked like a very sad and lonely man. Television did get his films in the end. He died soon after we visited him and his estate sold all his films to the big American networks.

When Tom died, I was promoted and given his job as Head of Light Entertainment. People talk casually about 'stepping into dead men's shoes'. That's what I did, and I bitterly re-gretted the necessity. I loved Tom and would happily have carried on as his deputy for years to come had he been given a few more years of life. But these matters are out of our hands.

It was decreed that I must abandon my freelance status and become a member of staff in order to take up the post, a small sacrifice of freedom for the huge security of a generous BBC pension. Thus began the most productive period of my years in BBC television. I was supported by a management team of unparalleled talents: Huw Wheldon was managing director with David Attenborough as his deputy; Paul Fox ran BBC1 and Robin Scott, BBC2. These were the true architects of BBC television's greatness and it was an honour to work for them.

I had my first bit of good fortune while attending the 1970 BAFTA award ceremony with Paul Fox, who as Controller of BBC1 paid most of my department's bills and bought our programme ideas. That year, the BAFTA show was being produced by London Weekend Television for ITV and was presented by David Frost. When LWT was given the franchise, they put out a David Frost show each evening of the weekend and, ever the entrepreneur, David persuaded Ronnie Barker and Ronnie Corbett, who'd worked with him on *The Frost Report*, to join him, though not as a double-act. Just as we waited for the BAFTA show to begin, there was a technical breakdown and the screens went blank. While we in the studio sat twiddling our thumbs, someone behind the scenes had the bright idea of sending out the Two Ronnies to do an ad hoc routine to keep us entertained. They were brilliant together, and on an impulse I turned to Paul and said, 'How would you like them on your network?' Paul was sceptical. 'You'll never swing that, they're tied to David Frost.' 'Don't worry about the details,' I replied. 'Would you be interested?' He nodded, somewhat sceptically.

The next morning I went to see David Frost's agent and put a proposition to him. What I didn't know was that Frost's programme was on the point of being dropped by LWT so Messrs Barker and Corbett would be out of work. I offered a comprehensive contract – thirteen shows a year starring Corbett and Barker together, and a series of half-hour situation comedies in which they appeared separately. It seems un-believable now, but the Two Ronnies themselves had never actually considered the possibility of working together. I knew that producing them was a job for Jimmy Gilbert. I gave him the project and he became the main creative force in bringing together all the elements that finally resulted not only in *The Two Ronnies* but also *Porridge* and *Open All Hours*.

I needed an assistant head who would do for me what I had done for Tom. After some of my most senior producers had turned down the job because they couldn't bear the idea of not being involved in making programmes, I turned to Tony Preston. Tony had been a POW in Korea and on his return joined the BBC. When he came to my notice he was the chief planner for BBC1. Almost immediately he earned his bread by introducing me to an old mate of his, Michael Parkinson, who was a well-established journalist and television performer and had done programmes for Granada TV as well as for BBC Current Affairs.

For some time I had been looking for a British equivalent of Jack Paar, the American chat-show host who combined wit, intelligence and human curiosity. I sounded out Paul Fox about Michael Parkinson; he was lukewarm. When Paul had been in charge of Current Affairs Michael had worked for him, and though Paul didn't doubt he had talent he felt Michael was also a little indolent. I pressed my case and Paul agreed that we go ahead. We found an ideal producer in Richard Drewett and before long Parky was established as a Saturday-night fixture, with most of the big stars making an appearance on his show.

Michael had his favourite guests – Billy Connolly, for instance. But Connolly could be near the knuckle and Richard Drewett was sufficiently worried about one of his jokes to refer it formally to me. Since the show was recorded earlier in the evening of its transmission there was time for judicious edits, and Richard felt he might have to use the razorblade to cut out a story Billy told about two Scotsmen in Glasgow drinking together. One says he's murdered his wife and buried her in the back yard. The other doesn't believe him so they go home and sure enough she's buried, but her bottom is sticking out. 'Why have you left her bum showing?' 'It's somewhere to park my bike!' The audience loved it and I decided it should stay in. If delivered badly the joke could be in doubtful taste, but told in Billy's inimitable style and at eleven o'clock at night, I thought it acceptable – not least because anyone likely to take offence would probably be in bed.

Once when Jimmy Tarbuck was a guest on the Michael's show he nearly gave me a seizure. I was at a dinner with some rather staid people one Saturday night and the conversation got round to my job, and eventually to *Parkinson*. Once dinner was over, the consensus round the table was that they would like to watch the show. It went well until at the end of his interview Michael asked Jimmy for a good story. Jimmy launched into the tale of a man who phoned an escort agency to ask if they had a woman six feet, six inches in height but weighing only six stone. They said they had and they would send her round. She duly arrived and the man told her to take her clothes off and kneel by the fire. He then opened the door of the room and in came an enormous Great Dane dog. At this point Jimmy looked up and said to the camera, 'If Bill Cotton's watching this, he'll be having a heart attack!' He wasn't far wrong – I could feel the atmosphere around me in the room getting more tense. Jimmy continued. 'The man takes the dog up to the woman, taps it sharply on the nose and says, "That's what you'll look like if you don't eat your Bonio."' I nearly banned Jimmy for life for advertising on the BBC and ruining my night out.

I sometimes used to entertain Parky's guests in my office while they were waiting to be called onto the set. I recall Nat King Cole telling me that even when he was the main attraction in some clubs in the American deep South, he was required to use the outside toilet. Bing Crosby confessed that for him Frank Sinatra was the greatest. 'Frank can generate more atmosphere from an audience even when he's still sitting in his dressing-room than I achieve at the high point of my act.' Then there was Dustin Hoffman, who was shown into my office accompanied by a lovely-looking woman whom he introduced to me as his wife. I made sure she felt welcome, and was suitably attentive. She wasn't a very loquacious conversationalist but the highly articulate Hoffman made up for that. As they got up to leave I said I'd been delighted to meet him and his wife. He paused and said, 'Actually, this is not my wife. I've never set eyes on her before. I believe she works for you.' Sure enough, it was one of our PAs on the show who had been too terrified to contradict him when he played the joke on me.

Parkinson dominated Saturday nights on BBC1 until the early eighties, when he was persuaded to join a group of television talents – David Frost, Angela Rippon, Anna Ford and Robert Kee – to become the founders of TV-AM, having won the franchise to operate ITV's breakfast show. The Famous Five, as they became known, all had a financial stake in the new company, and I thought they were taking a huge risk. After the deal had been announced but about a year before TV-AM was due on the air, I had lunch with Parky to discuss a timetable for his remaining months at the BBC. He said, 'You don't think I should do it, do you?' I told him I didn't think the precedents were good. The American film conglomerate United Artists was launched by a number of big stars, including Mary Pickford, Douglas Fairbanks, Charlie Chaplin and the film director D. W. Griffiths, who decided to pool their creative talent and run their own show instead of remaining the paid employees of other companies. But the performer's skills are quite different from those of the entrepreneur, and the project failed. The money-men had to come in to rescue and exploit it. London Weekend Television was launched on the same principle and suffered the same fate. I predicted the Famous Five might pull it off for a couple of years, but not more. In the event I was over-optimistic – they survived only months in partnership, though each resumed a successful solo career.

My father used to say success depended on three things: hard work, knowing what you are talking about, and a lot of luck. Serendipity certainly helped my career along. In 1970, through my contacts at the Montreux Festival I was invited to visit Dutch Television and was asked to give a talk to all their production staff. I was intrigued by a Dutch game show called *One out of Eight,* which was devised and presented by a lady called Mise Bowman. Four families, each represented by two members of different generations, had to copy a number of tasks set them by experts. One by one they were eliminated until only one family remained; a short question-and-answer round then decided which member of the winning family went on to the last round. A procession of prizes rolled past on a moving conveyor-belt and the winners were able to keep those items they could remember afterwards. It was all in Dutch, of course, but once I got the hang of it, I could see the basis of a new kind of game show. And I knew exactly who I wanted to star in it: Bruce Forsyth. He had become a megastar by presenting *Sunday Night at the London Palladium* on ITV but was not quite sure what to do next. I struck a deal with Mise Bowman. I wasn't exactly Father Christmas: I offered her twenty-five pounds a show for the copyright. Still, she did well. Once the format became a success in Britain she was able to offer it to German television for a thousand pounds a throw.

Bruce wasn't enthusiastic. He was worried about becoming

typecast as a game-show host when he had other talents as an all-round entertainer. But he had perhaps the best agent in the business, the legendary Billy Marsh, who immediately saw the possibilities of the format and persuaded Bruce to sign up. I decided we needed to do a pilot for what we called *The Generation Game*, and I asked Jim Moir and Colin Chalmers to produce it. Both had joined the department in 1964 when we expanded to cope with two channels, and in my view were outstanding talents.

Such programmes are called 'people' shows nowadays, and there are thousands of them. *The Generation Game* was the first, and I'm proud to have seen its potential. The pilot worked well. The producers over-recorded in order to try out as many games as possible and get the scoring system right. I couldn't attend the pilot because I was in hospital having a hernia operation, but I saw the recording and loved it – especially the final game. A well-known conjuror came on carrying two trays, one containing six glasses and another tray with six eggs on it. The trick was to knock the top tray out of the way and get the eggs to drop into the glasses. He did his patter and then to a roll of drums and the magic words 'All the eggs in the glasses!', he grasped the tray, gave it a tug and the eggs duly dropped into the glasses – but only at the third attempt. Then one of the contestants walked on, casually yanked the tray and to everyone's astonishment the eggs fell into the glasses. It was a magic moment and it brought the house down.

We recorded the show on a Thursday for transmission on the following Saturday evening. It was a disaster. We had tried to recreate the games that went well on the pilot and they just wouldn't work. It taught me that you can't create magic to order. After a lot of discussion, I decided to abandon the recording and ask the producers to edit down the original pilot from eighty to fifty minutes so we could show that. Bruce protested that this would make nonsense of the scoring system, but I pointed out that in the end the winner won. Nobody noticed the changes and the show went out to rave reviews.

We had an end-of-series party in the pub next door to the

Television Theatre on Shepherd's Bush Green, a favourite haunt of the Irish residents of the area. Bruce was our host and had determined to do things in style, so he booked a private room. We duly assembled at the pub after the recording and trooped up to the room to discover it had obviously just been vacated. We came upon two labourers in dirty T-shirts, red bandanas round their necks, dripping in perspiration, trying to sweep up the accumulated debris with stiff brooms. Bruce was apoplectic with rage, but Billy Marsh took in the situation immediately, advanced with a smile on his face and said, 'Which one of you is the wine waiter?' By his quick-wittedness, Billy turned what could have been a crisis into a farce. We all fell about laughing and the party was a roaring success.

Bruce and *The Generation Game* securely anchored the Saturday evening BBC1 schedules until 1978 when Michael Grade, at that time Director of Programming for London Weekend Television, persuaded him to do a two-hour extravaganza for them which was to be called *Bruce Forsyth's Big Night*. The idea was to utilise Bruce's talents not just as a game-show host but also as an interviewer, singer and dancer. It was no use pretending the loss of Bruce was anything other than a huge blow to the BBC, but I genuinely wished him well in this highly ambitious new project. And in a sense I owed Michael one, since he had pointed Morecambe and Wise in our direction. Michael and I had been good friends for much of our lives, but I knew his intention in this instance wasn't very friendly: he hoped to use Bruce to break the stranglehold the BBC had on Saturday nights by exploiting the star who'd helped to establish that very supremacy.

Unfortunately for LWT, *Bruce Forsyth's Big Night* turned out to be a damp squib. I didn't shed too many tears about that as we set about finding a replacement for Bruce, for we realised that the format was more enduring than any single star, however big. At the turn of the millennium it is still running with Jim Davidson in charge. By a strange turn of fate, the replacement we found for Bruce, Larry Grayson, had actually been discovered by Michael Grade in his days as a theatrical agent.

This time it was the pilot that was the disaster. Larry could do virtually anything on stage other than the thing which really mattered: explaining to the contestants in simple, clear English just what the games involved. We solved the problem by giving that task to Isla St Clair, a fresh-faced Scottish folk singer we'd booked as Larry's Girl Friday.

It wasn't roses all the way in my heady early days in charge of the Light Entertainment Group; we had our flops. One of the most painful resulted in my having to take off air an undisputed comedy genius, Peter Cook. When the run of *Not Only . . . But Also . . .* finished, Dudley Moore went off to Hollywood to do his own thing and became an unlikely sex-symbol, which left Peter Cook at a loose end. He decided he would like to do his own talk show. Peter had been a much sought-after guest on chat shows (it was a toss-up whether he or Kenneth Williams was the bigger draw), so Michael Mills assumed that Peter would have no difficulty in filling the other chair, that of interviewer. Trusting Michael's judgement, I booked Peter for eight shows.

I watched the first programme in the series and was inclined to cancel the whole deal. Peter was all over the place. He had none of the self-discipline of a good interviewer. He asked inane questions and didn't listen to the answers, then went into long rambling disquisitions about nothing in particular. I was appalled. Michael Mills persuaded me to stay my hand until they'd made a second and third show. He argued that Peter was in a fragile state psychologically and the humiliation of having his show taken off could destroy him. After the third show, I'd had enough and lowered the boom on the series.

Peter was an icon of the comedy world so my decision was greeted with incredulity and fury by his supporters, of whom there were many thousands. Peter himself took it very badly and appeared in my office with his lawyer who asked me why I had pulled the plug on the show. In response, I read the standard clause which appears in all contracts, giving the BBC the right to remove from the schedules any programme liable to bring the Corporation into disrepute. If Peter pursued his case, I had certainly no intention of paying for the five programmes that hadn't been made. As the discussion wore on, I began to suspect that money was at the root of Peter's attitude. Sure enough, his lawyer asked if he could talk to me privately. We went next door. 'Strictly off the record,' he said, 'my problem is that Peter has already spent the money.' 'Your problem's solved,' I replied. 'He can keep the money and owe the BBC a few performances at a reduced fee when his finances take a turn for the better.' We went back to my office. A beatific smile appeared on Peter's face as his lawyer explained the deal, and we went off to the bar swearing undying affection for each other.

The seventies was a golden era for comedy. The roll-call of winners was amazing: *Porridge, Sykes, Dad's Army, Till Death Do Us Part, Steptoe and Son, Fawlty Towers, Some Mothers Do 'Ave 'Em, Whatever Happened to the Likely Lads?, Last of the Summer Wine* and *The Good Life*. I had no responsibility for producing the actual programmes, but if anything went wrong – which usually meant crossing that vaguely defined boundary of taste between the acceptable and the unacceptable – I was the one the DG or the board of governors summoned onto the quarter deck for a keel-hauling.

Till Death Do Us Part got me into all kinds of trouble. One sequence in which Alf and his left-wing son-in-law had an argument about the Virgin Birth had the Head of Religious Broadcasting phoning me to protest at an appalling blasphemy. I'd been out and hadn't seen the previous evening's transmission, but it was practice to preview the entire series before transmission and though I am no theologian I couldn't recall anything remotely blasphemous in the three episodes I'd watched. 'What blasphemy?' I asked. 'The Virgin Mary on the pill,' was his succinct reply. I couldn't believe it, and said I'd phone him back. I rang the producer who admitted that because of technical problems they had changed the running-order and put out the programme containing the alleged blasphemy instead of one of those I'd previewed. We were in big trouble. I

Boo on the Adriatic Coast in Italy in 1955. Our drive across Europe to get there had its moments.

My three daughters – Kate, Lisa (Lulu) and Jane – at Lisa's wedding. Their motto could be the same as the Three Musketeers: 'All for one – and one for all'.

Father with the Mother Superior and Sister Ann Celine at a fête at St Anthony's Hospital, Cheam. In the background is his mate, Russ Conway.

Boo, Kate, Jane and Mother taken with the Polaroid camera Perry Como gave me. Boo and the children had spent Easter with Boo's mother in Majorca. They were away two weeks and I was very lonely. Lisa was born the following January.

The Val Doonican Show, 1982.

Dave Allen at Large, 1978.

This picture was taken in the Television Theatre at Shepherd's Bush, my second home for so many years, when I became Head of Variety.

To BILL COTTON
Best wishes
Ralph Richardson
'60

A signed memento of the first time Perry Como and Ralph Richardson met, during the filming for the show at eight forty-five on Easter morning.

Billie Anthony and RSM Brittain on *Off the Record* in 1957. It was by way of a reunion for the sergeant-major and me.

Tommy Cooper. A greatly missed comedian adored by the public and his fellow performers. We had a few jars together over the years.

Talking Shirley MacLaine into doing a show. The agent doesn't look too convinced.
I told him I wouldn't take advantage of her good nature, to which she said, 'Pity.'

Tom Sloan, George Inns and I discussing ideas for a show with Max Bygraves in 1965.
George was the executive producer of the *Show of the Week* series on BBC2.

The cast of *The Frost Report* prior to leaving for and winning the Golden Rose of Montreux, 1967.

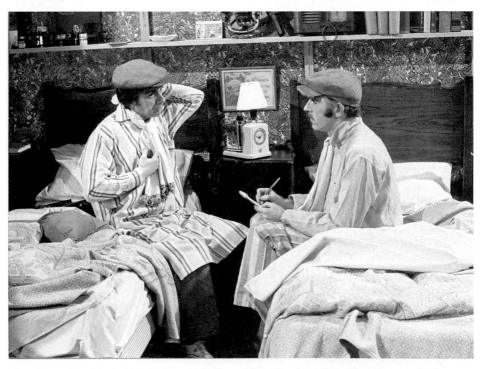

The Show of the Week: Not Only… But Also… Peter Cook and Dudley Moore, 1970. With *The Morecambe and Wise Show* and *The Two Ronnies,* this show made up a most powerful treble of doubles.

Kings of the Castle – Eric and Ernie.

Working the scoreboard on the programme to select the British entry for the 1970 Eurovision Song Contest. 'Congratulations' became the entry and a big hit, but didn't win the contest. Cliff Richard is holding the scoreboard up!

With Jimmy Savile on the set of *Jim'll Fix It*. In the background is Roger Ordish the producer, for whom the programme turned out literally to be his life's work.

asked for a play-back of the offending episode and a full script.

It was actually Alf's son-in-law who mooted the possibility of the Virgin Mary being on the pill – otherwise, he said, there would have been many more messiahs, and it was Alf who screamed with fury at this blasphemy and said that he would rot in hell for it. Curiously, all the complaints I got insisted that Alf Garnett had uttered the blasphemy, when in fact he reacted like a traditional believer. But whoever had said the fateful words, we ought not to have transmitted that sequence and I made a full apology and tightened up our previewing rules. Given the material routinely transmitted these days it would seem I overreacted, but I don't think so.

My dear friend Dave Allen frequently had the religious constituency in a state of righteous indignation, especially the Catholic bishops who were often the target of his good-natured lampooning. Dave specialised in dangerous subjects for humour: religion, death, sex and horror. When a comedian moves into areas such as these, he or she is bound to give offence to some viewers. Taste is such a subjective thing; what makes me laugh may leave you grimacing with disapproval. My job was to hold the ring, to allow talented comedians such as Dave the maximum freedom to explore their chosen themes – even occasionally letting them go just a little too far – but blowing the whistle if they made a habit of outraging the viewers. In matters of taste, it is only possible for scriptwriters and comedians to determine exactly where the frontiers of the permissible are by overstepping them from time to time.

Religion has been Dave's abiding obsession. Only a former Irish Catholic could be quite so witheringly accurate in his satire, which is probably why Dave was much admired by the then Director-General, Sir Charles Curran. He invited Alasdair Milne, then TV's Director of Programmes, and myself to attend him in his office to meet the Lord Provost of Edinburgh, who had asked for a meeting in order to complain about Dave Allen. The Lord Provost arrived in a wheelchair and began by saying that he was a devout Catholic and objected to the BBC giving Dave Allen a licence to undermine the Catholic Church. The

DG then revealed that he too was a Catholic, and since the Church had for two thousand years withstood persecution, martyrdom and war, he doubted it would wither under the assault of a few pointed jokes from a stand-up comedian. In a pause during the exchange Alasdair, trying to appeal to the Lord Provost's Scottish pride, made the point that all great comedians used controversial material, even Scotland's own Billy Connolly. The Lord Provost fixed him with a withering look and retorted, 'Billy Connolly is not invited to take tea with me.' Alasdair subsided. The meeting ended in deadlock but it was of great significance for Alasdair and myself because we had won the wholehearted endorsement of Sir Charles, a rather austere man whose background was that of an administrator rather than a programme-maker. Frankly, I expected him to be more guarded and less enthusiastic in his support for Dave Allen's comedy.

Because Dave's humour is based on aspects of the perennial human condition rather than strictly topical issues, his material hasn't dated. When I take down one of his early tapes and scan it, I am struck by the continuing relevance of his comments on the passing scene. One thing has changed: he used to smoke incessantly throughout his act, now he is a non-smoker which means he has to find some other way of drawing attention to that missing finger-joint, about the loss of which he has offered innumerable explanations. I don't know which version to believe so I've decided he had it cut off as a talking point.

Throughout the seventies my life was dominated by my work. The Cotton family moved first to a house in Lent Rise near Burnham Beeches which was big and comfortable and could hold a growing family, and then in 1975 to Sheen. By now, my mother was in a residential home nearby and all the girls had gone.

Sailing and golf have always been my main hobbies. I bought a boat from Ernie Wise and played golf at the Royal Mid Surrey in Richmond, a lovely flat course. My regular partner was Huw

Wheldon, who has been described as 'the last of the great actor-managers and the best Director-General the BBC never had'. Huw had been a genuine war hero. He served in the Royal Welch Fusiliers and was parachuted into France on D-Day, winning the MC. After he was demobbed he became publicity officer for the Festival of Britain, then in 1952 he joined the BBC Television service in the same capacity.

Huw was a restless, highly articulate Welshman with a booming voice and a sharp wit. He had that indefinable quality charisma, and it was inevitable that he would soon want to be where the action is in television – making programmes rather than getting publicity for them. He applied for a senior producer's post even though he hadn't the slightest experience in directing programmes. His articulateness and powers of leadership got him the job. Leonard Miall, then Head of Television Talks and Current Affairs, gave him a crash-course in television production, and Huw was off, blasting his way to the top in the BBC. He graduated from Children's Programmes to Music and Arts and worked for that formidable lady Grace Wyndham Goldie.

Huw was renaissance man – he was good at virtually everything he turned his hand to. Besides producing excellent programmes he was an equally good presenter, fronting programmes such as *Monitor*, the innovative arts programme which did so much to make music, painting and drama accessible to the general viewer. And when he leapfrogged several of his senior colleagues to become controller of programmes for BBC TV, he then proved himself to be a first-class administrator.

Huw and I had one thing in common: neither of us had joined the BBC by way of Oxbridge, unlike almost all of our contemporaries. And we both believed that the BBC's core duty was to entertain the public, for the simple reason that unless listeners and viewers found a programme agreeable they wouldn't stay with it long enough to be educated or informed. Granted, I was at what some would regard the vulgar end of the market, but Huw was never patronising about popular

155

entertainment, and I always felt I had his support when I waged an endless battle to correct the built-in bias the BBC had consistently shown towards news and current affairs.

Had there been any justice in the universe, Huw would have been made Director-General when Hugh Carleton Greene's term of office came to an end in 1968. However, the former Radio Doctor, Lord Hill of Luton, never a man to hide his light under a bushel, had been appointed chairman of the BBC governors the year before and had no intention of being overshadowed by any DG who was as big a personality as he was. He made sure that Huw was passed over in favour of Charles Curran, a highly competent administrator though a somewhat colourless individual.

One of my relaxations was football. I had a guaranteed seat in Harold Davison's box at Chelsea. He was a top theatrical agent and often entertained visiting stars there. One Saturday afternoon, I found myself sitting next to a good-looking American woman. We got into conversation and she asked me if I would explain the game of soccer to her. I said the only thing she needed to know was that the team that kicked, headed or in any other way except with the use of their hands got the ball into their opponents' goal the most times was the winner, and if anything else of interest cropped up, I'd let her know. At half-time, she went off to the powder room and I asked Harold who she was. 'Sorry I didn't introduce you,' he said. 'That's Mary Travers of Peter, Paul and Mary, a popular singing trio who regularly get to the top of the pops.' The upshot was she invited me that evening to be her guest at a club where Tom Paxton, a well-known folk-singer of the day, was performing.

Tom Paxton was his usual brilliant self, and after working for about an hour announced he was going to take a break but that he would like to introduce a young man who had written the Peter, Paul and Mary hit 'Trains and Boats and Planes'. On came this rather shy, somewhat academic-looking young man who announced he would sing a song he had composed called 'Wake Up Jimmy Newman'. It was a Vietnam anti-war song about two wounded soldiers lying on stretchers waiting to be helicoptered out of the frontline. When the helicopter arrives, one says to the other, 'Wake up, here's the chopper that's going to take us home.' No response: his mate is dead. The boy sang it with such intense emotion I found I had broken the pencil in my pocket while listening to it. It was greeted with sustained applause.

After the show Jerry Weintraub, Tom's agent, asked me about the possibility of the BBC doing a Tom Paxton series. I told him frankly I couldn't afford Tom, but I would be very interested in giving his writer a show on BBC2. He said, 'OK, but I hope you know what you're doing, he's had very little experience.'

And that's how John Denver got his first television series. It was produced by Stanley Dorfman and was received with critical acclaim. He became a big star but remained at heart a shy, unassuming character. Whenever he came to Britain he was happy to appear on the BBC and insisted that I paid him only as much as he got for his very first show. Tragically, out of due time he was killed in a plane crash.

In the continual search for fresh shows, I came up with an idea that seemed to me to be ideal for Harry Secombe. Years before, something like it had been done by Wilfred Pickles in a programme called *Ask Pickles*. I hopped on a train to Great Yarmouth where Harry was appearing. He was not in the best of moods; Britain was enjoying a heatwave and the theatre, not being air-conditioned, was like an oven. He was therefore less than enthusiastic when I told him my idea for a series in which he, like a genial magician, would make people's dearest wishes come true.

Harry hummed and hawed and finally agreed to give it a go, so I asked Stewart Morris to turn the idea into a programme. After a couple of weeks, Stewart came to see me looking very worried. 'How's it going?' I asked. He shook his head. 'He doesn't want to do it, does he?' I said. So we decided to release Harry from any contractual obligation and it seemed that a promising programme had bitten the dust.

But that same week I'd arranged to see Jimmy Savile to give

him some bad news. I'd decided to take off a series he'd been presenting called *Clunk Clink*. It hadn't worked because it depended on good interviewing and that wasn't Jimmy's thing – his larger-than-life personality had the effect of eclipsing his guests, which wasn't the point of the programme at all. But after I'd given him the bad news and we got on to discussing other projects that might suit him, it suddenly struck me that the idea I'd tried to sell to Harry Secombe might work for him, especially if children were involved – Jimmy could get kids to do anything. Jimmy's reaction was always the same: 'If you think it's a good idea, boss, I'll try it. Just don't take me off *Top of the Pops*.'

We decided to call the show *Jim'll Fix It*. Our initial concern had been that children at home might not write in with enough interesting notions to provide variety and interest. We needn't have worried. We soon discovered there are no limits to a child's imagination. The very first challenge came from a little girl whose dearest wish was to swim with a dolphin. We were away and running, and Jimmy was in his element. *Jim'll Fix It* ran and ran. It was what I called a proper television programme – a strong idea, a brilliant presenter and an endless supply of amazingly varied stunts. And it was ideally suited to early-evening family viewing.

One of the bonuses of helping to make stars such as John Denver and Jimmy Savile and employing many others was that I could call in favours when I needed them, and whenever the Royal Variety Performance came round I spent a lot of time on the telephone. It was originally called the Royal Command Performance with the implication being that all the artists had been chosen by the Royal Family, and since they were the usual mixed bag of good, bad and indifferent acts, I guess Buckingham Palace didn't want to take the blame for the dross, so that title was dropped.

The Royal Variety Performance was at first shown exclusively on ITV, master-minded by one of the Grade brothers, the theatre impresario Bernard Delfont, and transmitted by his brother Lew Grade's television company, ATV. After a couple of years, Bernie decided that as a national event it ought to alternate between ITV and the BBC and he invited the BBC to become involved. Lew was furious, but Bernie was unrepentant. The brothers were personally very close but when it came to business neither of them took any prisoners.

1966 was the BBC's first year and it fell to me to direct it. I'd been responsible for *The Billy Cotton Band Show* segment of the Royal Variety Performance when the Old Man was alive, but I'd never directed the whole evening. The first task of anyone responsible for televising the show was to get on good terms with the producer Robert Nesbitt, because the performance was actually staged in a theatre and Robert looked after that side of things. Technically speaking, the problem was to satisfy the requirements of both a theatre and television audience. Robert lit the theatre so as to suit the live audience, but this was a level of lighting much too weak for television – it looked as though the stars were performing in a coal cellar. Robert, an old Etonian with a very formal manner and a traditional approach to theatre, could be very prickly, but I discovered that a crate of champagne worked wonders on his temper. When we needed more light, I'd come in from the outside broadcast truck and plonk a bottle of bubbly on his makeshift desk in the amphitheatre and look pleadingly at him. He would raise one eyebrow and say, 'Oh, very well, then,' and turn up the lights.

One of the transatlantic stars that year was Jerry Lewis, who was a pain in the neck to cope with – that's if you got the chance to get near him at all, since his retinue behaved so protectively you'd have thought he was the US President. He didn't like the television lighting and agreed with Bob that it should be standard theatrical lighting. I thought we'd got a compromise but just before he went on stage he told the stage manager he wanted the lights brought down or he was going home. He got what he wanted and the television audience could barely see him through the gloom. My heart bled for him.

Everything went like clockwork for the big night. The cameramen and the rest of the crew were real professionals who knew exactly what they were doing and gave me every co-operation, so I sat in the scanner in my dinner jacket, quietly confident and calling the shots. Suddenly, in the middle of Frankie Howerd's performance all the cameras failed, and the bank of monitors at which I'd been staring went blank. Slowly the cameras came alive again one by one, though for some reason we couldn't fathom I found it impossible to move across the whole range of shots, and I'd lost some of my carefully composed pictures. I sweat easily, so by the time the show was over and I joined the presentation-line to meet the Queen Mother, my once immaculate shirt and dinner jacket were wringing wet.

In 1972 *Till Death Do Us Part* was getting huge ratings on television and someone had the bright idea that the show's writer, Johnny Speight, should produce a special sketch for Alf Garnett and Co. to perform before the Queen. I was asked my opinion. It was a tricky issue. Johnny had put some outrageous lines in the mouths of Alf and his socialist son-in-law on the precise subject of the monarchy. I decided there was no problem for television since the show was pre-recorded and we could therefore edit when necessary, but what about the live audience in the theatre, including members of the Royal Family?

Bernie solved the problem in his own inimitable way; he hadn't spent his whole life dealing with stars for nothing. On the morning of the performance he invited Johnny out for a spot of lunch. To Johnny's puzzlement, Bernie ordered a bottle of bubbly and announced that they had something to their mutual advantage to celebrate. He then leaned over the table and reminded Johnny that he, Bernie, was also the head of EMI Films and had come up with a brilliant idea for a feature film for which he wanted Johnny to write the script. As he left the restaurant with a dazed and gratified Johnny, Bernie said, 'By the way, John, we wouldn't want to embarrass anyone tonight, would we?'

1974 was a year in which there were two elections, both of them narrowly won for Labour by Harold Wilson. I first met him at a football match. He had agreed to attend a friendly game played between Fulham and Santos, and my dad's friend Eric Miller, a director of Fulham, invited me along. We watched the game from a club-room in the stand overlooking the pitch. When I arrived there was a group gathered around the Prime Minister at one end of the room. It seemed to be an all-male occasion except for the PM's advisor, Marcia Falkender, who was sitting watching the game on her own at the other end of the club-room from everyone else. I decided to join her. She asked me if I wouldn't prefer to be with the PM; I suggested he had quite enough people pounding his ear and said that if she didn't mind, I'd sit with her. We found plenty to talk about. I was surprised to hear that she had often been invited to visit commercial television companies, but had never received an invitation from the BBC. I said I was sure it was an oversight, and I'd put it right. She then went on to ask me if I could help get some stars to come to Number Ten when the Prime Minister held parties in aid of various charities. I told her that I was sure I could.

When the match finished she brought the Prime Minister over to where I was sitting. He was glad to hear I would help with those parties, and he would leave the selection of the stars to me. Over the next few years, I got many BBC stars to appear at Downing Street parties in aid of charities. In return, my wife and I were invited to watch the Trooping of the Colour and dine at Number Ten. I found Marcia a very attractive, highly intelligent person who was loathed in certain circles within both the Labour Party and Whitehall generally for her alleged un-healthy influence over Wilson. She seemed to be impervious to criticism, though some of it was so cruel that she must have been hurt by it.

Some weeks later at a Board of Governors' dinner I was describing a recent visit to Downing Street. I commented favourably about Marcia Falkender and expressed surprise that she had never been invited to the BBC, whereupon a governor's wife retorted, 'I should think *not*! She's got an illegitimate child.' 'You'd have preferred her to have an abortion, I presume?' I replied sarcastically. That was the end of that conversation. After the meal the DG, Charles Curran, came over to me and said, 'I heard what that woman said, and she does not speak for the BBC. You make the arrangements and I'll be delighted to meet her.'

When in 1976 Harold Wilson suddenly resigned, Marcia phoned to ask if I could come to a farewell party at Number Ten and bring along some of my showbiz mates who would create a jolly atmosphere and prevent the event from degenerating into a wake. It was a bizarre occasion. Nobody knew why Wilson had resigned and rumours were flying everywhere. At one point we had a sing-song round the piano. Later in the evening when the Prime Minister was mellow and good whisky had made me daring, I noticed him standing alone, went over and asked him why he had decided to quit. He puffed at his pipe and said, 'If you stay in this place you get more and more cut off from real life; you lose touch with what the people really think and want. I think I've reached that stage, so I'm going. It's as simple as that.'

I last saw him in the mid-nineties when he came along to Wesley's Chapel in City Road for their celebrity Christmas Carol Concert. He sat with a pleasant smile on his face, lost in some private world and utterly dependent on his wife, Mary.

One of the acts I had taken to Downing Street for Harold's charity parties was Morecambe and Wise. By now they had the world at their feet but for some reason they decided it was time they were recognised by their colleagues in the industry and so asked me to enter one of their shows for the Montreux Festival. I wasn't keen. Though the BBC still won prizes most years, the general view seemed to be that we'd got more of our fair share of major awards over the years and it was the turn of others. I told Eric and Ernie frankly I didn't think they would win. Still, Eric thought it would be fun and a day out for their wives. The day their show was viewed, all the Brits present at the Festival fell about roaring with laughter while the Continentals sat in stony silence – some kinds of British humour just do not travel well.

When it came to voting day, the rumour mill was working overtime. It was suggested that three shows were fighting it out for top honours: an Anne Bancroft show from America, ITV's *The Benny Hill Show,* and *Morecambe and Wise* from the BBC. There was a delay in the announcement of the winners and people kept sidling up to Eric and Ernie, congratulating them on what they were sure was a foregone conclusion. I became the resident pain in the neck, beseeching them not to get too excited. I'd been involved in Montreux for years and knew only too well that politics played as great a part as programme quality in determining winners and losers.

In the event Anne Bancroft's show, *Annie, the Woman in the Lives of Man,* won the Silver Rose and Morecambe and Wise didn't feature in the awards. We were pretty disconsolate at first but then wandered off to a restaurant and ordered fish and chips and plenty of wine. Slowly we all began to see the funny side of things, and Eric started doing his inimitable clowning act. The other diners watched entranced as we British did what we do best (because we've had so much practice at it) and celebrated our defeat.

In 1976 we entered a special edition of *The Two Ronnies* called *The Picnic.* Written by Ronnie Barker and directed by Terry Hughes, it was totally without dialogue other than endless grunts, groans and special effects. The BBC was responsible for the Two Ronnies' travel arrangements and when I was told there were no first-class air services to Geneva, I agreed that they should travel like the rest of us in economy class. As it happened a Swissair flight was more conveniently timed than any with BA, so they were booked economy class on that one, only to discover when they boarded the aircraft that not only did it have a first-class section, but the entire ITV delegation were travelling in it. Their tempers were not improved when Cyril Bennett, the Director of Programmes for LWT, sent a note back saying, 'Up front and loving it!' and, grinning hugely, kindly brought them the leftovers of his first-class meal.

The BBC was on an economy drive at the time, so I had no qualms about the bookings, but I probably went too far when I ruled that for the press dinner that evening the reporters present should pay for their meal – though the BBC would provide the wine. Ronnie Corbett, still slightly put out by the travel arrangements, thought this was a rotten idea; the BBC as the hosts should have paid for the whole thing. He was and is a great mate of mine but he has a fiery temper and we had a robust exchange of views. In retrospect I think he was right. By the time we walked back together to the hotel from the restaurant along the lake we were friends again, and *The Picnic* won the Bronze Rose, so it turned out reasonably well in the end.

Plenty was happening on the family front. By now my two elder daughters were doing their own thing. Jane had served an apprenticeship at Richmond Theatre and became an assistant stage manager for Southern TV and ATV. I was very anxious that she should train as a producer but she enjoyed her work on the studio floor and wasn't keen to disappear behind the glass in the control-room. She met and married a designer at ATV, Ken Wheatley, and had two sons: Tom, who is trying his hand with a pop group, and Leo, who in 1989 as a child actor co-starred, (as he likes to put it) with Charlton Heston in the film *The Little Kidnappers*. He was seven years old at the time and was heard to say to his co-star after a take, 'That was good for me, Chuck. How about you?' Nothing much has happened to him since, except school, but the world hasn't heard the last of him by any means. Jane's marriage broke up, she faced the tough challenges of being a single mum, became a Buddhist and through a shared faith met a writer, Billy Hamon, whom she married in 1996.

Kate had gone to work for the agents Plunkett Green. She was doing very well there but got itchy feet and asked me if I would help her to get to Australia. I didn't think for one moment she'd go through with it, but she did and I found myself at London airport seeing her off. I gave her the name of the BBC representative in Australia, Basil Sands. He met her at the airport and looked after her until she got herself sorted out. Eventually she met a fellow and toured around Australia and New Zealand. We wrote to each other regularly, but when I got through to her on the phone and heard her newly acquired

Australian accent I nearly had a fit. 'Dad you don't half sound English!' was her opening statement. 'I am English,' I replied, 'and I'll thank you to remember that you are too.' Some time later I was able to call in and see her in Australia on my way out to stay with Dave Allen in Hong Kong. The next time I spoke to her on the phone was to answer a call in the middle of the night from her chap, asking me if he could have her hand in marriage. In the end she decided she wasn't ready to settle down. Recently she married Matthew, a Brentford supporter, so he is nearly family.

Lisa (Lulu) was the daughter closest to my mother. They would talk for hours like two washerwomen. After leaving school she went to secretarial college and then got a job with Brent Walker, where she met Chris who is now her husband. They have four sons – Rory, Harry, Ben and Sam – each two years apart in age and a wonderful handful.

In the 1976 New Year Honours List I was made an OBE, and the investiture was set for 17 February. I was also due to be sworn in as a magistrate at Richmond around the same time, but at the end of January I passed blood in my water a couple of times and was advised to have an exploratory operation. I opted to get the two ceremonies over first and then go into King Edward VII Hospital to allow the surgeons to do their worst.

I was invited to become a JP as a result of a conversation with Frank Cassells, at that time a county-court judge. As chairman of the selection panel for JPs at Richmond, he asked if I was interested in becoming a magistrate. I said I was far too busy. He was not impressed and said that people like me, who were used to making decisions, had a duty to serve the public in this way, so I signed up.

After the excitement and pride of the investiture, I pitched up at the King Edward VII Hospital. The sister in charge of the ward settled me in and on leaving the room said, 'I understand you're in the entertainment business?' Cowed, I nodded, whereupon she snapped, 'Please inform your friends that this is a hospital not a hotel.' And swept out. I immediately christened her 'HMS Warspite'. My first visitor arrived at about seven o'clock and it was my old mate Johnny Johnston, who'd come armed with a magnum of champagne. I was just warning him about the resident battleship when the door opened and in she sailed. Johnny immediately tried to hide the bottle under his coat, but the shaking caused it to explode, the cork flew off, and in seconds Johnny was standing in a puddle of vintage champagne. 'I'll wipe it up!' he cried, terrified, pulling out his handkerchief. For an instant we were all frozen in time, then the sister burst out laughing. 'We don't expect you to wipe it up, we just don't want you to cover the floor with it,' she said. We got on like a house on fire after that, but I still called her Warspite!

The next morning I had the operation, which went well, though when I woke up I found a catheter in place, which when a few hours later I was able to guffaw caused me agony, so much so that I put up a notice – 'Please don't make me laugh' – which was no formality when I was being visited by some of the greatest wits in the business. I ran a competition between the nurses for the privilege of removing my catheter. The loser got the job.

EIGHT

By 1976 I had worked in BBC TV's Light Entertainment department for twenty years, and run it either as head or assistant head for fifteen. I was generally happy, though I'd been around so long that the same problems kept recurring year after year so I rarely felt the excitement of fresh challenges – I was beginning to get stale. I'd not been without offers to join the opposition and move over to ITV. In 1973 a major ITV company had offered me the job of Director of Programmes. I needed little encouragement to turn the job down because I didn't want to leave London.

Then in 1976 I received another phone call, this time from Howard Thomas who ran Thames Television. Over lunch he offered me the post of Director of Programmes at Thames with an understanding that I would become Managing Director after two years. Making the decision about this job was a bit more difficult. At that time, being in the public sector, the BBC was suffering a pay-freeze while ITV could pay whatever level of salaries it chose. This was a prime job in London with a television company highly respected for its entertainment programmes, and they were prepared to double my BBC salary. I really didn't want to go, because in truth I've never really worried about earning large amounts of money, but I was forty-eight years old and a little more financial security in my dotage would have been welcome.

I discussed the offer with Alasdair Milne who had just replaced David Attenborough as Director of Programmes, Television. He could do nothing about my salary but came up with an elegant arrangement that bolstered my pension. In any case, the wage-freeze was finally lifted and, though the BBC couldn't match ITV executive salaries, I got the kind of increase that was enough to hold me in a job I loved doing anyway.

A few months after I'd decided to stay at the BBC, I was at the Royal Albert Hall for a BAFTA awards ceremony when Jeremy Isaacs came over to thank me for turning down the Thames job. He'd been appointed in my place and was very happy. In truth, the food at BAFTA was so awful that I had compensated by drinking too much and when I stood up to greet him, I fell over. He didn't exactly smell my breath, but he must have thought Thames had had a lucky escape!

What turned out to be the last booking I made as Head of Light Entertainment followed lunch with an agent, Cyril Berlin, for whom I had a great deal of respect. The bane of an agent's life is an important client who is unhappy, and Cyril had on his books Des O'Connor, who had been doing well on ITV but for various reasons had not had his contract renewed. Cyril asked if I had any ideas, and I described a format I'd seen in America which might suit Des. It was a combination of a chat and variety show. Des would interview his guests and then introduce their act. If they were comedians they would share a settee with Des using him as an audience, while singers and dancers performed on the stage. Apart from anything else, it was an excellent vehicle for introducing new talent. Des was a most encouraging host and his warmth would help newcomers to get over their first-appearance nerves.

Des liked the format but bucked at the idea of the show going out on BBC2, still very much a minority channel. I pointed out that both Vera Lynn and Morecambe and Wise made regular appearances on BBC2, and that if the show went well a repeat on BBC1 was a real possibility. Des finally agreed and ever since has stuck to a formula that served him well on both BBC2 and BBC1 and now flourishes on ITV.

As it turned out, before 1977 was over any danger of my becoming stale vanished. It was all-change at the Beeb. There was to be a new Director-General, and as a consequence a re-shuffle. Having followed Hugh Wheldon as Managing Director of Television, Ian Trethowan was appointed DG and Alasdair

Milne took over his job. Bryan Cowgill moved up to become Director of News and Current Affairs, so the job of Controller of BBC1 was vacant. Alasdair asked me if I'd like to do it and I almost bit his hand off accepting it. I was just sorry that Dad wouldn't be there to see me become part of the BBC's senior-management team. He was always a little in awe of the BBC's top brass. I suspect it had something to do with his working-class upbringing. In fact, socially, Dad had a circle of friends that included royalty, members of the aristocracy and the wealthiest in the land, but in his own mind he was still a Cockney band-leader. So he would have been very proud of me *and* he was calculating enough to expect that having a son in a position to control BBC1's schedules wouldn't do his career any harm. We might have had some differences on that issue but alas, he wasn't around for me to fight with.

I left Light Entertainment in style. It was the Queen's Jubilee year so we decided to mount a special Royal Variety Show combining both circus and variety acts in Billy Smart's big top on The Meadows outside Windsor. During the week prior to the show I drove down to Windsor to see how things were going. I met Billy Smart Junior, and we wandered along to see the elephant Burma. She was a lovely but very jealous animal who had attached herself to Billy; he had to be careful he didn't show too much affection to any other females in the show – animal *or* human. We made a big fuss of her in her trailer and then toured the rest of the set-up.

The following day I went back to the circus and popped into Burma's trailer to say hello. I was stroking her ears when she suddenly leaned to one side and pinned me to the side of the trailer. For the first minute or two I wasn't too worried, but after a good ten minutes of fruitless cajoling I started fearing what would happen if she leaned a bit harder. I could only see one of her eyes and she never took it off me. Then I had a brainwave: looking towards the big top I shouted, 'Hi, Billy!' She immediately straightened up and turned her head in the direction from which she expected Billy, her favourite man, to appear. One frantic leap and I was free. Later Billy told me

Burma tended to lean on people who visited her when she was feeling lonely – 'But only if she likes you,' he assured me. That made me feel much better. What was being compressed into a block of corned beef compared to her affection?

The idea was that Burma would do a trick with Ronnie Corbett. A man would come into the ring leading a dog, lie down and let the dog jump over him. Ronnie the good sport would then also lie down, and instead of a dog Burma would gallop towards him. As often happens, the rehearsal went far better than the actual show, when the sight of Ronnie's face as two tons of elephant thundered towards him was a kaleidoscope of emotions, desperate jollity giving way to apprehension and then abject fear. Billy had assured him that never, ever would an elephant step on a prone human being, so why Ronnie should have been worried I can't imagine.

The show went well, but as usual we overran. There were a large number of six- to eight-minute acts performed by big stars giving their services free, most of whom were accustomed to being top of the bill where split-second timing is immaterial – if they were on a roll they'd go on for ever. But even a couple of minutes overrun here and there mounts up. At the interval I had to present to Prince Philip the artists who had already appeared. 'Overrunning again, I see,' he commented tartly. However, when I met the Queen at the end of the show she said, 'Don't take any notice of Philip. I loved every minute.'

So with royal approval ringing in my ears I moved from the fourth floor of Television Centre where Light Entertainment had its offices to the sixth floor where the top brass and the controllers presided. It was a big wrench. The group saw me off with a party and, looking round the room, I knew I would miss the camaraderie of the staff whom I had supervised for so long. In the room were senior producers, by then household names, whose careers I had helped to nurture from the day they first set foot in the BBC; that was one of the most rewarding parts of the job.

The job of Controller of BBC Television's main channel has been described as the most strategic post in the corporation.

One of my successors in the post, Michael Grade, rated it as more important than that of Managing Director or even Director-General because ultimately what viewers see on BBC Television either justifies the licence fee or makes them angry about being forced to pay it – and without the licence fee the entire BBC goes under. BBC Radio is very important to a considerable number of people, but few would be prepared to pay a licence fee just to receive radio programmes, however good. And while BBC2 offers high-quality minority pro-grammes, it is BBC1 which tackles the main opposition, ITV, head on; and how the BBC fares in this battle for ratings influences MPs both when they set the level of the licence fee and when, every few years, they vote on whether to renew the BBC's Charter. In my time, the magic figure was forty per cent – if the BBC's share of television audiences fell below that figure, alarm bells rang on the third floor of Broadcasting House and hands were wrung at the prospect of BBC's funding under the abolishment of the licence fee.

As Head of Light Entertainment I managed a large staff, whereas when I became Controller of BBC1 there was only my PA, Queenie, a couple of planners who did the detailed work on the schedules and a lovely lady, Eileen Philips, who looked after the finances – a tiny team in an organisation bursting with large empires. Paul Fox, who was Controller of BBC1 for six years, called it the loneliest job in the Corporation. But money is power, and a controller has loads and loads of it. When I did the job, I had something like £300 million a year to spend on buying in or financing programmes, and I could decide when those programmes would be transmitted – daytime or evening, in prime-time or on the outer fringes of popular viewing, late afternoon or late at night.

In the end, the key skill a channel controller must have or develop is programme judgement. Almost all channel con-trollers have previously been heads of output departments and are therefore experts in a single field – say, drama or sport, or, as in my case, light entertainment – but they must quickly develop an eye and an ear for programme quality right across

171

the board. Every year at what is called an offers meeting, a controller's office becomes a kind of Turkish market as all the heads of department appear to sell their wares, the programmes they wish to make in the coming year. Many of the programmes they offer will already be part of the schedules – *EastEnders* or *Match of the Day* or *Songs of Praise* – and the issues for discussion are whether the shows are still up to scratch and what budget changes have to be made. But roughly one third of the programmes on BBC1 will be new offerings, and this is where a controller must try to anticipate the viewing public's taste.

Having given the go-ahead for a new programme, a controller must then decide where to place it in the schedules – a brilliant show can die the death if it goes out at the wrong time or on the wrong day or against the wrong opposition on ITV. So we had to keep a wary eye on ITV's schedules too and try to read the minds of the executives who drew them up. Though we were in fierce competition, there was a point at which both sides recognised that going head to head with our strongest pro-grammes would be madness unless there was no alternative – hence when the BBC launched *EastEnders*, it was not placed opposite its great rival, *Coronation Street*. It wouldn't have mattered which of the two soap operas had won the ratings battle: the viewing public had to be the losers because many people might wish to watch both.

These were the sort of skills I had to pick up as quickly as possible, and I was helped by the BBC's audience-research department which monitored the viewers' actual choices in great statistical detail. Ultimately, though, public taste is so unpredictable that reading a chicken's entrails is probably as helpful as a mountain of statistics when trying to decide what will interest viewers in a year's time.

At least I had one hereditary advantage, an instinct nurtured from watching my father put together countless shows – picking the right numbers and getting them in the right order. Bradford on a wet Monday evening in winter is a universe away from the London Palladium at the height of the tourist season. The difference between Dad's choices as a band-leader and mine as a BBC controller was quite simply the degree of risk. If I got into the habit of scheduling badly, in its highly civilised way the BBC would probably give me a fancy title, more money and move me out of the way. However, if Dad had lost his rapport with theatre audiences, he'd have been landed with huge debts and twenty out-of-work musicians. So I had more awareness than most BBC executives about what was at stake in getting and hanging onto the loyalty of the viewing public.

There are television executives whose overriding aim seems to be to produce programmes that will earn the approval of their fellow producers within the industry, and if the viewers aren't impressed enough to watch then that's just too bad. I am and always have been an unashamed populist – how could I be anything else? I am my father's son; I respect minority audiences and believe their interests must be met, but I know that the BBC can only deserve a licence fee if it offers output that attracts the general public.

When a controller takes over a major television channel, he inherits a schedule for which programmes are already in the process of being made, so for the first eighteen months he cannot put his own distinctive stamp on the output. He gets the credit for good programmes he didn't commission and the blame for bad ones he never chose. In fairness to Bryan Cowgill, I inherited a schedule full of good things. The Head of the Drama Group, Shaun Sutton, had come up with a new series called *All Creatures Great and Small* based on the James Herriot books about the life and work of a vet in rural Yorkshire, and a wartime drama, *Secret Army*, which told true stories of airmen shot down during the war and the heroic efforts of the French Resistance to get them back to England.

David Croft used a parody of this plot-line in 1984 and produced the comedy *'Allo, 'Allo*. Set in a café used by the Resistance as the starting-point of an escape route for a hapless couple of British RAF types, it eventually became a comedy classic. When it was first shown, however, there were rumblings among the BBC governors and some members of the public who thought that portraying Gestapo members as figures of fun

and German officers in an affectionate light belittled the sufferings of the French during the Occupation. By then I had moved on and it fell to my successor, Alan Hart, to defend the series, which he did robustly. I would have done the same. Agreed, *'Allo, 'Allo* skirted the very boundaries of taste, but because of the brilliance of the writing and its sharply drawn bizarre characters it created a fantasy world that no viewers could mistake for real history.

Almost coinciding with my arrival, a hard-hitting drama series was launched. *Target* starred Patrick Mower as a macho detective in a regional police force and the series was intended to compete with ITV's *The Professionals*. As a concept it was gripping, but I thought there was too much violence in it so I refused to fund a second series. We replaced it with *Shoestring*, which featured Trevor Eve as a private detective who ran a phone-in programme on a local radio station. It become very popular, winning enormous viewing figures on a Sunday night. The problem was that we failed to sign Trevor Eve for more than one series and as a result we lost him, so *Shoestring* died an untimely death.

Jack Rosenthal's play *Spend, Spend, Spend*, which traced the disastrous life of Viv Nicholson who won £150,000 on the football pools (worth several million pounds in today's money), received the BAFTA award for best play in 1977. This was closely followed by *Pennies from Heaven*, Dennis Potter's play about a randy song-plugger who travelled around selling sheet-music. Naturally, both the subject and the hero rang a bell with me, given my early career! The audience's reaction to it was mixed. There were those who called it sheer filth, obnoxious and bordering on pornography, but a faithful audience of more than ten million viewers watched all six parts of it. It did the career of Bob Hoskins, who played the song-plugger, no harm at all – nor those of Cheryl Campbell and Gemma Craven.

The music was all from the thirties and featured the talents of Al Bowlly and Harry Roy and his band but, interestingly, Dennis didn't use any of my Dad's records. The story goes that he was nervous I might ban the play, so he'd taken out insurance: if I refused to transmit it, he could claim I had acted out of pique because none of my Dad's records had been chosen. As it happens Dad had a puritanical streak, and were he alive he would have objected most strongly if his music had been included in a play he thought obscene.

Dennis Potter's fears about my censorious tendencies were fuelled by the fact that I had already acted to ban one play, *Scum*, from BBC1. Set in a borstal, it had scenes of what to me were sickening violence, culminating in an assault where one of the inmates is beaten to a pulp with a makeshift weapon made by putting billiard balls in a sock. I felt that this scene was not just brutal, but that it would brutalise those who watched it. I called the production team into my office and explained my decision and the reasons behind it. The producer, Margaret Mattheson, argued her case with passion and great eloquence but to no avail. I have since wondered whether my decision not to show *Scum* was influenced by the fact that I was a magistrate and often had to hear cases of assault. Studying defendants in the dock, I used to wonder what had possessed them to behave so appallingly, and I had an uneasy niggle at the back of my mind that the television industry to which I had given my life might in some way be implicated. Anyway, *Scum* was made into an even more violent feature film and in a more permissive climate got shown on television. But I'm unrepentant.

My first Christmas as Controller of BBC1 was pretty hectic. Getting into shape a two-week schedule for the holiday period, even when the main ingredients had already been com-missioned by my predecessor, was hard work. It was in the 1970s a hallowed tradition in the broadcasting industry that all special occasions should be targeted by the trade unions for industrial action. As a result, we had to construct an extra schedule in case a strike took place. Though I have had my differences with Mrs Thatcher, there is no doubt that her trade-union legislation banning the closed shop and secondary picketing and introducing pre-strike ballots saved both the BBC and ITV from a union stranglehold on employment policy which was slowly throttling the industry to death. But when I became Controller of BBC1 Mrs Thatcher was still Leader of the Opposition and the sledgehammer impact of Thatcherism had not yet been felt, so we endured union-inspired misery.

I went along to the Light Entertainment Christmas party that year for the first time as a guest, and found myself chatting to Eric Morecambe and his wife, Joan. We'd had a few drinks and were larking about when Eric suddenly turned serious on me and asked if I'd heard that Thames Television had made him and Ernie a very generous offer to move channels. I said that I hadn't. When he mentioned the money involved, I assured him that the BBC would match it. We shook hands on it and went back to partying. I didn't bother my head about the matter any further over Christmas because I'd known Eric and Ernie for a very long time and felt that there was mutual trust between us. Admittedly, Ernie Wise was a close friend of Philip Jones, the Head of Entertainment at Thames Television, but I was sure Eric would talk his partner into staying with us.

After the Christmas break I went off to America to view and buy programmes. Hollywood was in the throes of an epidemic of Asian flu, and almost as soon as the plane landed I went down with it. I was lying in bed coughing and shivering when the phone rang. It was Queenie to tell me she had some bad news. 'Eric and Ernie have gone,' she said. I didn't take it in at first. 'Gone where?' I asked, having forgotten my conversation with Eric at the Christmas party. Then I remembered and told her I would phone her back. I put in a call to Eric and reached his wife, who said that he'd popped out for a moment and she'd get him to call me back. When the phone rang again, however, it was Billy Marsh, Eric and Ernie's agent. I asked him whether they had actually signed on the dotted line with Thames or if he was open to negotiation. He confirmed that the contract had been signed. There was nothing more to say.

I have lost many valued performers to the opposition in the course of my career; it is an occupational hazard in a high-profile, big-money business, but this was different. It felt more like a divorce than the end of a working partnership. In truth I felt badly done by. Over the years, as Head of Light Entertainment I had delivered to the Controller of BBC1 some of the best comedy seen on the BBC, pre-eminent among which was *The Morecambe and Wise Show*. Now I had barely taken up the job myself before they flew the coop. It couldn't have been a question of cash – I'd promised Eric I would match Thames pound for pound. So what was it? The only advantage Thames could offer them was the possibility of making feature films through its subsidiary, Euston Films. In one of the interviews that followed the news Morecambe and Wise were leaving the BBC, Eric was quoted as saying that when Bill Cotton left Light Entertainment to become Controller, he had been looking after himself and they were just doing the same. Of course, there was some truth in that. Show business is a tough world; if you don't look after yourself no one else will.

In a press statement, Ernie Wise said, 'To be leaving Bill Cotton is a matter of personal regret, but leaving the Corporation as such is a simple professional decision. Thames was offering a better deal so we accepted it.' But Eric and Ernie had to quit the BBC without their brilliant writer, Eddie Braben. He decided to stay on and signed another contract with us because he felt the BBC had been very good to him. He described working for the BBC as cosy, like wearing a well-worn cardigan, and felt it was an organisation that treated writers with respect, not just as accessories to the stars who spoke their lines. Eddie didn't want to work at Thames, and that was that, so Eric and Ernie would have to go through all the old traumas of finding writers who could exploit their very individualistic comic genius. Obviously, I am biased, but I don't believe they ever did quite recapture their great days in the BBC. Some critics described the Thames programmes as uninspired and vaguely cynical imitations of the original BBC *Morecambe and Wise Show*. I got no satisfaction from seeing them, as I believe, squandering their talent. The departure of Morecambe and Wise from the BBC cast a black cloud over my early days as Controller. I was very, very sad about it.

I hadn't been running BBC1 long before Brian Wenham

became Controller of BBC2, the minority channel. He had been editor of *Panorama* and Head of Current Affairs so he was a highly political animal. He was generally thought to be one of the most able figures in British broadcasting and his name was often mooted as a future DG. Because he had operated from Lime Grove where Current Affairs was based, I hadn't really come across him much at the Television Centre, but we were soon as thick as thieves. He had a deadpan wit and the ability to sum up complex political issues in devastating one-liners. He was brilliant, but he wasn't streetwise. He was generally suspected by some other BBC executives of being a conspirator, always plotting coups to advance his career. I never believed that. He just enjoyed the academic exercise of playing power games. Brian made an impact on the Corporation at many points but will probably always be associated with the development of snooker as a major television sport on BBC2. He played himself and knew a lot about the game, and he brilliantly exploited the flexibility of the BBC2 schedules to ensure that enthusiasts, of whom there were soon a growing number, could stay with protracted games until the very end without the channel having to break off and go to the next scheduled programme. As a result, in the 1980s snooker enjoyed some of the highest viewing figures ever recorded on BBC2.

Soon after Brian arrived, I put to him a proposition which would enable me to develop a new show. Sitting across my evening schedule was *24 Hours*, a regular current-affairs programme that went out five times a week. It was an important element in our overall output but it bisected the evening in such a way that I couldn't offer evening entertainment of a more relaxed kind suitable to the late hour. I wanted to transmit a five-nights-a-week chat show hosted by Michael Parkinson, along the lines of *The Jack Paar Show* on NBC in America. The Managing Director of Television and the Director-General thought my plan an experiment worth trying so, Brian being agreeable, it needed only the BBC governors to rubber-stamp the proposal and we were away.

Parky liked the idea so I booked him. Then I looked around for a producer. Derek Amoore had been a member of the *Tonight* team back in the sixties and had worked his way up the system to become Head of Television News. He was very clever but not always very wise. He drank a lot – at one party drank so much he was photographed blotto. The picture found its way back to the BBC and Derek was removed from Television News. In spite of his little weakness, I thought highly of him professionally and it seemed to me he had just that combination of programme flair and current affairs knowledge to give *The Parkinson Show* both pizazz and seriousness of purpose. Derek was kicking his heels doing nothing very much so he was delighted to be given something challenging to tackle.

I assumed the Director-General in supporting my plans had taken soundings with the governors, so I arrived at the board meeting full of confidence. I was rocked back on my heels when the vice-chairman, Mark Bonham-Carter, launched a full-scale attack on the whole idea. Though the term was not in common currency at the time, he thought that my proposal would dumb-down BBC1, removing from the nightly schedule a serious programme and replacing it with 'entertainment' – that dreaded concept some of the governors felt trivialised the output on a channel which ought to dedicate itself to esoteric programmes which they and their friends approved of and no one else watched. My choice of Derek Amoore to be executive producer added insult to injury in the eyes of the governors. They turned down the proposal flat. I was beside myself with fury and ended up in a worse position than I was before the idea was put to them, because the DG insisted that the move of the nightly current-affairs show to BBC2 should go ahead – I now had five late-night holes in my schedule I had to fill.

However, a few months before we moved *24 Hours* to BBC2, Robin Day had come to see me, complaining that he was finding it hard to get current-affairs editors and producers to employ him. I knew that he could be difficult to handle, but he was an undisputed star in the firmament of current affairs so I had a word with John Gau, who was then Head of Current

Affairs. He in turn talked to some of his producers, and one, Barbara Maxwell, came up with the idea of adapting the wide-ranging format of the radio show *Any Questions* for television with the title *Question Time*. It proved to be an ideal platform for Robin who, with his larger than life personality, had no difficulty in keeping heavyweights from the various political parties and obstreperous members of the audience in order. We ran it on Thursdays to fit in with the parliamentary week. I also went ahead with a week-night *Parkinson* on Wednesdays and a weekend version on Saturdays. Parky had been very dis-appointed at the turn of events in the governors' meeting, but he took it very well and tore up the original contract which had guaranteed him payment for five shows a week.

In those first few months as Controller, I was on a steep learning-curve. I came up against some very powerful interest-groups who kept an eagle eye open to see that their pet pro-grammes were given fair treatment. Religion had formidable champions, chief among whom was the Central Religious Advisory Committee on which sat representatives of most of the main Christian churches. Their particular concern was a religious documentary series called *Everyman*. My predecessor Bryan Cowgill had promised CRAC that these documentaries would be transmitted on Sundays during prime-time, at or before ten-thirty p.m. Nobody told me about this agreement so I went along merrily putting out *Everyman* after our main offering of the evening, which was of variable length and might be a film or play that usually ended nearer eleven p.m. than ten-thirty.

I knew I was in trouble when I had an invitation from the chairman of CRAC, the Bishop of St Albans (later to be Archbishop of Canterbury), Robert Runcie, to hear the com-mittee's views about religious programmes on BBC1. At the meeting, Bob introduced me and to my surprise explained to the committee that in his youth he had spent many hours dancing and listening to the music of the Billy Cotton Band, and he considered it quite a privilege to meet the great man's son. Under these circumstances, he trusted the committee would treat me gently. Good old Dad had come to my assistance again, this time from the other side of the grave, I was able to assure CRAC that I hadn't knowingly reneged on the agreement Bryan Cowgill had made and promised to put *Everyman* out as early as possible. Bob and I got on like a house on fire and we've been friends ever since.

The Royal Family is another powerful lobby. Soon after I became Controller of BBC1, I had a phone call from Buckingham Palace. Michael O'Shea, then the Queen's press secretary, was making a polite enquiry about whether or not we intended to go ahead with a drama series called *Blood Royal* about the kidnapping of a ten-year-old earl who was next in line to the throne. When I confirmed that we had such a series on the stocks, he expressed the sovereign's anxiety that the drama might encourage copycat action and put the younger members of the royal family in danger. So after some delicate negotiations with the producer and writer, the script was changed, the ten-year-old kidnap-victim became the son of a UN official and the series title became *Blood Money*. The writer Arden Linch understandably felt particularly aggrieved, because his book of the series, due to be released to coincide with the drama's transmission, had to be pulped. Given the present climate of mild scepticism about the monarchy, I wonder whether a present-day controller would feel he or she had to make such drastic changes.

I soon discovered how accountable the Controller of BBC1 is to all kinds of people, and in particular to the public. In a very special sense it is *their* channel, so I realised the importance of taking every opportunity to meet viewers at the public meetings the BBC organised around the country. These meetings were held in public halls, usually chaired by well-known television personalities such as Sue Lawley, Esther Rantzen or Terry Wogan to attract the crowds and advertised under the title *This is Your BBC*. A team of BBC executives representing a wide cross-section of the BBC's output on radio and television would put themselves in the firing-line and field a wide array of questions from the audience. Facing an audience in public didn't bother me in the least. This was the kind of occasion where my show business background was a great advantage to me.

Many of the questions were totally predictable. There was sure to be one about clashes between the TV coverage of different sports when there was a Test match or a golf championship being played that ran for a number of days. Why *didn't* we stay with the cricket or golf instead of breaking away to cover horse racing? Why *did* we stay with the cricket or golf and miss the three o'clock race at Haydock Park? Why were there no humanists or Buddhists on *Thought for the Day*? Why were the news bulletins bursting with stories of violence, disaster and death? What about some good news for a change? Then there was always at least one radio buff in the audience who got up and asked some fearfully technical question about wavelengths or transmitters. Then our engineering colleague who'd been dozing gently would spring up with a fanatical light in his eye and talk a totally foreign language for five minutes.

One of the interesting things we discovered through these meetings was just how unreliable the viewer's memory is about what he or she has seen. We would be attacked vehemently about poor taste or bad language in some drama or comedy which turned out to have been transmitted not by the BBC but by ITV. Or on more than one occasion a viewer expressed disgust or indignation at something he had seen or heard in a programme which proved not to have been there at all. I have sometimes played back a video and studied it frame by frame to make sure that my denial of an alleged enormity was correct. Sure enough, the viewer's imagination had supplied images that the programme's maker had left out.

By listening to viewers formally in public meetings and through hundreds of telephone calls and letters expressing strong opinions about programmes, I was serving my time in one of the black arts of television: reading the public's mind, trying to decide what will interest them in a couple of years. The staple ingredients of the television schedule didn't vary much from year to year, but it was when an output head confronted me with an exciting and risky programme idea which would demand big money and huge resources that I earned my salary – either by taking a chance or playing it safe. Either way there were no medals in it for me. If I played it safe, then the schedules were dismissed by the critics as boring and predictable; if I took a chance and it worked, then a new star shone in the firmament of television and the director, presenter and production team paraded at BAFTA to receive well-deserved awards.

Of all the programmes for which I was responsible as the Controller of BBC1, none gave me greater satisfaction than *Children in Need*. It had been running as an in-house charity for a number of years, and through the usual method of a broadcast appeal on Radio 4 had made a decent if not spectacular amount of money. But I noticed that it did nothing like as well as the television appeal organised by *Blue Peter* for Cambodia in 1979. Biddy Baxter, the founder of *Blue Peter*, had reacted to the awful pictures of refugee children starving in the Far Eastern country by organising a bring-and-buy sale on *Blue Peter* which by appealing to the imagination of children all over the country raised an astonishing three and three quarter million pounds.

I was delighted with this result but felt uneasy that our efforts on behalf of needy children in this country did so badly in comparison. I took a look at what was happening in other television systems. Both America and Australia had developed the telethon, a form of phone-in charity performance using big stars, popular comedians and well-known pop groups to attract huge audiences who were then persuaded to phone in financial pledges. Desmond Wilcox, Head of Television Features, had also been watching the rise of the telethon in the United States, and at a routine meeting raised with me the possibility of our trying the same thing in aid of Children in Need.

I had first to negotiate the proposal through the BBC Appeals Committee, a body set up almost as soon as the Corporation came into being to vet all the applications from charitable bodies

183

who wished to use the tremendous power of the airwaves to raise money. What we proposed was certainly an innovation. Broadcast appeals had traditionally been five-minute talks by well-known personalities describing the work of some worthwhile cause, whereas we intended to set aside a good part of a full evening's viewing on BBC1 for a showbiz spectacular. This was a radical change of scale and approach, but in the end the idea was approved.

Desmond and his producer, Mark Paterson, recruited a strong team of presenters which included his wife, Esther Rantzen, Terry Wogan and Sue Lawley, and the thing started to take shape. We were in the final planning stages when Thames Television stole a march on us and launched a telethon aimed at the London area. They deserve credit for being first in the field but, as is often the case, we benefited from their teething-troubles, especially the problems they had in actually getting their hands on the money promised over the telephone.

We decided to mount the show from the foyer of the Cunard Hotel in Hammersmith. On that night I was due to attend a dinner at my golf club and I felt I could not cry off because I had personally invited the guest speaker, the boxing commentator Harry Carpenter. During the day I called in at the Cunard Hotel several times to watch rehearsals for the show. Everything was going well, so I wished the production team good luck and said I'd be back that evening as soon as my dinner was over.

Harry Carpenter was in the middle of his speech when a waiter whispered in my ear that I was urgently required back at the Cunard Hotel. They had a problem – a nice one, but a problem all the same. Every one of the personalities who had been invited to perform had turned up and there were actually more of them than could be fitted into the running order. All producers of live programmes are terrified of having dead time on their hands so they usually book more artists than they strictly need – a disease which becomes most apparent in the studio discussion, where the panel always seems to have one too many on it so that no one gets the chance to develop his or her argument.

The foyer of the Cunard Hotel was bursting at the seams with the great and good of the showbiz world – pop stars, politicians, chat-show hosts, familiar faces from soap operas, sporting personalities – it was bedlam. I recall Sir Robin Day, who'd carefully prepared a much more light-hearted contribution than he usually made to current-affairs programmes, stumping around muttering words to the effect that he had brought his harp to the party and no one was asking him to play. Whereas I would usually have trod very delicately to placate such an array of television talent, I felt justified in pointing out that a little inconvenience was a small price for the affluent to pay to do something practical for the welfare of needy children. But we learned our lesson and in future years the running order was much more rigorously controlled so that guests were not kept hanging around. It is a tribute, though, to the innate generosity of the show business community that we had that problem at all on the first night.

That *Children in Need* evening raised in excess of a million pounds, which in 1980 was an enormous sum. It has gone from strength to strength in the years since and demonstrated the power of television as a socially constructive force. Live Aid, Band Aid and Comic Relief followed it. And one spin-off has been the growing sophistication of the phone-in system, which is now used in a number of mainstream programmes, such as *Crimewatch* and *Watchdog*.

The very first *Children in Need* programme and every one since was anchored and held together by Terry Wogan, and he does it so effortlessly that the sheer skill and nerve required to keep going for hours, switching from region to region and introducing one act after another is easily underestimated. And since timings cannot be exact, Terry has had to fill in countless longueurs with unscripted, witty chat – which requires both articulateness and intelligence.

It was around this time that I got to know Terry and his wife, Helen, quite well. He became one of my golfing partners and whenever we had a night off we indulged our common love of Chinese food. When things got fraught, one of us would ring the other and say, 'Let's go for a Chinese.' One evening after he and his wife had appeared in a show together, we had supper in a completely deserted Chinese restaurant. It can be very embarrassing, especially for celebrities like Terry, to eat in an empty restaurant, because your conversation echoes round the walls and every word is listened in to by the waiters standing about. We spent the evening whispering to one another.

It was the eve of my daughter Lulu's twenty-first birthday and she was in hospital at the time, so I asked if Terry would send her a birthday message on his Radio 2 breakfast show. I got up early the next morning and went along to the hospital carrying a radio, and insisted that Lulu listen to Radio 2. She was busy opening presents and didn't want to be bothered, but right on cue Terry delivered his message; Lulu dropped the gift she was examining when she suddenly heard her name issue from the radio. Everyone in the ward stared at her, astounded. Terry advised her, 'Don't let your dad take you to supper when you're better – you'll end up in an empty Chinese restaurant, whispering.' Lulu was a celebrity in the ward from then on.

I celebrated my fiftieth birthday on 23 April 1978. With an exquisite sense of timing, my wife Ann served divorce papers on me. She later withdrew them and the marriage staggered on for some years with us living under the same roof but barely on speaking terms. My old friend Johnny Johnston had insisted on holding a family party on the day itself, which was a Sunday. We all tramped off to the Portman Hotel where we had a marvellous lunch accompanied by excellent jazz and lots of drink. It went on until about five p.m. and ended with Johnny at the piano playing and singing all the songs we had published in our partnership together. I couldn't credit that I'd reached fifty, but looking round the table at my children in their late twenties and my mother in her early eighties it was not to be denied.

Landmark birthdays apart, I hadn't much time for socialising. Much of my spare time away from the Television Centre was spent as a magistrate on the bench at Richmond. Crime and punishment, the police and prisons featured largely in television dramas and documentaries, but the harsh reality was brought home to me with a vengeance as my two colleagues and I heard case after case where a spell in prison was one of the options open to us when defendants were found guilty. When the selection panel interviewed me about becoming a magistrate, one of the questions they asked was whether I'd mind sending someone to prison. I made what I suppose was the standard response – not if a criminal deserved it – but the reality was rarely as clear-cut as that. Depriving someone of his or her liberty is one thing, committing them to the Dickensian conditions of our prisons quite another.

I remember spending one Saturday sitting on my own hearing applications for remands. There were meant to be two of us, but the other magistrate had not turned up. An Asian man came up in front of me accused of interfering with young girls. The police asked for a remand in custody while the defendant's solicitor wanted bail – apparently there was someone in court willing to put up the money. The accused was either very reserved or a little simple-minded; he said little and didn't seem to know what was happening to him, and there was the hint of a suggestion that the girls had led him on. He had no fixed address and no one seemed to know where he would spend the weekend if I gave him bail. I was in a quandary. If I gave him bail and he offended again I would never forgive myself; on the other hand, prisoners suspected of sex offences can have a very bad time in prison. I discussed the case with the clerk of the court and in the end took the cautious and, for me, safest way out. I remanded him in custody, but the case worried me all weekend.

The following week, one of our most distinguished documentary-makers, Rex Bloomstein, came to see me with a proposal that he should do a series on life in Strangeways prison. He had got a promise of co-operation from the Home Office and had worked out meticulously what he wanted to do. The traumatic encounter with the man accused of sex offences at Richmond court was very much in my mind as I told him to go ahead. He spent three months filming the series, interviewing extensively prisoners and warders.

One of the interviews he conducted sticks in my mind because I decided that we could not show it. Rex had talked to a prisoner who was serving eighteen months for incest. He explained that while he was in the army his wife had deserted him, leaving behind their ten-year-old daughter. He resigned from the army to look after her and they moved into a tiny flat which was all he could afford. It had a single bedroom and one bed which he and his daughter had to share. As the years wore on, their relationship became that of man and wife and they had a family. They felt deep love for each other, and try as he might he could feel no shame about what they had done. His only concern was how they would make ends meet when he was released and how much harassment they might get from the police and neighbours. He pleaded, 'We love each other, and that can't be wrong.' It was unbearably poignant.

The decision whether or not to show this interview ended up on my desk because though both the prisoner and his daughter had given Rex permission to use the footage, the man had since died of cancer, which changed everything for his daughter and partner. She had been happy for the interview to be transmitted while he was still alive, but now he had died she wanted him to rest in peace. We were within our legal rights to show the interview because we had a piece of paper with the man's signature on it authorising us to do so, but I had no doubt about what was the compassionate thing to do so we agreed not to use the footage. Whether or not Rex Bloomstein's brilliant *Strangeways* series did anything to improve conditions in our prisons I very much doubt, but it made me see my work as a magistrate in a new light.

The early eighties saw another golden age of comedy for the BBC – and I can boast unashamedly about the quality of the output because I had nothing directly to do with its production, though much of it originated from my old department and I'd had a hand in training most of those who did. *Only Fools and Horses* was an immensely inventive series including some of the funniest visual gags ever seen on television. David Croft, the producer and co-writer of *Dad's Army,* came up with *Hi De Hi,* which was based on the experience of his co-writer Jimmy Perry who had worked as a Butlins red-coat after the war. The series went down well everywhere except in the boardrooms of some leisure companies who had been trying to live down the rather seedy reputation of the holiday camps of the fifties.

Then there was the comedy that caught Margaret Thatcher's eye, *Yes, Minister.* It was commissioned by Brian Wenham for BBC2 but was repeated on BBC1 and became a cult success. It was written by Jonathan Lynn and (later Sir) Tony Jay, who had worked in the old Talks group under Grace Wyndham Goldie and there learned a lot about the relationship between the ministers and their civil-service advisors. When the series ended Paul Eddington (who played the minister) and Nigel Hawthorne (his permanent secretary) were both given the CBE by the Prime Minister, whereas Derek Fowlds, who had been the junior civil servant in the minister's office, got no gong – an example of real life aping fiction, no doubt.

Not all our dealings with Mrs Thatcher were quite so amicable. She had become Prime Minister when the Conservatives won the 1979 general election. The coverage of a general election is always a nightmare for broadcasting organisations because the laws governing political impartiality are so stringent. Each political party monitors every radio and television programme – whatever its subject – for the slightest hint of bias. We got through the 1979 election campaign without making any waves until the very last moment when, through a misunderstanding for which we were not responsible, we ended our election coverage just before Mrs Thatcher arrived at Ten Downing Street and made her impassioned speech appealing for national unity. The BBC governors held an enquiry about the premature termination of the election coverage and it turned out that someone in Mrs Thatcher's office had got her timetable wrong and passed it on to us.

Whatever the reason, it meant that we started out on the wrong foot with the new Prime Minister and things didn't get any better from then on.

Northern Ireland was the source of many of our conflicts with Mrs Thatcher's government. One of the most serious concerned a *Panorama* team whose editor, Roger Bolton, decided to do a programme investigating the IRA. After being given a tip-off, they found the village of Carrickmore in County Tyrone, Northern Ireland, where masked IRA gunmen had set up road-blocks and were stopping and questioning car drivers. The IRA were making the point that the army and RUC did not control the border areas and they could, whenever they chose, take them over. The *Panorama* team shot some film without consulting their senior management, which was a breach of the rules.

John Gau, the Head of Current Affairs, told me of the incident. I realised the potential gravity of the situation, but since the film had not been transmitted I felt it was an internal matter of BBC procedures rather than a national security crisis. We agreed upon a statement to be issued to the press should the story be leaked. The matter did become public but in such an explosive way that it was all over the papers before I could issue any press statement.

The Prime Minister was beside herself with fury and asked the Home Secretary, Willie Whitelaw, to phone the BBC chairman, Sir Michael Swann, to express the government's outrage. He demanded an explanation from me. 'What have you got to say, Bill? After all, the film went out on your channel.' I pointed out that the film had never been developed, let alone transmitted on any channel and but for a press leak nothing more would have been heard about the incident.

The governors ordered an internal inquiry, which was headed by the acting DG, Gerard Mansell. He concluded that there had been a breach of the BBC's rules regarding the advance referral of all Northern Ireland issues to the NI Controller, but exonerated the *Panorama* team of any collusion with the IRA. Roger Bolton was taken out of Current Affairs and moved to a job in the secretariat and John Gau, who was utterly blameless, got an official reprimand. Though this was just a note on his record, it was to tell against him some years later when he was a candidate for my job as Controller of BBC1. Mrs Thatcher made it clear that she thought the BBC was a rogue force which had to be tamed, so the stage was set for stormy relations with the government from then on.

We had no sooner extricated ourselves from that mess than we found ourselves on collision course with the government over coverage of the 1980 Olympic Games, which were to be held in Moscow. The Americans decided to boycott the Games in protest against the Russian invasion of Afghanistan. Mrs Thatcher declared her support in principle for the American stand, so what was the BBC to do? We had made a huge investment in staff and resources, some of which could not be recouped, and there was great country-wide interest in the performance of British athletes such as Sebastian Coe, Steve Ovett and Daley Thompson. The governors were equivocal: having felt the Thatcher lash over Carrickmore they had no desire to incur her wrath again; on the other hand, for the BBC to demonstrate lack of support for the British team and also deny the public the chance to see the world's greatest athletes in action was unthinkable. Even Mrs Thatcher had not gone so far as to forbid the British team from competing, and it would be absurd for the BBC to have to rely on footage shot by foreign news agencies.

Alan Hart, the Head of Sport, and myself worked out a scheme which was in effect a compromise. Instead of the usual saturation coverage on both channels we would show about half the events, and to avoid being accused of transmitting pro-Soviet propaganda we would not show the closing ceremony which was bound to include some nationalistic material. Alan Hart argued the case in detail in front of the governors who were greatly impressed by him. When he became a candidate for my job, his performance in handling the 1980 Olympics was to be decisive.

I confess to finding the political ramifications of a controller's job a digression from my main concern: to get high-quality programmes on the air. I found wearisome the hostility of government, the constant lobbying of politicians, who saw political bias in almost every programme we transmitted, and the growing antagonism of the governors. We seemed to stagger from one public relations disaster to the next. Our organisational complexity was designed to create chaos. News and Current Affairs were two competing empires with their own convoluted lines of control, often clashing, neither knowing what the other was doing. There was a real necessity for bringing rationality to the operation by creating an effective News and Current Affairs directorate, but it would be some years before we got round to that.

One of my wilder ideas for BBC1 did actually involve a dramatic extension of our news coverage. One contact I had made on my programme-buying trips to America was Ted Turner. He had inherited from his father a successful billboard business but fell in love with television. He bought a local station in Atlanta and by transmitting its output via satellite created the first non-terrestrial TV station in America. By law, local TV stations could only transmit to a restricted geographical area, but Ted found a loophole in the legislation which enabled him to define his station's area as the satellite's footprint – which gave him a vast market for his television commercials. He then went on to launch CNN, the first twenty-four-hour news service. In its early years it swallowed up all his profits, but gave him power and made him a major player on the American television scene.

Ted and I had a meal together in Los Angeles and I was fascinated by his sheer enthusiasm and foresight. Here was a television entrepreneur prepared to put his money where his mouth was. I got carried away by his passion and drive, and before the meal was over I began to see visions and dream dreams. He had enormous respect for the BBC, so we hatched a plan for BBC1 to transmit CNN's continuous bulletins throughout the night when our screens were dark. I was keen that BBC1 should become the first twenty-four-hour news channel in the UK, and I knew from my travels in the US that in every country there are insomniac news freaks who will watch bulletins whenever they are transmitted.

My idea soon died the death when I got back to the BBC. It was considered unthinkable by top management that the Corporation should hand over editorial control of news bulletins to an American operator, even in the dead of night. The News and Current Affairs departments united in fierce opposition to my plans; and they had powerful friends among the governors. Ironically, a decade or so later the BBC *did* launch a twenty-four-hour news channel at prohibitive cost, eating up more than £50 million a year that could have been spent on programmes. But in the 1980s I was David fighting Goliath without even a catapult, so I conceded gracefully.

By 1981 I had been Controller of BBC1 for four years and had thoroughly enjoyed myself. However, that year saw the retirement of Robin Scott, who was BBC TV's deputy MD. I was asked if I would take the job and effectively serve as Head of the Television Service so that Alasdair could prepare himself to take over as Director-General when Ian Trethowan retired a year later. I agreed to give it a go for one year – with reluctance. I was a programme man first and last and found administration irksome but, in common with all Alasdair's friends, I had a vested interest in him becoming a great DG, so I agreed to do what I could.

My immediate concern was to help Alasdair to find someone to succeed me as Controller of BBC1. The board of governors made it clear that they wished to make the final selection themselves. To put it bluntly, they didn't trust top management to make an appointment of which they could approve. I saw no reason for the board to be involved – their sole and supremely important role in BBC appointments ought to be the choice of the Director-General; otherwise they should leave well alone. But they had so little confidence in us that they insisted on being in on the selection process for every member of the senior-management team. They were determined to stamp out rebelliousness and what they detected as a pronounced anti-Thatcher streak in their managers which was liable to put the Corporation even more directly on collision course with the government.

The board of management's favoured candidate for my old job was John Gau, Head of Current Affairs. It would not be a safe appointment: John had got across the DG on a couple of occasions when defending controversial *Panorama* programmes, one about the security services and another concerning allegations that doctors were transplanting organs from patients who were not clinically dead. In spite of this, Ian Trethowan agreed with Alasdair and myself that Gau was the obvious choice for the job. He had handled himself brilliantly in the most politically exposed job in the BBC; he was a vastly experienced programme-maker and commanded great respect throughout the Corporation.

George Howard had taken over from Sir Michael Swann as chairman of the governors and was determined from the outset to show who was in charge at the BBC. He still smarted from what he saw as the humiliation the governors had endured at the hands of the government, thanks to the indiscipline and irresponsibility of the News and Current Affairs departments over the matter of Carrickmore. So when Ian Trethowan suggested to him that my old job should go to John Gau without a contest, he wouldn't hear of it and told the DG to set up an appointments board which he would chair. Things began to look ominous for John Gau.

When the appointments board met, two of the four governors on it were George Howard and Lucy Faulkner, Gau's sternest critics over Carrickmore. The DG tried to get them to settle for Gau but they insisted on a shortlist of two, Gau and Alan Hart, Head of Sport, appearing before the full board, where Alan Hart prevailed and did a thoroughly decent job.

This time it was the board of management whose authority had been damaged. If the combined forces of the DG and his designed successor, not to mention what influence I had, could not persuade the governors to accept their judgement about a senior staff post, then we were in trouble. Certainly John Gau thought so. Plainly disillusioned at what he thought was weak management and unsympathetic governors, he left the BBC shortly afterwards and became a most distinguished independent programme-producer.

I'd barely settled into my new job before the outside broadcast cameramen began threatening industrial action. They claimed that they should be paid more than studio cameramen because they had to work outside in all kinds of weather, sometimes in dangerous places and keeping much more irregular hours. The union backed them, but I'd not the slightest doubt that were we to agree to this differential the same union officials would be back in my office in six months' time demanding a pay-rise for studio cameramen and we'd be back to square one in an ever escalating pay-cycle. The union officials had chosen the timing of the demand cunningly. Ahead of us lay a summer of important outside broadcast events: the FA Cup final, Wimbledon, Henley and, most important of all, the wedding of Prince Charles and Lady Diana Spencer. Our outside broadcast facilities would be stretched beyond the limit.

As management we were in a poor position to bargain, and during an informal meeting of cameramen and crews in one of the studios I told everyone so. I suggested a consultation process to identify the particular problems of OB cameramen, a proposal greeted by an uneasy and slightly surly silence which was broken by a strident voice from the back: 'That's all very well, Bill, but what are you going to do now for ageing cameramen?' 'What do they want?' I replied. 'Makeup?' There was then a roar of laughter which broke the tension and restored some goodwill.

By far the most significant event during my brief spell as deputy MD was the Papal visit to Britain in 1982. It fell to me to discuss the broadcast coverage of his trip with the Roman Catholic hierarchy, and to my astonishment I found myself dealing with an old friend with whom I'd had many professional dealings, Mark McCormack, a leading sports agent on both sides of the Atlantic. Apparently he'd offered his services to the Vatican to handle negotiations about fees and venues and degree of coverage. He is one of the sharpest and toughest bargainers in the business. I knew we'd have to watch ourselves, so I proposed to ITV that since this was a state visit we ought to operate together. Apart from anything else, Mark was quite capable of playing one of us off against the other in order to get the Vatican a better deal.

Sure enough, when we met Vatican officials they let McCormack's men do the talking, and they stated categorically that they would retain the rights to any filming we did. The pictures would belong to them and if we wished to repeat them in any subsequent programmes we would have to pay a royalty for each showing. I found this quite unacceptable. Not even in

A cartoon in the BBC house magazine *Aerial* suggesting a plea for divine intervention on behalf of our doomed satellite project.

wartime had the BBC surrendered editorial control and possession of its material. I explained to the senior Vatican official present that ITV and ourselves wished to give the Pope the maximum possible coverage and that we would treat him like any other head of state, covering his arrival at the airport, his trip into London and any other journey he made on the public highway. That was our right as a public service broadcaster. We would also ensure that his historic visit to Canterbury Cathedral was televised, but whatever else he did, such as celebrating mass and paying courtesy visits, we would regard as private business and keep well clear of it. All footage shot would remain either the BBC's or ITV's property. The McCormack representatives wanted to argue, but the Monsignor took our point immediately. He simply asked if the Vatican might be allowed to use any film we shot, and we were happy to agree. I went off to a lunch given by the Variety Club of Great Britain at the Dorchester and found myself sitting next to the Monsignor, who proved to be delightful company.

The Pope's visit was in every sense a great success; its climax in Canterbury Cathedral, when he and the Archbishop of Canterbury embraced and the congregation of thousands rose to give them a standing ovation, was a heart-stopping moment. Wherever he went, Pope John Paul II exuded piety and spiritual power.

Later that year, together with Bryan Cowgill, the Managing Director of Thames Television representing ITV, I travelled to St Peter's in Rome to present the Pope with a videotape compilation of the highlights of his visit to Britain. He kindly blessed two statues of St Anthony which I had brought with me to give to Ann Celine and Mary Perpetua, the two nursing nuns who had cared for Boo with such devotion in her last days. While in Rome we were entertained to dinner by Bishop Agnellus Andrew, a Scot with a wry wit who had worked for the BBC as Roman Catholic assistant to the Head of Religious Broadcasting before being posted to the Vatican in charge of media relations – a sort of ecclesiastical spin-doctor. He took us to a posh restaurant and insisted on picking up the bill, which he said with a chuckle he could afford to do because he enjoyed an index-linked pension from the BBC.

In 1982 the Independent Broadcasting Authority announced that it intended to issue a licence for breakfast-time television and invited bids for the franchise. Realistically, the BBC had to make some response. Historically we had covered the news and current affairs agenda in the early morning by means of Radio 4's *Today* programme, and I wondered whether we might trump ITV by going bi-media and producing a breakfast-time show which would be transmitted simultaneously on Radio 4 and BBC1, then the public could hear it in bed, watch it over the breakfast table and pick it up again on the car radio. Ian Trethowan, who was in his final year as DG, liked the idea but the two managing directors of Television and Radio respectively, Alasdair Milne and Aubrey Singer, thought that the effort to overcome the age-old competitiveness between radio and television staff and to batter down the defensiveness of News and Current Affairs staff would be too disruptive. They agreed to a feasibility study being undertaken by Monica Sims, the Controller of Radio 4, but nothing came of it.

There was a headlong race between the BBC and ITV to see who could get a breakfast show on the air first, which the BBC just won. *Breakfast Time* was presented from a sofa by Frank Bough and Selina Scott and produced by Ron Neil.

But where was the money coming from? Because we relied on the licence fee, the BBC's income was fixed and we spent it all each year. If we were to transmit three more hours of television between six and nine in the morning we would need extra resources, and so not for the first time we turned to Michael Checkland, who was responsible for the allocation of money and resources within the television service. We had worked together for years; when I was Controller of BBC1 I relied on Michael to find me the money to keep vastly expensive shows like *The Morecambe and Wise Show* on the air. To pay for *Breakfast Time* he somehow managed to squeeze the cash out of the system. With breakfast television a reality and all-day television just round the corner, the funding of the television service would become an increasingly critical matter which made Mike Checkland a key player in top management.

It was therefore essential we should keep him in the BBC. As Mike's public profile grew, he began to receive offers from ITV companies, one of which in particular attracted him: the offer to become Managing Director of Central Television which was based in Birmingham, Mike's home city. When he told me about the offer I begged him to do nothing until I'd had time to talk to Alasdair Milne, who was on holiday in Scotland. I tracked the DG down by telephone and told him that he had to fend off the Central offer at all costs. I put it bluntly: 'We cannot do without him. Everybody has his price. You've got to find out what Mike's is and give it to him.'

So Mike became Director of Resources for BBC TV and a member of the board of management. Later he was to be knighted as Director-General of the BBC after a period of tumultuous conflict leading to the firing of Alasdair Milne. In 1982, however, all that lay ahead of me.

Ian Trethowan retired as DG and a process of selection began for his post and for the managing directorships of Radio and Television. I really wanted the television job. In fact, I'd privately decided that if I didn't get it I would resign from the BBC and try my luck elsewhere.

Just at this moment I had a phone call from an old mate, Brian Tesler, who had been the first producer of *The Billy Cotton Band Show* and was now Managing Director of London Weekend Television. Michael Grade, their Director of Programmes, had decided to go off to Hollywood to seek his fortune, so how did I fancy taking his job for a couple of years? Then when the chairman, John Freeman, retired, Brian would take his place and I would take Brian's place as Managing Director. I appreciated his generous offer but I told him frankly I wanted to stick around the BBC to see whether they would make me Managing Director of Television. 'Oh, they'll never do that,' said Brian. I wondered what he knew that I didn't, but I wasn't to be moved so he asked me to keep our conversation secret since he would now offer the job to John Birt. 'I don't want him to know he was second choice. He has enough hang-ups as it is.'

To my surprise, I was asked by the chairman of the governors to apply for the post of Director-General. God knows why: it was an open secret they intended to give it to Alasdair. I took with me to the board the newspaper advertisement that asked for 'recommendations and applications' for the job. I pointed out that I was there not to apply for a job I didn't want but instead to recommend Alasdair. I had a very relaxed and chatty hour with the governors, spelling out what I regarded as Alasdair's qualifications, one of which was a general conviction within the BBC that since the 1950s, when he joined the organisation as a general trainee, he'd had the field marshal's baton in his knapsack. I said it was fated that he should get the top job, and suggested we get on with it. Ever after, Stuart Young, who attended that meeting as a governor but later became chairman, in conversation with me always referred to Alasdair as '*your* Director-General'.

So Alasdair Milne became DG and now had to put in place his immediate management team. Apparently, he told the board of governors that he wished to appoint Aubrey Singer as his deputy and myself as Managing Director of Television. However, the board, largely at the urging of the chairman, George Howard, decided to put the DG in his place and ignore his wishes. Aubrey Singer was to be Managing Director of BBC TV and I would be given the post of Managing Director of BBC Radio. When the proposal was put to me I turned it down flat. I knew nothing about BBC Radio – I was a television man bred in the bone and it was an insult to BBC Radio to fob me off on them in order to solve a problem of the governors' making.

Alasdair's reading of the governors' decision was that George Howard had accompanied Aubrey on a goodwill mission to China and been vastly impressed with him, so he resolved to champion his candidature for the television MD's job. I neither knew nor cared whether this story was true; I wished Aubrey well in the job but had no desire to continue as his deputy. I wouldn't flounce out of the BBC in a pet but did intend to leave in a dignified way within months. At that moment, I remembered Brian Tesler's comment and wished I'd taken him up on his offer.

Why beat about the bush? I was bitterly disappointed. My whole BBC career had been a preparation for the job. Quite apart from my personal feelings, it seemed to me ominous for the future of the BBC if Alasdair, as the newly appointed Director-General and still in the honeymoon period of his office, could not persuade the board of governors to appoint the team he wanted.

Alasdair seemed devastated at the turn of events and spent hours asking me not to leave the BBC. He had another proposal to put to me. Would I be prepared to become Director of Programmes in the television service and also Director of Development with a seat on the board of management? I couldn't see Aubrey being very happy about my retaining control of television programmes, and what exactly was the development I would be directing? In short, it was the task of setting up satellite television. Here was an irony indeed. Aubrey Singer had forgotten more about the technicalities of television than I would ever know. If the BBC intended to go along that route, Aubrey would have been the ideal executive to lead us there. So the governors had managed to get us in the wrong jobs – which didn't give any of us much confidence in their judgement.

In the event, because I really didn't want to leave the BBC, which I dearly loved, and because things were so volatile at the top that all kinds of changes might occur, I decided to stick around. The governors obviously didn't want to lose me because they made me Managing Director of Satellite Broadcasting. I got a hike in salary, a penthouse office in the 600 Building opposite the Television Centre and a seat on the board of management. I spent about eighteen months in a state of almost total frustration, reading endless reports and attending government working parties. The idea was that the BBC would get a satellite from a consortium of space companies to transmit programmes on a system which would require the public to get new TV sets in order to receive them – a problem compounded by the fact the Japanese showed no interest in manufacturing domestic receivers for this new system.

Things got incredibly complicated; there were problems not just about the basic technology but also the kind of programmes we would transmit from the silver bird if we ever got it into the air. I concluded that the BBC should withdraw from the project as elegantly as it could – a view which Alasdair and Stuart Young, by then chairman of the governors, came to share. We got out from under, and eventually the future of any British satellite system passed to a consortium which became known as BSB. I became an MD with nothing to manage.

I continued to serve as a magistrate, and at one of our annual dinners I found myself seated next to a lady called Kate Burgess whom I'd first met on the bench a couple of weeks before. She then told me that as the youngest magistrate on the bench she was required to make a speech at the annual dinner, and asked if I, as a fairly well-known public speaker, had any advice for her. I told her to make sure her speech had a beginning, a middle and an end, and said that if she told any funny stories she should attribute them to someone else so that if no one laughed it wouldn't be her fault. I listened with interest to her speech. She did tell a few jokes and assigned their authorship to her children, so she benefited from the 'Ah' factor. Afterwards, we had a couple of drinks together and passed a very pleasant evening. I gathered she was separated from her husband with a divorce soon to be made final. She had a very attractive personality, a good brain and a well-developed sense of humour, and I remember thinking as I drove home that if only I'd been ten years younger . . . We found a bond developing between us as we sat on the bench together, so my life was about to change again – in more ways than I could imagine.

NINE

At the beginning of 1984 Alasdair called me to his office and told me that he wanted me to be Managing Director of the Television Service in place of Aubrey Singer, who was taking early retirement to become an independent television producer. I had heard rumours that there were tensions between Aubrey and his two right-hand men, Michael Checkland, Director of Resources, and Brian Wenham, who had been promoted to become Director of Programmes, but I had my hands full with the satellite issue so I hadn't paid much attention to the gossip – tensions are inevitable in a highly creative business like television.

As I went back to Television Centre, I felt an immense sense of elation. Boo's prophecy made twenty years before had come true. But I tried to keep a sense of proportion. In four years' time I would walk out of the place for the last time and, as I always said, leaving the BBC is a little like withdrawing your hand from a bowl of water – the ripples quickly die away and it's as though you've never been there.

For the previous eighteen months I had sat in my office opposite Television Centre, watching the comings and goings in that semi-circular brick fortress where I spent nearly thirty of the happiest years of my life. I and my colleagues had worked away keeping programmes on the air while the building went up around us. Deep in the bowels of the building were the studios where some of the great shows for which Light Entertainment was responsible were made.

I *had* missed the old place, and although I found the work of investigating the BBC's future in satellite broadcasting fully absorbing I was glad to get back to my first love. And I walked straight back into a row that was in a strange way of my own making. Years before when I was Controller of BBC1, on one of my buying trips to America I had been very impressed with a proposal to make a mini-series based on Colleen McCullough's best-selling novel *The Thorn Birds*. It was to star Richard Chamberlain as a priest torn apart by love; it had a dashing hero, a beautiful heroine, a smattering of religion and a touch of lust – honest-to-God mainstream entertainment, neither a screen gem nor mere 'chewing gum for the eyes', as the tabloids liked to describe televised trash. Because we were in at the beginning of the project, we got offered a very good deal so I snapped it up.

By the time *The Thorn Birds* was made, I had moved on and my successor as Controller of BBC1 decided to transmit it a couple of weeks after Christmas 1983 on a Monday evening, which meant displacing *Panorama,* the BBC's Current Affairs weekly flagship programme. That was one mistake; the other was to run it very soon after Granada's adaptation of *The Jewel in the Crown,* undoubtedly a drama classic. The BBC was under regular attack from Thatcher's government and the showing of *The Thorn Birds* brought down on us the wrath of the Home Secretary Douglas Hurd, who quite unfairly compared *The Thorn Birds* with *The Jewel in the Crown* and accused the BBC of wasting the licence fee-payers' money. And he pointed out that to compound the offence, the BBC had shelved one of the few serious programmes on BBC1, *Panorama,* in favour of this imported pap.

Then a generally hostile press joined in. Max Hastings, editor of the *Daily Telegraph,* led the pack. He dismissed *The Thorn Birds* as 'one of the most paltry, tawdry imported soap operas any television channel had the contempt to inflict on the viewing public'. The fact that fifteen million members of the viewing public watched and enjoyed it made no dent in his argument. Quite fallaciously, he made *The Jewel in the Crown* and *The Thorn Birds* the benchmarks of the respective overall quality of the two broadcasting organisations. Neither Max Hastings nor Douglas Hurd seemed to have noticed that ITV also produced

The Price is Right while the BBC transmitted David Attenborough's *Life on Earth*.

We weathered that storm by defending without apology *The
Thorn Birds* as the staple diet of television fiction; *The Jewel in
the Crown* was a once-in-a-blue-moon event which demanded a
level of resources and cash no television channel could sustain
regularly. But we were resigned to the fact that if it hadn't been
The Thorn Birds it would have been something else. In Mrs
Thatcher's eyes, whatever the BBC did was wrong. She was
operating like a fast-bowler in cricket. First of all she dismissed
the Argentinians in the Falklands, then she smashed into the
unions, and now it was the broadcasters' turn. She had direct
power over the BBC only in Parliament, when the licence fee
had to be fixed or the BBC Charter was due for renewal. She
had no statutory authority to interfere in programme policy,
except in a national emergency, but she did have the right to
appoint those who had the final say about programmes: the
BBC's governors.

As the governors of the pre-Thatcher era retired, each was
replaced by someone who could be relied on to be 'one of us'.
Historically, the governors had been selected in such a way as to
achieve some kind of rough political balance, but by the 1980s,
even when she paid lip-service to the Labour Party's right to
representation, she carefully chose people on the right wing of
the party, such as the retired trade union leader Sir John Boyd,
or Lord Barnett, who as plain Joel Barnett had been Harold
Wilson's chief secretary to the Treasury. Consequently, any
programme that appeared to be critical of the government was
savaged by the governors. Whereas in times past the BBC's
board of management had felt that the governors were in place
to protect them from political interference by the government,
now the perception was that the governors were Mrs Thatcher's
agents within the Corporation.

If we in BBC management seemed paranoid about Mrs
Thatcher, it was with good cause. When the board of governors
entertained her to dinner in 1983, she regaled us with her
opinion of the BBC's behaviour during the Falklands War. She

went on for about twenty minutes without drawing breath and virtually accused us of subversion. When she paused, I asked her, 'Are you saying, Prime Minister, that the BBC acted treasonably in the Falklands? Because if you are, you are wrong.' She fixed me with her most forbidding look and replied, 'I have said all I intend to say.' We passed on to other things. After she'd left, the people round the table were split about my likely fate. One half told me not to bother decorating my office, the other half assured me she wouldn't mind at all because she liked people to stand up to her.

We had a return match in the latter part of 1984, when Mrs Thatcher invited some of us to Downing Street for lunch. It was just after the IRA bombing of the Grand Hotel in Brighton during the Conservative Party Conference, and as we drove to Number Ten I said to Alasdair that I thought it would be a very low-key affair – after all, she'd just escaped an assassination attempt. As we were having drinks, she strode into the room full of vim and vigour and in fighting form. She talked about her reactions when the bomb went off. She was in the bathroom, from where she rushed into the bedroom to see if her husband Denis was all right only to find him standing in unmatching pyjama trousers and top. He'd said he'd taken them out of the drawer. 'Rubbish,' she said, 'they're certainly not Mix 'n' Match.'

When we went into lunch I found myself seated next to her. My bottom had hardly touched the chair before she started bowling at me. 'How is television getting on?' she asked. 'Fine,' I replied. 'The figures have perked up and the viewers seem to be enjoying our programmes, though money is always a problem.' I thought I was getting in a gentle hint about the level of the licence fee, but then came the bouncer. 'Well, why don't you take some advertising?' I gulped and then said, 'Tell me, Prime Minister, did you see any of the Olympics?' I was referring to the recent Games in Los Angeles. 'Yes I did,' she replied, and I went on to ask her if she was watching during the wonderful moment in the opening ceremony when the entire audience held up the coloured discs they'd been given and made a huge picture of the flags of all the competing nations. 'Yes I did, and it was marvellous.' 'Well,' I said, 'British viewers saw that because we had our own coverage but the American audience couldn't see it because their network was showing a beer commercial at the time.' She smiled as though in acknowledgement that I'd made a fair debating point, and changed the subject.

Shortly after I took over at Television Centre, I had a long conversation with Brian Wenham in the garden of his home at Weybridge. I put to him a plan to strengthen BBC1's early-evening scheule. It involved moving the BBC news from five-forty p.m. to six o'clock, then after the regions had done their own thing at six-thirty we should schedule a newly developed soap opera, *EastEnders,* at seven o'clock on two evenings. *EastEnders* had been created by a team led by Jonathan Powell, Head of Drama. Julia Smith was to produce it, and the script would be supervised by Tony Holland, who had worked on *Z Cars* and *Angels.* To my successor at BBC1, Alan Hart, belonged the credit for commissioning and encouraging this BBC rival to ITV's *Coronation Street.*

I was not a great fan of soap operas and game shows, the staple diet of much US television – I felt they took up too much production time and resources and were better suited to commercial television; the BBC ought to develop other forms of high-quality entertainment. But *EastEnders* was on the stocks, it had already consumed considerable resources, offered employment to significant numbers of actors and was awaited with great anticipation throughout the industry. I knew doing my King Canute act would be pointless, so I reconciled myself to the inevitable.

For the other three midweek early evenings, I wanted to give Terry Wogan his own chat show. Originally my idea had been that Terry should do a late-night show along the lines of that hosted by Johnny Carson in the United States, but Terry preferred an earlier slot which had more chance of attracting his large Radio 2 morning-programme audience.

To make radical changes to the schedules we needed to look much more closely at the two channels' controllers. Brian's successor as Controller of BBC2 was Graeme MacDonald. His distinguished record as a drama producer had been followed by a spell as a highly successful Head of the Drama Group. Under his leadership BBC2 was blossoming. BBC1 was more problematic: Alan Hart had done the job for three years and had some outstanding successes, but I felt it was time he moved on – we needed to ratchet the channel up a gear. This observation led Brian to introduce Michael Grade's name into the conversation.

I had known Michael for much of my adult life. After a spell in London Weekend Television as Director of Programmes, Michael had gone off to seek his fortune in Hollywood as president of Embassy Television, a production house for situation comedies founded by the distinguished director Norman Lear. On one of his recent visits to America, Brian Wenham had met Michael and formed the impression that he wasn't very happy in Tinsel Town and might welcome an approach from the BBC.

In March 1984 I flew out to California and had a long discussion with Michael. He was quite honest with me; the job he would love to do at the BBC was to run both BBC1 and BBC2, but that would effectively have made redundant Brian Wenham as Director of Programmes, so I couldn't offer him that. However, I had the Director-General's agreement to talk about the BBC1 job. Michael had a number of problems, one of which was money. I could only offer him a pittance in comparison to the huge salary and bonuses Hollywood paid him, so he would have to make a severe financial sacrifice if he joined the BBC. Then there was his wife, Sarah, a lawyer turned television producer who loved her life and work in the United States and would be reluctant to move back to Britain. We agreed that Michael and Sarah should think things over and come to some conclusion. I pointed out there was a deadline. I needed to have his decision by midnight Hollywood time on 23 May because the next morning there was to be a meeting of the

BBC governors and I needed to tell them what had been decided. The chairman of the governors had already agreed that if Michael said yes, he would not be submitted to the charade of an appointments board.

At midnight on 23 May, Sarah phoned me. Apparently they had been arguing the matter for days with Michael veering to the view that since he'd taken Sarah out to Hollywood in the first place to suit his own career he couldn't well put pressure on her to return. She asked me one question: 'If he comes to the BBC, will you promise to look after him?' Getting the answer she wanted, she said, 'Well he's definitely coming.'

I was relying on the assurance of the chairman of the governors that Michael would not be subjected to a formal appointment interview, and he kept his word. Though I often found the governors *en masse* a pain in the neck, individually most of them were nice people with interesting backgrounds. For instance, Malcolm McAlpine (from the construction family) was a true-blue Tory, an intelligent, gentle man, and I was delighted when he invited me to the McAlpine box at Epsom to watch the Oaks. A few days before, after a meeting at Bush House, the home of the BBC's World Service, I went for a stroll down the Strand and there in the window of a menswear shop I saw a very well-made suit. It was a Chester Barrie in Prince of Wales check which I thought would be ideal for a day at the races. I tried it on, had it altered and bought it.

The following Saturday I arrived at the racecourse resplendent in my Prince of Wales check suit and cast an eye out for the McAlpines' man of affairs who was to greet me and bring me to their box. I was told he would be wearing a bowler hat and sporting a red carnation. I recognised him immediately because of the bowler hat and buttonhole, but he was also wearing an identical Chester Barrie Prince of Wales-check suit. We entered the McAlpine box looking like a couple of the Beverley Sisters.

I got on well personally with most of the governors, especially Stuart Young. Indeed when his predecessor, George Howard, retired and was elevated to the House of Lords, we in the board of management had discussed who we would like to see in the job – I suggested Stuart Young, who was already on the board. Some of my colleagues were highly sceptical. The chairmanship had always been an essentially establishment job, held by distinguished academics, retired senior civil servants or landed gentry. Stuart, though a top accountant, was in trade as a director of Tesco and British-Caledonian Airlines. That was a problem, but I felt it ought not to be decisive. In contrast to William Rees-Mogg, former editor of *The Times*, who had been appointed at the same time, we felt that Stuart had 'gone native' – he was on our side.

I knew we would only get someone of whom Mrs Thatcher approved, and Stuart fitted the bill. His brother, David, had been made a peer and had been appointed to Mrs Thatcher's cabinet, and she also knew Stuart well. I thought that Stuart and Alasdair as chairman and DG respectively would make an excellent team, Stuart keeping an eye on the finances while Alasdair looked after programmes.

To our delight, Stuart was appointed chairman, but our joy turned to horror within a matter of weeks when he was found to have lung cancer. He was operated on and had a course of chemotherapy. After a couple of months he seemed to make a full recovery, but his strength was impaired and we had the sense that he was living on borrowed time.

I often travelled with him, and Mike Checkland. When I became chairman of BBC Enterprises, the commercial wing of the BBC's operations, I frequently had to fly to America. I found a good way of getting myself on Concorde: on quick turnaround trips the BBC allowed us to travel first class, and when in New York if we turned up for our flight a couple of hours early – just before Concorde left – and volunteered to fly on the half-full supersonic airliner, thus leaving a first-class seat free on the plane we had planned to catch, British Airways would often agree. Mike and I used this wheeze coming back from one trip. I was having a wonderful time watching the curvature of the earth glide by beneath us when the stewardess asked me if I would join the captain on the flight-deck.

I was greeted in the cockpit by the captain, whose enormous pair of sunglasses meant I couldn't see his face. 'Hello, Bill,' he said. 'I thought you were going to ignore me.' He then showed me round the cockpit of this wonderful plane without revealing how he knew me. When I got back to my seat, I rang for the stewardess. 'What's the captain's name?' I asked. 'He seems to know me but I don't think I've ever met him.' She replied, 'His name's Arthur Budd but he's usually known as Leo.' Indeed I knew him. He was the son of our local publican at Old Windsor, and as a teenager during the war had served in the ATC at Windsor which my father commanded. Arthur didn't have the academic qualifications to become an RAF pilot, but my dad pulled some strings at the Air Ministry and helped to get him accepted. He never looked back and ended up as the senior Concorde captain.

It was back to serious work in September 1984, as the winter battle with ITV loomed ahead. But I would have Michael Grade as my right-hand man. He started work for the BBC on the anniversary of the day the Second World War broke out, 3 September – appropriate, as it turned out. And he arrived in a hail of press publicity which some of the BBC top brass at Broadcasting House found distasteful. Everything he said and did earned him headlines or mentions in the gossip columns of the tabloids; everything about him, down to his red braces and matching socks, were a matter of record. An off-the-cuff remark he made about the hairstyles of weather forecasters caused uproar and he also upset Sir Robin Day (which wasn't all that difficult to do). But people knew he was around, and he generated excitement and anticipation, which is exactly what I had hoped for. Of course, such a high profile was utterly at odds with the BBC's tradition of managers keeping their heads down and leaving it to the stars to get acres of newsprint. That was too bad – we were losing a propaganda war and badly needed the odd press victory.

Michael settled down in the BBC very quickly, though in

some quarters he was dismissed as a song and dance man, a commercial operator who would turn BBC1 into a vaudeville operation. In reality, he had a firmer grasp of the meaning of public-service broadcasting than most of his detractors. He gained the respect of the production staff by taking the trouble to watch their programmes and then ringing them up at home to offer words of congratulation and encouragement. His office door was always open to members of staff anxious to talk about their problems – a policy which reversed traditional manage-ment practice, where the more important you are in an organisation, the harder it is to get to see you.

And because he had worked as a sports journalist on the *Daily Mirror*, Michael knew how to handle the press. Instead of regarding them as enemies trying to undermine the BBC, he recognised that they had a job to do and that the Corporation had everything to gain by helping them to do it whenever possible. He put the BBC's case in public fearlessly and with good humour. We developed a good working relationship and he got on well with other members of television management, especially with his counterpart on BBC2, Graeme MacDonald. They began to work out a pattern of joint scheduling so that when BBC1 had a programme which was unlikely to be a crowd-puller, Michael would warn Graeme in advance to put one of his strongest programmes against it, thus making it more likely that some of the audience would stay with the BBC instead of turning over to ITV.

He was a brilliant scheduler. He was in his element when moving things around, taking things out, putting things in and generating an air of confidence. Perhaps his greatest coup in those early days was to persuade the staff of *Panorama*, who were hanging onto their eight–ten slot on a Monday evening like grim death, that the programme had to move because ratings were plummeting. *Panorama* was a sacred cow or, as someone called it, to change the metaphor, the Albert Hall monument of the BBC – untouchable, with a great history adorned by most distinguished journalists from Richard Dimbleby onwards.

Michael came to see me and told me that he wanted to move

Panorama from ten minutes past eight on Monday evenings to a spot after the nine o'clock news and cut down its length to forty minutes. I bowed my head gravely to accord him the respect due to a kamikaze pilot about to go off on a suicide mission. Some of the great names in the Corporation's history – giants of broadcasting – had stubbed their toes trying to move that same great monolith. I told him bluntly, 'You'll be taking on not only the governors but also all the BBC's journalists at Lime Grove, but if you're determined to try, start with the Lime Grove lot. If you can get them on side, I'm prepared to tackle the governors. God bless you and all who sail in you.'

Michael got together the journalists in their lair in that row of terraced Edwardian houses in Lime Grove, and after three stormy meetings convinced them that *Panorama* had to move or continue bleeding to death. We took the case to the governors who, once they were satisfied they wouldn't have to face a revolt of all the Corporation's journalists, agreed to the change. After the meeting, Alasdair took me on one side and confided that he was worried. He said there was a general feeling around the place that Michael Grade had taken over my job and was running the television service, and what was I going to do about it? 'Nothing,' I replied. 'Just so long as it's successful, I don't care who gets the credit, and Michael deserves a lot of it for what he's accomplished in these few months.'

In the throes of all this excitement, I got a letter from a parish priest in Bedford that brought Dad's family back into my life. He was writing on behalf of a Mrs Primrose Winterbottom who was not in the best of health and had asked to see me. It was Aunty Prim, my father's younger sister. I remembered her wedding. Dad couldn't attend because he and the band had an engagement somewhere, so my mother represented him and took me with her. I must have been about six at the time, and my child-like mind was much tickled by a family joke to the effect that Aunty Prim might now be a Winterbottom but she had a warm heart. Large families often drift apart, and I had heard nothing of her for years until this vicar's letter arrived out of the blue. I made contact with her immediately and arranged to go and see her the following weekend. I asked my nephew Tim, my brother Ted's son, if he'd like to come – 'After all – who knows? – maybe she's your long-lost wealthy great-aunt.'

When we drove into her road, I began to think that my facetious remark might be near the mark. The houses were huge, each with its own curving drive and extensive gardens. As we went down the road, though, the houses got smaller until we arrived at a semi-detached cottage whose front door opened immediately into the sitting-room. Aunty Prim came out to greet me. She was small and bird-like, quite unlike the rest of Joe and Susan Cotton's children, who were stocky like my father.

Aunty Prim had married late and there were no children, so to compensate she and her husband had become bird fanciers and there were cups and trophies all over the house. She'd evidently taken great pride in Dad. She produced a load of his showbiz memorabilia, including a scrapbook which not only told his story but also held press clippings about me. She wanted me to have it – 'I'm on my last legs, you see,' she said. She asked about the band and I told her most of them were long since dead, then I realised she was confusing me with my father.

Tim and I stayed for a couple of hours and promised to keep in touch. Prim faded fast and went into a nursing home, and at her request I obtained power of attorney to look after her affairs. She had circulation problems and the doctors thought her leg would have to be removed, but she would have none of it; she was going to die whole. The last time I saw her, she asked why I wasn't in uniform, obviously taking me for the young Billy Cotton back from the trenches in the First World War. She died a week later and left everything to a charity that cared for budgerigars. So passed the last of Dad's generation of Cottons.

But Cotton family matters of an altogether less wholesome kind suddenly became public. In November 1984 Alasdair and I, with other members of the board of management, were due to go to Hong Kong to attend the Commonwealth Broadcasting Conference. The day before we left there were headlines in both the *Daily Mail* and the *Sun* which put the spotlight on my failed marriage. My wife Ann and I had not lived under the same roof for about a year, and somehow the *Daily Mail* had got wind of the fact and doorstepped my wife. She got very upset, broke down and poured out her heart, accusing me of ingratitude and infidelity, naming Kate Burgess as my mistress. Kate then found her house in East Molesey under siege, reporters and photographers camped in her drive.

Usually this kind of stress would have driven me to reach for my fags – I was a three-packs-a-day man – but a few days before my departure for Hong Kong I'd developed a throat infection and my doctor advised me to give cigarettes a rest and to cancel my trip. I didn't feel I could do the latter as I was due to make a speech at the conference – and anyway, I was glad to dodge the attentions of the press for a while. However, the *Daily Mail* caught up with me in my Hong Kong hotel bedroom at two o'clock in the morning. The reporter expected me to have a protracted conversation with him about my wife's statement. Almost voiceless with jet lag and laryngitis, I disabused him with one short, sharp piece of advice.

The next morning I went to see a throat specialist recommended by the hotel. He was a grave young man in a white coat operating from a room behind a shop in the centre of the city. He examined my throat and said simply, 'You stop smoking or you die.' Over the years my doctors had advised me to give up smoking, and I'd made vague attempts now and again, but now in one sentence that young man stopped me dead. There was something about his matter-of-fact cold comment that frightened the life out of me. I have never smoked since.

On the flight back to Britain I had plenty of time to think and I realised I must sort out my marriage once and for all. It was fair to neither Kate nor to Ann to leave things as they were. I knew beyond a shadow of a doubt that my future lay with Kate. The press coverage had at least the advantage that there was no need for me to explain the breakdown of my marriage. My friends were very supportive, especially Alasdair Milne and his wife Sheila. They were *there* for me, with a meal and a bed when I needed them. Sheila, though very ill from time to time, was always a cheerful and gracious hostess. It was good to see

Alasdair happy in his own home; what with attacks from the government, the governors and the press, his life in the BBC was pretty miserable.

At first Kate and I didn't live together. I stayed at the Eccentric Club, which used to be in St James, or with one of my daughters, then every other weekend, when Kate's children went to stay with her ex-husband, we were free to go down to Deal where I had a flat by the sea. This was the time when I discovered who my real friends were. Richard Armitage was one of the very dearest. I'd known him since my late teens and we'd kept in touch regularly. Apart from anything else, as an agent he had a stable of stars the BBC engaged from time to time: David Frost, Rowan Atkinson, Stephen Fry, Hugh Laurie and Emma Thompson. We didn't just talk about my marital affairs, he had a burning desire to revive *Me and My Girl*, the musical composed by his father, Noel Gay. I had once put a proposition to Eric Maschwitz when he was Head of Light Entertainment that we should do a television version. Unfortunately *Charlie Girl*, a musical with a similar storyline, opened in London around the same time, and despite very poor reviews it did well – mainly because it starred Anna Neagle. So *Me and My Girl* went into the pending file. But in 1985 Richard was finally able to mount it, and after an out-of-town run in Leicester it opened at the Adelphi in London.

I put some money into the show, and only wish I had invested more because it was an enormous hit. Kate and I went to the opening night and she spent most of the time watching the reaction of Richard, who sat with us. It is fascinating to observe someone's dream come true. She and Richard had become good friends very quickly. They had a fondness for back-gammon and used to play into the small hours when we went to stay at the house in Stebbing that Richard was renovating. He had bought the place in a dilapidated state and was slowly restoring it with the help of his two sons, Charles and Alex.

The Old Rectory became a very comfortable country seat, complete with a magnificent swimming-pool in a converted barn. Every year Richard organised a house party which

It's goodnight from me . . .   and it's goodnight from him . . .

and her . . .   and her.

Ronnie Barker always said he didn't like dressing up as a woman. But then he wasn't as pretty as Ronnie Corbett.

Presenting a recording
of his visit to Britain to
the Pope.

An imposter making
a quick get-away
(Dave Allen and friends).

Sue Lawley and I on my little motor cruiser *Mabel Hope* at Poole in 1995.
I called the boat *Mabel Hope* after my mother. She loved Poole Harbour and boats!

Complete with red noses – Jonathan Ross, Griff Rhys Jones, Lenny Henry, Jonathan Powell, me and Alan Yentob at the inaugural Comic Relief.

When you've got to go, you've got to go.
Caught by the photographer in a tear-wiping
session. But having good friends helps.

Cilla   Mary and Parkie

Jim

Michael Checkland's board of management. I've included this picture because it will probably never happen again that three people from the entertainment side of broadcasting sit on the top table of the BBC controlling the programme output. Michael Grade (third from left), myself and David Hatch (third from right).

The last evening at the BBC. A young Marine presenting me with the BBC flag after they had beat 'Retreat' on the forecourt of Television Centre. He at the beginning of a career in the Marines, me at the end of a career at the BBC.

Michael Aspel confronted
me for *This is Your Life*
at Castle Ashby. John and
Jacqui Harris led me into
the trap.

Vera was the perfect person to be with me when Michael gave me the Red Book.
At the start of her career she sang with my father's band – in the fifties she made hit
records of two of the songs we published at Michael Reine Music Co. And she did
her last television series on BBC2 when I was Head of Light Entertainment.
My admiration for her is unbounded.

Celebrating the winning of Meridian's franchise. Next to me is Simon Aubrey, then Roger Laughton, Clive Hollick and Terry Jones.

Reunion of ex-BBC Heads of Variety at Montreux, 1997.
Left: Terry Hughes. Terry is now a top director in America with *Friends*, *Golden Girls* and *Third Rock from the Sun* among his credits.
Right: Jim Moir. Jim is now the very successful Controller of Radio 2, and is one of the most sought-after 'before dinner' or 'after dinner' speakers in the business.

Kathryn Mary Cotton and husband on holiday in Venice
– the good life continues.

included a cricket match for which he recruited many of his artists and other show business personalities. I hurled a bat at the bowling for a number of years and then decided to retire, whereupon I was presented with a cup by Hinge and Brackett and I didn't know whether to shake their hands or kiss them.

I have many happy memories of the Old Rectory. Richard discovered there had been a Roman lake in the grounds and he proceeded to excavate it. In the middle was an island which could be reached by a small rowing boat. On one occasion when I got into the skiff and pushed off, it started to wobble and take in water, and then it slowly sank. Kate and Richard clung to each other convulsed with laughter as the water slowly swallowed me up while I held my hand vertically in the air to protect a gold watch my father had given me. Soon, only my hand and arm remained rigid above water as though waiting for the great sword Excalibur to be thrust into it. No one made any serious attempt to rescue me.

The stars of *Me and My Girl*, Robert Lindsay and Emma Thompson, and the rest of the cast were guests at Richard's 1985 house party. Richard did his usual 'state of the union' speech which was followed by a wonderful spontaneous cabaret from Jake Thackray and Richard Stilgoe. I had to drive back to London that night and I'd been a real wet blanket at the dinner, drinking only water and pontificating about the dangers of drinking and driving. I pointed out pompously that a magistrate must be whiter than white. I then got into my car and drove off. Halfway down the drive I was temporarily blinded by one of the powerful lights illuminating the grounds and wrapped my car round a tree, to the enormous glee of the assembled company.

On the programme front, in the autumn of 1985 we ran into trouble with one of the programmes in our *Rough Justice* series. The purpose of the series, presented by David Jessel, was to investigate apparent miscarriages of justice in the courts. Obviously, in dealing with such sensitive matters meticulous research and sound legal advice were essential, and *Rough*

This Dave Allen cartoon makes the point very effectively.

Justice had an honourable track-record in getting wrongly convicted prisoners released. The producers became interested in a man called Anthony Mycock whom they decided was in prison for an offence he had not committed. The robbery victim on the weight of whose testimony Mycock had been found guilty was living in California. The production team went there to interview her and she confessed that she had lied in court. After the programme was transmitted, Anthony Mycock was released – apparently a resounding victory both for justice and for *Rough Justice*.

But things were not what they seemed. It turned out that the methods the team had used to extract the confession from the woman in California were so irregular that the Lord Chief Justice vigorously condemned both the BBC and programme in the High Court. Understandably, Alasdair Milne was furious.

He asked me as the team's head of establishment to discipline them. I interviewed the producer and the reporter and faced a moral dilemma. By patient research and much tenacity they had got an innocent man out of gaol, but they had used methods the BBC could not countenance and which had brought down on us a deluge of vilification from the press.

I suspended them both for three months without pay. Alasdair thought I had been too lenient – he felt they should have been fired. I could understand his feelings because he was the one at the sharp end, a target for constant press criticism. In one of his onslaughts, Max Hastings had described BBC management in general as 'bankrupt of ideas and pathetically inadequate' and Alasdair in particular as 'a hapless director general'. Perhaps I *was* too lenient but I had been in television a long time and I knew that creative programme-making always involves risks, especially in the area of investigative journalism. On balance I would rather producers pushed towards the frontiers of the acceptable even if they occasionally crossed them than stay in the safe hinterland and make bland programmes.

Snooker, thank God, never got the BBC into trouble with the Lord Chief Justice, but it threw up problems of a different kind. The World Championships held at the Crucible Theatre at Sheffield had become a major television event which attracted the attention of big companies eager to sponsor it. Imperial Tobacco had secured the sponsorship and named it the Embassy World Championship. In return for spending a hefty sum of money, the company naturally expected its name to be prominently displayed in strategic places around the Crucible where the television cameras could not miss it.

The sponsorship of the Championships was nothing to do with us – that was a matter between the company and the snooker authorities – but the presence of tobacco advertising on BBC TV did concern both us and the Ministry of Health. They disapproved of tobacco advertising but were very conscious of the vast revenue in duty which tobacco sales brought to the Treasury, so they were equivocal.

219

I had suggested that the easiest way to solve the problem was for the government to make tobacco advertising illegal, then all the Embassy logos in the Crucible Theatre would have to come down and the snooker authorities could look for sponsors whose products were more socially acceptable. But politicians are ever conscious of public reaction against the banning of anything that has popular support, so the government put the onus on the BBC to take action. At the request of the governors, I issued a set of guidelines setting out what could and could not be shown by way of advertising at the Championships. The governors would have preferred a set of rules rather than guidelines, but I was adamant. Guidelines would be just that – they gave the television producer advice, but ultimately, if any advertisement was too obtrusive he had the right to ban it, and that was that. A set of rules laying out sizes and positions of logos and the length of time the sponsor's name could be shown on screen would be an invitation to clever lawyers and advertising executives to find some loophole in our wording, and then we would have been bogged down in endless arguments and possible litigation.

I doubt Imperial Tobacco had a portrait of me in their boardroom, but it was an essentially professional disagreement. When I took Kate up to Sheffield to see how the guidelines were working in practice, the director of Imperial Tobacco could not have been more hospitable – and Kate hit it off a treat with his partner. The two finalists that year were Steve Davis and Dennis Taylor, and everybody who knew anything about snooker assured me that it was a foregone conclusion that Steve Davis would win comfortably. Rather than stay for a totally predictable final, Kate and I set off back to London and arrived at my daughter's flat after midnight only to be told the match was still on. We were just in time to see Dennis Taylor win on the final black.

It was a busy summer, what with Wimbledon, a Test match and a Royal Gala in Edinburgh, but the most significant event – which was to overshadow the BBC in the coming months – again occurred in Northern Ireland. It was a programme in our *Real Lives* series called *At the Edge of the Union* and featured a day in the life of two Ulster politicians, both of whom lived in Londonderry: Martin McGuinness, then deputy leader of Sinn Fein, and Gregory Campbell of the Democratic Unionist Party. It was a straight-forward, unsensational documentary – indeed, if anything, rather bland. But because it was about Northern Ireland the video had to be referred to senior management for approval before it was transmitted. Michael Grade saw it, told me he had viewed it and assured me he could see no problem.

Nor would there have been any problem had a *Sunday Times* reporter scanning the *Radio Times* not noticed that the BBC intended to put out a documentary featuring Martin McGuinness, a man with known IRA connections. He then extracted a comment from the Northern Ireland secretary, Douglas Hurd, who condemned the programme, whereupon the paper's Washington correspondent ratcheted up the story a notch by asking Mrs Thatcher, who was on a visit to the USA, what she thought of the idea of the BBC giving a platform to terrorists. The lady blew a fuse and the next thing we knew the chairman of the governors had a letter from the Home Secretary, Leon Brittan, asking him to ban the programme. Brittan had not actually seen the programme and he carefully denied that he was putting any pressure on the BBC; he merely expected the governors to do their patriotic duty. He later disingenuously claimed he was just acting as an ordinary citizen in making his protest to the BBC.

The governors reacted with varying degrees of panic or outrage, some of them seeing the issue as a glorious opportunity to demonstrate their loyalty to Mrs Thatcher and a chance to bring the board of management to heel. A minor issue was blowing up into a major crisis. *Real Lives* put two of my friends, Stuart Young, chairman of the governors (by now a very sick man), and the Director-General, Alasdair Milne, on collision course. And it was Sod's Law that Alasdair, who as editor in chief had the final word on the programmes that could be transmitted on the BBC's airwaves, was on holiday and virtually unreachable in Norway when the crisis occurred.

Disregarding all precedent, the governors insisted on seeing a video of the programme in advance of its transmission. We asked them not to do that because it would undermine Alasdair's editorial authority, but the government was breathing down the chairman's neck and he didn't see how he could make an intelligent response to the Home Secretary's letter if the board hadn't seen the video. There was some force in that argument, but I argued that they ought to trust the board of management's judgement. We *had* seen the video, and in our view, with minor changes, it was perfectly acceptable and in no way legitimised or encouraged terrorism.

By now Michael Checkland, who was acting DG, had managed to reach Alasdair by telephone. Alasdair conceded that the governors did have the right to view the video if they insisted, but devoutly hoped they wouldn't push the matter. Stuart Young for his part hoped that once the governors saw the programme they would be reassured and the problem would go away.

It didn't. The two boards saw the video together. The atmosphere was fraught, the hostility of certain governors palpable. Their body-language and murmurs of indignation every time McGuinness appeared on screen did not bode well for the discussion that was to follow. It was like Saturday morning at the flicks where the kids hissed every time the villain made an appearance. The vice-chairman, William Rees-Mogg, led the attack. His view was that the programme portrayed the IRA sympathetically and in particular made the false allegation that McGuinness represented all Northern Ireland Catholics. I'd seen the video two or three times but couldn't see the evidence for such an inference. One by one the governors made their contribution. All of them with the solitary exception of the Welsh governor, Alwyn Roberts, hated the film and were utterly opposed to it being transmitted. To me, they sounded and behaved more like a lynch-mob than the trustees of one of the nation's most important cultural institutions, and there was no doubt it was the absent DG whom they would have liked to see dangling on the end of their rope. Though Alasdair had no hand in setting up *Real Lives* and indeed did not even know of the existence of a programme called *At the Edge of the Union*, the clear implication was that this was the sort of subversive material which stemmed from his misguided or incompetent leadership.

The BBC journalists called a one-day strike and were supported by some of their ITV colleagues. I went to a meeting of production staff who were appalled at the decision to ban the programme and at the governors' insistence on viewing the video prior to transmission. I had to be frank with them. What would they do if the Home Secretary was demanding some response about a programme *they* hadn't seen but any number of other people had, including the *Real Lives* production team and God knows who else at the Television Centre? In fact, a pirate version of the programme was doing the rounds and many journalists had seen it. The urgent requirement wasn't to censure the governors for previewing the video but to get them to reverse their decision that the programme should not be transmitted.

On Alasdair's return, he saw the video and fully endorsed the board of management's view. He persuaded the board of governors, with the exceptions of William Rees-Mogg and Daphne Park, to agree to the programme being transmitted in the autumn, provided it was followed by a studio discussion.

The programme duly went out in October, and no one could see what all the fuss had been about. But relations between the two boards became even more strained, and the chief casualty was Alasdair. It was clear the governors wanted him out.

In the middle of this crisis, on 6 August we celebrated my mother's ninetieth birthday. She and Kate got on like a house on fire, so Kate threw a party for her. Joining all her family were Johnny Johnston, Queenie (now more a friend than a PA), and Annie and Gerry Kunz. My mother had suffered and survived the breakdown of her marriage and the death of her eldest son. In her mid-eighties when she really wasn't any longer able to look after herself, she had opted to go into Brinsworth, the home run by the Variety Artists' Federation. It took her a while to adjust, but her anxiety was greatly eased by my daughter Lulu visiting her every day for the first few weeks. I would take her out at the weekends. She became slightly institutionalised but retained her keen sense of humour and her optimism. She loved spending the day at Kate's house on Sundays because she was able to join in normal family activities, such as making marmalade and cleaning the silver and all the other chores that made her feel useful.

Like many elderly and housebound citizens, my mother relied greatly on television, and I had been doing some hard thinking about the quality of service BBC television offered to our viewers during the daytime. It had long been assumed that BBC Radio looked after the public during the day, but what about these housebound people who had bought television sets and paid their licence fee? They were hardly getting value for money. I asked the governors to give me extra funds to pay for daytime programmes. They approved the proposal and I appointed Roger Laughton, who had run a first-class Features department, to set about creating and scheduling a service across both BBC1 and BBC2 to run from the end of breakfast-time TV up to five-forty in the evening when the early-evening news was transmitted.

Roger exploited the talent and resources of the BBC regions to produce shows like *Open Air*, *The Clothes Show*, *Watchdog* and *Kilroy* and also established a BBC News bulletin at one o'clock. He also went on a scouting trip abroad, and I arranged to join him in Australia where I met an old friend of mine, producer and entrepreneur Reg Grundy. We watched a selection of his shows with a view to buying some. Roger had been particularly impressed with a soap opera which was doing good business on Australian television. Reg showed me a couple of episodes of *Neighbours* and we bought it on the spot. It was a show full of sunshine and vigorous young people, a cheerful, upbeat soap I knew would do well at lunchtime on a drab winter's day in Britain. And so it proved.

There was one slight hiccup. The show had started on Australia's Channel Seven and was then transferred to Channel Ten, at which point some of the sets and actors were changed.

DOUBLE BILL

We didn't know that when we put out back editions on BBC1, and were deluged with phone calls from viewers complaining about the lack of continuity. Indeed, there was such a huge response that Michael Grade quickly cottoned on to the fact that *Neighbours* was developing a cult following among the younger generations and moved the repeat from the following morning to five-thirty the same evening. It's ironic, given my reservations about soap operas, that the two which were launched during my spell in charge of the television service should still be going strong.

While I was away in Australia Kate, who had lived in East Molesey for a couple of years, moved into a larger house on the other side of the main road. It was a repossessed house of splendid proportions that had been empty for a year and it was in a fairly rough state. When I got back home, Kate took me to see the house and explained the alterations and renovations she planned. Frankly I thought she had bitten off a bit too much, and suggested she ought to rent somewhere while the builders gutted the place. Not at all – you don't make money out of restoring houses that way. She and her three teenaged children, Barnaby, Edmund and Elizabeth, literally camped out in the shell while the builders worked round them. They had a gasring, a few chairs, a dining-room table, a radio and television all in the front-room, and slept in sleeping bags in the unheated bedrooms. When the children needed a bath they used to take their soap and a towel along the road and found a friendly neighbour who would let them use the bathroom.

By Christmas Kate had created some sort of order in the house and the Cotton and Burgess families spent the holiday together. To brighten our festivities, a story in the tabloids alleged that I had raised a loan from the BBC to buy the house. (In fact, the house was paid for entirely by Kate who over the years had become pretty adept at buying and developing property.) Kate's divorce had long been declared final and I had reached a financial arrangement with Ann; it seemed pointless to go on living apart. We decided to move in together and get married as soon as possible.

There was still one hurdle to be surmounted. I'd met Kate's children but not her formidable mother, Enid Ralphs, who was chairman of the Magistrates' Association and also chairman of the Norwich Bench for many years. I gathered she viewed me with a somewhat jaundiced eye. When the relationship between Kate and myself hit the press, we both resigned from the magistrates' bench at Richmond, which was a blow to Enid since she was proud of her daughter's public service. Her husband, Sir Lincoln Ralphs, had been a member of the BBC's General Advisory Committee and they both had pronounced views on BBC Television. To cap everything, I was a married man and nearly nineteen years older than her daughter.

The first encounter between Lady Ralphs and myself took place at L'Ecu de France, a Jermyn Street restaurant that no longer exists. I chose the venue because its tables were arranged in alcoves and I thought if things got a bit rough at least we wouldn't be overheard by the rest of the diners. It turned out to be a very civilised and enjoyable meal. Kate had obviously smoothed the ground in advance by having a frank discussion with her mother about her feelings for me. Enid assured me that she intended to support Kate in whatever she wished to do; in turn, I assured her that I thought the world of her daughter and would do everything possible to make her happy. Having arrived at L'Ecu de France slightly apprehensively, I left with a smile of relief on my face and the waiter saw the benefit in the size of my tip.

I became part of a fascinating, highly intelligent family: there's Kate's brother David, a consultant surgeon, his wife, Diana, and their four sons, and Kate's elder sister, Anne, a barrister. Ralphs family gatherings are happy, argumentative affairs.

If a new era in my life was beginning with Kate, another was ending. December saw the last appearance at a Royal Television Society dinner of its retiring president, my great friend and mentor Huw Wheldon who'd made the rest of us who followed him as managing directors of the television service seem inadequate. The farewell was held at the Arts Club off

Piccadilly. Paul Fox, the incoming president, was in the chair and introduced Huw, and the Welsh wizard showed that age had not robbed him of his eloquence. He had a short and long version of every story he told and this, his valedictory appearance, was a night for the longer versions. He was followed by the head of the Birmingham centre of the BBC, Phil Sidey, who was a formidable after-dinner speaker. He had been preparing his speech for months, and it showed. It was a clever, witty performance and he finished to enormous applause. I'd drawn the short straw, being asked to speak last, after Phil. There's only one way out of a fix like that. I began by saying that Phil and I had met for a drink before dinner, and as a bit of fun decided to swap speeches; the assembled throng had already heard my speech and I would now deliver Phil's.

I only saw Huw once after that very emotional occasion. He had cancer at an advanced stage and I visited him at his home on Richmond Hill. We sat in the upstairs living-room with the River Thames stretching below us. He knew he was dying, and he didn't want to. There was so much he still longed to do. It wasn't to be. He died on 24 March 1986 and there was a crowded memorial service in Westminster Abbey a couple of months later, when the great American soprano Jessye Norman brought tears to everyone's eyes by singing Dido's lament from Purcell's *Dido and Aeneas* – a tremendous finale for a much loved and respected man, one of the giants of British broadcasting.

That year saw the fiftieth anniversary of the creation of BBC Television, and messages flooded in from many countries paying tribute to the world's first television service and praising the consistently high quality of its programmes – in stark contrast to Thatcher's government which carried on a campaign of constant denigration of the Corporation.

One thing at least probably pleased Mrs Thatcher: *Yes, Minister* was chosen as the BBC's entry for the Montreux Festival. The choice pleased me too because I can lay claim to saving the series for the BBC. When I first became Managing Director, I was told that there would be no further *Yes, Minister* because Light Entertainment had been unable to agree financial terms with the writers. I immediately invited Tony Jay and Jonathan Lynn to a meeting in my office. Tony's line quite simply was that market forces should prevail; there was a great demand for their product so they must take it wherever their terms could be met. I assured him that I too believed in the power of the market and said I would pay the sum they were asking if they would produce twenty-six shows by Christmas. This wasn't the line he had been expecting. I pointed out that if we were going to lay out expenditure of that order, which would be a significant slice of our Light Entertainment budget, there must be a sufficient number of shows to build up viewer expectations. It was a game of bluff and double-bluff. Tony and I both knew that a run of twenty-six programmes was out of the question – they had been writing them at the rate of seven a series, which though a rare treat didn't occupy enough screen time to realise the comedy's potential. We compromised on a run of fourteen programmes plus a Christmas special. And the title was to be changed. The eponymous minister Jim Hacker would by a fluke become Premier: hence *Yes, Prime Minister*.

I was delighted that the comedy had been nominated for Montreux, because that year I was invited to be the president of its jury (partly, I suspect, to recognise the BBC's fiftieth anniversary but also, I would like to think, acknowledging that I knew something about light entertainment). Kate and I drove to Montreux. The role of president was very demanding. Loaded to the gunnels with food and drink after hosting innumerable receptions, I had to sit through all the viewings – no sneaking off for the odd night on the town as I'd managed in 1967 when I was a mere juror. There are always political undertones to international festivals like these, but I had one vice-president from the Eastern Bloc and one from the Third World to help me hold the ring. It was demanding, but good fun.

I guess it is impossible to spend a lifetime dealing with comedy and comedians professionally without one's own sense of humour being affected. And I confess there were times when my sense of the ridiculous got me into trouble. The BBC had a great many women in critically important jobs but only a handful who had reached the level of senior management, and they felt the rest of us patronised them – as I discovered to my cost at a meeting where one asked me bluntly, 'Why do you call me "love"?' Actually, I call most women 'love', just as I call many men 'mate'. The reason is simple: my memory for names is atrocious and I find this form of address a way of avoiding seeming rude or offhand. I tried to explain this and was on the receiving end of an impassioned speech about the BBC's appalling attitude to women. The incident became part of the folklore of the BBC. Apparently, when she finished I replied, 'I think you've got a point there, darling.' When she complained to a male colleague he replied, 'That's nothing. He calls me "petal".'

I recall an exchange with one of the governors, Sir John Boyd, where my sense of humour fell on stony ground. In his day, Sir John had been one of the most powerful trade union bosses in the land and was a devout member of the Salvation Army. At one meeting of the board of governors, Sir John had made a plea for a television programme that would do for industry what *The Archers* had done for farming. I pointed out that there was already such a drama serial running on BBC1: *Howards' Way*, which was set in a small boatyard at the centre of a marina. Sir John confessed he hadn't seen it, perhaps because it went out on an early Sunday evening when he was at church. He promised to watch it. Four episodes later, he complained that *Howards' Way* was doing nothing for the ship-building industry; it was about sex, sex and more sex. 'You've missed the point, Sir John,' I said. 'It's not a show about boats, it's a show about beds. The furniture manufacturers love it.'

Sir John was not amused. As it turned out, the ship builders thought *Howards' Way* was giving a great boost to the sale of boats, and at the Boat Show some of them begged me not to take it off. But I felt that Sir John regarded me with some suspicion from then on.

And there was more programme trouble before 1986 was out. Ian Curteis had written some very distinguished drama scripts for the BBC, including *Suez 1956* and *Churchill and the Generals,* and had been semi-commissioned by Alasdair at a Writers' Luncheon Club meeting four years previously to write a play about the Falklands War. When he duly delivered the script, Alasdair asked me to read it. It was a pro-Thatcherite account of the conflict – which didn't worry me; a writer is entitled to a viewpoint, however partisan – but I felt it was not up to standard. However, I made no pretensions to being a qualified literary critic so without comment I handed it over to Michael Grade, who as Controller of BBC1 would have to make the drama resources available and schedule it. He was equally disappointed with the script and didn't feel he could justify spending a million pounds of the BBC's money on it. He made a valiant attempt through his Head of Drama, Peter Goodchild, to get Ian Curteis to rewrite it. Mr Curteis saw no reason why he should, and drew the conclusion that it was the script's pro-Thatcherite stance which had made it unacceptable to us.

At this point Alasdair stepped in and, hoping to save Ian Curteis's pride, wrote to him pointing out that there was a general election in the offing and a play glorifying the Prime Minister would get the BBC into serious trouble. Ian Curteis didn't believe him and the matter reached both the press and the board of governors. Quite independently, Michael Grade had been dealing with another script about the Falklands War, *Tumbledown,* about the experiences of Lieutenant Robert Lawrence MC, who had been badly wounded and then in the post-war desire to play down the suffering caused by the conflict felt he had been poorly treated. Michael was enthusiastic about this script by Charles Wood, though the coincidence in timing of the two accounts was unfortunate. That we should be enthusiastic about an anti-Thatcherite account of the Falklands War and refuse to take forward a pro-Thatcherite script confirmed the government's worst suspicions of the BBC. The possibility that we were making our judgement for strictly professional reasons never seemed to have occurred to them.

Some of the governors shared the government's sentiments and suggested a compromise: let the BBC make both and then the country could decide which was the more truthful account – an absurd proposition which both Michael Grade and I resisted. Three times the governors discussed the issue, but finally they gave in. *Tumbledown* was transmitted to great acclaim, Ian Curteis had his script serialised in the *Daily Mail*. It was another unfortunate episode that widened the gulf between the two boards and exposed Alasdair to even more political flak.

My life wasn't all BBC politicking and internal rows. My job gave me privileged access to great sporting occasions. Kate and I were invited to the directors' box at Wimbledon Football Club in Plough Lane, which is where Dad played for them as an amateur, before they moved to Selhurst Park. Wimbledon were playing Everton in an FA Cup-tie. During the interval, we were having a cup of tea in a room off the box when an Everton director came up to me and said, 'In my youth I used to dance to your band at the Rialto Ballroom in Liverpool.' As I was in my mid-fifties at the time and he was in his late seventies, I asked him to think about it. 'If I was who you think I am, I'd be over ninety now. Do I really look that old?' He laughed, and said, 'How stupid can I get?'

I was often mistaken for my father. He only began doing television shows when he was in his fifties so that's how the general public remember him – avuncular, bald with glasses – and since I was at the time roughly that age and avuncular, bald with glasses, people easily got confused. Even now, thirty years after his death, London cabbies often say as I'm paying the fare, 'You don't half look like your old man,' or 'Many's the time I took your father to his flat in Bury Street.' I appreciate the fact that Dad is still warmly remembered.

I've grown like him not just in appearance but in some of my ways. I used to pull his leg about his little quirks; now I find the laugh is on me. Like him, I'm getting hard of hearing and have a tendency to push my glasses up on to my forehead when I want to read something – the most famous photographic portrait of Dad, by Karsh of Ottawa, shows him looking quizzically at the camera with his glasses up on top of his head.

We share a tendency to hypochondria. He went everywhere with a briefcase filled with bottles of pills and herbal remedies rattling like a Caribbean maraca. I've been known to watch a medical drama and mysteriously develop the symptoms of some of the more rarefied diseases being treated. I'm also a creature of habit, sharing his tendency to nod off in cinemas, trains and when being driven anywhere. And I'm given to nostalgia, remembering warmly past times and regretting their passing.

A man once came up to me in a bar and said, 'My mate lived next door to your father in Liverpool, and they used to play together as kids.' Caught off my guard, I said, 'No, my father was a Londoner, born and brought up in Westminster.' He persisted aggressively. 'No, he wasn't a Londoner, he was my mate's next door neighbour in Liverpool.' 'Of course he was,' I replied. 'My mistake.' I drank up and left. These two Liverpudlians had probably dined out for years on the myth that one of them had lived next door to the famous band-leader Billy Cotton, and his mate wasn't going to let me ruin the story. And there was a sense in which Dad had belonged to the whole nation. He was one of the first stars to become a household name on both radio and television. Except for the purposes of historical record, it didn't matter a damn where he had been born.

TEN

At the beginning of 1986 there was another shake-up in top management. Somewhat reluctantly, Brian Wenham left the television service to become Managing Director of Radio. Because Wenham had spent his whole career in television, a real radio professional, David Hatch, who'd been in charge of Radio 4, was appointed his Director of Programmes to help him out, and this carried with it a seat on the board of management. I was delighted. David was an entertainment man through and through. He had been part of the very successful *Footlights* team while he was up at Cambridge along with John Cleese and a whole raft of very talented actors and comedians. After a short spell as an actor he joined the BBC as a radio producer and stayed with the wireless throughout his career.

So with Michael Grade combining his job as Controller of BBC1 with that of Director of Programmes for Television, we had for the first time in the Corporation's history three members of the board of management responsible for programmes whose backgrounds were in entertainment rather than journalism. It was generally accepted throughout the Corporation that Michael would succeed me as Head of the Television Service in a couple of years when I retired. At least, that was the theory – things turned out very differently.

In July, Kate celebrated her fortieth birthday, so we had what they call in the North Country a 'bit of a do'. It was a party for ninety members of our families and friends and the first of many parties we were to hold in a house that had very much become my home. That same month, the Commonwealth Games, for which we were doing the television coverage, opened in Edinburgh. The organisers had trouble finding the cash to

233

mount the Games, so larger than life newspaper tycoon and shady character Robert Maxwell came to the rescue flourishing his Mirror Group chequebook. In his own inimitable way he just took things over, and despite the fact he had broken his ankle was much in evidence when the Queen declared the Games open.

I went up to Edinburgh to make quite certain that Big Bob hadn't taken over the BBC operation as well. The day after the opening ceremony I had lunch with him and he insisted I flew back to London in his private jet. He had a coterie of attractive personal assistants who buzzed around him like flies, organising his life by the minute. Just before we were due to take off, the assistant in charge of arranging our flight discovered that her boss was missing. As I had a meeting in London later in the afternoon I said I'd better make use of my British Airways ticket and catch the shuttle to London. In tones of panic, she begged me to hang on, and a whole army of pretty girls combed the airport. After about ten minutes Maxwell limped into the room on his stick offering no explanation for where he had been or why he had kept us waiting. I gathered this was not unusual.

During the flight to London we chatted generally, then Maxwell asked me how I liked working for the BBC. I said I enjoyed it very much. I knew one of his hobbies was seducing successful executives from other companies into his employment in order to demonstrate his power, so in a semi-jocular tone I said I had a list of people I would never work for. My father headed it, Lew Grade was on it and so was he. He asked me if the people on the list were allowed to know why they had been black-balled. I replied that all the people on the list were marvellous at looking after themselves but if anything went wrong I wondered what would happen to me. Maxwell chuckled, though his eyes weren't smiling, and then conversation seemed to dry up. We read the papers for the rest of the flight.

In August the BBC received a body-blow. Stuart Young, the chairman of the governors, died. He came back from a trip to China and India with a hacking cough. His cancer had returned.

The board of management and he had had their differences, most notably over *Real Lives*, but we had all come to appreciate just what an enthusiastic and tough guardian of the BBC he had been during his years on the board. He had graduated from being a hard-nosed Thatcherite free marketeer into a champion of public service broadcasting funded by licence fee, and his credibility with the government had been a tremendous asset. I visited him in hospital the week before he died and he showed great courage, walking to the lift with me to demonstrate he was still in there fighting.

I was away on a week's holiday in Scotland when Stuart died, and caught the sleeper back to London to join the mourners at his funeral which, as he was Jewish, took place very quickly after his death. I was very fond of him, and later in the year had the privilege, along with Margaret Thatcher and Alasdair Milne, of speaking at a memorial service for him attended by the Princess of Wales at the Guildhall.

We waited with some apprehension to see who the Prime Minister would appoint as chairman in Stuart's place. Meanwhile, Joel Barnett as vice-chairman was looking after things and very quickly began to make his presence felt. Two years previously, *Panorama* had broadcast the programme *Maggie's Militant Tendency* which, after much meticulous research and legal vetting, exposed alleged links between some Tories and right-wing extremist organisations. Two of the MPs named in the programme sued the BBC for libel, and the case had been dragging its way through the legal process for two years. It finally came to court during the time Lord Barnett was filling the interregnum and as acting chairman he ordered Alasdair Milne to settle. The BBC apologised to the MPs, paid them damages and incurred legal costs of half a million pounds.

Libel is one of those areas of the law where the outcome is often unpredictable. Lord Barnett was entitled to his opinion and he had the power to enforce it, but the public and political consequences of the BBC being seen to cave in were very damaging. The integrity of BBC journalism was gleefully traduced by a hostile press, one hundred MPs called for

Alasdair's resignation and, yet again, the board of governors showed themselves mistrustful of the judgement of the professional broadcasters by unanimously endorsing Joel Barnett's decision. Another public-relations disaster was added to the long list of blunders laid by the governors at Alasdair's door, and I realised that he was living on borrowed time.

There was fevered speculation about the identity of the next chairman of the BBC. The press floated a number of names, the one most frequently mentioned being that of Lord King, the man who had sorted out British Airways. If the Prime Minister had decided on radical surgery, this was the man to wield the knife.

On the Tuesday of the Conservative Party Conference I went down to Bournemouth, where it was being held, in order to be host at the cocktail party the BBC gave at all these gatherings. Norman Tebbit, who was then chairman of the party, was one of the guests and on his high horse about the BBC. Besides the recent libel affair, he had been incensed by a news report from Libya by the BBC's chief news reporter Kate Adie, who had vividly but accurately described the damage an American bombing raid had done. Tebbit regarded the report as blatant pro-Gaddafi propaganda and he had said as much at the Tory Party Conference in the course of an anti-BBC tirade. He then proceeded to carry on the fight at the cocktail party and laid into us over the wine and canapés. I asked him if he would come to the BBC and have dinner with some of the people who were responsible for the television programmes to which he objected. 'You wouldn't like it if I did come,' was his reply. I countered with, 'I wouldn't have asked you if I was worried about that. The invitation stands.' He promised to get in touch, and some months later we had a very convivial meal with a number of managers and programme editors to whom he spoke frankly about what he perceived as anti-Tory party bias in our News and Current Affairs programmes. He got as good as he gave, but remained an outspoken critic of the Corporation.

Meanwhile I'd heard the name of Christopher Chataway mentioned vaguely here and there as a potential chairman.

Before he went into politics and became a Tory MP, Chris had made a great name for himself as a distance runner. None of my generation will forget his victory in the 10,000 metres against the Russian Vladimir Kuts at White City, fighting it out to the very end of the last lap, so close together the same spotlight beam caught them both. That night Chataway became a national hero to be spoken of in the same breath as Roger Bannister, who broke the four-minute mile. Chris had gravitated into television after his running career was over and became a newscaster on the newly formed ITN along with Robin Day and Alastair Burnet. He was then elected an MP for Chichester, and after a couple years in the House Ted Heath appointed him postmaster general – in those days the minister responsible for broadcasting.

Chris's name began to catch on and I heard it often enough at the Conservative Party Conference to phone Alasdair and tell him that all the smart money was on Chris Chataway's name being announced as the next chairman of the BBC governors.

The Home Secretary, Douglas Hurd, duly announced the name of the new chairman of the BBC. Not Chris Chataway but Marmaduke Hussey. 'Who he?' asked irreverent journalists of the *Private Eye* persuasion. Those who claimed to be in the know said the job had been offered to the vice-chairman, William Rees-Mogg, but he had other fish to fry and recommended his neighbour and former *Times* colleague Duke Hussey, who as the paper's managing director had presided over a year-long strike in 1978, and had had only a seat on the board since Rupert Murdoch's takeover. His wife was lady-in-waiting to the Queen and her brother was William Waldegrave, a Conservative cabinet minister.

The Labour opposition was outraged by the appointment, their media spokesman Gerald Kaufman assuring the press that when they came to power they would sack him. William Rees-Mogg, on the other hand, thought it was a brilliant appointment. 'Dukey', he said, was 'tough enough to resist the BBC's blandishment and subversion'. Before he'd even crossed the threshold of the BBC, Dukey was being cast as a new headmaster appointed to bring the unruly boys to order. I found it infinitely depressing. What we needed was a reconciler, someone who would win the confidence of both boards and could heal the growing rift which was paralysing us.

We were eventually summoned to the TV Centre's sixth-floor suite to meet Dukey. He was a big, shaggy man resting heavily on a stick to take the weight off an artificial limb. He had lost his leg during the war at Anzio. As a young second lieutenant in the Guards, he found himself on the wrong side of the frontline and tried to get back by using his hurdling skills to jump over a German slip trench containing a machine gun. He counted on surprise and almost made it. Unfortunately, he slipped on landing and received a burst of fire in his back and legs. Captured, he lay near death until a German army-doctor ended days of agony and saved his life by amputating the leg.

So no one was in any doubt about Dukey's physical courage, nor about his stoicism and humour. One of the first things I heard him say was, 'I fall over a lot, but don't worry, I always get up again.' He gave the impression of being an old buffer but beneath the huffing and puffing he was obviously no fool. It was a pleasant enough meeting, and along the lines of a commanding officer inspecting his troops he announced that he would embark on a series of organised visits to see the staff at work. We tried to make him welcome but we couldn't avoid the uneasy feeling that his friend Rees-Mogg could have already marked our cards and filled his head with unhelpful advice on how to deal with the mandarins of the BBC.

A fortnight later Kate and I spent the weekend with Richard Armitage at Stebbing. On the Sunday morning, Richard and I went for a walk and he asked me what I intended to do when I left the BBC. I replied that it was still eighteen months away and I hadn't given it much thought. He then suggested I might like to finish my working life where I started it, working for the Noel Gay Organisation. I remember saying, 'Provided you make me a rich man, I accept,' and we left it at that. But I was very touched by his offer, which relieved me of any worry about my future once I left the BBC.

The following week Michael Grade and I flew to America to attend celebrations being held by various entertainment organisations paying tribute to fifty years of BBC Television. We were guests of honour at a lunch given by the Council of the National Association of Television Arts and Sciences at the Coconut Grove. At our table were Tony Curtis, who was accompanied by a spectacular-looking raven-haired beauty who announced herself as Miss Hawaii Tropical and said nothing else, Charles Bronson and his wife, Jill Ireland, and the comedian Milton Berle, who was to provide the floor-show.

I had a tenuous link with Jill. Her ex-father-in-law, David McCullum, had been the leader of the London Symphony Orchestra and also moonlighted as one of a three-strong string-section which augmented Dad's band for his Sunday lunchtime broadcasts. Jill herself was making a recovery from breast cancer, a period of her life she documented well in her book *Life Wish*, a title she had chosen deliberately to resonate and contrast with her husband Charles Bronson's highly successful film *Death Wish*.

During the speeches, fulsome tributes were paid to the BBC and Michael and I were called on to reply. By now we had performed at so many similar functions that our double act was highly polished. We must have done pretty well because Milton Berle began his act by announcing, 'If I'd known I was following those two I wouldn't have taken the gig.'

The next day we flew to New York for a dinner with one of the leading networks, NBC, hosted by the network president, then on to Washington where the British ambassador Tony Acland was our host for a dinner at the British Embassy. I had become a fairly hard-bitten BBC type but it was deeply moving to realise just how enormous the Corporation's reputation was throughout the world thanks to the integrity, skill and dedication of thousands of employees. I just felt very sad that back at home Thatcher's government still viewed us with a jaundiced eye and lost no opportunity to belittle us.

On my return, still euphoric after my triumphal progress on behalf of the BBC through America, I went into the office in high spirits. Then I got a call from Richard Armitage's younger son, Alex. Richard had collapsed with a massive stroke and had died at Stebbing the night before. I was absolutely stunned. Richard had died in his early fifties at the height of his powers. He had a hit musical running in London and New York and he was about to launch his London production of *High Society*. His agency was booming and his musical company was on the up and up. It all seemed grotesquely unfair.

Richard was my very closest friend, and in the short time Kate had been part of my life the pair had formed a benign conspiracy to keep me in my place. I could only imagine the gap in the lives of his partner Lo and his two sons.

At the family's request, I gave the eulogy at his funeral which was held at the parish church in Stebbing where Richard often played the organ for Sunday services. Besides the family, in the congregation were some of the stars whose careers he had nurtured and cared for: Esther Rantzen, Emma Thompson, Robert Lindsay, Russ Conway and Stephen Fry. They were there primarily not to remember him as a great impresario but to pay tribute to a loveable human being.

In December there was a service in St Giles, which is just a stone's throw away from Richard's office in Denmark Street where he had spent all his working life and I had started mine. By now enough time had elapsed for the shock of his death to have subsided and given way to our wish to celebrate his life. Stephen Fry's contribution was a Dickensian pastiche so brilliantly written that at first it was impossible to distinguish it from the real thing. It was a tribute from a witty and talented performer to his mentor – Richard had employed him to rework the book of *Me and My Girl*.

We spent that Christmas at Beauchamp Place, the name of the house Kate had bought and renovated in East Molesey. My mother came to stay for the three days of the holiday. Kate's children had decorated the house, including our four-poster bed, and on Christmas morning we sat Mother in it and Kate gave her a specially made Christmas stocking. Mother was close to tears as she admitted it was the first Christmas stocking she'd ever been given in eighty years. She said it in no spirit of self-pity – she was just overwhelmed with delight. Dad had cared for her but he wasn't one to make a fuss of her, so Kate was delighted to do the honours.

A few weeks later there was a board of governors meeting preceded by a farewell dinner for Alwyn Roberts, the Welsh governor, whose term of office had ended. We had enormous affection and respect for him because he had often been the lone voice on the board in support of management. He would be sorely missed.

The board meeting next morning was just par for the course: endless nitpicking by the governors who disapproved of this, complained about that and generally harassed Alasdair; it seemed he could do nothing right. I remember Huw Wheldon once coming out of a similar meeting and exploding, 'Sodding governors!' Now I knew exactly what he meant.

After the meeting, Mike Checkland and Alasdair joined me in my office and we despaired of ever establishing a creative relationship with the governors. Then the secretary of the BBC, Patricia Hodgson, whose job was to head the secretariat of the board of governors, came in and said, 'Alasdair, the chairman would like to see you.' Alasdair said later he found it odd that Patricia Hodgson had called him by his Christian name. She always punctiliously addressed him as 'DG'.

Alasdair left and was back within five minutes, as white as a ghost. 'They've fired me,' he said tersely. I presumed he meant Hussey had told him the board would not be extending his contract when it lapsed in a year's time. Mike asked him, 'When?' Al replied, 'Now, but I haven't given them the pleasure of firing me, I've resigned, and I'm off home.' I just couldn't believe it. As chief executive of the most important cultural institution of Britain, the Director-General of the BBC had a symbolic as well as actual significance. I couldn't credit that he would be treated in such an insulting and demeaning manner.

Reflecting on the extraordinary events of that day, I wish Alasdair had refused to say or do anything other than ask for time to decide what his best course of action was. He could then have consulted his friends and even insisted on a meeting of the full board of governors immediately after lunch to see how many of them, face to face, would have told him to go. Individually, most of the governors were decent people but they were being led by a man who believed in exercising the full extent of his powers. Hussey was determined to show who was boss right from the outset. It's easy now to wonder whether Alasdair reacted in the wisest manner but the shock must have been incredible. And he was a proud, even impulsive man. I suspect Hussey and Barnett were banking on the fact that he would react the way he did.

Mike Checkland as deputy DG was sent for and told to keep the ship steady. Then it was my turn. Joel Barnett was in the room with Hussey, who opened the conversation by saying, 'Alasdair has decided to resign,' and handed me his signed note of resignation. Joel Barnett then said, 'It won't come as a surprise to you, Bill,' to which I replied, 'Well, let's say that when I woke up this morning Alasdair was the Director-General, and I had no reason to believe he would not be when I went to bed.' I took my leave.

I presumed the chairman would be telling each member of the board of management about the governors' action, but apart from Mike I was the only one he saw. I think I was seen as a second line of defence: if Mike Checkland refused to serve in the interregnum, I would have been asked to do the job. In the event Mike agreed. I didn't question the legal or moral right of the board of governors to get rid of any one of us, but they had fired Alasdair in such a way as to rob him of his dignity and I was disgusted. They could have talked to Alasdair in a civilised way and reached some agreement about a date for his departure which recognised the many years of distinguished service he had given to the Corporation.

I toyed with the idea of resigning in protest at the treatment of Alasdair but I was on the brink of retirement anyway, so it would have been little more than an empty gesture. I also realised I had a duty to stand by Mike and steady the nerves of the staff who would be shattered when they heard the news.

We then trooped into the dining-room for lunch. The chairman called for silence by tapping a glass, ordered the catering staff to leave and read out a statement about Alasdair's resignation. I noticed that the table had been laid without any place-cards so that no one would notice there was no card with Alasdair's name on it. The whole thing had been a well-prepared operation with every detail worked out in advance. I couldn't understand why we had gone through the charade of a board meeting at which the governors pretended that everything was normal when they knew they were about to throw the BBC into turmoil. Tapping on a glass to call for order became a BBC in-joke, but I never found it funny.

The staff of the Corporation was bewildered and saddened. Alasdair was a popular boss. He could be prickly and brusque but he was honest and fair and utterly devoted to the making of good programmes. He was not a systems man and found administration tiresome. He had the right priorities but he wasn't a natural politician; he had no interest or aptitude for the internal power game and he paid for it.

However great our shock and anger at the firing of Alasdair, our minds inevitably turned to the question of his successor. All the usual names – and some very unlikely ones – were mooted in the press. Michael Grade was outraged when there were strong rumours that the chairman's favoured candidate was the Current Affairs presenter David Dimbleby. Michael had nothing against him personally but felt that it would be a disaster for the BBC if he ended up as DG. He told me he intended to write to Hussey warning him that if Dimbleby was appointed he would leave the BBC. I told him frankly that if he intended to try to spike Dimbleby's guns then he had a moral responsibility to put his own hat in the ring, to mix a metaphor. I thought it was too early for Michael this time round, but that if he made his mark with the board during his interview it would put his appointment as my successor beyond doubt.

We then fell to discussing who we would like to see in the job, and our first choice was Paul Fox. He had been Head of Sport and Controller of BBC1 before leaving in 1973 for ITV, where he had become one of the major figures on the British broadcasting landscape. Paul is a big man in both senses of the word and we felt he could handle the board of governors and provide a counter-balance to Duke Hussey. We arranged to see the chairman privately in his London flat to lobby for Paul's appointment. Dukey was very affable but Michael and I both formed the impression that he had another candidate in mind – the rumours about Dimbleby were probably true. There also seemed to be a perception, shared by Joel Barnett, that Paul at sixty-two was too old – curious, then, that a year later they appointed him to be my successor as Managing Director of BBC Television.

The beauty-contest started. The internal candidates were Brian Wenham, Mike Checkland and Michael Grade. The outsiders were David Dimbleby, Jeremy Isaacs, the chief executive of Channel Four, and Anthony Smith, an academic who had been editor of *Panorama* and had something of a reputation as a television intellectual. Though Hussey was weighing in for Dimbleby and Barnett was said to favour Isaacs, the smart money was on the two insiders, Checkland and Wenham.

It was symbolic that during the run-up to the appointment of a new Director-General one of the greatest of the breed, Hugh Carleton Greene, died. He had been the principal architect of the modern BBC. After a career in journalism as the *Daily Telegraph*'s foreign correspondent in Europe during the 1930s, Greene was head of the BBC's German Service throughout the war. Then following a spell running the broadcasting service in Malaya he had been appointed Director-General in 1960. As all the obituaries pointed out, he opened windows at the BBC, sweeping away the Corporation's stuffy image and encouraging risky and innovative programme-making. I represented the BBC at his funeral which was held in Cockfield church in Suffolk.

Interestingly, Hugh was also a DG who was effectively removed from the job after clashes with the then chairman of the governors, Lord Hill. Hill, who made his name on BBC

Wireless as the Radio Doctor, had been chairman of the Independent Broadcasting Authority before the Prime Minister of the time, Harold Wilson, had parachuted him into the BBC to subdue a rebellious corporation. But in those days, the BBC was a much more civilised organisation and Hugh's departure was engineered with great panache.

A couple of days before his interview, Michael Grade asked if I would sit in with a group of people who would throw the sort of questions at him the board might ask. One of the other inquisitors was an old friend of his from LWT, John Birt. It was the first time I had come across him since Brian Tesler had mentioned his name when offering me the job of Director of Programmes at LWT. He demonstrated that he had a forensic mind and asked probing questions, though I thought him a little humourless – at least by my knockabout standards. Still, he was pleasant enough.

On the day the new DG was to be appointed, I was attending the BBC Enterprises' Showcase at the Grand Hotel in Brighton. This was an annual event where we showed off our programmes to other broadcasters in Europe in the hope they would buy some of them.

On the way back to London my carphone rang. The white smoke had gone up from Broadcasting House: Mike Checkland was to be the new DG despite the chairman's preferences. He did try to foist Dimbleby on Mike as his deputy, but Mike wasn't having it.

I was pleased for Mike, though I wondered whether he had the guns to stand up to the chairman and governors. I felt sorry for Brian Wenham. I had never rated his chances highly; he wasn't popular with the governors – he was much too quick-witted for some of them and had a streak of sardonic wit that made him enemies. He was not awfully discreet but undoubtedly had the best brain on the board of management and I realised that we were bound to lose him; there was nowhere else in the BBC for him to go. Sure enough he left soon afterwards.

The next day we went to a management weekend with the

board of governors at Ettington Park Hotel. I remember coming away from there with the distinct impression that the new chairman was thoroughly enjoying himself. After his ignominious exit from *The Times* it had looked as though he was going to fade into the sunset, then the Thatcher government raised him from the dead and gave him one of the most prestigious and powerful jobs in the land.

After that conference, Michael Grade was formally given the title of Managing Director (Designate). It was a move I welcomed. I was no longer interested in power and I could now relax and take things easier. I also looked forward to watching from the touchline the game being played out at Broadcasting House as a new team was being formed and players shuffled for position.

New DG Michael Checkland hadn't worked in the foothills of power for years without learning a thing or two about the endemic problems of the BBC, chief of which was the rivalry between News and Current Affairs that had contributed to a number of the most disastrous clashes between the Corporation and the government. The first item on his agenda was to sort out the BBC's journalism. Under Alasdair it had been handled by Alan Prothero as assistant DG. A first-class journalist with a marvellous sense of humour, Alan was a free-spirited Welshman who had been blamed by the governors when BBC *Breakfast Time* taped off-air an extract from an exclusive TV-AM interview with Princess Michael of Kent. This had been the last straw. He was already in deep trouble for an article he had written about the *Real Lives* fiasco which was published in the *Listener,* a journal funded by the BBC about aspects of broadcasting. Alan likened the Home Secretary thanking the governors for banning the programme to the White Star Line congratulating the iceberg for sinking the *Titanic.* It was a wonderful line to go out on, and out he went.

Meanwhile Michael Grade was very keen to get his friend, John Birt from London Weekend Television, into the BBC. The job on offer was to head both News and Current Affairs throughout the Corporation in a new structure which took all journalism out from under the control of Radio and Television's respective managing directors. The new directorate would have its own budget and air-time. Michael's whole philosophy of programme-making was diametrically opposed to that of John Birt. Birt thought that carefully planned policy would produce good programmes, whereas Michael believed good programmes ought to determine policy. Nevertheless, he much admired John's organisational ability and rigorous journalistic standards. I hardly knew John Birt but I trusted Michael's judgement and so supported the idea.

As it happened, John Birt had also been recommended to Duke Hussey. Eventually, Michael Checkland met him for the first time over lunch and on the strength of his initial impressions offered him the job. Somewhere in the discussions, it was also proposed that he become deputy DG, which made him nominally Michael Grade's superior. Michael wasn't worried about that as he'd got the impression from the DG that John would merely be standing in for Michael Checkland when he was away; he would have no operational control over the television service. I was quite easy about the appointment. I would be leaving the BBC in a year's time and recognised that Mike Checkland had to build a team for the future.

In that valedictory year I went to as many of the big occasions as possible, knowing that I would soon cease to be on the automatic invitation lists. I particularly relished the annual BAFTA Awards, and as usual had my own table to which I invited nominees for awards.

That year I noticed that Wendy Hiller had been nominated for Best Actress in a BBC play called *All Passion Spent*. In my youth she had been a star fantasised about. She was also unforgettable in the title role of the film version of *Major Barbara* in which she played opposite Rex Harrison. I arranged that she should join my party along with Michael Gambon and David Jason and their respective partners. As befitted her legendary status, she sat next to me and we had a thoroughly enjoyable conversation. When I brought up the subject of *Major*

Barbara she told me that she had never seen the picture. Apparently the producer had been so horrible to her during the shooting that she determined never to see his beastly film.

As the time for the announcement of the award in her category drew nearer, she got noticeably more nervous. She took out her powder compact and checked her hair and make-up in the mirror, then sat waiting expectantly, her gold-tipped walking-stick at the ready. The four nominations were announced and clips of their performances were shown. Then someone else was announced as the winner. She just sat looking straight ahead. Eventually she turned to me and said, 'They're quite boring these occasions, aren't they? I think I'll go home.' She gestured to her escort, a young writer who I guess had been recruited for the job by her agent, got to her feet and stalked out majestically, head held proudly in the air.

When her escort returned to our table, he said that someone had told Wendy that if she was invited to sit at my table, it meant she had won an award, and this was the only reason she'd agreed to come. I felt terrible, but I was completely in the dark about the awards. I chose my table-guests simply because they were interesting personalities and in one capacity or another had served the BBC well.

In the spring of that year, I had lunch with an old friend of mine from my music-business days. His name was Maurice Taylor and, like me, he had worked for Chappell's as a song-plugger. He then left to try his luck in America and did very well. When he came back to England he bought Thornbury Castle in the West Country which is now a successful hotel with an excellent restaurant. He also supported the Prince of Wales Charitable Trust in a voluntary capacity, and at the lunch told me he was sure the Prince together with Princess Diana would be prepared to be interviewed by the BBC if an appropriate fee went to the Trust. I thought this very unlikely and assured him that the heir to the throne did not give that sort of interview.

After the lunch, just to be sure I was right, I phoned Sir William Heseltine, the Queen's press secretary, and received an assurance that any such interview was out of the question.

Imagine my surprise later in the year when who should turn up on ITV but the Prince and Princess of Wales being interviewed by Sir Alastair Burnet?

The popular perception of the monarch was certainly beginning to change, so I was not too surprised when Hugh Williams, Head of BBC Operations in Manchester, came to see me and told me that Prince Edward had quit the Royal Marines and was looking for gainful employment as a television producer. He had told Stuart Hall, the veteran presenter of *It's a Knockout!*, that he would like to produce a royal version of the show. Would the BBC or any other broadcaster be interested in televising it? Apart from himself, the cast would include Princess Anne, the recently married Duke and Duchess of York, and of course stars of stage, screen and sport. The royals would captain the teams while the stars did the hard work. There was talk of selling the show to an American network, though all the proceeds would go to charity.

My immediate reaction was that this idea was fraught with danger, but Hugh was convinced that if we didn't do it ITV would; the Prince was a very determined young man. Once again I called Bill Heseltine to make sure the Palace was happy for the programme to go ahead. The show was to be recorded at Alton Towers, and during March I hosted a lunch with the Prince, John Bloom (the owner of Alton Towers), Michael Grade and Hugh Williams. I pointed out the danger of getting involved with an American network which in return for hard cash would demand full value from the royals – which might prove embarrassing.

We set about planning the programme. During the following weeks Dukey popped in to tell me how pleased the Queen was that I was taking a personal interest in the show (information presumably passed on by his wife, the Queen's lady-in-waiting). Then I got confused because Bill Heseltine phoned to tell me he had just been reprimanded by the Prince for discussing his business with me, and that the Queen had backed her son. I was glad that royal disapproval no longer entailed a spell in the Tower of London.

The day we were due to record the show dawned wet and miserable, but there was a two-hour window of fine weather during the afternoon so we got on with it. Royals and commoners alike threw themselves into the various games with unbounded enthusiasm; that said, I think that even Prince Edward, who is now a seasoned producer, will not look back on this show as any sort of breakthrough. Indeed, I read somewhere recently that it was the start of a downward trend in respect for the royal family because of the undignified way certain of the royals were alleged to have behaved. I doubt *It's a Royal Knockout* can be blamed for the rise of republicanism in Britain, but I don't think it added to the lustre of the monarchy.

The BBC had always had a special relationship with the royal family. Richard Cawston, once a first-class documentary-maker at the BBC and later Head of Documentaries, ought to have put up a 'By Royal Appointment' sign outside his office. He produced *The Royal Family*, the first behind-the-scenes, in-depth look at the British monarchy, which attracted twenty-three million viewers when it was first shown. He was also responsible for the Queen's Christmas message each year.

Then Richard left us and we had to find someone else to take on that role. I had the bright idea of asking David Attenborough. Little did I realise that David had been critical of Richard Cawston's film – not because of any technical imperfections but because as an expert on natural life he feels that the monarchy is a tribal thing that depends on mystique, on the general public not being allowed to see what goes on behind the scenes. So it was poetic justice that I asked him to do it, pointing out that if the Queen heard he had turned the offer down he would lose his knighthood. For a second his face dropped then he laughed and agreed. He did the job superbly.

Morbid though it might seem, the eventuality which was never far from the broadcasters' minds was the possibility of the Queen Mother's death. A whole protocol had been worked out and periodically we had rehearsals. Who would make the announcement? What sort of programmes would be suitable in the aftermath? How long would the mourning last? It was a measure of our affection and esteem for the Queen Mother that we were determined the ceremonial should be done with style and efficiency. Cash was put aside each year, and when I was running BBC1 and we were very short of money I used to raid the fund. 'Let's use the Queen Mum's money,' I'd say. 'She's not going anywhere. She'll live to be a hundred.' One of my better forecasts.

The process of sorting out the BBC's journalism started and John Birt began to make his presence felt. To me, he and the chairman had one thing in common: it seemed basically neither of them liked the BBC. This was shown not necessarily in what they did but in how they did it. Within a very short time of Birt's arrival I was reminded of Chester Wilmont's description in his book *Struggle for Europe* of General Montgomery's arrival at the American HQ during the successful German offensive in the Ardennes. He swept in like 'Christ come to cleanse the temple'.

John became very assertive about his title of Deputy Director-General and didn't confine his activities to News and Current Affairs, which we had assumed was the purpose of bringing him into the BBC. Michael Grade started getting notes from him criticising the output. Michael half-jokingly mentioned this to me and I told him to tear them up and, when he had enough to fill an envelope, return them to their sender. But what Michael took to be interference in his business began to get under his skin; he complained to Michael Checkland who had a word with Birt, and the notes stopped. However, there was something ominous about the way Birtism, as it soon became known, began to spread its tentacles throughout the Corporation.

I remember phoning a wise friend of mine in ITV and asking him what his opinion was of Birt. He said some nice things but added that John was obstinate and persistent and he needed someone to sit on him firmly from time to time otherwise he would grow like Topsy. Unfortunately, the only person who could sit on Birt – the chairman – was becoming his closest ally. This was an alliance that did not bode well for Michael Grade, but he'd survived in the rough, tough world of Hollywood so I wasn't too worried.

At the end of May, my PA, Queenie, retired. She'd really worked for only two people in the thirty-odd years she'd been in the television service: Tom Sloan and myself. She was a bit put out with me because she wanted to stay on until I went, but for various reasons I decided it would be in her best interests if she left before I did. To make clear how displeased she was, she announced that she didn't want a farewell party. I said that was fine; we would have a party without her and send her the photographs. Then she moved the goalposts and said that if she had a party, she didn't want me to make a speech or say anything publicly. I agreed. When the day came and a large number of her friends and colleagues gathered, I kept my promise and said not a word – instead I gestured on my fingers in mock sign language which Jim Moir, who was by now Head of Light Entertainment, interpreted in a brilliant speech.

Queenie knew more about me than I did. She was a confidante I could trust and rely on implicitly. She helped me through good times and bad and protected me when I needed it. I knew how discreet she was because I am sure she had the same relationship with Tom but she never discussed him with me.

Another party we held around that time was for Alasdair. We were all determined that his abrupt departure should not prevent us from having a proper celebration of all his work for the Corporation. He had – and has – a deep love of all things Scottish, especially the Gaelic language and piping, so, at the end of an evening when all his colleagues had dined him out, the lights were dimmed, the curtains of the sixth-floor suite at Television Centre were drawn back, and there, high on the opposite balcony, could be seen a line of pipers who played a lament. It was a moving occasion and the affection felt for Alasdair was palpable.

In July 1987 Margaret Thatcher won her third election, and yet again the BBC incurred the wrath of Norman Tebbit, the party chairman. Relying on the result of an exit poll immediately the voting finished, the BBC predicted a resounding Labour victory, but when the actual results began to flow in, it was obvious we'd got it wrong. Tebbit claimed the mistake had been wishful thinking. And once she'd settled in for her third term, the Prime Minister held a conference in Downing Street on broadcasting during which she laid about her with a will. This time it was ITV's turn to get a hand-bagging, so BBC types present kept their mouths shut and watched the slaughter.

Shortly after the election I went to Stuart Young's stone-setting. According to Jewish custom, this is done with due ceremony twelve months after burial. When the ceremony was over I was talking to Shirley Young, Stuart's widow, who introduced me to John Harris, a close family friend. John had built up a successful business in audio and video equipment, reviving the Alba brand name. During the conversation he asked me if after I'd retired from the BBC I would accept a non-executive directorship of Alba when the company went public. All of which duly transpired.

I already knew I wouldn't be idle when I left the BBC. Richard Armitage's two sons had come to see me a few weeks after his death and said they knew their fathers' plans and they wanted to stick to them; they asked if I would consider joining Noel Gay and running its television arm. I advised them to wait for six months to be sure that that was what they really wanted. Six months later they appeared again in my office and repeated the offer; I accepted, feeling that I was fulfilling the wishes of one of my dearest friends. My diary for 1988 was filling up nicely.

One of my final tasks at the BBC was to help Michael Grade to get his top management team in place at the Television Centre. Both controllerships were vacant, BBC1 because Michael was becoming Managing Director and BBC2 because Graeme MacDonald was retiring. There were four very strong candidates for the two jobs: Will Wyatt, Head of Features, Roger Laughton, Head of Daytime, Alan Yentob, Head of Music and Arts, and Jonathan Powell, Head of Drama.

I told Michael that he should make the final choice, since his career as well as theirs was on the line. Obviously, in accordance with BBC custom he would have to justify his choice to a selection board, but he should not be forced to appoint anyone in whom he did not have complete confidence.

When the selection board was convened, it turned out that John Birt was to be included in it. I therefore asked Michael Checkland why an ex-three-day-a-week controller of LWT was needed to choose controllers for the television service. He promised to sort matters out. Then Michael Grade and I were summoned to another meeting in the DG's office in which he made it clear that John Birt was exercising his right as deputy DG to be a member of the board, and what's more, the chairman wanted it that way. Then John Birt himself joined us. Michael Grade argued that it would send out all the wrong signals to the staff of the television service if Birt, who nominally outranked him, was to have a hand in choosing his closest colleagues. He ended by pleading with John to withdraw from the board. Birt was unrelenting. His contract stated that he was DG general and that is what he intended to be.

Michael and I left the DG's office full of foreboding, he about his future in the BBC and myself about the future of the BBC itself. I felt Michael Checkland had been lent on and had lost control of the game. He served his time as Director-General conscientiously and with a certain amount of success in overseeing necessary economies in a humane way, but increasingly Birt and Hussey were at the controls. What had been exposed was the Achilles' heel of the BBC. If a chairman and a Director-General or even a deputy Director-General have the same 'vision', they can take the BBC wherever they choose. Who can stop them?

This alliance proved its strength when Michael Checkland's contract was due for renewal in 1991. Birt was appointed over dinner at Broadcasting House without any other candidate being considered. John Birt has been quoted as saying he joined a corporation which had suffered a nervous breakdown. That was nothing compared to the nightmare the place lived through for the next decade.

The board to appoint the controllers took place. Alan Yentob and Jonathan Powell were appointed and within a matter of weeks Michael Grade had quit the BBC to become chief executive at Channel Four. I was bitterly disappointed, but I couldn't blame him. He would have been totally isolated in the Television Centre with Birt and Hussey calling the shots at Broadcasting House. In the interim, I was a lame duck running the television service with two brand-new controllers. We got by until Paul Fox was appointed, and the staff showed me every consideration.

One other incident was an ominous sign of the times. I had always objected to the idea of giving *Newsnight* on BBC2 an invariable starting time at ten-thirty. I didn't see why we needed yet another news programme at a fixed time in addition to the regular bulletins. It also made scheduling on BBC2 very difficult if we wanted to run a film or a major light-entertainment show at peak viewing-time. Indeed, *Newsnight* got its largest viewing figures when it was preceded by just such a programme.

When I got wind that there might changes afoot to the timing of *Newsnight*, I asked Michael Checkland to agree that no decision would be made until I had put my case to the governors. Then in the week between Christmas and New Year, the chairman, the DG and John Birt held a press conference in a studio at Television Centre. They didn't invite me to join them on the platform so I sat in the audience. They announced a number of future projects, then almost casually the DG said that from June *Newsnight* would start every night at ten-thirty p.m. The eyes of many of the staff present were on me and I was acutely uncomfortable. I felt a fool . . . no, it was stronger than that: I felt betrayed. I went back to my office and expected Checkland and Birt as a matter of courtesy to call in and explain their decision. No one appeared.

After the New Year, I received a letter from the chairman, dated 31 December, saying he appreciated how difficult, not to say unpleasant, it must have been for me to be confronted with this surprise decision, but that he and the DG had been afraid of press leaks. He invited me to lunch at Claridge's where we could talk things over. It was a convivial enough meal but I knew he didn't really want to hear what I'd got to say about the

Newsnight decision, so there was little point in discussing it.

Michael Checkland and I went back a long way together in the television service and he had been a loyal colleague and friend, but now everything had changed. He had thrown his lot in with Birt, and the *Newsnight* decision was inevitable. To this day I still don't understand why I wasn't allowed to put my case to the governors. It was no big deal. Against the Birt-Hussey axis I would probably have lost the argument but at least been spared the humiliation of that press conference.

Why end on a sour note? I had much to celebrate; the eighties produced many programmes to be proud of. *Child Watch* provided the basis for Esther Rantzen's Child Line, a phone-in service that to date has counselled more than one million children. Then in February 1988 we launched Comic Relief. The original idea came from Richard Curtis, the co-writer of *Blackadder* and many other successful comedies. What Bob Geldof and his fellow pop stars had done with Live Aid, Richard wanted comedians to emulate. He shared his thoughts with Jane Tewson who was working for Mencap at the time. They went off to Africa to do a recce and were horrified by what they saw in Somalia and Eritrea.

So Comic Relief was created, and the first effort was a three-night run of star-studded comedy at the Shaftesbury Theatre. It got television coverage through an *Omnibus* programme that went behind the scenes and looked at how the show was put together, then Noel Edmonds' *House Party* followed it up. Helen Fielding, later to write the Bridget Jones column and the best-selling books which flowed from it, worked tirelessly in the office. On 5 February, Comic Relief was officially launched and has since raised £160 million. One of the most moving and talked-about film clips it produced came out of a visit by Billy Connolly to Mozambique (referred to by Billy's children as 'Nose and Beak') where Comic Relief was financing work among displaced families. Billy was there when a father was reunited with his little son. He put his arms around both of them and for once the loquacious Glaswegian comedian was lost for words. There wasn't a dry eye in the house.

In March, Michael Checkland announced my successor. It was Paul Fox, so I was able to say I was making way for an older man. If anyone could compensate for the loss of Michael Grade on whom I had set such hopes, it was my friend Paul. Michael Checkland did sound me out about staying on as chairman of BBC Enterprises, but I had promised myself that I would leave the Corporation on my sixtieth birthday – and in truth, I'd had enough; I wanted to go.

I had still to face the ordeal of a whole welter of farewell ceremonies. There was a cocktail party in Television Centre to which many of my colleagues came to wish me well, then the board of governors gave a dinner for senior management, my family and some close friends. It was held in the Council Chamber at Broadcasting House around whose walls are portraits of all past Directors-General. The chairman made a very flattering speech and presented me with a number of presents. I was invited to reply and I did, at some length. At one stage I looked at the chairman, who because of his disability was in some discomfort, and said, 'I'm sorry about this, but I've been here quite a long time, and there's quite a lot to say.' Eventually I ran out of steam and I turned to look at Reith's portrait, which hangs over the fireplace. I addressed him thus: 'To you, sir, I would like to say just this. When we met you didn't particularly like me and I didn't particularly like you, but I am forever grateful to you for creating the finest broadcasting service in the world.'

Then it was the turn of the Light Entertainment department, among whom I had spent the happiest days of my life at the BBC. When Kate and I arrived in the reception at the Television Centre, we were announced by a fanfare from the State Trumpeters of the Household Cavalry. There were present retired heads of Light Entertainment from both ITV and the BBC and producers past and present. Jim Moir, Head of Light Entertainment, as is his habit, made a brilliant speech. He began by saying, 'Bill taught me all I know, but unfortunately not all he knows,' which though not strictly true was immensely flattering. Philip Jones, who was in charge of Thames Television Light Entertainment for so long, a professional rival and the man who enticed Eric and Ernie back to ITV from the BBC, also said a few words. When I rose to thank this good band of friends there was certainly a break in my voice.

The Variety Club of Great Britain decided to honour me with the Silver Heart at a lunch held in the Hilton Hotel in Park Lane. The event was televised and my old mate David Jacobs did the commentary. Esther Rantzen introduced speakers who spoke with great humour mixed with a little affectionate malice. Les Dawson, Mike Parkinson, Vera Lynn – who sang a chorus of 'Forget Me Not', my song-writing debut and finale – Noel Edmonds, Jimmy Savile, Colin Morris, Bruce Forsyth and Dave Allen all had their say. In my speech I reminded them that in 1962, the Variety Club of Great Britain had voted my father the Show Business Personality of the Year. I hope he would have been proud of me.

I've sometimes been described as a star-maker, but in my experience, talent will find its own level; all I could do, because I had access to air time, was to speed up the process. But as one after another of these showbiz personalities spoke, my chief feeling was one of gratitude to them – after all, besides giving me much friendship they had also paid my wages.

I had barely started my thank-you speech when I was interrupted by a waiter who began clearing away the dishes right under my nose. I looked more closely. It was Gorden Kaye in his guise as René, the café owner in the TV comedy *'Allo 'Allo*. I made some protesting noises but he swept them aside saying that he had to get things ready for an evening meal in honour of a really important man, Monsieur Paul Renard – or Paul Fox – my successor who now took priority over me because *he* could offer people work.

Friday 22 April arrived – the day I would be going into Television Centre for the last time as a member of the BBC. At lunchtime I took my PA, Rosemary, to lunch in the canteen.

When I first joined the BBC at Television Centre, the canteen was one of the first buildings to be erected; we had used it as a rehearsal-room until there were enough staff to put it to its proper use. Now it was packed full of people and there was about it the buzz of gossip and purposeful activity. I recalled my early days, when the entire staff was small enough for us all to be on first-name terms.

In the afternoon I had a final walk round the studios and the offices. I knew I would always carry good memories of my time there, the fun I had had and the many friendships I had made. And when disaster struck my life, it was the compassion, humanity and support of this place that had helped me through. I had given the BBC my best shot and I'd been very lucky the way the cards had fallen.

That evening Kate and I booked in at a nearby hotel so we could get changed into our gladrags for the final party. It was to be hosted by the Director-General and his wife, Michael and Sue Checkland. When Kate and I drew up on the forecourt of Television Centre, all the guests were standing outside in the chilly night air waiting to greet us. I was conducted to a podium, and wondered what would happen next. Suddenly there was a roll of drums, and then from round the corner the band of the Royal Marines appeared and began to beat 'Retreat' in front of the two flagpoles flying the BBC standard and the Union Jack. As they marched and counter-marched, they played a medley of the songs that Father had made famous, and I imagined that Billy Cotton, bandsman of the London Regiment, would be looking down approvingly.

Finally, the buglers sounded 'Sunset', the band played the 'Evening Hymn' and the BBC flag was lowered. Then 'Reveille'. The guests didn't seem to notice the cold; they were totally absorbed. The playing of the 'Last Post' and the slow lowering of the BBC flag was a heart-stopping moment. There is a film of the occasion which shows me in close-up shedding an unashamed tear as that haunting bugle call filled the air. Then two marines brought and presented to me the folded flag.

The party was held in the sixth-floor suite and was a very jolly occasion. In every part of my life, at boarding school, in the army and later in the BBC, there was always a special room to which you hoped one day to have access. The sixth-floor suite of the TV Centre was such a room. Its table will seat in excess of sixty people for dinner and it is often used for parties; but it's round this table too that the boards of governors and management had sometimes met and made decisions that affected my career. In the future, I would sit there only as a guest. There were speeches, nice things said, happy memories relived, but by now I was punch-drunk from the cascade of kind words everyone was showering on me and I barely remember what was said, though the warmth and affection stay with me.

Midnight came and my sixtieth birthday dawned, retirement-age in the BBC. They drank to my health and wished me a happy birthday. It was time to go. Seen off by our dear friends, Kate and I climbed into the car and drove out of the gates of Television Centre.

EPILOGUE

I had a riot of mixed feelings as I drove out of the BBC for the last time, but I knew everything would be all right because of the woman sitting next to me. Kate and I had been together for most of my time as MD and she had been a tremendous support to me through both good times and bad. I've had more than my fair share of luck, and never more so than when I invited her to share my life.

I had wondered if there was really life after the BBC. Having been fully absorbed in the world of entertainment, I was terrified of being at a loose end. As things turned out, a whole new phase of my life opened up. My job as chairman of Noel Gay Television brought me back to programme-making again. Almost as soon as I joined, the new satellite company BSB commissioned us to produce eight programmes a week for their Galaxy channel – this helped to establish the television side of Noel Gay under the leadership of Paul Jackson. And I persuaded my old mate Dave Allen to do a comedy series for us which was snapped up by ITV.

Another television colleague was Sue Lawley. She had decided to get off the treadmill of being a news presenter and concentrate on doing individual projects. She also wanted to spend more time with her family. Paul Fox suggested she talk to me about it. She had already become the presenter of *Desert Island Discs* on Radio 4 and wondered if I might be interested in advising her about this change of direction in her career. For the next ten years we thoroughly enjoyed ourselves. Not everything went according to plan, but by and large we won more than we lost. Sue and her husband, Hugh, became close friends of ours, and although we decided to end our formal business relationship at the beginning of 1999, our phone bills still reflect the long and sometimes scandalous conversations we regularly have.

Then there was a surprise phone call from my former colleague Roger Laughton, chief executive designate of a group bidding for the ITV franchise in the south of England, inviting me to become deputy to the chairman, Clive Hollick. On the day the award of the franchises was announced, the directors of the company stood round a lone fax machine in the middle of Roger's office waiting for it to spew out a document pronouncing on our future. We won, and eventually after MAI amalgamated with United Newspapers, Clive became chief executive of the group and I took over as chairman of Meridian.

A couple of years after I left the BBC I received the highest accolade my colleagues in the television industry could give me: the presidency of the Royal Television Society, in succession to Paul Fox. At the end of my term, they waved me goodbye with the Society's gold medal, which along with a statuette of the Fellowship of the British Academy of Film and Television Arts (BAFTA) now sits proudly on my desk at home.

Michael Aspel's red book is recognition of a different kind. One day in 1995 I drove up to Castle Ashby in the Midlands with John Harris, the chairman of Alba, and his wife, Jacqui. The growth of Alba has been the most spectacular success story I've been associated with since I left the BBC. I was appointed a non-executive director of a medium-size 'value for money' company selling radios and televisions, and it is now a major player in the industry.

As far as I knew that day our journey up the M1 was to attend a sales presentation by Bush, one of Alba's subsidiaries.

We arrived in the castle courtyard and as I stepped out of the car, a band suddenly struck up *Somebody Stole My Gal*, my father's old signature tune. I thought 'That's a strange tune to open a sales presentation', and found myself confronted by Michael Aspel and his big red book. I'd been well and truly had.

I sat in the *This is Your Life* studio humbled and amazed as a stream of show business stars paraded in to say nice things about my influence on their careers, among them Terry Wogan, Russ Conway, Bruce Forsyth, Esther Rantzen, Sue Lawley, Vera Lynn, Ernie Wise, Jimmy Tarbuck, Sandie Shaw, Cilla Black, Mike Yarwood, David Jacobs, Pete Murray and the Two Ronnies. And the special studio guests included television executives such as Paul Fox, Brian Tesler, Michael Grade and the great theatrical agent Billy Marsh. My only regret was that among this parade of famous and distinguished guests the producers did not give Kate, the most important person in my life, the opportunity of saying a few words.

I was particularly moved by the presence of Billy Marsh in the studio, frail and in a wheelchair. It must have been one of his last public appearances. When he died, his business partner, Jan Kennedy, who had cared deeply for him, invited me to become a director of Billy Marsh Associates. In his memory and out of deep admiration for her I gladly accepted and joined her husband, Tony, on the board.

My rehabilitation into the non-BBC world was made much easier by Kate's love and care. When we first met, she had a part-time job with Marie Curie Cancer Care in its education department; now she is a director of the ten centres they run throughout the United Kingdom, but she still finds time to look after me and our extended family. When I had a couple of operations on my carotid arteries she virtually lived in the hospital.

Kate organises great parties – surprises are her speciality. When I was awarded the CBE in 1989 I was sure she would insist on a party, but she merely suggested an extended lunch at the Ritz after our visit to the Palace. That, she said firmly, would be enough excitement for an elderly man in one day. I therefore accepted an invitation for us to have a drink with Paul Fox and some of my old colleagues at the Television Centre in the evening. We finally drove home at about seven o'clock and I opened the door to be confronted by a riot of friends filling the hall and spilling up the staircase.

For my seventieth birthday, Kate invited more than two hundred of our friends to the Whitehall Theatre and swore them to secrecy. I walked into the theatre expecting to see a show and found myself the main attraction. Sue Lawley conducted the proceedings and I was given a thorough but affectionate going-over by Jim Moir, Ben Elton, Alan Simpson (the writer of *Steptoe and Son*), Robert Lindsay, Dave Allen and Ashley Hill and Vernon Lawrence, two of my colleagues from television. After a cake was wheeled onto the stage by my two grandsons, Tom and Leo, we celebrated with a supper Kate had prepared herself.

It wasn't until 1990 that my divorce was finalised. My marriage with Ann lasted twenty-five years. Much water has flowed under the bridge since then and we have both found other partners. I wish her as much happiness as I have found.

The evening my decree became absolute, I suggested to Kate we should dress up and go out for dinner. Expectancy was in the air. I suspected Kate was ready to agree to any proposal I might make. We had a nice dinner and drove home without the subject being raised. When we got home and were having a nightcap, she said, 'You are going to ask me to marry you.' There was a laugh in her voice but it was definitely a statement and not a question. 'Oh, I didn't realise that's what you wanted,' I replied, 'but if you're asking me then my answer is yes.' We both collapsed in laughter.

Our wedding was held at Wesley's Chapel, City Road on 21 April 1990. Colin Morris and the chapel's minister, Paul Hulme, officiated. David, Kate's brother, gave the bride away, her sister Anne acted as matron of honour and Paul Fox was the best man. As we stood at the communion rail we were surrounded by our extended family – three generations of them, all come to wish us well. There were notable absentees too: my brother, my mother – who had died the previous year in her nineties – Kate's father and, of course, the senior partner of Double Bill.

We held the wedding reception in a marquee on the lawn of our home, and after we'd eaten Dave Allen spoke on behalf of the bride and Michael Grade spoke on behalf of the bridegroom.

And in the best fairy-story tradition, Kate and I lived happily ever after.

INDEX

'BC' indicates Bill Cotton

THE
PERFECT
ASSASSIN